# A Bibliography of
# American County Histories

*A Bibliography of*

# AMERICAN
# COUNTY
# HISTORIES

Compiled by
*P. William Filby*

Genealogical Publishing Co., Inc.
Baltimore                                    1987

Copyright © 1985 by
Genealogical Publishing Co., Inc.
Baltimore, Maryland
All Rights Reserved
Second Printing 1987
Library of Congress Catalogue Card Number 85-80029
International Standard Book Number 0-8063-1126-6
*Made in the United States of America*

# CONTENTS

# PREFACE

For many years I have been aware that Clarence S. Peterson's *Consolidated Bibliography of County Histories in Fifty States* (1961) did not meet its criteria and fell well below the accepted standards of scholarship. I knew Lt. Peterson during the time he was conducting research at the Peabody Institute Library in Baltimore and found him a dedicated worker, but since he was without the assistance now enjoyed by me and others in the field, he could not expect his bibliography to be complete. He also tended to include titles other than pure histories –vital records, for instance–so although he estimated that his book contained references to more than 3,000 county histories, the real number was probably closer to 2,000.

Some years ago Dr. Michael Tepper, president and managing editor of the Genealogical Publishing Company of Baltimore, asked me to produce an entirely new bibliography, but it was not until recently that I was able to undertake such an important assignment. This present work, I hope, will correct some of the many flaws in Peterson's work and make up for the long-standing deficiencies in the field of county history bibliography in general.

American county histories reached their high-water mark in the 1880s and 1890s, when publishers reckoned on making up their costs by including "biographies of prominent citizens." Such books were usually referred to as "mug books," either because of the portraits accompanying the biographies or because the biographies were copied by the publisher without any attempt to check the facts. Using these works today for family history research is a questionable practice, but I am always glad to find a mug book since often it is the *only* work available on a comparatively new state or county, and it gives some background to the biographies. These works pose a problem for the bibliographer, however. Books beginning with titles such as "Historical and Biographical . . ." can contain a history of the county and consist in the main of biographies, yet they are often the only histories available. For this reason I have included them in this bibliography. On the other hand, books entitled "Biographies of Prominent Men . . ." have been omitted, as have those bearing such titles as "Portrait and Biographical Histories. . . ."

It became clear from the start that I could not use Peterson as a base because he had paraphrased many titles, had often omitted the names of authors and compilers, and had left out much bibliographical data. Throughout this work I have made a fetish of gathering all the bibliographical data possible, paying special attention to the number of pages in a book so that the reader could know whether it was a short work of 40 pages or a substantial 600-page work. Unfortunately, I could not always achieve my goal.

After exhausting various library collections and examining state bibliographies, I appealed to librarians in every state, usually at the state historical society and/or the state archives. Replies varied. A few librarians could do no more than point to the standard bibliographies, but others entered into the spirit of the task and presented me with such formidable lists that I had to use discretion in selection. Many stayed with me all the way to press time, and I am much indebted to them.

*P. William Filby, F.S.G.*
Former Director,
Maryland Historical Society
Baltimore

# INTRODUCTION

The purpose of this work is to identify American county histories. Some degree of selection was necessary, particularly where four or five good histories existed, and thus, although I made no special attempt to omit histories of less than 100 pages or so, some weeding out was essential. For many of the western states, however, a bicentennial or centennial publication of less than fifty pages might be the only county history available, and therefore these apparent lightweights have been included. In the main, though, my intention has been to compile a work which contains bibliographical references to all county histories of any consequence up to the present time. The great periods of county history publishing, the late nineteenth century and the first twenty years of the twentieth century, have never been equalled, although the Bicentennial did cause an expected surge, but even then few definitive works were published. Essentially, the number of county histories of note–approximately 5,000–has increased little since 1919.

Since I had every intention of producing a scholarly bibliography, I have attempted to copy titles accurately and fully, although in the interest of space I have used ellipsis points if part of a title was not informative. I have also tried to give the place of publication, publisher, date of publication, and number of pages. In addition, I have made every attempt to record reprints and other editions. To accomplish this I used the extensive collection of county histories at the Library of Congress (which does not have anything like a complete collection, however, as so many county histories were published without copyright); the collection in the New York Public Library (possibly the best in the country); every state bibliography, although not every state has a good modern bibliography; and finally I relied on at least one librarian in every state. Some disappointment was in store when I checked the state bibliographies. Georgia bibliographies, for instance, failed to give the paginations; several bibliographies of other states were woefully out of date, and only a handful included works of the 1980s. Then I wrote to many librarians, listing my questions. Some answered the questions immediately, while others offered to share their knowledge with me as my work progressed. In all but a few cases the state lists compiled from collections in the Library of Congress and the New York Public Library swelled to double the number with use of bibliographies and the help of librarians. As a means of double-checking the years after the cut-off of the various bibliographies, I examined the book lists published in *The Genealogical Helper,* where the immaculate bibliographical descriptions of new county histories were invaluable. Publishers' catalogues also were helpful.

Weaknesses in a bibliography such as this are inevitable. Virtually all titles have been copied from secondary sources, that is, I have not sat with the books and copied the titles; instead I have relied on my correspondents and on bibliographies, library catalogues, card files, and other sources. In addition, it is probable that I overlooked some books which had been published after the cut-off date of the various state bibliographies.

## Scope

County histories in all but Alaska, Hawaii, and Puerto Rico are included. "Collective" histories–those in which a number of counties are treated –have also been included, but the publications of Goodspeed and others, covering nearly every county in a state, have merely been listed, and in such cases no attempt has been made to enter the counties in their appropriate place.

## Closing Date

December 1984.

## Arrangement

States are in alphabetical order, as are the counties within the states. Where more than one history for any county is given, they are listed in order of publication. Where two or more counties are treated in one title, the work is entered under the first county, with the second county cross-referenced. "Collective" works are found under the "Regional" heading at the beginning of the state lists, and where it is warranted the counties are cross-referenced, giving the page on which the title is located. In order to assist readers in finding an author quickly in a library catalogue, authors' given names are quoted in full, when known. Information appearing in brackets [ ] has been supplied from other sources.

## Reprints, Editions, Indexes

Since many county histories are out of print every attempt has been made to supply details of reprints, later editions, and indexes. This information appears in parenthesis ( ) following the main entry.

# ACKNOWLEDGEMENTS

When checking library catalogues I found references to a number of books with different spellings and dates. Bibliographies of some states were immaculate, while others were infuriatingly lacking in such details as name of publisher and number of pages. Very few state bibliographies went beyond 1979. It was therefore necessary to correspond with at least one librarian in every state, and to my delight every librarian replied. To all my friends and helpers I offer my heartfelt thanks in the realization that this bibliography could not have been compiled without them.

First, the following helped me develop a bibliographical structure for their states: Elizabeth C. Wells (Alabama), John L. Ferguson (Arkansas), J. Carlyle Parker (California), Thomas J. Kemp (Connecticut), Beatrice Millican, Hazel Purdie, and Mary Sue Farmer (Georgia), Carolynne L. Miller (Indiana), Portia Allbert (Kansas), Wiley Roger Pope (Minnesota), Anne Lipscomb (Mississippi), Ann Reinert and Sylvia Nimmo (Nebraska), Kathleen Stavec (New Jersey), Gunther E. Pohl (New York), Gerald G. Newborg and Richard J. Wolfert (North Dakota), Petta Khouw (Ohio), Betty J. Brown (Oklahoma), Donald R. Brown and John C. Fralish, Jr. (Pennsylvania), Fran Schell (Tennessee), David Putnam, Jr., Ruth Dorsett, and Steven R. Wood (Utah), Frank L. Green and Elaine Webster (Washington), James L. Hansen (Wisconsin), and Jean Brainerd (Wyoming).

The following answered my questions and supplied other information: Linda S. McCleary (Arizona), Brenda L. Tatum (Arkansas), Catherine T. Engel (Colorado), Dr. Barbara E. Benson (Delaware), Kimberly Baklarz (Florida), Elizabeth P. Jacox (Idaho), David T. Thackery (Illinois), Ray Gooldy (Ye Olde Genealogie Shoppe), The Bookmark (Indiana), Karen Laughlin (Iowa), Dorothy C. Rush (Kentucky), Ernest J. Brin and Florence M. Jumonville (Louisiana), Shirley Thayer (Maine), Anna R. Bryan (Maryland), David C. Dearborn (Massachusetts), Alice C. Dalligan (Michigan), Elizabeth Bailey (Missouri), David Walter (Montana), Lee Mortensen (Nevada), Jennifer Westover (New Hampshire), Dr. Donald R. Lavash (New Mexico), Walter Steesy (Heart of the Lakes Publishing Co.) (New York), Frank D. Gatton, Pam Toms, and Frances W. Kunstling (North Carolina), Annette Bartholomae (Oregon), Albert T. Klyberg (Rhode Island), Eleanor M. Richardson (South Carolina), Rosemary Evetts (South Dakota), Ann Graves (Texas), Marilyn Blackwell (Vermont), Donald Haynes (Virginia), Douglas A. Olson (Washington), Mary M. Jenkins (West Virginia), and Wendy Greathead.

In my many visits to the Library of Congress during 1984 I was pampered and assisted on the computers and in the stacks by the staff of the Local History and Genealogy Department: Judith P. Austin, Judith P. Reid, Samuel M. Andrusko, Virginia S. Wood, Thomas E. Wilgus, and Sandra M. Lawson. Their help was valuable and timely.

To all the above I express my thanks and as usual note that though they supplied much of the information in the book, the errors are entirely mine.

P.W.F.

# A Bibliography of
# American County Histories

# ALABAMA

## Autauga County

Autauga County; the First Hundred Years, 1818-1918, comp. by Daniel S. Gray. Prattville: Autauga County-Prattville Pub. Lib. [1972]. 181 pp.

## Baldwin County

A Brief History of Baldwin County . . . by Lydia J.N. Comings and M.M. Albers. Fairhope: Baldwin County Hist. Soc., 1928. 91 pp. (Repr. Fairhope: Baldwin County Hist. Soc. [1969].)

A History of Baldwin County, by Kay Nuzum. [Bay Minette: Baldwin Times, [1970.] 176 pp. ([2d ed.] [Bay Minette: Baldwin Times, 1971.])

## Barbour County

History of Barbour County, Alabama, by Mattie C. Thompson. Eufaula: N.p. [1939]. 574 pp.

Backtracking in Barbour County . . . by Anne K. Walker. Richmond, Va.: Dietz Pr., 1941. xxvii, 353 pp. (Repr. Eufaula: Heritage Assoc., 1967.)

## Bibb County

Alabama's Bibb County, by Mrs. Frank R. Stewart. Piedmont: Author, or Centre: Stewart Univ. Pr., 1983. 103 pp.

Bibb County, Alabama, the First Hundred Years, 1818-1918, by Rhoda C. Ellison. University: Univ. of Alabama Pr., 1984. xiii, 304 pp.

## Bullock County

Collections and Recollections of Bullock County History, by Bullock County Historical Society. [Montgomery: Herff-Jones Co., 1977.] 159 pp.

## Butler County

The History of Butler County, Alabama, from 1815 to 1885 . . . by John B. Little. Cincinnati, Ohio: Elm St. Pr. Co., 1885. 256 pp. (Repr. with added index. Greenville: J.G. Little, Jr., 1971. 271 pp.)

Butler County in the Nineteenth Century, by Marilyn D. Hahn. Easley, S.C.: Southern Hist. Pr., 1978. 209 pp.

## Calhoun County

Alabama's Calhoun County, by Mrs. Frank R. Stewart. Centre: Stewart Univ. Pr., 1976. 259 pp.

1

## Chambers County

Reminiscences of the Early Days in Chambers County, by Hon. E.C. Richards, 1942, *see* Randolph County.

The Reason for the Tears: a History of Chambers County, Alabama, 1832-1900, by Bobby L. Lindsey. West Point, Ga.: Hester Pr. Co., 1971. v, 319 pp.

## Cherokee County

Cherokee County History, 1836-1956, by Mrs. Frank R. Stewart. 2 vols. Centre: Stewart Univ. Pr., 1958-59.

## Chilton County

Chilton County and Her People: a Brief History, by Thomas E. Wyatt. [Clanton: Union Banner], 1940. 96 pp. (2d ed. [Clanton: Union Banner], 1950. 169 pp. [3d ed.?] [Clanton: Union Banner], 1960. 168 pp.)

## Choctaw County

Alokoli: the Choctaw County Bicentennial Book, assembled and pub. by the Choctaw County Bicentennial Commission. [Butler?:] The Comm., 1976. 233 pp.

## Clarke County

A Glance Into the Great South-east; or, Clarke County, Alabama, and Its Surroundings, from 1540 to 1877, by Timothy H. Ball. Grove Hill: N.p., 1882. 782 pp. (Repr. Tuscaloosa: Willo Pub. Co., 1962.)

History of Clarke County, by John S. Graham. Birmingham: Birmingham Pr. Co., 1923. 350 pp.

Historical Sketches of Clarke County, Alabama; a Story of the Communities of Clarke County, Alabama, by Clarke County Historical Society. Huntsville: Strode Pub. [1977]. 424 pp.

## Cleburne County

Alabama's Cleburne County; a History of Cleburne County and Her People, by Mrs. Frank R. Stewart. Centre: Stewart Univ. Pr., 1982.

## Coffee County

Piney Wood Echoes; a History of Coffee County, 1949, *see* Dale County.

Coffee Grounds; a History of Coffee County, Alabama, 1841-1970, by Fred S. Watson. Armiston: Higginbotham, 1970. 299 pp.

## Colbert County

Two Hundred Years at Muscle Shoals, being an Authentic History of Colbert County, 1700-1900 . . . by Nina Leftwich. Tuscumbia: N.p., 1935. 279 pp. (Index, by Thelma Goodloe. [Amarillo, Tex.: indexer, 1971.] 17 leaves.)

# Conecuh County

History of Conecuh County, Alabama . . . by Benjamin F. Riley. Columbus, Ga.: T. Gilbert, 1881. 233 pp. (Repr. with index, comp. by J. Vernon Brantley. Blue Hill, Maine: Weekly Packet Pr. [1964]. 246 pp.)

# Coosa County

History of Coosa County, by George E. Brewer. [Montgomery: N.p., 1942.] 285 pp. (From Alabama Historical Quarterly. Vol. 4:1-2, 1942.) (Index, comp. by William Colley, Jr. Aurora, Colo.: indexer [n.d.]; index, by Barbara E. Grether. Van Nuys, Calif.: indexer, 1973. 31 leaves.)

# Covington County

Early History of Covington County, Alabama, 1821-1871, by Wyley D. Ward. Bicentennial ed. Huntsville: Opp News [1976]. 382 pp.

Bicentennial Edition: a Historical Review of Covington County and Surrounding Communities. Opp: Opp News, 1976.

# Cullman County

Combing Cullman County, by Margaret J. Jones. Cullman: Modernistic Pr. [1972]. xvi, 222 pp.

Cullman County Across the Years, by Margaret J. Jones. Cullman: Modernistic Pr. [1975]. xii, 137 pp.

# Dale County

Piney Wood Echoes: a History of Dale and Coffee Counties, Alabama, by Fred S. Watson. Elba: Elba Clipper, 1949. 200 pp.

Forgotten Trails: a History of Dale County, Alabama, 1824-1966, by Fred S. Watson, ed. by William E. Snell. Birmingham: Banner Pr. [1968]. 288 pp.

# DeKalb County

Landmarks: a Pictorial History of DeKalb County, Alabama, by Landmarks of DeKalb County. Collegedale, Tenn.: Coll. Pr., 1971. 172 pp.

# Elmore County

Elmore County Heritage, 1972, by Elmore County Historical Society. Fort Toulouse: N.p. [1972]. 36 pp.

# Escambia County

History of Escambia County, Alabama, by Annie C. Waters. Huntsville: Strode Pub., 1983. 669 pp.

## Etowah County

A History of Etowah County, Alabama, by Etowah County Centennial Committee. [Birmingham: Roberts & Son, 1968.] 402 pp.

## Fayette County

History of Fayette County, Alabama, comp. and ed. by Herbert M. Newell, Jr. and Mrs. H.M. Newell. Fayette: Newell Offset Pr., 1960. 460 pp.

Fayette County History, by Fayette County Historical Society. 3 vols. [Fayette: The Soc., 1969-74.]

## Henry County

History of Henry County, Alabama, by Eva C. Scott. [Pensacola, Fla.?:] N.p., 1961. 506 pp.

Henry's Heritage: a History of Henry County, Alabama, comp. by Hoyt M. Warren. Abbeville: Henry County Hist. Soc., 1978. vi, 415 pp.

## Houston County

Hub of the Wiregrass; a History of Houston County, Alabama, 1903-72, by Fred S. Watson. Anniston: Higginbotham, 1972. 356 pp.

## Jackson County

History of Jackson County, by John R. Kennamer. Winchester, Tenn.: South Pr. and Pub. Co., 1935. 213 pp.

## Jefferson County

Jefferson County and Birmingham, Alabama: Historical and Biographical, ed. by John W. Du Bose. Birmingham: Temple & Smith, 1887. 595 pp. (Repr. Easley, S.C.: Southern Hist. Pr., 1976. 600 pp.)

The Valley and the Hills; an Illustrated History of Birmingham and Jefferson County, by Leah R. Atkins. Woodland Hills, Calif.: Windsor Pub., 1981. 247 pp.

## Lamar County

Lamar County History, by Joe G. Acee. 3d rev. ed. Vernon: Lamar Democrat, 1976. 188 pp.

## Lauderdale County

A History of Lauderdale County, Alabama, by Jill K. Garrett. [Columbia, Tenn.: N.p., 1964.] 264 pp.

Lauderdale County, Alabama in the 1870s. Columbia, Ind.: Mrs. P.C. Warren, 1981. 222 pp., plus surname index.

## Lawrence County

Early Settlers of Alabama, by James Saunders, with Notes and Genealogies by Elizabeth S.B. Stubbs. New Orleans, La.: L. Graham, 1899. 530, xxiv pp. (History of Northern Alabama, with detailed history of Lawrence County.) (Repr. 2 vols. Tuscaloosa: Willo Pub. Co., 1961. Repr. University: McEllhiney, 1963. Repr. Baltimore: Genealogical Pub. Co., 1969. Repr. Spartanburg, S.C.: Reprint Co., 1977.)

Life and Legend of Lawrence County, Alabama, by Dorothy Gentry. Tuscaloosa: Nottingham-SWS Inc., 1982. 235 pp.

## Lee County

The History of Opelika . . . Embracing More Particularly Lee and Russell Counties, from the Earliest Settlement . . . by F.L. Cherry. [Montgomery: N.p., 1953.] 537 pp.

## Limestone County

History of Limestone County, Alabama, by Robert H. Walker, Jr. N.p.: Limestone County Comm. and R.H. Walker, Jr., 1973. xv, 217 pp.

## Macon County

Historical Assets, Macon County, Alabama, by South Central Alabama Development Commission. Montgomery: N.p., 1975. ix, 290 pp.

## Madison County

Early History of Madison County, 1800-1840. (In Alabama Historical Quarterly, 1930. Vol. 1, pp. 101-11, 148-68, 308-17, 439-505. No more pub.)

A Dream Come True: the Story of Madison County . . . by James Record. 2 vols. Huntsville: N.p., 1970-76.

A History of Madison County and Incidentally of North Alabama, 1732-1840, by Judge Thomas J. Taylor, ed. by W.S. Hoole and A.S. Hoole. University: Confederate Pub. Co. [1976].

## Marion County

History of Marion County, Alabama, by County Teachers. [Hamilton?: N.p., 1959.] 78 pp.

## Marshall County

A History of Marshall County, Alabama, by Katherine McK. Duncan and L.J. Smith. Vol. 1, Prehistory to 1969 (all pub.). Albertville: Thompson Pr., 1969. 160 pp.

## Morgan County

A History of Morgan County, Alabama . . . by John Knox. [Decatur: Decatur Pr. Co., 1967.] 271 pp. (Surname index, comp. by Mrs. B.E. Breedlove. San Antonio, Tex.: comp., 1968. 18 leaves.)

## Pickens County

History of Pickens County, Alabama, from Its First Settlement in 1817 to 1856, by Nelson F. Smith. Carrollton: Pickens Republic Office, 1856. 272 pp. (Repr. included in Carl Elliott's Annals of Northwest Alabama. Tuscaloosa: Willo Pub. Co., 1958. 240 pp. Repr. with new index, by Mary B. Kirksey. Spartanburg, S.C.: Reprint Co., 1980. 283 pp.

The History of Pickens County, Alabama, 1546-1920, by James F. Clanahan. Carrollton: Clanahan Pub. [1964]. 422 pp.

## Pike County

Pioneer and Modern History of Pike County, by Mrs. Ella R. Hattaway. N.p.: Business Directory, 1937. 41 pp.

History of Pike County, Alabama, by Margaret P. Farmer. Troy: N.p., 1952. 144 pp.

One Hundred and Fifty Years in Pike County, Alabama, 1821-1971, by Margaret P. Farmer. Anniston: Higginbotham, 1973. 549 pp.

Alabama's Pike County, by Mrs. Frank R. Stewart, Containing a Reprint of Pioneer History of Pike County, 1921, by the Centennial Committee. 2 vols. Centre: Stewart Univ. Pr., 1976.

## Randolph County

History of Randolph County, by James M.K. Guinn. Reminiscences of the Early Days in Chambers County, by Hon. E.C. Richards. [Alabama Historical Quarterly. Vol. 4:3, 1942.] 159 pp.

A History of Randolph County, by Eugenia E. Smith. [Roanoke: Pr. of Roanoke Leader, 1978?] 63 pp.

1850 Randolph County, Alabama, comp. by Lynda S. Eller. Lanett: comp., 1982. 137 pp.

## Russell County

Russell County in Retrospect . . . by Anne K. Walker. Richmond, Va.: Dietz Pr., 1950. xxii, 423 pp.

The History of . . . Russell County, 1953, *see* Lee County.

The History of Russell County, Alabama, comp. by Russell County Historical Commission. Dallas, Tex.: National ShareGraphics, 1982. 382 pp.

## St. Clair County

History of St. Clair County, Alabama, by Mattie L.T. Crow. Huntsville: Strode Pr., 1971. x, 205 pp.

## Talladega County

Under Seven Flags, by Randolph F. Blackford. Birmingham: Birmingham Pr. Co., 1950. 76 pp.

Historic Tales of Talladega, by E. Grace Jemison. [Talladega?: N.p., 1959.] 356 pp.

## Tallapoosa County

A History of Tallapoosa County, by William P. Ingram. [Birmingham: N.p., 1951.] 119 pp.

## Tuscaloosa County

History of Tuscaloosa, Alabama, by Alton Lambert. 3 vols. Centre: Stewart Univ. Pr., 1977.

## Walker County

History of Walker County, Its Towns and People, by John M. Dombhart. Thornton, Ark.: Cayce Pub. Co. [1936]. 382 pp.

Dixie's Diverse Destiny, by Margery T. Lockhart. Huntsville: Strode Pub., 1979. 352 pp.

## Washington County

The History of Washington County: the First County in Alabama, by Jacqueline A. Matte. Chatom: Washington County Hist. Soc., 1982. xvi, 461 pp.

## Winston County

The Free State of Winston: a History of Winston County, Alabama, by Wesley S. Thompson. Winfield: Parell Pr. [1958]. xi, 220 pp.

Winston: Antebellum and Civil War History of a Hill County of Northern Alabama, by Donald B. Dodd and W.S. Dodd. Jasper: Carl Elliott [1972]. 319 pp.

# Arizona

## Apache County

History of Western Arizona Stake at Zion: Early Settlement of Apache County, by Joseph Fish. N.p., n.d. 121 leaves.

Apache County, Arizona Centennial Commission. Apache County, Arizona. N.p.: The Comm., 1979. 48 pp.

Apache County Centennial Committee. Lest Ye Forget. N.p., 1980. 224 pp.

## Cochise County

Cochise County, Arizona, Past and Present, by Ervin Bond. Douglas: N.p., 1982.

## Gila County

Honor the Past . . . Mold the Future, Gila Centennials, Inc. Globe: N.p., 1975. 134 pp.

## Graham County

Lest We Forget, ed. by Otto M. Marshall. Pima: N.p., 197-. 141 pp.

Graham County, Arizona, 1870-1977, by Graham County Historical Society. N.p.: Newsfoto, 1978. 416 pp.

## Greenlee County

Greenlee County: the Wonderland of Arizona. [Phoenix: Rush & Rush, 1922.] 48 pp.

Clifton Editor, by Al Fenn. Phoenix: Arizona Sun Pr., 1977. 95 pp. (Greenlee County history.)

## Maricopa County

History of Maricopa County, by Joseph Miller. News Articles Copied from the Weekly Phoenix Herald, 1883. Phoenix: N.p., n.d. 17 leaves.

The Commercial History of Maricopa County, by A. George Daws. Phoenix: N.p., 1919. 194 pp.

## Mohave County

Mohave County: Sketches of Early Days, by Roman Malach. Kingman: N.p., 1974. 142 pp.

Early Ranching in Mohave County, by Roman Malach. Kingman: Mohave County Bd. of Supervisors, 1978. 44 pp.

*Mohave County (cont.)*

Early Days in Mohave County, by Roman Malach. Kingman: Mohave County Bd. of Supervisors, 1979. 56 pp.

Mohave County Northland, by Roman Malach. Kingman: Mohave County Bd. of Supervisors, 1979. 44 pp.

Mohave County Album, by Roman Malach. Kingman: Mohave County Bd. of Supervisors, 1979. 52 pp.

Northland Pioneers in Mohave County. Kingman: H. & H. Pr., 1981. 48 pp.

## Pima County

An Englishman's Arizona; the Ranching Letters of Herbert H. Hislop, 1876-1878 . . . Tucson: Overland Pr., 1965. xxii, 74 pp.

## Pinal County

Cow-Country Counselor, by Tom Fulbright. New York: Exposition Pr., 1968. 196 pp.

## Santa Cruz County

Open Range and Hidden Silver: Arizona's Santa Cruz County, by Alma Ready. Nogales: Alto Pr., 1973. 178 pp.

## Yavapai County

One Last Frontier: a Story of Indians, Early Settlers and Old Ranches of Northern Arizona, by Pat Savage. New York: Exposition Pr. [1964]. 236 pp.

Old Timer Tales, by I. H. Parkman. Prescott: Sharlot Hall Historical Soc., 1972. (Ongoing ser., several vols.)

## Yuma County

Statistical Information Relating to the Mohawk Valley of Arizona . . . ed. by Frank V. McDonald. New York: Lehmaier & Bro., Pr., 1892. 61 pp.

# ARKANSAS

## Regional

A. Biographical and Historical Memoirs of Eastern Arkansas. Chicago: Goodspeed Pub. Co., 1890. 820 pp. (Includes Arkansas, Crittenden, Cross, Lee, Monroe, Phillips, Prairie, St. Francis, White, and Woodruff Counties.)

B. Biographical and Historical Memoirs of Northeast Arkansas. Chicago: Goodspeed Pub. Co., 1889. 981 pp. (Includes Clay, Craighead, Fulton, Greene, Independence, Izard, Jackson, Lawrence, Mississippi, Poinsett, Randolph, and Sharp Counties.)

C. Biographical and Historical Memoirs of Pulaski, Jefferson, Lonoke, Faulkner, Grant, Saline, Perry, Garland and Hot Spring Counties, Arkansas . . . Chicago: Goodspeed Pub. Co., 1889. 811 pp. (Biographical index, by Mrs. Leister E. Presley. Searcy: Presley [1973]. 32 pp.)

D. Biographical and Historical Memoirs of Southeastern Arkansas. Chicago: Goodspeed Pub. Co., 1890. 1,088 pp. (Includes Ashley, Bradley, Calhoun, Chicot, Clark, Cleveland, Columbia, Dallas, Desha, Drew, Hempstead, Howard, Lafayette, Lincoln, Little River, Miller, Nevada, Ouachita, Pike, Sevier, and Union Counties.)

E. Biographical and Historical Memoirs of Western Arkansas. Chicago: Southern Pub. Co., 1891. 497 pp. (Includes Johnson, Logan, Montgomery, Polk, Pope, Scott, and Yell Counties.)

F. History of Benton, Washington, Carroll, Madison, Crawford, Franklin and Sebastian Counties, Arkansas, from the Earliest Time to the Present . . . Chicago: Goodspeed Pub. Co., 1889. 1,382 pp. (Biographical index, by Mrs. Leister E. Presley. Searcy: Presley, 1973. 50 pp.)

G. The History of Lawrence, Jackson, Independence, and Stone Counties . . . by Sallie W. Stockard. Little Rock: Arkansas Democrat Co., 1904. 204 pp.

## Arkansas County

A Topographical Description and History of Arkansas County, Arkansas from 1541 to 1875, by William H. Halliburton. [De Witt?:] N.p., 1876. 190 pp. (Repr. Easley, S.C.: Southern Hist. Pr., 1978.)

Biographical and Historical Memoirs of Eastern Arkansas. Arkansas County, 1890, *see* A., above.

## Ashley County

Biographical and Historical Memoirs of Southeastern Arkansas. Ashley County, 1890, *see* D., above.

History of Ashley County, Arkansas, by Young W. Etheridge. Van Buren: Press-Argus, 1959. 173 pp.

## Baxter County

History of Baxter County, by Francis H. Shiras. Mountain Home: J.W. Daniel & Shiras Bros. [1939?]. 159 pp.

History of Baxter County, 1873-1973, by Mary A. Messick. Centennial ed. [Mountain Home: Mountain Home Chamber of Commerce, 1973.] xiv, 506 pp.

## Benton County

Benton County Directory and History . . . N.p.: Claud Coffelt, 1948. 125 pp.

History of Benton County, Arkansas, by J. Dickson Black. Dentonville: Author, 1975. 496 pp.

History of Benton County, 1889, *see* F., p. 10.

## Boone County

Boone County and Its People, by Ralph R. Rea. Van Buren: Press-Argus [1955]. 224 pp.

## Bradley County

Biographical and Historical Memoirs of Southeastern Arkansas. Bradley County, 1890, *see* D., p. 10.

A Bicentennial History of Bradley County, by Robert L. Gatewood. Warren: Warren & Bradley County Hist. Soc., 1976. 56 pp.

## Calhoun County

Biographical and Historical Memoirs of Southeastern Arkansas. Calhoun County, 1890, *see* D., p. 10.

## Carroll County

History of . . . Carroll County, 1889, *see* F., p. 10. (History of Carroll County, repr. arranged by O. Klute Braswell. Berryville: Braswell Pr. Co. [196-?]. Repr. with new material. 1978.)

An Outlander's History of Carroll County, Arkansas. Sesquicentennial ed., 1830-1983, by Jim Lair, with collaboration by O. Klute Braswell. Marceline, Mo.: Walsworth Pub. Co., 1983. 406 pp.

## Chicot County

Biographical and Historical Memoirs of Southeastern Arkansas. Chicot County, 1890, *see* D., p. 10.

## Clark County

Biographical and Historical Memoirs of Southeastern Arkansas. Clark County, 1890, *see* D., p. 10.

## Clay County

Biographical and Historical Memoirs of Northeast Arkansas. Clay County, 1889, *see* B., p. 10.

History of Clay County, by Robert T. Webb, Mountain Home: Shiras Bros. Pr. Shop, 1933. 85 pp.

## Cleburne County

Time and the River: a History of Cleburne County, by Evalene Berry. Little Rock: Rose Pub. Co., 1982. 392 pp.

## Cleveland County

Biographical and Historical Memoirs of Southeastern Arkansas. Cleveland County, *see* D., p. 10.

## Columbia County

Biographical and Historical Memoirs of Southeastern Arkansas. Columbia County, 1890, *see* D., p. 10.

History of Columbia County, by Nettie H. Killgore. [Magnolia?: N.p., 1947.] 231 pp.

## Conway County

Historical Reminiscences and Biographical Memoirs of Conway County, Arkansas. Little Rock: Hist. Pub. Co., 1890. 129 pp. (Repr. Van Buren: Press-Argus, 1960.)

## Craighead County

Biographical and Historical Memoirs of Northeast Arkansas. Craighead County, 1889, *see* B., p. 10. (Repr., with foreword by Hugh Park. Van Buren: Press-Argus, 1964. 64 pp.)

History of Craighead County, Arkansas, by Harry L. Williams. Little Rock: Parke-Harper Co., 1930. 654 pp. (Repr. of Craighead County, with index by Doris T. Thurman. Little Rock: Rose Pub. Co., 1977. 737 pp. Repr. Easley, S.C.: Southern Hist. Pr., 1979. 752 pp.)

The Story of Craighead County; a Narrative of People and Events in Northeast Arkansas, by Charles A. Stuck. [Jonesboro: N.p., 1960.] 335 pp. (Repr. White Bear Lake, Wis.: Author [1978].)

## Crawford County

History of . . . Crawford County, 1889, *see* F., p. 10.

History of Crawford County, Arkansas, by Clara B. Eno. Van Buren: Press-Argus, 1951. 499 pp.

*Crawford County (cont.)*

An Historical Salute to Crawford County, by Crawford County Bicentennial Commission. Van Buren: Pr. by the Courier, 1976. 106 pp.

## Crittenden County

Biographical and Historical Memoirs of Eastern Arkansas. Crittenden County, 1890, *see* A., p. 10.

## Cross County

Biographical and Historical Memoirs of Eastern Arkansas. Cross County, 1890, *see* A., p. 10.

History of Cross County, Arkansas, 1955 . . . by Robert W. Chowning. Wynne: Wynne Progress, 1955. 132 pp.

## Dallas County

Biographical and Historical Memoirs of Southeastern Arkansas. Dallas County, 1890, *see* D., p. 10.

## Desha County

Biographical and Historical Memoirs of Southeastern Arkansas. Desha County, 1890, *see* D., p. 10.

## Drew County

Biographical and Historical Memoirs of Southeastern Arkansas. Drew County, 1890, *see* D., p. 10.

Old Times Not Forgotten: a History of Drew County, by Rebecca DeArmond. Little Rock: Rose Pub. Co., 1980. 418 pp.

## Faulkner County

Biographical and Historical Memoirs of . . . Faulkner County, 1889, *see* C., p. 10.

The History of Faulkner County, Arkansas, by Alex McPherson. Conway: Conway Times Plant [1927]. 104 pp.

Conway and Faulkner County, Arkansas, 1800-1961, by Robert L. Gatewood. Conway: N.p., 1961. 95 pp.

Faulkner County, Arkansas, 1778-1964; a History in 3 Parts, by Robert L. Gatewood. Rev. and enl. [Conway: N.p., 1964.] viii, 188 pp.

## Franklin County

History of . . . Franklin County, 1889, *see* F., p. 10.

## Fulton County

Biographical and Historical Memoirs of Northeast Arkansas. Fulton County, 1889, *see* B., p. 10.

## Garland County

Biographical and Historical Memoirs of . . . Garland County, 1889, *see* C., p. 10.

## Grant County

Biographical and Historical Memoirs of . . . Grant County, 1889, *see* C., p. 10.

## Greene County

Biographical and Historical Memoirs of Northeast Arkansas. Greene County, *see* B., p. 10. (Repr. of Greene County, with a foreword by Hugh Park. Van Buren: Press-Argus, 1963. 76 pp.)

History of Greene County, Arkansas, by Vivian Hansborough. Little Rock: Democrat Pr. & Litho Co., 1946. 204 pp.

## Hempstead County

Biographical and Historical Memoirs of Southeastern Arkansas. Hempstead County, 1890, *see* D., p. 10.

## Hot Spring County

Biographical and Historical Memoirs of . . . Hot Spring County, 1889, *see* C. p. 10.

An Album of Yesteryears, 1876-1976, Centennial and Bicentennial ed. Malvern: Hot Spring County Hist. Soc., 1976. 40 pp.

## Howard County

Biographical and Historical Memoirs of Southeastern Arkansas. Howard County, 1890, *see* D., p. 10.

The Unfinished Story of North Howard County, comp. by Umpire High School, Naida Tyndall, et al., 1971-1981. Umpire: N. Howard County Youth Group for Hist. Research, 1971. 368 pp.

History of Howard County, Arkansas, 1873-1973, by Howard County Heritage Club. Nashville: Nashville News, 1973. 77 pp. (Rev. and updated. 1971-1981. Umpire: North Howard County Youth Group for Hist. Research, 1982. 368 pp.)

## Independence County

Biographical and Historical Memoirs of Northeast Arkansas. Independence County, 1889, *see* B., p. 10.

*Independence County (cont.)*

The History of . . . Independence County, 1904, *see* G., p. 10.

A History of Independence County, Arkansas, by A.C. McGinnis. Batesville: The Chronicle, 1976. 119 pp.

## Izard County

Biographical and Historical Memoirs of Northeast Arkansas. Izard County, 1889, *see* B., p. 10.

A History of Izard County, Arkansas, by Karr Shannon. Little Rock: Democrat Pr. & Litho Co. [1947]. vii, 158 pp.

Historical and Biographical Sketches of the Early Settlement of the Valley of White River, Together with a History of Izard County, by Augustus C. Jeffery. Reprint of a Series of Newspaper Accounts . . . 1800-1877, by A.C. Jeffery, ed. by Dale Hanks. Richmond, Va.: Jeffery Hist. Soc., 1973. 70 pp.

## Jackson County

Biographical and Historical Memoirs of Northeast Arkansas. Jackson County, 1889, *see* B., p. 10.

The History of . . . Jackson County, 1904, *see* G., p. 10.

## Jefferson County

Biographical and Historical Memoirs of . . . Jefferson County, 1889, *see* C., p. 10.

## Johnson County

Biographical and Historical Memoirs of Western Arkansas. Johnson County, 1891, *see* E., p. 10.

Johnson County, Arkansas, the First Hundred Years, by Ella M. Langford. [Clarksville: E.M. Langford, 1921.] 210 pp. (Repr. Clarksville: Johnson County Hist. Soc., 1976.)

## Lafayette County

Biographical and Historical Memoirs of Southeastern Arkansas. Lafayette, 1890, *see* D., p. 10.

## Lawrence County

Biographical and Historical Memoirs of Northeast Arkansas. Lawrence County, 1889, *see* B., p. 10.

The History of Lawrence County, 1904, *see* G., p. 10.

Centennial Memorial History of Lawrence County, by Walter E. McLeod. Russellville: Russellville Pr. Co., 1936. 163 pp.

## Lee County

Biographical and Historical Memoirs of Eastern Arkansas. Lee County, 1890, *see* A., p. 10.

## Lincoln County

Biographical and Historical Memoirs of Southeastern Arkansas. Lincoln County, 1890, *see* D , p. 10.

History of Lincoln County, Arkansas, 1871-1983. Dallas, Tex.: Taylor Pub. Co. for Lincoln County Hist. Comm., 1983. 320 pp.

## Little River County

Biographical and Historical Memoirs of Southeastern Arkansas. Little River County, 1890, *see* D., p. 10.

Little River County, by Bill Beasley. Ashdown: Little River County Hist. Soc., 1975. 209 pp.

## Logan County

Biographical and Historical Memoirs of Western Arkansas. Logan County, 1891, *see* E., p. 10.

## Lonoke County

Biographical and Historical Memoirs of . . . Lonoke County, 1889, *see* C., p. 10.

History of Lonoke County, Arkansas, by R.L. Young. Lonoke: N.p., 1917? 15 pp. (2d ed. Lonoke: N.p., 1924? 54 pp.)

## Madison County

History of . . . Madison County, 1889, *see* F., p. 10.

Early Days in the Ozarks, by Robert E. Sutton. Eureka Springs: Times-Echo Pr., 1950. 45 pp.

## Marion County

History of Marion County, by Earl Berry. Little Rock: Marion County Hist. Assoc., 1977. 523 pp.

## Miller County

Biographical and Historical Memoirs of Southeastern Arkansas. Miller County, 1890, *see* D., p. 10.

History of Texarkana and Bowie [Texas], and Miller [Arkansas] Counties, Texas-Arkansas, by Barbara Chandler and J.E. Howe. Texarkana: N.p., 1939. 375 pp.

## Mississippi County

Biographical and Historical Memoirs of Northeast Arkansas. Mississippi County, 1889, *see* B., p. 10. (Repr. of Mississippi County. Bragg City, Mo.: Priv. pr. by Mrs. Jeff Wade, Jr. and Mrs. R. Hasskarl, 1973. 126 pp.)

History of Mississippi County, Arkansas, comp. and ed. by Mabel F. Edrington. [Ocala? Fla.:] N.p., 1962. 428, 79 pp.

## Monroe County

Biographical and Historical Memoirs of Eastern Kansas, Monroe County, 1890, *see* A., p. 10.

## Montgomery County

Biographical and Historical Memoirs of Eastern Arkansas. Montgomery County, 1891, *see* E., p. 10.

## Nevada County

Biographical and Historical Memoirs of Southeastern Arkansas. Nevada County, 1890, *see* D., p. 10.

## Newton County

History of Newton County, Arkansas, by Walter F. Lackey. Independence, Mo.: Zion's Pr. & Pub. Co. [1950]. 432 pp.

## Ouachita County

Biographical and Historical Memoirs of Southeastern Arkansas. Ouachita County, 1890, *see* D., p. 10.

## Perry County

Biographical and Historical Memoirs of . . . Perry County, 1889, *see* C., p. 10.

## Phillips County

Biographical and Historical Memoirs of Eastern Arkansas. Phillips County, 1890, *see* A., p. 10.

## Pike County

Biographical and Historical Memoirs of Southeastern Arkansas. Pike County, 1890, *see* D., p. 10.

Early History of Pike County, Arkansas: the First 100 Years, comp. and pub. by Pike County Heritage Club. Murfreesboro: The Club, 1978. 230 pp.

## Poinsett County

Biographical and Historical Memoirs of Northeast Arkansas. Poinsett County, 1889, *see* B., p. 10.

## Polk County

Biographical and Historical Memoirs of Western Arkansas. Polk County, 1891, *see* E., p. 10.

## Pope County

Biographical and Historical Memoirs of Western Arkansas. Pope County, 1891, *see* E. p. 10.

David Porter West's Early History of Pope County . . . [Dover?: N.p., 1906?] 53 pp. (Repr. Little Rock: Foreman-Payne Pubs., 1968.)

Early History of Pope County; a History of Pope County in the Nineteenth Century, and in the Early Part of the Twentieth Century, by David L. Vance. Mabelvale: Foreman-Payne Pubs., 1970. 216 pp.

History of Pope County, Arkansas, by the Pope County Historical Association. 2 vols. Winston Salem, N.C. and Topeka, Kans.: The Assoc., 1979-1981. 544, 584 pp.

## Prairie County

Biographical and Historical Memoirs of Eastern Arkansas. Prairie County, 1890, *see* A., p. 10.

## Pulaski County

Biographical and Historical Memoirs of Pulaski County, 1889, *see* C., p. 10.

## Randolph County

Biographical and Historical Memoirs of Northeast Arkansas. Randolph County, 1889, *see* B., p. 10.

Directory of Randolph County, Arkansas, comp. by L.F. Blankenship. Pocahontas: Atar Herald Pr. Co., 1910. 111 pp. (Index, by Freda Roberts. Oklahoma City: Roberts, 1983. 44 pp.)

History of Randolph County, Arkansas, by Lawrence Dalton. Little Rock: Democrat Pr. and Litho. Co. [1946?]. 359 pp. (Repr., enl. Pocahontas: Herman Dalton, 1981. 394 pp. 2d pr. 1983. 400 pp.)

## St. Francis County

Biographical and Historical Memoirs of Eastern Arkansas. St. Francis County, 1890, *see* A., p. 10.

History of St. Francis County, Arkansas, by Robert W. Chowning. Forrest City: Times Herald Co., 1954. 156 pp.

## Saline County

Biographical and Historical Memoirs of . . . Saline County, 1889, *see* C., p. 10.

## Scott County

Biographical and Historical Memoirs of Western Arkansas. Scott County, 1891, *see* E., p. 10.

History of Scott County, Arkansas, by Henry G. McCutcheon. [Little Rock: Pr. by H.G. Pugh & Co., 1922.] 74 pp.

A History of the Early Events and Happenings in Scott and Sebastian Counties, Arkansas. Waldron: Advance Reporter, 1938. 86 pp.

A History of Scott County, Arkansas, by Norman Goodner. Siloam Springs, Bar D Pr., 1941. 89 pp.

## Searcy County

Searcy County, My Dear; a History of Searcy County, Arkansas, by Orville J. McInturff. Marshall Mountain Wave [1963]. 204 pp.

History and Folklore of Searcy County, Arkansas: Source Book, ed. by Mary F. Harrell. Harrison: New Leaf Pr., 1977. 481 pp.

## Sebastian County

History of . . . Sebastian County, 1889, *see* F., p. 10. (Repr. of Sebastian County. Columbia, Tenn.: Woodward & Stinson Pr. Co., 1977. 97 pp.)

A History of the Early Events in . . . Sebastian County, *see* Scott County.

The First Hundred Years of Sebastian County, by Norman M. Wilkinson. [Fort Smith?: N.p., 1951?] 90 pp.

## Sevier County

Biographical and Historical Memoirs of Southeastern Arkansas. Sevier County, 1890, *see* D., p. 10.

The History of Sevier County and Her People (1803-1936), researched by the Sevier County Historical Society, ed. and written by Netty McCommas. Dallas, Tex.: Taylor Pub. Co. and Sevier County Hist. Soc., 1980. 352 pp.

## Sharp County

Biographical and Historical Memoirs of Northeast Arkansas. Sharp County, 1889, *see* B., p. 10.

## Stone County

History of . . . Stone County, 1904, *see* G., p. 10.

# Union County

Biographical and Historical Memoirs of Southeastern Arkansas. Union County, 1890, *see* D., p. 10.

The History of Union County, Arkansas, by Juanita W. Green. [Stephens?:] N.p., 1954. 201 leaves.

# Van Buren County

A History of Van Buren County, 1833-1983, Sesquicentennial, ed. by Eleanor B. Ryman. Conway: River Road Pr., and Clinton: Clinton Lib., 1976. 213 pp. (2d ed. 1873-1983. Clinton: Maria Van Buren D.A.R. Chapter, 1982. 250 pp.)

# Washington County

A History of . . . Washington County, 1889, *see* F., p. 10. (Repr. of Washington County. Siloam Springs: J. Roger Huff, 1978 and 1981. 337 pp.)

# White County

Biographical and Historical Memoirs of Eastern Arkansas. White County, 1890, *see* A., p. 10. (Repr. of White County. [N.p., 19-.] 159 pp.)

The Humorous History of White County, Arkansas, by Claude E. Johnson. Searcy: Author, 1975. 132 pp.

# Woodruff County

Biographical and Historical Memoirs of Eastern Arkansas. Woodruff County, 1890, *see* A., p. 10.

# Yell County

Biographical and Historical Memoirs of Western Arkansas. Yell County, 1891, *see* E., p. 10.

The History of Yell County, Arkansas, by Wayne Banks. [Van Buren: Press-Argus, 1959.] 298 pp.

# CALIFORNIA

## Regional

Hand-book and Directory of San Luis Obispo, Santa Barbara, Ventura, Kern, San Bernardino, Los Angeles & San Diego Counties, comp. by Luther L. Paulson. San Francisco: Francis & Valentine, 1875. 534 pp.

Illustrated History of Southern California, Embracing the Counties of San Diego, San Bernardino, Los Angeles and Orange . . . Chicago: Lewis Pub. Co., 1890. 898 pp.

Memorial and Biographical History of the Counties of Merced, Stanislaus, Calaveras, Tuolumne and Mariposa, California . . . Chicago: Lewis Pub. Co., 1892. 408 pp. (Repr. Modesto: The Guild, McHenry Museum of Art & Hist., 1980. Includes a personal name index, ed. by J. Carlyle Parker. [Turlock:] Stanislaus State Coll. Lib., 1973.) [26 pp.]

Memorial and Biographical History of the Coast Counties of Central California . . . ed. by Henry D. Barrows and L.A. Ingersoll. (Includes Monterey, San Benito, Santa Cruz, San Mateo Counties.) Chicago: Lewis Pub. Co., 1893. 446 pp.

## Alameda County

The Centennial Year Book of Alameda, California . . . by William Halley. Oakland: Author, 1876. xv, 586 pp. (Index . . . comp. by Mabel W. Thomas and E. Blumann. Oakland: Oakland Pub. Lib., 1947. 140 leaves.)

History of Alameda County, California, by J.P. Munro-Fraser. Oakland: M.W. Wood, 1883. 1,001 pp. (Repr. Oakland: Holmes Book Co., 1969.)

Alameda County . . . California. A History of Alameda County from Its Formation to the Present. [Oakland:] Oakland Tribune, 1898. 248 pp.

Past and Present of Alameda County, California, ed. by Joseph E. Baker. 2 vols. Chicago: S.J. Clarke Pub. Co., 1914.

History of Alameda County, California, by Frank C. Merritt. 2 vols. Chicago: S.J. Clarke Pub. Co., 1928. (Index to Vol. 1, comp. by Marguerite E. Cooley. Oakland: W.P.A., 1939. 223 leaves.)

Historical Atlas and Landmarks of Alameda County, California, ed. by George Tays. Oakland: N.p., 1938. 349 leaves.

Alameda County Past and Present, by Leslie J. Freeman. San Leandro: Pr. of San Leandro Reporter, 1946. 159 pp.

## Alpine County

Report on the History of the Grover Hot Springs State Park Area and Surrounding Region of Alpine County, by W.T. Jackson. [Sacramento:] Dept. of Parks, 1964. 96 pp.

## Amador County

History of Amador County, California . . . [by Jesse D. Mason]. Oakland: Thompson & West, 1881. 344 pp. (Repr. Sacramento: California Traveler, 1965.)

Amador County History, ed. by Mrs. Elizabeth A. Sargent. N.p.: Amador County Federation of Women's Clubs, 1927. 127 pp.

## Butte County

History of Butte County, California: Vol. 1, History of California from 1513 to 1850, by Frank T. Gilbert. Vol. 2, History of Butte County . . . by Harry L. Wells. 2 vols. in 1. San Francisco: H.L. Wells, 1882. (Repr. Berkeley: Howell-North Books, 1873. 305 pp.)

A History of Butte County, California . . . by Joseph F. McGie and George C. Mansfield. Los Angeles: Hist. Record Co., 1918. 1,331 pp.

Here Is My Land; Sketches of Butte County, California, by the Butte County Branch of National League of American Penwomen. [Chicago: Hurst & Moore], 1940. 93 pp.

A History of Butte County: a Source Book for Teachers, by Jos. F. McGie. Rev. ed. Oroville: Butte County Office of Education, 1958. 333 pp. (3d ed., 1960.)

## Calaveras County

Memorial . . . History of . . . Calaveras County, 1892, in Memorial and Biographical History . . . 1892, *see* p. 21.

California Mother Lode Records, comp. by Edith G. Jensen. 3 vols. [San Leandro?:] N.p., 1962-63.

## Colusa County

Colusa County, California . . . with Historical Sketch of the County [by Will S. Green]. San Francisco: Elliott & Moore, 1880. 196 pp. (Repr. with suppl. Sacramento: Sacramento Lithograph Co., 1950. xxi, 196 pp.)

Colusa County, California . . . [by Ellis T. Crane]. 2d ed. Oakland: Pacific Pr. Pub. House, 1887. 104 pp.

Colusa County: Its History . . . by Justus H. Rogers. Orland: N.p., 1891. 473 pp.

History of Colusa and Glenn Counties, California . . . by Charles D. McComish and R.T. Lambert. Los Angeles: Hist. Record Co., 1918. 1,074 pp.

## Contra Costa County

History of Contra Costa County . . . by J.P. Munro-Fraser. San Francisco: W.A. Slocum, 1882. 710 pp. (Repr. Oakland: Brook-Sterling Co., 1974. xiii, 710 pp.)

The History of Contra Costa County, California, ed. by Frederick J. Hulaniski. Berkeley: Elms Pub. Co., 1917. xix, 635 pp.

History of Contra Costa County . . . Los Angeles: Hist. Record Co., 1926. 1,102 pp.

History of Contra Costa County, by Mae F. Purcell. Berkeley: Gillick Pr., 1940. 742 pp.

## Del Norte County

History of Del Norte County . . . [by Anthony J. Bledsoe]. Eureka: Wyman, 1881. 175 pp.

The History of Del Norte County . . . by Esther R. Smith. Oakland: Holmes Book Co., 1953. 224 pp.

## El Dorado County

Historical Souvenir of El Dorado County, comp. by Paolo Sioli. Oakland: Author, 1883. 227 pp.

Pioneers of El Dorado, by Charles E. Upton. Placerville: C.E. Upton, 1906. 201 pp.

California's El Dorado Yesterday and Today, by Herman D. Jerrett. Sacramento: Anderson Pr., 1915. 141 pp.

## Fresno County

History of Fresno County . . . by Wallace W. Elliott & Co. San Francisco: Elliott, 1882. 246 pp. (Repr. Fresno: Valley Pubs., 1973.)

Memorial and Biographical History of the Counties of Fresno, Tulare and Kern . . . Chicago: Lewis Pub. Co., 1892. 822 pp.

History of Fresno County . . . from Early Days, by Paul E. Vandor. 2 vols. Los Angeles: Hist. Record Co., 1919.

History of Fresno County and the San Joaquin Valley . . . by Lilbourne A. Winchell. Fresno: A.H. Cawston [1933]. 323 pp. (History of Fresno and Madera County, Jos. Bancroft ed. for Madera County. 344 pp. Apparently the same book with another title.)

The Fresno County Blue Book, Containing Facts and Impressions for the Better Understanding of Fresno County Past and Present . . . by Ben R. Walker. Fresno: A.H. Cawston, 1941. 555 pp.

Fresno County—the Pioneer Years, from the Beginnings to 1900, by Charles W. Clough and W.B. Secrest, Jr., ed. by Bobbye S. Temple. Fresno: Panorama West Books, 1984. ix, 362 pp.

## Glenn County

A Lemon Home in California, by Leigh H. Irvine. Orland: N.p., 1900. 77 pp.

History of . . . Glenn County, 1918, *see* Colusa County.

## Humboldt County

History of Humboldt County . . . [San Francisco: W.W. Elliott], 1881. 218 pp. (Repr. Fresno: Mid-Cal. Pubs., 1969.)

History and Business Directory of Humboldt County . . . pub. by Lillie E. Hamm. Eureka: Daily Humboldt Standard, 1890. 224 pp.

Souvenir of Humboldt County . . . pub. by Humboldt Chamber of Commerce. Eureka: Times Pub. Co., 1902. 192 pp. (2d ed. Eureka: Times Pub. Co., 1904. 210 pp.)

Humboldt County, California . . . by Charles W. Ward. [Eureka: Ward-Perkins-Gill Co.], 1915. 128 pp.

History of Humboldt County . . . by Leigh H. Irvine. Los Angeles: Hist. Record Co., 1915. xv, 1,290 pp.

California's Redwood Wonderland, Humboldt County, by Delmar L. Thornbury. [San Francisco: Sunset Pr., 1923.] 167 pp.

The Humboldt Bay Region, 1850-1875; a Study in the American Colonization of California, by Owen C. Coy. Los Angeles: California State Hist. Assoc., 1929. xiii, 346 pp.

The Quest for Qual-a-wa-loo (Humboldt Bay); a Collection of Diaries and Historical Notes Pertaining to . . . Humboldt County, ed. and pub. from MSS. by Clarence E. Pearsall, et al. [San Francisco: N.p., 1943.] 190 pp. (Repr. Oakland: Holmes Book Co., 1966.)

Lure of Humboldt Bay Region: Early Explorations, Discoveries, and Foundations Establishing the Bay Region, by Chad L. Hoopes. Dubuque, Iowa: W.C. Brown Book Co. [1966]. viii, 260 pp. (Rev. ed. Dubuque, Iowa: Kendall/Hunt Pub. Co. [1971]. x, 299 pp.)

## Imperial County

Imperial County: a Record of Settlement, 1913, *see* San Diego County.

The History of Imperial County, California, ed. by Finis C. Ferr. Berkeley: Elms and Frank, 1918. vi, 526 pp.

Imperial Valley, by Tracey Henderson. [San Diego: Neyenesch Pr., 1968.] 240 pp.

## Inyo County

The Story of Inyo, by Willie A. Chalfant. Chicago: Author, 1922. xvii, 358 pp. (Record of Inyo County, earlier than 1870.) (Rev. ed. . . . [Los Angeles: Citizens Pr. Shop], 1933. vi, 430 pp.; rev. ed. repr. [Bishop: Pinon Book Store, 1964.] vii, 430 pp.)

*Inyo County (cont.)*

Inyo, 1866-1966, sponsored by Inyo County Board of Supervisors. [Bishop?: Chalfant Pr., 1966.] 95 pp.

## Kern County

Hand-book and Directory of . . . Kern County, 1875, in Hand-book and Directory of San Luis Obispo . . . *see* p. 21.

History of Kern County . . . San Francisco: W.W. Elliott, 1883. [Repr. Bakersfield: Kern County Hist. Soc., 1965.] 226 pp. (Also bound with Tulare County, with different pagination.)

Memorial . . . of Kern County, 1892, *see* Fresno County.

History of Kern County . . . with Biographical Sketches . . . History, by Wallace M. Morgan . . . Los Angeles: Hist. Record Co., 1914. 1,556 pp.

History of Kern County . . . by Thelma B. Miller. 2 vols. Chicago: S.J. Clarke Pub. Co., 1929.

Where Rolls the Kern: a History of Kern County, California, by Herbert G. Comfort. Moorpark: Enterprise Pr., 1934. 241 pp.

Pioneer Days in Kern County, by Arthur S. Crites. Los Angeles: W. Ritchie Pr., 1951. 279 pp.

Early Days in Kern, by Eugene Burmeister. Bakersfield: Cardon House [1963]. 78 pp.

## Kings County

History of . . . Kings County, 1913, *see* Tulare County.

History of Kings County, California, by Kathleen E. Small. 2 vols. Chicago: S.J. Clarke Pub. Co., 1926.

History of Kings County, by Robert R. Brown. Hanford: A.H. Cawston, 1940. 385 pp.

The Story of Kings County, California, by J.L. Brown. Berkeley: Lederer, Street & Zeus Co., 1942. 126 pp.

## Lake County

Historical . . . Sketch Book of . . . Lake County, 1873, *see* Napa County.

Hand-book and Directory of . . . Lake County, 1874, in Hand-book . . . of Napa, *see* p. 21.

History of . . . Lake County, 1881, *see* Napa County.

History of . . . Lake County, 1914, *see* Mendocino County.

Your Lakes and Valleys and Mountains: History of Lake County, by Henry K. Mauldin, ed. by Ben S. Allen. San Francisco: East Wind Pr., 1960. Vol. 1 (no more pub.?).

## Lassen County

Illustrated History of . . . Lassen County, 1882, *see* Plumas County.

Fairfield's Pioneer History of Lassen County . . . 1870 . . . by Asa M. Fairfield. San Francisco: Author, 1916. xxii, 506 pp. (Index, comp. by Lassen County Free Lib. [Susanville], 1923. 62 leaves.)

## Los Angeles County

Hand-book and Directory of . . . Los Angeles County, 1875, in Hand-book and Directory of San Luis Obispo . . . *see* p. 21.

An Historical Sketch of Los Angeles County, California, from the Spanish Occupancy . . . 1771 to 1876 [by Juan J. Warner. Los Angeles: L. Lewin, 1876]. 88 pp. (Repr. Los Angeles: O.W. Smith, 1936. 159 pp. Added intro. by J.P. Widney.)

History of Los Angeles County . . . [by John A. Wilson]. Oakland: Thompson & West, 1880. 192 pp. (Repr. Berkeley: Howell-North Books, 1959. 192 pp.)

An Illustrated History of Los Angeles County . . . Chicago: Lewis Pub. Co., 1889. 835 pp.

Historical and Biographical Records of Los Angeles and Vicinity . . . by James M. Guinn. Chicago: Chapman Pub. Co., 1901. 940 pp.

Ingersoll's Century History, Santa Monica Bay Cities . . . [and] a Condensed History of Los Angeles County, 1542-1908 . . . Los Angeles: Ingersoll, 1908. 512 pp.

A History of California and an Extensive History of Los Angeles and Environs . . . [by James M. Guinn]. 3 vols. Los Angeles: Hist. Record Co., 1915.

Historical Record Souvenir, Los Angeles County, by Los Angeles County Pioneer Society. Los Angeles: Times Mirror Pr., 1923. 283 pp.

History of Los Angeles County, ed. by John S. McGroarty. 2 vols. Chicago: American Hist. Soc., 1923. (and The County of Los Angeles, by J.S. McGroarty. Chicago: American Hist. Soc., 1923. 183 pp.)

History and Reminiscences, Los Angeles City and County . . . comp. by William A. Spalding. 3 vols. Los Angeles: J.R. Finnell Pub. Co. [1931].

## Madera County

History of . . . Madera County, 1933, *see* Fresno County.

Madera, the Rich, Colorful and Exciting Historical Heritage of That Area Now Known as Madera County, California, by Charles W. Clough. [Madera: N.p., 1968.] 96 pp.

## Marin County

History of Marin County . . . by J.P. Munro-Fraser. San Francisco: Alley, Bowen & Co., 1880. 516 pp.

*Marin County (cont.)*

Early Marin, by Jack Mason. [Petaluma: House Pr., 1971.] xii, 212 pp.

Discovering Marin; Historical Tour by Cities and Towns, by Louise Teather. Fairfax: A. Philpott, 1974. 128 pp.

The Making of Marin (1850-1975), by Jack Mason. (Marin Co. Historical Society.) Inverness: North Shore Books [1975]. 217 pp.

## Mariposa County

Memorial . . . of County of Mariposa, 1892, in Memorial and Biographical History . . . of Merced, *see* p. 21.

California's Agua Fría; the Early History of Mariposa County, by Raymund F. Wood. Fresno: Academy Lib. Guild, 1954. 112 pp.

## Mendocino County

Historical . . . Sketch Book of Mendocino County, 1873, in Historical and Descriptive Sketch Book of Napa, *see* p. 21.

Hand-book and Directory of . . . Mendocino County, in Hand-book and Directory of Napa, *see* p. 21.

History of Mendocino County . . . by Lyman L. Palmer. San Francisco: Alley, Bowen, 1880. 676 pp. (Repr. [N.p.: Mendocino County Hist. Soc., 1967.] xviii, 799 pp.)

History of Mendocino and Lake Counties . . . History, by Aurelius O. Carpenter. Los Angeles: Hist. Record Co., 1914. 1,045 pp.

## Merced County

History of Merced County . . . San Francisco: Elliott & Moore, 1881. 232 pp. (Repr. Fresno: California Hist. Books, 1974.)

Memorial . . . of County of . . . Merced, 1892, in Memorial and Biographical History of . . . Merced, *see* p. 21.

History of Merced County, California, by John Outcalt. Los Angeles: Hist. Record Co., 1925. 913 pp.

History of Merced County, by Corwin Radcliffe. Merced: A.H. Cawston, 1940. 414 pp.

## Modoc County

California Northeast, the Bloody Ground, by William S. Brown. [Oakland: Bio-books, 1951.] xiv, 207 pp. [Annals of Modoc.]

## Mono County

The Story of Early Mono County . . . by Elia M. Cain. San Francisco: Fearon Pub., 1961. 166 pp.

## Monterey County

Handbook and Directory of . . . Monterey County, 1875, in Handbook and Directory of Santa Clara, *see* p. 21.

History of Monterey County [by James M. Guinn]. San Francisco: Elliott and Moore, 1881. (Repr. Prescott, Ariz.: Magee Pubs., 1983. 296 pp.; also bound with San Benito, 1881, with different pagination, 1983.)

Memorial . . . of Monterey County, 1893, in Memorial and Biographical History of the Coast Counties . . . *see* p. 21.

History and Biographical Record of Monterey and San Benito Counties . . . by J.M. Guinn. 2 vols. Los Angeles: Hist. Record Co., 1910. 764 pp.

History of Monterey, Santa Cruz, and San Benito Counties, ed. by Rolin G. Watkins and M.F. Hoyle. 2 vols. Chicago: S.J. Clarke Pub. Co., 1925.

Monterey, the Presence of the Past, by Augusta Fink. San Francisco: Chronicle Books [1972]. 254 pp.

History of Monterey County, California. Fresno: Valley Pubs., 1979. 197 pp.

## Napa County

Historical and Descriptive Sketch Book of Napa, Sonoma, Lake, and Mendocino Counties . . . by Campbell A. Menefee. Napa City: Reporter Pub. House, 1873. 356 pp. (Repr. Fresno: California Hist. Books, n.d.)

Hand-book and Directory of Napa, Lake, Sonoma and Mendocino Counties . . . by Luther L. Paulson. San Francisco: Author, 1874. xvi, 296 pp.

History of Napa and Lake Counties, by Lyman L. Palmer. San Francisco: Slocum, Bowen & Co., 1881. xvi, 600, 291 pp. (Repr. Fresno: Valley Pubs., 1974.)

History of Napa County . . . comp. by Tilliel Kanaga. [Oakland: Enquirer Pr., 1901.] 372 pp.

History of . . . Napa County, 1912, *see* Solano County.

Napa County, by H.L. Gunn. 2 vols. Chicago: J.S. Clarke Pub. Co., 1926. (Also pub. as History of Solano County, by Marguerite Hunt, and Napa County, by Harry L. Gunn.)

## Nevada County

Bean's History and Directory of Nevada County, California . . . comp. by Edwin F. Bean. Nevada: Daily Gazette Book & Job Office, 1867. 423 pp.

History of Nevada County, California . . . [by Harry L. Wells]. Oakland: Thompson & West, 1880. 234 pp. (Repr. Berkeley: Howell-North Books, 1970.)

History of . . . Nevada County, 1924, *see* Placer County.

## Orange County

Illustrated History of County of Orange, 1890, in Illustrated History of Southern California, *see* p. 21.

History of Orange County . . . Samuel Armor, supervising ed. Los Angeles: Hist. Record Co., 1911. 705 pp. (Rev. ed. Los Angeles: Hist. Record Co., 1921. 1,669 pp.)

History of Orange County, California, by Adalina B. Pleasants. 3 vols. Los Angeles: J.R. Finnel & Sons Pub. Co., 1931.

The Historical Volume and Reference Works: Orange County, ed. by Thomas T. Talbert. 3 vols. Whittier: Hist. Pub., 1963.

Orange County Through Four Centuries, by Leo J. Friis. Santa Ana: Pioneer Pr., 1965. xi, 225 pp.

Orange County Under Spain, Mexico and the U.S., by Don Meadows. Los Angeles: Dawson's Book Shop, 1966. 344 pp.

Rawhide and Orange Blossoms: Stories and Sketches of Early Orange County. Santa Ana: Pioneer Pr., 1967. xi, 359 pp.

## Placer County

Directory of the County of Placer for 1861; containing a History of the County . . . comp. by R.J. Steele, et al. San Francisco: C.F. Robbins, 1861. 208 pp.

History of Placer County, by Myron Angel and M.D. Fairchild. Oakland: Thompson & West, 1882. 436 pp.

History of Placer and Nevada Counties . . . by William B. Lardner and M.J. Brook. Los Angeles: Hist. Record Co., 1924. 1,225 pp.

## Plumas County

Illustrated History of Plumas, Lassen & Sierra Counties, with California from 1513 to 1850. San Francisco: Fariss & Smith, 1882. 507 pp. (Repr. Berkeley: Howell-North Books, 1971. 507 pp.)

## Riverside County

Riverside Community Book, by Arthur G. Paul. Riverside: A.H. Cawston, 1854. 496 pp.

History and Directory of Riverside County, 1893-94, by A.A. Byron & Son. Riverside: Riverside Daily Pr. Job Office, 1893. 152, 189 pp.

History of Riverside County, California . . . History, by Elmer W. Holmes. Los Angeles: Hist. Record Co., 1912. xii, 783 pp.

History of . . . Riverside County, 1922, *see* San Bernardino County.

History of Riverside City and County, by John R. Gabbert. Phoenix, Ariz.: Riverside (Calif.) Record Pub. Co., 1935. 615 pp.

## Sacramento County

History of Sacramento County . . . [ed. by George F. Wright]. Oakland: Thompson & West, 1880. 294 pp. (Repr. Berkeley: Howell-North Books, 1960.)

An Illustrated History of Sacramento County . . . by Winfield J. Davis. Chicago: Lewis Pub. Co., 1890. vii, 808 pp.

History of Sacramento County . . . History, by William L. Willis. Los Angeles: Hist. Record Co., 1913. xiv, 1,056 pp.

History of Sacramento County . . . ed. by G. Walter Reed. Los Angeles: Hist. Record Co., 1923. 1,004 pp.

## San Benito County

Handbook . . . of San Benito County, 1875, in Handbook and Directory Santa Clara, *see* p. 21.

History of San Benito County . . . San Francisco: Elliott & Moore, 1881. 188 pp. (Also bound with Monterey, 1881, but with different pagination.)

Memorial . . . of County of San Benito, 1893, in Memorial and Biographical History of the Coast Counties of Central California, *see* p. 21.

Historical . . . Record of . . . San Benito County, 1910, *see* Monterey County.

History of . . . San Benito County, 1925, *see* Monterey County.

## San Bernardino County

Hand-book . . . of San Bernardino County, 1875, in Hand-book and Directory of San Luis Obispo, *see* p. 21.

History of San Bernardino County . . . San Francisco: W.W. Elliott, 1883. 229 pp. (Repr. of History of San Bernardino and San Diego Counties . . . 1883. Includes material on present-day Riverside County. Riverside: Riverside Museum Pr., 1965. 204 pp.)

Illustrated History of . . . San Bernardino County, 1890, in Illustrated History of Southern California . . . *see* p. 21.

Ingersoll's Century Annals of San Bernardino County, 1769 to 1904 . . . by Luther A. Ingersoll. Los Angeles: Author, 1904. xxii, 887 pp. (Index to names, comp. by Mary L. Lewis. San Bernardino: N.p. [1967?]. 58 leaves.)

History of San Bernardino and Riverside Counties, by John Brown, Jr. and James Boyd. 3 vols. [Madison, Wis.:] Western Hist. Assoc., 1922. 1,538 pp.

Heritage of the Valley: San Bernardino's First Century . . . by George W. Beattie and H.L. Beattie. Pasadena: San Pasqual Pr., 1939. 459 pp. (Repr. Oakland: Biobooks, 1951.)

Raising the Dust, as Told to C. Hemphill-Gobar, by Julian S. Gobar. St. George, Utah: N.p., 1969. 374 pp.

Saga of the San Bernardinos, by Pauliena B. LaFuze. 2 vols. [Bloomington:] San Bernardino County Museum Assoc. [1971].

# San Diego County

Hand-book . . . of San Diego County, 1875, in Hand-book and Directory of San Luis Obispo . . . *see* p. 21.

History of San Diego County, California . . . San Francisco: W.W. Elliott, 1883. 204. pp. (Repr. History of San Bernardino and San Diego Counties, 1965.)

San Diego and Imperial Counties, California; a Record of Settlement . . . ed. by Samuel T. Black. 2 vols. Chicago: S.J. Clarke Pub. Co., 1913. (Compilation of data, much of which appears in Smythe's . . . History of San Diego, Vol. 2.)

The City and County of San Diego . . . [by Theodore S. Van Dyke]. [San Diego: Leberthon & Taylor, 1888.] 218 pp.

Illustrated History of . . . County of San Diego, 1890, in Illustrated History of Southern California . . . *see* p. 21.

City of San Diego and San Diego County . . . by Clarence A. McGrew. 2 vols. Chicago: American Hist. Assoc., 1922.

History of San Diego, by W. Davidson, Historian . . . San Diego: San Diego Pr. Club, 1936. 479, 314 pp.

# San Francisco County

The Annals of San Francisco . . . by Frank Soule, et al. New York: D. Appleton & Co., 1855. 824 pp. (Index, comp. under the direction of Charles F. Griffin. San Francisco: California Hist. Soc., 1935. 22 pp.; Index, ed. by Joseph Gaer. [San Francisco, 1935.] 96 pp.)

The Colonial History of . . . San Francisco . . . by John W. Dwinelle. San Francisco: Towne and Bacon, 1863. 102, 115 pp. ([2d ed.] San Diego: Frye & Smith, n.d. 124, 115 pp.; 3d ed. San Francisco: Towne & Bacon, 1866. 106, 391 pp.; 4th ed. San Francisco: Towne & Bacon, 1867. 34, 106, 365, 391 pp.)

San Francisco, a History of the Pacific Coast Metropolis, by John P. Young. 2 vols. San Francisco: Clatle [1912].

History of the San Francisco Bay Region . . . History and Biography . . . by Bailey Millard. 3 vols. San Francisco: American Hist. Soc., 1924.

The History of San Francisco . . . by Lewis F. Byington. 3 vols. Chicago: S.J. Clarke Pub. Co., 1931.

The Annals of San Francisco, comp. by Dorothy H. Harding. San Francisco: California Hist. Soc., 1939. Vol. 1 (no more pub.). (In the form of a continuation of Soule, 1855, above.)

# San Joaquin County

History of San Joaquin County, California, by Frank T. Gilbert. Oakland: Thompson & West, 1879. 142 pp. (Repr. Berkeley: Howell-North Books, 1968. 142 pp. Repr. also, 1973.)

An Illustrated History of San Joaquin County, California . . . Chicago: Lewis Pub. Co., 1890. 666 pp.

*San Joaquin County (cont.)*

The Counties of San Joaquin and Tuolumne in California . . . Stockton: N.p. [1902?].

History of San Joaquin County . . . by George H. Tinkham. Los Angeles: Hist. Record Co., 1923. 1,640 pp.

## San Luis Obispo County

Hand-book and Directory of San Luis Obispo . . . 1875, *see* p. 21.

History of San Luis Obispo County . . . by Myron Angel. Oakland: Thompson & West, 1883. 391 pp. (Repr. Berkeley: Howell-North Books, 1966. 391 pp.)

Memorial . . . of the County of San Luis Obispo . . . 1891, in Memorial and Biographical History of the Counties of Santa Barbara . . . *see* p. 21.

History of . . . San Luis Obispo County, 1917, *see* Santa Barbara County.

History of San Luis Obispo County and Its Environs . . . by Annie L. Morrison. Los Angeles: Hist. Record Co., 1917. 1,038 pp.

History of San Luis Obispo County, Its People and Resources, ed. by Christian N. Jesperson. [Los Angeles?:] H.M. Meier, 1939. 318 pp.

## San Mateo County

Handbook and Directory of . . . San Mateo County, 1875, *see* Santa Clara County.

Moore and DePue's Illustrated History of San Mateo County . . . San Francisco: G.T. Brown, 1878. 109 pp. (Repr. Woodside: G. Richards Pubs. [1974]. xii, 44 pp. 79 leaves.)

History of San Mateo County . . . San Francisco: B.F. Alley, 1883. 322 pp.

Memorial . . . of San Mateo County, 1893, in Memorial and Biographical History of the Coast Counties of Central California, *see* p. 21.

History of San Mateo County . . . comp. by Philip W. Alexander and C.P. Hamm. Burlingame: Burlingame Pub. Co., 1916. 204 pp.

History of San Mateo County . . . by Roy W. Cloud. 2 vols. Chicago: S.J. Clarke Pub. Co., 1928. (Index to the Chronology and County Events . . . San Mateo: N.p., 1939. 17 leaves.)

History of San Mateo County, by Frank M. Stanger. Narrative and Biographical . . . San Mateo: San Mateo Times, 1938. 425 pp.

Peninsula Community Book (San Mateo County) . . . N.p.: Cawston, 1946. 406 pp.

South from San Francisco, San Mateo County, California; Its History . . . by Frank M. Stanger. [San Mateo: San Mateo County Hist. Assoc., 1963.] 214 pp.

# Santa Barbara County

Hand-book . . . of Santa Barbara County, 1875, in Hand-book and Directory of San Luis Obispo . . . *see* p. 21.

History of Santa Barbara County . . . [by Jesse D. Mason]. Oakland: Thompson & West, 1883. 477 pp. (Repr. Berkeley: Howell-North Books, 1961. 477 pp.)

A Memorial and Biographical History of Santa Barbara, San Luis Obispo and Ventura . . . by Mrs. Yda A. Storke. Chicago: Lewis Pub. Co., 1891. 677 pp.

History of Santa Barbara, San Luis Obispo and Ventura Counties, California, by Charles M. Gidney, et al. 2 vols. Chicago: Lewis Pub. Co., 1917.

History of Santa Barbara County, California, by Michael J. Phillips. 2 vols. Chicago: S.J. Clarke Pub. Co., 1927.

History of Santa Barbara County, California, ed. by Owen H. O'Neill. Santa Barbara: H.M. Meier, 1939. 415, 496 pp.

# Santa Clara County

Handbook and Directory of Santa Clara, San Benito, Santa Cruz, Monterey, and San Mateo Counties . . . comp. by Luther L. Paulson. San Francisco: Compiler, 1875. 455 pp.

History of Santa Clara County . . . by J.P. Munro-Fraser. San Francisco: Alley, Bowen, 1881. 798 pp.

Pen Pictures from the Garden of the World, or Santa Clara County . . . Containing the History of Santa Clara County . . . ed. by H.S. Foote. Chicago: Lewis Pub. Co., 1888. 672 pp.

Santa Clara County and Its Resources; Historical . . . [San Jose: San Jose Mercury Pub. & Pr. Co., 1895.] 319 pp. (Repr. [San Jose:] N.p., 1896. 322 pp.)

History of Santa Clara County . . . History, by Eugene T. Sawyer. Los Angeles: Hist. Record Soc., 1922. 1,692 pp.

The Santa Clara County Book, by Nancy Fox and Ed Fox. [Los Altos:] Tafnews [1973]. 159 pp.

# Santa Cruz County

Handbook . . . of Santa Cruz County, 1875, *see* Santa Clara County.

Santa Cruz County, California . . . with Historical Sketch of the County. San Francisco: W.W. Elliott, 1879. 102 pp.

History of Santa Cruz County . . . by Edward S. Harrison. San Francisco: Pacific Press Pub. Co., 1892. 379 pp.

Memorial . . . of . . . County of Santa Cruz, 1893, in Memorial and Biographical History of the Coast Counties of Central California, *see* p. 21.

History of Santa Cruz County . . . History, by Edward Martin. Los Angeles: Hist. Record Co., 1911. 357 pp.

*Santa Cruz County (cont.)*

History of . . . Santa Cruz County, 1925, *see* Monterey County.

Annals of Santa Cruz, by Leon Rowland. Santa Cruz: [Branson Pub. Co., 1947.] 155 pp.

## Shasta County

The History and Business Directory of Shasta County, Comprising an Accurate Sketch of the County . . . comp. by B.F. Frank. Redding: Redding Independent Book & Job Pr. House [1881]. 180 pp.

Shasta County, California, a History, by Rosena A. Giles. Oakland: Biobooks, 1949. 301 pp.

In the Shadow of the Mountain: a Short History of Shasta County . . . by Edward Petersen. [Cottonwood?: N.p., 1965.] 183 pp.

## Sierra County

Illustrated History of . . . Sierra County, 1882, *see* Plumas County.

## Siskiyou County

History of Siskiyou County . . . [by H.L. Wells]. Oakland: D.J. Stewart, 1881. 218 pp.

## Solano County

History of Solano County [by J.P. Munro-Fraser]. San Francisco: Wood, Alley & Co., 1879. 503 pp.

History of Solano and Napa Counties . . . History, by Thomas J. Gregory. Los Angeles: Hist. Record Co., 1912. xiv, 1,044 pp.

History of Solano County, California, by Marguerite Hunt; and Napa County, by Harry L. Gunn. 2 vols. Chicago: Clarion Pub. Co., 1926.

## Sonoma County

Historical . . . Sketch Book of . . . Sonoma County, 1873, *see* Napa County.

Hand-book . . . of Sonoma County, 1874, *see* Napa County.

Historical and Descriptive Sketch of Sonoma County, California, by Robert A. Thompson. Philadelphia: L.H. Everts, 1877. 104 pp.

History of Sonoma County . . . [by J.P. Munro-Fraser]. San Francisco: Alley, Bowen, 1880. 717 pp.

An Illustrated History of Sonoma County . . . Chicago: Lewis Pub. Co., 1889. xiii, 737 pp.

*Sonoma County (cont.)*

History of Sonoma County . . . History, by Thomas J. Gregory. Los Angeles: Hist. Record Co., 1911. xv, 1,112 pp. (Same ed. without biographical section. N.d. 251 pp.)

History of Sonoma County, by Honoria R.P. Tuomey. 2 vols. Chicago: S.J. Clarke Pub. Co., 1926. 1,742 pp.

History of Sonoma County, California, Its People, Resources, ed. by Ernest L. Finley. Santa Rosa: Press Democrat Pub. Co., 1937. 453, 384 pp.

## Stanislaus County

History of Stanislaus County, California. San Francisco: Elliott & Moore, 1881. 254 pp. (Index, ed. by J. Carlyle Parker. [Turlock: Stanislaus State Coll. Lib., 1970.] 23 leaves. Repr. Evansville, Ind.: Unigraphic, 1974. Repr. Fresno: Valley Pubs., 1974.)

Memorial . . . of the County of Stanislaus, 1892, in Memorial and Biographical History of the Counties of Merced . . . *see* p. 21.

History of Stanislaus County . . . by George H. Tinkham. Los Angeles: Hist. Record Co., 1921. 1,495 pp.

Stories of Stanislaus; a Collection of Stories on the History . . . of Stanislaus County, by Solomon P. Elias. [Los Angeles: N.p., 1924.] 344 pp.

## Sutter County

History of Sutter County . . . [by William H. Chamberlain and H.L. Wells]. Oakland: Thompson & West, 1879. 127 pp. (Repr. Berkeley: Howell-North Books, 1974. 127 pp.)

History of . . . Sutter County, 1924, *see* Yuba County.

## Tehama County

Tehama County . . . San Francisco: Elliott & Moore, 1880. 166 pp. (Repr. Fresno: California Hist. Books, 1975.)

## Trinity County

The Annals of Trinity County, by Isaac Cox. San Francisco: Commercial Book & Job Steam Pr., 1858. 206 pp. (San Francisco eds. by James W. Bartlett. Weaverville, 1926 and 1940. 265, 283 pp.; Eugene, Ore.: printed for Harold C. Holmes by J.H. Nash. Univ. of Oregon Pr., 1940. 265 pp.)

## Tulare County

History of Tulare County . . . San Francisco: W.W. Elliott, 1883. 226 pp. (Repr. Fresno: California Hist. Books, 1975; also bound with Kern, 1883, but with different pagination.)

*Tulare County (cont.)*

Memorial . . . of County of Tulare, 1892, in Memorial and Biographical History of the Counties of Fresno . . . *see* p. 21.

History of Tulare and Kings Counties, California . . . History, by Eugene L. Menefee and Fred A. Dodge. Los Angeles: Hist. Record Co. [1913]. 890 pp.

History of Tulare County . . . by Kathleen E. Small; and Kings County . . . by J. Larry Smith. 2 vols. Chicago: S.J. Clarke Pub. Co., 1926.

A Modern History of Tulare County, by Annie R. Mitchell. Visalia: Ltd. Eds. of Visalia [1974]. 203 pp.

## Tuolumne County

A History of Tuolumne County . . . [by Herbert O. Lang?]. San Francisco: B.F. Alley, 1882. xi, 509, 48 pp. (Repr. Berkeley: Howell-North Books, 1940. Repr. Sonora: Tuolumne County Hist. Soc., 1960 and 1973.)

Memorial . . . of the County of . . . Tuolumne, 1892, in Memorial and Biographical History of the Counties of Merced . . . *see* p. 21.

County of . . . Tuolumne County, 1902?, *see* San Joaquin County.

The Saga of Old Tuolumne, by Edna B. Buckbee. New York: Pr. of the Pioneers, 1935. x, 526 pp.

Annals of Tuolumne, by Thomas R. Stoddart, with . . . index, by Carlo N. De Ferreri. [Sonora: Mother Lode Pr., Tuolumne County Hist. Soc., 1963.] 188 pp.

## Ventura County

Hand-book . . . of Ventura County, 1875, in Hand-book and Directory of San Luis Obispo . . . *see* p. 21.

History of . . . Ventura County, 1883, *see* Santa Barbara County.

Memorial . . . of the County of . . . Ventura, 1891, *see* Santa Barbara County.

History of . . . Ventura County, 1917, *see* Santa Barbara County.

History of Ventura County, California, by Solomon N. Sheridan. 2 vols. Chicago: S.J. Clarke Pub. Co., 1926. 1,034 pp.

History of Ventura County, by Elizabeth K. Ritter, ed. by E.M. Sheridan and M. Windsor. Los Angeles: H. McL. Meier, 1940. 403 pp.

## Yolo County

The Illustrated Atlas and History of Yolo County . . . 1825 to 1880 . . . [San Francisco:] De Pue & Co., 1879. iv, 105 pp.

History of Yolo County . . . History, by Thomas J. Gregory, et al. Los Angeles: Hist. Record Co. [1913]. xii, 889 pp.

History of Yolo County . . . by Nelle S. Coil, et al.; ed. by William O. Russell. Woodland: N.p., 1940. 573 pp.

# Yuba County

History of Yuba County . . . [by William H. Chamberlain and H.L. Wells]. Oakland: Thompson & West, 1879. 150 pp.

History of Yuba and Sutter Counties, by Peter J. Delay. Los Angeles: Hist. Record Co., 1924. 1,328 pp.

# COLORADO

## Regional

History of Clear Creek and Boulder Valleys, Containing . . . a History of Gilpin, Clear Creek, Boulder, and Jefferson Counties, and Biographical Sketches . . . Chicago: O.L. Baskin, 1880. 713 pp. (Index, by Sanford C. Gladden. [Boulder: Empire Reproduction and Pr. Co., 1970.] 37 pp.)

## Adams County

History of Adams County, Brighton and Fort Lupton, Colorado. Brighton: N.p., 1959? 34 pp.

## Arapahoe County

History of the City of Denver, Arapahoe County and Colorado . . . Chicago: O.L. Baskin, 1880. 652 pp. (Repr. D.A.R. Mount Rosa Chapter. Littleton: The Chapter, 1976. 652 pp.)

## Baca County

A History of Early Baca County . . . by J.R. Austin. N.p.: Author, 1936. 54 leaves.

A History of Baca County, by James H. Hill. Greeley: State College of Education, 1941. xviii, 215 leaves. (M.A. thesis)

A Place Called Baca, by Ike Osteen. Chicago: Adams Pr., 1980. 202 pp.

## Bent County

Historic Old Bent County, by Ruth R. Lytle. Denver: Univ. of Denver, 1931. 247 pp. (M.A. thesis)

The History of Bent County, Colorado, by Hugh M. Warren. Greeley: State College of Education, 1939. xxix, 197 pp. (M.A. thesis)

Bent County Pioneers, comp. by Jennie E. Stewart. Boulder: D.A.R., Colorado, Arapahoe Chapter, 1946-48. 219 pp.

## Boulder County

Boulder . . . County History, 1880, in History of Clear Creek and Boulder Valleys . . . see above.

## Chaffee County

A History of Chaffee County, comp. and ed. by June Shaputi and S. Kelly. Buena Vista: Buena Vista Heritage, 1982. 285 pp.

## Cheyenne County

Cheyenne County History. Cheyenne Wells: Eastern Colorado Hist. Soc., 1979. 432 pp.

## Clear Creek County

Clear Creek and Boulder County History, 1880, in History of Clear Creek and Boulder Valleys . . . *see* p. 38.

Annals of Clear Creek County, by Jesse S. Randall. 5 parts. Georgetown: Courier, n.d.

## Custer County

Custer County History, 1879, *see* Fremont County.

## Douglas County

A History of Douglas County, 1820-1910, by Anne Moore. Denver: Univ. of Denver, 1970. viii, 143 leaves. (M.A. thesis)

## Eagle County

A Descriptive History of Eagle County, Colorado . . . by William McCabe. Red Cliff: N.p., 1899. 63 pp.

Eagle County History, by Eagle County School Children and Teachers. Eagle: N.p., 194?, various paging.

## Elbert County

Biographies and History of Elbert County, by Students of Elbert County, comp. by Esther Carson. Elbert: N.p., 1971.

Western Pioneer Days: Biographies and Genealogies of Early Settlers, with History of Elbert County, Colorado, by Ethel R. Corbett. [Denver:] Author [1974]. xvii, 354 pp.

## Fremont County

Historical and Descriptive of Fremont and Custer Counties . . . Canon City: Binckley & Hartwell, 1879. 136 pp.

From Trappers to Tourists: Fremont County, Colorado, 1830-1950, by Rosemae (Wells) Campbell. Palmer Lake: Filter Pr., 1972. viii, 244 pp.

## Garfield County

Garfield County, Colorado, the First Hundred Years, 1883-1983, by Andrew Gulliford. Carbondale: C.R. Lilly, 1983. 46 pp.

## Gilpin County

Gilpin County History, 1880, in History of Clear Creek and Boulder Valleys . . . see p. 38.

Early Records of Gilpin County, Colorado, 1859-1861, ed. by Thomas M. Marshall. Boulder: N.p., 1920. xvi, 313 pp.

## Grand County

History of Grand County, Colorado, by R.C. Cohig. Denver: Univ. of Denver, 1939. 174 pp. (M.A. thesis)

Island in the Rockies: the History of Grand County, Colorado, to 1930, by Robert C. Black, III. Boulder: Pruett Pub. Co., 1969. 435 pp.

## Gunnison County

Gunnison County, by Betty Wallace [pseud. for Elizabeth V. Wallace]. Denver: Sage Books [1960]. 208 pp.

History with the Hide Off, by Betty Wallace [i.e. Elizabeth V. Wallace]. Denver: Sage Books [1964]. 276 pp. (Repr. in 1965 and 1966.)

Your Passport to the Gunnison Country; a Potpourri of Past and Present, by Charles A. Page. Gunnison: Page Books [1973]. 84 pp.

## Hinsdale County

Tiny Hinsdale of the Silvery San Juan, by Carolyn Wright and C. Wright. [Denver:] Big Mountain Pr. [1964]. 196 pp.

## Jackson County

History of Jackson County, Colorado . . . by Adah B. Bailey. [Walden: Jackson County Star, 1946.]

## Jefferson County

Jefferson County . . . History, 1880, in History of Clear Creek and Boulder Valleys . . . see p. 38.

History of Jefferson County, Colorado, by Ethel Dark. Greeley: State College of Education, 1939. xxiv, 253 pp. (M.A. thesis)

Jefferson County, Colorado, the Colorful Past of a Great Community, by Sara E. Robbins. Lakewood: Jefferson County Bank, 1962. 84 pp.

# Kiowa County

Kiowa County, by Roleta D. Teal. N.p.: Kiowa's County Bicentennial Comm., 1976. 432 pp.

# Lake County

History of Lake County, by R.G. Hill. (In Baskin's Arkansas Valley, Colorado. 1881. pp. 207- 414.)

# Larimer County

History of Larimer County, Colorado, collated and comp. by Ansel Watrous. Fort Collins: Courier Pr. & Pub. Co., 1911. 513 pp.

# Las Animas County

All About Trinidad and Las Animas County, Colorado; Their History . . . by Michael Beshoar. Denver: Times Pr. House, 1882. iv, 118 pp.

# Lincoln County

Where the Wagons Rolled: the History of Lincoln County . . . Before 1925, by Dale Cooley. Hugo: Lincoln County Hist. Soc., 1976.

# Logan County

A Brief History of Logan County, Colorado . . . by Emma B. Conklin. [Sterling: Elbridge Gerry Chapter, D.A.R., 1928.] 354 pp.

Where the Buffalo Roamed: an Historical Pageant of Logan County, Colorado, by Lela N. Brown. Denver: Univ. of Denver, 1949. 153 pp.

# Mesa County

History and Business Directory of Mesa County, Colorado . . . a Description . . . Grand Junction: Mesa County Democrat, 1886. 93 pp.

# Montezuma County

A History of Montezuma County, Colorado . . . by Ira S. Freeman. [Boulder: Johnson Pub. Co., 1958.] 323 pp.

# Park County

A History of Park County, Colorado, by Roy A. Davidson. Denver: Univ. of Denver, 1940. 168 pp. (M.A. thesis)

# Phillips County

Those Were the Days . . . Reminiscences of Early Days by Early Settlers, by Phillips County Historical Society. Holyoke: Holyoke Enterprises Pr. Co., 1973. 173 pp.

## Pueblo County

History of Pueblo County, by Pueblo Superintendent of Schools. Pueblo: N.p., 1928.

Pueblo County History, comp. by Mabel B. Bullen. Pueblo: Pueblo Chapter of D.A.R., 1939?

This Is Pueblo County, by League of Women Voters, Pueblo. Pueblo: Congress-Times Pr., 1965. 63 pp.

## Routt County

A History of Routt County, Colorado, by C. Lemont Montgomery. Greeley: State College of Education, 1938. 222 pp. (M.A. thesis)

## San Juan County

Pioneers of San Juan County . . . Durango: N.p., 1952. 192 pp.

## Sedgwick County

The History of Sedgwick County, Colorado, comp. by the Fort Sedgwick Historical Society. 2 vols. Dallas, Tex.: National ShareGraphics, 1982-83.

## Washington County

The Pioneer Book of Washington County, Colorado. Akron: Washington County Museum Assoc., 1959. 392 pp.

## Weld County

Under Ten Flags: a History of Weld County, Colorado, by Mary L. Geffs. Greeley: N.p., 1938. 318 pp.

South Platte Country; a History of Old Weld County, Colorado, 1739-1900, by Dean F. Krakel. Laramie, Wyo.: Powder River Pub., 1954. vi, 268, 47 pp. (Originally M.A. thesis, 1951. "Weld County in the Frontier Period.")

Into the Sunset, Reminiscent of Early Days [by George S. Ball]. [Greeley: Northern Weld County, 1966.] 184 pp.

Weld County Old and New: an Historical Gazetteer of Weld County, Colorado, 1836-1981, comp. and ed. by Carol R. Shwayder. Greeley: Unicorn Ventures, 1982.

# CONNECTICUT

## Regional

History of Eastern Connecticut, Embracing the Counties of Tolland, Windham, Middlesex, and New London . . . by Pliny LeR. Harwood. 3 vols. Chicago & New Haven: Pioneer Hist. Pub. Co., 1931-32.

## Fairfield County

History of Fairfield County, with Biographical Sketches . . . comp. under the supervision of D. Hamilton Hurd. Philadelphia: J.W. Lewis, 1881. 878 pp.

Leading Business Men of Fairfield County, and a Historical Review of the Principal Cities . . . Boston: Mercantile Pub. Co., 1887. 188 pp.

History of Fairfield County, Connecticut, 1639-1928, by Lynn W. Wilson. 3 vols. Chicago: S.J. Clarke Pub. Co., 1929.

## Hartford County

The Memorial History of Hartford County, 1633-1884, ed. by J. Hammond Trumbull. 2 vols. Boston: E.L. Osgood, 1886.

History of Hartford County, 1633-1928 . . . by Charles W. Burpee. 3 vols. Chicago: S.J. Clarke Pub. Co., 1928.

## Litchfield County

A Biographical History of the County of Litchfield . . . by Payne K. Kilbourne. New York: Clark, Austin & Co., 1851. 413 pp.

History of Litchfield County . . . Philadelphia: J.W. Lewis, 1881. xiii, 730 pp.

Litchfield County Sketches, by Newell M. Calhoun. Norfolk: Litchfield County View Club, 1906. 177 pp.

Rural Life in Litchfield County, by Charles S. Phelps. Norfolk: Litchfield County Univ. Club, 1917. 317 pp.

## Middlesex County

A Statistical Account of the County of Middlesex in Connecticut, by David D. Field. 1819. (Repr. Haddam: J.T. Kelsey, 1892. 186 pp.)

History of Middlesex County . . . New York: J.E. Beers, 1884. 579 pp.

History of . . . Middlesex County, 1931-32, in History of Eastern Connecticut, *see* above.

# New Haven County

Leading Business Men of New Haven County, and a Historical Review of the Principal Cities . . . [by William H. Beckford]. Boston: Mercantile Pub. Co., 1887. 270 pp.

History of New Haven County, Connecticut, ed. by J.L. Rockey. 2 vols. New York: W.W. Preston & Co., 1892.

A Modern History of New Haven and Eastern New Haven County, by Everett G. Hill. 2 vols. New York: S.J. Clarke Pub. Co., 1918.

History of New Haven County, Connecticut, by Mary H. Mitchell. 3 vols. Chicago: Pioneer Hist. Pub. Co., 1930.

# New London County

History of New London County . . . comp. under the supervision of D. Hamilton Hurd. Philadelphia: J.W. Lewis, 1882. 768 pp.

A Modern History of New London County, ed. in chief, Benjamin T. Marshall. 3 vols. New York: Lewis Hist. Pub. Co., 1922.

# Tolland County

History of Tolland County, Including Its Earliest Settlement . . . to the Present Time . . . by J.R. Cole. New York: W.W. Preston & Co., 1888. xi, 992 pp.

History of . . . Tolland County, 1931-32, in History of Eastern Connecticut, *see* p. 43.

# Windham County

History of Windham County, by Ellen D. Larned. 2 vols. Worcester, Mass.: Author, 1874-1880.

History of Windham County . . . ed. by Richard M. Bayles. New York: W.W. Preston & Co., 1889. xvi, 1,204 pp.

Historic Gleanings in Windham County, by Ellen D. Larned. Providence, R.I.: Preston & Rounds, 1899. 257 pp.

A Modern History of Windham County . . . ed. by Allen B. Lincoln. 2 vols. Chicago: S.J. Clarke Pub. Co., 1920.

History of . . . Windham County, 1931-32, in History of Eastern Connecticut, *see* p. 43.

# DELAWARE

## *Regional*

History of Delaware, 1609-1888 . . . by J. Thomas Scharf. 2 vols. Philadelphia: L.J. Richards & Co., 1888. (Repr. Port Washington, N.Y.: Kennikat Pr., 1972. 1,358 pp. Index, ed. by Gladys M. Coghlan and Dale Fields. Wilmington: Hist. Soc. of Delaware, 1976. 1,152 pp.) (Vol. 2 contains Histories of New Castle County, pp. 611-1,028; Kent County, pp. 1,028-1,200; Sussex County, pp. 1,200-1,346.)

## Kent County

[History of Kent County, 1888.] In History of Delaware, by J.T. Scharf, *see* above.

A History of Kent County, Delaware, by Harold B. Hancock. Dover: Kent County Bicentennial Comm., 1976. 72 pp.

## New Castle County

[History of New Castle County, 1888.] In History of Delaware, by J.T. Scharf, *see* above.

## Sussex County

[History of Sussex County.] In History of Delaware, by J.T. Scharf, *see* above.

The History of Sussex County, by Dick Carter. Rehoboth Beach: Community Newspapers, Inc., 1976. 72 pp.

The History of Sussex County, Delaware, by Harold B. Hancock. Georgetown, Del.: Sussex County Bicentennial Comm., 1976. 159 pp.

Folklore of Sussex County, Delaware, by Dorothy W. Pepper. Georgetown, Del.: Sussex County Bicentennial Comm., 1976. 116 pp.

# FLORIDA

## Alachua County

Alachua, the Garden County of Florida, Its Resources and Advantages. Gainesville: Alachua County Immigration Assoc. [1888]. 56 pp. ([Another ed.], by John W. Ashby. New York: South Pub. Co., 1898.)

Historic Alachua County, Florida, Narrative and Biographical, by Fritz W. Buchholz. St. Augustine: Record Co., 1929. 430 pp.

History of Alachua County 1824-1969, by Jesse G. Davis. Gainesville: N.p., 1970. 176 pp.

## Brevard County

Brief Description of Brevard County, Florida. Titusville: Star, 1889. 71 pp.

Tales of Old Brevard, by Georgiana Kjerulff. Melbourne: Kellersberg Fund, 1972. 142 pp.

## Collier County

Florida's Last Frontier; the History of Collier County, by Charlton W. Tebeau. [Coral Gables:] Univ. of Miami Pr., 1957. 260 pp. (Rev. ed., 1966. 278 pp.)

## Dade County

Dade County, by Ethan V. Blackman. Washington, D.C.: V. Rainbolt, 1921. 255 pp.

History of Dade County, Florida, by Tracy Hollingsworth. [Miami: Miami Post, 1936.] 151 pp. (Repr. Coral Gables: Glade House [1940]. 192 pp.)

## Duval County

History of Duval County, Florida, by Pleasant D. Gold. St. Augustine: Record Co., 1928. 693 pp.

## Escambia County

History of Escambia County, Narrative and Biographical, by H.C. Armstrong, et al. St. Augustine: Record Co., 1930. 483 pp.

## Gadsden County

History of Gadsden County, by J. Randall Stanley. Quincy: Gadsden County Hist. Comm., 1948. 208 pp.

# Hernando County

Brooksville and Hernando County, Florida, ed. by Mary K. Whitehurst. Brooksville: Brooksville Sun, 1936. 80 pp.

# Hillsborough County

History of Hillsborough County, Florida; Narrative and Biographical, by Ernest L. Robinson. Saint Augustine: Record Co., 1928. 424 pp.

# Jackson County

History of Jackson County, by J. Randall Stanley. [Marianna?: Jackson County Hist. Soc., 1950.] 281 pp.

# Jefferson County

History of Jefferson County, Florida, by Mary O. McRory and E.C. Barrows. Monticello: Kiwanis Club, 1958. 144 pp.

# Lake County

History of Lake County, Florida . . . ed. by William T. Kennedy. St. Augustine: Record Co., 1929. 311 pp.

# Manatee County

The Land of Manatee . . . by Morton M. Casseday. 3 vols. [New York: F. Presbrey Co., 1902.] (Reissue. [New York, 1905]. 3 vols.)

# Marion County

Ocali Country . . . a History of Marion County, Florida. Part 1, by Eloise R. Ott; Part 2, by Louis H. Chazal. [Oklawaha: Marion Pub., 1966.] 245 pp.

# Martin County

History of Martin County, comp. by Janet Hutchinson. Hutchinson Island: Martin County Hist. Soc., 1975. 419 pp.

# Monroe County

Yesterday's Florida Keys, by Stan Windhorn and W. Langley. Miami: E.A. Seamann Pub. [1974]. 128 pp.

# Orange County

Early Settlers of Orange County, by Clarence E. Howard. Orlando: Author, 1915.

History of Orange County, Florida, Narrative and Biographical, by William F. Blackman. De Land: E.O. Painter Pr. Co., 1927. 232, 208 pp. (Repr. Chuluota: Mickler House, 1973. 232, 208 pp.)

## Osceola County

History of Osceola County; Florida Frontier Life, by Minnie Moore-Willson. Florida ed. Orlando: Inland Pr., 1935. 59 pp.

## Palm Beach County

Pioneer Life in Southeast Florida, by Charles W. Pierce, ed. by D.W. Curl. Coral Gables: Univ. of Miami Pr. [1970]. 264 pp.

## Pasco County

Tales of West Pasco; Factual Stories Depicting the History . . . Covering More Than a Century . . . Hudson: A.J. Makovec, 1962. 108 pp.

## Pinellas County

History of Pinellas County, Florida, by W.L. Straub. St. Augustine: Record Co., 1929. 507 pp.

## Polk County

History of Polk County, Florida; Narrative and Biographical, by M.F. Hetherington. St. Augustine: Record Co., 1928. 379 pp. (Repr. Chuluota: Mickler House, 1971.)

## St. Lucie County

A Brief History of St. Lucie County, by Ada C. Williams. Fort Pierce: T.M. Field, 1963. 35 pp.

## Santa Rosa County

History of Santa Rosa County, a King's Country, by Martin L. King. [Milton: N.p., 1972.] xv, 140 pp.

## Suwannee County

The Story of Suwannee County, prepared by Suwannee Co. Extension Staff. [Live Oak, 1964?]. 68 pp.

## Volusia County

History of Volusia County, Florida, by Pleasant D. Gold. De Lane: E.O. Painter Pr. Co., 1927. 525 pp.

Volusia County, Past and Present, by Thomas E. Fitzgerald. Daytona Beach: Observer Pr., 1927. 222 pp.

Presenting Forty Years of Progress, 1901-1941, Volusia County, by Ianthe (Bond) Hebel. Daytona Beach: Fitzgerald Pubs., 1941. 205 pp.

Centennial History of Volusia County, Florida, 1854-1954, ed. by Ianthe (Bond) Hebel. Daytona Beach: College Pub. Co. [1955]. 205 pp.

## Walton County

History of Walton County, by John L. McKinnon. Atlanta, Ga.: Byrd Pr. Co., 1911. 389 pp.

# GEORGIA

## Appling County

Footprints in Appling County, 1818-1978, by Ruth T. Barron. Dallas, Tex.: Taylor Pub. Co., 1981. 384 pp.

## Atkinson County

Atkinson County, Georgia: a History, comp. for the Atkinson County Development Committee, by Sue K. McCranie. [Willacoochie: Author], 1966.

## Bacon County

The Alma-Bacon County Story: a Model for Rural America, by Robert E. Nipp. Washington, D.C.: Government Pr. Office, 1972. 55 pp.

## Baldwin County

History of Baldwin County, Georgia, by Mrs. Anna M.G. Cook. Anderson, S.C.: Keys-Hearn Pr. Co., 1925. 484 pp. (Repr. with new index, comp. by Mrs. Fred H. Hodges, Sr. Spartanburg, S.C.: Reprint Co., 1978. 521 pp.)

A Treasure Album of Milledgeville and Baldwin County, Georgia, by Nelle W. Hines. Macon: J.W. Burke Co., 1936. 52 pp.

History Stories of Milledgeville and Baldwin County, by Leola Beeson. Macon: J.W. Burke Co., 1943. xii, 202 pp.

Sesqui-centennial of Milledgeville and Baldwin County, Georgia, 1893-1953. Milledgeville: Old Capitol Hist. Soc., 1953.

Such Goings On, by Nelle W. Hines. (General History of Milledgeville and Baldwin County.) Macon: J.W. Burke Co., 1958. 283 pp.

## Banks County

History of Banks County, Georgia, 1858-1976, by Jessie J. Mize. Homer: Banks County Chamber of Commerce, 1977. 832 pp.

## Barrow County

Beadland to Barrow: a History of Barrow County, ed. by C. Fred Ingram. Atlanta: Cherokee Pub. Co., 1978. 427 pp.

Pictorial Review of Barrow County, by Barrow County Historical Society. Dallas, Tex.: Taylor Pub. Co. for the Hist. Soc., 1981. 240 pp.

## Bartow County

The History of Bartow County, Formerly Cass, by Lucy J. Cunyas. Cartersville: Tribune Pub. Co., 1933. xv, 343 pp. (Repr. with addenda. Easley, S.C.: Southern Hist. Pr., 1976. xvi, 404 pp.)

## Berrien County

Berrien County, 1856-1956, by Berrien County Centennial Historical Committee. Adel: Adel News, 1956. 82 pp.

History of Berrien County, by Berrien County Chamber of Commerce. Nashville, Tenn.: Nashville Pr. and Office Supply, 1979. 120 pp.

## Bibb County

The Founding Fathers of the County of Bibb and the Town of Macon, Georgia, 1823, by Eleanor D. McSwain. Macon: Author, 1977. ii, 44 pp.

## Bleckley County

History of . . . Bleckley County, 1957-58, *see* Pulaski County.

## Brooks County

The History of Brooks County, Georgia, 1858-1948, by Folks Huxford. Quitman: Hannah Clarke Chapter, D.A.R., 1948. xiii, 607 pp. (Repr. Spartanburg, S.C.: Reprint Co., 1978.)

## Bulloch County

The Story of Bulloch County, by Brooks and Leodel Coleman. Statesboro: Bulloch County Hist. Soc., 1973. 112 pp.

## Burke County

An Intelligent Student's Guide to Burke County, Georgia History, by Nell Baldwin and A.H. Hillhouse. Waynesboro: Authors, 1956. 203 pp.

## Butts County

History of Butts County, Georgia, 1825-1976, by Lois McMichael. Atlanta: Cherokee Pub. Co., 1978. 758 pp.

## Camden County

History of Camden County, Georgia, by James T. Vocelle. [Jacksonville, Fla.: Kennedy Brown-Hall Co., 1914.] 156 pp. (Repr. Kingsland: South Eastern Georgian, 1967. Repr. Ann Arbor, Mich.: Univ. Microfilms, 1970.)

Camden's Challenge: a History of Camden County, Georgia, by Marguerite Reddick. Woodbine: Camden County Hist. Comm., 1976. 606 pp.

# Carroll County

Carroll County and Her People, by Private Joe Cobb. N.p., 1907? vi, 149 pp. (Repr. N.p.: Carroll County Chamber of Commerce [1974?].)

History of Carroll County, Georgia, by Leon P. Mandeville. [Carrollton: G.F. Cheney Pub., 1910?])

Georgia's Last Frontier: the Development of Carroll County, by James C. Bonner. Athens: Univ. of Georgia Pr. [1971]. xii, 236 pp.

# Catoosa County

Official History of Catoosa County, Georgia, 1853-1953, by Susie B. McDaniel. Dalton: Gregory Pr. and Office Supply, 1953. 231 pp.

History in Catoosa County, by William H.H. Clark. [Ringgold: N.p., 1972.] vi, 298 pp.

# Charlton County

History of Charlton County, by Alex S. McQueen. Atlanta: Stein Pr. Co., 1932. 271 pp. (Repr. with new index, by Margaret H. Cannon. Spartanburg, S.C.: Reprint Co., 1978. 295 pp.)

Charlton County, Georgia: Historical Notes, 1972, Including Family Histories and Genealogies. [N.p.: Charlton County Hist. Comm., 1972.] 538 pp.

# Chattahoochee County

History of Chattahoochee County, Georgia, by Norma K. Rogers. [Columbus: Columbus Office Supply Co.], 1933. 404 pp. (Repr. with new index. Easley, S.C.: Southern Hist. Pr., 1976. Repr. Ann Arbor, Mich.: Univ. Microfilms, 1976.)

# Chattooga County

History of Chattooga County, by John H. Cook. Macon: Mercer Univ., 1931. (M.A. thesis)

# Cherokee County

The History of Cherokee County, by Rev. Lloyd G. Marlin. Atlanta: Pr. of Walter W. Brown Pub. Co. [1932]. xiii, 289 pp.

Yesterday in the Hills, by Floyd C. Watkins. Athens: Univ. of Georgia Pr., 1973. xiii, 184 pp.

# Clarke County

Clarke County, Georgia, and the City of Athens, by Charles M. Strahan. Athens: [Charles P. Byrd Pr.], 1893. 88 pp.

History of Athens and Clarke County, by Sylvanus Morris. Athens: H.J. Rowe, 1923. 180 pp.

*Clarke County (cont.)*

Survey of Athens and Clarke County, Georgia . . . 4 vols. Athens: Univ. of Georgia Pr. [1944-45].

Antebellum Athens and Clarke County, Georgia, by Ernest C. Hynds. Athens: Univ. of Georgia Pr., 1974. viii, 196 pp.

## Clay County

History of Clay County, by Priscilla N. Todd. Fort Gaines: Clay County Lib. Bd., 1976. 174 pp.

History of Clay County, Georgia, by Mrs. H.J. Sanders. Edison: N.p., 1977.

## Clayton County

Historic Clayton County: Home of "Gone With the Wind," by Terry Bakken. Jonesboro: Hist. Jonesboro, Inc., 1975. 93 pp.

History of Clayton County, Georgia, 1821-1983, ed. by Alice C. Kilgore. History, by Joseph N.N. Moore. Clayton City: Ancestors Unlimited, 1983. 697 pp.

## Clinch County

History of Clinch County, Georgia, rev. to date, Giving the Early History of the County Down to the Present Time [1916] . . . comp. and ed. by Folks Huxford. [Macon: J.W. Burke Co., 1916.] 309 pp. (Repr. Ann Arbor, Mich.: Univ. Microfilms, 1973. Repr. Homerville: Huxford Gen. Lib., 1983.)

## Cobb County

The First Hundred Years: a Short History of Cobb County in Georgia, by Sarah B.G. Temple. Atlanta: Walter W. Brown Pub. Co., 1935. xiii, 901 pp. (Repr. Covington, Va.: Cherokee Pub. Co., 1980.)

## Coffee County

Ward's History of Coffee County . . . by Warren P. Ward. [Atlanta: Pr. of Foote & Davies Co., 1930.] xiv, 354 pp. (Repr. with new index, by Margaret H. Cannon. Spartanburg, S.C.: Reprint Co., 1978. xiv, 388 pp.)

## Colquitt County

History of Colquitt County, Georgia, and Her Builders, by Mattie Coyle. Moultrie: Observer Pr., 1925. 62 pp.

History of Colquitt County, by W.A. Covington. Atlanta: Foote & Davies Co., 1937. xiv, 365 pp. (Index by Anne G. Foshee, et al. Moultrie: Colquitt-Thomas Regional Lib., 1976. 34 pp. Repr. with new index, by Anne G. Foshee. Spartanburg, S.C.: Reprint Co., 1980. 395 pp.)

## Cook County

The History of Cook County, Georgia . . . by June T. Parrish. [Adel: Adel News Pub. Co., 1968.] 132 pp.

## Coweta County

Coweta County Chronicles for 100 Years . . . ed. and comp. by Mary G. Jones and L. Reynolds for Sarah Dickinson Chapter, D.A.R. of Newnan, Georgia. Atlanta: Stein Pr. Co., 1928. xiv, 869 pp. (Repr. Easley, S.C.: Southern Hist. Pr., 1979. 888 pp.)

A History of Coweta County from 1825 to 1880, by W.U. Anderson. Newnan: Coweta Hist. Soc., 1977. 135 pp. (Index. Newnan: Coweta Hist. Soc., 1981.)

## Crawford County

History of Roberta and Crawford County, by Emmie C. Bankston. Macon: Omni Pr., 1976? 295 pp.

## Crisp County

Crisp County, Georgia Historical Sketches . . . by William P. Fleming. Vol. 1 (no more pub.). Cordele: Ham Pr. Co., 1932. 195 pp. (Repr. with new index, by Carlton J. Thaxton. Spartanburg, S.C.: Reprint Co., 1980. 228 pp.)

Crisp County's History in Pictures and Stories, by Cordele-Crisp County Historical Society. Atlanta: W.H. Wolfe Assoc., 1978. 666 pp.

## Decatur County

History of Decatur County, Georgia [by Frank S. Jones]. [N.p.: Author, 1971.] 420 pp. (Index, by Mrs. W.D. McCord. Monroe: Bainbridge S.W. Georgia Regional Lib., 1977. Repr. with new index, by Anne G. Foshee. Spartanburg, S.C.: Reprint Co., 1980. 463 pp.)

## DeKalb County

Historic DeKalb, by Percy Plant. [Decatur?: N.p., 1957.]

## Dodge County

History of Dodge County, by Mrs. Wilton P. Cobb. Atlanta: Foote & Davis Co., 1932. xiii, 256 pp. (Repr. with new index, by Margaret H. Cannon. Spartanburg, S.C.: Reprint Co., 1979. 312 pp.)

## Dooly County

Historical and Genealogical Collections of Dooly County, Georgia, comp. and ed. by Nora and Watts Powell. 3 vols. [Vienna: N.p., 1973-75.]

## Dougherty County

History and Reminiscences of Dougherty County, Georgia, comp. and ed. by Members of Thronateeska Chapter, D.A.R. Albany: [Herald Pub. Co.], 1924. xvi, 411 pp. (Repr. with new index, by Margaret H. Cannon. Spartanburg, S.C.: Reprint Co., 1978.)

# Early County

Some Pioneer History of Early County, 1818-1971, by Joel W. Perry. N.p.: Early County News, 1971. 59 pp.

Collections of Early County Historical Society, comp. by Mary G. Whitehead. 2 vols. Blakely: The Soc., 1971-79.

Early County in 1976. Blakely: Early County Hist. Soc., 1977. 118 pp.

Early Joel: on Joel Perry (Early County's first historian, and his columns, pub. in the Early County News), by Robert P. Dews. Chicago: Adams Pr., 1978. 118 pp.

# Echols County

History of Echols County, by Echols County Centennial Historical Committee, 1858-1958. N.p.: The Committee, 1958.

# Elbert County

The Official History of Elbert County, 1790-1935, by John H. McIntosh, Suppl., 1935-1939, by Stephen Heard Chapter, D.A.R. [Elberton: The Chapter, 1940.] x, 554 pp. (Repr. Atlanta: Cherokee Pub. Co., 1968.)

# Emanuel County

A Sketch of Emanuel County and Swainsboro, Georgia, by Mrs. G.A. Fountain. N.p., 1950.

Footprints Along the Hoopee: a History of Emanuel County, 1812-1900, by James E. Dorsey. Swainsboro: Emanuel County Hist. Preservation Soc., 1978. 258 pp.

# Evans County

A History of Our Locale, Mainly Evans County, Georgia, by Lucille Hodges. Macon: Southern Pr. [1965]. x, 322 pp.

# Fayette County

A Short History of Fayette County, Georgia, 1821-1877, by Francis Reeves. Inman: N.p., 1977.

History of Fayette County, 1821-1971, by Fayette County Historical Society, ed. by Carolyn C. Cary. Fayetteville: The Society, 1977. 768 pp.

# Floyd County

A History of Rome and Floyd County . . . 1540-1922 . . . by George M. Battey, Jr. Atlanta: Webb & Vary Co., 1922. 640 pp. (Repr. Dayton, Ohio: Morningside Bookshop, 1969. Repr. Covington, Va.: Cherokee Pub. Co., 1977.)

## Forsyth County

Pioneer History of Forsyth County, Georgia, by Don L. Shadburn. Sesquicentennial ed. Cumming: Forsyth Heritage Foundation, and Roswell: W.H. Wolfe Assoc., 1981. xiii, 715 pp.

## Fulton County

History of Fulton County, Georgia, Narrative and Biographical, by Lucian L. Knight. Atlanta: A.H. Cawston, 1930. 514 pp.

Official History of Fulton County, by Walter G. Cooper. [Atlanta: Walter W. Brown Pub. Co.], 1934. xvi, 912 pp. (Repr. with new index. Spartanburg, S.C.: Reprint Co., 1978.)

Fulton County Centennial, 1854-1954. Atlanta: Foote & Davies Co., 1954. 180 pp.

## Gilmer County

The Annals of Upper Georgia Centered in Gilmer County, by George G. Ward. Carrollton: Thomasson Pr. Co., 1965. viii, 692 pp.

A Little History of Gilmer County, by Lawrence L. Stanley. Ellijay: Author, 1975. viii, 215 pp.

## Glascock County

Centennial of Glascock County. Gibson: Glascock County Centennial Corp., 1957. 38 pp.

## Gordon County

History of Gordon County, Georgia, by Lulie Pitts. Calhoun: Pr. of Calhoun Times, 1933. 480 pp.

1976 Bicentennial History of Gordon County, 1830-1976, by Burton J. Bell. Calhoun: Gordon County Hist. Soc., 1976. 845 pp. [Includes repr. of Lulie Pitts' History of Gordon County, 1933.]

Stories of Gordon County and Calhoun, Georgia, by Jewell B. Reeve. Calhoun: Author, 1962. 304 pp. [Cover: Climb the Hills of Gordon.] (Repr. Easley, S.C.: Southern Hist. Pr., 1979.)

## Grady County

Grady County, Georgia, Some of Its History, by Yvonne Brunton. Vicksburg, Miss.: Author, 1979. 353 pp. (Rev. 2d ed. Danielsville: Heritage Papers, 1980.)

## Greene County

History of Greene County, Georgia, 1786-1886 . . . by Thaddeus B. Rice and C.W. Williams. Macon: J.W. Burke Co., 1961. 648 pp. (Repr. with index, by Margaret H. Cannon. Spartanburg, S.C.: Reprint Co., 1979.)

## Gwinnett County

History of Gwinnett County, 1818-1960, by James C. Flanigan. 2 vols. Vol. 1, Hapeville: Tyler & Co., 1943. 446 pp. Vol. 2, Hapeville: Longino & Porter, 1959. 629 pp. (Repr. 2 vols. in 1, Lawrenceville: Author, 1975.) )

## Hall County

Hall Through the Years, by Margaret Powell. Gainesville: W.O. Sexton Pr. Service [1968]. 150 pp.

This 'n That: History of Hall County, Georgia, by Sybil W. McRay. Vol. 1 (all pub.?). Gainesville: N.p., 1973.

## Hancock County

History of Hancock County, Georgia, by Elizabeth W. Smith and S.S. Carnes. 2 vols. Washington: Wilkes Pub. Co., 1974.

## Haralson County

Haralson County History Book, by Haralson County Historical Society. Dallas, Tex.: Taylor Pub. Co., 1983. 248 pp.

## Harris County

History of Harris County, Georgia, 1827-1961, by Louise Barfield. [Columbus: Coleman Office Supply House, 1961.] 766 pp. (Repr. Atlanta: W.H. Wolfe Assoc., 1980.)

## Hart County

History of Hart County, 1933, by John W. Baker. [Atlanta: Foote & Davies Co., 1933.] xii, 426 pp. (Surname index, by Bobbie O. Martin. Powder Springs: Author, 1980. 32 pp.)

## Henry County

Henry County, the Mother of Counties, by Vessie T. Rainer. [McDonough?: Henry County Hist. Foundation, 1971.] xxi, 374 pp.

## Houston County

A Land So Dedicated: Houston County, Georgia, by Bobbie S. Hickson. Perry: Houston County Lib. Bd., 1976. 316 pp.

First Hundred and Ten Years of Houston County, Georgia, 1822-1932. Warner Robins: Central Georgia Gen. Soc., 1983. 452 pp.

## Irwin County

History of Irwin County, by James B. Clements. [Atlanta: Foote & Davies Co., 1932.] 539 pp. (Repr. with new index, by Margaret H. Cannon. Spartanburg, S.C.: Reprint Co., 1978. 590 pp.)

## Jackson County

The Early History of Jackson County, Georgia: the Writings of the Late Gustavus J.N. Wilson . . . 1784-1914, ed. by W.E. White. [Atlanta: Foote & Davies Co., 1914.] 343 pp.

Historical Notes on Jackson County, Georgia, by Frary Elrod. [Jefferson: Author, 1967.] 243 pp.

## Jasper County

History of Jasper County. Monticello: Jasper County Hist. Foundation, 1984. 374 pp.

## Jefferson County

History of Jefferson County, by Mrs. Z.V. Thomas. Macon: Pr. of J.W. Burke Co., 1927. 144 pp. (Repr. with new index, by Margaret H. Cannon. Spartanburg, S.C.: Reprint Co., 1978. 154 pp.)

Jefferson County, Georgia, 1871-1900; a Collection of Newspaper Sources, comp. by James E. Dorsey. Swainsboro: Emanuel County Jun. Coll. Lib., 1979. 50 pp.

## Jones County

History of Jones County, Georgia, for 100 Years, 1807-1907, by Carolyn Williams. Macon: J.W. Burke Co., 1957. xxii, 103 pp. (Repr. Macon: J.W. Burke Co., 1976. Repr. with name index, by Margaret H. Stephens. Macon: Washington Memorial Lib., 1980. 214 pp.)

History of the People of Jones County, Georgia, by Frank M. Abbott. 4 vols. Macon: Lineage Unlimited, 1977.

## Lamar County

History of Lamar County [ed. by Augusta Lambdin]. Sponsored by Willie Hunt Smith Chapter, U.D.C. [Barnesville:] Barnesville News-Gazette, 1932. 516 pp. (Repr. Atlanta: William H. Wolfe Assoc., 1978. 563 pp.)

## Lanier County

Old Times Are Not Forgotten; a Story in Picture and Words of the People of Lanier County, by Lakeland-Lanier County Bicentennial Historical Committee. Lakeland: Carey Cameron Pub., 1978. 110 pp.

## Laurens County

Bird's Eye View of Dublin and Laurens County, Georgia. Dublin: Dublin and Laurens County Chamber of Commerce, 1920.

The Official History of Laurens County, Georgia, 1807-1941, by Bertha S. Hart, ed. by John Laurens Chapter, D.A.R. Dublin: The Chapter, 1941. xiii, 546 pp. (Repr. Atlanta: Cherokee Pub. Co., 1972.)

## Lee County

History of Lee County, Georgia, by Lee County Historical Society. Leesburg: The Society, 1983. 900 pp.

## Liberty County

Liberty County: a Pictorial History, by Virginia F. Evans. Statesville, N.C.: Brady Pr. Co., 1976. 176 pp. (Repr. Hinesville: Liberty County Pub. Lib., 1979.)

## Lincoln County

History of Lincoln County, Georgia, by Clinton J. Perryman. Ann Arbor, Mich.: Univ. Microfilms International, 1979. 261 pp. (Facsimile of MS. produced in 1933.)

## Lowndes County

History of Lowndes County, Georgia, 1825-1941. Valdosta: General James Jackson Chapter, D.A.R. [1942]. 407 pp. (Repr. with new index, comp. by Mrs. Fred H. Hodges, Sr. Spartanburg, S.C.: Reprint Co., 1978. 424 pp.)

Pines and Pioneers: a History of Lowndes County, Georgia, 1825-1900, by Jane T. Shelton. Atlanta: Cherokee Pub. Co., 1975. 306 pp.

A Pictorial History of Lowndes County, Georgia, 1825-1975. Valdosta: Lowndes County Hist. Soc., 1975. 80 pp.

## Lumpkin County

History of Lumpkin County for the First Hundred Years, 1832-1932, by Andrew W. Cain. Atlanta: Stein Pr. Co., 1932. 506 pp. (Repr. with new index, by Margaret H. Cannon. Spartanburg, S.C.: Reprint Co., 1978. 530 pp.)

## McDuffie County

A Handbook of History: McDuffie County, Georgia, 1870-1970, by Pearl Baker. Thomson: Progress-News Pub. Co., 1971. 238 pp.

## Macon County

History of Macon County, Georgia, by Louise F. Hays. Atlanta: Stein Pr. Co., 1933. 803 pp. (Repr. with new index. Spartanburg, S.C.: Reprint Co., 1979. 828 pp.)

History of Macon County, Georgia, by Ida Young. New York: Cholson & Hargrove, 1950. vii, 728 pp.

## Madison County

Sketches of Early History of Madison County, Georgia, by Grover H. Cartledge. Danielsville: N.p., 1967.

History of Madison County, Georgia, by Paul Tabor. N.p., 1974. 212 pp.

## Marion County

History of Marion County, Georgia, by Nettie Powell. Columbus: Hist. Pub. Co. [1931]. 178 pp.

## Meriwether County

Brooks of Honey and Butter: Plantations and People of Meriwether County, Georgia, by William H. Davidson. 2 vols. [Alexander City, Ala.: Outlook Pub. Co., 1971.]

Historical Account of Meriwether County, 1824-1974, by Regina P. Pinkston. Greenville: Meriwether Hist. Soc., 1974. 448 pp. (Repr. LaGrange: Family Tree, 1983.)

## Miller County

The History of Miller County, Georgia, 1856-1980, by Nellie C. Davis. Colquitt: Colquitt Garden Club, 1980. 560 pp.

## Mitchell County

History of Mitchell County, 1857-1976, by Margaret Spence and A.M. Fleming. N.p., 1976? 340 pp.

## Monroe County

Monroe County, Georgia: a History, by Monroe County Historical Association. Forsyth: W.H. Wolfe Assoc., 1980. x, 725 pp.

## Montgomery County

Montgomery County: a Collection of Newspaper Sources, 1873-1885, by James E. Dorsey. Swainsboro: Emanuel County Jun. Coll. Lib., 1980. 211 pp.

Montgomery County, Georgia; a Source Book of Genealogy and History, by James E. Dorsey and J.K. Derden. Swainsboro: Magnolia Pr., 1983. 292 pp.

## Morgan County

Rambles Through Morgan County; Her History . . . by Louise McH. Hicky. [Washington: Wilkes Pub. Co., and Madison: Morgan Hist. Soc., 1971.] xiii, 211 pp.

## Murray County

History of Murray County, by Charles H. Shriner. Dalton: A.J. Showalter Co., 1911. 48 leaves. (Repr. Dalton: Whitfield-Murray Hist. Soc., 1981. 115 pp.)

## Oglethorpe County

The History of Oglethorpe County, Georgia, by Florrie C. Smith. Washington: Wilkes Pub. Co., 1970. 288 pp. (Suppls. I and II, 1972, 1979.)

*Oglethorpe County (cont.)*

The Story of Oglethorpe County, by Lena S. Wise. Lexington: Hist. Oglethorpe Inc., 1980. (Repr. from thesis, A History of Oglethorpe County, Univ. of Georgia, Athens, 1953.) 102 pp.

## Paulding County

Paulding County, People and Places, by W.A. Foster. 2 vols. Atlanta: W.H. Wolfe Assoc., 1983. 846, 782 pp.

## Peach County

History of Peach County, Georgia . . . Gov. Treutlen Chapter, D.A.R. Atlanta: Cherokee Pub. Co., 1972. 591 pp.

## Pickens County

History of Pickens County, by Lucius E. Tate. Atlanta: W.W. Brown Pub. Co. [1935]. (Repr. with new index. Spartanburg, S.C.: Reprint Co., 1978.)

## Pierce County

History of Pierce County, Georgia, by Dean Broome. Vol. 1 (all pub.). Blackshear: Author, 1973. vii, 645 pp.

## Pike County

History of Pike County from 1822 to 1922, comp. by Rev. R.W. Rogers. Zebulon: Author, 1922? 72 pp.

History of Pike County, Georgia, 1822-1932, by Lizzie R. Mitchell. N.p., 1948. 160 pp. (Originally in Pike County Journal, 1932. Repr. with every-name index, by Margaret H. Cannon. Spartanburg, S.C.: Reprint Co., 1980. ix, 195 pp.)

Pike County, Georgia, Sesquicentennial, 1822-1972, ed. by Rubye S. Snead. Zebulon: Pike County Sesquicentennial Assoc., 1972. 96 pp.

## Pulaski County

History of Pulaski County, Georgia, comp. by Hawkinsville Chapter, D.A.R. Atlanta: W.W. Brown Pub. Co. [1935]. 599 pp. (Repr. Atlanta: Hawkinsville Chapter, D.A.R., 1976.)

History of Pulaski and Bleckley Counties, Georgia, 1808-1956. Update of 1935 History to Include Bleckley County. 2 vols. [Macon: J.W. Burke Co., 1957-58.]

## Rabun County

Sketches of Rabun County History, 1819-1948, by Andrew J. Ritchie. [Atlanta: Foote & Davies, 1948.] 503 pp. (Repr. Clayton: Author, 1959. Every-name index. Park, Utah: Hamilton Computer Services, 1977. 27 pp.)

## Randolph County

Randolph County, Georgia . . . by Iva P. Goolsby, et al. Columbus: Randolph County Hist. Soc., 1976. 670 pp.

## Richmond County

History of Richmond County. N.p.: Commercial Pr. Co., 1946. (Unfinished) (Repr. Univ. Microfilm International, n.d. 116 pp.?)

## Rockdale County

The Rockdale Citizen: Rockdale County Centennial ed., 1871-1971. Conyers: Citizen Pub. Co., 1971? 104 pp.

History of Rockdale County, ed. by Margaret G. Barksdale, et al. Conyers: Tom Hay Pr. Co., 1978 [i.e. 1979]. 213 pp.

## Schley County

History of Schley County, by Mrs. J.H. Williams. Ellaville: Author, 1933. 48 pp. (Repr. Ellaville: Schley County Preservation Soc., 1982.)

Ellaville and Schley County: an Historical Sketch, by Steve Gurr. Ellaville: Schley County Bicentennial Comm., 1976. 64 pp.

## Screven County

Pioneer Days: a History of the Early Years in Screven County, by Clyde D. Hollingsworth. [Sylvania: Author, 1947.] 72 pp.

## Stephens County

The History of Stephens County, Georgia, 1715-1972, by Kathryn C. Trogdon. Toccoa: Toccoa Woman's Club, 1973. xi, 568 pp.

## Stewart County

The History of Stewart County, Georgia . . . History, by Helen E. Terrill; Biographical Sketches, by Sara R. Dixon. 2 vols. Columbus: Columbus Office Supply, 1958. (Repr. Waycross: Dixon, 1975.)

## Talbot County

Handbook of Talbot County, by O.D. Gorman. Macon: J.W. Burke Co., 1888.

There Was a Land: a Story of Talbot County, Georgia . . . by Robert H. Jordan. Columbus: Columbus Office Supply Co., 1971. 383 pp.

## Tattnall County

Sketches of Bygone Days: Historical Facts of Tattnall County . . . by Joseph T. Grice. Glennville: Author, 1958. 58 pp.

# Telfair County

History of Telfair County from 1812 to 1949, comp. by Floris P. Mann. Macon: J.W. Burke Co. [1949]. xvi, 204 pp. (Repr. with new index, by Margaret H. Cannon. Spartanburg, S.C.: Reprint Co., 1978. xviii, 204 pp.)

# Terrell County

Terrell County's Centennial Panorama, 1856-1956, Dawson, Georgia. N.p., 1956. 76 pp.

History of Terrell County, by Stone Castle Chapter, D.A.R. Dawson: Kinchafoonee Regional Lib., 1980. 700 pp.

# Thomas County

Thomasville Among the Pines, and Thomas County, Georgia, by John Triplett. Thomasville: N.p., 1891. 48 pp. (3d pr. Thomasville: Thomasville-Thomas County Chamber of Commerce, 1967.)

History of Thomas County, Georgia, from the Time of De Soto to the Civil War . . . by William I. McIntyre. Thomasville: Times Enterprise, 1923. 66 pp.

Ante-Bellum Thomas County, 1825-1861, by William W. Rogers. Tallahassee: Florida State Univ. Pr., 1963. 136 pp.

Thomas County, 1865-1900, by William W. Rogers. Tallahassee: Florida State Univ. Pr. [1973]. xiv, 486 pp.

Heritage of Thomas County, Georgia, by R.W. Trefftz. Thomasville: N.p., 1976.

# Tift County

History of Tift County, ed. by Ida B. Williams. Macon: J.W. Burke Co. [1948]. xx, 503 pp. (Repr. Macon: J.W. Burke Co., 1979.)

# Toombs County

The History of Toombs County, by Amos M. Teasby. Athens: Univ. of Georgia, 1940. (M.A. thesis)

# Towns County

Early History of Towns County: Facts and Folklore, by J.K. Holmes. N.p., 1961.

Hearthstones of Home: Founders of Towns County, Georgia, by Jerry A. Taylor. N.p., 1983. 335 pp.

# Troup County

History of Troup County, by Clifford L. Smith. Atlanta: Foote & Davies Co., 1935. vii, 323 pp.

## Turner County

History of Turner County, by John B. Pate. Atlanta: Stein Pr. Co., 1933. 198 pp. (Repr. with new index, by Margaret H. Cannon. Spartanburg, S.C.: Reprint Co., 1979. 236 pp.)

## Twiggs County

History of Twiggs County, Georgia, Sesquicentennial 1809-1959 . . . comp. by J. Lanette O'N. Faulk and B.W. Jones. Jeffersonville: Major Gen. John Twiggs Chapter, D.A.R. [1960]. 479 pp. (Repr. Easley, S.C.: Southern Hist. Pr., 1969. 488 pp.)

Abstracts of Some Documents of Twiggs County, Georgia, Beginning About 1809 and Ending About 1900, comp. by Eleanor D. McSwain. [Macon?: National Pr. Co., 1972.] iii, 354 pp.

## Union County

Sketches of Union County, a Pictorial History of Union County, 1832-1976, by C.R. Collins, et al. 2 vols. Blairsville: Union County Hist. Soc., 1976. 88, 160 pp.

## Upson County

History of Upson County, Georgia, by Carolyn W. Nottingham and E. Hannah. Macon: J.W. Burke Co., 1930. 1,122 pp. (Repr. with title, Early History . . . Easley, S.C.: Southern Hist. Pr., 1969. Repr. Thomaston: Upson Hist. Soc., 1982.)

Sesquicentennial: Upson County, 1824-1974, by Mrs. J.M. Kellum. Thomaston, 1825, 1976. Thomaston: Upson Hist. Soc., 1975.

## Walker County

History of Walker County, Georgia, by James A. Sartain and A.M. Matthew. Vol. 1 (all pub.). Dalton: A.J. Showalter Co., 1932. 559 pp. (Index, by Flora D. Patterson, et al. Lafayette: Cherokee Regional Lib., 1978. 131 pp.)

Walker County, Georgia Heritage, 1833-1983. Lafayette: Walker County Hist. Comm., 1984. 456 pp.

## Walton County

History of Walton County, by John L. McKinnon. Atlanta: Byrd Pr., 1911. 389 pp.

Wayfarers in Walton: a History of Walton County, Georgia, 1818-1967, by Anita B. Sams. [Monroe:] General Charitable Foundation of Monroe [1967]. xvii, 885 pp. (Repr. Monroe: Walton Pr., 1980. 900 pp.)

## Ware County

History of Ware County, Georgia, by Laura S. Walker. Macon: J.W. Burke Co., 1934. xvii, 547 pp. (Repr. Easley, S.C.: Southern Hist. Pr., 1974. 560 pp.)

# Warren County

History of Warren County, Georgia, 1793-1974, by Virginia H. Wilhoit. Washington: Wilkes Pub. Co., 1976. 309 pp.

# Washington County

History of Washington County, by Ella Mitchell. Atlanta: Byrd Pr. Co., 1924. 171 pp. (Repr. Atlanta: Cherokee Pub. Co., 1973.)

# Webster County

History of Webster County, by Mrs. C. R. Merritt. Weston: Weston Woman's Club, and Roswell: W.H. Wolfe Assoc., 1980. 750 pp.

# White County

A History of White County, 1857-1980. Cleveland: White County Hist. Soc., 1980. 392 pp.

# Whitfield County

Official History of Whitfield County, Georgia, by Whitfield County Historical Commission. [Dalton: A.J. Showalter Co.], 1936. 238 pp. (Repr. Dalton: Whitfield-Murrens Hist. Soc., 1981.)

# Wilcox County

Our Heritage, Wilcox County, by Reuviel Roberts. Abbeville: Wilcox Heritage Assoc., 1975.

Passing of the Pines. Roswell: Wolfe Assoc., 1984. 589 pp.

# Wilkes County

The Story of Wilkes County, Georgia, by Eliza A. Bowen, ed. by Louise F. Hays. Marietta: Continental Book Co., 1950. iii, 192 pp.

We Have This Heritage: the History of Wilkes County, Georgia, Beginnings to 1860, by Robert M. Willingham, Jr. Washington: Wilkes Pub. Co., 1969. 234 pp.

Chronicles of Wilkes County, Georgia, from Washington [Georgia] Newspapers, 1889-1898, ed. by Mary B. Warren. Danielsville: Heritage Papers, 1978. 512 pp. (Includes Eliza Bowen's Story of Wilkes County.)

# Wilkinson County

History of Wilkinson County, by Victor Davidson. John Ball Chapter, D.A.R. Macon: J.W. Burke Co. [1930]. 645 pp. (Repr. with new index. Spartanburg, S.C.: Reprint Co., 1978.)

Wilkinson County, Georgia, Historical Collections, comp. by Joseph T. Maddox. Irwinton: Author [1973]. 1xvii, 431 pp. (Updated to 1978.)

## Worth County

History of Worth County, Georgia . . . 1854-1934 (1974), by Mrs. Lillie M. Grubbs. 2 vols. Vol. 1, 1854-1934; Vol. 2, 1934-1974. Macon: J.W. Burke Co., 1934; Ann Arbor, Mich.: Edwards Bros., 1975. xviii, 594, 731 pp. (Pub. for Barnard Trail Chapter, D.A.R. Repr. of Vol. 1. Sylvester: Barnard Trail Chapter, D.A.R., 1975. Rev. index, 1978.)

# IDAHO

## Regional

History of North Idaho, Embracing Nez Perce, Idaho, Latah, Kootenai and Shoshone Counties, State of Idaho, by William S. Shiach, J.M. Henderson, and H.B. Averill. Chicago: Western Hist. Pub., 1903.

## Adams County

History of Adams County, 1938, *see* Washington County.

## Alturas County

History of Alturas and Blaine Counties, Idaho, by George A. McLeod. Hailey: Hailey Times, 1930. 119 pp. (Rev. ed. Hailey: Hailey Times, 1938. xx, 192 pp. 3d ed. Hailey: Hailey Times, 1950. 215 pp.)

Memories of Old Alturas County, Idaho, by Lucille H. Hall. Denver, Colo.: Big Mountain Pr., 1956. 72 pp.

## Bannock County

The History of Bannock County, Idaho, by Arthur C. Saunders. Pocatello: Tribune Co., 1915. 143 pp.

History of Bannock County, Idaho, by Frank Hartkopf. Laramie, Wyo.: N.p., 1942. 156 pp. (M.A. thesis, Univ. of Wyoming)

## Bear Lake County

Tullidge's Histories. Vol. 2. Salt Lake City: Juvenile Instructor Pr., 1889. vi, 540, 372 pp. (Includes Oneida and Bear Lake Counties, Idaho.) (Vol. 1 is History of Salt Lake City.)

History of Bear Lake Pioneers . . . ed. by Frank R. Peterson. Salt Lake City: Daughters of Utah Pioneers, Bear Lake County, 1968. 915 pp.

## Bingham County

"Old Bingham", the Banner County of Idaho at the World's Columbian Exposition, 1893. Chicago: S.D. Childs [1893?].

## Blaine County

History of Blaine County, 1938, *see* Alturas County.

# Bonneville County

Bonneville County in the Making, by Barzilla W. Clark. Idaho Falls: Author, 1941. 140 pp.

Captain Bonneville's County, Idaho Falls, by Edith H. Lovell. Idaho Falls: Eastern Idaho Farmer, 1963. 275 pp.

# Camas County

A Brief History of Camas Prairie, Idaho, by Lucille M. Nelson. Caldwell: Caxton Pr., 1937. 119 pp.

A History of Camas Prairie, by John F. Ryan. Fairfield: Camas County Hist. Soc., 1975. 119 pp.

# Caribou County

Caribou County Chronology . . . by Verna I. Shupe. [Colorado Springs, Colo.: Print Craft Pr., 1930.] 64 pp.

# Cassia County

History of Cassia County and Burley, by Idaho Writers League, Burley Chapter. Rev. ed. N.p., n.d.

Western Saga Guide Book: Cassia County Crosstrails of the Pioneers, by Alson W. Dawson. [Burley: Cassia County Hist. Soc., 1974.] 90 pp.

# Custer County

History of Custer County, Idaho, by Jesse H. Black. Challis: Challis Messenger [1930].

Land of the Yankee Fork, by Esther Yarber. Denver: Sage Books [1963]. 207 pp.

# Elmore County

Elmore County, Its Historical Gleanings . . . comp. by Olive De E. Greefsema. [Mountain Home?:] Caxton Pr., 1949. xvii, 453 pp.

A Glimpse of Early Elmore County: 1963 Territorial Centennial. Mountain Home: N.p., 1963. 96 pp.

# Franklin County

History of Franklin County, Idaho, by W.H. Simons. N.p., 1936. (M.A. thesis, Colorado State Coll. of Education)

Hometown Album: a Pictorial History of Franklin County, Idaho . . . ed. by Newell Hart. Preston: Cache Valley Newsletter Pub. Co., 1973. 843 pp.

## Idaho County

History of . . . Idaho County, 1903, in History of North Idaho, *see* p. 67.

Pioneer Days in Idaho County, by Sister Alfreda Elsensohn. 2 vols. Caldwell: Caxton Pr., 1947-51. (Repr., 1984.)

## Kootenai County

History of . . . Kootenai County, 1903, in History of North Idaho, *see* p. 67.

## Latah County

History of . . . Latah County, 1903, in History of North Idaho, *see* p. 67.

A History of Latah County to 1900, by Lawrence R. Harker. Moscow: N.p., 1941. (M.A. thesis, Univ. of Idaho)

Latah County, Idaho, by Marvin A. Jagels. N.p., 1954.

They Came to a Ridge, by Ann N. Driscoll, ed. by Maryann McKie. Moscow: News Review Pub. Co., 1970. 96 pp. ([Repr.], 1973. 104 pp. 1975. 104 pp.)

## Lemhi County

History of Lemhi County, by George E. Shoup. Boise: Idaho State Lib., 1969. 34 pp.

## Madison County

Pioneering the Snake River Fork Country, by Louis J. Clements and H.S. Forbush. Rexburg: Eastern Idaho Pub. Co., 1972. xxii, 312 pp.

## Nez Perce County

History of . . . Nez Perce County, 1903, in History of North Idaho, *see* p. 67.

## Oneida County

Tullidge's Histories. Vol. 2. Salt Lake City: Juvenile Instructor Pr., 1889. vi, 540, 372 pp. (Includes Oneida and Bear Lake Counties, Idaho.) (Vol. 1 is History of Salt Lake City.)

## Owyhee County

A Historical, Descriptive and Commercial Directory of Owyhee County, Idaho, by Lem A. York. Silver City: Pr. of the Owyhee Avalanche, 1898. iv, 140, 16 pp.

Sketches of Owyhee County, by Helen Nettleton. N.p., 197-. (Index, by Quentin Tedquist. Williamsburg: Iowa Hist. Soc., 1981.)

## Payette County

All Along the River: Territorial and Pioneer Days on the Payette, by Nellie Mills. Montreal: Payette Radio, Ltd. [1963]. 320 pp.

## Shoshone County

History of . . . Shoshone County, in History of North Idaho, *see* p. 67.

Gems of Thought and History of Shoshone County, comp. and ed. by George C. Hobson. Kellogg: Kellogg Evening News Pr., 1940. 84 pp.

Beneath These Mountains, by Russell A. Bankson. New York: Vantage Pr., 1966. 228 pp.

## Twin Falls

A Folk History of Twin Falls County, comp. and ed. by the History Publication Committee. Twin Falls: Standard Pr. Co., 1962. 110 pp.

## Washington County

History of Washington and Adams County, by Frank Harris. Weiser: Weiser American, 1938? 74 pp. (Repr., 1983.)

# ILLINOIS

## *Regional*

History of Gallatin, Saline, Hamilton, Franklin and Williamson Counties, Illinois . . .
Chicago: Goodspeed, 1887. 961 pp. (Repr. Evansville, Ind.: Unigraphic, 1973.
Index. Winnetka Pub. Lib., 1973. 122 pp.)

## Adams County

The History of Adams County, Illinois . . . Chicago: Murray, Williamson &
Phelps, 1879. 971 pp.

Past and Present of the City of Quincy and Adams County, by William H.
Collins. Chicago: Clarke, 1905. 1,124 pp.

Quincy and Adams County History . . . ed. by David F. Wilcox. 2 vols. Chicago:
Lewis Pub. Co., 1919.

Quincy and Adams County . . . by Thad W. Ward. Quincy: N.p., 1936. 159 pp.

## Alexander County

History of Alexander, Union and Pulaski Counties, Illinois, ed. by William H.
Perrin. Chicago: O.L. Baskin, 1883. 588, 338 pp. (Index. Winnetka: Winnetka
Pub. Lib., 1973. 127 pp.)

## Bond County

History of Bond and Montgomery Counties, ed. by William H. Perrin. 2 parts.
Chicago: O.L. Baskin, 1882. 419, 333 pp.

The Past and Present of Boone County, Illinois, Containing a History of the
County . . . Chicago: H.F. Kett, 1877. 414 pp. (Repr. Evansville, Ind.:
Unigraphic, 1980.)

Historical Encyclopedia of Illinois . . . and History of Boone County, ed. by
Richard V. Carpenter. 2 vols. Chicago: Munsell Pub. Co., 1909.

## Brown County

History of Brown County, 1882, *see* Schuyler County.

## Bureau County

Reminiscences of Bureau County . . . by Nehemiah Matson. Princeton: Republican
Book and Job Office, 1872. 406 pp. (Repr.? Tiskilwa: Tiskilwa Chief Pr.
Office, 1937. 134 pp.)

History of Bureau County, Illinois, ed. by H.C. Bradsby. Chicago: World Pub. Co., 1885. 710 pp. (Repr. Evansville, Ind.: Unigraphic, 1979.)

Past and Present of Bureau County, Illinois, by George R. Harrison. Chicago: Pioneer Pub. Co., 1906. 968 pp.

Big Bureau and Bright Prairies; a History of Bureau County, Illinois, ed. by Doris P. Leonard. [Moline?: Bureau County Bd. of Supervisors, 1968.] viii, 260 pp.

## Calhoun County

History of Calhoun County, by George W. Carpenter. Jerseyville: Democrat Pr., 1934. 93 pp.

## Carroll County

The History of Carroll County, Illinois . . . Chicago: H.F. Kett, 1878. 501 pp.

Historical Encyclopedia of Illinois . . . and History of Carroll County, ed. by Charles L. Hostetter. 2 vols. Chicago: Munsell Pub. Co., 1913.

Carroll County—a Goodly Heritage, ed. by E. George Thiem. Mount Morris: Keble Pr. Co., 1968. ix, 485 pp.

## Cass County

History of Cass County, Illinois, ed. by William H. Perrin. Chicago: O.L. Baskin, 1882. 357 pp.

Historical Sketches, by James N. Gridley, et al. Virginia: Enquirer, 1907? 449 pp.

Historical Encyclopedia of Illinois . . . and History of Cass County, ed. by Charles E. Martin. 2 vols. Chicago: Munsell Pub. Co., 1915.

## Champaign County

History of Champaign County, Illinois . . . Philadelphia: Brink, McDonough, 1878. 194 pp.

Early History and Pioneers of Champaign County . . . by Milton W. Mathews. Urbana: Champaign County Herald, 1886. 126 pp.

Historical Encyclopedia of Illinois . . . and History of Champaign County, ed. by Joseph O. Cunningham. 2 vols. Chicago: Munsell Pub. Co., 1905. (Repr. with new subject and name indexes. Urbana: Champaign County Hist. Archives & Urbana Free Lib., 1984.)

A Standard History of Champaign County, Illinois . . . J.R. Stewart, supervising ed. 2 vols. Chicago: Lewis Pub. Co., 1918.

## Christian County

History of Christian County, Illinois . . . Philadelphia: Brink, McDonough, 1880. 259 pp.

*Christian County (cont.)*

Past and Present of Christian County, Illinois, by Hon. James C. McBride. Chicago: S.J. Clarke Co., 1904. 582 pp.

Historical Encyclopedia of Illinois . . . and History of Christian County, ed. by Henry L. Fowkes. 2 vols. Chicago: Munsell Pub. Co., 1918.

Illinois Sesquicentennial ed. of Christian County History . . . ed. by Dorothy D. Drennan. 2 vols. in 1. Jacksonville: Production Pr., 1968.

## Clark County

History of Clark County, 1883, *see* Crawford County.

## Clay County

History of Clay County, 1884, *see* Wayne County.

Biographical and Reminiscent History of . . . Clay County, 1909, *see* Richland County.

Gleanings from Old Newspapers, Clay and Richland Counties, Illinois, by Lois B. Taylor. Vol. 1. Olney: Taylor Pr. Shop, 1975. 376 pp. (Vol. 2 is Early Marriages of Richland County.)

## Clinton County

History of . . . Clinton County, 1881, *see* Marion County.

## Coles County

The History of Coles County, Illinois . . . Chicago: Le Baron, Jr., 1879. 695 pp.

Historical Encyclopedia of Illinois . . . with History of Coles County, ed. by Charles E. Wilson. Chicago: Munsell Pub. Co., 1906. 886 pp.

## Cook County

History of Cook County, Illinois from the Earliest Period to the Present Time . . . by Alfred T. Andreas. Chicago: A.T. Andreas, 1884. 888 pp. (Repr. with index. Evansville, Ind.: Unigraphic, 1980.)

Historical Encyclopedia of Illinois . . . Cook County ed. 2 vols. Chicago: Munsell Pub. Co., 1901-5. (Almost the same as 1900 ed. Vol. 2 has History of Chicago and Cook County.)

Historical Review of Chicago and Cook County, ed. by N. Waterman. 3 vols. Chicago: Lewis Pub. Co., 1908.

History of Cook County, Illinois . . . ed. by Weston A. Goodspeed, et al. 2 vols. Chicago: Goodspeed Hist. Assoc. [1911?].

## Crawford County

History of Crawford and Clark Counties, Illinois, ed. by William H. Perrin. Chicago: O.L. Baskin, 1883. 470, 374 pp. (Repr. with index to biographical sketches. Evansville, Ind.: Unigraphic, 1980.)

Historical Encyclopedia of Illinois . . . with History of Crawford County . . . ed. by Newton Bateman and Paul Selby. Chicago: Munsell Pub. Co., 1909. 840 pp. (Repr. of Crawford County. Evansville, Ind.: Unigraphic, 1979. 226 pp.)

Our Crawford County, Illinois Heritage, comp. by Donna G. Johnston. Casper, Wyo.: Compiler, 1983? x, 730 pp.

## Cumberland County

Counties of Cumberland, Jasper and Richland, Ill., Historical and Biographical. Chicago: F.A. Battey, 1884. 839 pp. (Repr. Olney: Hist. Soc. Pub., 1968. ii, 839 pp. 2d ed., comp. by Cumberland County Hist. and Gen. Socs. Greenup, 1974. Surname index, comp. by Mrs. Golden (Mary Todd) Greeson. Olney: H.S.P., 1969. 31 pp.)

Cumberland County History, comp. by Cumberland County Hist. and Gen. Socs. [Olney: Taylor Pr. Shop, 1968.] iv, 846 pp. (Repr. Olney: Taylor Pr. Shop, 1973. iv, 873 pp.)

## De Kalb County

History of De Kalb County, Illinois, by Henry L. Boies. Chicago: O.P. Bassett, 1868. 530 pp. (Repr. indexed. Evansville, Ind.: Unigraphic, 1980.)

Past and Present of De Kalb County, Illinois, by Prof. Lewis M. Gross, et al. 2 vols. Chicago: Pioneer Pub. Co., 1907.

From Oxen to Jets; a History of De Kalb County, 1835-1963, by Harriet (Wilson) Davy. Dixon: De Kalb County Bd. of Supervisors [1963]. xvii, 272 pp.

## De Witt County

History of De Witt County, Illinois . . . by W.R. Brink. [Philadelphia?: N.p., 1882?] 358 pp. (Name index, by Violet Taylor. Indianapolis, Ind.: Heritage House, 1978. 54 pp.)

History of De Witt County, Illinois . . . 2 vols. Chicago: Pioneer Pub. Co., 1910. (Complete-name index, comp. by Mrs. Harlan B. Taylor. Decatur: Vio-Lin Enterprises, 1973. 54 pp.)

## Douglas County

History of Douglas County, Illinois, comp. by Henry C. Niles. Tuscola: Converse & Parks, 1876. 79 pp.

County of Douglas, Illinois, Historical and Biographical. Chicago: F.A. Battey, 1884. 570 pp.

*Douglas County (cont.)*

Historical and Biographical Record of Douglas County, Illinois; comp. by John Gresham. [Logansport, Ind.: Wilson, Humphreys], 1900. 299 pp.

## Du Page County

A History of the County of Du Page, Illinois . . . by C.W. Richmond and H.F. Vallette. Chicago: Scripps, Bross & Spears, 1857. 212 pp.

History of Du Page County Illinois . . . Aurora: Knickerbocker & Hodder, 1877. 250 pp.

History of Du Page County, Illinois, by Rufus Blanchard. Chicago: O.L. Baskin & Co., 1882. 294, 247 pp. Part 1, historical.) (Index. Winnetka: Winnetka Pub. Lib., 1973. 41 pp.)

Historical Encyclopedia of Illinois . . . and History of Du Page County . . . 2 vols. Chicago: Munsell Pub. Co., 1913.

Du Page County, a Descriptive and Historical Guide, 1831-1939. Federal Writers' Project. Re-ed. by Marion Knoblauch. Elmhurst: L.A. Ruby [1948]. xvii, 253 pp. (Special rev. ed. 1925-50. Wheaton: Du Page Title Co. [1951]. xvii, 253 pp.)

## Edgar County

History of Edgar County, Illinois . . . Chicago: William Le Baron Co., 1879. 798 pp.

Historical Encyclopedia of Illinois . . . and History of Edgar County . . . Chicago: Munsell Pub. Co., 1905. 781 pp.

## Edwards County

Combined History of Edwards, Lawrence and Wabash Counties, Illinois . . . Philadelphia: J.L. McDonough, 1883. 377 pp. (Index. Knightstown, Ind.: The Bookmark, 1982. Repr. Albion: Edwards County Hist. Soc., 1981. 453, xiii pp., including index.)

Yester-years in Edwards County, Illinois . . . comp. by Edgar L. Dukes. 2 vols. Albion: N.p., 1945-48. (2d ed., with corrections and additions. [Albion:] N.p., 1946. 200 pp.; 3d ed. [Albion:] N.p. 1950.)

A History of Edwards County, Illinois. Albion: Edwards County Hist. Soc., 1980. 538 pp.

## Effingham County

History of Effingham County, Illinois, ed. by William H. Perrin . . . 2 vols. Chicago: O.L. Baskin, 1883. 286, 263, 79 pp.

Illinois Historical Encyclopedia . . . Effingham County . . . Chicago: Munsell Pub. Co., 1910. 893 pp. (Name index to hist. and biog. section. Evansville, Ind.: Unigraphic, 1979. 276 pp. Repr. Knightstown, Ind.: The Bookmark, 1982.)

*Effingham County (cont.)*

Effingham County, Illinois—Past and Present, ed. by Hilda E. Feldhake. Effingham: N.p., 1968. 418 pp.

The Sesquicentennial of Effingham County 1831-1981, comp. by Larry F. Banbury. Effingham: Banbury Pub. Co., 1982. 808 pp.

## Fayette County

Fayette County, Illinois. Philadelphia: Brink and McDonough, 1878. 108 pp. (Index. Winnetka: Winnetka Pub. Lib., 1974. 39 pp. Repr. Evansville, Ind.: Unigraphic, 1979.)

Historical Encyclopedia of Illinois . . . and History of Fayette County, ed. by Robert W. Ross and J.J. Bullington. 2 vols. Chicago: Munsell Pub. Co., 1910.

## Ford County

History of Ford County, Illinois, from Its Earliest Settlement to 1908, by E.A. Gardner. 2 vols. Chicago: S.J. Clarke Pub. Co., 1908.

## Franklin County

History of . . . Franklin County . . . 1887, *see* p. 71.

## Fulton County

Fulton County, Illinois, with Sketches . . . Peoria: C.C. Chapman, 1878. 1,090 pp.

Historical Encyclopedia of Illinois . . . and History of Fulton County, ed. by Jesse Heylin. Chicago: Munsell Pub. Co., 1908. 1,213 pp.

A History of Fulton County, Illinois . . . 1818-1968 . . . ed. by Helen H. Clark. N.p. [1969]. xiv, 297 pp.

Historic Fulton County: Sites and Scenes—Past and Present. Lewistown: Fulton County Hist. Soc., 1973. x, 326 pp.

## Gallatin County

History of Gallatin County, 1887, *see* p. 71.

Early Settlers' Records, Gallatin County, Illinois, copied by Lucy R. Bender. 6 vols. N.p., 1936.

Gallatin County; Gateway to Illinois, by Lucile Lawler. [Crossville: N.p., 1968.] 153 pp.

# Greene County

History of Greene County, Illinois . . . Chicago: Donnelley, Gassette & Loyd, 1879. 771 pp. (History, comp. by Clement L. Clapp.) (Repr. with index. Evansville, Ind.: Unigraphic, 1979. 800 pp. Index to biographical sketches, by Mildred Schulz. Springfield, 196-? 17 leaves.)

History of Greene and Jersey Counties . . . Sringfield: Continental Hist. Co., 1885. 1,156 pp.

Past and Present of Greene County, Illinois, by Hon. Edward Miner. Chicago: S.J. Clarke Pub. Co., 1905. 645 pp.

# Grundy County

History of Grundy County, Illinois . . . 2 parts. Chicago: O.L. Baskin, 1882. vi, 362, 156 pp.

Historical Encyclopedia of Illinois . . . and History of Grundy County . . . 2 vols. Chicago: Munsell Pub. Co., 1914.

# Hamilton County

History of Hamilton . . . County, 1887, *see* p. 71.

Hamilton County Sesquicentennial, 1821-1971. [McLeansboro: N.p., 1971.] 76 pp.

# Hancock County

History of Hancock County, Illinois . . . by Thomas Gregg. Chicago: C.C. Chapman, 1880. 1,036 pp. (Repr. Augusta: Tri-County Gen. Soc., 1984.)

Historical Encyclopedia of Illinois . . . and History of Hancock County, ed. by Charles J. Scofield. 2 vols. Chicago: Munsell Pub. Co., 1921.

This Is Hancock County, Illinois, an Up-to-date Historical Narrative . . . Chicago: Loree Co., 1955. vi, 570 pp.

# Hardin County

History of Hardin County, Illinois, by Ruby F. Hall. Carbondale: N.p. [1970]. v, 99 pp.

# Henderson County

History of Mercer County . . . Also a Short History of Henderson County. Chicago: H.H. Hill, 1882. 1,414 pp.

Historical Encyclopedia of Illinois . . . and History of Henderson County, ed. by James W. Gordon. 2 vols. Chicago: Munsell Pub. Co., 1911.

Recollections of Pioneer and Army Life, by Matthew H. Jamison. Kansas City: Hudson Pr. [1911]. 363 pp.

## Henry County

The History of Henry County, Illinois . . . Chicago: H.F. Kett, 1877. 589 pp.

History of Henry County, Illinois, by Henry L. Kiner. 2 vols. Chicago: Pioneer Pub. Co., 1910.

This is Henry County, Illinois; an Up-to-date Historical Narrative . . . Chicago: Loree Co., 1955. vi, 610 pp.

Corn, Commerce, and Country Living; a History of Henry County, ed. by Terry E. Polsen. [Moline: Desaulniers, 1968.] ix, 360 pp.

## Iroquois County

History of Iroquois County, Illinois . . . by H.W. Beckwith. Chicago: H.H. Hill & Co., 1880. 468, 671 pp. (Repr. with name index. Evansville, Ind.: Unigraphic 1980.)

Past and Present of Iroquois County, Illinois, by J.W. Kern. Chicago: S.J. Clarke Pub. Co., 1907. 741 pp.

## Jackson County

History of Jackson County, Illinois . . . Philadelphia: Brink, McDonough, 1878. 142 pp.

Historical Sketches of Jackson County, Illinois . . . by Edmund Newsome. Carbondale: E. Newsome, 1882. 140 pp. (Index, by Barbara B. Hubbs. Murphyshore: N.p., 1938. 37 leaves.)

## Jasper County

County of Jasper, Historical and Biographical, 1884, *see* Cumberland County.

## Jefferson County

History of Jefferson County, Illinois, ed. by William H. Perrin. Chicago: Globe Pub. Co., 1883. vii, 419, 149 pp.

Wall's History of Jefferson County, Illinois, by John A. Wall. Indianapolis, Ind.: B.F. Bowen, 1909. 618 pp.

History of Jefferson County, Illinois, 1810-1962, comp. by Continental Historical Bureau. Mount Vernon: Bureau, 1962.

## Jersey County

History of Jersey County, 1885, *see* Greene County.

History of Jersey County, Illinois, ed. by Oscar B. Hamilton. Chicago: Munsell Pub. Co., 1919. 673 pp. (Repr. Evansville, Ind.: Unigraphic, 1980.)

# Jo Daviess County

The History of Jo Daviess County, Illinois . . . Chicago: H.F. Kett, 1878. 853 pp. (Index. Winnetka: Winnetka Pub. Lib., 1973. 131 pp.)

Historical Encyclopedia of Illinois . . . and History of Jo Daviess County, ed. by Hon. William Spensley. Chicago: Munsell Pub. Co., 1904. 705 pp.

# Johnson County

A History of Johnson County, Illinois, by Mrs. P.T. Chapman. [Herrin: Herrin News, 1925.] 502 pp.

# Kane County

The Past and Present of Kane County, Illinois . . . Chicago: W. Le Baron, 1878. 821 pp.

Commemorative Portrait and Biographical Record of Kane and Kendall Counties, Illinois, by Pliny A. Durant, et al. Chicago: Beers, Leggett, 1888. 999 pp.

Historical Encyclopedia of Illinois . . . and History of Kane County, ed. by Gen. John S. Wilcox. Chicago: Munsell Pub. Co., 1904. 950 pp.

History of Kane County, Illinois, by Rodolphus W. Joslyn. 2 vols. Chicago: Pioneer Pub. Co., 1908.

# Kankakee County

Historical Encyclopedia of Illinois . . . and History of Kankakee County, ed. by William F. Kenaga and G.R. Letourneau. 2 vols. Chicago: Middle-West Pub. Co., 1906.

# Kendall County

History of Kendall County, Illinois, from the Earliest Discoveries to the Present Time, by Rev. Edmund W. Hicks. Aurora: Knickerbocker & Hodder, 1877. 438 pp.

Commemorative Portrait . . . of Kendall County, 1888, *see* Kane County.

Historical Encyclopedia of Illinois . . . and History of Kendall County . . . 2 vols. Chicago: Munsell Pub. Co., 1914. 1,078 pp.

# Knox County

History of Knox County, Illinois . . . by Charles C. Chapman & Co. Chicago: Blakely, Brown & Marsh, 1878. 718 pp. (Repr. Evansville, Ind.: Unigraphic, 1979.)

Historical Encyclopedia of Illinois . . . and History of Knox County, ed. by W. Selden Gale and G.C. Gale. 2 vols. Chicago: Munsell Pub. Co., 1899. 968 pp.

History of Knox County, Illinois . . . by Albert J. Perry. 2 vols. Chicago: S.J. Clarke Pub. Co., 1912.

Centennial Annals of Knox County, Illinois, 1818-1918 . . . by Ella P. Lawrence. [Galesburg?: Republican Register Pr., 1918.] 228 pp.

This is Knox County, Illinois; an Up-to-date Historical Narrative . . . Chicago: Loree Co., 1955. vi, 522 pp.

## Lake County

Historical and Statistical Sketches of Lake County . . . by Elijah M. Haines. Waukegan: E.G. Howe, 1852. 112 pp.

The Past and Present of Lake County, Illinois, Containing a History of the County . . . Chicago: William Le Baron, 1877. 501 pp. (Index, comp. by Mildred Schulz.)

Historical Encyclopedia of Illinois . . . and History of Lake County, ed. by Hon. Charles A. Partridge. Chicago: Munsell Pub. Co., 1902. 747 pp. (History of Lake County, pub. separately, pp. 619-747, 1902.) (Repr. Evansville, Ind.: Unigraphic, 1979. 747 pp.)

A History of Lake County, Illinois, by John J. Halsey. [Philadelphia:] R.S. Bates, 1912. xii, 872 pp. (Index. Winnetka: Winnetka Pub. Lib., 1973. 79 pp.)

## La Salle County

History of La Salle County . . . and a Sketch of the Pioneer Settlers of Each Town to 1840 . . . by Elmer Baldwin. Chicago: Rand, McNally, 1877. 552 pp.

The Past and Present of La Salle County, Illinois, Containing a History . . . Chicago: H.F. Kett, 1877. 653 pp. (Repr. Evansville, Ind.: Unigraphic, 1980.)

History of La Salle County, Illinois . . . 2 vols. Chicago: Inter-State Pub. Co., 1886.

History of La Salle County, Illinois, by W.J. Hoffman. Chicago: S.J. Clarke Pub. Co., 1906. 1,177 pp.

## Lawrence County

History of . . . Lawrence County, 1883, *see* Edwards County.

Historical Encyclopedia of Illinois . . . and History of Lawrence County, ed. by John W. McCleare. Chicago: Munsell Pub. Co., 1910. 760 pp.

## Lee County

History of Lee County . . . by Dr. Cochran, et al. Chicago: H.H. Hill, 1881. 873 pp.

Recollections of the Pioneers of Lee County, Illinois. Dixon: Inez A. Kennedy, 1893. 582 pp.

*Lee County (cont.)*

Historical Encyclopedia of Illinois . . . and History of Lee County, ed. by A.C. Bardwell. Chicago: Munsell Pub. Co., 1904. 831 pp. (Repr. Knightstown, Ind.: The Bookmark, 1978. Lee County, pp. 620-831.)

History of Lee County, Illinois, by Frank E. Stevens. 2 vols. Chicago: S.J. Clarke Pub. Co., 1914.

Early Lee County . . . ed. by William D. Barge. [Chicago: Barnard & Miller], 1918. 160 pp.

## Livingston County

History of Livingston County, Illinois . . . Chicago: William Le Baron, 1878. 896 pp.

Historical Encyclopedia of Illinois . . . and History of Livingston County, ed. by Christopher Straun, et al. 2 vols. Chicago: Munsell Pub. Co., 1909.

This Is Livingston County, Illinois; an Up-to-date Historical Narrative . . . Chicago: Loree Co., 1955. vi, 722, 62 pp.

## Logan County

History of Logan County, Illinois: Its Past and Present . . . Chicago: Donnelley, Loyd, 1878. 560 pp.

Logan County Directory . . . Containing a Brief History . . . comp. by James F. Hyde. Dwight: C.L. Palmer, 1880. 381 pp.

History of Logan County, Illinois . . . Chicago: Interstate Pub. Co., 1886. 909 pp. (Complete-name index, comp. by Linda S. Allison and Mrs. H.B. Taylor. N.p., 1972. 122 pp.)

History of Logan County, Illinois, by Lawrence B. Stringer. 2 vols. N.p., 1911. (Repr. 2 vols. Lincoln: Lincoln Pub. Lib., 1978.)

## McDonough County

History of McDonough County, Illinois . . . by S.J. Clarke. Springfield: D.W. Lusk, 1878. 692 pp.

History of McDonough County, Illinois . . . Springfield: Continental Hist. Co., 1885. xvi, 1,158 pp.

Historical Encyclopedia of Illinois . . . and History of McDonough County, ed. by Alexander McLean. 2 vols. Chicago: Munsell Pub. Co., 1907. 1,055 pp.

## McHenry County

History of McHenry County, Illinois . . . Chicago: Inter-State Pub. Co., 1885. 941 pp. (Index. Winnetka: Winnetka Pub. Lib., 1973. Repr. with every-name index. McHenry: McHenry County, Illinois Gen. Soc., 1983. 1,216 pp.)

McHenry County, Illinois, 1832-1968, ed. by Lowell A. Nye. Woodstock: McHenry County Bd. of Supervisors [1968]. ix, 972 pp.

## McLean County

A Gazetteer of McLean County . . . comp. by Bailey & Hair. Chicago: J.C.W. Bailey, 1866. xii, 276 pp.

The Good Old Times in McLean County, Illinois, Containing 260 Sketches of Old Settlers . . . by Dr. E. Duis. Bloomington: Leader Pub. & Pr. House, 1874. xvi, 865 pp. (2d ed. [Bloomington:] McKnight & McKnight Pub. Co., 1968. xi, 865 pp. Index, by Alice T. Steinberg. [Normal:] Normal Gen. Soc., 1959. 45 pp.)

The History of McLean County, Illinois . . . Chicago: William Le Baron, 1879. 1,078 pp.

Historical Encyclopedia of Illinois . . . and History of McLean County, ed. by Ezra M. Prince and J.H. Bunham. 2 vols. Chicago: Munsell Pub. Co., 1902.

History of McLean County, Illinois, by Jacob L. Hasbrouck. 2 vols. Indianapolis, Ind.: Hist. Pub. Co., 1924.

The Way It Was in McLean County . . . by H. Clay Tate. [Bloomington:] McLean Co. '72 Assoc., 1972. xvi, 402 pp.

## Macon County

History of Macon County, Illinois . . . by John W. Smith. Springfield: Rokker's Pr. House, 1876. 304 pp.

History of Macon County, Illinois. Philadelphia: Brink, McDonough & Co., 1880. 242 pp. (Repr. Evansville, Ind.: Unigraphic, 1972.)

Past and Present of the City of Decatur and Macon County, Illinois . . . Chicago: S.J. Clarke Pub. Co., 1903. 885 pp.

Centennial History of Decatur and Macon County, comp. and rewritten by Mabel E. Richmond. Decatur: Decatur Review, 1930. 470 pp.

This Is Macon County, Illinois: an Up-to-date Historical Narrative . . . Chicago: Loree Co., 1954. x, 366 pp.

History of Macon County, 1976, by Oliver T. Banton. Decatur: Macon Hist. Soc., 1976. iv, 555 pp.

## Macoupin County

History of Macoupin County, Illinois . . . Philadelphia: Brink, McDonough & Co. 1879. 288 pp.

Record of Macoupin County . . . by John Moran. Carlinville: Springfield State Register, 1897. 201 pp.

History of Macoupin County, Illinois . . . Hon. Charles A. Walker, supervising ed. 2 vols. Chicago: S.J. Clarke Pub. Co., 1911.

## Madison County

History of Madison County, Illinois . . . Edwardsville: W.R. Brink, 1882. 603 pp. (Index, prepared by Katharine Moorhead. [Edwardsville: Madison County Hist. Soc., n.d.] 26 leaves.)

*Madison County (cont.)*

Centennial History of Madison County, 1812-1912, by W.T. Norton, et al. 2 vols. Chicago: Lewis Pub. Co., 1912. (Repr. 2 vols. in 1. Evansville, Ind.: Unigraphic, 1970. xlix, viii, 1,208 pp.)

## Marion County

History of Marion and Clinton Counties, Illinois . . . Philadelphia: Brink, McDonough & Co., 1881. 316 pp. (Repr. Evansville, Ind.: Unigraphic, 1979.)

Brinkerhoff's History of Marion County, Illinois, by Prof. J.H.G. Brinkerhoff. Indianapolis, Ind.: B.F. Bowen, 1909. 862 pp. (Repr. with every-name index. Salem: Marion County Gen. and Hist. Soc., 1979. 908 pp.)

Biographical and Reminiscent History of . . . Marion County, 1909, *see* Richland County.

## Marshall County

The History of Marshall County, 1860, *see* Putnam County.

Records of the Olden Time, Embracing Sketches of . . . County of Marshall, 1880, *see* Putnam County.

## Mason County

Centennial History of Mason County . . . by Joseph Cochrane. Springfield: Rokker's Pr. House, 1876. 352 pp.

The History of Mason County, 1879, *see* Menard County.

Pioneers of Mason County, 1902, *see* Menard County.

## Massac County

History of Massac County, Illinois . . . by Oliver J. Page. [Metropolis: N.p., 1900?] 383 pp.

History of Massac County, Illinois, by George W. May. Galesburg: Wagoner Pr. Co. [1955]. 232 pp.

## Menard County

The History of Menard and Mason Counties, Illinois . . . Chicago: O.L. Baskin, 1879. 871 pp. (Menard County, by Rev. R.D. Miller; Mason County, by Gen. J.M. Ruggles.) (Index. Winnetka: Winnetka Pub. Lib. [196-].)

Pioneers of Menard and Mason Counties . . . by Thompson G. Onstot. Forest City: T.G. Onstot, 1902. 400 pp. (Index to pioneers, prepared by Havana, Illinois Members of the Church of Jesus Christ, LDS, 1984. 19 pp.)

*Menard County (cont.)*

Past and Present of Menard County, Illinois, by Rev. Robert D. Miller. Chicago: S.J. Clarke Pub. Co., 1905. 549 pp.

## Mercer County

History of Mercer County . . . Containing Also a Short History of Henderson County. Chicago: H.H. Hill, 1882. 1,414 pp.

Historical Encyclopedia of Illinois . . . and History of Mercer County, ed. by Col. William A. Lorrimer. Chicago: Munsell Pub. Co., 1903. 798 pp.

Past and Present of Mercer County, Illinois, by Isaac N. Bassett. 2 vols. Chicago: S.J. Clarke Pub. Co., 1914.

History of Mercer County, Illinois, 1882-1976 . . . by Daniel T. Johnson. [Aledo:] Mercer County Bicentennial Comm., 1977. 820 pp.

## Monroe County

History of Monroe County, 1883, *see* Randolph County.

Arrowheads to Aerojets [Monroe County, Illinois, 1673-1966 . . . comp. by Monroe County Historical Society. Valmayer: Myron Roever Assoc., 1967.] 959 pp.

## Montgomery County

History of . . . Montgomery County, 1882, *see* Bond County.

Past and Present of Montgomery County, Illinois, by J.L. Traylor. Chicago: S.J. Clarke Pub. Co., 1904. 770 pp.

Historical Encyclopedia of Illinois . . . and History of Montgomery County, ed. by Alexander T. Strange. 2 vols. Chicago: Munsell Pub. Co., 1918.

## Morgan County

History of Morgan County, Illinois; Its Past and Present . . . Chicago: Donnelley, Loyd, 1878. 768 pp. (Index. Winnetka: Winnetka Pub. Lib., 196-. Repr. with index. Evansville, Ind.: Unigraphic, 1980.)

Historic Morgan and Classic Jacksonville, comp. by Charles M. Eames. Jacksonville: Daily Journal Pr. Office, 1885. 336, xxviii pp.

Historical Encyclopedia of Illinois . . . and History of Morgan County, ed. by William F. Short. Chicago: Munsell Pub. Co., 1906. 984 pp.

## Moultrie County

History of Moultrie County, 1881, *see* Shelby County.

## Ogle County

Sketches of the History of Ogle County, Illinois [by Henry R. Boss]. Polo: H.R. Boss, 1859. 90 pp.

*Ogle County (cont.)*

The History of Ogle County, Illinois . . . Chicago: H.F. Kett, 1878. 858 pp.

Portrait and Biographical Album of Ogle County, Illinois . . . Also Containing a History of the County . . . Chicago: Chapman Bros., 1886. 905 pp.

Historical Encyclopedia of Illinois . . . and History of Ogle County, ed. by Horace G. Kauffman and R.H. Kauffman. 2 vols. Chicago: Munsell Pub. Co., 1909.

## Peoria County

The History of Peoria County, Illinois . . . Chicago: Johnson & Co., 1880. 851 pp. (Repr. with index. Peoria: Peoria County Gen. Soc., 1981. 680 pp.)

This Is Peoria County, Illinois; an Up-to-date Historical Narrative . . . ed. by John Drury. Chicago: Loree Co., n.d. vi, 482, 62 pp.

Peoria City and County, Illinois . . . by Col. J.M. Rice. 2 vols. Chicago: S.J. Clarke Pub. Co., 1912.

Students' History of Peoria County, Illinois, by George W. May. Galesburg: Wagoner Pr. Co. [1968]. 321 pp.

## Perry County

History of . . . Perry County, 1883, *see* Randolph County.

Students' History of Perry County, by John W. Neville. [N.p., 1945.] 68 leaves.

## Piatt County

History of Piatt County . . . by Emma C. Piatt. [Chicago: Shepard & Johnston, 1883.] 643 pp. (Repr. with every-name index. Evansville, Ind.: Unigraphic, 1979.)

Past and Present of Piatt County, Illinois . . . ed. by Charles McIntosh. Chicago: S.J. Clarke Pub. Co., 1903. 517 pp.

Historical Encyclopedia of Illinois . . . and History of Piatt County, ed. by Francis M. Shonkwiler. 2 vols. Chicago: Munsell Pub. Co., 1917.

The Good Life in Piatt County; a History of Piatt County, Illinois, ed. by Jessie B. Morgan. Moline: Desaulniers [1968]. vi, 287 pp.

## Pike County

History of Pike County, by W.A. Grimshaw. Pittsfield: Democratic Pr., 1877. 46 pp.

History of Pike County, Illinois . . . Chicago: C.C. Chapman, 1880. 966 pp.

Past and Present of Pike County, Illinois, by Melville C. Massie. Chicago: S.J. Clarke Pub. Co., 1906. 751 pp.

*Pike County (cont.)*

This Is Pike County, Illinois; an Up-to-date Historical Narrative, ed. by John Drury. Chicago: Loree Co., 1955. vi, 522 pp.

## Pulaski County

History of Pulaski County, 1883, *see* Alexander County.

History of Pulaski County, 1843-1943 . . . by W.N. Moyers. Mound City: Enterprise, 1943. 100 pp.

## Putnam County

The History of Putnam and Marshall Counties . . . by Henry A. Ford. Lacon: Author, 1860. vii, 160 pp.

Records of the Olden Time . . . Embracing Sketches of the Discovery, Explorations and Settlement of the Counties of Putnam and Marshall . . . by Spencer Ellsworth. Lacon: Home Journal Steam Pr., 1880. 772 pp.

## Randolph County

A Directory and Business Mirror, and Historical Sketches of Randolph County, by E.J. Montague. Alton: Courier Steam Book and Job Pr. House, 1859. 246 pp.

Combined History of Randolph, Monroe and Perry Counties, Illinois . . . Philadelphia: J.L. McDonough & Co., 1883. 510 pp.

## Richland County

County of . . . Richland, Illinois, Historical . . . 1884, *see* Cumberland County.

Biographical and Reminiscent History of Richland, Clay and Marion Counties, Illinois . . . Indianapolis, Ind.: B.G. Bowen, 1909. 608 pp.

Gleanings from Old Newspapers . . . Richland County, 1975, *see* Clay County.

## Rock Island County

The Past and Present of Rock Island County, Illinois, Containing a History . . . Chicago: H.F. Kett, 1877. 480 pp. (Repr. Evansville, Ind.: Unigraphic, 1979.)

Early Rock Island, by William A. Meese. Moline: Desaulniers & Co., 1905, 97 pp.

Historic Rock Island County . . . Rockland: Kramer & Co., 1908. 184 pp.

Historical Encyclopedia of Illinois . . . and History of Rock Island County . . . 2 vols. Chicago: Munsell Pub. Co., 1914.

The High Prairie; the Story of the Early Settlers of Upper Rock Island County, Illinois, by Louis D. Hauberg. [Rock Island?: N.p., 1962?] 142 pp.

## St. Clair County

History of St. Clair County, Illinois . . . Philadelphia: Brink, McDonough & Co., 1881. 371 pp.

Historical Encyclopedia . . . and History of St. Clair County, ed. by A.S. Wilderman. 2 vols. Chicago: Munsell Pub. Co., 1907.

## Saline County

History of Saline County, 1887, *see* p. 71.

Saline County, a Century of History, 1847-1947 . . . [Harrisburg?: N.p., 1947.] 327 pp.

## Sangamon County

History of the Early Settlers of Sangamon County, Illinois . . . by John C. Power. Springfield: E.A. Wilson, 1876. 797 pp. (Repr. N.p.: Phillips Bros., 1970. 27, 797 pp.)

History of Sangamon County, Illinois . . . Chicago: Inter-State Pub. Co., 1881. 1,067 pp.

Past and Present of the City of Springfield and Sangamon County, Illinois, by Joseph Wallace. 2 vols. Chicago: S.J. Clarke Pub. Co., 1904.

Historical Encyclopedia of Illinois . . . and History of Sangamon County, ed. by Paul Selby. 2 vols. in 4. Chicago: Munsell Pub. Co., 1912.

## Schuyler County

Combined History of Schuyler and Brown Counties, Illinois . . . Philadelphia: W.R. Brink & Co., 1882. 412 pp.

Historical Encyclopedia of Illinois . . . and History of Schuyler County, ed. by Howard F. Dyson. Chicago: Munsell Pub. Co., 1908. 975 pp.

## Shelby County

Combined History of Shelby and Moultrie Counties . . . Edwardsville: Brink, McDonough & Co., 1881. 333 pp. (Repr. Knightstown, Ind.: The Bookmark, 1982.)

Historical and Biographical Album of Shelby County. Shelbyville: Wilder, 1900. 313 pp.

Historical Encyclopedia of Illinois . . . and History of Shelby County, ed. by George D. Chafee. 2 vols. Chicago: Munsell Pub. Co., 1910.

## Stark County

Stark County and Its Pioneers, by Mrs. Eliza J. (Hall) Shallenberger. Cambridge: B.W. Seaton, 1876. 327 pp. (Index. Winnetka: Winnetka Pub. Lib., 1973. 26 pp.)

*Stark County (cont.)*

Documents and Biography Pertaining to the Settlement and Progress of Stark County, Illinois . . . Chicago: M.A. Leeson, 1887. 708 pp.

This Is Stark County, Illinois: an Up-to-date Historical Narrative, by John Drury. Chicago: Loree Co., 1955. vi, 218 pp.

## Stephenson County

The History of Stephenson County, Illinois . . . Chicago: Western Hist. Co., 1880. 786 pp.

History of Stephenson County, Illinois . . . by Addison L. Fulwider. 2 vols. Chicago: S.J. Clarke Pub. Co., 1910.

Sketches of the History of Stephenson County, Illinois, by William J. Johnston. Freeport: Burnside, 1954. 102 pp. (Repr. in Illinois State Historical Society Trans., 1923, pp. 217-320.)

History of Stephenson County, 1970. [ed. by Mrs. John W. Barrett]. Freeport: County of Stephenson Soc. [1972]. 679 pp.

## Tazewell County

History of Tazewell County, Illinois . . . Chicago: C.C. Chapman, 1879. 794 pp. (Index. Winnetka: Winnetka Pub. Lib., 1973. Repr. Pekin: Tazewell County, Illinois, Gen. Soc., 1982.)

Historical Encyclopedia of Illinois . . . and History of Tazewell County, ed. by Ben C. Allensworth. 2 vols. Chicago: Munsell Pub. Co., 1905.

## Union County

History of . . . Union County, 1883, *see* Alexander County.

## Vermilion County

Vermilion County, Historical, Statistical, and Descriptive . . . Danville: H.A. Coffeen, 1870. 116 pp.

History of Vermilion County . . . by Hiram W. Beckwith. Chicago: H.H. Hill, 1879. 1,041 pp. (Index. Winnetka: Winnetka Pub. Lib., 1973. 105 pp.)

The Past and Present of Vermilion County, Illinois . . . Chicago: S.J. Clarke Pub. Co., 1903. 1,158 pp.

History of Vermilion County, Illinois . . . by Lettie E. Jones. 2 vols. Chicago: Pioneer Pub. Co., 1911.

Stories of Historical Days in Vermilion County, Illinois . . . comp. for school libraries, by L.A. Tuggle. [Danville: Inter-State Pr. Co., 1940?] 102 pp.

Vermilion County Pioneers, comp. by James V. Gill. 2 vols. Danville: Heritage House, 1969-70.

## Wabash County

History of . . . Wabash County, 1883, *see* Edwards County.

Journal of Mary Hallock Shearer; Early History from Southeastern Illinois' Wabash County. [St. Louis?: N.p., 1967.] xiv, 169 pp.

## Warren County

The Past and Present of Warren County, Containing a History of the County . . . Chicago: H.F. Kett, 1877. 352 pp. (Index. Winnetka: Winnetka Pub. Lib., 197-.)

Historical Encyclopedia of Illinois . . . and History of Warren County, ed. by Hugh R. Moffett and T.H. Rogers. 2 vols. Chicago: Munsell Pub. Co., 1903.

Historical and Biographical Record of Monmouth and Warren County, Illinois, ed. by Luther E. Robertson. 2 vols. Chicago: Munsell Pub. Co., 1927.

## Washington County

History of Washington County, Illinois. Philadelphia: Brink, McDonough & Co., 1879. 96 pp. (Index. Winnetka: Winnetka Pub. Lib., 1973. 39 pp. Repr. Evansville, Ind.: Unigraphic, 1974.)

## Wayne County

History of Wayne and Clay Counties, Illinois. Chicago: Globe Pub. Co., 1884. 474, 242, 28 pp. (Repr. with added index for Wayne County. Evansville, Ind.: Unigraphic, 1970. Repr. with added index. Fairfield: Bland Books, 1983.)

Wayne County, Illinois, Newspaper Gleanings, 1855-1875, comp. by Doris E.W. Bland. Fairfield: Bland Books, 1974. 129 pp.

## White County

History of White County, Illinois. Chicago: Inter-State Pub. Co., 1883. 972 pp. (Repr. N.p.: White County Hist. Soc., 1966, lacking pp. 1-188, History of Illinois.)

## Whiteside County

History of Whiteside County, Illinois, from Its First Settlement to the Present Time . . . ed. by Charles Bent. [Clinton, Iowa: L.P. Allen], 1877. 536 pp.

History of Whiteside County, Illinois . . . by William H. Davis. 2 vols. Chicago: Pioneer Pub., 1908.

Whiteside County, by Wayne Bastian. Morrison: Whiteside County Bd. of Supervisors, 1968. 480 pp.

## Will County

The History of Will County, Illinois . . . Chicago: William Le Baron, Jr., 1878. 995 pp. (Index. Winnetka: Winnetka Pub. Lib., 197-. Repr. with index. Evansville, Ind.: Unigraphic, 1973. iv, 995, 101 pp.)

*Will County (cont.)*

Souvenir of Settlement and Progress of Will County, Illinois . . . Chicago: Hist. Directory Pub. Co., 1884. 485 pp.

Past and Present of Will County, Illinois, by W.W. Stevens, et al. 2 vols. Chicago: S.J. Clarke Pub. Co., 1907.

History of Will County, by August Maue. 2 vols. Topeka, Kans.: Hist. Pub. Co., 1928.

## Williamson County

The History of Williamson County, Illinois . . . by Milo Erwin. Marion: N.p., 1876. viii, 286 pp. (Repr. Herrin: Herrin News, 1914.)

History of Williamson County, 1887, *see* p. 71.

Pioneer Folks and Places: an Historic Gazetteer of Williamson County, Illinois, by Barbara B. Hubbs. [Herrin: Herrin Daily Journal, 1939.] 249 pp.

## Winnebago County

The History of Winnebago County, Illinois, Its Past and Present . . . Chicago: H.F. Kett, 1877. 672 pp. (Index. Winnetka: Winnetka Pub. Lib., 1974. 156 pp.)

History of Rockford and Winnebago County, Illinois, from the First Settlement in 1834 to the Civil War, by Charles A. Church. Rockford: New England Soc. of Rockford, 1900. 386 pp.

Past and Present of the City of Rockford and Winnebago County, Illinois, by Charles A. Church. Chicago: S.J. Clarke Pub. Co., 1905. 684 pp. (Repr. Rockford: Rockford Hist. Soc., 1978.)

Historical Encyclopedia of Illinois . . . and History of Winnebago County, ed. by Charles A. Church. 2 vols. Chicago: Munsell Pub. Co., 1916.

This Is Winnebago County, Illinois; an Up-to-date Historical Narrative, by John Drury. Chicago: Island Photo Co., 1956. vi, 386 pp.

## Woodford County

History of Woodford County . . . by Benjamin J. Radford. Peoria: W.T. Dowdall, 1877. 78 pp.

The Past and Present of Woodford County, Illinois; Containing a History . . . comp. by W.H. Perrin and H.H. Hill. Chicago: William Le Baron, Jr., 1878. 660 pp. (Repr. with new name index. Evansville, Ind.: Unigraphic, 1979.)

History of Woodford County, by Roy L. Moore. Eureka: Woodford County Republican, 1910. 248 pp.

This is Woodford County, Illinois; an Up-to-date Historical Narrative, by John Drury. Chicago: Loree Co., 1955. vi, 410 pp.

The Woodford County History, comp. by Woodford County Sesquicentennial History Committee, ed. by William Yates. Bloomington: Woodford County Bd. of Supervisors, 1968. 212 pp.

# INDIANA

## Regional

Counties of Warren, Benton, Jasper and Newton, Indiana, Historical and Biographical, by Weston A. Goodspeed . . . Chicago: F. A. Battey, 1883. 810 pp. (Repr. Evansville: Unigraphic, 1979.)

Biographical and Historical Souvenir for the Counties of Clark, Crawford, Harrison, Floyd, Jefferson, Jennings, Scott and Washington, Indiana . . . comp. by John M. Gresham & Co. Chicago: Gresham & Co., 1889. 289, 300 pp.

History of Wayne, Fayette, Union and Franklin Counties. 2 vols. Chicago: Lewis Pub. Co., 1899.

History of Northeast Indiana: Lagrange, Steuben, Noble and De Kalb Counties, ed. by Ira Ford. 2 vols. Chicago: Lewis Pub. Co., 1920.

## Adams County

Biographical and Historical Record of Adams and Wells Counties, Indiana . . . Chicago: Lewis Pub. Co., 1887. 1,025 pp.

Reminiscences of Adams, Jay and Randolph Counties, comp. by Martha C. Lynch. [Fort Wayne: Lipes, Nelson & Singmaster, 1896.] 352 pp. (Repr. with new index. Knightstown: The Bookmark, 1980. 400 pp.)

Snow's History of Adams County, Indiana, by John F. Snow. Indianapolis: B. F. Bowen, 1907. 477 pp.

Standard History of Adams and Wells Counties, Indiana, ed. by John W. Tyndall and O. E. Leah. 2 vols. Chicago: Lewis Pub. Co., 1918. (Repr. Evansville: Unigraphic, 1980. 984 pp.)

A Short, Short Story of Adams County, Indiana. Berne: Economy Pr. Concern [1936]. 142 pp. (Repr. Decatur: [American Legion, 1956].)

The 1979 History of Adams County, Indiana, ed. by Dick D. Heller, Jr. Decatur: Adams County Hist. Soc., 1980. 786 pp.

## Allen County

History of Allen County, Indiana . . . [ed. by Thomas B. Helm]. Chicago: Kingman Bros., 1880. 188 pp.

History of the Maumee River Basin . . . by Charles E. Slocum [and R. S. Robertson]. 3 vols. Indianapolis: Bowe & Slocum [1905?]. (The Organization of Allen County, by R. S. Robertson, 1954. 49 pp. Originally Vol. 2 of History of Maumee River Basin.)

## Bartholomew County

The People's Guide . . . Also, a Historical Sketch of Bartholomew County . . . ed. by Cline & McHaffie. Indianapolis: Indianapolis Pr. & Pub. House, 1874. 400 pp.

History of Bartholomew County, Indiana. Chicago: Brant & Fuller, 1888. 892 pp.

## Benton County

County of . . . Benton, 1883, in Counties of Warren . . . *see* p. 91.

Annals of Benton County, by Elmore Barce. Fowler: Benton Review Shop, 1925. 134 pp.

History of Benton County, Indiana, by Elmore Barce and R. A. Swan. 3 vols. Fowler: Benton Review Shop, 1930-32.

Persons and Firms in the Benton County Histories, comp. by W.P.A. Knightstown: The Bookmark [1941?].

History of Benton County and Historic Oxford, by Jesse S. Birch. Oxford: Craw & Craw [1942]. xii, 386 pp.

## Blackford County

Biographical and Historical Record of Blackford County, 1887, *see* Jay County.

Blackford and Grant Counties, ed. by Benjamin G. Shinn. 2 vols. Chicago: Lewis Pub. Co., 1914.

## Boone County

People's Guide . . . to Boone County, Indiana, by Cline & McHaffie. Indianapolis: Indianapolis Pr. & Pub. House, 1874. 248 pp.

Early Life and Times in Boone County, Indiana . . . from the First Down to 1886 . . . comp. by Samuel Harden and D. Spahr. [Indianapolis: Carlon & Hollenbeck Pr., 1887.] 498 pp. (Repr. Evansville: Unigraphic, 1979.)

History of Boone County . . . by Leander M. Crist. 2 vols. Indianapolis: A.W. Bowen [1914].

## Brown County

Counties of Morgan, Monroe and Brown, by C. Blanchard. Chicago: F.A. Battey, 1884. 800 pp. (Repr. of Brown County part, with new index. Evansville: Unigraphic, 1979?)

Tales and Trails of Brown County, Indiana, by Frances C. Feare. [Nashville:] Brown County Business & Prof. Women's Club [1965]. 60 pp.

## Carroll County

Recollections of the Early Settlement of Carroll County, Indiana, by James H. Stewart. Cincinnati: Hitchcock & Walden, 1872. 372 pp. (Repr. Knightstown: The Bookmark, 1977. 401 pp.)

History of Carroll County, Indiana . . . [ed. by Thomas B. Helm]. Chicago: Kingman Bros., 1882. 352 pp. (Repr. Knightstown: Eastern Indiana Pub. Co., 1966. 352 pp.)

History of Carroll County, Indiana . . . by John C. Odell. Indianapolis: B.F. Bowen, 1916. 679 pp. (Repr. with new index. Evansville: Unigraphic, 1973. 679, 42 pp.)

## Cass County

History of Cass County, Indiana, by Thomas B. Helm. Chicago: Kingman Bros. 1878. 63 pp.

History of Cass County . . . by Thomas B. Helm. Chicago: Brant & Fuller, 1886. 976 pp.

History of Cass County, Indiana, from Its Earliest Settlement to the Present Time . . . ed. by Jehu Z. Powell. 2 vols. Chicago: Lewis Pub. Co., 1913.

## Clark County

Biographical and Historical Souvenir for the County of Clark, 1889, *see* p. 91. (Repr. of Clark County part. Knightstown: The Bookmark, 1977. 158 pp.)

Baird's History of Clark County, Indiana, by Captain Lewis C. Baird. Indianapolis: B.F. Bowen, 1909. 919 pp.

## Clay County

Counties of Clay and Owen, Indiana, Historical and Biographical, ed. by Charles Blanchard. Chicago: F.A. Battey, 1884. 966 pp.

A History of Clay County, Indiana, Closing for the First Century's History . . . by William Travis. 2 vols. New York: Lewis Pub. Co., 1909.

## Clinton County

History of Clinton County, Indiana . . . Chicago: Inter-State Pub. Co., 1886. 924 pp.

History of Clinton County, Indiana . . . by Hon. Joseph Claybaugh. Indianapolis: A.W. Bowen & Co., 1913. 982 pp.

## Crawford County

Biographical and Historical Souvenir for the County of . . . Crawford, 1889, *see* p. 91. (Repr. of Crawford County part. Knightstown: The Bookmark, 1977. 106 pp.)

A History of Crawford County, Indiana, by Hazen H. Pleasant. Greenfield: Mitchell Pr. Co., 1926. viii, 644 pp.

## Daviess County

History of Daviess County, 1886, *see* Knox County.

History of Daviess County, Indiana, ed. by Alva Fulkerson. Indianapolis: B.F. Bowen, 1915. (W.P.A. index; index of Persons and Firms in Four Daviess County Atlases, Histories, etc. Knightstown: The Bookmark, 197-. 212 pp.)

## Dearborn County

History of Dearborn and Ohio Counties, Indiana, from Their Earliest Settlement . . . Chicago: F.E. Weakley, 1885. 987 pp. (Repr. Evansville: Unigraphic, 1979.)

History of Dearborn County . . . ed. by Archibald Shaw. Indianapolis: B.F. Bowen, 1915. 1,072 pp. (Repr. Evansville: Unigraphic, 1980.)

## Decatur County

History of Decatur County, Indiana . . . by Lewis A. Harding. Indianapolis: B.F Bowen, 1915. 1,216 pp.

## De Kalb County

Pioneer Sketches, Containing Facts and Incidents of the Early History of De Kalb County, by S.W. Widney. Auburn: W.T. & J.M. Kimsey, 1859. xlvi, 53 pp.

History of De Kalb County . . . Chicago: Inter-State Pub. Co., 1885. 1,028 pp. (Repr. with all-name index. Knightstown: The Bookmark, 1978. 1,072 pp.)

History of De Kalb County, Indiana . . . Indianapolis: B.F. Bowen, 1914. 1,004 pp.

History of . . . De Kalb County, 1920, in History of Northeast Indiana, *see* p. 91.

## Delaware County

History of Delaware County, Indiana . . . [by Thomas B. Helm]. Chicago: Kingman Bros., 1881. 303 pp. (Repr. Evansville: Unigraphic, 1979.)

Our County: Its History and Early Settlement . . . by John S. Ellis. [Muncie: Neely Pr. Co., 189-.] 194 pp.

A Twentieth Century History of Delaware County, Indiana . . . ed. by General William H. Kemper. 2 vols. Chicago: Lewis Pub. Co., 1908.

History of Delaware County, Indiana, ed. by Frank D. Haimbaugh. 2 vols. Indianapolis: Hist. Pub. Co., 1924.

Muncie and Delaware County: an Historical Sketch, by Richard A. Greene. Muncie: Delaware County Hist. Soc., 1965.

## Dubois County

History of Dubois County, 1885, *see* Pike County.

History of DuBois County from Its Primitive Days to 1910 . . . by George R. Wilson. Jasper: Author, 1910. 412 pp.

Teder's History of DuBois County, by John H. Teder. [Jasper?: N.p., 1964.] 224 pp.

A History of Northeast DuBois County, by Alves J. Kreitzer. DuBois: N.p., 1970. xi, 458 pp.

## Elkhart County

History of Elkhart County, Indiana . . . Chicago: C.C. Chapman, 1881. 1,181 pp.

A Twentieth Century History . . . of Elkhart County, Indiana, ed. by Anthony Deahl. Chicago: Lewis Pub. Co., 1905. xii, 793 pp.

A Standard History of Elkhart County, Indiana . . . ed. by Abraham E. Weaver. 2 vols. Chicago: American Hist. Soc., 1916.

Pioneer History of Elkhart County, Indiana, with Sketches . . . by Henry S.K. Bartholomew. [Goshen: Goshen Pr., 1930.] xvi, 337. (Repub. under title, Stories and Sketches of Elkhart County . . . [Nappanee: E.V. Pub. House, 1936.] xi, 336 pp.)

## Fayette County

History of Fayette County, Indiana . . . Chicago: Warner, Beers, 1885. 331 pp.

History of . . . Fayette County, 1899, in History of Wayne . . . County, *see* p. 91.

The History of Fayette County, ed. by Frederick I. Barrows. [Indianapolis: B.F. Bowen], 1917. 1,159 pp. (Repr. Knightstown: The Bookmark, 1982.)

## Floyd County

Biographical and Historical Souvenir for the County of . . . Floyd, 1889, *see* p. 91. (Repr. of Floyd County part. Knightstown: The Bookmark, 1977. 154 pp.)

## Fountain County

History of Fountain County, Together with Historic Notes on the Wabash Valley . . . Fountain County, by T.F. Davidson, and Wabash Valley, by H.W. Beckwith. Chicago: H.H. Hill & N. Iddings, 1881. 264, 494, 224 pp. (Also has section on Montgomery County, by P.S. Kennedy.) (Repr. Covington: D.A.R., Richard Henry Lee Chapter, 1970. Repr. with name index. Evansville: Unigraphic, 1979. 982 pp.)

Past and Present of Fountain and Warren Counties, Indiana, ed. by Thomas A. Clifton. Indianapolis: B.F. Bowen, 1913. 987 pp.

## Franklin County

History of . . . Franklin County, 1899, in History of Wayne . . . County, *see* p. 91.

History of Franklin County . . . by August J. Reifel. Indianapolis: B.F. Bowen, 1915. 1,475 pp. (Repr. Evansville: Unigraphic, 1971.)

## Fulton County

Fulton County: the Pictorial Story of America, Containing the Romantic Incidents of History . . . by Elia W. Peattie. 3 parts in 1 vol. Chicago: National Pub. Co., 1896.

## Gibson County

History of Gibson County, Indiana. Edwardsville: James T. Tartt & Co., 1884. 244 pp. (Repr. Evansville: Unigraphic, 1978.)

History of Gibson County . . . by Gilbert R. Stormont. Indianapolis: B.F. Bowen, 1914. 1,076 pp. (Repr. Evansville: Unigraphic, 1979.)

## Grant County

History of Grant County, Indiana, from Earliest Times to the Present . . . Chicago: Brant & Fuller, 1886. 944 pp. (Repr. Evansville: Unigraphic, 1974. Repr. Knightstown: The Bookmark, 1982.)

Grant County [History], 1914, *see* Blackford County.

Centennial History of Grant County, 1812 to 1912 . . . ed. by Rolland L. Whitson. 2 vols. Chicago: Lewis Pub. Co., 1914. 1,429 pp.

## Greene County

The Early History of Greene County, Indiana . . . comp. by Jack Baber. Worthington: Milleson, 1875. (Repr. Indianapolis: Hoosier Bookshop, 1962. 96 pp.)

History of Greene and Sullivan Counties, Indiana . . . Chicago: Goodspeed Bros., 1884. 824 pp. (Repr. with index. Evansville: Unigraphic, 1975. 881 pp. Repr. Sullivan: Sullivan County Hist. Soc., 1984. 873 pp.)

Pioneer Days: a History of Early Bloomfield and Greene County. Bloomfield: N.p., 1959. 109 pp.

## Hamilton County

The People's Guide . . . Also a Historical Sketch of Hamilton County . . . by Cline & McHaffie. Indianapolis: Indianapolis Pr. & Pub. House, 1874. 411 pp.

History of Hamilton County, Indiana, by Thomas B. Helm. Chicago: Kingman Bros., 1880. 148 pp. (Repr. with added appendix of sesquicentennial items. Evansville: Unigraphic, 1973. 148, 30 pp.)

*Hamilton County (cont.)*

A History of the Formation, Settlement and Development of Hamilton County, Indiana, from 1818 to the Close of the Civil War, by Augustus F. Shirts. N.p., 1901. 370 pp.

History of Hamilton County, Indiana . . . by John F. Haines. Indianapolis: B.F. Bowen, 1915. 1,001 pp.

## Hancock County

History of Hancock County, Indiana, from Its Earliest Settlement . . . in 1818, Down to 1882 . . . by John H. Binford. Greenfield: King and Binford, 1882. 536 pp.

The Pioneer, comp. by Samuel Harden, 1895, *see* Madison County.

History of Hancock County, Indiana, by George J. Richmond. Indianapolis: Federal Pub. Co., 1916. 1,155 pp. (Repr. Knightstown: The Bookmark, 1982.)

The Hancock County Kaleidoscope, by Dorothy J. Williams. N.p.: Hancock County Hist. Soc., 1976. 607 pp.

## Harrison County

Biographical and Historical Souvenir for the County of . . . Harrison, 1889, *see* p. 91. (Repr. of Harrison County part. Knightstown: The Bookmark, 1977. 186 pp.)

Illustrated Atlas and History of Harrison County, Indiana, comp. by F.A. Bulleit. Corydon: F.A. Bulleit, 1906. 78 pp.

History of Harrison County, by William H. Roose. New Albany: Tribune, 1911. 78 pp.

Indiana's Birthplace: a History of Harrison County, Indiana, originally comp. by William H. Roose (1911), rev. in 1966, by Arville L. Funk. Chicago: Adams Pr., 1966. 92 pp.

Harrison County in the Indiana Sesquicentennial Year, by Arville L. Funk. Chicago: Adams Pr. [1967]. 79 pp.

## Hendricks County

The People's Guide . . . Also a Historical Sketch of Hendricks County . . . by Cline & McHaffie. Indianapolis: Indianapolis Pr. and Pub. House, 1874. 400 pp.

History of Hendricks County, Indiana. Chicago: Inter-State Pub. Co., 1885. 755 pp.

History of Hendricks County, Indiana . . . ed. by John V. Hadley. Indianapolis: B.F. Bowen, 1914. 845 pp.

History of Hendricks County, 1914-1976, ed. by John R. McDowell, Jr. Danville: Hendricks County Hist. Soc., 1976. 640 pp.

## Henry County

Henry County Past and Present: a Brief History of the County from 1821 to 1871, by Edward Pleas. New Castle: Pleas Bros., 1871. iv, 148 pp. (Repr. Knightstown: Eastern Indiana Pub. Co., 1967.)

The People's Guide . . . Also a Historical Sketch of Henry County . . . by Cline & McHaffie. Indianapolis: Indianapolis Pr. & Pub. House, 1874. 400 pp.

History of Henry County, Indiana . . . by Edward Pleas. Chicago: Inter-State Pub. Co., 1884. 912 pp. (Repr. Knightstown: The Bookmark, 1966.) (Omitting state history, 558 pp.)

Hazzard's History of Henry County, Indiana, 1822-1906 . . . by George Hazzard. 2 vols. New Castle: G. Hazzard, 1906.

Index to Histories, etc. W.P.A. N.p., 194-. 482 pp.

## Howard County

Counties of Howard and Tipton, Indiana, Historical and Biographical . . . ed. by Charles Blanchard. Chicago: F.A. Battey, 1883. 453 pp. (Repr. Howard County part. Knightstown: The Bookmark, 1979. 497 pp.)

History of Howard County, Indiana, by Jackson Morrow . . . 2 vols. Indianapolis: B.F. Bowen [1909?]. 1,078 pp.

Howard County W.P.A. Index: Names of Persons and Firms That Appear in Howard County Histories. [N.p., 1941.] 256 pp. (Repr. Knightstown: The Bookmark, 1979.)

## Huntington County

History of Huntington County, Indiana, from the Earliest Time to the Present . . . Chicago: Brant & Fuller, 1887. 883 pp.

History of Huntington County, Indiana, comp. by Frank S. Bash. 2 vols. Chicago: Lewis Pub. Co., 1914.

## Jackson County

History of Jackson County, Indiana. Chicago: Brant & Fuller, 1886. 760 pp. (Repr. Evansville: Unigraphic, 1979.)

Early History of Jackson County, by Holmes W. Chadwick. [Brownstown: The Banner, 1943.] 73 pp.

Historical and Genealogical Records Pertaining to Jackson County, Indiana, by D.A.R., Fort Vallonia Chapter. Seymour: The Chapter, 1952. 237 pp.

## Jasper County

County of . . . Jasper, 1883, in Counties of Warren . . . *see* p. 91. (Repr. Jasper County part. Knightstown: The Bookmark, 1981. 214 pp.)

Standard History of Jasper and Newton Counties . . . ed. by Louis R. Hamilton and W. Darroch. 2 vols. Chicago: Lewis Pub. Co., 1916. (2d pr., with personal name index [comp. by Mark Marler. Nashville, Tenn.: N.p., 1971.] 52 pp.) (Omits prominent men of Indiana.)

Jasper County History, by Milton Jay. N.p., 1922. (Repr. with new name index. Knightstown: The Bookmark, 1979. 498 pp.)

Jasper County W.P.A. Index. Names of Persons and Firms That Appear in Jasper County Histories, Atlases or Other Source Books. N.p., 194-. (Repr. Knightstown: The Bookmark, 1979. 161 pp.)

## Jay County

History of Jay County, Indiana, by W.W. Montgomery. Chicago: Author, 1864? 288 pp.

Historical Hand-atlas and History of Jay County, Indiana. Chicago: H.H. Hardesty, 1881. 228 pp.

Biographical and Historical Record of Jay and Blackford Counties, Indiana . . . Chicago: Lewis Pub. Co., 1887. 901 pp. (Repr. of Jay County part. Knightstown: The Bookmark, 1979. 514 pp. Index, comp. by Debra J. LeCount. Knightstown: The Bookmark, 1976. 41 pp.)

Reminiscences of . . . Jay County, 1897, *see* Adams County.

History of Jay County, Indiana, by Milton T. Jay. Indianapolis: Hist. Pub. Co., 1922. 262 pp. (Repr. with new name index. Knightstown: The Bookmark, 1979. 498 pp.)

History of Jay County, Indiana. Portland: Jay County Hist. Book, 1983.

## Jefferson County

Biographical and Historical Souvenir for the County of . . . Jefferson, 1889, *see* p. 91. (Repr. of Jefferson County part. Knightstown: The Bookmark, 1977. 228 pp.)

A History of Jefferson County . . . by Emory O. Muncie. Bloomington: Indiana Univ., 1932. 169 pp. (thesis)

## Jennings County

Biographical and Historical Souvenir for the County of . . . Jennings, 1889, *see* p. 91. (Repr. of Jennings County part. Knightstown: The Bookmark, 1977. 125 pp.)

## Johnson County

The People's Guide . . . of Johnson County, Indiana, by Cline & McHaffie. Indianapolis: Indianapolis Pr. and Pub. House, 1874. 399 pp.

A Historical Sketch of Johnson County, Indiana, by David D. Banta. Chicago: J.H. Beers & Co., 1881. 170 pp.

History of Johnson County, from the Earliest Time to the Present . . . Chicago: Brant & Fuller, 1888. 918 pp.

History of Johnson County, Indiana, by Elba L. Branigin. Indianapolis: B.F. Bowen, 1913. 863 pp.

## Knox County

History of Knox and Daviess Counties, from Earliest Times . . . Chicago: Goodspeed Pub. Co., 1886. 914 pp. (Outline index, by Elsie Adams, et al. [Vincennes:] Vincennes Hist. & Antiquarian Soc. [1973]. 448 pp.)

History of Old Vincennes and Knox County, Indiana, by George E. Greene. 2 vols. Chicago: Clark, 1911. 893 pp.

## Kosciusko County

Biographical and Historical Record of Kosciusko County . . . Chicago: Lewis Pub. Co., 1887. 734 pp.

Kosciusko County, Indiana: Early History . . . comp. by L.B. Hillis. Warsaw: Reub Williams & Sons, 1911. 24 pp.

A Standard History of Kosciusko County . . . by Hon. Lemuel W. Royse. 2 vols. Chicago: Lewis Pub. Co., 1919. 709 pp.

## Lagrange County

Counties of Lagrange and Noble, Indiana, Historical and Biographical . . . Chicago: F.A. Battey, 1882. 441, 502 pp.

History of . . . Lagrange County, 1920, in History of Northeast Indiana, *see* p. 91.

Lagrange County Centennial History, comp. by John W. Hanan, 1828-1928. Lagrange: Lagrange Pub. Co. [1929]. 121 pp.

## Lake County

Lake County, Indiana, from 1834 to 1872, by Rev. Timothy H. Ball. Chicago: J.W. Goodspeed, 1873. 364 pp.

County of Lake, 1882, *see* Porter County.

Lake County, Indiana, 1884; an Account of the Semi-centennial Celebration . . . with Historical Papers . . . Old Settler & Historical Association of Lake County, Indiana, ed. by T.H. Ball. Crown Point: T.H. Ball, 1884. 486 pp.

Encyclopedia of Genealogy and Biography of Lake County, with a Compendium of History . . . Chicago: Lewis Pub. Co., 1904. 674 pp. (Repr. Evansville: Unigraphic, 1979.)

*Lake County (cont.)*

A Standard History of Lake County, Indiana, ed. by William F. Howab. 2 vols. Chicago: Lewis Pub. Co., 1915.

History of the Lake and Calumet Regions of Indiana, Embracing the Counties of Lake, Porter and LaPorte . . . comp. by Thomas H. Cannon. 2 vols. Indianapolis: Hist. Assoc., 1927.

The First Hundred Years of Lake County, Indiana, by Sam B. Woods. [Crown Point?: N.p.], 1938. 418 pp.

This Is Lake County, Indiana: an Up-to-date Historical Narrative . . . by John Drury. Chicago: Inland Photo Co., 1956. vi, 250 pp.

## LaPorte County

History of LaPorte County, Indiana . . . by Jasper Packard. LaPorte: S.E. Taylor, 1876. 467 pp.

History of LaPorte County, Indiana . . . Chicago: C.C. Chapman & Co., 1880. 914 pp.

A Twentieth Century History . . . of LaPorte County, Indiana, by E.D. Daniels. Chicago: Lewis Pub. Co., 1904. xiv, 813 pp.

History of the County of . . . LaPorte, 1927, *see* Lake County.

## Lawrence County

History of Lawrence and Washington Counties, Indiana . . . Chicago: Goodspeed, 1884. 937 pp.

History of Lawrence and Monroe Counties, Indiana . . . Indianapolis: B.F. Bowen & Co., 1914. 764 pp.

Thirty-three Years in the History of Lawrence County, Indiana, 1884-1917, by James M. Guthrie. Bedford: N.p., 1958. 223 pp.

## Madison County

History of Madison County, Indiana, from 1820 to 1874 . . . comp. by Samuel Harden. Markleville: N.p., 1874. 411 pp.

History of Madison County . . . [ed. by Thomas B. Helm]. Chicago: Kingman, 1880. 128 pp. (Repr. Evansville: Unigraphic, 1971. Bound in is a repr. of Atlas and Directory of Madison County, Indiana. Cleveland: American Atlas Co., 1901. 218 pp.)

The Pioneer, comp. by Samuel Harden. Greenfield: William Mitchell Pr. Co., 1895. 457 pp. (Account of the pioneers of Madison and Hancock Counties, Indiana.) (Repr. with index. Evansville: Unigraphic, 1970. 488 pp.)

Historical Sketches and Reminiscences of Madison County . . . by John L. Forkner and B.H. Dyson. [Logansport: Pr. of Wilson, Humphreys], 1897. 1,038 pp.

History of Madison County, Indiana . . . comp. by John L. Forkner. 2 vol Chicago: Lewis Pub. Co., 1914. 791 pp. (Repr. 2 vols. in 1. Evansvill Unigraphic, 1970.)

Centennial History of Madison County, Indiana, 1823-1923, ed. by James . Netterville. 2 vols. Anderson: Hist. Assoc., 1925.

Madison County, W.P.A. Index. Names of Persons and Firms That Appear i Madison County Histories, Atlases or Other Source Books. [Indianapoli: W.P.A., 1941.] 708 pp.

## Marion County

History of Indianapolis and Marion County, Indiana, by Berry R. Sulgrove Philadelphia: L.H. Everts, 1854. x, 666 pp. (Repr.? 1884.)

The People's Guide . . . Also a Historical Sketch of Marion County . . . by Cline & McHaffie. Indianapolis: Indianapolis Pr. & Pub. House, 1874. 600 pp.

Greater Indianapolis . . . Marion County, by Jacob P. Dunn. 2 vols. Chicago: Lewis Pub. Co., 1910. (Repr. Evansville: Unigraphic, 1977. Repr. Knightstown: The Bookmark, 1982. 1,300 pp.)

A Home in the Woods; Oliver Johnson's Reminiscences of Early Marion County, as Related by Howard Johnson. Indianapolis: Indiana Hist. Soc., 1951. (In Indiana Hist. Soc. Pub., Vol. 16:2, pp. 143-234.)

## Marshall County

Holland's Plymouth City Directory for 1876-77, and History of Marshall County, Indianapolis. Chicago: Western Pub. Co., 1876. 168 pp.

History of Marshall County, Indiana, 1836-1880, by Daniel McDonald. Chicago: Kingman Bros., 1881. 154 pp.

A Twentieth Century History of Marshall County, Indiana, comp. by Hon. Daniel McDonald. 2 vols. Chicago: Lewis Pub. Co., 1908. (Repr. 2 vols. Indianapolis: Hoosier Heritage Pr. [1973]. xiv, 648 pp.)

The Story of Marshall County, by Minnie H. Swindell. [Plymouth:] N.p., 1923. 87 pp.

Marshall County, W.P.A. Inventory: History and Records. N.p., 1941. 465 pp.

## Martin County

History of Martin County, Indiana, by Harry Q. Holt. 2 vols. Paoli: Stout's Pr. Shop, 1953, 1966.

## Miami County

History of Miami County, from the Earliest Time to the Present . . . Chicago: Brant & Fuller, 1887. 812 pp. (Name index. Peru: American Pub., 1977.)

*Miami County (cont.)*

History of Miami County, Indiana, by John H. Stephens. Peru: Author, 1896. 380 pp. (Repr. Evansville: Unigraphic, 1976.)

History of Miami County, Indiana . . . ed. by A.L. Bodurtha. 2 vols. Chicago: Lewis Pub. Co., 1914.

## Monroe County

County of . . . Monroe, 1884, *see* Morgan County. (Repr. of Monroe County part. Knightstown: The Bookmark, 1978. 316 pp.)

History of Monroe County, 1914, *see* Lawrence County.

Historic Treasures, True Tales of Deeds with Interesting Data in the Life of Bloomington, Indiana, and Monroe County, comp. by Forest M. Bell. Bloomington: Indiana Univ. Pr., 1922. 182 pp. (Repr. Indianapolis: Ye Olde Gen. Shoppe, 1979.)

## Montgomery County

People's Guide . . . of Montgomery County, by Cline & McHaffie. Indianapolis: Indianapolis Pr. and Pub. House, 1874. 400 pp.

Montgomery County . . . History, by P.S. Kennedy, 1881, *see* Fountain County.

History of Montgomery County, Indiana . . . 2 vols. Indianapolis: A.W. Bowen & Co., 1913.

Sugar Creek Saga: a History and Development of Montgomery County, by Theodore G. Gronert. Crawfordsville: Wabash Coll., 1958. 496 pp.

## Morgan County

The People's Guide . . . Also, a Historical Sketch of Morgan County . . . by Cline & McHaffie. Indianapolis: Indianapolis Pr. and Pub. House, 1874. 406 pp.

Counties of Morgan, Monroe and Brown . . . ed. by Charles Blanchard. Chicago: F.A. Battey, 1884. 800 pp. (Repr. Evansville: Unigraphic, 1969. Index, by Esther A. Watts. Whittier, Calif.: Author, 1972. 163 pp. Repr. of Morgan County part. Knightstown: The Bookmark, 1978. 316 pp.)

The Pioneers of Morgan County: Memoirs of Noah J. Major, ed. by Logan Esarey. Indianapolis: E.J. Hecker, 1915. (Indiana Hist. Soc., Pub., Vol. 5:5, pp. 231-516.)

One Hundred Men: a Legislative History of Morgan County, Indiana, by Noble K. Littell. N.p., 1970. 135 pp.

## Newton County

County of . . . Newton, 1883, in Counties of Warren, *see* p. 91. (Repr. of Newton County part. Knightstown: The Bookmark, 1979. 259 pp.)

Newton County, by John Ade; a Collection of Historical Facts . . . Concerning Newton County, from 1853 to 1911. Indianapolis: Bobbs-Merrill Co. [1911]. 320 pp.

Standard History of Newton County, 1916, *see* Jasper County.

100 Years of Newton County History, 1860-1960, by John M. Connell. [Brook: Brook Reporter, 1940.] 40 pp.

## Noble County

County of Noble, 1882, *see* Lagrange County.

County of Noble, 1882, *see* Whitley County.

Alvord's History of Noble County . . . by Samuel E. Alvord. Logansport: Bowen, 1902. 602 pp.

History of . . . Noble County, 1920, in History of Northeast Indiana, *see* p. 91.

Noble County and the Indiana Sesquicentennial; Decades of Decision and History of Noble County from Prehistoric Times to the Present, by Norman J. Carter. [Ligonier:] N.p., 1966. 96 pp.

## Ohio County

History of Ohio County, 1885, *see* Dearborn County.

## Orange County

History of . . . Orange County, 1884, *see* Lawrence County.

History of Orange County, Indiana. Paoli: Stout's Pr. Shop, 1965. (Repr. from History of Lawrence, Orange and Washington Counties, 1884, pp. 355-670.)

History of Orange County, Indiana. Paoli: Paoli Business & Prof. Women's Club, 1950. 320 pp.

Orange County Heritage, comp. by Arthur L. Dillard. Paoli: Stout's Pr. Shop, 1971. 240 pp.

## Owen County

County of Owen, Historical, 1884, *see* Clay County.

History of Owen County, ed. by Charles Blanchard. 2 vols. Spencer: First Pioneer Days Festival, 1962-63.

Fact and Folklore of Owen County, Indiana, by Dixie Kline. 2 vols. Spencer: Author, 1976-82.

## Parke County

History of Parke County, 1880, *see* Vigo County. (Repr. of Parke County part. Knightstown: The Bookmark, 1979. 504 pp.)

*Parke County (cont.)*

History of Parke and Vermillion Counties, Indiana, with Historical Sketches . . . Indianapolis: B.F. Bowen, 1913. 816 pp.

Parke County, Indiana, Centennial Memorial . . . Rockville: [Rockville Chautauqua Assoc., 1916]. 128 pp.

## Perry County

History of . . . Perry County, 1885, *see* Warrick County.

Perry County: a History, by Thomas J. de la Hunt. Indianapolis: W.K. Stewart Co., 1916. xii, 350 pp.

## Pike County

History of Pike and DuBois Counties, Indiana . . . Chicago: Goodspeed Bros., 1885. 786 pp. (Repr. Evansville: Unigraphic, 1965. Repr. Pike County part. Knightstown: The Bookmark, 1979. 296 pp.)

Pike County History: Bicentennial ed., 1776-1976, comp. by Ruth M. McClellan. Petersburg: Pike County Hist. Soc., 1976. 501 pp.

Our People of Pike County, Indiana, by Ruth M. McClellan. Evansville: Unigraphic, 1978. 248 pp.

## Porter County

Counties of Porter and Lake, Indiana, Historical and Biographical . . . ed. by Weston A. Goodspeed and Charles Blanchard. Chicago: F.A. Battey, 1882. 771 pp.

History of Porter County . . . by Harry G. Cutler. 2 vols. Chicago: Lewis Pub. Co., 1912. 881 pp.

History of the County of . . . Porter, 1927, *see* Lake County.

This is Porter County; an Up-to-date Historical Narrative . . . by John Drury. Chicago: Inland Photo Co., 1956. iv, 356 pp.

## Posey County

History and Directory of Posey County . . . by William P. Leonard. Evansville: A.C. Isaacs, 1882. 264 pp. (Repr. Evansville: Unigraphic, 1979.)

History of Posey County . . . Chicago: Goodspeed, 1886. 714 pp. (Repr. with index. Evansville: Unigraphic, 1974. Repr. Knightstown: The Bookmark, 1982.)

The History of Posey County, by J.C. Leffel. Chicago: Standard Pub. Co., 1913. 401 pp.

## Pulaski County

County of Pulaski, Historical, 1883, *see* White County.

A Century of Achievement in Pulaski County, Indiana, 1839-1939, by John G. Reidelbach. Winamac: N.p., 1939. 146 pp. (Repr., 1972.)

## Putnam County

Biographical and Historical Record of Putnam County, Indiana . . . Chicago: Lewis Pub. Co., 1887. 522 pp. (Repr. Knightstown: Eastern Indiana Pub. Co., 1967. Personal index. [Nashville: M. Marler, 1971.] 52 pp. Repr. with index. Knightstown: The Bookmark, 1975.)

Weiks' History of Putnam County, Indiana, by Jesse Weiks. Indianapolis: B.F. Bowen & Co., 1910. 785 pp.

A Journey Through Putnam County History, by Putnam County Sesquicentennial Committee. N.p. [1966]. 444 pp.

## Randolph County

Directory and Historical Sketches of Randolph County, Illinois. N.p.: Montague, 1859. 250 pp. (Repr. Evansville: Unigraphic, 1979.)

History of Randolph County, Indiana, by Ebenezer Tucker. Chicago: Kingman Bros., 1882. 512 pp. (Repr. with new added surname index. Winchester: Randolph County Hist. Soc., 1984.)

Reminiscences of . . . Randolph County, 1897?, *see* Adams County.

Randolph County, Indiana Past and Present, by John L. Smith and L.L. Driver. Indianapolis: Bowen, 1914. 1,603 pp. (Repr. 2 vols. Lynn: Randolph Southern Hist. Soc., 198-?)

## Ripley County

History and Directory of Ripley County, by Edward C. Jerman. [Versailles: Republican Pr., 1888.] 88 pp.

History of Ripley County, Indiana, by Indiana Federation of Business and Professional Women's Clubs. Batavia, Ohio: Clermont Pub. Co., 1968. 137 pp.

## Rush County

History of Rush County, Indiana . . . Chicago: Brant & Fuller, 1888. 867 pp. (Repr. Knightstown: Eastern Indiana Pub. Co., 1966. 629 pp.)

Sketches of Rush County, Indiana, ed. by Mary M. Alexander and C.G. Dill. Rushville: Jacksonville Pub. Co., 1915. 100, xxxiv pp.

Centennial History of Rush County, Indiana, ed. by Abraham L. Gary and E.B. Thomas. 2 vols. Indianapolis: Hist. Pub. Co., 1921. (Repr. 2 vols. Knightstown: Mayhill Pub. Co., 197-. 1,200 pp.)

Rush County History, 1822-1972 . . . [ed. by Eleanor Arnold]. [Sesquicentennial ed.] [Richville: Rush County Sesquicentennial, 1972?] 96 pp.

## St. Joseph County

History of St. Joseph County, Indiana . . . Chicago: C.C. Chapman, 1880. 971 pp. (Repr. Knightstown: The Bookmark, 1982.)

A History of St. Joseph County, Indiana, by Timothy E. Howard. 2 vols. Chicago: Lewis Pub. Co., 1907.

An Account of St. Joseph County from Its Organization . . . by John B. Stoll. Dayton: Dayton Hist. Pub. Co., 1923. 565 pp. (Issued as Vol. 3 of Logan Esarey's History of Indiana . . . to 1922.)

## Scott County

Biographical and Historical Souvenir for the County of . . . Scott, 1889, *see* p. 91. (Repr. Scott County part. Knightstown: Mayhill Pub., 1977. 74 pp.)

## Shelby County

History of Shelby County, Indiana, from 1822 to 1876 . . . Shelbyville: R. Spicer, 1876. 40 pp.

History of Shelby County, Indiana . . . Chicago: Brant & Fuller, 1887. 794 pp. (Repr. Knightstown: Eastern Indiana Pub. Co., 1968. 547 pp.)

Chadwick's History of Shelby County, Indiana, by Edward H. Chadwick. Indianapolis: B.F. Bowen, 1909. 982 pp. (Repr. Evansville: Unigraphic, 1979.)

Biographical and Historical Sketches of Shelby County, comp. from William Hacker's Historical Records, La Fayette & Shelby Lodge no. 28, F. & A.M., 1879, comp. by Claude J. Haymond. Indianapolis: Indiana Hist. Soc., 1930. 74 pp.

## Spencer County

History of Spencer County, 1885, *see* Warrick County.

## Starke County

McCormick's Guide to Starke County . . . by Chester A. McCormick. [Knox:] Author, 1902. 102 pp. (Repr. Indianapolis: Hoosier Bookshop, 1962.)

Standard History of Starke County . . . by Joseph N. McCormick. Chicago: Lewis Pub. Co., 1915. 747 pp.

## Steuben County

History of Steuben County, Indiana . . . Chicago: Inter-State Pub. Co., 1885. 868 pp.

The County of Steuben, Indiana. Angola: Imperial Pub. Co., 1898. 99 pp.

History of . . . Steuben County, 1920, in History of Northeast Indiana, *see* p. 91.

The 1955 History of Steuben County, Indiana . . . ed. by Harvey W. Morley. [Angola:] H.W. Morley, 1956. xv, 610 pp.

## Sullivan County

History of Sullivan County, 1884, *see* Greene County.

A History of Sullivan County, Indiana, Closing of the First Century's History of the County . . . ed. by Thomas J. Wolfe. 2 vols. New York: Lewis Pub. Co., 1909.

## Tippecanoe County

Past and Present of Tippecanoe County, Indiana, ed. by Richard P. De Hart. 2 vols. Indianapolis: B.F. Bowen, 1909.

A History of Tippecanoe County and the Wabash Valley. Dayton, Ohio: National Hist. Assoc., 1928. 204, 136 pp.

## Tipton County

County of Tipton, Historical, 1883, *see* Howard County. (Repr. Tipton County part. Knightstown: The Bookmark, 197-. 451 pp.)

Tipton County, Her Land and People. Tipton: Tipton County Pub. Co., 1976. 832 pp.

## Union County

History of . . . Union County, 1899, in History of Wayne . . . County, *see* p. 91.

## Vanderburgh County

History of Vanderburgh County, Indiana, from Earliest Times to the Present . . . [Madison, Wis.] Brant & Fuller, 1889. 675 pp. (Repr. Evansville: Unigraphic, 1980.)

A History of Evansville and Vanderburgh County, Indiana, . . . by Jospeh P. Elliott. Evansville: Keller Pr. Co., 1897. 499 pp.

History of the City of Evansville and Vanderburgh County, Indiana, by Frank M. Gilbert. 2 vols. Chicago: Pioneer Pub. Co., 1910.

## Vermillion County

The People's Guide . . . with . . . a Historical Sketch of Vermillion County . . . by Cline & McHaffie. Indianapolis: Indianapolis Pr. and Pub. House, 1874. 399 pp.

Biographical and Historical Record of Vermillion County, Indiana . . . Chicago: Lewis Pub. Co., 1888. 520 pp.

History of Vermillion County, 1913, *see* Parke County.

## Vigo County

History of Vigo and Parke Counties . . . by Hiram W. Beckwith. Chicago: H.H. Hill & N. Iddings, 1880. 264, 504, 525 pp. (Repr. of Vigo County part. Knightstown: Mayhill Pub., 1977. 533 pp.)

History of Vigo County, Indiana . . . by Henry C. Bradsby. Chicago: S.B. Nelson & Co., 1891. 1,018 pp.

Greater Terre Haute and Vigo County . . . by Charles C. Oakey. 2 vols. Chicago: Lewis Pub. Co., 1908.

An Account of Vigo County . . . by William F. Cronin. Dayton, Ohio: Hist. Pub. Co., 1922. 496 pp.

## Wabash County

History of Wabash County, Indiana . . . by Thomas B. Helm. Chicago: J. Morris, 1884. 492 pp. (Complete name index, comp. by Doris R. Binnie and L.H. Binnie. Fort Wayne: Fort Wayne Pub. Lib., 1971. 156 pp.)

History of Wabash County . . . by Clarkson W. Weesner. 2 vols. Chicago: Lewis Pub. Co., 1914. 970 pp.

A Brief Centennial History of Wabash County, 1835-1935, by Otho Winger. [North Manchester: N.p., 1935.] 44 pp.

Wabash County History: Bicentennial ed., 1976, ed. by Linda Robertson. Marceline, Mo.: Walsworth Pub. Co., 1976. 608 pp.

## Warren County

Past and Present of Warren County, 1913, *see* Fountain County.

Warren County Centennial, 1827-1927. Williamsport, Pa.: N.p., 1927. 93 pp.

County of Warren . . . 1883, *see* p. 91. (Repr. Warren County part. Knightstown: The Bookmark, 1978. 211 pp.)

## Warrick County

A History of Warrick County . . . by Edwin Adams. Crescent City: Job Pr. Office, 1868. 80 pp. (Repr. with index. Evansville: Unigraphic, 1976. 80, 12 pp.)

Warrick and Its Prominent People. A History of Warrick County, Indiana, from the Time of Its Organization and Settlement . . . ed. by Will Fortune. [Evansville: Courier Co.], 1881. 179 pp.

History of Warrick, Spencer and Perry Counties, Indiana . . . Chicago: Goodpseed Bros., 1885. 837 pp.

History of Warrick and Its Prominent People, from the Earliest Time to the Present . . . by Monte N. Katterjohn. Boonville: Crescent Pub. Co., 1909. 106 pp.

## Washington County

History of Washington County, 1884, *see* Lawrence County.

History of Washington County, Indiana. Paoli: Stout's Pr. Shop, 1965. (Pp. 667-937 of Lawrence, Orange, and Washington Counties, 1884.)

Biographical and Historical Souvenir for the County of . . . Washington, *see* p. 91.

Centennial History of Washington County, by Warder W. Stevens. Indianapolis: Bowen, 1917. 1,060 pp. (Repr. Evansville: Unigraphic, 1967. Index 76 pp.)

A History of Washington County, by Washington County Historical Society. Evansville: Unigraphic, 1976. 593, 86 pp.

## Wayne County

History of Wayne County, Indiana, from Its First Settlement to the Present Time . . . by Andrew W. Young. Cincinnati, Ohio: R. Clarke & Co., 1872. 459 pp.

History of Wayne County, Indiana . . . 2 vols. Chicago: Inter-State Pub. Co., 1884. 1,736 pp. (Repr. 2 vols., with Indiana History omitted. Knightstown: Bookmark, 1979. 1,305 pp.)

History of Wayne County, 1899, *see* p. 91.

History of Wayne County, Indiana . . . Logansport: B.F. Bowen, 1903. 597 pp.

Memoirs of Wayne County and the City of Richmond, Indiana . . . by Henry C. Fox. 2 vols. Madison, Wis.: Western Hist. Assoc., 1912.

## Wells County

Historical Hand Atlas and History of Wells County, Indiana. Chicago: H.H. Hardesty, 1881. 231 pp.

Biographical and Historical Record of Wells County, 1887, *see* Adams County.

Standard History of Wells County, 1918, *see* Adams County.

## White County

Counties of White and Pulaski, Indiana, Historical and Biographical . . . Chicago: F.A. Battey, 1883. 772 pp. (County Histories, by W.A. Goodspeed.) (Repr. Knightstown: The Bookmark, 1981.)

Standard History of White County . . . ed. by W.H. Hamelle. 2 vols. Chicago: Lewis Hist. Co., 1915. 915 pp. (Repr. Knightstown: The Bookmark, 1981. 1,034 pp.)

## Whitley County

Counties of Whitley and Noble, Indiana, Historical and Biographical . . . ed. by Charles Blanchard, Historical ed., Weston A. Goodspeed. 2 parts. Chicago: F.A. Battey, 1882. 428, 502 pp. (Repr. of Whitley County part. Knightstown: The Bookmark, 1977. 428 pp. Index, by Donald E. Gradeless. Racine, Wis.: Author, 1980. Repr. with index. Knightstown: The Bookmark, 1980. 506 pp.)

History of Whitley County, by S.P. Kaler and R.H. Maring. Indianapolis: B.F. Bowen, 1907. 861 pp.

# IOWA

## Adair County

Adair County History, 1884, *see* Guthrie County.

Adair County History, 1892, *see* Montgomery County.

History of Adair County, Iowa . . . Lucian M. Kilburn, supervising ed. 2 vols. Chicago: Pioneer Pub. Co., 1915.

## Allamakee County

Allamakee County History, 1882, *see* Winneshiek County.

Past and Present in Allamakee County, by Ellery M. Hancock. 2 vols. Chicago: S.J. Clarke Pub. Co., 1913.

## Appanoose County

The History of Appanoose County, Iowa . . . Chicago: Western Hist. Co., 1878. 624 pp.

Appanoose Biographical and Historical Record, 1886, *see* Wayne County.

Biographical and Genealogical History of Appanoose and Monroe Counties, Iowa. New York: Lewis Pub. Co., 1903. 623 pp.

Past and Present of Appanoose County, Iowa . . . ed. by L.J. Taylor. 2 vols. Chicago: S.J. Clarke Pub. Co., 1913.

## Audubon County

History of Audubon County, Iowa . . . ed. by Henry F. Andrews. Indianapolis, Ind.: B.F. Bowen, 1915. 876 pp.

## Benton County

The History of Benton County, Iowa . . . Chicago: Western Hist. Co., 1878. 641 pp.

History of Benton County, by Luther B. Hill. 2 vols. Chicago: Lewis Pub. Co. [1910]. 900 pp.

Pioneer Recollections . . . Depicting the Early History . . . of Benton County . . . Vinton: Hist. Pub. Co., 1941. 392 pp.

## Black Hawk County

The History of Black Hawk County, Iowa . . . Chicago: Western Hist. Co., 1878. 602 pp.

Historical and Biographical Record of Black Hawk County, Iowa. Chicago: Inter-State Pub. Co., 1886. 619 pp.

History of Black Hawk County, Iowa . . . ed. by Isaiah Van Metre. Chicago: Biographical Pub. Co., 1904. 801 pp.

History of Black Hawk County, Iowa, and Its People. John C. Hartman, supervising ed. 2 vols. Chicago: S.J. Clarke Pub. Co., 1915.

## Boone County

The History of Boone County, Iowa, Containing . . . Biographical Sketches . . . Des Moines: Union Hist. Co., 1880. 680 pp.

History of Boone County, Iowa. Nathan E. Goldthwait, supervising ed. 2 vols. Chicago: Pioneer Pub. Co., 1914.

## Bremer County

Bremer County History, 1883, *see* Butler County.

## Buchanan County

History of Buchanan County, Iowa . . . ed. by C.S. Percival and E. Percival. Cleveland: Williams Bros., 1881. 437, 99 pp.

History of Buchanan County, Iowa . . . by Harry Church and Katharyn J. Chappell. 2 vols. Chicago: S.J. Clarke Pub. Co., 1914.

## Buena Vista County

Past and Present of Buena Vista County, Iowa, by C.H. Wegerslev and Thomas Walpole. Chicago: S.J. Clarke Pub. Co., 1909. 659 pp.

Buena Vista County History, Iowa, comp. by the . . . W.P.A., Iowa. Storm Lake: 1942. 87 pp. (Typescript)

## Butler County

History of Butler and Bremer Counties, Iowa, Together with Biographies . . . Springfield, Ill.: Union Pub. Co., 1883. 1,323 pp.

History of Butler County, Iowa . . . by Irving H. Hart. 2 vols. Chicago: S.J. Clarke Pub. Co., 1914.

## Calhoun County

Past and Present of Calhoun County, Iowa . . . Beaumont E. Stonebraker, supervising ed. 2 vols. Chicago: Pioneer Pub. Co., 1915.

## Carroll County

Carroll Biographical and Historical Record, 1887, *see* Greene County.

History of Carroll County, Iowa . . . by Paul Maclean. 2 vols. Chicago: S.J. Clarke Pub. Co., 1912.

## Cass County

History of Cass County, Iowa, Together with Brief Mention of Old Settlers, by Lafe Young. Atlantic: Telegraph Steam Pr. House, 1877. 126 pp.

History of Cass County, Iowa . . . Springfield, Ill.: Continental Hist. Co., 1884. 910 pp.

## Cedar County

The History of Cedar County, Iowa . . . Chicago: Western Hist. Co., 1878. 729 pp.

A Topical History of Cedar County, ed. by Clarence R. Aurner. 2 vols. Chicago: S.J. Clarke Pub. Co., 1910.

## Cerro Gordo County

Cerro Gordo County History, 1883, *see* Franklin County.

History of Cerro Gordo County, Iowa . . . ed. and comp. by J.H. Wheeler. 2 vols. Chicago: Lewis Pub. Co., 1910. 795 pp.

## Cherokee County

History of Cherokee County, Iowa, by Thomas McCulla. 2 vols. Chicago: S.J. Clarke Pub. Co., 1914. 925 pp.

Cherokee County, Iowa, comp. by W.P.A. [Des Moines:] N.p., 1940. 58 leaves.

## Chickasaw County

History of Chickasaw and Howard Counties, Iowa, by W.E. Alexander. Decorah: Western Pub. Co., 1883. 629 pp.

Historical and Reminiscences of Chickasaw County, Iowa, by Julius H. Powers. Des Moines: Iowa Pr. Co., 1894. 332 pp.

History of Chickasaw and Howard Counties, Iowa, by Robert H. Fairbairn. 2 vols. Chicago: S.J. Clarke Pub. Co., 1919.

## Clarke County

Biographical and Historical Record of Clarke County, Iowa. Chicago: Lewis Pub. Co., 1886. 531 pp. (Every-name index, by Mrs. Lester Saffell, Jr., Renton, Wash., 1977.)

## Clay County

The History of Clay County, Iowa . . . by W.C. Gilbreath. [Dubuque?: Smith, Mathis, 1889?] 272 pp.

History of Clay County, from Its Earliest Settlement to 1909, by Samuel Gillespie and J.E. Steele. Chicago: S.J. Clarke Pub. Co., 1909. 682 pp.

Remember When . . . by Don Buchan. [Spencer: N.p.], 1964. 103 pp.

## Clayton County

History of Clayton County, Iowa . . . Chicago: Inter-State Pub. Co., 1882. 1,144 pp.

History of Clayton County, Iowa, by Realto E. Price. 2 vols. Chicago: Robert O. Law Co., 1916. (Repr. Evansville, Ind.: Unigraphic, 1979.)

History of Clayton County, Iowa. Elkader: Clayton County Gen. Soc., 1984. 900 pp.

## Clinton County

The History of Clinton County, Iowa . . . Chicago: Western Hist. Co., 1879. 817 pp.

Portrait and Biographical Album of Clinton County . . . Containing a History . . . Chicago: Chapman Bros., 1886. 706 pp.

Wolfe's History of Clinton County, Iowa, ed. by P.B. Wolfe. 2 vols. Indianapolis, Ind.: B.F. Bowen, 1911.

Clinton County History, Written for the Children of Clinton County, by Estelle G. Le Prevost. Clinton: Allen Pr. Co., 1930. 128 pp. (Rev. and enl. [Clinton?: N.p.], 1948. 176 pp.)

## Crawford County

History of Crawford County, Iowa . . . by F.W. Meyers. 2 vols. Chicago: S.J. Clarke Pub. Co., 1911.

Early Days in Iowa, by Lon F. Chapin. (Covering Crawford and Ida Counties.) Pasadena, Calif.: Southwest Pub. Co. [1931]. xiv, 226 pp.

Crawford County History, Iowa, comp. by W.P.A. [Denison: N.p.], 1941. 88 leaves.

# Dallas County

The History of Dallas County, Iowa . . . Des Moines: Union Hist. Co., 1879. 647 pp.

Past and Present of Dallas County, Iowa, by Robert F. Wood. Chicago: S.J. Clarke Pub. Co., 1907. 795 pp.

# Davis County

History of Davis County, Iowa . . . Des Moines: State Hist. Co., 1882. 751 pp.

The Rise and Progress of Civilization in the Hairy Nation . . . a Brief History of Davis County, Iowa, by Henry C. Ethell. Bloomfield: H.C. Ethell, 1883. 144 pp.

# Decatur County

Biographical and Historical Record of Decatur County, 1887, *see* Ringgold County.

History of Decatur County, Iowa . . . J.M. Howell and H.C. Smith, supervising eds. 2 vols. Chicago: S.J. Clarke Pub. Co., 1915.

Down One Hundred Years, by Lawrence D. Ahern. Des Moines: Wallace-Homestead Co., 1938. 266 pp.

# Delaware County

The History of Delaware County, Iowa . . . Chicago: Western Hist. Co., 1878. 707 pp.

History of Delaware County, Iowa . . . Captain John F. Merry, supervising ed. 2 vols. Chicago: S.J. Clarke Pub. Co., 1914.

Stories of the Beginning of Delaware County [1834-1870] . . . Written for the Youth of Today . . . by Belle Bailey. 2 vols. Manchester: Author, 1932-1935.

# Des Moines County

The History of Des Moines County, Iowa . . . Chicago: Western Hist. Co., 1879. 727 pp.

History of Des Moines County, Iowa, ed. by Augustine M. Antrobus. 2 vols. Chicago: S.J. Clarke Pub. Co., 1915.

# Dickinson County

A History of Dickinson County, Iowa . . . by Roderick A. Smith. Des Moines: Kenyon Pr. & Mfg. Co., 1902. 598 pp.

History of Dickinson County, 1917, *see* Emmet County.

## Dubuque County

The History of Dubuque County, Iowa . . . Chicago: Western Hist. Co., 1880. 977 pp.

History of Dubuque County, Iowa, by Weston A. Goodspeed, ed. by F.T. Oldt. Chicago: Goodspeed Hist. Assoc. [1911?]. 943 pp.

Dubuque County History, Iowa, comp. by W.P.A. [Dubuque: N.p.], 1942. 99 leaves.

## Emmet County

History of Emmet County and Dickinson County, Iowa . . . 2 vols. Chicago: Pioneer Pub. Co., 1917.

## Fayette County

The History of Fayette County, Iowa . . . Chicago: Western Hist. Co., 1878. 758 pp.

Past and Present of Fayette County, Iowa . . . 2 vols. Indianapolis, Ind.: B.F. Bowen, 1910.

## Floyd County

History of Floyd County, Iowa . . . Chicago: Inter-State Pub., 1882. 1,142 pp.

History of Floyd County, Iowa, by Clement L. Webster. Charles City: Intelligencer Pr. [1897]. 67 pp.

## Franklin County

History of Franklin and Cerro Gordo Counties . . . Springfield, Ill.: Union Pub. Co., 1883. xvi, 1,005 pp. (Index, ed. by Margaret Burmeister, et al. Hampton: Franklin County Gen. Soc., 1983.)

History of Franklin County, Iowa . . . by I.L. Stuart. 2 vols. Chicago: S.J. Clarke Pub. Co., 1914.

Franklin County History, Iowa, comp. by . . . W.P.A. [Des Moines?: N.p.], 1941. 73 leaves.

## Fremont County

History of Fremont County, Iowa . . . Hamburg: Democrat Pr. [1876]. 62 pp.

History of Fremont County, Iowa . . . Des Moines: Iowa Hist. Co., 1881. viii, 778 pp.

History of Fremont and Mills Counties. Chicago: Lewis Pub. Co., 1901.

## Greene County

Biographical and Historical Record of Greene and Carroll Counties, Iowa . . . Chicago: Lewis Pub. Co., 1887. 707 pp.

Past and Present of Greene County, Iowa . . . by Edwin B. Stillman. Chicago: S.J. Clarke Pub. Co., 1907. 664 pp. (Repr. with new index. Jefferson: Greene Co. Gen. Soc., 1979.)

## Guthrie County

Centennial History of Guthrie County, Iowa . . . Des Moines: Carter, Hussey & Curl, 1876. 215 pp.

History of Guthrie and Adair Counties, Iowa . . . Springfield, Ill.: Continental Hist. Co., 1884. 1,105 pp. (Repr. Evansville, Ind.: Unigraphic, 1979.)

Past and Present of Guthrie County, Iowa . . . Chicago: S.J. Clarke Pub. Co., 1907. 879 pp.

## Hamilton County

History of Hamilton County, Iowa, by Jesse W. Lee. 2 vols. Chicago: S.J. Clarke Pub. Co., 1912.

## Hancock County

History of Hancock County, 1884, *see* Kossuth County.

History of Hancock County, 1917, *see* Winnebago County.

## Hardin County

History of Hardin County, Iowa . . . Springfield, Ill.: Union Pub. Co., 1883. 984 pp.

Past and Present of Hardin County, Iowa, ed. by William J. Moir. Indianapolis: B.F. Bowen, 1911. 1,051 pp. (Repr. Evansville, Ind.: Unigraphic, 1979.)

## Harrison County

History and Description of Harrison County . . . by G.F. Waterman. Magnola: Western Star Book & Job Office, 1868. 64 pp.

History of Harrison County, Iowa . . . by Joe H. Smith. Des Moines: Iowa Pr. Co., 1888. 491 pp.

History of Harrison County, Iowa. Chicago: National Pub. Co., 1891. 1,000 pp. (Repr. Evansville, Ind.: Unigraphic, 1979.)

History of Harrison County, Iowa . . . by Hon. Charles W. Hunt and W.L. Clark. Indianapolis, Ind.: B.F. Bowen, 1915. 987 pp.

## Henry County

The History of Henry County, Iowa . . . Chicago: Western Hist. Co., 1879. 667 pp.

The History of Henry County, Iowa, comp. by the Henry County Bicentennial Commission. Vol. 1. Dallas, Tex.: National ShareGraphics, 1982. 460 pp.

## Howard County

History of Howard County, 1883, *see* Chickasaw County.

History of Howard County, 1919, *see* Chickasaw County.

## Humboldt County

History of Humboldt County, 1884, *see* Kossuth County.

History of Humboldt County . . . Chicago & Cedar Rapids: Hist. Pub. Co. [1901]. 659 pp.

## Ida County

Early Days in Iowa [Ida County], 1931, *see* Crawford County.

## Iowa County

The History of Iowa County, Iowa . . . Des Moines: Union Hist. Co., 1881. 774 pp.

History of Iowa County, Iowa . . . by James G. Dinwiddie. 2 vols. Chicago: S.J. Clarke Pub. Co., 1915.

## Jackson County

The History of Jackson County, Iowa . . . Chicago: Western Hist. Co., 1879. 783 pp.

Annals of Jackson County, Iowa . . . Nos. 1-7 (all pub.). Maquoketa: Jackson County Hist. Soc., 1905-13.

History of Jackson County, Iowa, by Hon. James W. Ellis. 2 vols. Chicago: S.J. Clarke Pub. Co., 1910.

Jackson County History, Iowa, comp. by W.P.A. N.p., 1942. 111 leaves.

## Jasper County

The History of Jasper County, Iowa . . . Chicago: Western Hist. Co., 1878. 674 pp. (Repr. Newton: Jasper County Gen. Soc., 1978.)

Past and Present of Jasper County, Iowa, Gen. James B. Weaver, ed. in chief. 2 vols. Indianapolis, Ind.: B.F. Bowen, 1912.

Recollections and Sketches of Northwest Jasper . . . [Baxter: Baxter Centennial Comm., 1972.] 136 pp.

# Jefferson County

Jefferson County, Iowa; Centennial History, 1776-1876 . . . Fairfield: Ledger Office, 1876. 35 pp.

The History of Jefferson County, Iowa . . . Chicago: Western Hist. Co., 1879. 603 pp.

History of Jefferson County, Iowa . . . by Charles J. Fulton. 2 vols. Chicago: S.J. Clarke Pub. Co., 1914.

# Johnson County

History of Johnson County, Iowa . . . from 1836 to 1882 . . . Iowa City: [N.p.], 1883. 966 pp.

Leading Events in Johnson County, Iowa, by Charles R. Aurner. 2 vols. Cedar Rapids: Western Hist. Pr., 1912-13.

Johnson County History, comp. . . . by W.P.A. Iowa City: [N.p.], 1941. 100 leaves.

# Jones County

The History of Jones County, Iowa . . . Chicago: Western Hist. Co., 1879. 705 pp.

History of Jones County, Iowa . . . R.W. Corbit, ed. in chief. 2 vols. Chicago: S.J. Clarke Pub. Co., 1910.

# Keokuk County

The History of Keokuk County, Iowa . . . Des Moines: Union Hist. Co., 1880. 822 pp.

A Brief History of Keokuk County . . . Sigourney: The News, 1897.

# Kossuth County

History of Kossuth, Hancock and Winnebago Counties . . . Springfield, Ill.: Union Pub. Co., 1884. 933 pp.

History of Kossuth and Humboldt Counties, Iowa. Springfield, Ill.: Union Pub. Co., 1884. 911 pp.

History of Kossuth County, Iowa . . . by Benjamin F. Reed. 2 vols. Chicago: S.J. Clarke Pub. Co., 1913. 1,462 pp.

# Lee County

The History of Lee County . . . Chicago: Western Hist. Co., 1879. 887 pp.

Story of Lee County, Iowa, ed. under the supervision of Nelson C. Roberts. 2 vols. Chicago: S.J. Clarke Pub. Co., 1914.

Lee County History, Iowa, comp. . . . by W.P.A. [Keokuk?: N.p.], 1942. 99 leaves.

## Linn County

The History of Linn County, Iowa . . . Chicago: Western Hist. Co., 1878. 816 pp. (Repr. with every-name index. Cedar Rapids: Linn County Heritage Soc., 1980. 816, 111 pp.)

History of Linn County, Iowa . . . by Luther A. Brewer and B.L. Wick. 2 vols. Cedar Rapids: Torch Pr., 1911.

## Louisa County

A History of Louisa County from Earliest Settlement to 1912, by Arthur Springer. 2 vols. Chicago: S.J. Clarke Pub. Co., 1912. (Index, comp. by Louisa County Hist. Soc. Wapello: Wapello Pub. Lib., 1968.)

The Newspaper Accounts of B.F. Wright . . . and Others of Louisa County, Iowa, by Robert L. Johnson. Denver: Robela Pub. Co., 1967. 172 pp.

## Lucas County

History of Lucas County, Iowa . . . Des Moines: State Hist. Co., 1881. 743 pp.

Past and Present of Lucas and Wayne Counties, Iowa, by Theodore M. Stuart. 2 vols. Chicago: S.J. Clarke Pub. Co., 1913.

History of Lucas County, Iowa, 1978. Produced by Lucas County Genealogy Soc. Marcelline, Mo.: Walsworth Pub. Co., 1978. 782 pp.

## Lyon County

Historical Sketch of Lyon County, Iowa . . . by S.C. Hyde. Lemars: Sentinel Pr., 1872. 40 pp.

Compendium of History, Reminiscences and Biography of Lyon County, Iowa. Chicago: Ogle Co., 1904-5. 530 pp.

Early History of Lyon County, by George Monlux. Rock Rapids: [N.p.], 1909. 150 pp.

## Madison County

History and Business Directory of Madison County, Iowa . . . by J.J. Davies. Des Moines: Mills & Co., 1869. 254 pp.

The History of Madison County, Iowa . . . Des Moines: Union Hist. Co., 1879. 657 pp.

History of Madison County, Iowa, and Its People, ed. by Herman A. Mueller. 2 vols. Chicago: S.J. Clarke Pub. Co., 1915. (Repr. Winterset: Mary A. Banks, 1983.)

## Mahaska County

The History of Mahaska County . . . Des Moines: Union Hist. Co., 1878. 724 pp.

Proud Mahaska, 1843-1900 . . . by Semira A. Phillips. Oskaloosa: Herald Pr., 1900. 383 pp.

*Mahaska County (cont.)*

History of Mahaska County . . . by Manoah Hedge. [Oskaloosa: Author, 1905?] 139 pp.

Past and Present of Mahaska County, by Manoah Hedge. Chicago: S.J. Clarke Pub. Co., 1906. 576 pp.

Roustabout's History of Mahaska County, by Roustabout [pseud. for Phil Hoffman]. [Oskaloosa?: N.p., 1916.] 102 pp.

## Marion County

Pioneers of Marion County, Consisting of a General History . . . by William M. Donnel. Des Moines: Republican Steam Pr. House, 1872. 346 pp.

The History of Marion County, Iowa . . . Des Moines: Union Hist. Co., 1882. 807 pp.

The History of Marion County, Iowa . . . John W. Wright and W.A. Young, supervising eds. 2 vols. Chicago: S.J. Clarke Pub. Co., 1915.

## Marshall County

History of Marshall County, Iowa, by Mrs. Nettie Sanford. Clinton: McAllaster & Co., 1867. 157 pp.

The History of Marshall County, Iowa . . . Chicago: Western Hist. Co., 1878. 696 pp.

Past and Present of Marshall County, Iowa, by Judge William Battin. 2 vols. Indianapolis, Ind.: B.F. Bowen, 1912.

History of Marshall County, Iowa, by Gerard Schultz. Marshalltown: Marshall Pr. Co., 1955. 244 pp.

## Mills County

History of Mills County, Iowa . . . Des Moines: State Hist. Co., 1881. viii, 722 pp.

History of Mills County, 1901, *see* Fremont County.

## Mitchell County

History of Mitchell and Worth Counties, Iowa . . . [ed. by J.E. Clyde and H.A. Dwelle]. Springfield, Ill.: Union Pub. Co., 1884. 986 pp. (Repr. 2 vols. Chicago: S.J. Clarke Pub. Co., 1918.)

The Story of Mitchell County, 1851-1973, comp. by Mitchell County Historical Society. Mason City: Klito Pr. Co. [1973?]. xx, 513 pp.

## Monona County

History of Monona County, Iowa . . . Chicago: National Pub. Co., 1890. 661 pp.

# Monroe County

The History of Monroe County, Iowa . . . Chicago: Western Hist. Co., 1878. 507 pp.

An Illustrated History of Monroe County, Iowa . . . to 1896 . . . by Frank Hicklooper. [Albia:] N.p., 1896. 360 pp.

Biographical and Genealogical History of Monroe County, 1903, *see* Appanoose County.

Monroe County History, Iowa, comp. . . . by W.P.A. [Des Moines?: N.p.], 1940. 87 pp.

# Montgomery County

History of Montgomery and Adair Counties. Chicago: Lewis Pub. Co., 1892.

History of Montgomery County, Iowa . . . Des Moines: Iowa Hist. and Biographical Co., 1881. vii, 741 pp. (Index of persons mentioned . . . comp. by the Red Oak Public Library, 1963.)

A History of the County of Montgomery . . . to 1906, by William W. Merritt, Sr. Red Oak: Express Pub. Co., 1906. xvi, 343 pp.

# Muscatine County

The History of Muscatine County, Iowa . . . Chicago: Western Hist. Co., 1879. 692 pp.

History of Muscatine County, Iowa . . . ed. by Irving B. Richman. 2 vols. Chicago: S.J. Clarke Pub. Co., 1911.

# O'Brien County

History of O'Brien County . . . by D.A.W. Perkins. Sioux Falls, S.Dak.: Brown & Saenger, 1897. viii, 485 pp.

Past and Present of O'Brien and Osceola Counties, Iowa, by Hon. John L.E. Peck for O'Brien County, and Hon. William J. Miller for Osceola County. 2 vols. Indianapolis, Ind.: B.F. Bowen, 1914. 1,300 pp. (Repr. Evansville, Ind.: Unigraphic, 1979.)

# Osceola County

History of Osceola County, Iowa . . . by D.A.W. Perkins. Sioux Falls, S.Dak.: Brown & Saenger, 1892. 269, 27 pp.

Past and Present of Osceola County, by Hon. William J. Miller, 1914, *see* O'Brien County.

Osceola County History, Iowa, comp. . . . by W.P.A. Sibley: N.p., 1942. 56 leaves.

## Page County

The History of Page County, Iowa, from . . . 1843 to 1876 . . . Clarinda: Herald Book & Job Office, 1876. 99 pp.

History of Page County . . . Des Moines: Iowa Hist. Co., 1880. 806 pp. (Repr. Marceline, Mo.: Walsworth Pub. Co.)

History of Page County, Iowa . . . by W.L. Kershaw, et al. 2 vols. Chicago: S.J. Clarke Pub. Co., 1909.

Page County History, Iowa, comp. by W.P.A. Clarinda: N.p., 1942. 99 leaves.

## Palo Alto County

History of Palo Alto County, Iowa, by J.L. Martin. Emmetsburg: N.p., 1877. 22 pp. & unpaged.

History of Palo Alto County, Iowa, by Dwight G. McCarty. Cedar Rapids: Torch Pr., 1910. 201 pp.

## Plymouth County

History of Plymouth County, 1890-91, *see* Woodbury County.

History of Plymouth County, Iowa . . . ed. by William S. Freeman. 2 vols. Indianapolis, Ind.: B.F. Bowen, 1917.

## Pocahontas County

The Pioneer History of Pocahontas County, Iowa . . . by Robert E. Flickinger. Fonda: G. Sanborn, 1904. xxiv, 909 pp.

Pocahontas County, Iowa History, comp. in 1981 by Pocahontas County Historical Society Members and Friends. Rolfe: The Soc., and Dallas, Tex.: Taylor Pub. Co., 1982. 774 pp.

## Polk County

Early Sketches of Polk County, Iowa, by Mrs. Netti Sanford. Newton: Charles A. Clarke, 1874. 152 pp.

Centennial History of Polk County, Iowa, by J.M. Dixon. Des Moines: State Register, 1876. 339 pp.

The History of Polk County, Iowa . . . Des Moines: Union Hist. Co., 1880. 1,037 pp.

Annals of Polk County, Iowa . . . by Will Porter. Des Moines: Geo. A. Miller Pr. Co., 1898. 1,064 pp.

Pioneers of Polk County, Iowa, and Reminiscences of Early Days, by L.F. Andrews. 2 vols. Des Moines: Baker-Trisler Co., 1908.

Historical Polk County . . . prepared by W.P.A. Nos. 1-2 (no more pub.). [Des Moines: N.p., 1940-41.]

*Polk County (cont.)*

History of Des Moines and Polk County, by Johnson Brigham. 2 vols. Chicago: S.J. Clarke Pub. Co., 1911.

Historical Highlights of Polk County, Iowa, by Robert R. Denny. [N.p., 1973]. 73, 22 pp.

## Pottawattamie County

History of Pottawattamie County, Iowa . . . 2 parts. Chicago: O.L. Baskin & Co., 1883. 364, 277 pp.

Notes on the History of Pottawattamie County, by D.C. Bloomer. Annals of Iowa, Vols. 9-12. 1874.

History of Pottawattamie County, Iowa . . . to 1907, by Homer H. Field and J.R. Reed. 2 vols. Chicago: S.J. Clarke Pub. Co., 1907.

## Poweshiek County

The History of Poweshiek County, Iowa . . . Des Moines: Union Hist. Co., 1880. 975 pp.

History of Poweshiek County, Iowa . . . by Leonard F. Parker. 2 vols. Chicago: S.J. Clarke Pub. Co., 1911.

## Ringgold County

Biographical and Historical Record of Ringgold and Union Counties . . . Chicago: Lewis Pub. Co., 1887. 737 pp.

Biographical and Historical Record of Ringgold and Decatur Counties, Iowa . . . Chicago: Lewis Pub. Co., 1887. 796 pp.

Early History of Ringgold County, 1844-1937, by Mrs. B.M. (Mary) Lesan. [Mount Ayr:] Author, 1937. 259 pp.

Ringgold County History, Iowa, comp. . . . by W.P.A. Mount Ayr: N.p., 1942. 65 leaves.

## Sac County

History of Sac County, Iowa, by William H. Hart. Indianapolis, Ind.: B.F. Bowen, 1914. 918 pp.

## Scott County

History of Scott County, Iowa . . . Chicago: Inter-State Pub. Co., 1882. 1,265 pp.

History of Davenport and Scott County, Iowa, by Harry E. Downer. 2 vols. Chicago: S.J. Clarke Pub. Co., 1910.

Scott County History, Iowa, comp. by W.P.A. [Davenport?: N.p.], 1942. 135 leaves.

## Shelby County

Past and Present of Shelby County, Iowa, by Edward S. White. Indianapolis, Ind.: B.F. Bowen, 1915. 1,511 pp. (Repr. 2 vols. Evansville, Ind.: Unigraphic, 1978.)

## Sioux County

The Story of Sioux County, by Charles L. Dyke. [Sioux City: Verstegen Pr. Co.], 1942. vii, xvi, 567, 62 pp. (2d ed. called Later Gleanings.) [Orange City: N.p.], 1943. 568-577 pp.

## Story County

A History of Story County, Iowa . . . by William G. Allen. Des Moines: Iowa Pr. Co., 1887. 485 pp. (Repr. Ames: Irene Crippen, 1984?)

Biographical and Historical Memoirs of Story County, Iowa . . . Chicago: Goodspeed Pub. Co., 1890. 460 pp.

History of Story County, Iowa . . . by William O. Payne. 2 vols. Chicago: S.J. Clarke Pub. Co., 1911.

## Tama County

History of Tama County, Iowa . . . by Samuel D. Chapman. [Toledo:] Toledo Times Office, 1879. 296 pp.

History of Tama County, Iowa . . . Springfield, Ill.: Union Pub. Co., 1883. 1,081 pp.

Those Were the Days, 1873-1973. Traer Centennial History Committee. [Cedar Falls: Congdon Pr. Co., 1973.] 184 pp.

## Taylor County

History of Taylor County, Iowa . . . Des Moines: State Hist. Co., 1881. 828 pp.

History of Taylor County, Iowa, by Frank E. Crossen. Chicago: S.J. Clarke Pub. Co., 1910.

## Union County

Illustrated Centennial Sketches . . . of Union County, Iowa. Creston: C.J. Colby, 1876. 145 pp. (Repr. Evansville, Ind.: Unigraphic, 1979.)

Biographical and Historical Record of Union County, 1887, *see* Ringgold County.

History of Union County, Iowa, by George A. Ide. Chicago: S.J. Clarke Pub. Co., 1908. 836 pp. (Repr. Evansville, Ind.: Unigraphic, 1979.)

## Van Buren County

The History of Van Buren County, Iowa . . . Chicago: Western Hist. Co., 1878. 606 pp.

*Van Buren County (cont.)*

Van Buren County, comp. . . . by W.P.A. Farmington: T.L. Keith, 1940. 148 pp.

## Wapello County

The History of Wapello County, Iowa . . . Chicago: Western Hist. Co., 1878. 670 pp.

History of Wapello County, Iowa . . . ed. and comp. by Capt. Samuel B. Evans. Chicago: Biographical Pub. Co., 1901. 670 pp.

History of Wapello County, Iowa, Harrison L. Waterman, supervising ed. 2 vols. Chicago: S.J. Clarke Pub. Co., 1914.

## Warren County

History of Warren County . . . Des Moines: Union Hist. Co., 1879. vi, 743 pp. (Repr. Evansville, Ind.: Unigraphic, 1979. 800 pp.)

History of Warren County, Iowa . . . to 1908, by Rev. W.C. Martin. Chicago: S.J. Clarke Pub. Co., 1908. 997 pp. (Repr. with surname index added. Evansville, Ind.: Unigraphic, 1978.)

History of Warren County, Iowa, comp. by Gerard Schultz. Indianola: Record and Tribune Co., 1953. 355 pp.

## Washington County

History of Washington County, Iowa . . . Des Moines: Union Hist. Co., 1880. 702 pp.

History of Washington County, Iowa, from the First White Settlements to 1908, by Howard A. Burrell. 2 vols. Chicago: S.J. Clarke Pub. Co., 1909.

## Wayne County

Biographical and Historical Record of Wayne and Appanoose Counties, Iowa . . . Chicago: Inter-State Pub. Co., 1886. 746 pp.

Past and Present of Wayne County, by T.M. Stuart, 1913, *see* Lucas County.

## Webster County

Centennial History of Webster County . . . by Erastus G. Morgan. Fort Dodge: Times Job Pr. Rooms, 1876. 73 pp.

History of Fort Dodge and Webster County, Iowa, by Harlow M. Pratt. 2 vols. Chicago: Pioneer Pub. Co., 1913.

## Winnebago County

History of Winnebago County, 1884, *see* Kossuth County.

History of Winnebago County and Hancock County, Iowa . . . 2 vols. Chicago: Pioneer Pub. Co., 1917.

## Winneshiek County

History of Winneshiek County . . . by Charles H. Sparks. Decorah: J.A. Leonard, 1877. xii, 156 pp.

History of Winneshiek and Allamakee Counties, Iowa, by W.E. Alexander. Sioux City: Western Pub. Co., 1882. 739 pp.

Past and Present of Winneshiek County, Iowa, by Edwin C. Bailey. 2 vols. Chicago: S.J. Clarke Pub. Co., 1913.

## Woodbury County

History of the Counties of Woodbury and Plymouth, Iowa [by Will L. Clark, et al.]. Chicago: A. Warner & Co., 1890-91. 1,022 pp.

Past and Present of Sioux City and Woodbury County, Iowa, ed. by Hon. Constant R. Marks. Chicago: S.J. Clarke Pub. Co., 1904. 826 pp.

Woodbury County History, Iowa, comp. by W.P.A. Sioux City: N.p., 1942. 174 leaves.

The History of Woodbury County, Iowa, comp. by Woodbury County Gen. Soc. Dallas, Tex.: National ShareGraphics, 1984. 700 pp.

## Worth County

History of Worth County, 1884, *see* Mitchell County.

## Wright County

History and Business Directory of Wright County, Iowa. Des Moines: Author, 1870. 92 pp.

History of Wright County, Iowa . . . ed. by Hon. B.P. Birdsall. Indianapolis, Ind.: B.F. Bowen, 1915. 1,061 pp.

# KANSAS

## Allen County

History of Allen and Woodson Counties, Kansas, ed. by Lew W. Duncan and
C.F. Scott. Iola: Iola Register, 1901. 894 pp.

## Anderson County

First History of Anderson County . . . to the Centennial Year of 1876, by
William A. Johnson. Garnett: Kansas Journal, n.d. 40 pp. (Repr., *see* below.)

History of Anderson County . . . to 1876 . . . by Judge James Y. Campbell.
[Garnett:] Garnett Weekly Journal Pr. [1876?]. 86 pp. (Repr., *see* below.)

The History of Anderson County, Kansas . . . to 1876, by William A. Johnson.
[Garnett:] Kauffman & Iler, 1877. 289 pp. (Repr., *see* below.)

A History of Anderson County, Kansas . . . by Harry Johnson. Garnett: Garnett
Review Co., 1936. xi, 383 pp. (Repr., *see* below.)

Anderson County Histories, by Anderson County Historical Society. Garnett: The
Soc., 1977. 823 pp.

Anderson County, Kansas Histories. Garnett: Anderson County Historical Soc.,
1977. (Repr. of Campbell, Harry Johnson and W.A. Johnson Histories of
Anderson Co.) (Original Histories, *see* above.)

## Atchison County

History of Atchison County, Kansas, by Sheffield Ingalls. Lawrence: Standard
Pub. Co., 1916. 887 pp.

Atchison Centennial, 1854-1954; a Historic Album of Atchison County, comp.
by Catherine Roe and B. Roe. [N.p.: Lockwood Co., 1954.] 64 pp.

## Barber County

Chosen Land: a History of Barber County, Kansas [by Barber County History
Committee]. Medicine Lodge: Barber County Hist. Soc., 1876. 82 pp. (Repr.
Morrill: Free Pub. Lib., Bd. of Trustees, 1982.)

## Barton County

Biographical History of Barton County, Kansas . . . Great Bend: Great Bend
Tribune, 1912. 318 pp.

## Bourbon County

History of Bourbon County, Kansas, to the Close of 1865, by Thomas F. Robley. Fort Scott: [Pr. of Monitor Book & Pr. Co.], 1894. vii, 210 pp. (Repr. with index additions. Fort Scott: Sekan Pr. Co., 1975.)

## Brown County

History and Statistics of Brown County, Kansas . . . comp. by Major E.N. Morrill. Hiawatha: Kansas Herald Book, News & Job Office, 1876. 82 pp.

Annals of Brown County, Kansas . . . to 1900, comp. and pub. by Grant W. Harrington. Hiawatha: Harrington Pr. Co., 1903. 564 pp.

A.N. Ruley's History of Brown County. [Hiawatha: The World, 1930.] 416 pp. (Repr. Morris: Free Pub. Lib., 1976.)

## Butler County

History of Butler County, Kansas, by Volney P. Mooney. Lawrence: Standard Pub. Co., 1916. 869 pp.

Butler County's Eighty Years, 1855-1935, by Jessie P. Stratford. [El Dorado: Butler County News, 1934.] 408 pp.

The Kingdom of Butler, 1857-1870; a History of Butler County, Kansas, by Jessie P. Stratford. El Dorado: Butler County Hist. Soc. [1970]. vi, 218 pp.

True Tales of the Kingdom of Butler, by Lawrence P. Klintworth. El Dorado: Butler County Hist. Soc., 1981. 228 pp.

## Chase County

Chase County Historical Sketches. 2 vols. N.p.: Chase County Hist. Soc., 1940-48.

Chase County Centennial, Chase County Courthouse Centennial, 1872-1972. N.p. [1972?] 185 pp.

## Cherokee County

History of Cherokee County, Kansas, and Representative Citizens, by Nathaniel T. Allison. Chicago: Biographical Pub. Co., 1904. 630 pp.

Illustrated Cherokee County, Kansas, 1866-1923, comp. by Galena Weekly Republican. Galena: The Republican, 1923. 56 pp.

## Clark County

Notes on Early Clark County, Kansas, by Clark County Chapter, Kansas State Historical Society. 4 vols. (Repr. from The Clark County Clipper, 1939-1945.) Ashland: The Soc.

## Clay County

Clay County Illustrated, comp. by Clay Center Dispatch. Clay Center: The Dispatch, 1901. 73 pp.

## Cloud County

The Blade Annual and History of Cloud County . . . by J.M. Hagaman. Concordia: Blade Steam Pr. House, 1884. 78 pp.

Biographical History of Cloud County, Kansas . . . Mrs. E.F. Hollibaugh, biographer and historian. [Chicago: Lewis Pub. Co.? 1903.] 919 pp.

## Coffey County

Early Day History of Coffey County, Dating Back to the 1870's . . . Burlington: Burlington Daily Republican [1966]. 144 pp.

First Hand Historical Episodes of Early Coffey County, from the Pens of George Throckmorton . . . and Many Other Pioneers. Comp. by John Redmond. N.p., n.d. 144 pp.

## Comanche County

Comanche County History, Comanche County, Kansas, by Comanche County Hist. Soc. Dallas, Tex.: Taylor Pub. Co., 1981. 816 pp.

## Cowley County

History of Cowley County, Kansas, comp. by Winfield Courier, by A.A. Millington up to 1882, and Brought Down to . . . 1901, by E.P. Greer. Winfield, 1901. 129 pp.

## Crawford County

A Twentieth Century History and Biographical Record of Crawford County, Kansas. Chicago: Lewis Pub. Co., 1905. 656 pp. (Repr. [Clinton, Mo.: The Printery, and Pittsburgh, Pa.: Crawford County Gen. Soc.], 1976. Indexed. 683 pp.)

## Decatur County

Decatur County, Kansas [by Decatur County Historical Book Committee]. [Lubbock, Tex.: Specialty Pub., 1983.] 512 pp. (General index [by Wilma Wallsmith]. [Levant: Author, 1983?] 8 leaves.)

## Doniphan County

. . . Doniphan County, Kansas, History and Directory for 1868-69 . . . ed. by R.F. Smith. [Wathena:] Smith, Vaughan, 1868. xlviii, 349 pp.

Gray's Doniphan County History. A Record of . . . Half a Hundred Years, by Patrick L. Gray. Bendenna: Roycroft Pr., 1905. 84, 166 pp.

. . . Illustrated Doniphan County, 1837-1916 . . . 79 Years of Progress . . . [Troy: N.p., 1916.] 384 pp. (Repr. Troy: Montgomery, 1984?)

## Edwards County

The Kinsley-Edwards County Centennial, from Prairie to People, 1873-1973, ed. by Myron G. Burr and E.A. Burr. [Kinsley-Edwards County Centennial Committee.] Kinsley & Medicine Lodge: Noland Pub., 1973. 414 pp.

Oft Told Tales: a History of Edwards County, Kansas to 1900, by Myrtle H. Richardson. [Lewis: Lewis Pr., 1976.] 224 pp.

The Great Next Year Country: a History of Edwards County, Kansas . . . 1901 to 1925, by Myrtle H. Richardson. [Lewis: Lewis Pr., 1983.] 464 pp.

## Elk County

Pioneer Days: Interesting Incidents and History of Early Days in Elk County, comp. by Frederick C. Flory. Howard: N.p., n.d. 48 pp.

Elk County: a Narrative History of Elk County and Its People, by Elk County Historical Society Book Committee. N.p.: The Soc., 1979. 260 pp.

## Ellis County

Conquering the Wind, by Amy B. Toepfer and A.C. Dreiling, ed. by Victor G. Leiker. [Garwood, N.J.: Editor, 1966.]

## Ellsworth County

. . . Compendious History of Ellsworth County, Kansas . . . Ellsworth: Reporter Office, 1879. 60 pp.

A History of Ellsworth County, Kansas, by Francis L. Wilson. N.p.: Ellsworth County Hist. Soc., n.d. 68 pp.

## Finney County

Directory of Finney County, Kansas, Containing . . . a Short Descriptive History of Finney County . . . First biennial vol. Salina: Kansas Directory Co., 1886. 284 pp.

History of Finney County, Kansas, comp. by Finney County Historical Society. [Garden City?:] N.p., 1950-54. 2 vols.

## Ford County

Early Ford County, by Ida E. Rath. North Newton: Mennonite Pr. [1904]. xx, 267 pp.

Saga of Sawlog, by Kate W. Krumrey. Denver, Colo.: Big Mountain Pr. [1965]. 417 pp.

## Geary County

Garden of Eden, comp. and ed. by John B. Jeffries and Irene Jeffries. Junction City: Geary County Hist. Soc., 1978. 146 pp. [Cover: Pictorial History of Geary County, Kansas.]

## Gove County

History of Gove County, Kansas, to . . . 1886, by W.P. Harrington. Gove City: Republican Gazette Office, 1920. 32 pp. (Repr. Gove City: Republican Gazette Office, 1930. 70 pp.; Repr. Scott City: News Chronicle Pr. Co., for Gove County Hist. Assoc., 1973. 74 pp.)

History and Heritage of Gove County, Kansas, ed. and comp. by Albert B. Tuttle and M.T. Tuttle. Gove: Gove County Bicentennial Comm., and Gove Co. Hist. Assoc., n.d. 279 pp.

## Graham County

Graham County, Kansas; Location, Description, Adaptation . . . Hill City: N.p., 1904? 41 pp.

## Grant County

History of Grant County, Kansas, by Robert R. Wilson and E.M. Sears. [Wichita?: N.p., 1950.] 278 pp.

Grant County, Kansas [by Grant County Historical Commission]. [Dallas, Tex.: Taylor Pub. Co., 1982.] 584 pp.

## Greeley County

History of Early Greeley County, a Story of Its Tracks, Trails and Tribulations. Vol. 1. Tribune: Greeley County Hist. Soc., 1981.

## Greenwood County

History of Greenwood County as Published in the Centennial Issue of the Eureka Herald, July 4, 1968. [Cover: A Century of Greenwood County History.] N.p. [Greenwood County Hist. Soc.?], n.d. 88 pp.

## Harper County

The Harper County Story, by Gwendoline Sanders and Paul Sanders. [North Newton: Mennonite Pr.], 1968. 213 pp.

## Hodgeman County

History of Hodgeman County, Kansas, by H.C. Norman. Kinsley: N.p., 1941. 52 leaves.

## Jackson County

History and Statistics of Jackson County, Kansas . . . comp. by Judge Ward S. Hoaglin. Holton: Recorder and Express Book and Job Rooms, 1876. 31 pp.

# Jewell County

History of Jewell County, Kansas . . . by M. Winsor. Jewell City: Diamond Pr. Office, 1878. 36 pp.

What Price White Rock? a Chronicle of Northwestern Jewell County, by Harry E. Ross. Burr Oak: Burr Oak Herald [1937]. vii, 152 pp.

# Johnson County

History of Johnson County, Kansas, by Ed Blair. Lawrence: Standard Pub. Co., 1915. 469, 67 pp. (Repr. Shawnee Mission: Johnson County Gen. Soc., 1976.)

Historic Johnson County . . . Shawnee Mission: Neff Pr. [1969]. 52 pp.

# Kearny County

History of Kearny County, Kansas, by Kearny County Historical Society. 1 vol. [Lakin: The Soc., 1964.]

# Kingman County

A History of Kingman County, Kansas, 1871-1969, by Fred Hurd. [North Newton: Mennonite Pr., 1970.] 198 pp.

# Labette County

History of Labette County, Kansas . . . to 1892, by Nelson Case. Topeka: Crane & Co., 1893. 372 pp.

History of Labette County, Kansas, and Representative Citizens. Chicago: Biographical Pub. Co., 1901. 825 pp.

Our Heroes in Our Defense, Labette County, Kansas [by W.H. Lightfoot]. [Parsons: Commercial Pub. Co., 1921.] 196 pp.

# Leavenworth County

Early History of Leavenworth City and County . . . by Henry M. Moore. Leavenworth: Dodsworth Book Co., 1906. 339 pp. (Repr. Marceline, Mo.: Walsworth Pub. Co., 1975.)

History of Leavenworth County, Kansas, by Jesse A. Hall and L.T. Hand. Topeka: Hist. Pub. Co., 1921. 680 pp.

# Lincoln County

A Souvenir History of Lincoln County, Kansas, by Elizabeth N. Barr. [Topeka: Kansas Farmer Job Office], 1908. 123 pp. (Repr. with errata and addenda. Salina: Consolidated, 1976. 134 pp. Surname index to 1976 repr., by Elizabeth N. Barr. Salina: Smoky Valley Gen. Soc., 1976. 8 pp.)

Lincoln, That County in Kansas, by Dorothe L.T. Homan. Lindsborg: D.C. Homan, 1979. 389, vii pp.

# Linn County

Linn County, Kansas; a History by William A. Mitchell. Kansas City, Mo.: N.p., 1928. 404 pp.

From Pioneering to the Present; Linn County, Its People, Events, and Ways of Life. 2 vols. Pleasanton: Linn County Hist. Soc., 1976-78.

# Lyon County

Annals of Emporia and Lyon County: Historical Incidents of the First Quarter of a Century, 1857-1882, by Jacob Stotler. Emporia [1898]. 100 pp.

History of Emporia and Lyon County, by Laura M. French. Emporia: Emporia Gazette Pr., 1929. 292 pp.

# McPherson County

Pioneer Life and Lore of McPherson County, Kansas, by Edna Nyquist. McPherson: Democrat-Opinion Pr., 1932. 164 pp.

# Marion County

Marion County, Kansas, Past and Present, by Sondra Van Meter. [Marion:] Board of Directors of Marion County Hist. Soc. [1972]. xiii, 344 pp.

# Marshall County

Illustrated ed. of Marysville, and Marshall County, Kansas, comp. by True Republican. [Marysville:] Clark & Runneals [1890]. 92 pp.

History of Marshall County, Kansas . . . by Emma (Calderhead) Forter. Indianapolis, Ind.: B.F. Bowen, 1917. 1,041 pp.

# Meade County

A History of Meade County, Kansas, by Frank S. Sullivan. Topeka: Crane & Co., 1916. 184 pp.

Pioneer Stories of Meade County, by Meade County Council of Women's Clubs. 2 vols. [Marceline, Mo.: Walsworth Bros.], 1950-65. (Repr. with additions, comp. by Meade Council of Women's Clubs. Meade, 1974. 314 pp.)

# Montgomery County

History of Montgomery County, Kansas . . . comp. by Lew W. Duncan. Iola: Iola Register, 1903. 852 pp.

Who's Who? a History of Kansas and Montgomery County . . . by Charles C. Drake. Coffeyville: Coffeyville Journal Pr., 1943. 276 pp.

## Morris County

History of Morris County, 1820-1890, by John Maley. N.p. [Morris County Hist. Soc., 1981]. 124 pp. (Repr. of his earlier newspaper columns.)

## Nemaha County

Old Settlers' Tales . . . Settlers of . . . Southwestern Nemaha County . . . 1902, *see* Pottawatomie County.

History of Nemaha County, Kansas, by Ralph Tennal. Lawrence: Standard Pub. Co., 1916. 816 pp.

## Neosho County

Gleanings from Western Prairies, by Rev. William E. Youngman. Cambridge: Jones & Pigott, 1882. xv, 214 pp. (Repr. Freeport, N.Y.: Books for Libraries Pr. [1971]. xv, 214 pp.)

History of Neosho and Wilson Counties, Kansas, by Lew W. Duncan. Fort Scott: Monitor Pr. Co., 1902. 922 pp. (Repr. Chanute: Chanute Gen. Soc., 1977. 1,001 pp.)

History of Neosho County, by William W. Graves. 2 vols. St. Paul: Journal Pr., 1949-51.

## Ness County

Hand-book of Ness County, Kansas, by ed. of the Dairy World, Chicago. Chicago: C.S. Burch Co., 1887. 36 pp.

Ness, Western County, Kansas . . . by Minnie (Dubbs) Millbrook. Detroit: Millbrook Pr. Co. [1955]. 319 pp.

## Norton County

The History of the Early Settlement of Norton County, Kansas, by Hon. Francis M. Lockard. Norton: Champion [1894?]. 294 pp. (Repr. Norton: Daily Telegram, 1967.)

Seventy Years in Norton County, Kansas, 1872-1942, by Darius N. Bowers. Norton: Norton County Champion, 1942. 238 pp.

## Osage County

The Early Years of Osage County, by Roger Carswell. North Newton: Mennonite Pr., 1982. 88 pp.

## Osborne County

Osborne County Revisited, by Gladys B. Enoch. N.p., 1971. [Cover: 1871-1971.] 106 pp.

Loom of a Century . . . 1871-1971 . . . [Osborne County Centennial Book Committee.] N.p. [1971]. 80 pp.

*Osborne County (cont.)*

Osborne County, Kansas. 2 vols. Osborne: Osborne County Gen. and Hist. Soc., 1977.

## Pawnee County

Progress in Pawnee County: 80th Anniversary ed., comp. by Tiller and Toiler. Larned: N.p., 1952. 142 pp.

## Phillips County

Phillipsburg-Phillips County Centennial, 1872-1972, ed. and comp. by Cecil Kingery. N.p., 1972.

Phillips County, Kansas Settlers Prior to 1900, comp. by the Phillips County Genealogical Society. Phillipsburg: Phillips County Gen. Soc., 1977. 216 pp.

## Pottawatomie County

Old Settlers' Tales: Historical and Biographical Sketches of the Early Settlement and Settlers of Northeastern Pottawatomie and Southwestern Nemaha Counties, Kansas . . . to 1877, by Ferdinand F. Crevecoeur. [Onaga: N.p., 1902.] 162 pp.

Early History of Pottawatomie County. Centennial ed., 1854-1954, by Pottawatomie County Historical Research Committee. N.p., 1954. 40 pp.

## Pratt County

Pioneer Saints and Sinners; Pratt County from Its Beginnings to 1900, by John R. Gray. [Pratt: Rotary Club, 1968.] 165 pp.

## Rawlins County

An Old Time History of Rawlins County, Kansas, by Alfaretta Courtright. [Omaha, Nebr.?: N.p., 1961.] 60 pp.

The Time That Was: the Courageous Acts and Accounts of Rawlins County, Kansas, 1875-1915. Colby: H.F. Davis Memorial Lib., Colby Community Coll., 1973. xv, 215 pp.

## Reno County

History of the City of Hutchinson and Reno County, Kansas, comp. by Hutchinson News. Hutchinson: N.p. [1896?]. 126 pp.

History of Reno County, Kansas . . . by Sheridan Ploughe, with Biographical Sketches . . . 2 vols. Indianapolis, Ind.: B.F. Bowen, 1917.

When the Prairies Were New; Life with the Homesteaders, by Alfred B. Bradshaw. Turon: A.J. Allen, 1959. 94 pp.

## Republic County

A History of Republic County, Kansas . . . to 1883 . . . Topeka: Daily Capital Pr. House, 1883. 106 pp.

A History of Republic County, Kansas . . . from Its First Settlement Down to June 1, '01 . . . by Isaac O. Savage. Beloit, Wis.: Jones & Chubbic, 1901. 321 pp.

History of Republic County, 1868-1964, comp. by Anona S. Blackburn and M.S. Cardwell. [Belleville: Belleville Telescope, 1964.] 520 pp.

## Rice County

The Story of Early Rice County, by Horace Jones. [Wichita: Wichita Eagle Pr.], 1928. 135 pp. (Repr. Lyons: Paul E. Jones, 1959. 141 pp.)

Up from the Sod: the Life Story of a Kansas Prairie County, by Horace Jones. Lyons: Coronado Pub. [1968]. 207 pp.

Rice County Centennial, Land of Quivera, 1871-1971 [by Rice County Centennial Book Committee]. N.p. [1971].

## Riley County

An Illustrated Sketch Book of Riley County, Kansas, the "Blue Ribbon County" ... Manhattan: Nationalist, 1881. 140 pp.

Riley County, Kansas; a Story of Early Settlements . . . by Winifred N. Slagg. Manhattan: N.p. [1968]. xvi, 255 pp.

## Rooks County

Lest We Forget, by Rooks County Historical Society. 2 vols. Osborne: Osborne County Farmer, 1980.

## Rush County

Rush County History Book, a Century in Story and Pictures. Rush County Book Comm. N.p.: Rush County Hist. Soc., 1976. 265 pp. (Index, prepared by Dorothy Richards, et al.)

## Saline County

Pictorial History of Saline County. Saline County Historical Society. Vol. 1: As We Were . . . [Salina], 1976.

## Scott County

History of Early Scott County. Scott City: Scott County Hist. Comm., 1977. 527 pp.

## Sedgwick County

History of Wichita and Sedgwick County, Kansas . . . by Orsemus H. Bentley. 2 vols. Chicago: C.F. Cooper & Co., 1910.

## Seward County

Seward County, Kansas, comp. by the Seward County Historical Society, ed. by Pauline Toland. Liberal: K.C. Printers, 1979. 446 pp.

## Shawnee County

Historical Sketch of Shawnee County, Kansas . . . 1876 [by Frye W. Giles]. Topeka: Commonwealth Pr. House, 1876. 68 pp.

History of Shawnee County, Kansas, and Representative Citizens, ed. and comp. by James L. King. Chicago: Richmond & Arnold, 1905. 628 pp.

Witness of the Times, a History of Shawnee County, by Roy D. Bird and D.H. Wallace. [Topeka: Shawnee County Hist. Soc., 1976.] 376 pp.

## Sherman County

The Prairie Pioneers of Western Kansas and Eastern Colorado, by John C. Jones and Winona C. Jones. Boulder, Colo.: Johnson Pub. Co. [1956]. 136 pp.

They Came to Stay: Sherman County and Family History. 3 vols. Goodland: Sherman County Hist. Soc., 1980-81.

## Smith County

Home on the Range, by Margaret A. Nelson. Boston: Chapman & Grimes [1948]. 285 pp. (Commemorative ed. [Burbank, Calif.?:] F.E. Sterba [1971]. 285 pp.)

## Stafford County

A History of Stafford County, by Frank A. Steele. [Stafford: Stafford County Hist. Soc., 1982.] 142 pp.

## Stevens County

History of Stevens County, Kansas, by Edith Thomson. N.p. [1967]. 165 pp.

The History of Stevens County and Its People. Hugoton: Stevens County Hist. Assoc. [1979]. 653 pp.

## Sumner County

The Sumner County Story, by Gwendoline Sanders and Paul Sanders. North Newton: Mennonite Pr., 1966. 190 pp.

## Thomas County

A Brief Sketch of Thomas County, Kansas . . . [by Eugene Worcester]. [Colby:] Thomas County Cat., 1887. 92 pp.

The Golden Jubilee Anniversary of Thomas County and Its Neighbors [comp. by George H. Kinkel and C.A. Jones]. [Rexford: Rexford News, 1935.] 6, 188 pp.

Thomas County, Kansas; the First One Hundred Years, by Cline C. Curtiss. Colby: Prairie Pr., 1973. 130 pp.

Land of the Windmills, Thomas County, Kansas, ed. by Ronald I. Bruner. History and Commentary, by Helen Schnellbacher Frahm. Vol. 1. Colby: Thomas County Hist. Soc., 1976. 180 pp.

Golden Heritage of Thomas County [by Thomas County Historical Society]. N.p. [1978]. 429 pp.

## Wabaunsee County

Early History of Wabaunsee County, Kansas . . . by Matt Thomson. Alma: N.p., 1901. viii, 368 pp. (Repr. Manhattan: A.G. Pr. [1979].)

Business Directory and History of Wabaunsee County . . . Topeka: Kansas Directory Co., 1907. 104 pp.

New Branches from Old Trees, a New History of Wabaunsee County. [comp. by Wabaunsee County Hist. Soc., 1976.] 911 pp. (Surname index, by Alice E. Soldan. n.d. 27 leaves.)

## Wallace County

Wallace County History . . . Sharon Springs: Sharon County Historians, 1979. 400 pp.

## Wichita County

History of Wichita County, Kansas, by Wichita County Historical Association. Vol. 1. North Newton: Mennonite Pr., 1980.

## Wilson County

History of . . . Wilson County, 1902, *see* Neosho County.

In the Heart of the Oil Field [by F.O. Williams]. [Fredonia: Author], 1904. 138 pp. (Repr. Fredonia: Carl Shoaf, 1983.)

## Woodson County

History of . . . Woodson County, 1901, *see* Allen County.

## Wyandotte County

Wyandotte County and Kansas City, Kansas, Historical and Biographical . . . Chicago: Goodspeed Pub. Co., 1890. 895 pp.

History of Wyandotte County, Kansas, and Its People, ed. and comp. by Perl W. Morgan. 2 vols. Chicago: Lewis Pub. Co., 1911.

Historic Spots or Mile-Stones in the Progress of Wyandotte County, Kansas, by Grant W. Harrington. [Merriam?:] N.p., 1935. 360 pp.

# KENTUCKY

## Regional

History of Bourbon, Scott, Harrison and Nicholas Counties, Kentucky . . . ed. by William H. Perrin. Chicago: O.L. Baskin, 1882. 815 pp. (Repr. Cincinnati, Ohio: Art Guild Inc., 1968. Repr. with new index. Easley, S.C.: Southern Hist. Pr., 1979. 888 pp.)

Kentucky: a History of the State . . . by William H. Perrin, J.H. Battle and G.C. Kniffin. Louisville, 1888. (Repr. Easley, S.C.: Southern Hist. Pr., 1979.) This work was published in eight editions, each treating several counties, but since their publication chiefly concerned biographies, it is not proposed to cross-reference each county treated under the appropriate county. Most counties are treated, and to get a bibliography of the whole set, see Filby's *American & British Genealogy & Heraldry*, 3d ed., 1983, nos. 3071-3094, pp. 182-83.

🌱          🌱          🌱

## Anderson County

A History of Anderson County, Begun in 1884 by Major Lewis W. McKee, Concluded in 1936 by Mrs. Lydia K. Bond, 1780-1936 . . . Frankfort: Roberts Pr. Co. [1936]. iii, 223 pp. (Repr. Baltimore: Regional Pub. Co., 1975.)

## Barren County

The Times of Long Ago, Barren County, Kentucky, by Franklin Corin. Louisville: J.P. Morton & Co., 1929. 131 pp.

Barren County and Its People, by L.K. McGhee. Louisville: N.p., 1956.

## Bath County

An Outline History of Bath County, from 1811 to 1876. Lexington: Transylvania Pr. and Pub. Co., 1876. 54 pp.

A History of Bath County, Kentucky; with Historical and Biographical Sketches . . . by John A. Richards. Yuma, Ariz.: Southwest Pr., 1961. 592 pp.

## Bell County

History of Bell County, Kentucky, by Henry H. Fuson. 2 vols. New York: Hobson Book Pr., 1947. x, 634 pp. (Index, prepared by Annie W. Burns. [N.p., 1961]. 40, 25 pp.)

## Boone County

History of Boone County, Kentucky, by A.M. Yealey. Reprint of Articles Pub. in Newspapers over a Period of 50 Years. Florence: William Fitzgerald, 1960. 32 pp.

## Bourbon County

History of Bourbon County . . . 1882, *see* History of Bourbon, Scott . . . Counties, p. 141.

Historical Pageant of Bourbon County, Kentucky, 1785-1929. Millersburg: Bourbon County High School, 1929.

## Boyle County

History of . . . Boyle County, 1924, *see* Mercer County.

## Breathitt County

Bloody Breathitt, by E.L. Noble. 3 vols. Jackson: Jackson Times Pr. Co. [1936]-47.

In the Land of Breathitt, comp. . . . by W.P.A. Northport, N.Y.: Bacon, Percy & Daggett [1941]. 172 pp.

## Breckinridge County

History and Legend of Breckinridge, Kentucky, by William Thompson. N.p. [1972]. 170 pp.

## Bullitt County

A History of Bullitt County, Kentucky, by Bullitt County Historical Commission. Vine Grove: Ancestral Trails Hist. Soc., 1974. 64 pp.

## Caldwell County

First History of Caldwell County, Kentucky, by Clausine R. Baker. Madisonville: Commercial Pr., 1936. 219 pp.

## Calloway County

History of Calloway County, Kentucky, Together with Sketches of Its Prominent Citizens . . . comp. and pub. by Ledger & Times. [Murray: Ledger & Times, 1931?] 64 pp. (Repr. Murray: Kentucky Repr. Co., 1972.)

## Carlisle County

History and Memories of Carlisle County, by Ran Graves. Wickliffe: Advance-Yeoman Pub., 1958. 82 pp.

## Casey County

Celeste and Other Sketches, by Peter B. Riffe. Lebanon: Standard Pr., 1876. 179 pp.

The Men, Women, Events, Institutions and Lore of Casey County, Kentucky, collected by Willie M. Watkins. Louisville: Standard Pr. Co. [1939]. xiii, 223 pp.

## Christian County

County of Christian, Kentucky, Historical and Biographical, ed. by William H. Perrin. 2 vols. Chicago: F.A. Battey, 1884. 320, 319 pp. (Repr. Evansville, Ind.: Unigraphic, 1972. Repr. with new index. Spartanburg, S.C.: Reprint Co., 1979. 656 pp.)

County of . . . Christian . . . 1884, *see* Todd County.

A History of Christian County, Kentucky, from Oxcart to Airplane, by Charles M. Meacham. Nashville, Tenn.: Marshall & Bruce Co., 1930. xiv, 695 pp.

## Clark County

Early Clark County, Kentucky; a History, 1674-1824, by Willard R. Jillson. Frankfort: Roberts Pr., 1966. 99 pp.

## Clay County

History of Clay County, Kentucky, by Mr. and Mrs. Morgan. Manchester: Morgan Book Co., 1976. 577 pp.

## Cumberland County

History of Cumberland County, by Joseph W. Wells. Louisville: Standard Pr. Co., 1947. xiii, 480 pp.

## Daviess County

History of Daviess County, Kentucky . . . Chicago: Inter-State Pub. Co., 1883. 870 pp. (Repr. Evansville, Ind.: Unigraphic, 1966.)

History of Owensboro and Daviess County, Kentucky, by Hugh O. Potter. N.p.: Daviess County Hist. Soc., 1974. 265 pp.

## Elliott County

Elliott County, by Mary Vansant. Morehead: Morehead Independent, 1934. 40 pp.

## Estill County

Historical Records of Estill County, Irvine, Kentucky, by Annie W. Burns. Washington, D.C.: L.K. McGhee [1953?]. 50, 45 pp.

History of Estill County, by Hallie T. Johnstone. Irvine: Kentucky Citizens, 1974. vi, 80 pp.

## Fayette County

History of Fayette County, Kentucky, by Robert Peter, ed. by William H. Perrin. Chicago: O.L. Baskin, 1882. 905 pp. (Repr. with full-name index. Easley, S.C.: Southern Hist. Pr., 1979. 905 pp.)

## Fleming County

Condensed History of Fleming County, Kentucky, by Dan T. Fisher. Flemingsburg: Author, 1908. 24 pp.

Early Fleming County, Kentucky Pioneers Historical Facts, by Wade Cooper. [Flemingsburg:] Author [1974]. 244 pp.

## Floyd County

Historic Floyd, 1800-1950. Floyd County Sesquicentennial, by Henry P. Scalf. [Prestonburg?:] N.p., 1950. 132 pp.

Annals of Floyd County, Kentucky, 1800-1826, by Charles C. Wells. Paintsville: Author, and Baltimore: Gateway Pr., 1983. 365 pp.

## Franklin County

The History of Franklin County, Kentucky, by Lewis F. Johnson. Frankfort: Roberts Pr. Co., 1912. 289, xviii pp.

Early Frankfort and Franklin County, Kentucky . . . 1750-1850, by Willard R. Jillson. Louisville: Standard Pr. Co., 1936. xvi, 182 pp.

Filling the Chinks, by Ermina J. Darnell. Frankfort: Roberts Pr. Co., 1966. 211 pp.

## Gallatin County

History of Gallatin County, Kentucky, by Gypsy M. Gray. Covington: N.p. [1968]. 123 pp.

## Garrard County

Looking Backward: Historical Sketches of Lancaster and Garrard County, by J.B. Kinnaird. [Lancaster: Central Record, 1924.] 32 pp.

History of Garrard County, Kentucky, and Its Churches, by Forrest Calico. New York: Hobson Book Pr., 1947. x, 513 pp.

Patches of Garrard County, 1796-1974: a History, comp. and ed. by the Lancaster Woman's Club. Lancaster: The Club, 1974. v, 410 pp.

## Green County

Green County Historical Factbook, comp. . . . by Marshall Lowe. Greensburg: Greensburg Pr. & Office Supply, 1970. 57 pp.

## Greenup County

History of Greenup County, Kentucky, by Nina M. Biggs and M.L. Mackay. [Louisville?:] Franklin Pr., 1951. xii, 345 pp. (Suppl. ed. New York: Vantage Pr., 1962.)

# Hardin County

A Series of Monographs Concerning the Lincolns and Hardin County, Kentucky, by R. Gerald McMurtry. Elizabethtown: Enterprise Pr., 1938. 133 pp.

Chronicles of Hardin County, Kentucky, 1766-1974, comp. by Mrs. Thomas D. Winstead. Bicentennial ed. [Elizabethtown?: N.p., 1974.] x, 77 pp.

# Harlan County

Harlan County, Kentucky, by Elmon Middleton. Big Laurel, Va.: J.T. Adams, 1934. 57, iv pp.

A History of Harlan County, by Mabel G. Condon. Nashville, Tenn.: Parthenon Pr. [1962]. 216 pp.

Historical Statistics of Harlan County, Kentucky . . . [Washington, D.C.: N.p., 1964.] 105 leaves.

My Appalachia; a Reminiscence . . . by Rebecca Caudill. New York: Holt, Rinehart & Winston [1966]. 90 pp.

# Harrison County

History of . . . Harrison County, 1882, *see* History of Bourbon . . . p. 141.

# Henderson County

History of Henderson County, Kentucky, by Edmund L. Starling. Henderson: N.p., 1887. 840 pp. (Repr. Evansville, Ind.: Unigraphic, 1965.)

The Annals and Scandals of Henderson County, Kentucky, by Maralee Arnett. Corydon: Fremar Pub. Co., 1976. 387 pp.

# Henry County

History of Henry County, Kentucky, by Maude (Johnson) Drane. [Louisville: Franklin Pr. Co.], 1948. xii, 274 pp.

# Hickman County

Hickman County, Kentucky, History. Clinton: Hickman County Hist. Soc., 1983. 430 pp.

# Hopkins County

History of Hopkins County, Kentucky, by Maurice K. Gordon. Madisonville: Hopkins County Gen. Soc., 1978. 389 pp.

# Jefferson County

History of the Ohio Falls Cities and Their Counties . . . 2 vols. Cleveland, Ohio: L.A. Williams, 1882.

A History of Early Jeffersontown and South Eastern Jefferson County, Kentucky, by Robert C. Jobson. Jeffersontown: Author, 1977. 259 pp.

## Jessamine County

A History of Jessamine County, Kentucky, from Its Earliest Settlement to 1898, by Bennett H. Young. Louisville: Currier-Journal Job Pr., 1898. 288 pp. (Repr. Utica, N.Y.: Cook & McDowell, 1979. 319 pp.)

## Johnson County

Johnson County History, by Mitchell Hall: a History of the County . . . to 1927. 2 vols. Louisville: Standard Pr., 1928. 1,260 pp.

A Short History of Paintsville and Johnson County. Paintsville: Paintsville Herald, for Johnson County Hist. Soc., 1962?

## Kenton County

Little Switzerland, by Milton H. McLean. Covington: Wolff's Standard Pr. Works, 1943. 62 pp.

## Lee County

The Romance of Lee County, by Nevyle Shackelford. Beattyville: Beattyville Enterprise [1947]. 116 pp.

Remembering Lee County; a Story of the Early Days, by Bernice C. Caudill. Danville: Bluegrass Pr. Co. [1968]. 65 leaves.

## Letcher County

History of Letcher County, Kentucky . . . [by Isaac A. Bowles]. [Hazard: Author, 1949.] 75 pp.

Letcher County, Kentucky: a Brief History, by William T. Cornett. Prestonsburg: State-wide Pr. Co., 1967. 40 pp.

## Lewis County

History of Lewis County, Kentucky, by O.G. Ragan. Cincinnati, Ohio: Jennings & Graham [1912]. 504 pp. (Repr. Evansville, Ind.: Unigraphic, 1979.)

## Livingston County

Chronicles of a Kentucky Settlement (Livingston County and Smithland), by William C. Watts. New York: Putnam, 1897. xiii, 490 pp.

## Logan County

The History of Russellville and Logan County, Which Is to Some Extent a History of Western Kentucky, by Alex C. Finley. 3 vols. (5 parts). Russellville: O.C. Rhea, 1878, 1879, 1890. 60, 100, 63 pp.

The Story of Logan County, by Edward Coffman. Russellville: N.p., 1962. 303 pp.

## Lyon County

One Century of Lyon County History [by Malvena Wiseman, et al.]. Eddyville: Young Pr. Co., 1964. 113 pp.

## Madison County

A Glimpse at Historic Madison County and Richmond, Kentucky, by Jonathan T. Dorris. Richmond: Richmond Daily Register Co., 1934. 65 pp.

Glimpses of Historic Madison County, Kentucky, by Jonathan T. Dorris. Nashville, Tenn.: Williams Pr. Co., 1955. 334 pp.

## Marshall County

Lemon's Hand Book of Marshall County Giving Its History . . . by James R. Lemon. Benton: N.p., 1894. 172 pp. (Repr. N.p.: Kentucky Reprint Co., 1971. 172 pp.)

History of Marshall County, Kentucky, by Leon L. Freeman and E.C. Olds. Benton: Tribune Democrat, 1933. 252, 52, 40 pp.

## Mason County

A Historical Sketch of Mason County, Kentucky, by Lucy C. Lee. Louisville: Pr. of Masonic Home J1 [1928]. 46 pp.

History of Nashville and Mason County, Kentucky, by Glenn Clift. Vol. 1 (no more pub.). Lexington: Transylvania Pr. Co., 1936. ix, 461 pp. (Repr. Evansville, Ind.: Unigraphic, 1980.)

## Meade County

Early Times in Meade County, Kentucky, by George L. Ridenour. Louisville: Western Recorder, 1929. 107 pp. (Repr. with index. Vine Grove: Ancestral Trails Hist. Soc., 1984. 129 pp.)

## Mercer County

Historical Sketch of Mercer County, by A.B. Rue. Harrodsburg: A.B. Rue Pub., 1904. 72 pp.

History of Mercer and Boyle Counties, by Mrs. Maria (Thompson) Daviess. Vol. 1 (no more pub.). Harrodsburg: Harrodsburg Herald, 1924. 179 pp. (Repr. Utica, N.Y.: Cook & McDowell Pub., 1979.)

## Montgomery County

Historical Sketches of Montgomery County, by Richard Reid. Mt. Sperling: Democrat Job Rooms Pr., 1882. 69 pp. (Repr. [Lexington: James M. Byrnes Co., 1926.])

Montgomery County, Kentucky Bicentennial, 1774-1974. [Mt. Sterling:] Montgomery County Bicentennial Comm., 1976. 142 pp.

## Morgan County

Morgan County, Kentucky, 1823-1923. West Liberty: Licking Valley Courier, 1923. 32 pp.

A Brief History of Our Early Life and Morgan County, Kentucky, by Harlan R. Brown. Ashland: Author, 1950. 83 pp.

Early Morgan County; a Historical Novel by Arthur C. Johnson. [West Liberty: N.p., 1974.] 351 pp.

## Muhlenberg County

A History of Muhlenberg County, by Otto A. Rothert. Louisville: John P. Norton, 1913. xvii, 496 pp. (Repr. N.p., 1964.)

Some Sketches of the History of Greenville and Muhlenberg County, by Gayle R. Carver. Greenville: Greenville Leader Pr. [1936-37]. 30 leaves.

## Nelson County

Early Historical Incidents in Nelson County, by Laura W. Brown. [Elizabethtown: N.p., 1920.]

Historic Nelson County, by Sarah B. Smith. Louisville: Gateway Pr., 1971. 407 pp.

## Nicholas County

History of . . . Nicholas County, 1882, *see* History of Bourbon . . . County, p. 141.

History of Nicholas County, by Joan W. Conley. N.p.: Nicholas County Hist. Soc., 1976. 549 pp.

## Ohio County

Ohio County, Kentucky in the Olden Days . . . Newspaper Sketches . . . by Harrison D. Taylor. Louisville: J.P. Morton, 1926. 204 pp. (Repr. Baltimore: Regional Pub. Co., 1969.)

Fogle's Papers, a History of Ohio County, Kentucky, comp. from the Writings of McDowell A. Fogle, Which Appeared Originally in the Rough River Ripples Column of Ohio County News, Hartford, Ky. Hartford: McDowell Pub., for the Ohio County Hist. Soc., 1977. 452, xx pp.

## Owen County

History of Owen County, Kentucky, by Miriam S. Houchens. Owenton: Owen County Hist. Soc., 1976. 413 pp.

## Perry County

History of Perry County, Kentucky . . . by Hazard Chapter, D.A.R., comp. by Eunice T. Johnson. [Hazard: D.A.R., 1953.] xiv, 286 pp.

## Pike County

One Hundred and Fifty Years, Pike County, Kentucky, 1822-1972, ed. by Leonard Roberts, et al. Pikeville: Pike County Hist. Soc., 1976. 102 pp.

## Pulaski County

A History of Pulaski County, Kentucky, by Alma (Owens) Tibbals. Bagdad & Louisville: G.O. Moore and Franklin Pr., 1952. 272 pp.

## Scott County

History of . . . Scott County, 1882, *see* History of Bourbon . . . p. 141. (Perrin's History of Scott County, taken from History of Bourbon . . . County, 1882.) Georgetown: The Graphic, n.d. See also second entry on p. 141.

The B.O. Gaines History of Scott County, by B.O. Gaines. 3 vols. Georgetown: B.O. Gaines Pr., 1905. 764 pp. (Repr. Georgetown: The Graphic, 1957. 820 pp.)

Pageant of Scott County History, 1774-1924, by F.E. Eberhardt, et al. Georgetown: Georgetown Coll., 1924. 55 pp.

## Shelby County

History of Shelby County, Kentucky . . . comp. and ed. by George L. Willis, Sr. Louisville: C.T. Dearing Pr. Co., 1929. 268 pp. (Repr. Utica, N.Y.: Cook & McDowell, 1979. 313 pp.)

## Taylor County

Early Taylor County History, by Robert L. Nesbitt. Campbellsville: News-Journal, 1941. 176 pp.

## Todd County

Sketches of the Early Settlement of Todd County, by Urban E. Kennedy. (First printed in Todd County Witness, 1872.) N.p., n.d. 80 pp.

Counties of Todd and Christian, by J.H. Battle and W.H. Perrin. Chicago & Louisville: F.A. Battey Pub. Co., 1884. 328 pp. (Repr. Spartanburg, S.C.: Reprint Co., 1979.)

The Story of Todd County, Kentucky, 1820-1970, by Frances M. Williams. [Nashville, Tenn.: Parthenon Pr., 1972.] 547 pp.

## Trigg County

County of . . . Trigg, 1884, *see* Christian County.

The Statistician Handbook of Trigg County, the Gateway to the Jackson Purchase in Kentucky and Tennessee, by Eurie P. (Wilford). Nashville, Tenn.: Rich Pr. Co., 1961. xv, 548 pp.

History of Trigg County, Historical and Biographical, ed. by W.H. Perrin. Chicago: F.A. Battey Pub. Co., 1884. 293 pp. (Repr. Spartanburg, S.C.: Reprint Co., 1979. 306 pp.)

## Union County

History of Union County, Kentucky, by Charles J. O'Malley. Evansville, Ind.: Courier Pr. Co., 1886. 896 pp. (Repr. Evansville, Ind.: Unigraphic, 1969.)

Union County, Past and Present, comp. . . . by W.P.A. Louisville: Schuhmann Pr. Co., 1941. 245, xxxii pp. (Repr. Evansville, Ind.: Unigraphic, 1972.)

## Warren County

The Times of Long Ago, Warren County, Kentucky, by Franklin Gorin. Louisville: J.P. Morton, 1936. 31 pp.

Early History of Warren County, by Will T. Hale, ed. by J.W. Womack, Jr. McMinnville, Tenn.: Standard Pr. Co., 1970.

Do You Remember When?, by Warren County Historical Comm. Bowling Green: Citizens National Bank, 1970.

## Washington County

Early Times in Washington County, Kentucky, by Orval W. Baylor. Cynthiana: Hobson Pr., 1942. 158 pp.

Pioneer History of Washington County, Kentucky, as comp. from Newspaper Articles, by Orval W. Baylor, et al. Ed. and indexed by Michael L. Cook and Bettie A. Cook. Owensboro: Cook & McDowell Pubs., 1979. 456 pp.

## Wayne County

A Century of Wayne County, Kentucky, 1800-1900, by Augusta P. Johnson. Louisville: Standard Pr. Co. [1939]. 281 pp. (Repr. Evansville, Ind.: Unigraphic, 1979.)

Glimpses of Historical Wayne County, Kentucky, by Bobby G. Edwards. Monticello: N.p., 1970. xiii, 111 pp.

## Whitley County

History of . . . Whitley County, 1938, *see* Campbell County, Tennessee.

## Wolfe County

Early and Modern History of Wolfe County, Kentucky, comp. by Wolfe County Woman's Club, 1958. [Campton?: The Club, 1958.] 340 pp.

## Woodford County

History of Woodford County, by William E. Railey. Frankfort: Roberts Pr. Co., 1928. 408 pp. (Repr. from Kentucky Historical Society Register, 1920-26.) New ed., 1938. (Repr. of 1938 ed. Baltimore: Regional Pub. Co., 1975. 449 pp.)

# LOUISIANA

## Acadia Parish

Acadia Parish, Louisiana: a History to 1900, by Mary A. Fontenot and P.B. Freeland. Baton Rouge: Claitor's Book Store, 1976. 377, 369 pp.

## Ascension Parish

The Story of Ascension Parish, Louisiana, by Sidney A. Marchand. [Baton Rouge:] Ortlieb Pr. Co., 1931. 194 pp.

The Flight of a Century (1800-1900) in Ascension Parish, by Sydney A. Marchand. Donaldsonville: N.p., 1936. 240 pp.

## Avoyelles Parish

History of Avoyelles Parish, Louisiana, by Corinne L. Saucier. New Orleans: Pelican Pub. Co., 1943. 569 pp.

Histoire et Géographie des Avoyelles en Louisiane. New Orleans: Pelican Pub. Co. [1956]. 111 pp. (*See* also entry above.)

Traditions de la Paroisse des Avoyelles en Louisiane, by Corinne L. Saucier. Philadelphia: American Folklore Soc., 1956, 62 pp.

La Commission des Avoyelles; and Avoyelles Parish, Crossroads of Louisiana: Where All Cultures Meet, by Sue L. Eakin. Baton Rouge: Moran Pub. Co., 1981. 217 pp.

## Beauregard District

Early Annals of Beauregard Parish, by Mrs. Lily Fraser. New Orleans: Louisiana State Univ., 1933. 70 pp. (thesis)

Beauregard Parish Sesquicentennial Celebration, 1818-1968. N.p.: Beauregard Parish Hist. Soc. [1968]. 32 pp.

## Bienville Parish

Ante-Bellum Bienville Parish, by Philip C. Cook. Ruston: Louisiana Polytechnic Inst., 1965. 182 pp. (M.A. thesis)

## Caddo Parish

Caddo: 1,000; a History of the Shreveport Area from the Time of the Caddo Indians to the 1970s, by Viola Carruth. Shreveport: Shreveport Magazine, 1970. 233 pp. (Much about Caddo Parish History.)

## Caldwell County

Caldwell Parish in Slices, 1838-1971, by H. Ted Woods. Baton Rouge: Claitor's Book Store, 1972.

## Claiborne Parish

The History of Claiborne Parish, Louisiana, from Its Incorporation in 1828 to . . . 1885 . . . comp. by D.W. Harris. New Orleans: Stansbury Pr., 1886. 263 pp.

## Concordia Parish

A History of Concordia Parish, by Robert D. Calhoun. [New Orleans, 1932]. 204 pp. (Repr. from Louisiana Hist. Soc. Quarterly.)

## De Soto Parish

De Soto Parish History and Cemetery Records, by J.A.H. Slawson. Center, Tex.: N.p., 1967. 114 pp.

## East Baton Rouge Parish

The Plains and the People; a History of Upper East Baton Rouge Parish, by Virginia Jennings. New Orleans: Pelican Pub. Co., 1962. 396 pp.

## East Feliciana Parish

East Feliciana, Louisiana, Past and Present. Sketches of the Pioneers, by Henry Skipwith. New Orleans: Hopkins Pr. Office, 1892. 61 pp. (Repr. Baton Rouge: Claitor's Book Store, for East Feliciana Pilgrimage and Garden Club, Clinton, 1957. 61 pp.)

The Felicianas of Louisiana, by Miriam G. Reeves. Baton Rouge: Claitor's Book Store, 1967. iii, 126 pp.

## Evangeline Parish

A History of Evangeline: Its Land, Its Men, and Its Women Who Made It a Beautiful Place to Live, by Robert Gahn. Baton Rouge: Claitor's Pub. Div. [1972]. xiii, 146 pp. (thesis)

## Grant Parish

Grant Parish, Louisiana; a History, by Mabel F. Harrison and L.M. McNeely. Baton Rouge: Claitor's Pub. Div., 1969. 312 pp.

## Iberia Parish

They Tasted Bayou Water, a Brief History of Iberia Parish, by Maurice Bergerie. New Orleans: Pelican Pub. Co., 1962. 162 pp.

## Iberville Parish

The Heart of the Sugar Bowl; the Story of Iberville, by Albert L. Grace. Plaquemine: [Baton Rouge: Franklin Pr.], 1946. 249 pp.

Plantation Life on the Mississippi, by William E. Clement. New Orleans: Pelican Pub. Co. [1952]. xvii, 212 pp. (Repr. New Orleans: Pelican Pub. Co., 1961.)

## Jackson County

Jackson Parish, Louisiana, ed. by Sharon Brown and M. Asken. Jonesboro: Jackson Parish Chamber of Commerce, 1982. 402 pp.

## Jefferson County

Historic Jefferson Parish, from Shore to Shore, by Betsy Swanson. Gretna: Pelican Pub. Co., 1975. xvi, 176 pp.

## Lafayette Parish

The Attakapas Trail; a History of Lafayette Parish . . . [Morgan City: King Hannaford Co., 1923.] 48 pp.

The Attakapas County; a History of Lafayette Parish, Louisiana, by Harry L. Griffin. New Orleans: Pelican Pub. Co. [1959]. 263 pp. (Repr. New Orleans: Pelican Pub. Co., 1974. 261 pp.)

Here Is South Louisiana, by Frances T. Love and John Love. Lafayette: Tribune Pr. Plant, 1965. 79 pp.

The Serpent and the Dove, by Francis J. Kichak. Hicksville, N.Y.: Exposition Pr., 1975. 186 pp.

## La Salle Parish

History of La Salle Parish, Louisiana, by L.H. Taylor and M.E. Plummer. Jena: Jena Louisiana Times, 1959-60.

## Lincoln Parish

Notes on a History of Lincoln Parish, Louisiana, by Kathleen Graham. 2d ed. Ruston: Louisiana Polytechnic Inst., 1945? 90 pp.

Historical Studies of Lincoln Parish, by Mary F. Fletcher. Ruston: N.p. [1960?]. 64 pp.

## Morehouse Parish

The Economic and Social History of Morehouse Parish, Louisiana, to 1900, by Scott D. Swanson. Munro: Letter Service Bureau, 1978. 228 pp.

## Natchitoches Parish

Natchitoches: the Up-to-date Oldest Town in Louisiana, by Germaine Portre-Bobinski. New Orleans: Dameron-Pierson, 1936. 238 pp.

Natchitoches Parish Cultural and Historical Resources, by H.F. Gregory, J.L. McCorkle, and H.K. Curry. Natchitoches: Natchitoches Parish Planning Comm., 1979. 84 pp.

## Plaquemines Parish

Plaquemines: the Empire Parish, by J. Ben Meyer. Buras?: Author, 1981. 97 pp.

## Pointe Coupee Parish

A History of Pointe Coupee Parish and Its Families, ed. by Judy Riffel. Baton Rouge: Le Comité des Archives de la Louisiane, and Dallas: National ShareGraphics, 1983. 363 pp.

## Rapides Parish

Rapides Parish, Louisiana; a History. [Baton Rouge: Alexandria Comm. of the Nat. Soc. of Colonial Dames in the State of Louisiana, 193-.] 192 pp. (Repr. from the Louisiana Historical Quarterly, 1932-35.)

Rapides Remembers, 1875-1975; a Chronicle, comp. by G.M.G. Kramer. Baton Rouge: Franklin Pr., 1975. 48 pp.

## Sabine County

History of Sabine Parish, Louisiana, by John G. Belisle; from the First Explorers and Settlers to the Present. [Many:] Sabine Banner Pr., 1912. 319 pp.

Sabine Parish, Louisiana Story; "Land of the Green Gold," by Amos L. Armstrong. Shreveport: Jones & Stringfellow, 1958. 273 pp.

Early Sabine Parish; Including the 1850 Sabine Parish Census & Early Towns, by Elias W. Sandel. N.p., 1972.

## St. Charles Parish

A History of St. Charles Parish to 1973, by Henry E. Yoes, III. Norco and Hahnville: St. Charles Herald Pubs., 1973. iv, 237 pp.

## St. James Parish

Cabanocey; the History, Customs, and Folklore of St. James Parish, by Lillian C. Bourgeois. New Orleans: Pelican Pub. Co. [1957]. 211 pp.

## St. John the Baptist Parish

A History of St. John the Baptist Parish, with Biographical Sketches, comp. and ed. by Jean M. Eyraud and D.J. Millet. Narrero: Hope Haven Pr., 1939. 143 pp.

Saint John the Baptist Parish on the Corridor of History. Baton Rouge: N.C. Ferachi, 1974. 62 pp.

## St. Mary Parish

Annotated Abstracts of the Successions of St. Mary Parish, Louisiana, by Mary E. Sanders. [Lafayette?: N.p.], 1972. x, 231 pp.

A History of St. Mary Parish, by Bernard Broussard. Baton Rouge: Claitor's Pub. Div., 1977. 196 pp.

## Vernon Parish

A Brief History of Vernon Parish, Louisiana, from the First Known Settlers of the Parish to the Present Time, by John T. Cupit. Rosepine: N.p., 1963. 137 pp.

Tall Pines, the Story of Vernon Parish, by Erbon W. Wise. Sulphur: West Calcasieu Pr. [1971]. 90 leaves.

## West Baton Rouge Parish

Chronicles of West Baton Rouge Parish, by Elizabeth Kellough and L. Mayeux. Baton Rouge: Kennedy Pr. Shop, 1979. 266 pp.

## West Feliciana Parish

West Feliciana, a Glimpse of Its History, by Louise Butler N.p.: True Democrat, 19--. 32 pp.

Plantation Life in the Florida Parishes of Louisiana, 1836-1846 . . . by Edwin A. Davis. New York: Columbia Univ. Pr., 1943. xvi, 457 pp. (Repr. New York: A.M.S. Pr., 1967. xvi, 457 pp.)

## Winn Parish

Briley's Memorial History . . . of Winn Parish, Louisiana, by Richard Briley, III. Montgomery: Mid-South Pub. [1966]. 287 pp.

# MAINE

## Androscoggin County

Atlas and History of Androscoggin County. Philadelphia: Sanford, Everts & Co., 1873. 120 pp.

History of Androscoggin County, Maine . . . ed. by Georgia D. Merrill. Boston: W.A. Fergusson & Co., 1891. 879 pp.

## Aroostook County

History of Aroostook, comp. by Hon. Edward Wiggin. Vol. 1 in 2 parts (no more pub.) [Presque Isle: Star-Herald Pr., 1922.] 306, 122 pp.

Aroostook: Our Last Frontier . . . by Charles M. Wilson. Brattleboro, Vt.: Stephen Daye Pr. [1937]. 240 pp.

100th Anniversary of Aroostook County. Houlton: Houlton Pioneer Times, 1939. 52 pp.

## Cumberland County

History of Cumberland County, by W. Woodford Clayton. Philadelphia: Everts & Peck, 1880. 456 pp.

## Franklin County

Franklin County, Maine, by Janice Durrell. Portland: Goss & Allen [1973?]. 72 pp.

## Hancock County

A Survey of Hancock County, Maine, by Samuel Wasson. Augusta: Sprague, Owen & Nash, 1878. 91 pp.

Register of the Towns of Sedgewick, Brooklin, Deer Isle, Stinington, and Isle au Haut, 1910, comp. . . . by Chatto and Turner, by Clarence I. Chatto. [Repr.?] Brooklin: Friend Memorial Public Lib. [1972]. 243 pp. (Partial coverage of Hancock County.)

## Kennebec County

Illustrated History of Kennebec County, Maine, 1625-1729-1892, by Henry D. Kingsbury, Simeon L. Deyo (et al.). 2 vols. New York: H.W. Blake, 1892. 1,273 pp.

A Northern Countryside, by Rosalind Richards. New York: Holt & Co., 1916. 210 pp.

*Kennebec County (cont.)*

Kennebec Yesterdays, by Ernest C. Marriner. Waterville: Colby College Pr., 1954. 320 pp.

## Knox County

Chronicles of Knox County, comp. by Robert B. Fillmore. [Rockland: N.p.], 1922. 106 pp. (Additions, 1923. 20 pp.)

## Lincoln County

Chronicles of Lincoln County, comp. by Robert B. Fillmore. Augusta: Kennebec Journal Pr. Shop, 1924. 152 pp.

Lincoln County, Maine 1760-1960, by Howard A. Maple. Rockland: Seth Low Pr. [1960]. (Unpaged)

## Oxford County

Sketches of Oxford County, by Thomas T. Stone. Portland: Shirley & Hyde, 1830. 111 pp.

## Penobscot County

History of Penobscot County [by Henry A. Ford?]. Cleveland: Williams, Chase & Co., 1882. 922 pp.

Penobscot County, Maine, by Richard W. Baker. Portland: Gross & Allen, 1973. 75 pp.

## Piscataquis County

History of Piscataquis County, by Rev. Amasa Loring. Portland: Hoyt, Fogg & Donham, 1880. vii, 340 pp.

Historical Collections of Piscataquis County . . . Papers . . . of Piscataquis County Historical Society . . . Vol. 1 (all pub.). Dover: Observer Pr., 1910. vi, 522 pp.

## Somerset County

The East Somerset County Register, 1911-12, by Clarence I. Chatto. Auburn: Chatto & Turner, 1912. 539 pp.

## Waldo County

A Survey of Waldo County, Maine: Historical . . . by John W. Lang. Augusta: Sprague, Owen & Nash, 1873. 131 pp.

## Washington County

Calais, Eastport and Vicinity, Their Points of Interest . . . by Geo. F. Bacon. Newark, N.J.: Glenwood Pub. Co., 1892. 119 pp.

*Washington County (cont.)*

An International Community on the St. Croix (1604-1930). Orono: Univ. Pr., 1950. 412 pp.

## York County

History of York County, Maine . . . by W. Woodford Clayton. Philadelphia: Everts & Peck, 1880. 445 pp.

The History of York County, Maine . . . by Ralph S. Bartlett. [Boston:] Jerome Pr. [1938]. 21 pp.

York County, by Adelaide E. Perry. Portland: Gross and Allen [1971]. 72 pp.

# MARYLAND

## Regional

History of Western Maryland; Being a History of Frederick, Montgomery, Carroll, Washington, Allegany, and Garrett Counties, from the Earliest Period to the Present Day, Including Biographical Sketches . . . by John T. Scharf. 2 vols. Philadelphia: L.H. Everts, 1882. (Repr. 2 vols. Baltimore: Regional Pub. Co., 1968.)

❧　　　❧　　　❧

## Allegany County

History of . . . Allegany County, 1882, in History of Western Maryland . . . by John T. Scharf, *see* above.

History of Allegany County . . . by James W. Thomas (and T.J.C. Williams). 2 vols. [Cumberland?:] L.R. Titsworth, 1923. (Repr. 2 vols. Baltimore: Regional Pub. Co., 1969.)

## Anne Arundel County

The Founders of Anne Arundel and Howard Counties, Maryland, by J.D. Warfield. Baltimore: Kohn & Pollock, 1905. 543, lvi pp. (Repr. Baltimore: Genealogical Pub. Co., 1980.)

A History of Anne Arundel County, Adapted for School Use, by Elihu S. Riley. Annapolis: C.G. Feldmeyer, 1905. vi, 169 pp.

## Baltimore County

History of Baltimore City and County [Maryland] . . . by John T. Scharf. Philadelphia: L.H. Everts, 1881. 947 pp. (Repr. with rearranged index. 1 vol. bound in 2. Baltimore: Regional Pub. Co., 1971.)

Baltimore County, Its History . . . by Thieman S. Offutt, et al. Towson: Jeffersonian Pub. Co. [1916]. 180 pp.

Real Stories from Baltimore County History . . . rev. and adapted by Isobel Davidson. Baltimore: Warwick & York, 1917. 282 pp. (Repr. with new preface, by Harry Bard. Hatboro, Pa.: Tradition Pr., 1967. vii, 296 pp.)

Here Is Baltimore County [by E. Bennett Bowen, et al.]. Towson: Board of Education of Baltimore County [1956]. 55 pp.

Baltimore County in the State and Nation. Towson: Board of Education of Baltimore County, 1957. 263 pp.

*Baltimore County (cont.)*

300th Anniversary Book of Baltimore County, Established 1659; a Reference Book of History . . . Baltimore: County Directories of Maryland [1959]. 308 pp.

Sidelights on the History of Baltimore County, articles by Joseph P. Connor [et al.], ed. by Edwin K. Gontrum. Towson: N.p. [1966]. 44 leaves.

## Calvert County

A History of Calvert County, by Charles F. Stein. Baltimore: Author, 1960. xv, 404 pp. (2d ed. Baltimore, 1961. xv, 404 pp. 3d ed. with Bicentennial Suppl. Baltimore: Author, 1976. xv, 484 pp.)

## Caroline County

An Outline of Caroline County, Maryland, History, by Edward M. Noble. N.p., 1918. 85 pp.

History of Caroline County . . . rev. and suppl. by Laura C. Cochrane, et al. [Federalsburg: J.W. Stowell Pr. Co., 1920.] xvi, 348 pp. (Repr. with an added index, by Emory Dobson. Baltimore: Regional Pub. Co., 1971. xvi, 359 pp.)

## Carroll County

History of . . . Carroll County, 1882, in History of Western Maryland . . . by John T. Scharf, *see* p. 159.

A Hundred Years of Carroll County, 1837-1937, by Branford G. Lynch. Westminster: Democratic Advocate Co., 1939. 125 pp.

Carroll County, Maryland: a History, 1837-1976, by Nancy M. Warner [et al.]. [Westminster:] Carroll County Bicentennial Comm., 1978. 225 pp.

## Cecil County

History of Cecil County . . . with Sketches of Some of the Old Families . . . by George Johnston. Elkton: Author, 1881. xi, 548, xii pp. (Repr. Baltimore: Regional Pub. Co., 1972.)

Cecil County, a Reference Book of History, Business, and General Information. Baltimore: County Directors of Maryland, 1956. 298 pp.

Cecil County, Maryland, 1608-1850: as Seen by Some Visitors, and Several Essays on Local History, collected by George E. Gifford, Jr. Rising Sun: George E. Gifford Memorial Comm., Calvert School, 1974. xxi, 241 pp.

## Charles County

The History of Charles County . . . by Margaret B. Klapthor. La Plata: Charles Co. Tercentenary, 1958. xi, 204 pp.

## Dorchester County

History of Dorchester County, Maryland, by Elias Jones. Baltimore: Williams & Wilkins, 1902. 473 pp. (Rev. History of Dorchester County. Baltimore: Read-Taylor Pr., 1925. 603 pp. New Rev. History of Dorchester County . . . Cambridge: Tidewater Pub., 1966. 603 pp.)

Footnotes to Dorchester History, by Walter E. Ruelle. Cambridge: Tidewater Pub., 1969. vii, 85 pp.

## Frederick County

The Centennial Celebration in Frederick County . . . Frederick: Baughman Bros., 1879. 64 pp.

History of Frederick County, 1882, in History of Western Maryland . . . by John T. Scharf, *see* p. 159.

History of Frederick County, from the Earliest Settlements to the Beginning of the War Between the States, by Thomas J.C. Williams, continued by Folger McKinsey. 2 vols. Frederick: L.R. Titsworth, 1910. 1,635 pp. (Repr. with added index, by Jacob M. Holdcraft. 2 vols. Baltimore: Regional Pub. Co., 1979. xxxii, 1,724 pp.)

A Textbook History of Frederick County, by Paul P. Gordon and Rita S. Gordon. Frederick: Board of Education of Frederick Co., 1975. 243 leaves.

## Garrett County

History of . . . Garrett County, 1882, in History of Western Maryland . . . by John T. Scharf, *see* p. 159.

## Harford County

History of Harford County, from 1608 . . . to the Close of the War of 1812, by Walter W. Preston. Baltimore: Press of the Sun Book Office, 1901. 360, xix pp. (Index . . . by Hilda Chance. Huntsville, Ark.: Century Enterprises, 1968. 35 pp. Repr. Baltimore: Regional Pub. Co., 1972. vii, 360, xix pp.)

Historical Sketches of Harford County, by Samuel Mason, Jr. Lancaster, Pa.: Intelligencer Pr. Co., 1940. 119 pp. ([2d ed.] Darlington: Little Pines Farm, 1955. 177 pp.)

Our Harford Heritage: a History of Harford County, by C. Milton Wright. [N.p., 1967]. 460 pp.

## Howard County

The Founders of . . . Howard County, by J.D. Warfield, 1905, *see* Anne Arundel County.

Origin and History of Howard County, Maryland, by Charles F. Stein. Baltimore: Author, 1972. xv, 383 pp.

## Kent County

Old Kent: the Eastern Shore of Maryland . . . and Genealogical Histories of Old . . . Families, etc., by George A. Hanson. Baltimore: J.P. Des Forges, 1876. vii, 383, xxxvi pp. (Repr. Chestertown: R.H. Collins & Sons, 1936. vi, 248, 45, 80 pp. Repr. Baltimore: Regional Pub. Co., 1967. vii, 383, xxxvi pp.)

History of Kent County, 1630-1916, by Fred G. Usilton. [N.p., 1916?]. 250 pp.

The Government of Kent County, Historical and Descriptive, by William R. Howell. Chestertown: Washington College, 1931. 199 pp.

## Montgomery County

The History of Montgomery County, from . . . 1650 to 1879 . . . Sketches of the Prominent Men . . . comp. by Thomas H.S. Boyd. Clarksburg: [Baltimore: W.K. Boyle], 1879. 168 pp. (Repr. with a new index. Baltimore: Regional Pub. Co., 1972. x, 187 pp.)

History of . . . Montgomery County, 1882, in History of Western Maryland . . . by John T. Scharf, *see* p. 159.

Historic Montgomery County Old Homes and History, by Roger B. Farquhar. Silver Spring: N.p. [1952]. 373 pp. (Repr. Silver Spring: N.p., 1962. x, 366 pp.)

## Prince George's County

Across the Years in Prince George's County . . . by Effie G. Bowie. Richmond, Va.: Garrett & Massie, 1947. xx, 904 pp. (Repr. Baltimore: Genealogical Pub. Co., 1975. xx, 904 pp.)

Prince George's County, Past and Present. Washington, D.C.: Federal Lithograph Co. [1962]. 64 pp. (3d pr., with revisions. Washington, D.C.: Federal Litho-graph Co. [1964]. 64 pp.)

Prince George's Heritage: Sidelights on the Early History of Prince George's County, Maryland, from 1696 to 1800, by Louise J. Hinton. [Baltimore:] Maryland Hist. Soc. [1972]. ix, 223 pp.

Prince George's County: a Pictorial History, by Alan Virta. Norfolk, Va.: Donning Co., 1984.

## Queen Anne's County

Queen Anne's County, Its Early History and Development . . . by Frederick Emory. Baltimore: Maryland Hist. Soc., 1950. xii, 629 pp.

## St. Mary's County

History of St. Mary's County, Maryland, by Regina C. Hammett. [Leonardtown:] St. Mary's Co. Bicentennial Comm. [and Ridge, Md.: Author], 1977. 546 pp. (3d pr. Ridge, Md.: Author, 1980. 546 pp.)

## Somerset County

Old Somerset on the Eastern Shore of Maryland . . . by Clayton Torrence. Richmond, Va.: Whittet & Shepperson, 1935. xvi, 583 pp. (Repr. Baltimore: Regional Pub. Co., 1979.)

Maryland's Historic Somerset: Somerset Board of Education. Prince Anne: The Board, 1955. 108 pp.

## Talbot County

History of Talbot County, 1661-1861, comp. . . . by Oswald Tilghman. 2 vols. Easton: Williams & Wilkins Co., 1915. (Repr. 2 vols. Baltimore: Regional Pub. Co., 1967.)

## Washington County

History of . . . Washington County, 1882, in History of Western Maryland . . . by John T. Scharf, *see* p. 159.

A History of Washington County, from the Earliest Settlements to the Present Time . . . by Thomas J.C. Williams. 2 vols. [Chambersburg, Pa.:] J.M. Runk & L.R. Titsworth, 1906. (Repr. 2 vols. Baltimore: Regional Pub. Co., 1968.)

## Wicomico County

What's Past Is Prologue: a History of Wicomico County, Maryland . . . Wicomico County Centennial, 1867-1967, ed. by Jane W. Bailey. Salisbury: Wicomico County Centennial, Inc., 1967. 207 pp.

## Worcester County

Worcester County Past and Present. 4 vols. Snow Hill: Board of Education of Worcester Co., 1956. 144 pp. total.

Worcester; a Pictorial Review, by Curtis J. Badger. Accomac, Va.: Eastern Shore News, 1974. 104 pp.

Worcester County—Maryland's Arcadia, by Reginald V. Truitt and M.G. Les Callette. Bicentennial ed. Snow Hill: Worcester County Hist. Soc., 1977. xxii, 579 pp.

# MASSACHUSETTS

## Regional

Inland Massachusetts Illustrated: a Concise Resume of the Natural Features and Past History of the Counties of Hampden, Hampshire, Franklin, and Berkshire . . . Springfield: Elstner Pub. Co., 1890. 272 pp. ([Central ed.] 1891. 292 pp.)

🌿     🌿     🌿

## Barnstable County

The History of Cape Cod: the Annals of Barnstable County . . . by Frederick Freeman. 2 vols. Boston: For Author, by G.C. Rand & Avery, 1858-62.

Historical Sketches of Towns in . . . Barnstable County, 1873, *see* Plymouth County.

History of Barnstable County, 1620-1637-1686-1890, ed. Simpson L. Deyo. New York: H.W. Blake, 1890. xii, 1,010 pp.

History of . . . Barnstable County, 1928, *see* Plymouth County.

## Berkshire County

A History of the County of Berkshire . . . by Gentlemen in the County, ed. by David D. Field and Chester Dewey. Pittsfield: S.W. Bush, 1829. iv, 468 pp.

History of Berkshire County . . . ed. by Thomas Cushing and E.A. Smith. 2 vols. in 1. New York: J.B. Beers & Co., 1885.

Natural Features and Past History of County of . . . Berkshire, 1890, in Inland Massachusetts Illustrated, *see* above.

Picturesque Berkshire . . . by Charles F. Warner. 2 vols. Northampton: W.F. Adams Co. [1893].

Historic Homes and Institutions and Genealogical and Personal Memoirs of Berkshire County. 2 vols. New York: Lewis Pub. Co., 1906.

Berkshire County: a Cultural History, by Richard D. Birdsall. New Haven, Conn.: Yale Univ. Pr., 1959. 401 pp.

## Bristol County

History of Bristol County . . . comp. under the supervision of D. Hamilton Hurd. Philadelphia: J.W. Lewis, 1883. xii, 922 pp.

Our County and Its People; a Descriptive and Biographical Record of Bristol County . . . [Boston:] Boston Hist. Co., 1899. xii, 799, 418 pp.

A History of Bristol County, ed. in chief, Frank W. Hutt. 3 vols. New York: Lewis Hist. Pub. Co., 1924.

## Essex County

Essex County History and Directory . . . Boston: C.A. & J.F. Wood, 1870. 621 pp.

Standard History of Essex County, Embracing a History of the County from Its Settlement to the Present Time . . . by Cyrus M. Tracy. Boston: C.F. Jewett, 1878. 424 pp.

History of Essex County . . . comp. under the supervision of D. Hamilton Hurd. 2 vols. Philadelphia: J.W. Lewis, 1888.

Municipal History of Essex County. Tercentenary ed. Benj. F. Arrington, ed. in chief. 4 vols. New York: Lewis Hist. Pub. Co., 1922.

The Story of Essex County, ed. in chief, Claude M. Fuess, comp. by Scott H. Paradise. 4 vols. New York: American Hist. Soc. [1935].

## Franklin County

Natural Features and Past History of County of . . . Franklin, 1890, in Inland Massachusetts Illustrated, *see* p. 164.

## Hampden County

Natural Features and Past History of County of . . . Hampden, 1890, in Inland Massachusetts Illustrated, *see* p. 164.

"Our County and Its People"; a History of Hampden County, ed. by Alfred M. Copeland. 3 vols. [Boston:] Century Memorial Pub. Co., 1902.

Hampden County, 1636-1936, by Clifton Johnson. 3 vols. New York: American Hist. Soc., 1936.

## Hampshire County

Natural Features and Past History of County of . . . Hampshire, 1890, in Inland Massachusetts Illustrated, *see* p. 164.

Picturesque Hampshire; a Suppl. to the Quarter-Centennial . . . Journal, by Charles F. Warner. Northampton: Wade, Warner & Co., 1890. 112 pp.

Historic Hampshire in the Connecticut Valley . . . from the Time of the Dinosaur Down to About 1900, by Clifton Johnson. Springfield: Milton Bradley [1932]. 410 pp.

The Hampshire History, Celebrating 300 Years of Hampshire County, comp. by . . . Lawrence E. Wickander, et al. Northampton: Hampshire County Comm., 1964. xiv, 364 pp.

## Middlesex County

Historic Fields and Mansions of Middlesex, by Samuel A. Drake. Boston: J.R. Osgood, 1874. xiv, 442 pp. (Later called "Old Landmarks".)

*Middlesex County (cont.)*

Old Landmarks and Historic Fields of Middlesex . . . by Samuel A. Drake. Boston: Roberts Bros., 1876. xiv, 442 pp. (Previously pub. as Historic Fields and Mansions of Middlesex. 3d ed. Boston: Roberts Bros., 1895; new and rev. ed., now called Historic Mansions and Highways Round Boston. Boston: Little, Brown, 1899; rev. ed. Rutland, Vt.: C.E. Tuttle [1971].)

History of Middlesex County, Containing Carefully Prepared Histories of Every City and Town in the County, by . . . Samuel A. Drake. 2 vols. Boston: Estes & Lauriat, 1880.

History of Middlesex County . . . by Duane H. Hurd. 3 vols. Philadelphia: J.W. Lewis, 1890.

Beneath Old Roof Trees, by Abram E. Brown. Boston: Lee & Shepard, 1896. xiii, 343 pp.

Beside Old Hearth-Stones, by Abram E. Brown. Boston: Lee & Shepard, 1897. xvii, 367 pp.

Ancient Middlesex . . . by Levi S. Gould. Somerville: Somerville Journal Pr., 1905. 336 pp.

Historic Homes and Places and Genealogical and Personal Memoirs Relating to the Families of Middlesex County . . . prepared under the supervision of William R. Cutter. 4 vols. New York: Lewis Hist. Pub. Co., 1908.

Middlesex County and Its People: a History, by Edwin P. Conklin. 4 vols. New York: Lewis Hist. Pub. Co., 1927.

## Nantucket County

History of Nantucket County, Island and Town, by Alexander Starbuck. Boston: C.E. Goodspeed & Co., 1924. 871 pp. (Repr. Rutland, Vt.: Tuttle, 1969.)

## Norfolk County

History of Norfolk County . . . comp. under the supervision of D. Hamilton Hurd. Philadelphia: J.W. Lewis, 1884. x, 1,001 pp.

History of Norfolk County, 1622-1918, Louis A. Cook, supervising ed. 2 vols. New York: S.J. Clarke Pub. Co., 1918.

History of . . . Norfolk County, *see* Plymouth County.

## Plymouth County

The Plymouth County Directory and Historical Register of the Old Colony, Containing an Historical Sketch of the County . . . Middlesboro: Pratt, 1867.

Historical Sketches of Towns in Plymouth and Barnstable Counties. Boston: Dudley & Co., 1873, from Directory and History of Plymouth and Barnstable Counties, 1873 (pp. 77-150.)

History of Plymouth County . . . comp. under the supervision of D. Hamilton Hurd. Philadelphia: J.W. Lewis, 1884. viii, 1,199 pp.

*Plymouth County (cont.)*

History of Plymouth, Norfolk and Barnstable Counties, by Elroy S. Thompson. 3 vols. New York: Lewis Hist. Pub. Co., 1928.

## Suffolk County

Professional and Industrial History of Suffolk County, Massachusetts, ed. by William T. David. 3 vols. Boston: Hist. Co., 1894.

## Worcester County

The History of the County of Worcester . . . by Peter Whitney. Worcester: Isaiah Thomas, 1793. 339 pp.

Historical Collections, by Holmes Ammidown. 2 vols. New York: Author, 1874. (2d ed. 2 vols. New York, 1877.)

History of Worcester County, Embracing a Comprehensive History of the County from Its First Settlement to the Present Time . . . 2 vols. Boston: C.F. Jewett, 1879.

History of Worcester County . . . comp. under the supervision of D. Hamilton Hurd. 2 vols. Philadelphia: J.W. Lewis, 1889.

Historic Homes and Institutions and Genealogical and Personal Memoirs of Worcester County . . . prepared under ed. supervision of Ellery B. Crane. 4 vols. New York: Lewis Pub. Co., 1907.

History of Worcester County, supervising ed. in chief, Ellery B. Crane. 3 vols. New York: Lewis Pub. Co., 1924.

Worcester County: a Narrative History, by John Nelson. 3 vols. New York: American Hist. Soc., 1934.

# MICHIGAN

## Allegan County

History of Allegan and Barry Counties, Michigan . . . Philadelphia: D.W. Ensign, 1880. 521 pp. (Repr. Evansville, Ind.: Unigraphic, 1980.)

Index to State of Michigan, County of Allegan, 1895, by Marilynn F. Starring. Fennville: Indexer, 1984. 103 pp. (From Kace's Illustrated Atlas, 1895.)

A Twentieth Century History of Allegan County, Michigan . . . comp. by Henry F. Thomas. Chicago: Lewis Pub. Co., 1907. xv, 655 pp.

## Alpena County

Complete History of Alpena County, Michigan, by William Boulton. Alpena: Argus Book & Job Rooms, 1876. 54 pp. (Repr. Mount Pleasant: Clarke Hist. Lib., Central Michigan Univ., 1964.)

Centennial History of Alpena County, Michigan . . . 1837-1876, by David D. Oliver. Alpena: Argus Pr. House, 1903. 186 pp. (Repr. Mount Pleasant: Clarke Hist. Lib., Central Michigan Univ., 1968.)

## Barry County

History of Barry County, 1880, *see* Allegan County.

History of Barry County . . . by William W. Potter. Grand Rapids: Reed-Tandler Co. [1912]. 269 pp.

Years Gone By; an Illustrated Account of Life in . . . Barry County, Michigan in the 19th and 20th Centuries, comp. by Prosper G. Barnard. [Kalamazoo:] Priv. pr., Sequoia Pr., 1967. 228 pp.

## Bay County

History of Bay County, 1883, *see* Tuscola County.

History of Bay County . . . Chicago: H.R. Page, 1883. 281 pp.

History of Bay County . . . ed. and comp. by Capt. Augustus H. Ganser. Chicago: Richmond & Arnold, 1905. 726 pp.

Bay County, Past and Present . . . comp. by Bay City Public Schools, ed. by Geo. E. Butterfield. Bay City: C. & J. Gregory, 1918. 212 pp.

Bay County, Past and Present, by George E. Butterfield. Centennial ed. Bay City: Bd. of Education [1957]. 242 pp.

## Berrien County

Berrien County Directory and History . . . ed. by Edward B. Cowles. Buchanan: Record Steam Pr. House, 1871. 384 pp.

*Berrien County (cont.)*

History of Berrien and Van Buren Counties, Michigan . . . by Franklin Ellis, et al. Philadelphia: D.W. Ensign, 1880. 548 pp. (Repr.? 1978.)

A Twentieth Century History of Berrien County, Michigan, ed. by Judge Orville W. Coolidge. Chicago: Lewis Pub. Co., 1906. x, 1,007 pp.

Berrien County, a 19th Century Story, by Albert Chauncey. Benton Harbor: Burch Pr., 1955. 123 pp.

## Branch County

Branch County Directory and Historical Record. Ann Arbor: Courier Steam Pr. House, 1871. 315 pp.

History of Branch County, Michigan . . . [by Crisfield Johnson]. Philadelphia: Everts & Abbott, 1879. 347 pp.

A Twentieth Century History . . . of Branch County, Michigan, ed. by Rev. Henry P. Collin. New York: Lewis Pub. Co., 1906. xvi, 879 pp.

## Calhoun County

Directory and History of Calhoun County, Michigan, by E.G. Rust. Battle Creek: Rust, 1869. 426 pp.

History of Calhoun County, Michigan . . . Philadelphia: L.H. Everts, 1877. 212 pp.

History of Calhoun County, Michigan . . . by Washington Gardner. 2 vols. Chicago: Lewis Pub. Co., 1913. 1,365 pp.

## Cass County

History of Cass County, from 1825 to 1875, by Howard S. Rogers. Cassopolis: W.H. Mansfield, 1875. 406 pp.

History of Cass County, Michigan . . . [by Alfred Mathews]. Chicago: Waterman-Watkins, 1882. 432 pp. (Repr. Evansville, Ind.: Unigraphic, 1971.)

A Twentieth Century History of Cass County, Michigan, ed. by Lowell H. Glover. Chicago: Lewis Pub. Co., 1906. xiv, 782 pp.

## Charlevoix County

Homecoming: Program of Events and History of the County. Charlevoix: N.p., 1935. 75 pp.

## Cheboygan County

History of Cheboygan and Mackinac Counties . . . comp. by George Robinson and R.A. Sprague. Detroit: Union Job Pr. Co., 1873. 45 pp.

The Centennial History of Cheboygan County . . . by W.H. Ware. Cheboygan: Northern Tribune Pr., 1876. 106 pp.

## Chippewa County

Story of Sault Ste. Marie and Chippewa County, by Stanley Newton. Sault Ste. Marie: News Pr. Co., 1923. 199 pp.

## Clinton County

History of Clinton County, 1880, *see* Shiawassee County.

Past and Present of Clinton County, Michigan, by Judge S.B. Daboll. Chicago: S.J. Clarke Pub. Co., 1906. 575 pp.

## Delta County

Souvenir of Delta County, Michigan, by C.O. Stiles. Iron Mountain: N.p., n.d. 42 pp.

## Eaton County

History of Eaton County, 1891, *see* Ingham County.

Past and Present of Eaton County, Michigan . . . ed. by Walcott B. Williams. 2 vols. Lansing: Hist. Pub. Assoc. [1906]. 663 pp.

Pioneer History of Eaton County, Michigan, by Daniel Strange, 1833-1866. [Charlotte:] Eaton County Pioneer & Hist. Soc., 1923. 192 pp.

## Genesee County

History of Genesee County, Michigan . . . [by Franklin Ellis]. Philadelphia: Everts & Abbott, 1879. 446 pp.

History of Genesee County, Michigan, by Edwin O. Wood. 2 vols. Indianapolis, Ind.: Federal, 1916.

## Grand Traverse County

Sprague's History of Grand Traverse and Leelanau Counties, Michigan . . . by E.L. Sprague and Mrs. G.N. Smith. Indianapolis, Ind.: B.F. Bowen, 1903. 806 pp.

## Gratiot County

Gratiot County, Historical . . . by Willard D. Tucker. Saginaw: Pr. of Seamann & Peters, 1913. 1,353 pp.

## Hillsdale County

History of Hillsdale County, Michigan . . . Philadelphia: Everts & Abbott, 1879. 334 pp.

Compendium of History and Biography of Hillsdale County, Michigan, ed. by E.G. Reynolds. Chicago: A.W. Bowen & Co. [1903]. 460 pp.

## Huron County

Pioneer History of Huron County, Michigan, by Lorence McK. Gwinn. [Bad Axe:] Huron County Pioneer and Hist. Soc., 1922. 100 pp.

Huron County Centennial History, 1859-1959 . . . by Chet Hey (Chester A. Hey). [Harbor Beach: Harbor Beach Times, 1959.] 84 pp.

## Ingham County

History of Ingham and Eaton Counties, Michigan . . . by Samuel W.D. Durant. Philadelphia: D.W. Ensign & Co., 1880. 586 pp.

Past and Present of the City of Lansing and Ingham County, Michigan . . . by Albert E. Cowles. Lansing: Michigan Hist. Pub. Assoc. [1905?]. 583 pp.

Pioneer History of Ingham County, comp. and arranged by Mrs. Franc L.Adams. Lansing: Wynkoop Hallenbeck Crawford Co., 1923. 856 pp.

## Ionia County

History and Directory of Ionia County, Michigan . . . by G.D. Dillenback. Grand Rapids: N.p. [1872]. 195 pp.

History of Ionia and Montcalm Counties, Michigan . . . by John S. Schenck. Philadelphia: D.W. Ensign, 1881. 502 pp.

History of Ionia County, Michigan, by Rev. Elam E. Branch. 2 vols. Indianapolis, Ind.: B.F. Bowen, 1916. 1,035 pp.

## Iron County

A History of Iron County, Michigan, by Jack Hill. [Iron River: Report Pub. Co., 1955.] 129 pp.

## Isabella County

Portrait and Biographical Album of Isabella County, Michigan . . . Also Containing a Complete History. Chicago: Chapman Bros., 1884. 589 pp.

Past and Present of Isabella County, Michigan, by Hon. Isaac A. Fancher. Indianapolis, Ind.: B.F. Bowen & Co., 1911. 729 pp.

## Jackson County

History of Jackson County, Michigan . . . Chicago: Inter-State Pub. Co., 1881. 1,156 pp. (Repr. 2 vols. Evansville, Ind.: Unigraphic, 1980.)

De Land's Jackson County, Michigan . . . comp. by Colonel Charles V. De Land. [Logansport? Ind.:] B.F. Bowen, 1903. 1,123 pp.

## Kalamazoo County

History of Kalamazoo County, Michigan . . . [comp. by Samuel W. Durant]. Philadelphia: Everts & Abbott, 1880. 552 pp. (Repr. with name index. Evansville, Ind.: Unigraphic, 1980.)

Compendium of History and Biography of Kalamazoo County, Michigan . . . ed. by David Fisher and F. Little. Chicago: A.W. Bowen [1906]. 571 pp.

## Kalkaska County

Early Days and Early Ways, by Lyle McCann. Kalkaska: N.p. [1972]. vi, 294 pp.

## Kent County

History and Directory of Kent County, Michigan . . . comp. and ed. by Dillenback & Leavitt. Grand Rapids: Daily Eagle Steam Pr. House, 1870. 319 pp.

History of Kent County, Michigan . . . by M.A. Leeson, et al. Chicago: C.C. Chapman, 1881. 1,426 pp.

The City of Old Rapids and Kent County, Michigan. Logansport, Ind.: A.W. Bowen, 1900.

Grand Rapids and Kent County, Michigan, Historical Account . . . ed. by Ernest B. Fisher. 2 vols. Chicago: Law, 1918. 1,105 pp.

## Lapeer County

History of Lapeer County, Michigan . . . Chicago: H.R. Page, 1884. 211 pp.

## Leelanau County

A History of Leelanau County, by A.H. Johnson. Traverse Bay: N.p., 1880. 60 pp.

History of Leelanau County, 1903, *see* Grand Traverse County.

The Story of Leelanau, by Julia T. Dickinson. Omena: Solle's Bookstore, 1951. 59 pp.

100 Years in Leelanau, by Samuel M. Littell. Leland: Print Shop, 1965. 80 pp.

## Lenawee County

History and Biographical Record of Lenawee County, Michigan, Containing a History . . . comp. by William A. Whitney. 2 vols. Adrian: W. Stearns & Co., 1879-80.

Illustrated History and Biographical Record of Lenawee County, Michigan . . . by John I. Knapp and R.I. Bonner. Adrian: Time Pr. Co., 1903. 511 pp.

Memoirs of Lenawee County, Michigan . . . ed. by Richard I. Bonner. 2 vols. Madison, Wis.: Western Hist. Assoc., 1909.

History of Lenawee County, 1928, *see* Saginaw County.

## Livingston County

History of Livingston County, Michigan . . . Philadelphia: Everts & Abbott, 1880. 462 pp. (Repr. with new index, Livingston County Hist. Soc. Evansville, Ind.: Unigraphic, 1974. 462, 96 pp.)

## Mackinac County

History of Mackinac County, 1873, *see* Cheboygan County.

Old and New Mackinac . . . by Rev. J.A. Van Fleet. 3d ed. Grand Rapids: Lever Book and Job Office, 1880. 173 pp.

Mackinac, Formerly Michilmackinac, by John R. Bailey. 4th ed. Lansing: R. Smith Pr. Co., 1899. 246 pp. (5th ed. Ann Arbor: Richmond & Backus Co., 1904. 231 pp.)

Historic Mackinac, by Edwin C. Wood. 2 vols. New York: MacMillan, 1918.

Ancient and Modern Michilmackinac . . . by James J. Strang, ed. by George S. May. Mackinac Island: W.S. Woodfill, 1959. xii, 100 pp. (Repr. from 1854, 1894 eds.)

## Macomb County

History of Macomb County, Michigan . . . by M.A. Leeson, et al. Chicago: Leeson, 1882. 924 pp.

Past and Present of Macomb County, Michigan, by Robert I. Eldredge. Chicago: S.J. Clarke Pub. Co., 1905. 712 pp.

## Manistee County

History of Manistee, Mason, and Oceana Counties, Michigan. [Chicago: H.R. Page & Co., 1882.] 154, 88 pp.

## Marquette County

Beard's Directory and History of Marquette County . . . Detroit: Badger & Bryce, 1873. xiii, 240 pp.

## Mason County

History of Mason County, 1882, *see* Manistee County.

Historic Not-ape-ka-gpn; an Individualized History of Mason County, Michigan, by Russell F. Anderson. [Ludington: Lakeside Pr. Co.], 1933. 137 pp.

## Menominee County

Centennial History of Menominee County, by Hon. Eleazer S. Ingalls. Menominee: Herald Power Pr., 1876. 76 pp.

Menominee County Book for Schools, ed. by Ethel Schuyler. Menominee: Menominee County Schools Comm., 1941. 400 pp.

## Monroe County

History of Monroe County, Michigan . . . ed. by Talcott E. Wing. New York: Munsell & Co., 1890. 606, 53 pp.

History of Monroe County, Michigan . . . by John McC. Bulkley. 2 vols. Chicago: Lewis Pub. Co., 1913.

Bay Settlement of Monroe County, Michigan, by Lambert M. La Voy. [Monroe?: N.p., 1971.] x, 309 pp.

## Montcalm County

History of Montcalm County, 1881, *see* Ionia County.

History of Montcalm County . . . by John W. Dasef. 2 vols. Indianapolis, Ind.: B.F. Bowen, 1916.

## Muskegon County

History of Muskegon County, Michigan . . . Chicago: H.R. Page & Co., 1882. 151 pp. (History of Ottawa County . . . 1882, appended.)

## Oakland County

History of Oakland County, Michigan [by Samuel W. Durant]. Philadelphia: L.H. Everts, 1877. 334, xxv pp.

History of Oakland County, Michigan . . . comp. and ed. by Thaddeus D. Seeley. 2 vols. Chicago: Lewis Pub. Co., 1912. 903 pp.

## Oceana County

History of Oceana County, 1882, *see* Manistee County.

Oceana County Pioneers . . . History . . . by Louis M. Hartwick. Pentwater: Pentwater News Steam Pr., 1890. 432 pp.

## Ontonagon County

This Ontonagon Country . . . by James K. Jamison. Ontonagon: Ontonagon Herald Co. [1939]. 269 pp. (3d ed. Ontonagon: Ontonagon Herald Co. [1948]. 240 pp. Repub. by Roy W. Drier. Calumet: N.p., 1965. 286 pp.)

## Osceola County

Portrait and Biographical Album [of Osceola County] . . . Also . . . a Complete History of the County . . . Chicago: Chapman Bros., 1884. 422 pp.

## Ottawa County

History of Muskegon County . . . Chicago: H.R. Page & Co., 1882. 151 pp. (History of Ottawa County . . . 1882, appended.)

*Ottawa County (cont.)*

Historical and Business Compendium of Ottawa County, Michigan . . . [by Hiram Potts]. 2 vols. in 1. Grand Haven: Potts & Conger [1892].

Historic Grand Haven and Ottawa County, by Leo C. Lillie. Grand Haven: N.p., 1931. xx, 304 pp.

## Saginaw County

History of Saginaw County, from 1819 Down to the Present, by Truman B. Fox. East Saginaw: Enterprise Pr., 1858. 80 pp. (Repr. Mount Pleasant: N.p., 1963.)

History of Saginaw County, Michigan . . . [by Michael A. Leeson]. Chicago: C.C. Chapman, 1881. 960 pp. (Repr. Evansville, Ind.: Unigraphic, 1980.)

History of Saginaw County; Historical, Biographical . . . by James C. Mills. 2 vols. Saginaw: Seemann & Peters, 1918.

## St. Clair County

History of St. Clair County, Michigan . . . Chicago: Andreas & Co., 1883. 790 pp.

St. Clair County, Michigan, Its History and People . . . by William L. Jenks. 2 vols. Chicago: Lewis Pub. Co., 1912.

## St. Joseph County

History of St. Joseph County, Michigan . . . Philadelphia: L.H. Everts, 1877. 232 pp.

History of St. Joseph County, Michigan . . . ed. by Harry G. Cutler. 2 vols. Chicago: Lewis Pub. Co. [1911].

St. Joseph in Homespun; a Centennial Souvenir, by Sue I. Silliman. Three Rivers: Three Rivers Pub. Co., 1931. 213 pp.

## Sanilac County

Portrait and Biographical Album of Sanilac County, Containing . . . a Complete History of the County. Chicago: Chapman Bros., 1884. 546 pp.

## Shiawassee County

History of Shiawassee and Clinton Counties, Michigan . . . by Franklin Ellis, et al. Philadelphia: D.W. Ensign, 1880. 541 pp.

Past and Present of Shiawassee County, Michigan . . . Lansing: N.p., n.d. 557 pp.

## Tuscola County

History of Tuscola and Bay Counties, Michigan . . . Chicago: H.R. Page, 1883. 211, 83 pp.

## Van Buren County

History of Van Buren County, 1880, *see* Berrien County.

History of Van Buren County, Michigan . . . by Capt. Goran W. Rowland. 2 vols. Chicago: Lewis Pub. Co., 1912. 1,158 pp.

## Washtenaw County

History of Washtenaw County, Michigan . . . Chicago: C.C. Chapman, 1881. 1,452 pp.

Past and Present of Washtenaw County, Michigan, by Samuel W. Beakes. Chicago: S.J. Clarke Pub. Co., 1906. 817 pp.

## Wayne County

History of Detroit [and Wayne County] and Michigan . . . by Silas Farmer. Detroit: S. Farmer & Co., 1884. xlvi, 1,024 pp. (2d ed., rev. and enl. 2 vols. Detroit: Farmer, 1889. 3d ed., rev. and enl. 2 vols. Detroit: Farmer for Munsell, N.Y., 1890. Repr. of 3d ed. Detroit: Gale Pub. Co., 1970.)

Chronography of Notable Events in the History of the Northwest Territory and Wayne County . . . 1531-1890 . . . comp. by Fred. Carlisle. Detroit: O.S. Gulley, Bornman and Co., 1890. 484 pp.

Landmarks of Wayne County . . . by Robert B. Ross and G.B. Catlin. Detroit: Evening News Assoc., 1898. xx, 872, 320 pp.

Compendium of History of the City of Detroit and Wayne County, Michigan. N.p.: Taylor, 1909. 719 pp.

History of Wayne County and City of Detroit, ed. by Clarence M. Burton. 5 vols. Chicago: S.J. Clarke Pub. Co., 1930.

## Wexford County

History of Wexford County, Michigan, comp. by J.H. Wheeler. Logansport, Ind.: B.F. Bowen, 1903. 557 pp.

# MINNESOTA

## Anoka County

History of Anoka County . . . Minnesota, by Albert M. Goodrich. Minneapolis: Hennepin Pub. Co., 1905. 327 pp. (Repr. N.p.: Anoka County Bicentennial Comm., 1976.)

Anoka County, Minnesota: a Collection of Historical Sketches and Family Histories, comp. by Members and Friends of Anoka County Historical Society. Anoka: Anoka County H.S., 1982. 317 pp.

## Becker County

A Pioneer History of Becker County, Minnesota . . . Historical Information . . . by Mrs. Jessica C. West. St. Paul: Pioneer Pr., 1907. 757 pp.

## Beltrami County

A Brief History of Beltrami County, by Charles W. Vandersluis. [Bemidji:] Beltrami County Hist. Soc., 1963. 40 pp.

## Benton County

History of . . . Benton County, 1972, see Morrison County.

## Big Stone County

Big Stone County History . . . by Lydia S. Wulff. [Ortonville: L.A. Kaercher 1959.] 122 pp.

## Blue Earth County

History of Blue Earth County . . . by Thomas Hughes. Chicago: Middle-West Pub. Co. [1909]. 622 pp. (Repr. Marceline, Mo.: Walsworth Pub. Co. [1976].)

## Brown County

History of Brown County, Minnesota . . . ed. by Lewis A. Fritsche. 2 vols. Indianapolis, Ind.: B.F. Bowen & Co., 1916. (Repr. in 1 vol. Marceline, Mo.: Walsworth Pub. Co. [1976].)

## Carver County

Compendium of History and Biography of Carver and Hennepin Counties, Minnesota, ed. by R.I. Holcombe and W.H. Bringham. Chicago: Henry Taylor, 1915. 542 pp.

## Chippewa County

History of Chippewa and Lac Qui Parle Counties, Minnesota . . . ed. by Lycurgus R. Moyer and O.G. Dale. 2 vols. Indianapolis, Ind.: B.F. Bowen & Co., 1916. (Repr. 2 Vols. [Marceline, Mo.: Walsworth Pub. Co., 1980?])

## Chisago County

Chisago County Bicentennial Committee: an Early Look at Chisago County. N.p., 1976. 294 pp.

## Clay County

Clay County Illustrated, Minnesota . . . Moorhead: D.W. Meeker, 1916. 136 pp.

History of Clay and Norman Counties, Minnesota . . . 2 vols. John Turner and C.K. Semling. Indianapolis, Ind.: B.F. Bowen & Co., 1918.

Here-There-Everywhere in Clay County, Minnesota, by Glenn E. Johnson. Hawley: Hawley Herald, 1972. 162 pp.

## Clearwater County

The Story of Clearwater County, 1902-1952, by Ralph A. Larson. Bagley: Farmers Pub. Co., 1952. 36 pp.

## Cottonwood County

History of Cottonwood and Watonwan Counties, Minnesota, by John A. Brown. 2 vols. Indianapolis, Ind.: B.F. Bowen & Co., 1916.

The Centennial History of Cottonwood County, Minnesota. [Windon?:] Cottonwood County Hist. Soc., 1970. 701 pp.

## Crow Wing County

History of . . . Crow Wing County, 1972, *see* Morrison County.

## Dakota County

Dakota County; Its Past and Present . . . by W.H. Mitchell. Minneapolis: Tribune Pr. Co., 1868. vi, 161 pp.

History of Dakota County . . . by Rev. Edward D. Neill. Minneapolis: North Star Pub. Co., 1881. vi, 551 pp.

History of Dakota and Goodhue Counties . . . Franklyn Curtiss-Wedge, ed. in chief. 2 vols. Chicago: H.C. Cooper, Jr. & Co., 1910.

## Dodge County

An Historical Sketch of Dodge County, Minnesota . . . Rochester: Federal Union Book & Job Pr. Office, 1870. 124 pp.

History of Dodge County . . . 1884, *see* Winona County.

*Dodge County (cont.)*

Dodge County: 125 Years of Growth, by Harold Severson. Manterville: Dodge County Century & Quarter Club, 1979. 258 pp.

## Douglas County

History of Douglas and Grant Counties, Minneapolis . . . Constant Larson, ed. in chief. 2 vols. Indianapolis, Ind.: B.F. Bowen & Co., 1916.

Douglas County: Album of the Ages, by Douglas County Historical Society. Dallas, Tex.: Taylor Pub. Co. [1980?]. 616 pp.

## Faribault County

Memorial Record of the Counties of Faribault, Martin, Watonwan and Jackson, Minnesota. Chicago: Lewis Pub. Co., 1895. 766 pp.

The History of Faribault County, Minnesota, from Its First Settlement to . . . 1879 . . . by Jacob A. Kiester. Minneapolis: Harrison & Smith, 1896. 687 pp.

Faribault County Bicentennial Commission: Faribault County, 1855-1976; a Panorama. Marceline, Mo.: Walsworth Pub. Co., 1977. 299 pp.

## Fillmore County

History of Fillmore County, Minnesota . . . by Judson W. Bishop. Chatfield: Holley & Brown, 1858. 40 pp. (Repr. Chatfield: News, 1980.)

History of Fillmore County . . . by Rev. Edward D. Neill. Minneapolis: Minnesota Hist. Co., 1882. 626 pp.

History of Fillmore County, Minnesota, comp. by Franklyn Curtiss-Wedge. 2 vols. Chicago: H.C. Cooper, Jr. & Co., 1912.

## Freeborn County

History of Freeborn County . . . by Rev. Edward D. Neill. Minneapolis: Minnesota Hist. Co., 1882. 548 pp.

History of Freeborn County, Minnesota, ed. by Franklyn Curtiss-Wedge. Chicago: H.C. Cooper, Jr. & Co. [1911]. 883 pp. (Repr. [Marceline, Mo.: Walsworth Pub. Co., 1976.].)

## Goodhue County

History of Goodhue County . . . Red Wing: Wood, Alley & Co., 1878. iv, 664 pp.

Goodhue County, Minnesota, Past and Present . . . by an Old Settler. Red Wing: Red Wing Pr. Co., 1893. vi, 349 pp.

History of . . . Goodhue County, 1910, *see* Dakota County.

History of Goodhue County, Minnesota, by Christian A. Rasmussen. [Red Wing: Red Wing Pr. Co.], 1935. viii, 336 pp.

## Grant County

History of . . . Grant County, 1916, *see* Douglas County.

## Hennepin County

Geographical and Statistical History of the County of Hennepin . . . by W.H. Mitchell and J.H. Stevens. Minneapolis: Russell & Beljoy, 1868. 149 pp.

History of Hennepin County . . . by Rev. Edward D. Neill. Minneapolis: North Star Pub. Co., 1881. iv, 713 pp.

Compendium of History and Biography of Minneapolis and Hennepin County, Minnesota, ed. by R.I. Holcombe and W.H. Bingham. Chicago: Henry Taylor & Co., 1914. 584 pp. (Same history appears without biographical sketches in Compendium of History and Biography of Carver and Hennepin Counties.)

History and Biography of . . . Hennepin County, 1915, *see* Carver County.

Hennepin County History: an Illustrated Essay, by Gustav R. Svendsen. Minneapolis: Hennepin County Hist. Soc., 1976. 95 pp.

## Houston County

History of Houston County . . . by Rev. Edward D. Neill. Minneapolis: Minnesota Hist. Co., 1882. 526 pp.

History of Houston County, Minnesota, ed. by Franklyn Curtiss-Wedge. Chicago: H.C. Cooper, Jr. & Co., 1919. (Repr.? Winona: H.C. Cooper, Jr. & Co., 1979. 824 pp.)

Houston County History, comp. by the Houston County Historical Society. Dallas, Tex.: Taylor Pub. Co., 1982. 459 pp.

## Itasca County

Pines, Mines and Lakes: the Story of Itasca County, Minnesota, by James E. Rothsolk. Grand Rapids, Mich.: Itasca County Hist. Soc., 1960. 155 pp.

## Jackson County

Memorial Record of the County of . . . Jackson, 1805, *see* Faribault County.

An Illustrated History of Jackson County, Minnesota, by Arthur F. Rose. Jackson: Northern Hist. Pub. Co., 1910. 586 pp. (Repr. N.p.: Jackson County Hist. Soc. [1979?].)

Jackson County History. Lakefield: Jackson County Hist. Soc., 1979. 432 pp.

## Kanabec County

"Ken-a-big": the Story of Kanabec County: an Illustrated History of Kanabec County: Its Early Years, by Frank Ziegler. Mora: B. & W. Pr., 1977. 225 pp.

## Kandiyohi County

Illustrated History and Descriptive and Biographical Review of Kandiyohi County, Minnesota . . . comp. by Victor E. Lawson. St. Paul: Pioneer Pr., 1905. 446 pp.

Round Robin of Kandiyohi County, Centennial Year, 1858-1958, ed. by Karl Thurn and Helen Thurn. [Wilmar: Raymond Pr., 1958.] 253 pp.

The Centennial History of Kandiyohi County, 1870-1970. Willmar: Color Pr., 1970. 341 pp.

## Kittson County

Our Northwest Corner: Histories of Kittson County, Minnesota, comp. by Kittson County Historical Society and the Red Valley Historical Society. 2 vols., Dallas, Tex.: Taylor Pub. Co., 1976-79.

## Koochiching County

Koochiching: Pioneering Along the Rainy River Frontier, by Hiram M. Drache. Danville, Ill.: Inter-State Pr. & Pub., 1983. xiv, 340 pp.

History of Koochiching County . . . comp. and ed. by History Book Committee. Dallas, Tex.: Taylor Pub. Co., for Koochiching County Hist. Soc., 1983. 304 pp.

## Lac Qui Parle County

History of . . . Lac Qui Parle County, 1916, *see* Chippewa County.

Fire on the Prairie: Memories of Lac Qui Parle, by Ray P. Herriges. Madison: Heritage Pr., 1980. 349 pp.

## Le Sueur County

History of . . . Le Sueur County, 1916, *see* Nicollet County.

## Lincoln County

Early History of Lincoln County, by A.E. Tasker. [Lake Benton:] Lake Benton News Pr., 1936. 352 pp. (Repr. Lake Benton News Pr., 1973.)

Lincoln County Centennial History Committee: Lincoln County, Minnesota, 1873-1973. Lake Benton: Journal Pr. Co. [1974?]. 210 pp.

## Lyon County

History and Description of Lyon County, Minnesota . . . by Christopher F. Case. [Marshall: Messenger Pr. House, 1884.] 97 pp.

A Illustrated History of Lyon County, Minnesota, by Arthur P. Rose. Marshall: Northern Hist. Pub. Co., 1912. 616 pp. (Repr. Marceline, Mo.: Walsworth Pub. Co., 1977.)

*Lyon County (cont.)*

The Centennial History of Lyon County, by Torgnyw Anderson. Marshall: Henle Pub. Co., 1970. 306 pp.

## McLeod County

History of McLeod County, Minnesota, Franklyn Curtiss-Wedge, ed. in chief, Chicago: H.C. Cooper, Jr. & Co., 1917. xix, 862 pp.

Know Your Own Country: a History of McLeod County, Minnesota, by Arthur M. Nelson. [Fairmont?:] Priv. Pr. [1947?]. 65 pp.

McLeod County History Book, 1978. Dallas, Tex.: Taylor Pub. Co., 1979. 684 pp.

## Marshall County

Self Portrait of Marshall County . . . ed. by Nancy Solum. Dallas, Tex.: Taylor Pub. Co., 1976. 808 pp.

## Martin County

Memorial Record of the County of . . . Martin, 1895, *see* Faribault County.

History of Martin County . . . to 1880, by William H. Budd. [Fairmont: Independent, 1897.] 124 pp. (Suppl. notes, by Walter Carlson, 1973. [Trimont?] N.p. [1974]. 119 pp.)

## Meeker County

A Random Historical Sketch of Meeker County, Minnesota, from Its First Settlement to 1876, by Abner C. Smith. Litchfield: Belfoy & Joubert, 1877. 160 pp.

Album of History and Biography of Meeker County, Minnesota . . . comp. by Alden Publishing Co. Chicago: Alden, Ogle & Co., 1888. 610 pp.

Meeker County History . . . 1855-1937, ed. and comp. by Frank B. Lamson. Dassel: Dassel Dispatch Pr., 1937. 71 pp.

Condensed History of Meeker County, 1855-1939 . . . comp. and pub. by Frank B. Lamson. Litchfield: Brown Pr. Co. [1939]. 240 pp.

The First 100 Years of Meeker County, by Patrick J. Casey. N.p.: Priv. pub., 1968. 233 pp.

## Morrison County

History of Morrison and Todd Counties, Minnesota . . . by Clara K. Fuller. 2 vols. Indianapolis, Ind.: B.F. Bowen & Co., 1915.

*Morrison County (cont.)*

The Land Called Morrison; a History of Morrison County, with Brief Sketches of Benton, Crow Wing and Todd Counties, by Harold L. Fisher. St. Cloud: Volkmuth Pr. Co. [1972]. 216 pp. (2d ed. St. Cloud: Volkmuth Pr. Co., 1976. 216 pp.)

## Mower County

History of Mower County, Minnesota . . . comp. by Inter-State Historical Society. Mankato: Free Pr. Pub. House, 1884. 610 pp.

The History of Mower County, ed. by Franklyn Curtiss-Wedge. Chicago: H.C. Cooper, Jr. & Co., 1911. xv, 1,006 pp.

## Murray County

A History of Western Murray County from 1688 to Dec. 1946 . . . N.p.: Priv. pr., 1947? 203 pp.

A History of Murray County: Murray County, Minnesota, comp. by the Book Committee in cooperation with the Murray County Historical Society, Slaton. Marceline, Mo.: Walsworth Pub. Co., 1982. 601 pp.

## Nicollet County

History of Nicollet and Le Sueur Counties . . . Hon. William G. Gresham, ed. in chief. 2 vols. Indianapolis, Ind.: B.F. Bowen & Co., 1916.

## Nobles County

An Illustrated History of Nobles County, Minnesota, by Arthur P. Rose. Worthington: Northern Hist. Pub. Co., 1908. 637 pp. (Repr. Marceline, Mo.: Walsworth Pub. Co. [1976]. 637, 77 (index) pp.)

Nobles County History . . . ed. by Al Goff. [Worthington:] Nobles County Hist. Soc., 1958. vii, 280, 47 pp.

85th Anniversary, 1872/3-1957/58, Minnesota Centennial, 1858-1958. Worthington: Worthington Daily Globe, 1958. 80 pp. in 5 sections.

## Norman County

History of . . . Norman County, 1918, *see* Clay County.

A Short History of Norman County, by Norman School Statehood Centennial Committee. [Ada?:] Priv. pub. [1958]. 124 pp.

In the Heart of the Red River Valley: a History of the People of Norman County, Minnesota, ed. by Dorothy D. Olson and L.I. Johnson. Dallas, Tex.: Taylor Pub. Co., 1976. 550 pp.

## Olmsted County

Geographical and Statistical History of the County of Olmsted . . . by W.H. Mitchell. Rochester: Shaver & Eaton [1866]. 121 pp. (Repr. N.p.: Olmsted County Hist. Soc. [1977].

History of . . . Olmsted County, 1883, *see* Winona County.

History of Olmsted County, Minnesota, Together with Sketches of Its Pioneers . . . Chicago: Goodspeed Hist. Assoc., 1910. 674 pp.

## Otter Tail County

History of Otter Tail County, Minnesota . . . ed. by John W. Mason. 2 vols. Indianapolis, Ind.: B.F. Bowen & Co., 1916.

Ancient History of Otter Tail and Surrounding Counties . . . by Albert Pries. Waseca: Walter's Pub. Co. [1978]. 105 pp.

East Otter Tail County History, by East Otter Tail Historical Society. Dallas, Tex.: Taylor Pub. Co., 1978. 335 pp.

## Pennington County

Pennington County Historical Society: Pioneer Tales: a History of Pennington County, Minnesota. Dallas, Tex.: Taylor Pub. Co., 1976. 568 pp.

## Pine County

100 Years in Pine County: Pine County Historical Society. [Askov: Priv. pub., 1963.] 144 pp.

The Homesteaders: the Experiences of Early Settlers in Pine County, Minnesota, by O. Bernard Johnson. Staples: Nordell Graphic Communications, 1973. 110 pp.

## Pipestone County

History of Pipestone County: Pipestone County Statehood Central Committee. [Pipestone:] Priv. pub. [1958]. 96 pp.

Illustrated History of the County of . . . Pipestone, 1911, *see* Rock County.

## Polk County

Compendium of History and Biography of Polk County, Minnesota, Major R.I. Holcombe, historical ed., William H. Bingham, general ed. Minneapolis: W.H. Bingham & Co., 1916. 487 pp.

Centennial History of Polk County, by Thomas M. McCall. [Crookston:] Priv. pub., 1961. 103 pp.

## Ramsey County

A History of the City of St. Paul, and of the County of Ramsey, Minnesota, by John F. Williams. Saint Paul: The Society, 1876. 475 pp.

History of Ramsey County and the City of St. Paul . . . by Rev. Edward D. Neill. Minneapolis: North Star Pub. Co., 1881. 650 pp.

Northern Ramsey County: Portrait of a Community. St. Paul: St. Paul Community Planning Organization, 1978. 94 pp.

## Red Lake County

A History of Red Lake County, Minneapolis, ed. by Anne Healy and S. Kankel. Dallas, Tex.: Taylor Pub. Co., 1976. 374 pp.

## Redwood County

The History of Redwood County, Minnesota, comp. by Franklyn Curtiss-Wedge. 2 vols. Chicago: H.C. Cooper, Jr. & Co., 1916.

Redwood: the Story of a County, by Wayne E. Webb. [Redwood Falls:] N.p., 1964. 570 pp.

## Renville County

The History of Renville County, Minnesota, comp. by Franklyn Curtiss-Wedge. 2 vols. Chicago: H.C. Cooper, Jr., & Co., 1916.

Renville County History Book, 1980: Renville County Historical Society. Dallas, Tex.: Taylor Pub. Co., for the Society, 1981. 542 pp.

## Rice County

History of Rice County . . . by Rev. Edward D. Neill. Minneapolis: Minnesota Hist. Co., 1882. 603 pp.

History of Rice and Steele Counties, Minnesota, comp. by Franklyn Curtiss-Wedge. 2 vols. Chicago: H.C. Cooper, Jr. & Co., 1910.

Early Pioneers and Indians of Minnesota and Rice County, by Lillie C. Berg. San Leandro, Calif.: Author, 1959. 221 pp.

Rice County Families: Their History, Our Heritage; a Project of the Rice County Historical Society. (Marceline, Mo.: Walsworth Pub. Co., 1981. 829 pp.)

## Rock County

An Illustrated History of the Counties of Rock and Pipestone, Minnesota, by Arthur P. Stone. Luverne: Northern Hist. Pub. Co., 1911. 802 pp. (Repr. N.p.: Rock and Pipestone County Hist. Societies [1980?].)

A History of Rock County, Rock County Historical Society. Luverne: The Society, 1977. 546 pp.

## Roseau County

Minnesota's Last Frontier, by Jeremiah W. Durham. (A Brief History of Roseau County.) [Minneapolis?: Priv. pub., 1925.] 48 pp.

The North Land, by Hazel H. Wahlberg; a History of Roseau County. [Roseau:] Roseau County Hist. Soc., 1975. 224 pp.

## St. Louis County

History of Duluth and St. Louis County, Past and Present, ed. by Dwight E. Woodbridge and J.S. Pardee. 2 vols. Chicago: H.C. Cooper, Jr. & Co., 1910.

Duluth and St. Louis County, Minnesota . . . ed. by Walter Van Brunt. 3 vols. Chicago: American Hist. Soc., 1921.

## Sherburne County

The Growth of Sherburne County, 1875-1975; as Seen Through Local News-papers, ed. by Cynthia Seelhammer and M.J. Mosher. Becker: Sherburne County Hist. Soc. [1975]. 663 pp.

## Sibley County

Historical Facts of Sibley County . . . 1853-1949. Sibley County Centennial Committee. [Henderson?:] Priv. pub., 1949. 47 pp.

## Stearns County

History of Stearns County, Minnesota, by William F. Mitchell. 2 vols. Chicago: H.C. Cooper, Jr. & Co., 1915.

## Steele County

Geographical and Statistical History of Steele County from Its Earliest Settlement to the Present Time . . . by W.H. Mitchell. Minneapolis: Tribune Pr. Co., 1868. 97 pp.

History of Steele and Waseca Counties, Minnesota . . . Chicago: Union Pub. Co., 1887. 756 pp.

History of . . . Steele County, 1910, *see* Rice County.

## Stevens County

Historical Contributions Concerning the Settlement and Development of West Central Minnesota, Stevens County, and the City of Morris, by Hon. Calvin L. Brown. (Repr. from Morris Tribune, 1922-23. [Morris: Morris Tribune, 1923?] 62 pp.)

The History of Stevens County, by Edna M. Busch. [Morris?:] Priv. pub., 1976. 192 pp.

## Swift County

History of Swift County . . . by Stanley H. Anonsen. Benson: Swift County Hist. Soc. [1929?]. 77 pp. (Originally M.A. thesis, Univ. of Minnesota)

Swift County History, Minnesota: a Collection of Historical Sketches. Benson: Swift County Hist. Soc., 1979 (with surname index). 962 pp. (Also by Taylor Pub. Co., Dallas, Tex.)

## Todd County

History of . . . Todd County, 1915, *see* Morrison County.

History, with Brief Sketches of Todd County, 1972, *see* Morrison County.

Todd County Histories . . . Original Histories of Todd County. Long Prairie: Todd County Bicentennial Comm., 1976. 441 pp.

## Wabasha County

Geographical and Statistical Sketch of the Past and Present of Wabasha County . . . by W.H. Mitchell and U. Curtis. Rochester: Federal Union Book & Job Pr. House, 1870. 164 pp.

History of Wabasha County, Together with Biographical Matter . . . Chicago: H.H. Hill & Co., 1884. 1,340 pp. (History of Winona County, pp. 17-435.)

History of Wabasha County, Minnesota, ed. by Franklyn Curtiss-Wedge. Winona: H.C. Cooper, Jr. & Co., 1920. 781 pp.

## Waseca County

History of . . . Waseca County, 1887, *see* Steele County.

Child's History of Waseca County, Minnesota, from Its First Settlement in 1854 to . . . 1904 . . . by James E. Child. [Owatonna: Pr. of Owatonna Chronicle], 1905. 847 pp.

## Washington County

History of Washington County . . . by Rev. Edward D. Neill. Minneapolis: North Star Pub. Co., 1881. 636 pp.

Washington: a History of the Minnesota County, ed. by Willard E. Rosenfelt. Stillwater: Croixside Pr., 1977. 332 pp.

## Watonwan County

Memorial Record of . . . Watonwan County, 1895, *see* Faribault County.

History of . . . Watonwan County, 1916, *see* Cottonwood County.

# Wilkin County

Wilkin County Family History Book, 1977: a History of Wilkin County, Minnesota, by Wilkin County Historical Society. Dallas, Tex.: Taylor Pub. Co., 1977. 437 pp.

# Winona County

History of Winona and Olmsted Counties . . . Chicago: H.H. Hill & Co., 1883. 1,140 pp. (Shorter versions are in History of Winona, Olmsted and Dodge Counties . . . Chicago: H.H. Hill & Co., 1884.)

History of Winona County, Together with Biographical Matter. Chicago: H.H. Hill & Co., 1883. 966 pp.

The History of Winona County, Minnesota, comp. by Franklyn Curtiss-Wedge. 2 vols. Chicago: H.C. Cooper, Jr. & Co., 1913.

# Wright County

History of Wright County, Minnesota, by Franklyn Curtiss-Wedge. 2 vols. Chicago: H.C. Cooper, Jr. & Co., 1915. (Repr. Buffalo: Wright County Hist. Soc., 1977.)

Condensed History of Wright County, 1851-1935, comp. by C.A. French (and Frank B. Lamson). Delano: Eagle Pr. Co., 1935. 228 pp.

Farnham's History of Wright County Illustrated, by David R.D. Farnham. Buffalo: Wright County Hist. Soc., 1976. 416 pp. (Originally newspaper articles.)

# Yellow Medicine County

An Illustrated History of Yellow Medicine County, Minnesota, by Arthur P. Stone. Marshall: Northern Hist. Pub. Co., 1914. xi, 562 pp.

A History of Yellow Medicine County, Minnesota, 1872-1972, by Carl Narvestad and Amy Narvestad. Granite Falls: Yellow Medicine County Hist. Soc., 1972. xiii, 870 pp.

# MISSISSIPPI

## Adams County

A History of Adams County, Mississippi, 1799-1964, by John A. Robertson. Clinton: Mississippi Coll., 1965. 143 pp.

## Alcorn County

The History of Alcorn County, Mississippi, comp. by the Alcorn County Historical Association. Dallas, Tex.: National ShareGraphics, 1983. 645 pp.

## Amite County

Amite County, Mississippi, 1699 (-1890), by Albert E. Casey. 4 vols. Birmingham, Ala.: Amite County Hist. Fund, 1948-69. 665, 696, 750, 465 pp.

Amite County and Liberty, Mississippi Sesquicentennial, 1809-1959. Gloster: Amite County Sesquicentennial Comm., 1959. (unpaged)

## Attala County

History of Kosciusko and Attala County, by L.L. Henderson, or Kosciusko-Attala History. Marceline, Mo.: Walsworth Pub. Co., for Kosciusko-Attala Hist. Soc., 1976? 314 pp.

## Bolivar County

Imperial Bolivar, by William F. Gray. Cleveland: Bolivar Commercial, 1923. 94 pp.

A Social and Economic History of Ante-Bellum Bolivar County, Mississippi, by Anna A. Kemper. University, Ala.: N.p., 1942 [i.e. 1956?]. vi, 124 leaves.

History of Bolivar County, Mississippi, comp. by Florence W. Sillers. Jackson: Hederman Bros., 1948. 636 pp. (Repr. with index. Spartanburg, S.C.: Reprint Co., 1976.)

## Calhoun County

History of Calhoun County, Mississippi, by Dennis Murphree. N.p., 1948? 90 pp. (Expansion of 1904 ed., by J.S. Ryan and T.M. Murphree.)

A History of Calhoun County, Mississippi, by David G. Sansing. Clinton: Mississippi Coll., 1959. 109 pp. (M.A. thesis)

## Carroll County

History of Carroll County . . . by William F. Hamilton, in Carroll Conservative. N.p.: Carroll County Conservative, 1901? 98 pp.

A History of Carroll County for 1871. Oxford: N.p., 1933. 61 leaves.

## Chickasaw County

A History of Chickasaw County to the Civil War, by James R. Atkinson. Fulton: Northwest Mississippi Hist. Soc., 1968. 68 pp.

## Choctaw County

Choctaw County Chronicles; a History of Choctaw County, Mississippi, 1830-1973, by J.P. Coleman. Ackermann: N.p., 1974. 484 pp. (Repr. Spartanburg, S.C.: Reprint Co., 1981. 484, li pp.)

## Claiborne County

Claiborne County, Mississippi, the Promised Land, by Katy McC. Headley. Port Gibson: Port Gibson-Claiborne County Hist. Soc., 1976. 542 pp.

## Clay County

A History of Clay County, Mississippi, Prior to 1900, by Anne G. Calvert. State College: Mississippi State Univ., n.d. 97 pp. (M.A. thesis)

The History of Clay County, by Richie N. Franks, ed. by Mary C. Landin, written in 1936-38. Utica, N.Y.: Landin, 1982. 167 pp.

## Coahoma County

Clarksdale-Coahoma County, 1836-1936, Centennial ed. Clarksdale: Ellwood Dillon & Delta Staple Cotton Festival Assoc., 1936. 74 pp.

Clarksdale and Coahoma County: a History, by Linton Weeks. Clarksdale: Carnegie Pub. Lib., 1982. 265 pp.

## Copiah County

Copiah County, Mississippi, Quarter Century Resource ed. Crystal Springs: H.W. Mason? 1920. 112 pp.

History of Copiah County to 1900, by John R. Sartin. Clinton: Mississippi Coll., 1959. 111 pp.

## De Soto County

Our Heritage: De Soto County, Mississippi, the North Mississippi Times. Memphis, Tenn.: Frank Myers & Assoc., n.d. 210 pp.

## Franklin County

History of Franklin County, Mississippi, from 1809 to 1899, by W.W. Lambright. McComb City: Special Job Office Pr., 1899. 100 pp.

A History of Franklin County, Mississippi, to 1865, by John W. Hadskey. State College: Mississippi State Univ., 1954. 268 pp. (M.S. thesis)

## George County

By the River of Water: History of George County, Mississippi, by W. Harvell Jackson. 2 vols. Pascagoula: Lewis Pr. Service, 1978-82. 274, 744 pp.

## Grenada County

A History of Grenada County, by J.C. Hathorn. Grenada: Elizabeth Jones Lib., 1968? 229 pp.

## Hancock County

Next Door to Heaven, ed. by Samuel G. Thigpen. Kingsport, Tenn.: Kingsport Pr., 1965. 247 pp.

## Harrison County

Facts About the Gulf Coast: the Book of Harrison County, Mississippi . . . Gulfport: W.A. Cox and E.F. Martin, 1905. 92 pp.

History of Harrison County, Mississippi, by John H. Lang. Gulfport: Dixie Pr., 1936. viii, 303 pp.

## Hinds County

History of Hinds County, Mississippi, 1821-1922 . . . by Mrs. Dunbar Rowland. Jackson: Jones Pr. Co. [1922]. 63 pp.

The History of Hinds County, Mississippi, Before 1860, by Hazel S. Ruff. Durham, N.C.: Duke Univ., 1941. 180 pp. (M.A. thesis)

The History of Hinds County During Reconstruction, 1865-1875, by Charles M. Bacon. Clinton: Mississippi Coll., 1959. 96 pp. (M.A. thesis)

## Holmes County

A History of Holmes County, Mississippi, by Spiro P. Cora. [Clinton:] Mississippi Coll., 1969. 135 leaves, (M.A. thesis)

## Itawamba County

Itawamba: a History; Story of a County in Northeast Mississippi, by Forrest F. Reed. Nashville, Tenn.: Reed & Co., 1966. x, 186 pp.

## Jackson County

Four Centuries on the Pascagoula, ed. by Cyril E. Cain. 2 vols. [State College: Mississippi State Univ.? 1953-62.]

A History of Jackson County, Mississippi, by William L. Ziglar. Clinton: Mississippi Coll., 1961. 175 pp. (M.A. thesis)

A Pictorial Walk Through ol' High Jackson, by Walt Hammer. Collegedale, Pa.: College Pr. [1967]. 130 pp.

## Jasper County

A History of Jasper County, Mississippi. State College: Mississippi State Univ., 1954. 155 pp.

Jasper County: a Prospect, 1833-1968, by Gabriel C. Green. Clinton: Mississippi Coll., 1968. vi, 120 leaves. (M.A. thesis)

## Jefferson County

A Short History of Jefferson County, Mississippi, by Norma L. Norton. Clinton: Mississippi Coll., 1960. 103 pp. (M.A. thesis)

## Jefferson Davis County

History of Jefferson Davis County, Mississippi. N.p., 1962.

## Jones County

A History of Jones County, Mississippi, by Suzanne Spell. Clinton: Mississippi Coll., 1961. 105 pp. (M.A. thesis)

A Mind-Confederacy; the Free State of Jones, 1862-186-; a Source Book, ed. by Mary H. Kitchens and T. Blackledge. Ellisville: Progress-Item [1971]. 112 pp.

## Kemper County

A Social and Economic History of Kemper County, Mississippi, in the Ante-Bellum Period, by Anel D. Bassett. [University, Ala.:] Univ. of Alabama, 1947. 110 leaves. (M.A. thesis)

A History of Kemper County, Mississippi, 1860-1910, by Charles R. Fulton. State College: Mississippi State Univ., 1968. 85 leaves. (M.A. thesis)

Southeast Kemper: Its People and Communities, by Louis Parmer. Livingston, Ala.: Sumter Graphics, 1982. 261 pp.

Kemper County: the Pioneer Days, by Louis Parmer. Livingston, Ala.: Sumter Graphics, 1983. 215 pp.

## Lafayette County

Faulkner's County: Yoknapatawpha, by Martin J. Dain. New York: Random House [1964]. 159 pp.

A History of Lafayette County, Mississippi, by C. John Sobotka, Jr. Oxford: Rebel Pr., 1976. 126 pp.

## Lamar County

Lamar County Heritage, by Leonard L. Slade, Sr. Baltimore: Gateway Pr., 1978. 261 pp.

## Lauderdale County

A History of Lauderdale County, Mississippi, by Dorothy L. Smith. Clinton: Mississippi Coll., 1961. 102 pp. (M.A. thesis)

## Lee County

A History of Lee County, Mississippi, by Ulvie Pitts. Clinton: Mississippi Coll., 1961. 135 pp. (M.A. thesis)

## Leflore County

A History of Leflore County, Mississippi, by Mary G. McCarty. University: Mississippi Univ., 1966. 92 leaves. (M.A. thesis)

Leflore County, Mississippi Centennial, 1871-1971. Greenwood: Centennial Book Comm., 1971. 68 pp.

## Lowndes County

A Pictorial History of the People of Lowndes County, Mississippi. N.p.: Lowndes County Dept. of Archives & Hist., 1981. 548 pp.

## Madison County

A History of Madison County, Mississippi from Its Earliest Times Through the Civil War. Clinton: Mississippi Coll., 1967. 115 pp.

## Marion County

History of Marion County, Mississippi. Marceline, Mo.: Walsworth Pub. Co. for Marion County Hist. Soc., 1976. 198 pp.

## Marshall County

History of Marshall County, Mississippi: 1836 - One Hundred Years - 1936. N.p.: The Garden Club of Marshall County, 1936. 48 pp.

## Monroe County

A Brief History of Aberdeen and Monroe County, Mississippi, 1821-1900, by Bertie (Shaw) Rollins. [Aberdeen?: N.p., 1957.] 128 pp.

## Newton County

History of Newton County from 1834 to 1894, by A.J. Brown. Jackson: Clarion Ledger Co., 1894. 472 pp. (Repr. Fulton: Itawamba County Times, 1964.)

The Newton Record. Newton County Centennial ed., 1836-1936. Newton: Newton Record, 1926. (v.35:12 of Newton Record, 1936.)

# Noxubee County

Historical Notes of Noxubee County, Mississippi, by John A. Tyson. Macon, Ga.: N.p., 1928. 287 leaves.

# Oktibbeha County

Historical Sketches of Oktibbeha County, Mississippi, by Thomas B. Carroll. Gulfport: Dixie Pr., 1931. xviii, 263 pp.

# Panola County

History of Panola County. Sardia: Southern Reporter, 1908-9. 47 pp.

A History of Panola County, 1836-1860, by Lula M. Fowler. University: Mississippi Univ., 1960. 100 pp.

# Pearl River County

Pearl River: Highway to Glory Land, by Samuel G. Thigpen. Kingsport, Tenn.: Kingsport Pr., 1965. 185 pp.

# Pike County

Pike County, Mississippi, 1798-1876; Pioneer Families and Confederate Soldiers, Reconstruction and Redemption, by Luke W. Conerly. Nashville, Tenn.: Brandon Pr. Co., 1909. 368 pp. (Repr. with additional records, by E.R. Williams. Easley, S.C.: Southern Hist. Pr. [1978]. 368, 38 pp.)

# Pontotoc County

Story of Pontotoc, part I-(III) . . . by Edmund T. Winston. [Pontotoc:] Pontotoc Progress Pr., 1931. 319 pp.

From These Hills: a History of Pontotoc County, by Callie B. Young. Pontotoc: Women's Club, 1976. 702 pp.

# Prentiss County

History of Prentiss County, by Reuben L. Bolton. Oxford: Univ. of Mississippi, 1935. 131 leaves. (M.A. thesis)

History of Booneville and Prentiss County, by Howard Carpenter. Booneville: Milwick Pr. Co., 1956. 134 pp.

# Rankin County

An Economic History of Rankin County, by Charles J. Silbernagel. Clinton: Mississippi Coll., 1966. 116 leaves. (M.A. thesis)

# Scott County

A History of Scott County, Mississippi, by Eugene R. Brown. Clinton: Mississippi Coll., 1967. (M.A. thesis)

## Simpson County

A History of Simpson County, Mississippi, to 1865, by James H. McLendon. Austin: Univ. of Texas, 1936.

A History of Simpson County, Mississippi, 1824-1862, by Richard T. Bennett. Clinton: Mississippi Coll., 1962. 142 leaves.

Simpson County, "Honoring the Past"; a Brief History, written and comp. by Simpson County Book Committee. Simpson County Sesquicentennial Celebration, July 27-Aug. 1974. N.p., n.d. 52 pp.

## Smith County

History of Smith County, Mississippi: 1976 Bicentennial History Comm. of Smith County. N.p., n.d. 127 pp.

## Sunflower County

A History of Sunflower County, Mississippi, by Sherry M. Donald. University: Mississippi Univ., 1968. 67 leaves.

Fevers, Floods and Faith; a History of Sunflower County, Mississippi, 1844-1976, by Marie M. Hemphill. Indianola: N.p., 1980. 849 pp.

## Tate County

A History of Tate County, by Howard Carpenter. Senatobia: B/C Pr. Co., 1975? 358 pp.

## Tippah County

The Historical Origins of Tippah County, by Reuben W. Griffith. University: Mississippi Univ., 1939. 116 leaves.

History of Tippah County, Mississippi: the First Century, by Andrew Brown. Ripley, Mo.: Tippah County Hist. and Gen. Soc., 1976. 321 pp.

The History of Tippah County, Mississippi, comp. by the Tippah County Historical and Genealogical Society. Dallas, Tex.: National ShareGraphics, 1981. 723 pp.

## Tishomingo County

History of Old Tishomingo County, 1832-1940, comp. by S.M. Nabors. [Corinth: N.p.], 1940. 108 pp. (Repr. [Corinth: J. Lipford, 1980.] 116 pp.)

Tishomingo County, 1836-1940, by Mary F. Sumners. University: Mississippi Univ., 1957. 154 leaves.

History of Old Tishomingo County, Mississippi Territory, comp. and ed. by Alexander Cochran. N.p., 1911. 277 pp. (Repr. Oklahoma City, Okla.: Barnhart Pr. Co., 1980.)

## Warren County

A History of Warren County, Mississippi, to 1860, by William H. Bunch, Jr. [Clinton], 1965. 108 pp. (M.A. thesis)

## Washington County

Washington County, Mississippi, by Edgar J. Cheatham. New Orleans: Tulane Univ., 1950? 160 leaves.

Memoirs of Henry Tillinghast Ireys: Papers of the Washington County Historical Society, 1910-1915, ed. by W.D. McCain and C. Capers. Jackson: Mississippi Dept. of Archaeology & Hist., 1954. 423 pp.

A History of Washington County, Mississippi, by Bern Keating. N.p.: Greenville Junior Auxiliary, 1976. 95 pp.

## Webster County

History of Webster County from 1874 to 1935, by Bernice W. Cox. University: Mississippi Univ., 1968. 54 leaves.

## Winston County

A History of Winston County, by William T. Lewis. N.p., 1938.

The Centennial History of Winston County, Mississippi, by William T. Lewis. Pasadena, Tex.: Glove Pub. Int. [1972]. 216 pp.

Winston County and Its People, by Nancy R. Parkes. Louisville, Ky.: Winston County Gen. & Hist. Soc., 1980. 320 pp.

## Yalobusha County

Organization and Early History of Yalobusha County, by Hiram P. Hathorn. Oxford: Univ. of Mississippi, 1933. 106 leaves.

The History of Yalobusha County, Mississippi, comp. by Yalobusha County Historical Society. Water Valley: Gurner, 1982. 527 pp.

## Yazoo County

Yazoo County Story: a Pictorial History of Yazoo County, Mississippi . . . Fort Worth, Tex.: Univ. Supply & Equipment Co., 1958. 184 pp.

Yazoo: Its Legends and Legacies, by Harriet Decelle and J. Pritcher. Yazoo: Delta Pr., 1976. 515 pp.

# MISSOURI

## Regional

A. History of Adair, Schuyler, Sullivan and Putnam Counties. Chicago: Goodspeed Pub. Co., 1888. 1,225 pp.

B. History of Cole, Moniteau, Morgan, Benton, Miller, Maries and Osage Counties, from the Earliest Time to the Present . . . Chicago: Goodspeed Pub. Co., 1889. 1,172 pp.

C. History of Franklin, Jefferson, Washington, Crawford and Gasconade Counties, Missouri, from the Earliest Time to the Present . . . Chicago: Goodspeed Pub. Co., 1888. 1,131 pp. (Repr. Cape Girardeau: Ramfre Pr., 1970. Index, comp. by Felix E. Snider. Cape Girardeau: Ramfre Pr., 1970. 92 pp.)

D. History of Hickory, Polk, Cedar, Dade and Barton Counties, Missouri . . . Chicago: Goodspeed Pub. Co., 1889. 967 pp.

E. History of Laclede, Camden, Dallas, Webster, Wright, Texas, Pulaski, Phelps and Dent Counties, Missouri. Chicago: Goodspeed Pub. Co., 1889. 1,219 pp.

F. History of Lewis, Clark, Knox and Scotland Counties, Missouri, from the Earliest Time to the Present . . . St. Louis: Goodspeed Pub. Co., 1887. 1,229 pp. (Repr. Marceline: Missouri Hist. Pr., 1982. 1,100 pp.)

G. History of Newton, Lawrence, Barry and McDonald Counties, Missouri, from the Earliest Time to the Present . . . Chicago: Goodspeed Pub. Co., 1888. 1,092 pp. (Biographical index, by Mary L. Palmer. N.p., 1966. 64 leaves.)

H. History of Southeast Missouri, Embracing an Historical Account of the Counties of Ste. Genevieve, St. Francois, Perry, Cape Girardeau, Bollinger, Madison, New Madrid, Pemiscot, Dunklin, Scott, Mississippi, Stoddard, Butler, Wayne and Iron . . . Chicago: Goodspeed Pub. Co., 1888. 1,215 pp. (Index, comp. by Felix E. Snider. Cape Girardeau: Ramfre Pr., 1964.) (Unpaged)

*Biographical indexes to many of the county histories were comp. by Elizabeth Prather Ellsberry in the 1960s and 1970s. They are not listed below, but are still available from the compiler.*

🌿      🌿      🌿

## Adair County

History of Adair County, 1888, *see* A., above.

History of Adair County, by Eugene M. Violette. ed. by C.N. Tolman. Kirksville: Denslow Hist. Co., 1911. xvi, 1,188 pp.

A Book of Adair County History . . . N.p.: Adair County Bicentennial Comm., 197-. 448 pp.

## Andrew County

History of Andrew and De Kalb Counties, Missouri. Chicago: Goodspeed Pub. Co., 1888. 591 pp.

## Atchison County

History of . . . Atchison County, 1882, *see* Holt County.

Biographical History, Atchison County, Missouri . . . Rock Port: N.p., 1905. 797 pp.

## Audrain County

History of Audrain County, Missouri . . . St. Louis: National Hist. Co., 1884. vi, 973 pp. (Repr. Clinton: The Printery, 1975.)

History of Audrain County, by G. Robertson. N.p., 1913.

Centennial History of Audrain County, by Herschel Schooley. Mexico: McIntyre Pub. Co. [1937]. 304 pp.

## Barry County

History of . . . Barry County, 1888, *see* G., p. 197.

Historic Spots in Old Barry County, by Nellie A. Mills. [Monett: N.p., 1952.] 154 pp.

Early Barry County, by Addam L. Matthews. North Newton, Kans.: Barry County Hist. Soc. [1965]. 334 pp.

## Barton County

History of . . . Barton County, 1889, *see* D., p. 197.

The Story of Barton County; a Complete History, 1855-1972, by Marvin L. Van-Gilder. [Lamar?:] Reiley Pub. [1972]. 48 pp.

## Bates County

The History of . . . Bates County, 1883, *see* Cass County.

The Old Settler's History of Bates County, Missouri, from Its First Settlement to Jan. 1900, by S.L. Tathwell. Amsterdam: Tathwell & Maxey, 1900. 284 pp.

History of Bates County, Missouri, by William O. Atkeson. Topeka, Kans.: Cleveland Hist. Pub. Co., 1918. 983 pp.

## Benton County

A Sketch of the History of Benton County, Missouri, by James H. Lay. Hannibal: Winchell & Ebert Pr. & Litho. Co., 1876. 76 pp.

History of . . . Benton County, 1889, *see* B., p. 197.

*Benton County (cont.)*

The History of Benton County, Missouri, by Kathleen K. White and K.W. Miles. 2 vols. Clinton: The Printery, 1969.

## Bollinger County

Historical Account of the County of . . . Bollinger, 1888, in History of Southeast Missouri, *see* H., p. 197.

"Bits of History"; Beginning, Growth & Folklore of Bollinger County, Missouri, by Mary L. Hahn. Cape Girardeau: Ramfre Pr., 1972. 208 pp. (More Bits, *see* below.)

Bollinger County: 1851-1976, a Bicentennial Commemorative, ed. by Mary L. Hahn. Marceline: Walsworth Pub. Co., 1977. 1,000 pp. (Repr. Marble Hill: Bollinger County Hist. Soc., 1981.)

"More Bits of History," by Mary L. Hahn. Marble Hill: Bollinger County Hist. Soc., 1982. (Bits of History, *see* above.)

## Boone County

History of Boone County, Missouri . . . St. Louis: Western Hist. Co., 1882. vii, 1,144 pp. (Repr. Cape Girardeau: Ramfre Pr., 1970.)

## Buchanan County

The History of Buchanan County, Missouri . . . St. Joseph: Union Hist. Co., 1881. viii, 1,073 pp. (Repr. Cape Girardeau: Ramfre Pr., 1974. 1,130 pp.)

The Daily News' History of Buchanan County and St. Joseph, Missouri . . . to 1898 . . . comp. by Christian L. Rutt. St. Joseph: Hardman Pr. [1898]. 571 pp.

History of Buchanan County and St. Joseph . . . 1826-1904, comp. and ed. by C.L. Rutt. Chicago: Biographical Pub. Co., 1904. 723 pp.

The History of Buchanan County, Missouri, comp. by Missouri River Heritage Assoc. Dallas, Tex.: National ShareGraphics, for the Assoc., 1984. 525 pp.

## Butler County

Historical Account of the County of . . . Butler, 1888, in History of Southeast Missouri, *see* H., p. 197.

History of Butler County, Missouri . . . by David B. Deem. 2d ed. Poplar Bluff: Bluff Pr. Co., 1940. 211 pp.

## Caldwell County

History of Caldwell and Livingston Counties, Missouri . . . St. Louis: National Hist. Soc., 1886. xiv, 1,227 pp. (Index to Biographies . . . comp. by Ora M.H. Pease. [Salem, Oreg., 1949.] 21 leaves.)

*Caldwell County (cont.)*

History of . . . Caldwell County, 1923, *see* Clinton County.

## Callaway County

History of Callaway County, Missouri . . . St. Louis: National Hist. Co., 1884. vii, 954 pp.

A History of Callaway County, Missouri. Fulton: Kingdom of Callaway County Hist. Soc., 1983. 564 pp.

## Camden County

History of . . . Camden County, 1889, *see* E., p. 197.

## Cape Girardeau County

Historical Account of the County of . . . Cape Girardeau, 1888, in History of Southeast Missouri, *see* H., p. 197.

## Carter County

History of Carter County; Carter County Centennial . . . by Eunice Pennington. N.p., 1959. 70 pp.

## Cass County

The History of Cass and Bates Counties, Missouri . . . St. Joseph: National Hist. Co., 1883. xi, 1,414 pp. (Computerized index. Park City, Utah: Hamilton Computer Service, 1978. 172 pp.)

History and Directory of Cass County, Missouri [by A.L. Webber]. Harrisonville: Cass County Leader, 1908. 408 pp.

## Cedar County

History of . . . Cedar County, 1889, *see* D., p. 197.

Historical Sketches of Cedar County, Missouri, by Clayton Abbott. [Stockton: N.p., 1967.] 276 pp.

Missouri History of Cedar County, by Clayton Abbott and L.B. Hoff. [Greenfield: Vedette Pr. Co., 1971.] 600 pp.

## Chariton County

History of . . . Chariton County, 1883, *see* Howard Co.

Historical, Pictorial and Biographical Record of Chariton County, Missouri . . . Salisbury: Pictorial and Biog. Pub. Co., 1896. 248 pp.

*Chariton County (cont.)*

History of Chariton and Howard Counties, Missouri. Howard County, by T. Berry Smith; Chariton County, by Pearl S. Gehrig. Topeka, Kans.: Hist. Pub. Co., 1923. 856 pp.

## Christian County

Christian County, Its First 100 Years. Ozark: [N.p., 1959]. 212 pp.

## Clark County

History of . . . Clark County, 1887, *see* F., p. 197.

## Clay County

History of Clay and Platte Counties, Missouri . . . St. Louis: National Hist. Co., 1885. xvi, 1,121 pp.

History of Clay County, Missouri, by William H. Woodson. Indianapolis: Hist. Pub. Co., 1920. 777 pp.

Clay County, Missouri . . . 1822-1972, by Alexander Doniphan Chapter, D.A.R. [Liberty:] Al's Pr. Service, 1972. 291 pp.

Clay County, Missouri Sesquicentennial Souvenir Book, History, 1822-1972. Liberty: Mrs. A.L. Reppert, 1982.

## Clinton County

History of Clinton County, Missouri. St. Joseph: National Hist. Co., 1881. 505, 264 pp.

History of Clinton and Caldwell Counties, Missouri: Clinton County, by Carrie P. Johnston; Caldwell County, by W.H.S. McGlumphy. Topeka, Kans.: Hist. Pub. Co., 1923. 836 pp.

## Cole County

History of Cole County, 1889, *see* B., p. 197.

## Cooper County

A History of Cooper County, Missouri, from the First Visit of White Men, 1804 - to 1876, by Henry C. Levens. St. Louis: Perrin & Smith, 1876. 231 pp.

History of . . . Cole County, 1883, *see* Howard County.

History of Cooper County, Missouri, by William F. Johnson. Topeka, Kans.: Hist. Pub. Co., 1919. 1,167 pp. (Repr. with every-name index. 2 vols. Fort Worth, Tex.: VKM Pub. Co., 1978. 1,468 pp.)

Melton's History of Cooper County, Missouri; an Account from the Early Times to the Present . . . by Elston J. Melton. Columbia: E.W. Stephens Pub. Co., 1937. 584 pp.

## Crawford County

History of . . . Crawford County, 1888, *see* C., p. 197.

Crawford County and Cuba, Missouri . . . by James I. Breier. Cape Girardeau: Ramfre Pr., 1972. 570 pp.

## Dade County

History of . . . Dade County, 1889, *see* D., p. 197.

History of Dade County and Her People. Greenfield: Pioneer Hist. Co., 1917.

## Dallas County

History of . . . Dallas County, 1889, *see* E., p. 197.

Early Days in Dallas County, by Elva Hemphill. N.p., 1954. 115 pp.

The Dallas County, Missouri Story, 1841-1971. Buffalo, N.Y.: Dallas County Hist. Soc., 1974. 434 pp.

## Daviess County

The History of Daviess County, Missouri. Kansas City: Birdsall & Dean, 1882. 868 pp.

Memories . . . being a Story of Early Times in Daviess County, Missouri, by John F. Jordin. Gallatin: Missourian Pr. [1904]. 206 pp.

History of Daviess and Gentry Counties, Missouri, by John C. Leopard, et al. Topeka, Kans.: Hist. Pub. Co., 1922. 1,039 pp.

## De Kalb County

History of . . . De Kalb County, 1888, *see* Andrew County.

A History of De Kalb County, Missouri, 1845-1981, ed. by Lora R. Lockhart and staff. Maysville: De Kalb County Hist. Soc., 1981. 409 pp.

## Dent County

History of . . . Dent County, 1889, *see* E., p. 197.

## Dunklin County

Historical Account of the County of . . . Dunklin, 1888, in History of Southeast Missouri, *see* H., p. 197.

History of Dunklin County, Missouri, 1845-1895 . . . by Mary F. Smyth-Davis. St. Louis: Nixon-Jones Pr. Co., 1896. 290 pp.

## Franklin County

History of Franklin . . . County, 1888, *see* C., p. 197.

*Franklin County (cont.)*

Historical Review of Franklin County, Missouri, 1818-1868, ed. by Melvin B. Robles and V.L. Osick. Union: Franklin County Sesquicentennial Corp. [1968]. 68 pp.

## Gasconade County

History of . . . Gasconade County, 1888, *see* C., p. 197.

## Gentry County

The History of Gentry and Worth Counties, Missouri. St. Joseph: National Hist. Co., 1882. 839 pp. (Repr. [Albany: N.p., 1954?])

History of . . . Gentry County, 1922, *see* Daviess County.

## Greene County

History of Greene County, Missouri . . . St. Louis: Western Hist. Co., 1883. viii, 919 pp. (Repr. Clinton: The Printery, 1969, with 28 pp. index.)

Past and Present of Greene County, Missouri: Early and Recent History . . . by Jonathan Fairbanks and C.E. Tuck. 2 vols. Indianapolis, Ind.: A.W. Bowen, 1915. 1,933 pp.

## Grundy County

The History of Grundy County, Missouri . . . Kansas City: Birdsall & Dean, 1881. 739 pp. (Repr. Trenton: Grundy County Hist. Soc., 1972.)

A History of Grundy County . . . [by James E. Ford]. Trenton: New Pub. Co., 1908. 875 pp.

Centennial History of Grundy County, Missouri, 1839-1939, by William R. Denslow. Trenton: Author, 1939. vii, 402 pp.

## Harrison County

History of Harrison and Mercer Counties, Missouri. Chicago: Goodspeed Pub. Co., 1888. 758 pp. (Repr. Princeton, N.J.: Mercer County Hist. Soc., 1972.)

History of Harrison County, Missouri, by George W. Wanamaker. Topeka, Kansas: Hist. Pub. Co., 1921. 855 pp.

## Henry County

The History of Henry and St. Clair Counties, Missouri . . . St. Joseph: National Hist. Co., 1883. xii, 1,224 pp. (Repr. Clinton: Henry County Hist. Soc., 1968.)

## Hickory County

History of Hickory . . . County, 1889, *see* D., p. 197.

*Hickory County (cont.)*

Wilson's History of Hickory County. [Hermitage?:] N.p., 1909? 189 pp.

Tales of Old Hickory County . . . by Opal S. Butts. Dallas, Tex.: Royal Pub. Co. [1966]. 83 pp.

## Holt County

The History of Holt and Atchison Counties, Missouri . . . St. Joseph: National Hist. Co., 1882. 1,036 pp.

## Howard County

History of Howard and Chariton Counties, Missouri. St. Louis: National Hist. Co., 1883. 1,225 pp.

History of Howard and Cooper Counties, Missouri . . . St. Louis: National Hist. Co., 1883. ix, 1,167 pp. (Repr. with new index. Keytesville: Keytesville Lib., 1983. 1,268 pp.)

History of . . . Howard County, 1923, *see* Chariton County.

## Iron County

Historical Account of the County of . . . Iron, 1888, in History of Southeast Missouri, *see* H., p. 197.

## Jackson County

The History of Jackson County, Missouri . . . Kansas City: Union Hist. Co., 1881. x, 1,006 pp. (Repr., indexed. Cape Girardeau: Ramfre Pr., 1966.)

A Memorial and Biographical Record of Kansas City and Jackson County, Missouri . . . Chicago: Lewis Pub. Co., 1896. 671 pp.

History of Jackson County, Missouri, by W.Z. Hickman. Topeka, Kans.: Hist. Pub. Co., 1920. 832 pp.

Jackson County, Missouri, Its Opportunities and Resources [by M.E. Ballou]. [Kansas City: N.p., 1926.] 324 pp.

## Jasper County

The History of Jasper County, Missouri . . . Des Moines, Iowa: Miller & Co., 1883. 1,065 pp.

A History of Jasper County, Missouri, and Its People, by Joel T. Livingston. 2 vols. Chicago: Lewis Pub. Co., 1912.

## Jefferson County

History of . . . Jefferson County, 1888, *see* C., p. 197.

Jefferson County, Missouri, in Story and Pictures, by Mary J. Boyer. [Imperial: N.p., 1958.] 179 pp.

Historic Sites of Jefferson County, Missouri, by Walter L. Eschbach and M.C. Drummond. [St. Louis:] Bartholomew & Assoc. [1968]. 178 pp.

Our Jefferson County Heritage; Reminiscences of Early Missouri, by Zoe B. Rutledge. Cape Girardeau: Ramfre Pr., 1970. 247 pp.

## Johnson County

The History of Johnson County, Missouri, Including a Reliable History of the Townships, Cities and Towns . . . Kansas City: Kansas City Hist. Co., 1881. xii, 989 pp. (Repr., index added. Clinton: The Printery, 1970. xii, 989, 89 pp.)

History of Johnson and Pettis Counties, Missouri. Chicago: Chapman Pub. Co., 1895. 665 pp.

History of Johnson County, by Ewing Cockrell. Topeka, Kans.: Hist. Pub. Co., 1918. 1,144 pp.

## Knox County

History of . . . Knox County, 1887, *see* F., p. 197.

Early History of Knox County. Edina: Edina Sentinel, 1916. 162 pp.

## Laclede County

History of Laclede County, 1889, *see* E., p. 197.

A History of Laclede County, Missouri, from 1820 to 1926, by Leo Nyberg. Lebanon: Rustic Pr., 1926. 178 pp.

History of Laclede County, Missouri, comp. by Lois R. Beard and Heritage Pub. Co. Dallas, Tex.: National ShareGraphics, 1979. 651 pp.

## Lafayette County

History of Lafayette County, Missouri . . . St. Louis: Missouri Hist. Co., 1881. 702 pp. (Repr. Warrensburg: West Central Gen. Soc., 1980.)

Young's History of Lafayette County, Missouri, by Hon. William Young. 2 vols. Indianapolis, Ind.: B.F. Bowen, 1910.

Tattle-tales . . . Stories About the Clinton, Missouri Area Since It Was Part of Lillard County [later Lafayette County] Since 1830 . . . comp. by Kathleen W. Miles and K.K. White. Clinton: Democrat Pub. Co., 1967. 107 pp.

## Lawrence County

History of . . . Lawrence County, 1888, *see* G., p. 197.

History of Mt. Vernon and Lawrence County, 1831-1931, by Mrs. L.S. Hurley? [Mt. Vernon: The Record, n.d.]

Lawrence County, Missouri, 1845-1970; a Brief History, by Lawrence County Historical Society. [Mt. Vernon: The Soc., 1970.] 143 pp.

## Lewis County

History of Lewis County, 1887, *see* F., p. 197.

## Lincoln County

History of Lincoln County, Missouri, from the Earlier Time to the Present. Chicago: Goodspeed Pub. Co., 1888. 637 pp. (Repr. Clinton: The Printery, 1969.)

## Linn County

The History of Linn County, Missouri . . . Kansas City: Birdsall & Dean, 1882. 883 pp.

Compendium of History and Biography of Linn County, Missouri . . . Chicago: H. Taylor [1912]. xiv, 791 pp.

## Livingston County

History of . . . Livingston County, 1886, *see* Caldwell County.

Past and Present of Livingston County, Missouri . . . by Major Albert J. Roof. 2 vols. Chicago: S.J. Clarke Pub. Co., 1913.

History of Livingston County, Missouri, ed. by Grace A. Boehner. Chillicothe: Livingston County Central Comm., 1937. 167 pp.

150 Years in Livingston County, Missouri. Chillicothe: R.S.V.P. Hist. Book, 1981.

## McDonald County

History of . . . McDonald County, 1888, *see* G., p. 197.

Illustrated History of McDonald County, Missouri, from the Earliest Settlement to the Present Time . . . ed. and comp. by J.A. Sturges. Pineville: N.p., 1897. viii, 344 pp.

McDonald County, Missouri: a Pictorial Interpretation . . . comp. by Larry C. Bradley. [Noel: McDonald Co. Pr., 1972.] 88 pp.

## Macon County

History of . . . Macon County, 1884, *see* Randolph County.

General History of Macon County, Missouri. Chicago: H. Taylor, 1910. xvi, 945 pp.

## Madison County

Historical Account of the County of . . . Madison, 1888, in History of Southeast Missouri, *see* H., p. 197.

## Maries County

History of . . . Maries County, 1889, *see* B., p. 197.

History of Maries County, by Everett M. King, ed. by K.L. King. Cape Girardeau: Ramfre Pr., 1963. 829 pp.

## Marion County

History of Marion County, Missouri . . . St. Louis: E.F. Perkins, 1884. x, 1,003 pp.

Portrait and Biographical Record of Marion, Ralls and Pike Counties . . . Chicago: C.O. Owen, 1895. 802 pp. (Repr. with rev. and new every-name index. New London: Ralls Book Co., 1982. 800 pp.)

A History of Marion County, by Kate Kuhn. [Hannibal?: N.p.], 1963. 224 pp.

## Mercer County

History of . . . Mercer County, 1888, *see* Harrison County.

Souvenir History of Mercer County, Missouri. Trenton: W.B. Rogers Pr. Co., 1911.

## Miller County

History of . . . Miller County, 1889, *see* B., p. 197.

A History of Miller County, Missouri, by Gerard Schultz. Jefferson City: Midland Pr. Co. [1933]. 176 pp.

Judge Jenkins' History of Miller County, Missouri . . . ed. by Clyde L. Jenkins. Vol. 1. (all pub.) Tuscumbia: N.p., 1971. (Index, by Peggy H. Gregory. Houston, Tex.: Author, 1972.)

## Mississippi County

Historical Account of the County of . . . Mississippi, 1888, in History of Southeast Missouri, *see* H., p. 197.

## Moniteau County

History of . . . Moniteau County, 1889, *see* B., p. 197.

A History of Moniteau County, Missouri, by James E. Ford. California: H. Crawford, 1926. 530 pp.

## Monroe County

History of Monroe and Shelby Counties . . . St. Louis: National Hist. Co., 1884. xiii, 1,176 pp.

## Montgomery County

Montgomery County, by L.A. Thompson. Montgomery City: N.p., 1879.

History of . . . Montgomery County, 1885, *see* St. Charles County.

## Morgan County

History of . . . Morgan County, 1889, *see* B., p. 197.

## New Madrid County

Historical Account of the County of . . . New Madrid, 1888, in History of Southeast Missouri, *see* H., p. 197.

## Newton County

History of . . . Newton County, 1888, *see* G., p. 197.

History of Newton, by Walter F. Lackey. Independence: Zion, 1950.

## Nodaway County

The History of Nodaway County, Missouri . . . St. Joseph: National Hist. Co., 1882. 1,034 pp.

## Oregon County

Oregon County's Three Flags, Six County Seats, Via the Horse and Buggy, by Lewis A.J. Simpson, ed. by Keith Johnson. Thayer: Thayer News [1971]. xiv, 97 pp.

## Osage County

History of . . . Osage County, 1889, *see* B., p. 197.

## Pemiscot County

Historical Account of the County of . . . Pemiscot, 1888, in History of Southeast Missouri, *see* H., p. 197.

## Perry County

Historical Account of the County of . . . Perry, 1888, in History of Southeast Missouri, *see* H., p. 197.

## Pettis County

The History of Pettis County, Missouri . . . [N.p., 1882.] 1,108 pp.

History of Pettis County, 1895, *see* Johnson County.

History of Pettis County, Missouri, by Mark A. McGruder. Topeka, Kans.: Hist. Pub. Co., 1919. 835 pp.

## Phelps County

History of . . . Phelps County, 1889, *see* E., p. 197.

## Pike County

The History of Pike County, Missouri . . . Des Moines, Iowa: Mills & Co., 1883. 1,038 pp. (Repr. with name index. Marceline: Missouri Hist. Pr., 1982. 1,100 pp.)

Portrait and Biographical Record of . . . Pike County, 1895, *see* Marion County.

## Platte County

Memories That Never Die, by Maude Mark (née Ingram). Perkins, Okla.: N.p., 1884. 123 pp.

History of . . . Platte County, 1885, *see* Clay County.

Annals of Platte County, Missouri . . . to 1897 . . . by W.M. Paxton. Kansas City: Hudson-Kimberly Pub. Co., 1897. 1,182 pp. (Repr. Cape Girardeau: Ramfre Pr., 1965.)

## Polk County

History of . . . Polk County, 1889, *see* D., p. 197.

## Pulaski County

History of . . . Pulaski County, 1889, *see* E., p. 197.

Lest We Forget: a History of Pulaski County, Missouri . . . by Mabel Mottas. [Springfield: N.p.], 1960. 81 pp.

## Putnam County

History of . . . Putnam County, 1888, *see* A., p. 197.

## Ralls County

Portrait and Biographical Record of . . . Ralls County, 1895, *see* Marion County.

Early Ralls County, by N.D. Norton. New London: N.p., 1945. 104 pp.

## Randolph County

History of Randolph and Macon Counties, Missouri . . . St. Louis: National Hist. Co., 1884. xiii, 1,223 pp. (Repr. with complete-name index. Marceline: Missouri Hist. Pr., 1983. 1,348 pp.)

History of Randolph County, Missouri. Topeka, Kans.: Hist. Pub. Co., 1920. 852 pp.

## Ray County

History of Ray County, Missouri . . . St. Louis: Missouri Hist. Co., 1881. 818 pp.

## St. Charles County

History of St. Charles, Montgomery and Warren Counties, Missouri . . . St. Louis: National Hist. Co., 1885. xvi, 1,131 pp.

Portrait and Biographical Record of St. Charles, Lincoln, and Warren Counties, Missouri . . . Chicago: Chapman Pub. Co., 1895. 573 pp.

## St. Clair County

The History of . . . St. Clair County, 1883, *see* Henry County.

## St. Francois County

Historical Account of the County of . . . St. Francois, 1888; in History of Southeast Missouri, *see* H., p. 197.

## St. Louis County

Early History of St. Louis City and County, by J.T. Scharf. 2 vols. Philadelphia: L.H. Everts & Co., 1877. 988 pp.

History of St. Louis County, Missouri . . . by William L. Thomas. 2 vols. St. Louis: S.J. Clarke Pub. Co., 1911.

## Ste. Genevieve County

Historical Account of the County of Ste. Genevieve, 1888, in History of Southeast Missouri, *see* H., p. 197.

## Saline County

History of Saline County, Missouri . . . St. Louis: Missouri Hist. Co., 1881. 974 pp. (Computerized index. Park City, Utah: Hamilton Computer Service, 1978.)

Past and Present of Saline County, Missouri, by Hon. William B. Napton. Indianapolis, Ind.: B.F. Bowen, 1910. 932 pp.

History of Saline County, ed. by A.H. Orr, et al. [N.p., 1967.] 546 pp. (Repr. Marceline: Walsworth Pub. Co., 1967.)

## Schuyler County

History of . . . Schuyler County, 1888, *see* A., p. 197.

A History of Schuyler County, Missouri. N.p.: Swanson & Ford, 1909-10.

## Scotland County

History of . . . Scotland County, 1887, *see* F., p. 197.

## Scott County

Historical Account of the County of . . . Scott, 1888, in History of Southeast Missouri, *see* H., p. 197.

## Shelby County

History of . . . Shelby County, 1884, *see* Monroe County.

General History of Shelby County, Missouri. Chicago: H. Taylor & Co., 1911. xvi, 671 pp.

## Stoddard County

Historical Account of the County of . . . Stoddard, 1888, in History of Southeast Missouri, *see* H., p. 197.

## Sullivan County

History of . . . Sullivan County, 1888, see A., p. 197.

## Texas County

History of . . . Texas County, 1889, *see* E., p. 197.

## Warren County

History of . . . Warren County, 1885, *see* St. Charles County.

Portrait and Biographical Record of . . . Warren County, 1895, *see* St. Charles County.

## Washington County

History of . . . Washington County, 1888, *see* C., p. 197.

## Wayne County

Historical Account of the County of . . . Wayne, 1888, in History of Southeast Missouri, see H., p. 197.

Wayne County, Missouri, by Rose F. Cramer. Cape Girardeau: Ramfre Pr., 1972. 734 pp.

## Webster County

History of . . . Webster County, 1889, *see* E., p. 197.

History of Webster County, 1855-1955, by F.W. George. [Springfield?: N.p., 1956?] 264 pp.

A History of Webster County; Commemorating the Celebration of Webster County's Centennial, 1955. Seymour: J.D. Stanard, 1961. 76 leaves.

## Worth County

The History of . . . Worth County, 1882, *see* Gentry County.

## Wright County

History of . . . Wright County, 1889, *see* E., p. 197.

# MONTANA

## Regional

Illustrated History of the Yellowstone Valley, Embracing the Counties of Park, Sweet Grass, Carbon, Yellowstone, Rosebud, Custer and Dawson, State of Montana. Spokane, Wash.: Western Hist. Pub. Co., 1907. xxi, 669 pp.

## Big Horn County

Lookin' Back, Big Horn County, by Big Horn County Historical Society. Hardin: Western Pubs., 1976. 338 pp.

## Blaine County

In the Land of Chinook; or, the Story of Blaine County, by Alva J. Noyes. Helena: State Pub. Co., 1917. 152 pp.

Trial and Triumph: 101 Years in North Central Montana, by Janet S. Allison. [Chinook?:] North Central Montana Cowbelles [1968]. iv, 211 pp. (Blaine, Hill and Northern Chouteau Counties.)

## Broadwater County

Broadwater Bygones: a History of Broadwater County, by Broadwater County Historical Society. Bozeman: Color World of Montana, 1977. 309 pp.

## Carbon County

History . . . of Carbon County, 1907, in Illustrated History of Yellowstone Valley, *see* above.

## Carter County

The Big North, by James B. Armstrong. [Helena, 1965]. 106, 70 pp.

## Chouteau County

Trails, Trials and Tributes. N.p.: Egly Country Club, 1958. 104 pp.

[History of . . . Chouteau County], 1968, *see* Blaine County.

## Custer County

History . . . of Custer County, 1907, in Illustrated History of Yellowstone Valley, *see* above.

213

*Custer County (cont.)*

Fanning the Embers. [Billings: Gazette Pr. & Litho., 1971.] xii, 580 pp.

## Daniels County

Daniels County History, by Daniels County History Committee. Great Falls: Blue Pr. and Letter Co., 1977. 1,014 pp.

## Dawson County

History . . . of Dawson County, 1907, in Illustrated History of Yellowstone Valley, *see* p. 213.

## Deer Lodge County

In the Shadow of Mount Haggin: the Story of Anaconda and Deer Lodge County, 1863-1976, by Deer Lodge Historical Group. Anaconda: Leader Pubs., 1975. 228 pp.

## Fergus County

A History of Fergus County, Montana, 1879-1915, by Anna Zellick. Chicago: Univ. of Chicago, 1945. (M.A. thesis)

## Flathead County

The Story of the Tobacco Plains Country: the Autobiography of a Community, ed. by Olga Weydemeyer Johnson, et al. [Rexford:] N.p., 1950. x, 273 pp.

## Gallatin County

Early History of Gallatin County, by Lina E. Houston. Bozeman: Bozeman Chronicle Pr., 1933. 58 pp.

Gallatin: a Century of Progress, by Morrill G. Burlingame. Bozeman: Artcraft Pr., 1964. 106 pp.

Gallatin County's Heritage: a Report of Progress, 1805-1916. Bozeman: Gallatin County Bicentennial Comm., 1976. 106 pp.

## Garfield County

Garfield County, the Golden Years, by Fern E. Schilreff and J.M. Shawver. Jordan: Tribune Pubs., 1969. 445 pp.

Garfield County, 1919-1969, by Garfield County High School. Jordan: N.p., n.d. 226 pp.

## Golden Valley

Dawn in Golden Valley: a County in Montana, by Albie Gordon, et al. N.p., 1971. 375 pp.

## Granite County

The Silver Empire, by Garnet Stephenson. [N.p., 1966.] 58 pp.

## Hill County

[History of Hill County], 1968, *see* Blaine County.

Grit, Guts and Gusto: a History of Hill County, by Hill County Centennial Comm. Havre: N.p., 1976. 505 pp. (Index. Havre: Fort Assiniboine Gen. Soc., 1984.)

## Judith Basin County

Furrows and Trails in Judith Basin. Bicentennial History. N.p., 1976. 309 pp.

## Lewis & Clark County

Twentieth Century Souvenir, Lewis and Clark County. N.p., n.d. 191 pp.

## Liberty County

Our Heritage in Liberty County. Chester: Liberty Co. Museum, 1976. 511 pp.

## Madison County

Pioneer Trails and Trials: Madison County, 1863-1920. Bicentennial ed. Virginia City: N.p., 1976. 1,029 pp.

## Meagher County

Meagher County: an Early-Day Pictorial History, 1867-1967 . . . White Sulphur Springs: Meagher Co. News [1968]. 76 pp.

## Mineral County

108 Years of History, by Montana Historical Society of Mineral County. Superior: Independent Pubs., 1976. 85 pp.

## Park County

History . . . of Park County, 1907, in Illustrated History of Yellowstone Valley, *see* p. 213.

## Petroleum County

The Creation of Petroleum County . . . by Joanne M.G. Hassing. Missoula: Univ. of Montana, 1966. 187 pp.

## Phillips County

The Yesteryears, comp. by Phillips County Historical Society. Malta: The Soc., 1978. 583 pp.

## Pondera County

Pondera, a County History, by Pondera History Association. Great Falls: Blue Pr. and Letter Co., 1968. 179 pp.

## Powder River County

Echoing Footsteps: Powder River County . . . [Butte: Ashton Pr. & Engr. Co., 1967.] xxiv, 719 pp.

## Roosevelt County

Roosevelt County's Treasured Years: a History, 1800-1976, by Leota Hoye. Great Falls: Blue Pr. and Letter Co., 1976. 1,084 pp.

## Rosebud County

History . . . of Rosebud County, 1907, in Illustrated History of Yellowstone Valley, *see* p. 213.

They Came and They Stayed, a Rosebud County History, by Rosebud Co. Bicentennial Historical Committee. Billings: Western Pr. and Litho., 1977. 424 pp.

## Sheridan County

Sheridan's Daybreak; a Story of Sheridan County and Its Pioneers, comp. by Magnus Aasheim. [Great Falls: Blue Pr. and Letter Co., 1970.] vi, 1,007 pp.

## Sweet Grass County

History . . . of Sweet Grass County, 1907, in Illustrated History of Yellowstone Valley, *see* p. 213.

Pioneer Society of Sweet Grass County. Pioneer Memories. Bozeman: Bozeman Business Service, 1960. 285 pp.

## Toole County

Echoes from the Prairies . . . History of North Toole County, by Prairie Homemakers. Shelby: Shelby Promoter [1976]. 668 pp.

## Treasure County

Tales of Treasure County, ed. by Ruth Carrington and E. Mackley. Billings: Times Pubs., 1976. 151 pp.

## Valley County

Local Community History of Valley County. Glasgow: Federation of Women's Clubs, 1925. 78 pp.

## Wheatland County

Yesteryears and Pioneers [Wheatland County], by Harlowton Women's Club Pioneer History Committee. Harlowton: N.p., 1972. 417 pp.

## Wibaux County

Wibaux's Golden Jubilee, by Wilbaux Golden Jubilee Committee. Wibaux: Gazette Pubs., 1961. 136 pp.

Trails Along Beaver Creek: a Chronicle of Wibaux, Montana, by Irene J. Jones. Wibaux: Wibaux Pioneer Gazette, 1976. 229 pp.

## Yellowstone County

History . . . of Yellowstone County, 1907, in Illustrated History of Yellowstone Valley, *see* p. 213.

# NEBRASKA

## Regional

Biographical and Historical Memoir of Adams, Clay, Hall and Hamilton Counties, Nebraska . . . Chicago: Goodspeed Pub. Co., 1890. 784 pp.

History of Elkhorn Valley: an Album of History and Biography . . . of Dodge, Cuming, Stanton, Madison, Antelope and Holt Counties, by C.H. Scoville. Chicago: National Pub. Co., 1892. xii, 779 pp. (Repr. with name index. Evansville, Ind.: Unigraphic, for Eastern Nebraska Gen. Soc., 1977. xxvi, 779, 125 pp.)

History of Western Nebraska and Its People, General History, Cheyenne, Box Butte, Deuel, Garden, Sioux, Kimball, Morrill, Sheridan, Scotts Bluff, Banner, and Dawes Counties . . . by Grant L. Shumway. 3 vols. Lincoln: Western Pub. & Engraving Co., 1921. (Originally Julius S. Morton's Illustrated History of Nebraska.)

History of Box Butte County, Nebraska . . . from 1886 to 1938, Its Neighboring Counties of Dawes, Sioux, Scotts Bluff, Morrill and Sheridan . . . by Anna N. Phillips and V.D. Ball. [Hemingford: Leger Pr., 1939.] 230 pp.

A History and Historic Sites Survey of Johnson, Nemaha, Pawnee and Richardson Counties in Southeastern Nebraska, by John Q. Magie. Lincoln: Nebraska State Hist. Soc., 1969. xv, 158 leaves.

☙　　☙　　☙

## Adams County

Biographical and Historical Memoir of Adams County, 1890, *see* above.

Past and Present of Adams County, Nebraska, by Judge William R. Burton and D.J. Lewis. 2 vols. Chicago: S.J. Clarke Pub. Co., 1916. 475, 324 pp. (Index to Vol. 1. Hastings: Adams County Hist. Soc., 1978. 53 pp.)

Adams County; the People, 1872-1972, ed. by Dorothy W. Creigh. Hastings: Hastings Centennial Comm., 1971. vi, 311 pp.

Adams County: a Story of the Great Plains, 1872-1972, by Dorothy W. Creigh. Hastings: County-Hastings Centennial Comm., 1972. xii, 1,106 pp.

## Antelope County

History of . . . Antelope County, 1892, in History of Elkhorn Valley, *see* above.

History of Antelope County, Nebraska, from . . . 1868 to . . . 1883, by A.J. Leach. [Chicago: R.R. Donnelley & Sons Co.], 1909. 262 pp. (Repr. Louisville, Ky.: Lost Cause Pr., 1976.)

*Antelope County (cont.)*

Early Day Stories, by A.J. Leach. Norfolk: Huse Pub. Co., 1916. 244 pp.

History of Antelope County, 1883-1973. Neligh: Service Pr., 1976. 136 pp.

## Arthur County

Arthur County History, by W.H. Dorris. Arthur: Author, 1962. 36 pp.

## Banner County

History of . . . Banner County, 1921, in History of Western Nebraska, *see* p. 218.

Banner County and Its People. 2 vols. Marceline, Mo.: Walsworth Pub. Co., for Banner County Hist. Soc., 1982. 555, 429 pp.

Banner County, by M. George. David: C. & D. Pr., 1983. 373 pp.

## Blaine County

Settlement of Blaine County, 1977, *see* Loup County.

## Boone County

Pioneers of the West . . . by John Turner. Cincinnati, Ohio: Jennings & Pye [1903]. 404 pp. (Experiences of an English family in early days of Boone County.)

## Box Butte County

History of . . . Box Butte County, 1921, in History of Western Nebraska, *see* p. 218.

History of Box Butte County . . . 1886 to 1938, *see* p. 218.

## Boyd County

History of Boyd County, Nebraska, comp. by Luree Snider. [Lynch: Lynch Herald], 1938. 99 pp.

## Brown County

Days of Yore: Early History of Brown County, Nebraska, by Lillian L. Jones. Ainsworth: Author, 1937. 56 pp.

Pioneer Stories of Brown, Keya Paha and Rock Counties, by Shirley M. Skinner. Ainsworth: Brown County Hist. Soc., 1980. 769 pp.

## Buffalo County

Buffalo County, Nebraska . . . by Samuel C. Bassett. 2 vols. Chicago: S.J. Clarke Pub. Co., 1910. 392, 451 pp.

*Buffalo County (cont.)*

Where the Buffalo Roamed; Stories of Early Days in Buffalo County, Nebraska. Nebraska Centennial, 1867-1967, comp. by Kearney Business and Professional Women's Club. [Shenandoah, Iowa: World Pub. Co., 1967.] 543 pp.

## Burt County

Victory: Burt County, Nebraska, in the World War . . . Tekamah: Burt County Herald, 1919. 160 pp.

A History of Burt County, Nebraska from 1803 to 1929, by Douglas C. Sutherland. Wahoo: Ludi Pr. Co., 1929. 283 pp.

## Butler County

The Centennial History of Butler County, Nebraska, by George L. Brown. Lincoln: Journal Co., 1876. 34 pp.

Butler County History. Dallas, Tex.: Taylor Pub. Co., for Butler County Hist. Soc., David City, 1982. 306 pp.

## Cass County

Early History of Cass County, by Alice P. Perry. (Pp. 63-188 of Premium List, 1967, Cass County Fair.) N.p.: Cass County Agricultural Soc., 1967. 200 pp.

Centennial History of Plattsmouth City and Cass County, Nebraska . . . comp. by Albert L. Child. Plattsmouth: Herald Book & Job Pr., 1877. 84 pp.

Pioneer Stories of Cass County, by Cass County Historical Society. Nehawka: Nehawka Enterprise, 1936? 100 pp.

Early Settlement in Eastern Nebraska: a Study of Cass County, by Milton E. Holtz. Lincoln: Univ. of Nebraska, 1964. 182 pp. (M.A. thesis)

## Cedar County

History of Cedar County, Nebraska, by J. Mike McCoy. N.p.: Priv. pr., 1937. 189 pp.

## Chase County

Chase County History. Centennial ed. Vol. 1, 1st pr., 1938, 2d, 1963, 3d, 1965, 29 pp.; Vol. 2, 1965, 84 pp.; Vol. 3, 1969, 60 pp.; Vol. 4, 1971, 59 pp. Imperial: Chase County Hist. Soc., 1938-71.

## Cherry County

A History of Cherry County, Nebraska . . . by Charles S. Reece. [Simeon: N.p., 1945.] 173 pp.

North Country; The Old Town, 1880-1889, by Olive Van Metre. History of Cherry County, Nebraska. Lincoln: Ethel Dedring, 1984. 238 pp.

# Cheyenne County

History of Cheyenne County, 1921, in History of Western Nebraska, *see* p. 218.

# Clay County

Biographical and Historical Memoirs of . . . Clay County, 1890, *see* p. 218.

History of . . . Clay County, 1921, *see* Hamilton County.

# Colfax County

Colfax County, the Best County in the Best State in the Union, by Fred L. Wertz. Schuyler: Wertz Pr. & Bindery, 1902. 75 pp.

History of Colfax County, Nebraska's Centennial Year, 1867-1967. [Schuyler: N.p.], 1957. 32 pp.

# Cuming County

History of Cuming County, Nebraska, by E.N. Sweet. Lincoln: Journal Co., 1876. 52 pp.

History of Cuming County, Nebraska . . . by Bartlett O'Sullivan. Fremont: Fremont Tribune, 1884. 176 pp.

History of . . . Cuming County, 1892, in History of Elkhorn Valley, *see* p. 218.

# Custer County

Solomon Devore Butcher's Pioneer History of Custer County . . . Broken Bow [Denver, Colo.: Merchant's Pub. Co.], 1901. 403 pp. (Repr. Denver, Colo.: Sage Books, 1965. x, 410 pp.)

History of Custer County, Nebraska, by W.L. Gaston and A.R. Humphrey. Lincoln: Western Pub. and Engraving Co., 1919. 1,175 pp.

Pioneer Stories of Custer County, Nebraska . . . comp. by Emerson R. Purcell. Broken Bow: E.R. Purcell, 1936. 193 pp.

Clear Creek Echoes: History of Westerville and Custer County Area, by Charles Myers. Arcadia: N.p., 1977. 330 pp.

# Dakota County

Warner's History of Dakota County, Nebraska . . . with Biographical Sketches . . . by Moses M. Warner. Lyons: Mirror Job Office, 1893. 387 pp. (Repr. Evansville, Ind.: Unigraphic, 1974.)

Dakota County History, by George Molstad. Dakota City: Dakota County Hist. Soc., and Dallas, Tex.: Taylor Pub. Co., 1982. 383 pp.

# Dawes County

History of . . . Dawes County, 1921, in History of Western Nebraska, *see* p. 218.

*Dawes County (cont.)*

History of the County of Dawes, 1939, in History of Box Butte, *see* p. 218.

## Deuel County

History of . . . Deuel County, 1921, in History of Western Nebraska, *see* p. 218.

## Dixon County

History of Dixon County, Nebraska . . . by William N. Huse. Norfolk: Daily New Pr., 1896. 372 pp.

Dixon County, comp. by Dixon County Book Committee. Dallas, Tex.: Taylor Pub. Co., 1982. 348 pp.

## Dodge County

History . . . of Dodge County, 1892, in History of Elkhorn Valley, *see* p. 218.

Progressive Men of Nebraska. Dodge County ed. . . . with Historical Review, ed. by Daniel M. Carr. Fremont: Progress Pub. Co., 1902. 170 leaves.

History of Dodge and Washington Counties, by William H. Buss and T.T. Osterman. 2 vols. Chicago: American Hist. Soc., 1921. 455, 921 pp. (Index. Fremont: Eastern Nebraska Gen. Soc., 1982. 98 pp.)

## Douglas County

Omaha and Douglas County, by Arthur C. Wakeley. 2 vols. Chicago: S.J. Clarke, 1917. 472, 997 pp.

Omaha and Douglas County: a Panoramic History, by Dorothy D. Dustin. Woodland Hills, Calif.: Windsor Pubs., 1980. 199 pp.

## Dundy County

Dundy County Heritage: a Bicentennial Commemorative Edition. 2 vols. N.p.: Dundy County Extension Council, 1976. 492 pp.

## Fillmore County

Pioneer Stories of the Pioneers of Fillmore and Adjoining Counties, by George R. McKeith. Exeter: Pr. of Fillmore County News [1915]. 82 pp.

The Fillmore County Story, ed. by Wilbur G. Gaffney. Geneva: Geneva Community Grange No. 403, 1968. vi, 398 pp.

## Franklin County

History of Franklin County . . . by Michael O'Sullivan. Lincoln: State Journal Co., 1873. 74 pp.

Historical Highlights of Franklin County, 1867-1967, by Barbara Bonham. Campbell: C. & L. Pub., 1967. 146 pp.

# Furnas County

Building a New Empire, by Nathaniel M. Ayers. New York: Broadway Pub. Co. [1910]. 221 pp. (Early Days in Furnas County.)

Pioneer Stories of Furnas County, Nebraska, comp. from the files of the Beaver City Times-Tribune. University Place: Claflin Pr. Co., 1914. 212 pp.

Where the Wind Blows Free, by Burhl Gilpin and Burhl B. Gilpin. New York: Greenwich Book Pub. [1965]. 172 pp.

# Gage County

History of Gage County, Nebraska . . . by Hugh J. Dobbs. Lincoln: Western Pub. & Engraving Co., 1918. 1,100 pp.

Gage County History, by Gage County Historical Society. Dallas, Tex.: Taylor Pub. Co., 1983. 363 pp.

# Garden County

History of . . . Garden County, 1921, in History of Western Nebraska, *see* p. 218.

# Garfield County

Garfield County Roundup: a History, 1867-1967, comp. by Garfield County Historical Society. [Ord: Quiz Graphic Arts], 1967. 450 pp.

# Gosper County

Proud Heritage: Early History of Gosper County, by Gladys Shafer. Elwood: Elwood Bulletin Pr., 1969. 48 pp.

# Grant County

Grant County Neighbors and Friends, comp. by Grant County Historical Society. Hyannis: The Soc., 1980. 453 pp.

# Greeley County

The Pioneer History of Greeley County, Nebraska, by Edith S. McDermott. [Greeley: Citizen Pr. Co., 1939.] 174 pp. (Repr., 1977.)

# Hall County

Biographical and Historical Memoir of . . . Hall County, 1890, *see* p. 218.

Geschichte der ersten Ansiedlung von Hall County in Nebraska von 1857 . . . Grand Island: Staats-Anzeiger und Herold, 1907. 117 pp.

History of Hall County, Nebraska . . . by August F. Buechler and R.J. Barr. Lincoln: Western Pub. and Engraving Co., 1920. xxii, 965 pp.

# Hamilton County

Biographical and Historical Memoir of . . . Hamilton County, 1890, *see* p. 218.

History of Hamilton and Clay Counties, Nebraska, comp. by Dale P. Stough, ed. by George L. Burr and O.O. Buck. 2 vols. Chicago: S.J. Clarke Pub. Co., 1921. 850, 650 pp.

Centennial History of Hamilton County, comp. by Mrs. Bertha G. Bremer. [Aurora: Hamilton County Centennial Assoc.], 1967. 263.

# Hitchcock County

A Century of Progress: Hitchcock County, 1873-1973 . . . ed. by Lester C. Powers and D.I. Powers. Trenton: Hitchcock County News, 1973. 108 pp.

# Holt County

History of . . . Holt County, 1892, in History of Elkhorn Valley, *see* p. 218.

Rime of the Sandhills; a True Picture of Old Holt County Horsethief-Vigilante Days, by Will H. Spindler. Mitchell, S. Dak.: Educator Supply Co., 1941. 346 pp.

# Howard County

Life in an American Denmark, by Alfred C. Neilsen. Des Moines, Iowa: Bookstore, Grand View Coll. [1962]. 142 pp.

# Jefferson County

Pioneer Tales of the Oregon Trail and of Jefferson County, by Charles Dawson. Topeka, Kans.: Crane & Co., 1912. 488 pp.

Jefferson County: the Historic and Educational Spot of Nebraska, comp. by Levi Bloyd. 5 books. Fairbury: Author, 1955. 4, 12, 18, 20, 24 pp.

# Johnson County

Johnson County Centennial, 1856-1956. Tecumseh: Tecumseh Chieftain, 1956. 50 pp.

History . . . of Johnson County, 1969, in History and Historic Sites Survey . . . *see* p. 218.

# Kearney County

Heroes Without Medals; a Pioneer History of Kearney County, Nebraska, by Roy T. Band. Minden: Warp Pub. Co. [1952]. vii, 286 pp.

# Keya Paha County

Pioneer Stories of . . . Keya Paha County, 1980, *see* Brown County.

## Kimball County

History of . . . Kimball County, 1921, in History of Western Nebraska, *see* p. 218.

## Knox County

An Historical Sketch of Knox County, Nebraska, by Solomon Draper. Niobrar: Pioneer Pub. House, 1876. (Index, by Lela S. Rickerson. Omaha [1983]. With descriptive pamphlet of Knox County. Niobrar: Santee & Hill, 1883. With index, by Lela S. Rickerson. Omaha [1983]. 58 pp.)

## Lancaster County

Lincoln, the Capital City and Lancaster County, Nebraska, ed. by Andrew J. Sawyer. 2 vols. Chicago: S.J. Clarke Pub. Co., 1916. 358, 811 pp.

History of Lancaster County, Then and Now, by Elinor L. Brown. [Lincoln: N.p., 1971.] 244 pp.

## Lincoln County

An Illustrated History of Lincoln County, Nebraska . . . ed. by Ira L. Bare, et al. 2 vols. Chicago: American Hist. Soc., 1920. 418, 416 pp.

Settlement and Economic Development of Lincoln County, by Louis Breternitz. Boulder, Colo.: Univ. of Colorado, 1931. 161 pp. (M.A. thesis)

## Logan County

Logan County Through the Years, by Mrs. Jim Sturtz, et al., comp. by Historical Committee of the Logan County Extension Council. Logan: Logan County Extension Council, Hist. Comm. [1963]. [119] pp.

## Loup County

Settlement of Loup and Blaine Counties, by Colleen Switzer. Broken Bow: Purcell's Inc., 1977. 409 pp.

## Madison County

History of . . . Madison County, 1892, in History of Elkhorn Valley, *see* p. 218.

## Merrick County

History of Merrick County, by Clark E. Persinger. Central City: Nonpareil Pr., 1898. 111 pp.

Merrick County's 100th Year, 1858-1958 [by Miner Harris], for Merrick County Centennial Association. Central City: Assoc., 1958. 72 pp.

History of Merrick County, comp. by Merrick County History Book Committee. Central City: Merrick County Hist. Soc., 1981; Dallas, Tex.: Taylor Pub. Co., 1981. 417 pp.

# Morrill County

History of . . . Morrill County, 1921, in History of Western Nebraska . . . *see* p. 218.

History of . . . Morrill County, 1939, in History of Box Butte County . . . *see* p. 218.

# Nemaha County

Nemaha County, by John H. Dundas. [Auburn: N.p., 1902.] 220 pp.

History . . . of Nemaha County, 1969, in History and Historic Sites Survey, *see* p. 218.

# Nuckolls County

Pioneer Sketches, Nebraska and Texas [comp. by William W. Straley]. Rico, Tex.: Rico Pr. Co., 1915. 61 pp. (Contains sketches of Nuckolls County.)

A History of Nuckolls County, Nebraska, by V.R. Wilcox. Greeley, Colo.: Colorado State Coll., 1935. 178 pp. (M.A. thesis)

From "Hoppers to Copters," Stories of Nuckolls County for 100 Years. [N.p.: Nuckolls County Centennial Comm., 1967.] 136 pp.

100 Years of Progress: a History of the First 100 Years of Nuckolls County, Nuckolls County Centennial. Superior: Superior Express, 1971. 78 pp.

# Otoe County

Otoe County, Nebraska, Written by the People of Otoe County, comp. by the Otoe County Historical Society, Otoe County Museum Society. Nebraska City: Otoe County Hist. Soc., 1983; Dallas, Tex.: Taylor Pub. Co., 1983. 301 pp.

# Pawnee County

Centennial History of Pawnee County, by Jos. L. Edwards. [Pawnee City:] N.p., 1876.

History . . . of Pawnee County, 1969, in History and Historic Sites, *see* p. 218.

Bicentennial Album of Pawnee County. McPherson, Kans.: Brand Iron, 1976. 400 pp.

# Perkins County

Memories of Perkins County, by J. Morgan Stevens. Astoria, Ill.: Stevens Pub., 1972? 121 pp.

# Phelps County

Complete Directory of Phelps County, Nebraska, comp. and pub. by W.H. Arnold. Kearney: Compiler, 1909. 186 pp.

*Phelps County (cont.)*

Early History of Phelps County, Nebraska, by Joseph G. Mitchell. Lincoln: Univ. of Nebraska, 1927. 97 pp. ts.

Heritage Progress, 1873-1980: a History of Phelps County, Nebraska. Dallas, Tex.: Taylor Pub. Co., for Phelps County Hist. Soc., Holdrege, 1981. 695 pp.

## Pierce County

Along Pioneer Trails in Pierce County, Nebraska, by Esther K. Hansen. [Pierce?: N.p., 1940.] 114 pp.

## Platte County

Past and Present of Platte County, Nebraska . . . George W. Phillips, supervising ed. 2 vols. Chicago: S.J. Clarke Pub. Co., 1915. 396, 668 pp.

History of Platte County, Nebraska, by Margaret Curry. Culver City: Murray & Gee, 1950. 1,011 pp.

## Polk County

Early Days in Polk County, by Mildred N. Flodman. Lincoln: Union Coll. Pr. [1966]. vii, 453 pp.

Our Polk Heritage. Osceola: Osceola Centennial Comm., 1975. 329 pp.

## Richardson County

History of Richardson County, Nebraska, by Lewis C. Edwards. Indianapolis, Ind.: B.F. Bowen, 1917. 1,417 pp. (Repr. 2 vols. Evansville, Ind.: Unigraphic, 1978.)

History . . . of Richardson County, 1969, in History and Historic Sites . . . *see* p. 218.

## Rock County

Those Who Came Before Us: a History of Rock County. Bassett: N.p., 1976. 162 pp.

Pioneer Stories of . . . Rock County, 1980, *see* Brown County.

## Saline County

Saline County: Nebraska History, Beginning in 1858, comp. by J.W. Kaura. Lincoln: Nebraska-Farmer Co. [1962]. 211 pp.

## Saunders County

Past and Present of Saunders County, Nebraska . . . Charles Perky, supervising ed. 2 vols. Chicago: S.J. Clarke Pub. Co., 1915. 290, 655 pp.

*Saunders County (cont.)*

Saunders County, Nebraska, sponsored by the Saunders County Historical Society, written by the People of Saunders County, Nebraska. Wahoo: Saunders County Hist. Soc., 1983. 519 pp.

## Scotts Bluff County

History of . . . Scotts Bluff County, 1921, in History of Western Nebraska, *see* p. 218.

Scotts Bluff and the North Platte Valley, comp. by Thomas L. Greene. Scotts Bluff: Scottsbluff Star Herald Pr. Co., 1950. 99 pp.

History of . . . Scotts Bluff County, 1939, in History of Box Butte County, *see* p. 218.

## Seward County

History of Seward County, Nebraska . . . by William W. Cox. Lincoln: State Journal Co., 1888. 290 pp. (2d ed. University Place: J.L. Claflin, 1905. 455, 223 pp.)

General History of Seward County, Nebraska, by John H. Waterman. Beaver Crossing: N.p., 1916. 291 pp. ([Rev. ed.] Beaver Crossing: N.p., 1927. 348 pp.)

Early Days in Seward County, Nebraska, by William H. Smith. [Seward:] Author, 1937. 103 pp.

On a Bend of the River: the Story of Seward and Seward County, Nebraska . . . by Jane Graff, ed. by S.J. Korinko. Henderson: Service Pr., 1967. 220 pp.

## Sheridan County

History of . . . Sheridan County, 1921, in History of Western Nebraska, *see* p. 218.

History of . . . Sheridan County, 1939, in History of Box Butte County, *see* p. 218.

Recollections of Sheridan County, Sheridan County Historical Society. N.p.: Iron Man Industries, 1976. 670 pp.

## Sherman County

A Brief History of Sherman County, Nebraska, by Meroe J. Owens. [Norfolk:] Norfolk Daily News, 1952. 258 pp.

## Sioux County

History of . . . Sioux County, 1921, in History of Western Nebraska, *see* p. 218.

History of . . . Sioux County, 1939, in History of Box Butte County, *see* p. 218.

Sioux County: Memoirs of Its Pioneers . . . ed. by Ruth Van Ackeren. [Harrison: Harrison Sun-News, 1967.] v, 304 pp.

## Stanton County

History of . . . Stanton County, 1892, in History of Elkhorn Valley, *see* p. 218.

A History of Stanton County, Nebraska, by Meroe J. Outhouse (Meroe J. Owens). Greeley, Colo.: Colorado State Teachers Coll., 1944. 165 pp. (M.A. thesis) (Repr.? Loup City: Author, 1969. 244 pp.)

## Thayer County

Brief Description of Thayer County, Nebraska . . . by Erasmus M. Correll. Hebron: Journal Steam Pr. House, 1885. 48 pp.

## Thomas County

Thomas and Surrounding Counties, collected by Willard J. Lynch, comp. by Sherrill F. Daniels. Omaha: Lynch, 1980. 163 pp.

## Valley County

History of Valley County, by Elizabeth Shaver. Lincoln: Univ. of Nebraska, n.d. 153 pp. (M.A. thesis)

## Washington County

History of Washington County, Nebraska . . . by John T. Bell. Omaha: Herald Pr. House, 1876. 64 pp.

History of . . . Washington County, 1921, *see* Dodge County.

A History of Washington County, Nebraska, by Forrest B. Shrader. [Omaha: Magic City Pr. Co., 1937.] iv, 350 pp.

Portal to the Plains: a History of Washington County, Nebraska, by Niel M. Johnson. Lincoln: North Pr. [1974]. 48 pp.

Washington County History: the People of Washington County. Fort Calhoun: Washington County Hist. Assoc., 1980. 464 pp.

## Wayne County

History of Wayne County, Nebraska . . . with a View of the Territory in 1938, by Dorothy Nyberg. Wayne: Wayne Herald, 1938. 306 pp.

Wayne County History, by the People of Wayne County. Dallas, Tex.: Taylor Pub. Co., for Wayne County Hist. Soc., 1981. 320 pp.

## Webster County

A History of Webster County, Nebraska, by Edyth L. Beezley. Lincoln: Univ. of Nebraska, 1937. 142 [5] leaves. (M.A. thesis)

80 Years in Webster County . . . by Elmer A. Thomas. [Hastings?: Author, 1953.] 148 pp.

## Wheeler County

Wheeler County Story Book, by Barbara Day and K. Keinzan. N.p., 1977. 210 pp.

## York County

Old Settlers' History of York County . . . [York:] N.p., 1913. 175 pp.

York County, Nebraska and Its People . . . with a Condensed History, by T.E. Sedgwick. 2 vols. Chicago: S.J. Clarke Pub. Co., 1921.

Cradle Days in York County. A Compilation of Historical Sketches First Published in The York Republican. York: York Republican, 1937. 108 pp.

# NEVADA

## Churchill County

Dig No Graves, by Marcia De Braga. [Sparks: N.p., 1964.] 75 pp.

## Elko County

The History and Development of Elko County, by Lulu H. Hurley. [Reno: Univ. of Nevada], 1910. (B.A. thesis)

Aged in Sage, by Jean McElrath. [Wells?: Recorder, 1964.] xiii, 174 pp.

Nevada's Northwest Frontier, by Edna B. Patterson, et al. Sparks: Western Pr. Pub. Co., 1969. (Much on Elko County.)

## Eureka County

Eureka and Its Resources, a Complete History of Eureka County, Nevada . . . by Molinelli, Lambert & Co. San Francisco: H. Keller & Co., 1879. 109 pp.

## Lander County

The History of Lander County, by Buster L. King. [Reno:] Univ. of Nevada, 1954. (M.A. thesis)

## Lincoln County

Lincoln County, Nevada, 1864-1909; History of a Mining Region, by James W. Hulse. Reno: Univ. of Nevada Pr., 1971. 89 pp.

## Pershing County

Ghosts of Humboldt Region; a Glimpse of Pershing County's Past, by Dave Basso. [Sparks: Western Pr. Pub. Co., 1970.] x, 189 pp.

## Washoe County

General History and Resources of Washoe County, Nevada, comp. by N.A. Hummel. Reno: Evening Gazette Job Pr., 1888. (Repr. Verdi: Sagebrush Pr., 1969.)

## White Pine County

White Pine Lang Syne; a True History of White Pine County, Nevada, by Effie Read. Denver, Colo.: Big Mountain Pr. [1965]. 318 pp.

# NEW HAMPSHIRE

## Belknap County

History of . . . Belknap County, 1885, *see* Merrimack County.

## Carroll County

History of Carroll County . . . ed. by Georgia D. Merrill. Boston: W.A. Fergusson & Co., 1889. xiii, 987 pp. (Repr. Somersworth: New Hampshire Pub. Co., 1971.)

## Cheshire County

Gazetteer of Cheshire County, 1736-1885 . . . by Hamilton Child. 2 parts in 1. Syracuse, N.Y.: Child, 1885. 560, 272 pp.

History of Cheshire and Sullivan Counties, by Duane H. Hurd. 2 vols. in 1. Philadelphia: J.W. Lewis & Co., 1886.

Historic Homes of Cheshire County, New Hampshire, by Marjorie W. Smith. 2 vols. [Brattleboro, Vt.: Griswold Offset Pr., 1968-71.] (From Keene Evening Sentinel, 1962-.)

## Coos County

Historical Sketches . . . in Coos County and Vicinity . . . 1754-1785, by Grant Powers. Haverhill: J.F.C. Hayes, 1841. 240 pp. ([Repr.?] Haverhill: H. Merrill, 1880.)

History of Coos County . . . [comp. by Mrs. Georgia D. Merrill]. Syracuse, N.Y.: W.A. Fergusson & Co., 1888. 956 pp. (Repr. Somersworth: New Hampshire Pub. Co., 1972.)

Spiked Boots, Sketches of the North Country, by Robert E. Pike. [Eatontown, N.J.: N.p., 1959.] 193 pp. ([New ed.?] 1961. 266 pp.)

## Grafton County

Gazetteer of Grafton County, New Hampshire, 1709-1886 . . . comp. by Hamilton Child. 2 parts in 1. Syracuse, N.Y.: Child, 1886. 644, 380 pp.

## Hillsborough County

History of Hillsborough County, comp. under the supervision of Duane Hamilton Hurd. Philadelphia: J.W. Lewis & Co., 1885. ix, 748 pp.

## Merrimack County

History of Merrimack and Belknap Counties . . . ed. by Duane Hamilton Hurd. Philadelphia: J.W. Lewis & Co., 1885. x, 933 pp.

## Rockingham County

History of Rockingham and Strafford Counties . . . comp. under the supervision of Duane Hamilton Hurd. Philadelphia: J.W. Lewis & Co., 1882. xiv, 890 pp.

History of Rockingham County, and Representative Citizens, by Charles A. Hazlett. Chicago: Richmond-Arnold Pub. Co., 1915. 1,306 pp.

## Strafford County

History of . . . Strafford County, 1882, *see* Rockingham County.

History of Strafford County, and Representative Citizens, by John Scales. Chicago: Richmond-Arnold Pub. Co., 1914. 953 pp.

## Sullivan County

History of . . . Sullivan County, 1886, *see* Cheshire County.

History of Sullivan County and Claremont, New Hampshire. N.p., n.d.

Sullivan County Recollections, by Henry H. Metcalf. Rev. N.p., 189-? 146 pp. and repub. from the Argus-Champion. Newport: Argus Pr., 1926. 140 pp.

# NEW JERSEY

## Regional

Reminiscences of Old Gloucester, or, Incidents in the History of the Counties of Gloucester, Atlantic and Camden . . . by Isaac Mickle. Philadelphia: T. War, 1845. (2d ed. Camden: Philotechnic Inst., 1877. 106 pp.)

History of the Counties of Gloucester, Salem and Cumberland . . . by Thomas Cushing and Charles E. Sheppard. Philadelphia: Everts & Peck, 1883. xiv, 728 pp. (Repr. Woodbury: Gloucester County Hist. Soc., 1974. 740 pp. Index, by Donald A. Sinclair. Woodbury: Gloucester County Hist. Soc., 1975. 272 pp.)

Biographical and Portrait Cyclopedia of the Third Congressional District of New Jersey, Comprising Middlesex, Monmouth and Somerset Counties, Together with an Historical Sketch of Each County, ed. by Samuel T. Riley. Philadelphia: Biographical Pub. Co., 1896. 1,039 pp.

Biographical, Genealogical and Descriptive History of the First Congressional District of New Jersey . . . 2 vols. New York: Lewis Pub. Co., 1900. (Includes Counties of Camden, Cape May, Cumberland, Gloucester, and Salem.)

Northwestern New Jersey: a History of Somerset, Morris, Hunterdon, Warren and Sussex Counties, ed. by A. Van Doran Honeyman. 4 vols. New York: Lewis Hist. Pub. Co., 1927.

The Jersey Shore: a Social and Economic History of the Counties of Atlantic, Cape May, Monmouth and Ocean, by Harold F. Wilson. 3 vols. New York: Lewis Hist. Pub. Co., 1953.

🌿          🌿          🌿

## Atlantic County

History of County of . . . Atlantic, 1845, in Reminiscences of Old Gloucester, *see* above.

The Daily Union History of Atlantic City and County, New Jersey . . . by John F. Hall. Atlantic City: Daily Union Pr. Co., 1900. 517 pp.

Early History of Atlantic County, pub. by Atlantic County Historical Society. Kutztown, Pa.: Kutztown Pub. Co., 1915. 179 pp.

Social and Economic History of County of Atlantic, 1953, in The Jersey Shore, *see* above.

Absegami Yesteryear: History of Atlantic County, by Jack Boucher. [Somers Point:] Atlantic County Hist. Soc., 1963.

## Bergen County

History of Bergen and Passaic Counties . . . comp. under the supervision of W.W. Clayton. Philadelphia: Everts & Peck, 1882. 577 pp.

*Bergen County (cont.)*

Genealogical History of . . . Bergen County, 1900, *see* Hudson County.

History of Bergen County . . . by J.M. Van Valen. New York: New Jersey Pub. & Engr. Co., 1900. 691 pp.

Old Bergen: History and Reminiscences . . . by Daniel Van Winkle. Jersey City: J.W. Harrison [1902]. ix, 319 pp.

History of Bergen County, 1630-1923, Frances A. Westervelt, supervising ed. 3 vols. New York: Lewis Hist. Pub. Co., 1923.

Three Hundred Years; the Story of the Hackensack Valley, Its Settlement and Growth, by Francis C. Koehler. Chester: L. Biebigheiser Pr. [1940]. 128 pp.

The History and Government of Bergen County . . . prepared by the New Jersey Historical Records Survey Project . . . W.P.A. Newark: Hist. Records Survey, 1941. 182 pp.

Bergen County Panorama . . . by Writer's Program, W.P.A. [Elizabeth: Colby & McGowan, 1941.] x, 356 pp.

Beautiful Bergen: the Story of Bergen County. [Ridgewood: J.L. Sheridan, 1962.] 51 pp.

## Burlington County

History of Burlington and Mercer Counties . . . by E.M. Woodward and J.F. Hageman. Philadelphia: Everts & Peck, 1883. viii, 888 pp.

## Camden County

History of County of . . . Camden, 1845, in Reminiscences of Old Gloucester, *see* p. 234.

The History of Camden County, by George R. Prowell. Philadelphia: L.J. Richards, 1886. x, 769 pp.

History of . . . County of Camden, 1900, in Biographical . . . History of the First Congressional District of New Jersey, *see* p. 234.

The Civil and Political History of Camden County and Camden City, by Charles S. Boyer. [Camden: Priv. pr., 1922.] 56 pp.

Camden County, 1681-1931; 250th Anniversary; the Story of an Industrial Empire, by Paul F. Cranston. Camden: Camden County Chamber of Commerce, 1931. v, 193 pp.

Camden County Centennial, comp. by A.C. Corotis. 1844-1944. [Camden: Board of Chosen Freeholders, 1944.] 144 pp.

## Cape May County

Sketch of the Early History of Cape May County . . . by Maurice Beesley. Trenton: Office of the True American, 1857. 208 pp.

*Cape May County (cont.)*

The History of Cape May County, from the Aboriginal Times to the Present Day . . . by Lewis T. Stevens. Cape May: L.T. Stevens, 1897. 479 pp. (Index, comp. by Robert P. Baker. Bound Brook: Gen. Soc. of New Jersey, 1982. 48 pp.)

History of . . . County of Cape May, 1900, in Biographical . . . History of the First Congressional District of New Jersey, *see* p. 234.

Social and Economic History of County of . . . Cape May, 1953, in The Jersey Shore, *see* p. 234.

## Cumberland County

History of the Early Settlement and Progress of Cumberland County . . . by Lucius C. Elmer. Bridgeton: G.F. Nixon, 1869. 142 pp.

History of the County of . . . Cumberland, 1883, *see* p. 234.

History of . . . County of . . . Cumberland, 1900, in Biographical . . . History of the First Congressional District of New Jersey, *see* p. 234.

Historical Tales of Cumberland County . . . Comprehensive Enough to Cover the County's Early History, comp. by William C. Mulford. Bridgeton: Evening News Co. [1941]. 197 pp.

The Great Wilderness, by Margaret L. Mints. Millville: Wheaton Hist. Assoc. [1968.] 148 pp.

## Essex County

History of Essex and Hudson Counties, comp. by William H. Shaw. 2 vols. Philadelphia: Everts & Peck, 1884.

Essex County Illustrated . . . a Brief Sketch of the Early Settlement of Essex County . . . by Merit H.C. Vail. Newark: Pr. of L.J. Hardhaw, 1897. 266 pp.

The Municipalities of Essex County, 1666-1924 . . . ed. by Joseph F. Folsom. 4 vols. New York: Lewis Hist. Pub. Co., 1925.

Red Lion Rampant: an Informal History of Essex County, New Jersey, by Mary Arny. Montclair: N.p., 1965. 100 pp.

## Gloucester County

History of County of Gloucester, 1845, in Reminiscences of Old Gloucester, *see* p. 234.

History of County of Gloucester, 1883, *see* p. 234.

History of County of . . . Gloucester, 1900, in Biographical . . . History of the First Congressional District of New Jersey, *see* p. 234.

Under Four Flags, Old Gloucester County, 1686-1964; a History of Gloucester County, ed. by Hazel B. Simpson. Woodbury: Board of Chosen Freeholders, Gloucester Co. [1965]. xi, 125 pp.

*Gloucester County (cont.)*

Notes on Old Gloucester County, New Jersey, comp. and ed. by Frank H. Stewart. 4 vols. Camden and Woodbury: N.p., 1917-1964. (Repr. 4 vols. in 2. Baltimore: Genealogical Pub. Co., 1977. 662, 947 pp.)

## Hudson County

History of the County of Hudson, New Jersey . . . by C.H. Winfield. New York: Kennard & Hay, 1874. vii, 568 pp.

History of Hudson County, 1884, *see* Essex County.

Genealogical History of Hudson and Bergen Counties, New Jersey, by Cornelius B. Harvey. New York: New Jersey Gen. Pub. Co., 1900. 627 pp. (First 48 pp. are history, remainder "mug" book.)

Hudson County Today; Its History, People, Trades, Commerce, Institutions and Industries, comp. by Robert R. Stinson, ed. by R. Rieser. Union: Hudson Dispatch [1914]. 162 pp.

History of the Municipalities of Hudson County, New Jersey, 1630-1923, ed. by Daniel Van Winkle. 3 vols. New York: Lewis Hist. Pub. Co., 1924.

## Hunterdon County

The First Century of Hunterdon County . . . by George S. Mott. Flemington: E. Vosseller, 1878. 54 pp. ([Repr.] Flemington: Hunterdon County Hist. Soc., 1961.)

History of Hunterdon and Somerset Counties . . . comp. by James P. Snell. Philadelphia: Everts & Peck, 1881. 864 pp.

History of . . . Hunterdon County, 1927, in Northwestern New Jersey, *see* p. 234.

Traditions of Hunterdon, by John W. Lequear (or Jacob Magill?). Flemington: D.H. Moreau, 1957. 210 pp.

The First 250 Years of Hunterdon County, 1714-1964 . . . [Flemington: N.p. 1964?] 105 pp.

## Mercer County

History of Mercer County, 1883, *see* Burlington County.

A Sketch of Mercer, New Jersey, 1838-1928. Camden: N.p., 1928.

## Middlesex County

History of Middlesex County, 1882, *see* Union County.

History of Middlesex County, 1896, in Biographical . . . Cyclopedia of the Third Congressional District of New Jersey, *see* p. 234.

History of Middlesex County, 1664-1920, ed. by John P. Wall and H.E. Pickersgill. 3 vols. New York: Lewis Hist. Pub. 1921.

## Monmouth County

Old Times in Old Monmouth; Historical Reminiscences of Old Monmouth County . . . Now Monmouth and Ocean Counties . . . by Edwin Salter and G.C. Beekman. Freehold: Monmouth Democrat, 1874. 477 pp. (Repr. Freehold: James S. Yard, 1887. Repr. of 1887 ed., by Edwin Salter and G.C. Beekman. Baltimore: Genealogical Pub. Co., 1980. 474 pp.)

History of Monmouth County . . . by Franklin Ellis. Philadelphia: R.T. Peck, 1885. x, 902 pp.

A History of Monmouth and Ocean Counties . . . by Edwin Salter. Bayonne: E. Gardner, 1890. 442, lxxx pp.

History of . . . Monmouth County, 1896, in Biographical . . . Cyclopedia of the Third Congressional District of New Jersey, *see* p. 234.

History of Monmouth County, 1664-1920. 3 vols. New York: Chicago: Lewis Hist. Pub. Co., 1922.

From Indian Trail to Electric Rail: History of the Atlantic Highlands . . . by Thomas H. Leonard. Atlantic Highlands: Atlantic Highlands Journal, 1923. xvii, 66 pp.

This Old Monmouth of Ours, by William S. Hornor. Freehold: Moreau Bros., 1932. 444 pp. (Repr. Allenhurst: Morris Gen. Lib., 1974.)

Social and Economic History of the County of . . . Monmouth, 1953, in The Jersey Shore, *see* p. 234.

## Morris County

Annals of Morris County, by Joseph F. Tuttle. [N.p., 1876.] 127 pp.

History of Morris County . . . by Edmund D. Halsey, et al. New York: W.W. Munsell, 1882. 407 pp. (Repr. Morristown: Morris County Hist. Soc., 1967. Index of names to 1882, ed. by Ernest M. Hart. New Brunswick: Gen. Soc. of New Jersey, 1978.)

A History of Morris County . . . 1710-1913 . . . ed. by Henry C. Pitney, Jr. 2 vols. New York: Lewis Hist. Pub. Co., 1914.

History of . . . Morris County, 1927, in Northwestern New Jersey, *see* p. 234.

Archives and Historical Sketch, Morris County, prepared by Historical Records Survey, W.P.A. Morristown: Board of Chosen Freeholders, 1937. 135 pp.

Washington Valley: an Informal History, Morris County, by Barbara Hoskins, et al. Morristown?: N.p., 1960. 329 pp.

## Ocean County

Old Times in Old Monmouth . . . Now Monmouth and Ocean Counties, 1874, *see* Monmouth County.

Centennial History of Ocean County; Historical Reminiscences of Ocean County . . . by Edwin Salter. Toms River: New Jersey Courier, 1878. 84 pp.

*Ocean County (cont.)*

A History of Ocean County, 1890, *see* Monmouth County.

Social and Economic History of the County of . . . Ocean, 1953, in The Jersey Shore, *see* p. 234.

## Passaic County

Historical Sketch of the County of Passaic, Especially the First Settlements and Settlers, by William Nelson. Paterson: Chiswell & Wurts, 1877. 39 pp.

History of Passaic County, 1882, *see* Bergen County.

History of the City of Paterson and the County of Passaic, by William Nelson. Paterson: Press Pr. and Pub. Co., 1901. viii, 448 pp.

Short Sketches on Passaic County History, by Edward M. Graf. Paterson: Priv. pr., 1935. 27 nos.

## Salem County

History and Genealogy of Fenwick's Colony, by Thomas Shourds. Bridgetown: G.F. Nixon, 1876. 553 pp. (Index, comp. and pub. by Elizabeth Livermore. [Ann Arbor, Mich.: Univ. Microfilms, 1962.] 121 pp. Index of names . . . by William Patterson. Salem County Hist. Soc. Pubs., No. 2, 1961.) (Repr. with added index, by William Patterson. Baltimore: Genealogical Pub. Co., 1976. 581 pp.)

History of the County of . . . Salem, 1883, *see* p. 234.

History of . . . County of Salem, 1900, in Biographical . . . History of the First Congressional District of New Jersey, *see* p. 234.

Salem County in the Revolution, by Frank H. Stewart. [Camden: Sinnickson Chew, 1932.] 102 pp.

The History of Salem County, being the Story of John Fenwick's Colony . . . by Joseph S. Sickler. Salem: Sunbeam Pub. Co. [1937]. 390 pp.

Fenwick's Colony: Salem County Pictorial, 1675-1964. [Salem: Salem County Tercentenary Comm., 1964.] 191 pp.

## Somerset County

Centennial History of Somerset County, by Abraham Messler. Somerville: C.M. Jameson, 1878. 190 pp.

History of Somerset County, 1881, *see* Hunterdon County.

History of . . . Somerset County, 1896, in Biographical . . . Cyclopedia of the Third Congressional District of New Jersey, *see* p. 234.

First Things in Old Somerset: a Collection of Articles Relating to Somerset County, by Abraham Messler. Somerville: Somerville Pub. Co., 1899. 172 pp.

*Somerset County (cont.)*

Within a Jersey Circle: Tales of the Past, Grave and Gay . . . by George Quarrie. Somerville: Unionist-Gazette Assoc. [1910]. 332 pp.

History of Somerset . . . County, 1927, in Northwestern New Jersey, *see* p. 234.

Somerset County, 250 Years . . . Somerville: Somerset Pr. [1938]. 192 pp.

Historic Somerset, comp. by J. Van Horn. N.p.: Pub. by comp. for Hist. Societies of Somerset County, 1965. xxii, 223 pp.

## Sussex County

The Historical Directory of Sussex County, Containing a Brief Summary of Events from Its First Settlement . . . comp. and ed. by Edward A. Webb. [Andover?:] N.p., 1872. 142 pp.

History of Sussex and Warren Counties . . . comp. by James P. Snell, et al. Philadelphia: Everts & Peck, 1881. 748 pp. (Index, comp. by Beatrice M. Adams. Livingston: N.p., 1964. Repr. with index. 2 vols. Washington: Virginia A. Brown, 1982.)

Sussex County Sesqui-centennial, 1903 . . . ed. by Jacob L. Burnell. Newton: New Jersey Herald Pr. [1903]. 157 pp.

Memoirs and Reminiscences, Together with Sketches of the Early History of Sussex County, by Rev. Caspar Schaeffer. Hackensack: Priv. pr., 1907. 187 pp.

History of . . . Sussex County, 1927, in Northwestern New Jersey, *see* p. 234.

Sussex County; a History, by Warren D. Cummings. For the Rotary Club of Newton. [Newton?: N.p., 1964.] 68 pp.

## Union County

History of Union and Middlesex Counties . . . ed. by W. Woodford Clayton. Philadelphia: Everts & Peck, 1882. 885 pp.

History of Union County . . . ed. by Frederick W. Ricord. Newark: East Jersey Hist. Co., 1897. xiii, 656 pp.

History of Union County, 1664-1923, ed. by A. Van Doran Honeyman. 3 vols. New York: Lewis Hist. Pub. Co., 1923.

## Warren County

History of Warren County, 1881, *see* Sussex County.

History of Warren County, by George W. Cummins. New York: Lewis Hist. Pub. Co., 1911. vii, 433 pp.

History of . . . Warren County, 1927, in Northwestern New Jersey, *see* p. 234.

History and Directory of Warren County, comp. by Frank Shampanore. Washington: Shampanore & Sons, 1931. 706 pp.

# NEW MEXICO

## Regional

These Also Served: Brief Histories of Pioneers, Short Stories and Pictures Relative to Catron, Grant, Sierra, Socorro, and Valencia Counties of New Mexico, by Susan E. Lee. Las Lunas: S.E. Lee, 1960. xiv, 208 pp. (The counties are not listed below.)

🌿       🌿       🌿

## Bernalillo County
Bernalillo County, a Description of the Smallest and Richest County of New Mexico . . . [Santa Fe: N.p.], 1906. 45 pp.

## Chaves County
Chaves County Historical Encyclopedia, ed. by Elvis E. Fleming. N.p., 1974.

## Colfax County
Out in God's Country: a History of Colfax County, New Mexico, by Lawrence R. Murphy. [Springer: Springer Pub. Co., 1969.]

## Curry County
A Biographical History of Curry County, New Mexico, by Norrell G. Tate. Albuquerque: Univ. of New Mexico, 1934. (M.A. thesis)

Curry County, New Mexico; a Collection of Historical Material. High Plains Historical Foundation. Dallas, Tex.: Taylor Pub. Co., 1978. 572 pp.

## Eddy County
Eddy County, New Mexico to 1981. South Eastern New Mexico Historical Society. Carlsbad: Pr. of Craftsman Pr., 1982. 496 pp.

## Lincoln County
Violence in Lincoln County, 1869-1881; a New Mexico Item, by William A. Keleher. Albuquerque: Univ. of New Mexico Pr. [1957]. 390 pp.

History of the Lincoln County War, by M.G. Fulton, ed. by Robert M. Mullin. Tucson: Univ. of Arizona Pr., 1968. 433 pp.

Looking Over My Shoulder; Seventy-five Years in the Pecos Valley, by Cecil Bonney. Boswell: Hall-Poorbaugh Pr., 1971. xiv, 235 pp.

My Girlhood Among Outlaws, by Lilly Klasner, ed. by Eve Ball. Tucson: Univ. of Arizona Pr. [1972]. vi, 336. (Excerpts from J.S. Chisum's diary, 1878.)

## Luna County

The History of Luna County. Denning: N.p., 1978. 320 pp.

## McKinley County

Encounter with the Frontier, by Gary Tietjen. Los Alamos: N.p., 1969. 141 pp. (History of McKinley County and some of Valencia County.)

## Mora County

A History of Mora, 1835-1887, by Eugene J. Hanosh. Las Vegas: Highlands Univ., 1967. (M.A. thesis)

## Otero County

A Personalized History of Otero County, New Mexico, by Emily K. Lovell. Alamogordo: Star Pub. Co., 1963. 39 pp.

## Roosevelt County

A Brief History of Roosevelt County, New Mexico, by Maryl L. Robinson. N.p.: Univ. of Texas, 1947. (M.A. thesis)

Roosevelt County History and Heritage . . . ed. by Jean Burroughs. Portales: Bishop Pr. Co., 1975. xvi, 361 pp.

Early Settlers of Roosevelt County, New Mexico, ed. by Dona L. Stone and P.S. Grove. Portales: El Portal Chapter, D.A.R., 1977. vii, 166 pp.

## San Juan County

The San Juan Basin: My Kingdom Was a County, by Eleanor D. MacDonald and John B. Arrington. Denver: Green Mountain Pr. [1970]. xviii, 247 pp.

## Santa Fe County

Santa Fe County, the Heart of New Mexico, Rich in History and Resources. Santa Fe: Bureau of Immigration, 1906. 145 pp.

History of Santa Fe County, by Sierra County Historical Society. N.p.: Truth or Consequences, 1979. 360 pp.

## Socorro County

Socorro: the Oasis, by F. Stanley. Denver: N.p., 1950. 221 pp.

Socorro, a Historic Survey, by John P. Conron. Albuquerque: Univ. of New Mexico Pr., 1980. viii, 124 pp.

## Torrance County

History of Torrance County, by Torrance County Historical Society. Estanvia?: N.p., 1980. 360 pp.

## Union County

Stories of Early Days in and Around Union County. N.p., n.d.

Settlement and Economic Development of Union County, New Mexico, by Berry N. Alvis. Boulder: Univ. of Colorado, 1934. 99 pp. (M.A. thesis)

Not So Wild, the Old West, by Clara T. Harvey. Denver, Colo.: Golden Bell Pr., 1961. 398 pp.

A History of Union County, 1803-1980 . . . Dallas, Tex.: Taylor Pub. Co., 1980. 296 pp.

## Valencia County

History of Valencia County, 1969, *see* McKinley County.

# NEW YORK

## *Regional*

Central New York, an Inland Empire, Comprising Oneida, Madison, Onondaga, Cayuga, Tompkins, Cortland, Chenango Counties and Their People . . . by William F. Galpin. 4 vols. New York: Lewis Hist. Pub. Co. [1941].

History of Central New York, Embracing Cayuga, Seneca, Wayne, Ontario, Tompkins, Cortland, Schuyler, Yates, Chemung, Steuben and Tioga Counties . . . by Harry R. Melone. 3 vols. Indianapolis: Hist. Pub. Co., 1932.

History of the Genesee Country (Western New York), Comprising the Counties of Allegany, Cattaraugus, Chautauqua, Chemung, Erie, Genesee, Livingston, Monroe, Niagra, Ontario, Orleans, Schuyler, Steuben, Wayne, Wyoming and Yates, ed. by Lockwood R. Doty. 4 vols. Chicago: S.J. Clarke Pub. Co., 1925.

History of the Mohawk Valley, Gateway to the West, 1614-1925; Covering the Six Counties of Schenectady, Schoharie, Montgomery, Fulton, Herkimer and Oneida, ed. by Nelson Greene. 4 vols. Chicago: S.J. Clarke Pub. Co., 1925.

History of the Pioneer Settlement of Phelps and Gorham's Purchase and Morris' Reserve, Embracing the Counties of Monroe, Ontario, Livingston, Yates, Steuben, Most of Wayne and Allegany, and Parts of Orleans, Genesee and Wyoming. To Which is Added, a Suppl. or Extension of the Pioneer History of Monroe County . . . by Orsamus Turner. Rochester: W. Alling, 1851. 624 pp. (Another ed., 1852. xv, 588 pp. Index, prepared by George E. Lookup. Lyons: Wayne County Hist. Soc., 1973. 256 pp.)

History of the Valley of the Hudson . . . 1609-1930, ed. by Nelson Greene, Covering the Sixteen New York State Hudson River Counties of New York, Bronx, Westchester, Rockland, Orange, Putnam, Dutchess, Ulster, Greene, Columbia, Albany, Rensselaer, Saratoga, Washington, Warren, Essex . . . 5 vols. Chicago: S.J. Clarke Pub. Co., 1931.

History of Tioga, Chemung, Tompkins and Schuyler Counties, New York . . . by Henry B. Peirce. Philadelphia: Everts & Ensign, 1879. 687 pp. (Name index, alphabetized by Nellie M. Sheldon. N.p., 1965.)

The North Country; a History, Embracing Jefferson, St. Lawrence, Oswego, Lewis and Franklin Counties, by Harry F. Landon. 3 vols. Indianapolis: Hist. Pub. Co., 1932.

An Outline History of Tioga and Bradford Counties in Pennsylvania; Chemung, Steuben, Tioga, Tompkins and Schuyler in New York . . . by John L. Sexton, Jr. [Elmira: Gazette Co., 1885.] 283 pp.

Southeastern New York, a History of the Counties of Ulster, Dutchess, Orange, Rockland and Putnam, comp. and ed. by Louise H. Zimm, et al. 3 vols. New York: Lewis Hist. Pub. Co. [1946].

## Albany County

Bi-centennial History of Albany: History of the County of Albany, N.Y. from 1609 to 1886 . . . by G.R. Howell and J. Tenney. New York: W.W. Munsell, 1886. xxx, 997 pp. (Includes history of County of Schenectady.)

Landmarks of Albany County, ed. by Amasa J. Parker. 2 vols. Syracuse: D. Mason & Co., 1897. vi, 557, 172, 418 pp.

History of . . . County of . . . Albany, 1931, in History of the Valley of the Hudson, *see* p. 244.

## Allegany County

History of the . . . County of . . . Allegany, 1851, in History of the Pioneer Settlement of Phelps and Gorham's Purchase, *see* p. 244.

History of Allegany County . . . 1806-1879. New York: F.W. Beers, 1879. 392 pp. (Repr. Ovid: W.E. Morrison & Co., 1978. Name index, by Robert French. Interlaken: Heart of the Lakes Pub., 1978. 46 pp.)

Allegany County and Its People: a Centennial Memorial History of Allegany County, ed. by Mrs. Georgia D. Merrill. Alfred: W.A. Fergusson, 1896. 951 pp. (Name index. Interlaken: Heart of the Lakes Pub., 1983.)

Recollections of the Log School House Period, and Sketches and Life and Customs in Pioneer Days, by Jno. S. Minard. Cuba: Free Pr., 1905. 146 pp. (Name index, by Francis Hoy. N.p., 1983. 160 pp.)

History of the . . . County of Allegany, 1925, in History of the Genesee Country, *see* p. 244.

## Bronx County

History of the . . . County of . . . Bronx, 1931, in History of the Valley of the Hudson, *see* p. 244.

## Broome County

History of Broome County . . . ed. by Henry P. Smith. 2 vols. Syracuse: D. Mason & Co., 1885. 630 pp. (Name index, by John J. Tyne. Interlaken: Heart of the Lakes Pub., 1979. 131 pp.)

Binghampton and Broome County, New York, by William F. Seward. 3 vols. New York: Lewis Hist. Pub. Co., 1924. 1,145 pp.

## Cattaraugus County

Cattaraugus County . . . comp. by John Manly. Little Valley: Author, 1857. 136 pp.

History of Cattaraugus County, by Franklin Ellis. Philadelphia: L.H. Everts, 1879. 512 pp. (Repr. Evansville, Ind.: Unigraphic, 1980.)

Historical Gazetteer and Biographical Memorial of Cattaraugus . . . ed. by William Adams. 2 vols. Syracuse: Lyman, Horton, 1893. vi, 1,164 pp.

History of . . . the County of . . . Cattaraugus, 1925, in History of the Genesee Country, *see* p. 244.

Cattaraugus County Sesquicentennial, 1808-1958, by J. Pierce. N.p., 1958.

Historical Review of Cattaraugus, by Michael C. Donovan. [N.p., 1959?] 128 pp.

## Cayuga County

History of Cayuga County, 1789-1879 . . . by Elliot G. Storke, assisted by James H. Smith. Syracuse: D. Mason & Co., 1879. viii, 518, xxxviii pp. (Repr. Interlaken: Heart of the Lakes Pub., 1978. All-name index, by Leslie L. Luther. Interlaken: Heart of the Lakes Pub., 1979. 76 pp.

History of Cayuga County, New York . . . from Papers in Cayuga County Historical Society . . . 1775-1908 . . . ed. by B. Snow. Auburn: N.p., 1908. xvi, 598 pp.

History of . . . Cayuga . . . County, 1932, in History of Central New York, *see* p. 244.

[History of] Cayuga . . . County, 1941, in Central New York, *see* p. 244.

## Chautauqua County

Sketches of the History of Chautauqua County, by Emory F. Warren. Jamestown: J.W. Fletcher, 1846. 159 pp.

History of Chautauqua County, New York, from Its First Settlement to the Present Time . . . by Andrew W. Young. Buffalo: Matthews & Warren, 1875. 672 pp. (Complete index to more than 10,000 names, comp. by Ridgway McNallie. Buffalo: Compiler, 1948. 117 pp. Microfilm ed. Cleveland: Bell & Howell, 1964.)

Biographical and Portrait Cyclopedia of Chautauqua, with a Historical Sketch of the County by Hon. Obed Edson, ed. by Butler F. Dilley. Philadelphia: J.M. Gresham, 1891. 730 pp.

History of Chautauqua County . . . Hon. Obed Edson, historian, ed. by Georgia D. Merrill. 2 vols. Boston, Mass.: W.A. Fergusson, 1894. 983 pp.

The Centennial History of Chautauqua County: a Story of 100 Years of Development. 2 vols. Jamestown: Chautauqua Hist. Co., 1904. 698, 1,173 pp.

History of Chautauqua County, New York and Its People, ed. by John P. Downs, et al. 3 vols. Boston, Mass.: American Hist. Soc., 1921.

History of the . . . County of . . . Chautauqua, 1925, in History of the Genesee Country, *see* p. 244.

Chautauqua County, a History, by Helen G. McMahon. Buffalo: H. Stewart [1958]. 339 pp.

## Chemung County

History of . . . Chemung . . . County, 1879, *see* p. 244. (Also repr. Ovid: W.E. Morrison & Co., 1981. 286 pp.)

An Outline History of . . . County of . . . Chemung, 1885, *see* p. 244.

Our County and Its People; a History of the Valley and County of Chemung, from the Closing Years of the Eighteenth Century, by Ausburn Towner. Syracuse: D. Mason & Co., 1892. 702, 160 pp.

A Brief History of Chemung County, for the Use of Grade Schools, by Ausburn Towner. New York: A.S. Barnes, 1907. 103 pp.

History of . . . the County of . . . Chemung, 1925, in History of the Genessee Country, *see* p. 244.

History of . . . Chemung . . . County, 1932, in History of Central New York, *see* p. 244.

## Chenango County

History of Chenango County, Containing the Divisions of the County and Sketches of the Towns . . . by Hiram C. Clark. Norwich: Thompson & Pratt, 1850. 119 pp.

History of Chenango and Madison Counties . . . by James H. Smith. Syracuse: D. Mason & Co., 1880. 760, xxix pp. (Name index, by John J. Tyne. Interlaken: Heart of the Lakes Pub., 1978. 210 pp.)

[History of] Chenango . . . County, 1941, in Central New York, *see* p. 244.

## Clinton County

A New Geography and History of Clinton County, New York, comp. by Henry K. Averill, Jr. Plattsburgh: Telegram Pr. House, 1879. 17 pp. (2d ed., rev. and enl. Plattsburgh: Telegram Pr. House, 1880. 32 pp. Another ed., 1885?)

History of Clinton and Franklin Counties . . . by Duane H. Hurd. Philadelphia: J.W. Lewis, 1880. 508 pp.

## Columbia County

History of Columbia County . . . by Franklin Ellis. Philadelphia: Everts & Ensign, 1878. 451 pp. (Personal name index. [N.p., 1959.] unpaged. Repr. with name index. Interlaken: Heart of the Lakes Pub., 1982.)

Columbia County at the End of the Century; a Historical Record of Its Formation and Settlement . . . 3 parts in 2 vols. Hudson: Record Pr. & Pub. Co., 1900.

History of the . . . County of . . . Columbia, 1931, in History of the Valley of the Hudson, *see* p. 244.

## Cortland County

Pioneer History; or, Cortland County and the Border Wars of New York . . . by H.C. Goodwin. New York: A.B. Burdick, 1859. 456 pp.

History of Cortland County . . . ed. by H.P. Smith. Syracuse: D. Mason & Co., 1885. 552 pp. (Repr. Interlaken: Heart of the Lakes Pub., 1983.)

"Grip's" Historical Souvenir of Cortland [by Edgar L. Welch]. [Cortland: Standard Pr., 1899.] 234 pp.

History of . . . Cortland . . . County, 1932, in History of Central New York, *see* p. 244.

Stories of Cortland County for Boys and Girls, by Bertha E. Blodgett. N.p.: Cortland County Hist. Soc., 1932. 287 pp. (Another ed. N.p., 1952. 307 pp.)

The Geography and History of Cortland County . . . by Cornelia B. Cornish. Ann Arbor, Mich.: Edwards Bros., 1935. v, 60 pp. (From M.A. thesis, Cornell Univ., 1929.)

[History of] Cortland . . . County, in Central New York, *see* p. 244.

Sesquicentennial Celebration, 1808-1958. N.p., 1958. 192 pp.

## Delaware County

History of Delaware County, and Border Wars of New York, Containing a Sketch of the Early Settlements . . . by Jay Gould. Roxbury: Keeny & Gould, 1856. xvi, 426 pp. (Repr. New Orleans: Polyanthos, 1973.)

History of Delaware County, ed. by W. Munsell. New York: W.W. Munsell, 1880. 363 pp. (Repr. Ovid: W.E. Morrison & Co., 1976.)

Delaware County, New York; History of the Century, 1797-1897. Centennial Celebration, ed. by D. Murray. Delhi: W. Clark, 1898. 604 pp. (Index of names, comp. by John J. Tyne. Sidney: Comp., 1973. 35 leaves. Name index. Interlaken: Heart of the Lakes Pub., 1979. 33 pp.)

Three Centuries in Delaware County, by J. DeVine. New York: N.p., 1933. 88 pp.

Chapters in the History of Delaware County, New York, by John D. Monroe. [Margaretville?:] Delaware County Hist. Assoc., 1949. 132 pp.

## Dutchess County

Dutchess County: Local Tales and Historical Sketches, by Henry D.B. Bailey. Fishkill Landing: J.W. Spaight, 1874. 431 pp.

General History of Dutchess County, from 1609 to 1876 . . . by Philip H. Smith. Pawling, N.H.: Author, 1877. 507 pp. (Index, by Grace M. Pierce. [N.p., 1916?] 70 pp.)

History of Dutchess County . . . by James H. Smith, et al. Syracuse: D. Mason & Co., 1882. 562, xxx pp. (Repr. with added index. Interlaken: Heart of the Lakes Pub., 1981. 809 pp. Pub. also without index, 1981. 720 pp. Name index. 1981. 86 pp.)

The History of Dutchess County, ed. by Frank Hasbrouck. 2 vols. Poughkeepsie: S.A. Matthieu, 1909. 791, xxxii pp.

*Dutchess County (cont.)*

Historical and Genealogical Record, Dutchess and Putnam Counties. Poughkeepsie: Oxford Pub. Co., 1912. xvi, 476 pp.

History of . . . the County of . . . Dutchess, 1931, in History of the Valley of the Hudson, *see* p. 244.

Dutchess County . . . Philadelphia: W.P.A. and William Penn Assoc. of Philadelphia, 1937. vii, 166 pp.

History of the County of . . . Dutchess, 1946, in Southeastern New York, *see* p. 244.

Old Dutchess Forever! The Story of an American County, by Henry N. MacCracken. New York: Hastings House [1956]. viii, 503 pp.

Blithe Dutchess, the Flowering of an American County from 1812, by Henry N. MacCracken. N.Y.: N.p., 1958. 495 pp.

## Erie County

Centennial History of Erie County; being Its Annals from the Earliest Recorded Events to the 100th Year of American Independence, by Crisfield Johnson. Buffalo: Matthews & Warren, 1876. 512 pp.

History of Buffalo and Erie County . . . by H. Perry Smith. 2 vols. Syracuse: D. Mason & Co., 1884. Vol. 1, History of Erie County; Vol. 2, History of Buffalo. (Early Settlers of Erie County, being a Complete Name Index to History of Buffalo and Erie County. N.p., 1950. Repr. 2 vols. Knightstown, Ind.: The Bookmark, 1982.)

Our County and Its People; a Descriptive Work on Erie County, ed. by Truman C. White. 2 vols. [Boston, Mass.:] Boston Hist. Co., 1898.

History of Buffalo and Erie County, 1914-1919, comp. by Daniel J. Sweeney. [Buffalo: N.p., 1920.] 733 pp.

History of the . . . County of . . . Erie, 1925, in History of the Genesee Country, *see* p. 244.

History of Erie County, 1870-1970, ed. by Walter S. Dunn, Jr., [Buffalo:] Buffalo and Erie County Hist. Soc. [1972]. 462 pp.

## Essex County

History of Essex County . . . ed. by H. Perry Smith. 2 vols. Syracuse: D. Mason and Co., 1885. 754 pp. (Index, comp. by Ruth G. Harris and S.B. Harris. Glens Falls: Compilers, 1978. 99 pp.)

History of the . . . County of . . . Essex, 1931, in History of the Valley of the Hudson, *see* p. 244.

Love of an Adirondack County (Essex). Ithaca: Cornell Pr., 1944. 86 pp.

The Sticks: a Profile of Essex County, by Barton Bernstein. New York: Mead [1972]. 175 pp.

## Franklin County

History of Franklin County, 1853, *see* St. Lawrence County.

History of Franklin County, 1880, *see* Clinton County.

Historical Sketches of Franklin County . . . by Frederick J. Seaver. Albany: J.B. Lyon & Co., 1918. xii, 819 pp.

History of . . . Franklin County, 1932, in The North Country, *see* p. 244.

## Fulton County

History of Fulton County, 1878, *see* Montgomery County.

History of Fulton County . . . by Washington Frothingham. Syracuse: D. Mason & Co., 1892. 635, 177 pp.

History of the . . . County of . . . Fulton, 1925, in History of the Mohawk Valley, *see* p. 244.

## Genesee County

History of the . . . County of . . . Genesee, 1851, in History of the Pioneer Settlement of Phelps and Gorham's Purchase, *see* p. 244.

1890 Gazetteer and Biographical Record, History and Directory of Genesee County, New York, 1788-1890. New York: F.W. Beers, 1890. 859 pp. (Repr. Knightstown, Ind.: The Bookmark, 1977.)

Our County and Its People, ed. by S. North. Boston, Mass.: N.p., 1899. 731 pp.

History of the . . . County of . . . Genesee, 1925, in History of the Genesee Country, *see* p. 244.

The Sesquicentennial of Genesee County, 1802-1952. [Batavia, N.p., 1952.] 119 pp.

## Greene County

History of Greene County . . . by H. Brace, et al. New York: J.B. Beers, 1884. 462 pp. (Repr. Cornwallville: Hope Farm Pr., 1969. Complete name index, by Jean D. Worden. Franklin, Ohio: Worden, 1984.)

Dear Old Greene County . . . [by Frank A. Gallt]. Catskill: N.p., 1915. 521 pp. (Another ed. Catskill: N.p., 1922. 580 pp.)

History of Greene County . . . by Jesse Van Vechten Vedder. Vol. 1 (all pub.): 1651-1800. [Catskill: N.p., 1927.] 207 pp. (2d ed. Priv. pr., 1928.)

History of . . . the County of . . . Greene, 1931, in History of the Valley of the Hudson, *see* p. 244.

## Hamilton County

Tales from an Adirondack County, by Ted Aber and Stella King. Prospect: Prospect Books, 1961. 208 pp.

The History of Hamilton County, by Ted Aber and Stella King. Lake Pleasant: Great Wilderness Books, 1965. xx, 1,209 pp.

# Herkimer County

A History of Herkimer County, Including the Upper Mohawk Valley, from the Earliest Period to the Present Time . . . by Nathaniel S. Benton. Albany: J. Munsell, 1856. 497 pp.

History of Herkimer County, 1791-1879. New York: F.W. Beers, 1879. 289 pp.

History of Herkimer County . . . ed. by George A. Hardin and F.H. Willard. 2 vols. Syracuse: D. Mason & Co., 1893. 550, 276 pp.

History of the . . . County of . . . Herkimer, 1925, in History of the Mohawk Valley, *see* p. 244.

# Jefferson County

A History of Jefferson County . . . from the Earliest to the Present Time, by Franklin B. Hough. Albany: J. Munsell, 1854. 601 pp.

History of Jefferson County . . . [by Samuel W. Durant]. Philadelphia: L.H. Everts, 1878. 593 pp.

Geographical Gazetteer of Jefferson County, New York, 1684-1890, by W.H. Horton. 2 parts in 1 vol. Syracuse: Hamilton Child, 1890. 887, 315 pp.

The Growth of a Century: as Illustrated in the History of Jefferson County, from 1793 to 1894 . . . comp. by John A. Haddock. Albany: Weed-Parsons, 1894. 842 pp. (2d ed. Albany: Weed-Parsons, 1895. 920 pp.)

Our County and Its People; a Descriptive Work on Jefferson County, ed. by Edgar C. Emerson. [Boston, Mass.:] Boston Hist. Co., 1898. xiii, 936, 318 pp.

Jefferson County Centennial, 1905 . . . comp. by Jere Coughlin. Waterton: Hungerford-Holbrook Co., 1905. 440 pp.

A History of . . . Jefferson . . . County, 1932, in The North Country, *see* p. 244.

# Kings County

The Civil, Political, Professional and Ecclesiastical History . . . of the County of Kings and the City of Brooklyn from 1683 to 1884, ed. by Henry R. Stiles, et al. 2 vols. New York: W.W. Munsell [1884]. 1,408 pp.

Historic Homesteads of Kings County . . . by Charles A. Ditmas. Brooklyn: Compiler, 1909. 120 pp.

# Lewis County

A History of Lewis County . . . from the Beginning of Its Settlement to the Present Time, by Franklin B. Hough. Albany: Munsell & Rowland, 1860. iv, 319 pp. (Another ed., with biographical sketches, by Franklin B. Hough. Syracuse: D. Mason & Co., 1883. 606, xxxvii pp.)

A History of . . . Lewis . . . County, 1932, in The North Country, *see* p. 244.

History of Lewis County, 1880-1965, ed. by G. Byron Bowen. [Lowville: Bd. of Legislators of Lewis County, 1970.] 563 pp.

## Livingston County

History of . . . Livingston County, 1851, in History of the Pioneer Settlement of Phelps and Gorham's Purchase, *see* p. 244.

A History of Livingston County: from Its Earliest Traditions, to Its Part in the War of Our Union . . . by Lockwood R. Doty. Genesee: E.E. Doty, 1876. xxvi, 685 pp.

History of Livingston County, 1687 . . . by James H. Smith. Syracuse: D. Mason & Co., 1881. 490 pp.

History of Livingston County, from Its Earliest Traditions to the Present Time . . . ed. by Lockwood R. Doty. Jackson, Mich.: Q.J. Van Deusen, 1905. 1,016 pp.

History of the County of . . . Livingston, 1925, in History of the Genesee Country, *see* p. 244.

## Madison County

History of Madison County, by Mrs. L.M. Hammond Whitney. Syracuse: Truair, Smith, 1872. 774 pp. (Another ed. Syracuse: Truair, Smith [1900].)

History of Madison County, 1880, *see* Chenango County.

Our Country and Its People: a Descriptive and Biographical Record of Madison County, ed. by John E. Smith. 2 vols. [Boston, Mass.:] Boston Hist. Co., 1899. x, 649, 239 pp.

[History of] Madison . . . County, 1941, in Central New York, *see* p. 244.

Madison County Today, ed. by Karl H. Lehman. Oneida Castle: N.p., 1943. 214 pp.

## Monroe County

History of the . . . County of Monroe, 1851, in History of the Pioneer Settlement of Phelps and Gorham's Purchase, *see* p. 244.

History of Monroe County, New York [1783-1877] . . . [by W.H. McIntosh]. Philadelphia: Everts, Ensign & Everts, 1877. 320 pp. (Name index, comp. by Monroe County Historian's Office. Rochester, 1966. 143 pp.)

Landmarks of Monroe County [by W.E. Peck, et al.]. 2 vols. Boston, Mass.: Boston Hist. Co., 1895. xi, 492, 103, 339 pp.

History of Monroe County, 1908, *see* Rochester County.

History of the . . . County of . . . Monroe, 1925, in History of the Genesee Country, *see* p. 244.

Pleasant Valley: an Early History of Monroe County and Region, 1650-1850, by Florence Lee. New York: Carlton Pr. [1970]. 321 pp.

Monroe County, 1821-1971: the Sesquicentennial Account of the History of Monroe County, by Howard C. Hosmer. Rochester: Rochester Museum and Science Center, 1971. 327 pp.

*Monroe County (cont.)*

Northfield on the Genesee . . . Early Times in Monroe County, New York. 1796-1814 . . . by Margaret S. MacNabb, et al. Rochester: County of Monroe, 1981. 368 pp.

## Montgomery County

History of Montgomery and Fulton Counties . . . New York: F.W. Beers, 1878. 252 pp. (Repr. with added index. Interlaken: Heart of the Lakes Pub., 1978. 432 pp. Name index, by Al Chambers, available separately. 72 pp.)

History of Montgomery County . . . by Washington Frothingham. Syracuse: D. Mason & Co., 1892. 460, 349 pp.

History of the . . . County of . . . Montgomery, 1925, in History of the Mohawk Valley, *see* p. 244.

Outlines of History, Montgomery County, State of New York, 1772-1972, by Hugh P. Donlon. Bicentennial ed. [Amsterdam: Noteworthy Co., 1973.] xi, 203 pp.

## Nassau County

Nassau, Suburbia, U.S.A.: the First Seventy-Five Years of Nassau County, New York, 1899-1974, by Edward J. Smits. Syosset: Friends of the Nassau County Museum, 1974. x, 303 pp.

## New York County

History of the . . . County of New York, 1931, in History of the Valley of the Hudson, *see* p. 244.

## Niagara County

History of Niagara County . . . by Orsamus Turner, et al. New York: Sanford & Co., 1878. 397 pp.

Landmarks of Niagara County, ed. by William Pool. Syracuse: D. Mason & Co., 1897. vi, 447, 254 pp.

Souvenir History of Niagara County, Commemorative of the 25th Anniversary of the Pioneer Association of Niagara County. [Lockport: Lockport Journal], 1902. 228 pp.

Niagara County, New York . . . a Concise Record of Her Progress and People, 1821-1921, Published During Its Centennial Year, by Edward T. Williams. 2 vols. Chicago: J.H. Beers, 1921.

History of the . . . County of . . . Niagara, 1925, in History of the Genesee Country, *see* p. 244.

Outpost of Empires; a Short History of Niagara County, by John Aiken, et al. Phoenix: F.E. Richards, 1961. 152 pp.

## Oneida County

Annals and Recollections of Oneida County . . . by Pomroy Jones. Rome: Author, 1851. xvi, 893 pp.

History of Oneida County [by Samuel W. Durant]. Philadelphia: Everts & Fariss, 1878. 678 pp. (Repr. with added name index. Interlaken: Heart of the Lakes Pub., 1984.)

Our County and Its People: a Descriptive Work on Oneida County, ed. by Daniel E. Wager. 3 parts. Boston, Mass.: Boston Hist. Co., 1896. xi, 411, 636, 180 pp. (Index to parts 2-3, "Family Sketches," by Elizabeth Edmunds. Lee Center: Author, 1981. 138 pp.)

Things Worth Knowing About Oneida County, by William W. Canfield and J.E. Clark. Utica: T.J. Griffiths, 1909. 148 pp.

History of Oneida County, from 1700 to the Present Time, by Henry J. Cookinham. 2 vols. Chicago: S.J. Clarke Pub. Co., 1912.

History of the . . . County of . . . Oneida, 1925, in History of the Mohawk Valley, *see* p. 244.

[History of] Oneida . . . County, 1941, in Central New York, *see* p. 244.

## Onondaga County

Onondaga; or, Reminiscences of Earlier or Later Times . . . by Joshua V.H. Clark. 2 vols. Syracuse: Stoddard and Babcock, 1849. (Index. [Syracuse, N.p., 1934?] 51 leaves. (Repr. 2 vols. Millwood: Kraus Reprint Co., 1973.)

History of Onondaga County, New York . . . by W. Woodford Clayton. Syracuse: D. Mason and Co., 1878. iv, 430 pp.

Onondaga's Centennial; Gleanings of a Century, ed. by Dwight H. Bruce. 2 vols. [Boston, Mass.:] Boston Hist. Co., 1896.

Pioneer Times in the Onondaga Country, by Carroll E. Smith. Syracuse: C.W. Bardeen, 1904. 415 pp. (Originally pub. in Syracuse Sunday Herald, 1899.)

Past and Present of Syracuse and Onondaga County, from Prehistoric Times to the Beginning of 1908, by Rev. William M. Beauchamp. 2 vols. New York: S.J. Clarke Pub. Co., 1908.

[History of] Onondaga . . . County, 1941, in Central New York, *see* p. 244.

Onondaga County, a Vanished World, by Anne G. Sneller. [Syracuse:] Syracuse Univ. Pr., 1964. x, 365 pp.

Onondaga Landmarks: a Survey of Historic and Architectural Sites in Syracuse and Onondaga County . . . Syracuse: Cultural Resources Council of Syracuse & Onondaga County, 1975. vii, 109 pp.

## Ontario County

History of the . . . County of . . . Ontario, 1851, in History of the Pioneer Settlement of Phelps and Gorham's Purchase, *see* p. 244.

*Ontario County (cont.)*

History of Ontario County, with Illustrations Descriptive of Its Scenery . . . [by W.H. McIntosh]. Philadelphia: Everts, Ensign & Everts, 1876. 276, xcvi pp.

History of Ontario County . . . ed. by George S. Conover, comp. by Lewis C. Aldrich. 2 vols. Syracuse: D. Mason & Co., 1893. 518, 396 pp.

A History of Ontario County and Its People, by Charles F. Milliken. 2 vols. New York: Lewis Hist. Pub. Co., 1911.

History of the . . . County of . . . Ontario, 1925, in History of the Genesee Country, *see* p. 244.

History of . . . Ontario . . . County, 1932, in History of Central New York, *see* p. 244.

## Orange County

An Outline History of Orange County . . . by Samuel W. Eager. Newburgh: S.T. Callahan, 1846-47. 652 pp. (Index, by Lilliam O. Estabrook. Rutland, Vt.: Tuttle Pub. Co. [1940]. 48 pp. Repr. [Middletown: T.E. Henderson, 1969.] 652, 16 pp.)

History of the County of Orange, by E.M. Ruttenber. Newburgh: Author, 1875. 424 pp.

History of Orange County . . . comp. by E.M. Ruttenber and L.H. Clark. 2 vols. Philadelphia: Everts & Peck, 1881. xii, 820 pp. (Orange County index. Chester: Orange County Gen. Soc., 1979. 262 pp. Repr. 2 vols. Interlaken: Heart of the Lakes Pub., 1980.)

The History of Orange County, ed. by Russel Headley. Middletown: Van Deusen and Elms, 1908. 997, xviii pp.

Orange County: a Narrative History . . . comp. by Almet S. Moffat. Washington-ville: N.p., 1928. 87 pp.

History of the . . . County of . . . Orange, 1931, in History of the Valley of the Hudson, *see* p. 244.

Outposts of History in Orange County, by Dwight Akers. Washingtonville: Blooming Grove Chapter, D.A.R., 1937. 116 pp. (2d ed., 1937.)

History of the County of . . . Orange, 1946, in Southeastern New York, *see* p. 244.

Orange County: a Journey Through Time. A Text on Local History, prepared by Orange-Ulster Board of Cooperative Educational Services. Goshen: The Board, 1983. 203 pp.

## Orleans County

History of the . . . County of . . . Orleans, 1851, in History of the Pioneer Settlement of Phelps and Gorham's Purchase, *see* p. 244.

Pioneer History of Orleans County . . . by Arad Thomas. Albion: H.A. Bruner, 1871. 463 pp. (Repr. Knightstown, Ind.: The Bookmark, 1980. Name index, by Evelyn R. Smith. Interlaken: Heart of the Lakes Pub., 1982. 29 pp.)

*Orleans County (cont.)*

Historical Album of Orleans County, 1824-1879. New York: Sanford & Co., 1879. 320 pp. (Repr. Ovid: W.E. Morrison & Co., 1970.)

Landmarks of Orleans County . . . ed. by Hon. Isaac S. Signor, et al. 3 parts. Syracuse: D. Mason & Co., 1894. viii, 688, 48, 242 pp.

History of the . . . County of . . . Orleans, 1925, in History of the Genesee Country, *see* p. 244.

## Oswego County

History of Oswego County . . . [by Crisfield Johnson]. Philadelphia: L.H. Everts, 1877. 449 pp.

Landmarks of Oswego County, ed. by John C. Churchill, et al. 3 parts. Syracuse: D. Mason & Co., 1895. xi, 843, 72, 348 pp. (Index to Part 3, "Family Sketches," comp. by Mrs. Cyril (Elizabeth) M. Edmunds. Lee Center: N.p., 1979. 78 pp.)

A History of . . . Oswego . . . County, 1932, in The North Country, *see* p. 244.

History of Oswego County, with Notes About the Several Towns in the County [by Ralph M. Faust]. Oswego: N.p., 1934. 107 pp. (Another ed., rev. and enl. N.p., 1948. 112 pp.)

## Otsego County

Reminiscences, Personal and Other Incidents; Early Settlement of Otsego County . . . by Levi Beardsley. New York: Pr. by C. Vinten, 1852. x, 575 pp.

History of Otsego County [by Duane H. Hurd]. Philadelphia: Everts & Fariss, 1878. 378 pp. (Name index, by John J. Tyne. Interlaken: Heart of the Lakes Pub., 1976. 124 pp.)

Otsego County: Geographical and Historical, from the Earliest Settlement to the Present Time . . . ed. by E. Bacon. Oneonta: Oneonta Herald, 1902. 85 pp.

The Legends and Traditions of a Northern County, by James F. Cooper. New York: G.P. Putnam's Sons, 1921. xi, 263 pp.

## Putnam County

The History of Putnam County . . . by William J. Blake. New York: Baker & Scribner, 1849. 368 pp.

History of Putnam County, New York . . . by W.S. Pelletreau. Philadelphia: Preston & Co., 1886. x, 771 pp.

Historical and Genealogical Record of Putnam County, 1912, *see* Dutchess County.

History of the . . . County of . . . Putnam, 1931, in History of the Valley of the Hudson, *see* p. 244.

*Putnam County (cont.)*

History of the County of . . . Putnam, 1946, in Southeastern New York, *see* p. 244.

Putnam County History, the Last 100 Years . . . Vol. 1 (all pub.). [Patterson: N.p., 1957.] 119 leaves.

## Queens County

Queens County in Olden Times; being a Supplement to the Several Histories Thereof, by Henry Onderdonk. Jamaica: C. Welling, 1865. 122 pp.

History of Queens County, 1683-1882 . . . New York: W.W. Munsell, 1882. 472 pp.

## Rensselaer County

History of Rensselaer County . . . by Nathaniel Sylvester. Philadelphia: Everts & Peck, 1880. 564 pp.

Landmarks of Rensselaer County, by George B. Anderson. 2 vols. Syracuse: D. Mason & Co., 1897. xi, 735, 460 pp.

Troy and Rensselaer County, New York; a History, by Rutherford Rayner. 3 vols. N.p.: Lewis Hist. Co., 1925.

History of the . . . County of . . . Rensselaer, 1931, in History of the Valley of the Hudson, *see* p. 244.

Our Yesterdays, a History of Rensselaer County, by Stephanie H. Craib and Roderick H. Craib. [Troy?: N.p.], 1948. 121 leaves.

## Richmond County

History of Richmond County, New York, by Nathaniel B. Sylvester. Philadelphia: N.p., 1880. 564 pp.

History of Richmond County, Staten Island, New York, from Its Discovery to the Present Time, ed. by Richard M. Bayles. 2 vols. New York: L.E. Preston & Co., 1887. ix, 741 pp.

## Rockland County

History of Rockland County . . . 1686-1884, ed. by Rev. David Cole. New York: J.B. Beers, 1884. 344, 75 pp. (Repr. Nyack: Rockland County Pub. Librarians Assoc., 1969. 344, 75 pp.)

The History of Rockland County, by Frank B. Green. New York: A.S. Barnes, 1886. vi, 444 pp. (Repr. [N.p., 1970?].)

Historical Record at the Close of the Nineteenth Century of Rockland County . . . ed. by Arthur S. Tompkins. 2 parts. Nyack: Van Deusen & Joyce, 1902. 577, 192 pp.

*Rockland County (cont.)*

History of the . . . County of . . . Rockland, 1931, in History of the Valley of the Hudson, *see* p. 244.

Now and Then and Long Ago in Rockland County, comp. by Cornelia F. Bedell [Duffern:] Priv. pr. [The Ramapo Valley Independent], 1941. xvii, 368 pp. (Repr.? [Orangeburg?: Hist. Soc. of Rockland County, 1968.] xvii, 399 pp.)

History of the County of . . . Rockland, 1946, in Southeastern New York, *see* p. 244.

The History of Rockland County, by W. Hasselbarth, pub. in Rockland County Journal, 1855-56. Cleveland, Ohio: Bell & Howell, 1964. 234 pp.

The Way It Was in North Rockland, by Norman R. Baker. Orangeburg: Hist. Soc. of Rockland County, 1973. 72 pp.

## St. Lawrence County

A History of St. Lawrence and Franklin Counties, from the Earliest Period to the Present Time, by Franklin B. Hough. Albany: Little & Co., 1853. 719 pp. (Repr. Baltimore: Regional Pub. Co., 1970. xv, 719 pp. Repr. with index. Harrison: Harbor Hill Books, 1980.)

History of St. Lawrence County, New York, 1748-1878 [by Samuel W. Durant]. Philadelphia: L.H. Everts, 1878. 521 pp. (Name index. N.p., 1982. 76 pp. Repr. with added name index. Interlaken: Heart of the Lakes Pub., 1983.)

Our Country and Its People: a Memorial Record of St. Lawrence County, N.Y., by G. Curtis. 2 vols. Syracuse: D. Mason & Co., 1894. 372, 720, 66 pp.

Fortune's Wheel, by Martha Gray. New York: The Abbey Pr. [1901]. viii, 275 pp.

A History . . . of St. Lawrence . . . County, 1932, in The North Country, *see* p. 244.

St. Lawrence County History . . . Canton: St. Lawrence County Hist. Assoc., 1975. 64 pp.

## Saratoga County

History of Saratoga County . . . by Nathaniel B. Sylvester. Philadelphia: Everts & Ensign, 1878. 514 pp. (Repr. Richmond, Ind.: Gresham Pub. Co., 1893. 635 pp. Index of names. Charlton: N.p., 1950. Index of names, by J. Cornelius Durkee, completed by H.I. Becker. N.p., 1965. 151 pp. Repr. with all-name index. Interlaken: Heart of the Lakes Pub., 1979. 750 pp.)

Our County and Its People; a Description and Biographical Record of Saratoga County, New York . . . [comp. by George B. Anderson]. 2 vols. [Boston, Mass.:] Boston Hist. Co., 1899. xi, 584, 203 pp.

History of the . . . County of . . . Saratoga, 1931, in History of the Valley of the Hudson, *see* p. 244.

## Schenectady County

History of the County of Schenectady, from 1662 to 1886 . . . by G. Howell and W. Munsell. New York: W.W. Munsell, 1886. vi, 218 pp.

History of Schenectady County, 1886, in Bi-centennial History of Albany . . . *see* Albany County.

A History of the County of Schenectady, comp. by C. Van Santvoord. Schenectady: Barhyte & Birch for Schenectady County Teachers' Assoc., 1887. 54 pp.

Schenectady County, New York; Its History to the Close of the Nineteenth Century, ed. by Austin A. Yates. New York: New York Hist. Co., 1902. viii, 463, 258 pp.

History of the . . . County of Schenectady, 1925, in History of the Mohawk Valley, *see* p. 244.

## Schoharie County

History of Schoharie County . . . by Jeptha R. Simms. Albany: Munsell & Tanner, 1845. 672 pp.

The Frontiersmen of New York . . . by Jeptha R. Simms. 2 vols. Albany: G.C. Riggs, 1882-83. (Enl. from History of Schoharie, 1845, *see* above.)

History of Schoharie County, 1713-1882 . . . by William E. Roscoe. Syracuse: D. Mason & Co., 1882. 470, xxviii pp. (Repr. with added index. Interlaken: Heart of the Lakes Pub., 1983.)

A Summary of Schoharie County . . . County Teachers' Association . . . by Solomon Sias. Middleburgh: P.W. Danforth Pr., 1904. 154 pp.

History of the . . . County of . . . Schoharie, 1925, in History of the Mohawk Valley, *see* p. 244.

The Little Hill Farm: or Cruisings in Old Schoharie, by John Van Schalck, Jr. Boston, Mass.: Universalist Pub. House [1930]. 179 pp.

A History of Schoharie County, ed. by Marion F. Noyes. [Richmondville:] Richmondville Phoenix, 1964. 184 pp.

## Schuyler County

History of . . . Schuyler County, 1879, *see* p. 244.

An Outline History of . . . County of . . . Schuyler, 1885, *see* p. 244.

History of the . . . County of . . . Schuyler, 1925, in History of the Genesee Country, *see* p. 244.

History of . . . Schuyler . . . County, 1932, in History of Central New York, *see* p. 244.

## Seneca County

History of Seneca County, New York, 1786-1876. Philadelphia: Everts & Ensign, 1876. 170 pp. (Index and suppl. Ovid: W.E. Morrison & Co., 1976. 86 pp.)

History of . . . Seneca . . . County, 1932, in History of Central New York, *see* p. 244.

Between the Lakes: the Settlement and Growth of South Seneca County, New York . . . comp. and ed. by Maurice L. Patterson. Interlaken: I.T. Pub. Corp., 1976. vi, 264 pp. (Repr. Interlaken: Author, 1983. 276 pp.)

The County Between the Lakes; a Public History of Seneca County, New York, 1876-1982, by Hilda R. Watrous. Interlaken: Seneca County Bicentennial Comm., 1983.

## Steuben County

History of the . . . County of . . . Steuben, 1851, in History of the Pioneer Settlement of Phelps and Gorham's Purchase, *see* p. 244.

History of the Settlement of Steuben County . . . by Guy H. McMaster. Bath: R.S. Underhill, 1853. iv, 318 pp. (Repr. Rochester: N.p., 1893. iv, 207 pp.)

History of Steuben County, New York . . . by W. Woodford Clayton. 2 vols. Philadelphia: Lewis, Peck & Co., 1879. 460 pp.

An Outline History of . . . Steuben . . . County, 1885, *see* p. 244.

Historical Gazetteer of Steuben County . . . comp. and ed. by Millard F. Roberts. 2 vols. in 1. Syracuse: M.F. Roberts, 1891. 592, 354 pp. (Repr. with every-name index. 2 vols. Bath: Steuben County Hist. Soc., 1979. 1,122 pp.)

Landmarks of Steuben County, ed. by Hon. Harlo Hakes, et al. Syracuse: D. Mason & Co., 1896. vii, 379, 80, 530 pp.

A History of Steuben County, and Its People, by Irvin W. Near. 2 vols. Chicago: Lewis Pub. Co., 1911.

History of the . . . County of . . . Steuben, 1925, in History of the Genesee Country, *see* p. 244.

History of . . . Steuben . . . County, 1932, in History of Central New York, *see* p. 244.

Pioneer History and Atlas of Steuben County, comp. by W.B. Thrall. [Perry:] N.p., 1942. 98 pp.

## Suffolk County

Historical and Descriptive Sketches of Suffolk County . . . by Richard M. Bayles. Fort Jefferson: Author, 1874. 424, ix pp. (Repr. Port Washington: N.p., 1962.)

History of Suffolk County . . . by J. Cooper, et al. New York: W.W. Munsell, 1882. 488 pp.

*Suffolk County (cont.)*

History of Suffolk County . . . ed. by S. Titus. Babylon: Budget Steam Pr., 1885. 125 pp.

Know Suffolk, the Sunrise County, Then and Now, by Nathaniel R. Howell. Islip: Buys Bros., 1952. 181 pp.

Suffolk County, by Charles J. McDermott. New York: J.H. Heineman [1965]. xiii, 86 pp.

## Sullivan County

History of Sullivan County . . . by James E. Quinlan. Liberty: Beebe & Morgans, 1873. 700 pp. (Repr. S. Fallsburg: N.p., 1965-66.)

## Tioga County

History of Tioga . . . County, 1879, *see* p. 244. (Also repr. Ovid: W.E. Morrison & Co., 1980. 212 pp.)

An Outline History of . . . Tioga . . County, 1885, *see* p. 244.

Historical Gazetteer of Tioga County, New York, 1785-1888, comp. and ed. by William B. Gay and M.F. Roberts. 2 vols. Syracuse: W.B. Gay & Co. [1887]. 493, 245 pp. (Repr. Evansville, Ind.: Unigraphic, 1980.)

Our County and Its People, ed. by L. Kingman. 2 vols. Elmira: N.p., 1897.

History of . . . Tioga County, 1932, in History of Central New York, *see* p. 244.

## Tompkins County

History of . . . Tompkins . . . County, 1879, *see* p. 244.

An Outline History of . . . Tompkins . . . County, 1885, *see* p. 244.

Landmarks of Tompkins County . . . ed. by John H. Selkreg. 3 parts. Syracuse: D. Mason & Co., 1894. viii, 704, 71, 276 pp. (Repr. Evansville, Ind.: Unigraphic, 1980.)

History of . . . Tompkins . . . County, 1932, in History of Central New York, *see* p. 244.

[History of] Tompkins . . . County, 1941, in Central New York, *see* p. 244.

## Tryon County

Annals of Tryon County . . . by William W. Campbell. New York: J. & J. Harper, 1831. (2d ed., called "The Border Warfare of New York . . ." Cherry Valley: Cherry Valley Gazette, 1849. 396 pp. [3d ed.] Cherry Valley: Cherry Valley Gazette, 1880. 312 pp. [4th ed.] New York: Dodd, Mead & Co., 1924. 257 pp.)

## Ulster County

History of Ulster County . . . by Nathaniel B. Sylvester. 2 vols. Philadelphia: Everts & Peck, 1880. 211, 229 pp. (Complete-name index, by Jean D. Worden. Franklin, Ohio: Worden, 1983. 204 pp. Repr. with added index. Interlaken: Heart of the Lakes Pub., 1983.)

The History of Ulster County, ed. by Alphonse T. Clearwater. Kingston: W.J. Van Deusen, 1907. 712, xii pp.

A History of Ulster County Under the Dominion of the Dutch, by Augustus H. Van Buren. Kingston: N.p., 1923. 146 pp.

History of the . . . County of . . . Ulster, 1931, in History of the Valley of the Hudson, *see* p. 244.

History of the County of Ulster, 1946, in Southeastern New York, *see* p. 244.

## Warren County

History of Warren County . . . ed. by Henry P. Smith. Syracuse: D. Mason & Co., 1885. 702 pp. (Repr. with added index, by Robert McAlear. Interlaken: Heart of the Lakes Pub., 1981. 808 pp.)

History of the . . . County of . . . Warren, 1931, in History of the Valley of the Hudson, *see* p. 244.

Warren County; a History and Guide, comp. by W.P.A. Glens Falls: Glens Falls Post Co., 1942. 275 pp.

History of Warren County, ed. by William H. Brown. Glens Falls: Bd. of Supervisors of Warren Co., 1963. 302 pp.

Backward Glances: Reminiscences of Warren County, by H. Mason. 3 vols. N.p., 1963-65. 1,138, 146, 111 pp. (Based on articles in Glens Falls newspapers.)

## Washington County

Gazette of the County of Washington, New York . . . by Allen Corey. Schuylerville: N.p., 1849. 264 pp.

History of Washington County . . . [by Crisfield Johnson]. Philadelphia: Everts & Ensign, 1878. 504, 131 pp. (Repr. Interlaken: Heart of the Lakes Pub., 1979. 704 pp.)

History and Biography of Washington County . . . Chicago: Gresham Pub. Co., 1894. 436 pp.

Washington County: Its History to the Close of the Nineteenth Century . . . by William L. Stone. 2 parts. New York: New York Hist. Co., 1901. xiii, 570, 318 pp.

History of the . . . County of . . . Washington, 1931, in History of the Valley of the Hudson, *see* p. 244.

History of Washington County, comp. by W. Hill. Fort Edward: comp., 1932. 298 pp.

## Wayne County

History of the . . . County of . . . Wayne, 1851, in History of the Pioneer Settlement of Phelps and Gorham's Purchase, *see* p. 244.

History of Wayne County . . . 1789-1877, by W. McIntosh. Philadelphia: Everts & Ensign, 1877. 216 pp. (Repr. Centennial ed. Pultneysville: Yankee Peddler Bookshop, 1975. Repr. Ovid: W.E. Morris & Co., 1976.)

Landmarks of Wayne County . . . ed. by Hon. George W. Cowles, et al. Syracuse: D. Mason & Co., 1895. viii, 437, 41, 343 pp.

History of the . . . County of . . . Wayne, 1925, in History of the Genesee Country, *see* p. 244.

History of . . . Wayne . . . County, 1932, in History of Central New York, *see* p. 244.

Historical Sketch of Wayne County, by D.A.R. N.p., 1940. 137 pp.

## Westchester County

A History of the County of Westchester, from Its First Settlement to the Present Time, by Robert Bolton, Jr. 2 vols. New York: A.S. Gould, 1848. (Carefully rev. by author. 2 vols. N.Y.: C.F. Roper, 1881. 3d ed. 2 vols. New York: N.p., 1905.)

History of Westchester County . . . by J. Thomas Scharf. 2 vols. Philadelphia: L.E. Preston, 1886. 893, 772 pp.

Manual of Westchester County, Past and Present . . . by Henry T. Smith. 3 vols. White Plains: H.T. Smith, 1898-1913. 300, 330, 335 pp.

Biographical History of Westchester County. 2 vols. Chicago: Lewis Pub. Co., 1899. 992 pp.

History of Westchester County, from Its Earliest Settlement to the Year 1900, by Frederic Shonnard and W.W. Spooner. New York: New York Hist. Co., 1900. vi, 638 pp. (Repr. Harrison: Harbor Hill Books, 1974 and 1983.)

History of Westchester County, New York, Alvah P. French, ed. in chief. 5 vols. New York: Lewis Hist. Pub. Co., 1925-27.

History of the . . . County of . . . Westchester, 1931, in History of the Valley of the Hudson, *see* p. 244.

Historic Westchester, 1683-1933. Glimpses of County History, by Elisabeth Cushman and J. Nichols. [Tarrytown: N.p., 1933.] 135 pp.

Westchester County and Its People, a Record . . . ed. under the direction of Ernest F. Griffin. 3 vols. New York: Lewis Hist. Pub. Co. [1946].

Westchester County, a Pictorial History, by Susan C. Swanson and E.G. Fuller. Norfolk, Va.: Donning Co., 1982. 200 pp.

Westchester County: the Past Hundred Years, 1883-1983, ed. by Marilyn E. Weigold. Harrison: Harbor Hill Books for Westchester County Hist. Soc., Valhalla, 1984. 368 pp.

## Wyoming County

History of the . . . County of . . . Wyoming, 1851, in History of the Pioneer Settlement of Phelps and Gorham's Purchase, *see* p. 244.

History of Wyoming County . . . New York: F.W. Beers, 1880. 310 pp. (Complete-name index, comp. by Laverne C. Cooley and R.M. French. Batavia: Cooley [1949]. 83 pp. Name index. Interlaken: Heart of the Lakes Pub., 1983. 40 pp.)

History of the . . . County of . . . Wyoming, 1925, in History of the Genesee Country, *see* p. 244.

## Yates County

History of the . . . County of . . . Yates, 1851, in History of the Pioneer Settlement of Phelps and Gorham's Purchase, *see* p. 244.

History and Directory of Yates County . . . by Stafford C. Cleveland. Vol. 1 (all pub.). Penn Yan: N.p., 1873. (Repr. 2 vols. Penn Yan: C.L. Wheeler, 1951. xxiii, 1,168 pp. (Vol. 2 not previously pub.; only Part 1 was ever pr., ends at p. 1,168 in mid-sentence.) Index, comp. by F. E. Bootes. Middlesex: Bootes, 1954. 25 leaves.)

History of Yates County . . . ed. by Lewis C. Aldrich. Syracuse: D. Mason & Co., 1892. 671 pp.

Students' Handbook of Yates County, ed. by W. Stork. Penn Yan: N.p., 1898. 158 pp.

History of the . . . County of . . . Yates, 1925, in History of the Genesee Country, *see* p. 244.

History of . . . Yates . . . County, 1932, in History of Central New York, *see* p. 244.

# North Carolina

## Alamance County

The History of Alamance . . . by Sallie W. (Stockard) Magness. Raleigh: Capital Pr. Co., 1900. 166 pp.

Centennial History of Alamance County, 1849-1949, by Walter Whitaker. Burlington: Burlington Chamber of Commerce, and Charlotte: Dowd Pr., 1949. 270 pp.

## Alexander County

Historical Sketches of Alexander County, North Carolina . . . by Rev. A.L. Crouse. Hickory: A.L. Crouse & Son, 1905. 124 pp.

Prologue: a History of Alexander County, by Ben L. Pittard. Taylorsville: N.p., 1958. 67 pp.

## Alleghany County

Alleghany County Heritage, ed. by Alleghany Historical Genealogical Society. Winston-Salem: Hunter Pub. Co., 1983. 555 pp.

## Anson County

History of Anson County, North Carolina, 1750-1976, by Mary L. Medley. Wadesboro: Anson County Hist. Soc., 1976. xvii, 417 pp.

## Ashe County

Ashe County, a History, by Arthur L. Fletcher. Jefferson: Ashe County Research Assoc. [1963]. xvi, 403 pp.

## Avery County

History of Avery County, North Carolina, by Horton Cooper. Asheville: Biltmore Pr. [1964]. 100 pp.

## Beaufort County

Some Colonial History of Beaufort County, North Carolina [by Francis H. Cooper]. Chapel Hill: The University, 1916. 45 pp.

Beaufort County, Two Centuries of Its History, by C. Wingate Reed. [Raleigh:] N.p., 1962. vi, 244 pp.

## Bertie County

Colonial Bertie County, North Carolina, abstracted and indexed by Mary B. Bell. 4 vols. Windsor: N.p., 1963-65.

Bertie County: a Brief History, by Alan D. Watson. Raleigh: Div. of Archives and History, 1982. vii, 91 pp.

## Buncombe County

Asheville and Buncombe County, by Foster A. Sondley; Genesis of Buncombe County, by Theodore F. Davidson. Asheville: The Citizen, 1922. 200 pp.

A History of Buncombe County, North Carolina, by Foster A. Sondley. 2 vols. in 1. Asheville: Miller Pr. Co., 1930. (Repr. Spartanburg, S.C.: Reprint Co., 1977. 919 pp.)

Historical Facts Concerning Buncombe County Government, by George A. Digges. Asheville: Biltmore Pr., 1935. 316 pp.

The Heritage of Old Buncombe County, North Carolina, ed. by Doris C. Ward. Asheville: Old Buncombe County Gen. Soc., 1983. 524 pp.

## Burke County

Burke County: a Brief History, by Edward W. Phifer, Jr. Raleigh: Div. of Archives and History, 1979. viii, 144 pp.

The Heritage of Burke County, North Carolina, ed. by Jean C. Ervin and N.M. Triebert. Morganton: Burke County Hist. Soc., 1981. 524 pp.

## Cabarrus County

Historical Shadows of Cabarrus County, North Carolina, by Jordon K. Rouse. Charlotte: Crabtree Pr., 1970. xi, 132 pp.

## Caldwell County

Annals of Caldwell County, by William W. Scott. Lenoir: News-Topic Pr., 1930. 174 pp.

Here Will I Dwell; the Story of Caldwell County, by Nancy Alexander. [Salisbury: Rowan Pr. Co., 1956], and Lenoir: Author, 1956. 230 pp.

## Camden County

Three Hundred Years Along the Pasquotank; a Biographical History of Camden County, by Jesse F. Pugh. Old. Trap: [Author, 1957]. xi, 249 pp.

## Carteret County

Carteret County Economic and Social, by Aleeze Lefferts, et al. Chapel Hill: Univ. of North Carolina Pr., 1926. 100 pp.

Portsmouth Island: Short Stories and History, by Ben B. Salter. [Atlantic?: N.p., 1972.] 72 pp.

*Carteret County (cont.)*

The Heritage of Carteret County, North Carolina, ed. by Pat Davis and Kathy Hamilton. Beaufort: Carteret County Hist. Research Assoc., 1982. 520 pp.

## Catawba County

A History of Catawba County, ed. by Charles J. Presler, Jr. Catawba County Historical Association. Salisbury: Rowan Pr. Co., 1954. 526 pp.

## Chatham County

Chatham County, 1771-1971, ed. by Wade Hadley, et al. [N.p.: Chatham County Hist. Soc., 1971.] 487 pp.

## Cherokee County

Our Heritage, the People of Cherokee County, North Carolina, 1540-1955, by Margaret Freel. Asheville: Miller Pr. Co., 1956. xiv, 407 pp.

The Cherokee Indians and Those Who Came After; Notes for a History of Cherokee County, North Carolina, 1835-1860, by Nathaniel C. Browder. Hayesville: Browder, 1973. 408 pp.

## Chowan County

Economic and Social History of Chowan County, North Carolina, 1800-1915, by W.S. Boyce. New York: Columbia Univ., 1917. (Ph.D. thesis)

## Cleveland County

The Living Past of Cleveland County, a History, by Lee B. Weathers. [Shelby: Star Pub. Co., 1956.] 269 pp. (Repr. with new index. Spartanburg, S.C.: Reprint Co., 1980.)

The Heritage of Cleveland County, North Carolina, ed. by Jim Marler. Shelby: Cleveland County Heritage Comm., 1982. 683 pp.

## Columbus County

Columbus County, North Carolina, by James A. Rogers. Whiteville: News Reporter, 1946. 108 pp.

## Cumberland County

Short History of Cumberland County and the Cape Fear Section, by James H. Myrover. Fayetteville: [Baptist Pub. Co., 1905]. 32 pp.

## Dare County

Fabulous Dare: the Story of Dare County, Past and Present, by David Stick. Kitty Hawk: Dare Pr. [1949]. 71 pp. (Repr. Raleigh: North Carolina Div. of Archives & Hist., 1970. 64 pp.)

*Dare County (cont.)*

Some Whisper of Our Name . . . by Neil W. Wechter. Manteo: Times Pr. Co. [1975].

## Davidson County

Davidson County, Economic and Social, by M. Jewell Smith. Chapel Hill: Univ. of North Carolina, 1925. 86 pp.

Centennial History of Davidson County, North Carolina, by Rev. Jacob C. Leonard. Raleigh: Edwards & Broughton Co., 1927. xvi, 270 pp.

Pathfinders Past and Present: a History of Davidson County, North Carolina, by M. Jewell Smith. High Point: Hall Pr. Co., 1972. vi, 461 pp.

The Heritage of Davidson County, North Carolina, ed. by Mary J. Shoaf and Katherine Skipper. Lexington: Gen. Soc. of Davidson County, 1982. 800 pp.

## Davie County

History of Davie County in the Forks of the Yadkin, by James W. Wall. Mocksville: Davie County Hist. Pub. Assoc. [1969]. viii, 406 pp.

Davie County . . . a Brief History, by James W. Wall. Raleigh: North Carolina Div. of Archives & Hist., 1976. 128 pp.

## Duplin County

Flashes of Duplin's History and Government, ed. by Faison W. McGowen. Kenansville: N.p., 1971. xv, 569 pp.

## Durham County

Durham County, Economic and Social, by W.M. Upchurch and M.B. Fowler. Chapel Hill: Univ. of North Carolina, 1918. 93 pp.

## Edgecombe County

History of Edgecombe County, North Carolina, by J. Kelly Turner and J.L. Bridgers, Jr. Raleigh: Edwards & Broughton Co., 1920. 486 pp.

Edgecombe County: a Brief History, by Alan D. Watson. Raleigh: Div. of Archives and History, 1979. ix, 109 pp.

## Forsyth County

Forsyth County, by Adelaide L. Fries. Salem: Stewart's Pr. House, 1898. 135 pp.

Forsyth County, Economic and Social, by Charles N. Siewers. New Bern: O.G. Dunn, 1924, and Chapel Hill: Univ. of North Carolina, 1924. 110 pp.

Forsyth, a County on the March, by Adelaide L. Fries, et al. Chapel Hill: Univ. of North Carolina Pr., 1949. vii, 248 pp.

## Franklin County

Historical Sketches of Franklin County, by Edward H. Davis. Raleigh: Edwards & Broughton Co., 1948. 298 pp.

## Gaston County

Gastonia and Gaston County, North Carolina; Past and Present, Future, by Joseph H. Separk. [Kingsport, Tenn.: Kingsport Pr., 1936.] 174 pp.

History of Gaston County, by Minnie S. Puett. Charlotte: Observer Pr. House, 1939. 218 pp.

Gastonia and Gaston County, 1849-1949. Gastonia: N.p., 1949. 237 pp.

Early History of Belmont and Gaston County, North Carolina, by R.L. Stowe. N.p., 1951. 61 pp.

The County of Gaston; Two Centuries of a North Carolina Region, by Robert F. Cope and M.W. Wellman. [Gastonia?:] Gaston County Hist. Soc., 1961. 274 pp.

## Granville County

Granville County, North Carolina. Notes and Memoranda for the History of Granville County and Genealogies, by Thomas M. Owen. 3 vols. Montgomery, Ala.: N.p. [190-].

A History of Granville County, North Carolina . . . Chapel Hill: Univ. of North Carolina, 1950. 268 pp. (dissertation)

Granville County, North Carolina Potpourri, comp. by Virginia R. Lyle. Nashville, Tenn.: Vee El Ancestral Studies, 1969. 178 leaves.

## Greene County

History of Greene County, North Carolina, by James M. Creech. Baltimore: Gateway Pr., 1979. 705 pp.

## Guilford County

The History of Guilford County, North Carolina, by Sallie W. Magness. Knoxville, Tenn.: Gaut-Ogden Co., 1902. 197 pp.

## Halifax County

History of Halifax County, by W.C. Allen. Boston: Cornhill Co. [1918]. xvi, 235 pp.

Halifax County, Economic and Social, by S.B. Allen and R.S. Travis, Jr. Chapel Hill: Univ. of North Carolina, 1920. 106 pp.

The Spirit of Roanoke; a Pageant of Halifax County History . . . Roanoke Rapids: Herald Pub. Co., 1921. 78 pp.

## Harnett County

They Passed This Way; a Personal Narrative of Harnett County History, by Malcolm Fowler. Centennial ed. [Lillington?:] Harnett County Centennial Inc., 1955. 167 pp.

## Haywood County

Centennial of Haywood County and Its County Seat, Waynesville, North Carolina, 1808-1908. Waynesville: Courier Pr. Co., 1908. 184 pp.

The Annals of Haywood County, North Carolina; Historical, Sociological, Biographical, and Genealogical, by William C. Allen. N.p., 1935. 628 pp. (Repr. Spartanburg, S.C.: Reprint Co., 1982. 714 pp. With new genealogical index, by Lois S. Neal.)

The Middle History of Haywood County, with Story Supplement, by W. Clark Medford. Waynesville: N.p., 1968. xi, 165 pp.

Haywood's Heritage and Finest Hour, by W. Clark Medford. Waynesville: N.p., 1971. vii, 112 pp.

## Henderson County

The Story of Henderson County, by Sadie S. Patton. Asheville: Miller Pr. Co. [1947]. (Repr. Spartanburg, S.C.: Reprint Co., 1982. xv, 290 pp.)

Postmarks: a History of Henderson County, North Carolina, 1787-1867, by Lenoir Ray. Chicago: Adams Pr., 1970. 412 pp.

## Hertford County

History of North Carolina, with Special Reference to the Annals of Hertford County and the Albemarle Country, by John W. Moore. 3 vols. Extracted from the Murfreesboro Inquirer, 1877-78. N.p., n.d.

The Colonial and State Political History of Hertford County, North Carolina, by Benjamin B. Winborne. [Murfreesboro?:] Edwards & Broughton Co., 1906. 348 pp. (Repr. with added foreword. Baltimore: Genealogical Pub. Co., 1976. 356 pp..)

## Iredell County

The Heritage of Iredell County, North Carolina, by Mildred Miller. Statesville: Gen. Soc. of Iredell County, 1980. 648 pp.

## Johnston County

Johnston County, Economic and Social, by William Sanders, Jr., and G.Y. Ragsdale. Smithfield: Smithfield Observer, 1922. 95 pp.

## Lenoir County

The Story of Kinston and Lenoir County, by Talmage C. Johnson and C.R. Holloman. Raleigh: Edwards & Broughton Co., 1954. xv, 413 pp.

*Lenoir County (cont.)*

Annals of Progress, the Story of Lenoir County and Kinston, North Carolina, by William S. Powell. Raleigh: North Carolina Div. of Archives & Hist., 1963. 107 pp.

The Heritage of Lenoir County, North Carolina, ed. by Mildred Matthis and Ed. Cooper. Kinston: Lenoir Co. Hist. Assoc., 1981. 564 pp.

## Lincoln County

Annals of Lincoln County, North Carolina . . . Lincoln County History Through the Years 1749 to 1937, by William L. Sherrill. Charlotte: Observer Pr. House, 1937. 536 pp. (Repr. Baltimore: Regional Pub. Co., 1972.)

## Macon County

Macon County, North Carolina, by Henry Stewart, Jr. Highlands: Blue Ridge Pr., 1902. 30 pp.

## Madison County

The Kingdom of Madison; a Southern Mountain Fastness and Its People . . . by Manly W. Wellman. Chapel Hill: Univ. of North Carolina Pr. [1973]. x, 222 pp.

This is Madison County, by Jinsie Underwood. Mars Hill: Underwood [1974]. 71 leaves.

## Martin County

Martin County History, by Francis M. Manning and W.H. Booker. Williamston: Enterprise Pub., 1977. 337 pp.

The Heritage of Martin County, North Carolina, ed. by Selby J.N. Hughes. Williamston: Martin County Hist. Soc., 1980. 776 pp.

## Mecklenburg County

The History of Mecklenburg County from 1740 to 1900, by John B. Alexander. Charlotte: Observer Pr. House, 1902. iv, 481 pp.

History of Mecklenburg County and the City of Charlotte, from 1740 to 1903, by Daniel A. Tompkins. 2 vols. Charlotte: Observer Pr. House, 1903.

Hornets' Nest; the Story of Charlotte and Mecklenburg County, by LeGette Blythe and C.R. Brockman. Charlotte: Pub. Lib. of Charlotte & Mecklenburg County, by McNally, 1961. 511 pp.

Mecklenburg: a Bicentennial Story, by Dannye Romine. Charlotte: Independence Square Assoc. [1975]. 84 pp.

## Montgomery County

The Heritage of Montgomery County, North Carolina, ed. by Mrs. Winnie Richter. Mount Gilead: Montgomery County Hist. Soc., 1981. 480 pp.

## Moore County

A History of Moore County, North Carolina, 1747-1847, by Blackwell P. Robinson. Southern Pines: Moore County Hist. Assoc., 1956. 270 pp.

The County of Moore, 1847-1947; a North Carolina Region's Second Hundred Years, by Manly W. Wellman. Southern Pines: Moore County Hist. Assoc., 1962. viii, 254 pp.

The Story of Moore County; Two Centuries of a North Carolina Region, by Manly W. Wellman. [Southern Pines:] Moore County Hist. Assoc., 1974. x, 190 pp.

## New Hanover County

A History of New Hanover County and the Lower Cape Fear Region, 1723-1800, by Alfred M. Waddell. Vol. 1 (no more pub.). [Wilmington?: N.p., 1909.] 232 pp.

Pictorial and Historical New Hanover County and Wilmington, North Carolina, 1723-1938, by W.L. De Rossett. Wilmington: N.p., 1938. 110 pp.

New Hanover County: a Brief History, by Lawrence Lee. Raleigh: North Carolina Div. of Archives & Hist., 1971. xiv, 124 pp. (Rev. and repr. Raleigh: North Carolina Div. of Archives, 1977.)

## Onslow County

The Commonwealth of Onslow; a History, by Joseph P. Brown. New Bern: O.G. Dunn, 1960. v, 434 pp.

The Heritage of Onslow County, ed. by The Onslow County Historical Society. Winston-Salem: Hunter Pub. Co., 1983. 515 pp.

## Orange County

Orange County, 1752-1952, ed. by Hugh Lefler and P. Wager. Chapel Hill: N.p., 1953. x, 389 pp.

## Pamlico County

A Glimpse of Pamlico County, comp. by Marion W. Hardy. Oriental: N.p., 1978. 152 pp.

## Pender County

History of Pender County, North Carolina, by Mattie Bloodworth. Richmond, Va.: Dietz Pr., 1947. x, 240 pp.

## Perquimans County

History of Perquimans County . . . from 1681 . . . by Ellen G. (Watson) Winslow. Raleigh: Edwards & Broughton Co., 1931. xi, 488 pp. (Repr. Baltimore: Regional Pub. Co., 1974.)

## Person County

Reminiscences: a Sketch and Letters Descriptive of Life in Person County in Former Days, by Alexander R. Foushee. Durham: Seeman Pr., 1921. 81 pp.

The Heritage of Person County, North Carolina, ed. by Mrs. Madeleine Eaker. 2 vols. Roxboro: Person County Hist. Soc., 1981-83.

## Pitt County

Sketches of Pitt County, a Brief History of the County, 1704-1910, by Henry T. King. Raleigh: Edwards & Broughton Co., 1911. 263 pp.

Pitt County, Economic and Social, by Pitt County Club. Chapel Hill: Univ. of North Carolina Pr., 1920. 78 pp.

The Heritage of Pitt County, North Carolina, ed. by Elizabeth Copeland. Greenville: Pitt County Hist. Soc., 1982. 888 pp.

## Polk County

Sketches of Polk County History, by Sadie S. Patton. [Hendersonville:] N.p., 1950. xiv, 161 pp. (Repr. Spartanburg, S.C.: Reprint Co., 1976. 175 pp.)

## Randolph County

Reminiscences of Randolph County, by Joseph A. Blair. Greensboro: Reece & Elam, 1890. 57 pp.

Randolph County, Economic and Social, by Fred Burgess. Chapel Hill: Univ. of North Carolina, 1924. 90 pp.

Randolph County, 1779-1979. Asheboro: Randolph County Hist. Soc., 1980. 304 pp.

## Robeson County

The State of Robeson . . . by Robert C. Lawrence. [New York: J.J. Little & Ives, 1939.] xiii, 279 pp.

## Rockingham County

Rockingham County, Economic and Social, by Rockingham Club. Chapel Hill: Univ. of North Carolina, and Raleigh: Edwards & Broughton Co., 1918. 84 pp.

Rockingham County: a Brief History, by Lindley S. Butler. Raleigh: Div. of Archives and History, 1982. xiv, 92 pp.

The Heritage of Rockingham County, North Carolina, ed. by Charles D. Rodenbough. Winston-Salem: Hunter Pub. Co., 1983. 759 pp.

# Rowan County

A History of Rowan County, North Carolina, by Rev. Jethro Rumple. Salisbury: J.J. Bruner, 1881. vii, 408, x pp. (Repr. with new index, by Edith M. Clark. N.p., 1929; Repr. with new index, by Edith M. Clark. Bicentennial ed. Baltimore: Regional Pub. Co., 1978. 434 pp.)

A Colonial History of Rowan County, North Carolina [by Samuel J. Ervin, Jr.]. Chapel Hill: Univ. of North Carolina Pr., 1917.

The Rowan Story, 1753-1953; a Narrative History of Rowan County, North Carolina. Salisbury: Rowan Pr. Co., 1953. 402 pp.

Rowan County, a Brief History, by James S. Brawley. Raleigh: North Carolina Div. of Archives & Hist., 1974. xi, 178 pp.

# Rutherford County

Rutherford, Economic and Social, by R.E. Price. Chapel Hill: Univ. of North Carolina, 1918. 76 pp.

History of Old Tryon and Rutherford County, North Carolina, 1730-1936, by Clarence W. Griffin. Asheville: Miller Pr. Co., 1937. xv, 640 pp. (Repr. Spartanburg, S.C.: Reprint Co., 1982, xv, 640, 41 pp., index.)

History of Rutherford County, 1937-1951, by Clarence W. Griffin. Asheville: The Inland Pr., 1952. 136 pp.

# Sampson County

Sampson County, Economic and Social, by North Carolina Club of University of Carolina. Chapel Hill: Univ. of North Carolina, 1917. 68 pp.

The Heritage of Sampson County, ed. by Oscar M. Bizzell. Winston-Salem: Hunter Pub. Co., 1983. 771 pp.

# Stanly County

Stanly County, U.S.A.: the Story of an Era and an Area, 1841-1872, by Ivey L. Sharpe. 2d ed. Greensboro: Piedmont Pr., 1972. v, 264 pp.

# Stokes County

The Heritage of Stokes County, North Carolina, ed. by John Woodard. Germanton: Stokes County Hist. Soc., 1981. 548 pp.

# Surry County

History of Surry County, or Annals of Northwest North Carolina, by Jesse G. Hollingsworth. [Greensboro: W.H. Fisher, 1935.] 284 pp.

The Heritage of Surry County, North Carolina, ed. by Mrs. Hester Jackson. Dobson: Surry County Gen. Assoc., 1983. 690 pp.

## Tyrrell County

History of Tyrrell County, by David E. Davis. Norfolk, Va.: J. Christopher Pr. [1963]. iii, 98 pp.

## Union County

A Story of Union County and the History of Pleasant Grove Camp Ground, by George T. Winchester. Mineral Springs: Author, 1937. 104 pp.

History of Union County, by H. Nelson Walden. Monroe: N.p., 1964. 79 pp.

## Vance County

"Zebs Black Baby"; Vance County, North Carolina, by Samuel T. Peace. Henderson: Author, 1955. 457 pp.

## Wake County

Historical Raleigh with Sketches of Wake County and Its Important Towns, by Moses N. Amis. Raleigh: Commercial Pr. Co., 1902. 289 pp. (Rev. and enl., 1913.)

History of Wake County, North Carolina . . . by Hope S. Chamberlain. Raleigh: Edwards & Broughton Co., 1922. 302 pp.

The Heritage of Wake County, ed. by Lynne Belvin and H. Riggs. Winston-Salem: Hunter Pub. Co., 1983. 670 pp.

## Warren County

The County of Warren, North Carolina, 1586-1917, by Manly W. Wellman. Chapel Hill: Univ. of North Carolina Pr. [1959]. 282 pp.

## Watauga County

A History of Watauga County, North Carolina . . . by John P. Arthur. Richmond, Va.: Everett Waddey & Co., 1915. x, 364 pp. (Repr. with new index. Easley, S.C.: Southern Hist. Pr., 1979. 443 pp.)

History of Watauga County, by Daniel J. Whitener. Souvenir of Watauga Centennial, Boone, North Carolina. Boone: N.p., 1949. 112 pp.

## Wayne County

The Heritage of Wayne County, North Carolina, coordinated by Mary Johnstone. Goldsboro: Wayne County Hist. Assoc., 1982. 544 pp.

## Wilkes County

Historical Sketches of Wilkes County, by John Crouch. Wilkesboro: J. Crouch, 1902. 145 pp.

The Land of Wilkes, by Johnson J. Hayes. Wilkesboro: Wilkes County Hist. Soc., 1962. xii, 577 pp.

*Wilkes County (cont.)*

The Heritage of Wilkes County, North Carolina, ed. by Mrs. W.O. Absher. North Wilkesboro: Wilkes Gen. Soc., 1983. 528 pp.

## Yadkin County

Yadkin County Record Book. Yadkinville: James Williams Pr. Co., 1939. 97 pp.

An Illustrated History of Yadkin County, 1850-1965 [by William E. Rutledge, Jr.]. [Yadkinville: N.p., 1965.] 180 pp.

The Heritage of Yadkin County, North Carolina, ed. by Frances H. Casstevens. Yadkinville: Yadkin County Hist. Soc., 1981. 776 pp.

## Yancey County

History and Geography of Yancey County. Teacher Training Class, Burnsville. Burnsville: Edwards Pr. Co. [1930]. 70 pp.

# NORTH DAKOTA

## Adams County

Adams County Founding, 1937, *see* Hettinger County.

Prairie Pioneers; a Story of Adams County, ed. by Mrs. Harley Erickson and Mrs. D. Merwin. Bismarck: Taylor Pub. Co., 1976. 653 pp.

Pioneer Sons and Daughters: History of Adams County, ed. by Marjorie Erickson and G. Olson. Sponsored by Dakota Buttes Historical Society. [Hettinger:] The Society [1980]. 248 pp.

## Barnes County

Barnes County History: Barnes County, North Dakota. Dallas, Tex.: Taylor Pub. Co. for Barnes County Hist. Soc., Valley City, 1976. 360 pp.

## Billings County

Echoing Trails: Billings County History. [Fargo: Knight Pr. Co., for Billings County Hist. Soc., Medora, 1979.] 635 pp.

## Bottineau County

En norske bygds historie: nordre Bottineau County, North Dakota, av Olav Redal. [One Norwegian Town's History, District of Bottineau County.] [Stanley:] Fortfatterens Forlag [Forefathers Pr.], 1917. 240 pp.

Historical Highlights of Bottineau County. [N.p.:] Bismarck Quality Pr., for Bottineau County Hist. Soc. [1977]. 151 pp.

## Bowman County

Prairie Tales. [Sioux Falls, S. Dak.: Midwest-Beach Pr. Co., 1965.] 388 pp.

## Burke County

Burke County and White Earth Valley Historical Society, 1971. [Bismarck: Quality Pr. Co., 1972.] 1,288 pp. (Covers years 1896-1971.)

## Burleigh County

Present Burleigh County and Bismarck, North Dakota. [Bismarck:] League of Women Voters of Bismarck, 1964. 54 pp.

Burleigh County: Prairie Trails to Hi-Ways, comp. and ed. by Beth H. Bauman and D.J. Jackson. Bismarck: Bismarck-Mandan Hist. and Gen. Soc., by Taylor Pub. Co., Dallas, Tex. [1978]. iv, 627 pp.

## Cass County

Rural Cass County: the Land and People, by David Staples. Dallas, Tex.: Taylor Pub. Co., for Cass County Hist. Soc., 1976. 944 pp.

## Dickey County

A History of Dickey County, North Dakota . . . ed. by R.M. Black. Ellendale: Dickey County Hist. Soc., 1930. 333 pp.

History of the Finnish Settlement in Brown, South Dakota and Dickey, North Dakota, Counties of South and North Dakota, 1881-1955. 2d ed. [Savo, S. Dak.: Savo Finnish Hist. Soc., 1956.] 128 pp.

History of Dickey County. [Oakes: Oakes Times? for Dickey County Hist. Soc., 1976.] 95 pp.

Once in a Hundred, 1882-1982. [Dickey: Dickey Centennial Hist. Book Comm., by Litchfield Bull., 1982.] 170 pp.

## Divide County

Stories and Histories of Divide County, written by the Participants or Relatives. [Marceline, Mo.: Walsworth Pub. Co., 1964.] 474 pp. (Repr. [Crosby: Divide County Book Comm.], 1974. 9,414 pp.)

## Emmons County

Emmons County History, comp. for the Bicentennial, 1976, ed. by Ellen Woods and E. Wenzel. [Linton: Emmons Co. Record?], 1976. 206 pp.

## Foster County

A History of Foster County, comp. by Foster County History Book Committee. Foster: The Comm., 1983. iv, 457, 113, 22 pp.

## Golden Valley County

Golden Valley County Pioneers, by Herman F. Dietz. Sentinel Butte: Centennial Comm., 1976. 431 pp.

## Grand Forks County

History of Grand Forks County . . . by Henry V. Arnold. Larimore: Pioneer Office, 1900. iv, 128 pp. (Repr.?: Author, 1918.)

Forty Years in North Dakota in Relation to Grand Forks County. Larimore: Arnold, 1921. 176 pp.

History of Grand Forks County, North Dakota, Assembled by Kempton Homemakers Club, 1964, updated and ed. by Mrs. Gilmore Lee. [Arville: The Club, 1974.] 32 pp.

*Grand Forks County (cont.)*

Grand Forks Heritage Book: a History of Rural Grand Forks County, North Dakota. 2 vols. Dallas, Tex.: Taylor Pub. Co., for Grand Forks County Heritage Book Comm., 1977-78.

## Grant County

Grant County, North Dakota, the Best of the Best. Carson: Carson Pr., 1925.

Prairie Pioneers, 1976. History of Grant County. New Leipzig: Grant County Hist. Soc., Quentin T. Michelson, 1976.

## Griggs County

Griggs County Heritage (Griggs County, North Dakota, 1879-1976). Dallas, Tex.: Taylor Pub. Co., 1976. 528 pp.

## Hettinger County

Thirtieth Anniversary Booklet in Commemoration of the Founding of Hettinger and Adams Counties, 1907-1937, comp. and pub. by the Adams County Record. (History of Adams County, by Jacob Sonderall.) N.p. [1938?].

50th Anniversary, Hettinger County, North Dakota . . . 50 Years of Progress, ed. by Ralph Shultz. [Mott: Mott Pioneer Pr., 1957.] 124 pp.

Our Hettinger County Heritage, by Enid Bern. Mott: Mott Pioneer Pr., 1975. 111 pp.

## La Moure County

The History of La Moure. La Moure: La Moure Chronicle, 1957. 124 pp.

La Moure County Bicentennial Celebration. La Moure: La Moure Chronicle, and Fargo: Kaye's Inc., 1976.

A History of La Moure, North Dakota, 1882-1982 (Jane Potts, Centennial Book Committee, Chairman). [La Moure?: Book Comm., 1982.] [Grafton: Grand Forks Assoc. Pr., 1982.] xiv, 372 pp.

## McIntosh County

Along the Trails of Yesterday, a Story of McIntosh County, by Nina F. Wishek. [Ashley:] Ashley Tribune, 1941. xv, 437 pp.

## McKenzie County

Early McKenzie County, North Dakota, by G.F. Shafer. N.p., 1913. 57 pp.

## McLean County

McLean County Heritage; McLean County, North Dakota, ed. by Stella Robinson and D. Staehr. Dallas, Tex.: Taylor Pub. Co., for McLean County Hist. Soc., 1978. 1,000 pp.

## Mercer County

Mercer County, by C.B. Heinemeyer. [Hazen:] Hazen Star [1942?].

## Morton County

Historic Mandan and Morton County, Early Days to 1970, by Palma Fristad. [Mandan: Mandan Chamber of Commerce, 1970.] 68 pp.

Morton Prairie Roots, comp. and ed. for the Morton County Historical Society's American Revolution Bicentennial Heritage Project, by Marion P. Peterson. Dallas, Tex.: Taylor Pub. Co. for the Heritage Project, 1975. vi, 846 pp.

## Mountrail County

Tales of Mighty Mountrail: a History of Mountrail County, North Dakota. Dallas, Tex.: Taylor Pub. Co., 1979. 632 pp.

## Oliver County

Oliver County History, 1906-1956. [Mandan: Young's] for North Dakota Old Settlers' 50th Anniversary Hist. Comm., 1956.

## Pembina County

A History of Pembina County, Pembina Centennial Committee. [N.p., 1967.] 60 pp.

Pembina County — "Then and Now" Heritage '76, pub. under auspices of the Pembina County Commissioners and the Pembina County Historical Society. Cavalier: Pembina Centennial Book Co., 1975. 200 pp.

## Pierce County

Fifty Years in Pierce County, by O.T. Tofsrud. [Rugby: Rachel Lindberg, 1943.]

A History of Pierce County, by O.T. Tofsrud. Rugby: N.p., 1936. 176 pp.

## Ramsey County

Ramsey County, North Dakota: 1883-1983, sponsored by the Lake Region Chautauqua Corp., comp. by the Centennial Heritage Book Committee, and written by the People of Ramsey County, North Dakota. 2 vols. N.p.: Lake Reg. Chautauqua Corp., by Dallas, Tex.: Taylor Pub. Co., 1982.

## Ransom County

The Early History of Ransom County, Including References to Sargent County, 1835-1885, by Henry V. Arnold. Larimore: Arnold, 1918. 74 pp.

Ransom County History, by Snorri M. Thorfinnson. Fort Ransom: Ransom County Hist. Soc., 1975.

## Renville County

Renville County History [1901-1976]. Mohall: Renville County Old Settlers' Assoc., 1976. 832 pp.

## Richland County

A History of Richland County . . . Early Settlers . . . [by Horace B. Crandall]. Colfax: Author, 1886. 144 pp.

A History of Richland County and the City of Wahpeton, North Dakota, by F.G. Callan. [Wahpeton: Globe Gazette, 1938?] 28 pp.

Richland County History. Wahpeton: Richland County Hist. Soc., 1976.

History of Richland County, North Dakota. Dallas, Tex.: Taylor Pub. Co. for Richland County Hist. Soc., 1977. 632 pp.

## Rolette County

History of Rolette County, North Dakota, by Laura T. Law. Minneapolis: Lund Pr. [1953]. 276 pp.

## Sargent County

The Early History of Ransom County, Including References to Sargent County, 1835-1885, by Henry V. Arnold. Larimore: Arnold, 1918. 74 pp.

Sargent County History, by Snorri M. Thorfinnson. N.p.: Sargent County Comm. [1976?]. 220 pp.

## Sheridan County

Sheridan County Heritage, '76, by Jim Wills. McClusky: McClusky Gazette, 1976. 210, 18 pp.

## Stark County

Stark County: Heritage and Destiny, ed. by Shirley Gilles, et al. Comp. and ed. by Stark County Historical Society. Bismarck: Taylor Pub. Co., 1978. viii, 792 pp.

## Steele County

Steele County, 1883-1983: a Centennial Commemoration, Steele County Historical Society. Finley: Steele Co. Pr., 1983. 440, 127 pp.

## Stutsman County

Glimpses of Jamestown and Stutsman County, by Mrs. W.F. Cushing. [Jamestown?: N.p.], 1915. 76 pp.

## Traill County

History of Traill County, by Clarence Anderson? Hillsboro: Author, 1976.

## Walsh County

Walsh Heritage; a Continued Story of Walsh County and Its Pioneers . . . [ed. by Mrs. Myrtle Balkee]. 2 vols. Centennial issue. [Grafton?:] Walsh County Hist. Soc., 1981, and Grafton Assoc. Pr., 1964.

Walsh Heritage: the Story of Walsh County and Its Pioneers, ed. by Gunder V. Berg, Walsh County Historical Society. 2 vols. Grafton: Grafton Assoc. Pr., 1976.

## Ward County

Ward County Diamond Jubilee, 1961. Minot: Ward County Diamond Jubilee, 1961. 78 pp.

## Wells County

The History of Wells County, North Dakota, and Its Pioneers . . . by Walter E. Spokesfield. [Valley City: N.p., 1929.] 804 pp.

## Williams County

Wonder of Williams: a History of Williams County, North Dakota. 2 vols. Williston: Williams County Hist. Soc., 1973.

# OHIO

## Regional

History of North Central Ohio, Embracing Richland, Ashland, Wayne, Medina, Lorain, Huron, and Knox Counties . . . by William A. Duff. 2 vols. Topeka, Kans.: Hist. Pub. Co., 1931.

Howe Historical Collections of Ohio. (Reprints of many county beginnings, town histories, some biographies, and sketches. Mostly about 20 pp. in length. Eighty-eight counties reprinted. Indianapolis, Ind.: Ye Olde Genealogie Shoppe, 1980s.)

## Adams County

A History of Adams County, Ohio, from Its Earliest Settlement to the Present Time . . . by Nelson W. Evans. West Union: E.B. Stivers, 1900. vii, 946 pp. (Repr. Evansville, Ind.: Unigraphic, 1979.)

## Allen County

History of Allen County, Ohio . . . Chicago: Warner, Beers, 1885. 824 pp.

History of Allen County, Ohio . . . ed. and comp. by Charles C. Miller. Chicago: Richmond & Arnold, 1906. 872 pp.

A Standard History of Allen County, Ohio; an Authentic Narrative of the Past . . . ed. by William Rusler. 2 vols. Chicago: American Hist. Soc., 1921.

A Guide to Lima and Allen County, Ohio, prepared by W.P.A. Lima: Lima Better Business Bureau, 1938. 64 pp.

## Ashland County

A History of the Pioneer and Modern Times of Ashland County, from the Earliest to the Present Date, by Horace S. Knapp. Philadelphia: Lippincott, 1863. 550 pp. (Index, by Elyzabeth S. McCorkle. [N.p., n.d.] 39 leaves.)

History of Ashland County, Ohio . . . by George W. Hill. [Cleveland:] Williams Bros., 1880. 408 pp.

Centennial Biographical History of . . . Ashland County, 1901, *see* Richland County.

History of Ashland County, Ohio, by Abraham J. Baughman. Chicago: S.J. Clarke Pub. Co., 1909. 864 pp. (Repr. Evansville, Ind.: Unigraphic, 1979.)

History of . . . Ashland County, 1931, in History of North Central Ohio, *see* above.

## Ashtabula County

History of Ashtabula County . . . by William W. Williams. Philadelphia: Williams Bros., 1878. 256 pp. (Repr. Evansville, Ind.: Unigraphic, 1974. Repr. Evansville, Ind.: Whipporwill, 1981. Repr. with every-name index. Jefferson: Ashtabula County Gen. Soc., 1983. 356 pp.)

Biographical History of Northwestern Ohio, Embracing the Counties of Ashtabula, Geauga and Lake. Chicago: Lewis Pub. Co., 1893. 1,028 pp.

Biographical History of Northeastern Ohio, Embracing the Counties of Ashtabula, Trumbull and Mahoning. Chicago: Lewis Pub. Co., 1893. 735 pp. (Repr., by John S. Stewart. 3 vols. N.p., 1935. 1,118 pp.)

History of Ashtabula County, Ohio, by Moina W. Large. 2 vols. Topeka, Kans.: Hist. Pub. Co., 1924.

## Athens County

Walker's History of Athens County . . . by Charles W. Walker. Cincinnati: R. Clarke, 1869. viii, 600 pp.

A Brief History of Athens County, by Clement L. Martzolff. Athens: Author, 1916. 40 pp.

Athens County, Ohio, by William E. Peters. Vol. 1 (no more pub.?). [Athens?:] N.p., 1947.

## Auglaize County

History of Auglaize County . . . by Robert Sutton. Wapakoneta: R. Sutton, 1880. 206 pp.

Early History of Auglaize County, by Joshua D. Simkins. St. Marys: Author, 1901. vi, 119 pp.

History of Western Ohio and Auglaize County . . . by C.W. Williamson. Columbus: Pr. of W.M. Linn, 1905. iii, 860 pp. (Repr. Evansville, Ind.: Unigraphic, 1974.)

History of Auglaize County, Ohio, ed. by William J. McMurray. 2 vols. Indianapolis, Ind.: Hist. Pub. Co., 1923. 1,240 pp.

A History of Auglaize County, Ohio, comp. by the Auglaize County Historical Society. Defiance: The Society, 1980. xii, 496 pp.

## Belmont County

History of Belmont and Jefferson Counties . . . by John A. Caldwell. Wheeling, W. Va.: Hist. Pub. Co., 1880. 611, xxx pp. (Repr. Evansville, Ind.: Unigraphic, 1976.)

Centennial History of Belmont County . . . ed. and comp. by Hon. A.T. McKelvey. 1801-1901. Chicago: Biographical Pub. Co. [1903?]. 833 pp. (Repr. Knightstown, Ind.: The Bookmark, 1977.)

## Brown County

The History of Brown County . . . Chicago: W.H. Beers, 1883. vii, 703, 308 pp.

History of . . . Brown County, 1913, *see* Clermont County.

Historical Collections of Brown County . . . comp. by Carl N. Thompson. Piqua: Hammer Graphics [1969]. xxxvi, 1,340 pp. (Repr. Ripley: N.p., 1971.)

## Butler County

A History and Biographical Cyclopaedia of Butler County, Ohio . . . Cincinnati: Western Biog. Pub. Co., 1882. xi, 666 pp.

Memorial Record of Butler County . . . Chicago: Record Pub. Co., 1894. 447 pp.

Centennial History of Butler County, Ohio, ed. by Hon. Bert S. Bartlow, et al. Indianapolis, Ind.: B.F. Bowen & Co., 1905. 989 pp.

## Carroll County

History of Carroll and Harrison Counties, Ohio, under ed. supervision of Judge H.J. Eckley. 2 vols. Chicago: Lewis Pub. Co., 1921.

Early History of Carroll County, by Velma Griffin. 2d ed. Carrollton: Carroll County Hist. Soc., 1973. 28 pp.

## Champaign County

The History of Champaign and Logan Counties, from Their First Settlement, by Joshua Antrim. Bellefontaine: Press Pr. Co., 1872. 460 pp.

The History of Champaign County . . . Chicago: W.H. Beers, 1881. 921 pp.

A Centennial Biographical History of Champaign County . . . New York: Lewis Pub. Co., 1902. 724 pp.

History of Champaign County, Ohio, by Evan P. Middleton. 2 vols. Indianapolis, Ind.: B.F. Bowen, 1917.

Urbana and Champaign County, comp. by W.P.A. Urbana: Gamner Pub. Co. [1942]. 147 pp.

## Clark County

History of Clark County, Ohio . . . Chicago: W.H. Beers, 1881. 1,085 pp. (Repr. Evansville, Ind.: Unigraphic, 1975. 1,085 pp. plus 92 pp. index.)

20th Century History of Springfield and Clark County, Ohio . . . ed. and comp. by William M. Rockell. Chicago: Biographical Pub. Co., 1908. 1,054 pp. (Repr. Evansville, Ind.: Unigraphic, 1976.)

A Standard History of Clark County and Springfield, by B.F. Prince. 2 vols. Chicago: American Hist. Soc., 1922.

Springfield and Clark County, Ohio, comp. by W.P.A. [Springfield:] Springfield Tribune Pr. Co. [1941]. 136 pp.

## Clermont County

History of Clermont County . . . [by J.L. Rockey]. Philadelphia: L.H. Everts, 1880. 557 pp. (Repr. Evansville, Ind.: Unigraphic, 1979. Index. N.p., n.d. 172 pp.)

Thirey & Mitchell's Encyclopedic Directory and History of Clermont County. [Cincinnati: S. Rosenthal, 1902.] 208 pp. (Repr. Knightstown, Ind.: The Bookmark, 1982.)

History of Clermont and Brown Counties, from the Earliest Times Down to the Present . . . by Byron Williams. 2 vols. Milford: Hobart Pub. Co., 1913.

Clermont County, Ohio. 1980. Batavia: Clermont County Gen. Soc., 1984. 300 pp.

## Clinton County

The History of Clinton County . . . Chicago: W.H. Beers, 1882. 1,180 pp.

History of Clinton County, Ohio, by Albert J. Brown. Indianapolis, Ind.: B.F. Bowen, 1915. 967 pp.

Clinton County, Ohio: a Collection of Historical Sketches and Family Histories, comp. by members and friends of the Clinton County Historical Society. Wilmington, Ohio: The Society, 1982. 315 pp.

## Columbiana County

History of Columbiana County . . . [by Horace Mack]. Philadelphia: D.W. Ensign, 1879. (Repr. with every-name index. Evansville, Ind.: Unigraphic, 1976.)

History of the Upper Ohio Valley, with Historical Account of Columbiana County. 2 vols. Madison, Wis.: Brant & Fuller, 1891.

History of Columbiana County . . . comp. by William B. McCord. Chicago: Biographical Pub. Co., 1905. 848 pp.

History of Columbiana County, Ohio, by Harold B. Barth. 2 vols. Topeka, Kans.: Hist. Pub. Co., 1926. 1,032 pp.

## Coshocton County

Historical Collections of Coshocton County . . . from the Time of the Earliest Known Occupants Unto the Present Time, 1764-1876 . . . by William E. Hunt. Cincinnati: R. Clarke, 1876. vii, 264 pp.

History of Coshocton County, Ohio, Its Past and Present, 1740-1881 . . . comp. by Norman N. Hill, Jr. Newark: A.A. Graham, 1881. 833 pp.

Centennial History of Coshocton County, Ohio, by William J. Bahmer. 2 vols. Chicago: S.J. Clarke Pub. Co., 1909. (Repr. 2 vols. in 1. Coshocton: Coshocton County Chapter, Ohio Gen. Soc., 1982.)

## Crawford County

History of Crawford County and Ohio . . . from Earliest Settlement to the Present Time . . . by William H. Perrin, et al. Chicago: Baskin & Battey, 1881. 1,047 pp.

A Centennial Biographical History of Crawford County . . . Chicago: Lewis Pub. Co., 1902. 868 pp.

History of Crawford County . . . by John E. Hopley. Chicago: Richmond-Arnold Pub. Co. [1912]. 1,254 pp.

## Cuyahoga County

History of Cuyahoga County, Ohio . . . comp. by Crisfield Johnson. [Philadelphia:] D.W. Ensign, 1879. 534 pp. (Repr. Evansville, Ind.: Whipporwill Pubs., 1984. 534, 110 pp.)

Memorial Record of the County of Cuyahoga and City of Cleveland . . . Chicago: Lewis Pub. Co., 1894. 924 pp.

A History of Cuyahoga County . . . by William R. Coates, et al. 3 vols. Chicago: American Hist. Soc., 1924.

## Darke County

The History of Darke County . . . Chicago: W.H. Beers, 1880. 772 pp. (Repr. Evansville, Ind.: Unigraphic, 1979.)

A Biographical History of Darke County, Ohio . . . Chicago: Lewis Pub. Co., 1900. 758 pp. (Repr. Evansville, Ind.: Unigraphic, 1973.)

History of Darke County, from Its Earliest Settlement to the Present Time . . . 2 vols. in 1. Milford: Hobart Pub. Co., 1914. 1,194 pp.

## Defiance County

History of Defiance County, Ohio . . . Chicago: Warner, Beers, 1883. 374 pp.

## Delaware County

History of Delaware County and Ohio . . . Containing a Brief History . . . Chicago: O.L. Baskin, 1880. 885 pp. (Repr., Evansville, Ind.: Unigraphic, 1975.)

Memorial Record of the Counties of Delaware, Union and Morrow. Chicago: Lewis Pub. Co., 1895. 501 pp.

20th Century History of Delaware County, Ohio . . . ed. and comp. by James R. Lytle. Chicago: Biographical Pub. Co., 1908. 896 pp.

Berlin Township and Delaware County, Ohio History, Told by Contemporaries, ed. by Anna C.S. Pabst. 6 vols. Delaware: N.p., 1955-59.

## Erie County

History of the Fire-Lands, Comprising . . . Erie County, 1879, *see* Huron County.

History of Erie County, Ohio, ed. by Lewis C. Aldrich. Syracuse, N.Y.: D. Mason, 1889. 653 pp. (Repr., indexed. Evansville, Ind.: Unigraphic, 1978. 653, 58 pp.)

A Standard History of Erie County . . . by Hewson L. Peeke. 2 vols. Chicago: Lewis Pub. Co., 1916.

The Centennial History of Erie County, Ohio, by Hewson L. Peeke. 2 vols. [Cleveland: Pentagon Pr. Co.], 1925. 746 pp.

## Fairfield County

History of Fairfield and Perry Counties, Ohio, Their Past and Present . . . comp. by Albert A. Graham. Chicago: W.H. Beers, 1883. 1,186 pp. (Repr. of Genealogies, Fairfield County, with index. Knightstown, Ind.: The Bookmark, 1980. 476 pp.)

A Complete History of Fairfield County, Ohio, by Hervey Scott, 1795-1876. Columbus: Siebert & Lilley, 1877. vi, 304 pp. (Repr., indexed. Lancaster: Fairfield County Chapter, Ohio Gen. Soc., 1983. 360 pp.)

Pioneer Period and Pioneer People of Fairfield County, Ohio, by Charles M.L. Wiseman. Columbus: F.J. Heer Pr. Co., 1901. 430 pp. (Repr. with index. Lancaster: Fairfield County Gen. Soc., 1984. 420 pp.)

A Biographical Record of Fairfield County, Ohio. New York: S.J. Clarke Pub. Co., 1902. 483 pp. (History of Perry County, biographical, pp. 407-482.)

History of Fairfield County . . . by Charles C. Miller. Chicago: Richmond-Arnold Pub. Co. [1912]. 820 pp.

## Fayette County

Pioneer Record . . . of Fayette County, Ohio, by Rufus Putnam. Cincinnati: Applegate, Pounsford, 1872. 120 pp. (Repr. Washington Court House: Jack Wheeler, 1974.)

History of Fayette County, by R.S. Dills. Dayton: Odell & Mayer, 1882. 1,039 pp. (Repr. Evansville, Ind.: Unigraphic, 1979. 1,039 pp., plus 52 pp. index.)

History of Fayette County, Ohio . . . ed. by Frank M. Allen. Indianapolis, Ind.: B.F. Bowen, 1914. 756 pp.

Fayette County, Ohio History. Washington, Ohio: Fayette County Gen. Soc., 1983.

## Franklin County

History of Franklin County . . . by William T. Martin. Columbus: Follett, Foster, 1858. v, 449 pp.

History of Franklin and Pickaway Counties . . . [Cleveland:] Williams Bros., 1880. 593 pp. (Repr. Evansville, Ind.: Unigraphic, 1979.)

*Franklin County (cont.)*

Franklin County at the Beginning of the Twentieth Century . . . comp. by Historical Publishing Company. Columbus: Hist. Pub. Co., 1901. 460 pp.

A Centennial Biographical History of the City of Columbus and Franklin County, Ohio . . . Chicago: Lewis Pub. Co., 1901. 1,012 pp.

Centennial History of Columbus and Franklin County, Ohio, by William A. Taylor. 2 vols. Chicago: S.J. Clarke Pub. Co., 1909. 1,652 pp.

History of Franklin County, Ohio, by Opha Moore. 3 vols. Topeka and Indianapolis: Hist. Pub. Co., 1930. 1,424 pp.

## Fulton County

History of . . . Fulton County, 1888, *see* Henry County.

The County of Fulton: a History of Fulton County, Ohio from the Earliest Days . . . ed. by Thomas Mikesell. Madison: Northwestern Hist. Assoc., 1905. 661 pp. (Repr. [with new index added]. Evansville, Ind.: Whipporwill, for Fulton County Gen. Soc. [1983?]. 661, 41 pp.)

A Standard History of Fulton County, Ohio . . . under ed. supervision of Frank H. Reighard. 2 vols. Chicago: Lewis Pub. Co., 1920.

## Gallia County

History of Gallia County, Ohio. N.p., 1882. (Repr. Evansville, Ind.: Unigraphic, 1976.)

History of . . . Gallia County, 1882, *see* Lawrence County.

History of Gallia County. Bicentennial ed. Gallipolis: N.p., 1976. xxx, 45 pp.

Gallia County, Ohio: People in History to 1980. [Gallipolis?:] Gallia Hist. Soc., 1980. 383 pp.

## Geauga County

History of Geauga and Lake Counties . . . Philadelphia: Williams Bros., 1878. 259 pp. prepared by A.G. Riddle, et al. (Index. [comp. by Mrs. Margaret O. Collacott, et al.]. Mentor: Lake County Hist. Soc., 1964. 100 leaves. Repr. Evansville, Ind.: Unigraphic, 1973.)

Pioneer and General History of Geauga County . . . [Burton?:] Hist. Soc. of Geauga County, 1880. 822 pp. (Repr. Evansville, Ind.: Unigraphic, 1979. 822 pp., 66 pp. index.) (Continuation of 1880 History. Columbus: Geauga County Hist. and Memorial Soc., 1953. xiv, 783 pp.)

Biographical History of . . . Geauga County, 1893, *see* Ashtabula County.

## Greene County

History of Greene County, by R.S. Dills. Dayton: Odell & Mayer, 1881. (Repr. Evansville, Ind.: Unigraphic, 1974. 1,018 pp.)

*Greene County (cont.)*

History of Greene County . . . 1803 to 1840 . . . with Roster of 10,000 of the Early Settlers . . . by George F. Robinson. Chicago: S.J. Clarke Pub. Co., 1902. 927 pp.

Greene County, 1803-1908, ed. by a Committee of the Home Coming Association. Xenia: Aldine Pub. House, 1908. x, 226 pp.

Out of the Wilderness; an Account of Events in Greene County, Ohio, ed. by Greene County Sesquicentennial Organization. Ann Arbor, Mich.: Edwards Bros., 1953. 306 pp.

## Guernsey County

History of Guernsey County, Ohio, by Col. Cyrus P.B. Sarchet. 2 vols. Indianapolis, Ind.: B.F. Bowen & Co., 1911. 975 pp. (Repr. 2 vols. in 1. Cambridge: Guernsey County Gen. Soc., 1983, and Columbus: Walsworth Pub. Co., 1983.)

Stories of Guernsey County, Ohio . . . by William G. Wolfe. Cambridge: Author, 1943. 1,093 pp.

Guernsey County, Ohio: a Collection of Historical Sketches and Family Histories, comp. by Members and Friends of the Guernsey County Genealogical Society. Cambridge: Guernsey County Chapter, Ohio Gen. Soc., 1979. 347 pp.

## Hamilton County

History of Hamilton County, Ohio . . . comp. by Henry A. Ford. Cleveland: L.A. Williams, 1881. 432 pp. (Repr. Evansville, Ind.: Unigraphic, 1974.)

History of Cincinnati and Hamilton County, Ohio, Their Past and Present . . . Cincinnati: S.B. Nelson, 1894. 1,056 pp.

## Hancock County

History of Hancock County from Its Earliest Settlement to the Present Time . . . by Daniel B. Beardsley. Springfield: Republic Pr. Co., 1881. 472 pp.

History of Hancock County . . . by C.R. Brown. Chicago: Warner, Beers, 1886. 880 pp. (Index, comp. by Hancock County Chapter, Ohio Genealogical Society. Findlay: Hancock County Gen. Soc., 1982. 76 pp. Evansville, Ind.: Unigraphic, 1979.)

History of Hancock County . . . by Jacob A. Spaythe. Toledo: B.F. Wade Pr. Co., 1903. 312 pp.

A Centennial Biographical History of Hancock County, Ohio . . . New York: Lewis Pub. Co., 1903. 595 pp.

20th Century History of Findlay and Hancock County, by J.A. Kimmel. Chicago: Lewis Pub. Co., 1910. 656 pp.

Across the Years in Findlay and Hancock County, by R.L. Heminger. Findlay: [Republic-Courier, 1965]. 205 pp.

## Hardin County

The History of Hardin County . . . partly comp. by R.C. Brown. Chicago: Warner Beers, 1883. 1,064 pp. (Repr. with index. Evansville, Ind.: Unigraphic, 1980.)

A Twentieth Century History of Hardin County, Ohio . . . by Minnie I. Kohler. 2 vols. Chicago: Lewis Pub. Co., 1910. 898 pp.

Centennial History of Hardin County . . . 1913, by Herbert T.O. Blue. [Canton: Rogers-Miller Co., 1933.] 180 pp.

Hardin County, Ohio: a Historical Update with Family Histories, by Book Committee, Hardin County Archaeological and Historical Society. Dallas, Tex.: Taylor Pub. Co., 1983. 407 pp., 16 pp. index.

## Harrison County

A Brief History of Harrison County, Ohio, by Samuel B. McGavran. Cadiz: Harrison Tribune, 1894. 55 pp.

Historical Collections of Harrison County, Ohio, with Lists [of vital records] and Genealogies, by Charles A. Hanna. New York: Priv. pr., 1900. viii, 636 pp. (Repr. Baltimore: Genealogical Pub. Co., 1975.)

History of . . . Harrison County, 1921, *see* Carroll County.

History of Harrison County, by Helen C. Bullock. [Cadiz:] Cadiz Pub. Lib., 1961. 48 pp.

## Henry County

History of Henry and Fulton Counties . . . ed. by Lewis C. Aldrich. Syracuse, N.Y.: Mason, 1888. 713 pp.

Henry County, Ohio: A Collection of Historical Sketches and Family Histories, comp. by Members and Friends of the Henry County Historical Society. 3 vols. Napoleon: The Society, 1976.

## Highland County

The History of the County of Highland, from Its Creation to . . . 1876 . . . by James H. Thompson. Hillsboro: Hillsboro Gazette, 1878. 132 pp.

History of . . . Highland County, 1880, *see* Ross County.

A History of the Early Settlement of Highland County, Ohio, by Daniel Scott. Hillsboro: Gazette Office, 1890. 192 pp. (Repr. with addendum, by Dorothy V. Majoewsky. Hillsboro: Southern Ohio Gen. Soc., 1983.)

State Centennial History of Highland County, Ohio, by J.W. Klise. Madison, Wis.: Northwestern Hist. Assoc., 1902. 535 pp. (Repr. Hillsboro: Southern Ohio Gen. Soc., 1980. Index, by Barbara J. Carmean. Owensboro, Ky.: Cook & McDowell, 1980.)

## Holmes County

History of Holmes County, Ohio, by G.F. Newton. Millersburg: N.p., 1889. 160 pp. (Repr., 1952.)

Historical Study of Holmes County, Ohio, by F.W. Almendinger. Millersburg?: Lib. Archives of Holmes Co., 1962. 105 pp.

Holmes County, Ohio, Flashes from the Past, by Donald Egger. Millersburg?: Lib. Archives of Holmes Co., 1963. 75 pp.

## Huron County

History of the Fire-Lands, Comprising Huron and Erie Counties, Ohio . . . [by William W. Williams]. Cleveland: Leader Pr. Co., 1879. 524 pp.

History of Huron County, Ohio, by Abraham J. Baughman. 2 vols. Chicago: S.J. Clarke Pub. Co., 1909.

History of . . . Huron County, 1931, in History of North Central Ohio, *see* p. 283.

## Jackson County

A History of Jackson County, by David W. Williams. Jackson: N.p., 1900. 188 pp.

Early Jackson, by Romaine Aten-Jones. [Jackson: N.p., 1942.] 70 pp.

History of Jackson County, ed. by Romaine Aten-Jones and A.M. Jenkins. Jackson: N.p., 1953. 91 pp.

## Jefferson County

History of . . . Jefferson County, 1880, *see* Belmont County.

20th Century History of Steubenville and Jefferson County . . . by Joseph B. Doyle. Chicago: Richmond-Arnold Pub. Co., 1910. 1,196 pp. (Repr. Evansville, Ind.: Unigraphic, 1976.)

Pioneer Days, by Mary (Donaldson) Sinclair. Steubenville: N.p., 1962. 172 pp.

## Knox County

A History of Knox County, Ohio, from 1779 to 1862 Inclusive . . . [by Anthony B. Norton]. Columbus: R. Nevins, 1862. 424 pp.

History of Knox County, Ohio, Its Past and Present . . . comp. by Norman N. Hill, Jr. Mt. Vernon: A.A. Graham, 1881. 854 pp.

Past and Present of Knox County, Ohio, Albert B. Williams, ed. in chief. 2 vols. Indianapolis, Ind.: B.F. Bowen, 1912.

History of . . . Knox County, 1931, in History of North Central Ohio, *see* p. 283.

## Lake County

History of . . . Lake County, 1878, *see* Geauga County.

Biographical History of . . . County of . . . Lake, 1893, *see* Ashtabula County.

Lake County History, comp. by Workers of the Writers' Program of W.P.A., Ohio. [Mentor: N.p., 1941.] 100 pp.

Here Is Lake County, Ohio, by Lake County Historical Society. Cleveland: H. Allen, 1964. 134 pp.

The Latch String Is Out; a Pioneer History of Lake County, Ohio, by Harry F. Lupold. Mentor: Lakeland Community Coll. Pr. [1974]. 163 pp.

## Lawrence County

Atlas and History of Lawrence County . . . Chicago: H.H. Hardesty & Co., 1882. 222, xxxii pp.

Historical Hand-Atlas . . . and Histories of Lawrence and Gallia Counties, Ohio . . . Chicago: Hardesty, 1882. 344 pp.

A Story About Lawrence County, Ohio. Huntington, W.Va.: P. Brown Pub. Co., 1966.

## Licking County

History of Licking County, repr. from the 1875 Atlas, with two new indexes. Knightstown, Ind.: The Bookmark, 1975. 202 pp.

Centennial History of Licking County, Ohio . . . by Isaac Smucker. Newark: Clark & Underwood, 1876. 80 pp. (Repr. Evansville, Ind.: Unigraphic, 1976.)

History of Licking County, Ohio, Its Past and Present . . . Containing a Complete History . . . comp. by Norman N. Hill, Jr. Newark: A.A. Graham, 1881. 822 pp.

Memorial Record of Licking County, Ohio. Chicago: Record Pub. Co., 1894. 1,191 pp. (Repr., 1976.)

Centennial History of the City of Newark and Licking County, Ohio, by Edwin M.P. Brister. 2 vols. Chicago: S.J. Clarke Pub. Co., 1909. 1,452 pp. (Repr. with every-name index. Newark: Licking County Gen. Soc., 1982.)

Licking County, Ohio. Newark: Licking County Gen. Soc., 1982.

## Logan County

The History of . . . Logan County, 1872, *see* Champaign County.

History of Logan County [by W.H. Perrin and J.H. Battle]. Chicago: O.L. Baskin, 1880. 840 pp.

The Historical Review of Logan County, by Robert P. Kennedy. Chicago: S.J. Clarke Pub. Co., 1903. 823 pp.

*Logan County (cont.)*

Logan County, 1982: a Collection of Historical Sketches and Family Histories, comp. by Logan County Genealogical Society. Bellefontaine: The Society, 1983, and Defiance: Hubbard Co., 1983.

## Lorain County

History of Lorain County . . . Philadelphia: Williams Bros., 1879. 373 pp.

A Standard History of Lorain County . . . ed. by George F. Wright. 2 vols. Chicago: Lewis Pub. Co., 1916.

History of . . . Lorain County, 1931, in History of North Central Ohio, *see* p. 283.

## Lucas County

History of the City of Toledo and Lucas County . . . ed. by Clark Waggoner. New York: Munsell & Co., 1888. xii, 956 pp.

Memoirs of Lucas County and City of Toledo . . . Harvey Scribner, ed. in chief. 2 vols. Madison, Wis.: Western Hist. Assoc., 1910. 1,311 pp.

Toledo and Lucas County, 1623-1923, ed. by John M. Killits. 3 vols. Chicago: S.J. Clarke Pub. Co., 1923.

Lucas County Historical Series, by Randolph C. Downes. 4 vols. [Toledo:] Hist. Soc. of Northwestern Ohio, 1948-54. (Repr. 4 vols. in 1. [Maumee: Maumee Valley Hist. Soc., 1968.])

## Madison County

The History of Madison County . . . by R.C. Brown, et al. Chicago: W.H. Beers, 1883. 1,165 pp.

Madison County, by C.E. Bryan. Indianapolis, Ind.: B.F. Bowen & Co., 1915. 942 pp.

A Chronicle of Our Time . . . Madison Seventy-Six, Madison County Bicentennial Committee. Marceline, Mo.: Walsworth Pub. Co., for Madison County Pub. Comm., 1978. 431 pp.

## Mahoning County

History of . . . Mahoning County, 1882, *see* Trumbull County.

Biographical History of . . . County of . . . Mahoning, 1893, *see* Ashtabula County.

20th Century History of Youngstown and Mahoning County, ed. by Thomas W. Sanderson. N.p., 1907. 1,030 pp.

## Marion County

The History of Marion County, Ohio . . . Chicago: Leggett, Conaway, 1883. 1,031 pp.

*Marion County (cont.)*

History of Marion County . . . ed. by J. Wilbur Jacoby. Chicago: Biographical Pub. Co., 1907. 834 pp. (Repr. Evansville, Ind.: Unigraphic, 1976.)

Marion County 1979 History, ed. by Treilia H. Romaine. Marion: Marion County Hist. Soc., 1979. 848 pp.

## Medina County

Pioneer History of Medina County, by Nira B. Northrop. Medina: G. Redway, 1861. 224 pp.

History of Medina County and Ohio . . . Chicago: Baskin & Battey, 1881. 922 pp. (Repr. Evansville, Ind.: Unigraphic, 1972.)

History of . . . Medina County, 1931, in History of North Central Ohio, *see* p. 283.

## Meigs County

Historical and Geographical Encyclopaedia of Meigs County . . . Chicago: H.H. Hardesty & Co., 1883. (Repr. containing outline map and history of the County . . . Defiance: Hubbard Co., 1982. Varied paging. Expanded index (every name), by Mrs. Jane Whiteman. Tulsa, Okla.: Author, 1982. 48 pp.)

The Pioneer History of Meigs County, by Stillman C. Larkin. Columbus: Berlin Pr. Co., 1908. 208 pp. (Repr. Pomeroy: Meigs County Pioneer & Hist. Soc., 1979.)

Pioneer History of Meigs County, Ohio, to 1949 . . . by Edgar Ervin. [N.p., 1949?] 514 pp.

Meigs County, Ohio History Book, by Meigs County Pioneer and Historical Society. [Pomeroy:] The Society, 1979.

## Mercer County

History of . . . Mercer County, 1882, *see* Van Wert County.

History of Mercer County, ed. by S.S. Scranton. Chicago: Biographical Pub. Co., 1907. 751 pp.

## Miami County

The History of Miami County . . . Chicago: W.H. Beers, 1880. 880 pp.

Centennial History: Troy, Piqua and Miami County . . . Compendium of National Biography [ed. and comp. by Thomas C. Harbaugh]. Chicago: Richmond-Arnold Pub. Co. [1909]. 857 pp.

The History of the County of Miami. Richmond, Ind.: Rerick Bros., 1894.

A History of Miami County, by Francis M. Sterrett. 3 vols. Troy: Montgomery Pr. Co., 1917. 684 pp.

A History of Miami County, Ohio, 1807-1953 . . . written under the supervision of Leonard U. Hill. [Piqua: Miami Co. Sesquicentennial Hist., 1953.] xii, 403 pp.

Historic Notes of Miami County, by William R. Kinder. Troy: Troy Foundation, 1953. viii, 213 pp.

## Monroe County

Souvenir of Woodsfield and Monroe County. Woodsfield: Monroe County Republican, 1906. 77 pp.

## Montgomery County

The History of Montgomery County, Ohio . . . Chicago: W.H. Beers, 1882. viii, 760 pp. (Repr., with index, Evansville, Ind.: Unigraphic, 1973. 760, 98 pp.)

History of the City of Dayton and Montgomery County, Ohio, by Rev. A.W. Drury. 2 vols. Chicago: S.J. Clarke Pub. Co., 1909.

Dayton and Montgomery County . . . ed. by Charlotte Conover. 4 vols. New York: Lewis Pub. Co., 1932.

## Morgan County

History of Morgan County . . . by Charles Robertson, rev. and extended by publishers. Chicago: L.H. Watkins, 1886. 538 pp. (Repr. Evansville, Ind.: Unigraphic, 1977. Index. McConnelsville: Morgan County Hist. Soc., 1980.)

The History of Morgan County, Ohio, 1980, by the People of Morgan County. McConnelsville: Morgan County Hist. Soc., 1980. 336 pp.

Historical Reminiscences of Morgan County, by Hon. James M. Gaylord. (Repr. McConnelsville: Morgan County Hist. Gen. Soc., Ohio Gen. Soc. Chapter, 1984. 92 pp.)

## Morrow County

History of Morrow County and Ohio . . . comp. by W.H. Perrin. Chicago: O.L. Baskin, 1880. 838 pp.

Memorial Record of County of . . . Morrow, 1895, *see* Delaware County.

History of Morrow County . . . by Abraham J. Baughman. 2 vols. Chicago: Lewis Pub. Co., 1911. 939 pp.

## Muskingum County

History of Muskingum County . . . by J.F. Everhart. [Columbus:] J.F. Everhart & Co., 1882. 480 pp.

The Biographical and Historical Memoirs of Muskingum County, Ohio. Chicago: Goodspeed, 1892. 620 pp. (Repr. Evansville, Ind.: Unigraphic, 1979.)

Zanesville and Muskingum County, Ohio, by T.W. Lewis. 3 vols. Chicago: S.J. Clarke Pub. Co., 1927. 547 pp.

Y-Bridge City: the Story of Zanesville and Muskingum County, by Norris F. Schneider. Zanesville: Muskingum Chapter, Ohio Gen. Soc., 1950. 437 pp. (2d pr., 1974; 3d pr., 1980. 4th pr., 1983.)

## Noble County

History of Noble County, Ohio . . . Chicago: Watkins, 1887. 597 pp. (Repr. Evansville, Ind.: Unigraphic, 1979.)

The County of Noble, ed. by Frank M. Martin. Madison, Wis.: Selwyn A. Brant, 1904.

## Paulding County

Historical Atlas of Paulding County . . . comp. by O. Morrow and F.W. Bashore. Madison, Wis.: Western Pub. Co., 1892. 109 pp. (Repr. Dallas, Tex.: Taylor Pub. Co., for John Paulding Hist. Soc., 1978.)

## Perry County

History of . . . Perry County, 1883, *see* Fairfield County.

A Biographical Record of Fairfield County . . . New York: S.J. Clarke Pub. Co., 1902. 483 pp. (History of Perry County, pp. 407-483.)

History of Perry County, Ohio, by Clement L. Martzolff. New Lexington: Ward & Weiland, 1902. xii, 195 pp.

History of Perry County, Ohio . . . 1980. [Somerset?:] Perry County Hist. Soc., 1980. 304 pp.

## Pickaway County

History of . . . Pickaway County, 1880, *see* Franklin County.

History of Pickaway County . . . by Aaron R. Van Cleaf. Chicago: Biog. Pub. Co., 1906. 882 pp. (Repr. Evansville, Ind.: Unigraphic, 1972.)

## Pike County

History of Pike County, Ohio, by Mrs. H. McCormick. [Waverly:] Pike Co. Comm., 1958. 42 pp.

## Portage County

History of Portage County . . . by R.C. Brown, et al. Chicago: Warner, Beers, 1885. 927 pp. (Repr., with index by Mrs. R.S. Winnagle. Revenna: Portage County Hist. Soc., 1972. 927, 187 pp.)

*Portage County (cont.)*

Portage Heritage; a History of Portage County . . . ed. by James B. Holm. [Ravenna:] N.p., 1957. 824 pp.

## Preble County

History of Preble County . . . Cleveland: H.Z. Williams & Bros., 1881. 337, 106 pp. (Repr. Evansville, Ind.: Unigraphic, 1980.)

A Biographical History of Preble County . . . Chicago: Lewis Pub. Co., 1900. 573 pp.

History of Preble County, Ohio, by R.E. Lowry. Indianapolis, Ind.: B.F. Bowen, 1915. 889 pp.

## Putnam County

Putnam County Centennial History, by Edwin Sommers, 1834-1934. N.p.: D.A.R., Putnam County, 1934. 176 pp.

Putnam County Pioneer Association Centennial History, 1873-1973. Ottawa: Audrey S. Carroll, 1974. 209 pp.

## Richland County

History of Richland County . . . Its Past and Present . . . comp. by Albert A. Graham. Mansfield: A.A. Graham, 1880. 941 pp. (Repr. Evansville, Ind.: Unigraphic, 1977.)

Philip Seymour, or Pioneer Life in Richland County, Ohio . . . by James F. M'Gaw. 2d ed. Mansfield: The Herald, 1883. 432 pp.

A Centennial Biographical History of Richland and Ashland Counties, Ohio . . . ed. by Abraham J. Baughman. Chicago: Lewis Pub. Co., 1901. 831 pp. (Repr. Evansville, Ind.: Unigraphic, 1979. 696, 37 pp.)

History of Richland County, Ohio, from 1880 to 1908 . . . ed. by Abraham J. Baughman. 2 vols. Chicago: S.J. Clarke Pub. Co., 1908. 1,175 pp.

History of . . . Richland County, 1931, in History of North Central Ohio, *see* p. 283.

## Ross County

Pioneer Record and Reminiscences of the Early Settlers and Settlement of Ross County, Ohio, by Isaac J. Finley. Cincinnati: R. Clarke & Co., 1871. 148 pp.

History of Ross and Highland Counties . . . Cleveland: Williams Bros., 1880. 532 pp. (Repr. Evansville, Ind.: Unigraphic, 1979.)

The County of Ross: a History of Ross County, by Henry H. Bennett. 2 vols. Madison, Wis.: S.A. Brant, 1902. (Repr. of Vol. 2, with new name index . . . Baltimore: Gateway Pr., 1981. 736, 109 pp.) (Also with title: State Centennial History of the County of Ross.)

*Ross County (cont.)*

A Standard History of Ross County . . . under ed. supervision of Lyle S. Evans. 2 vols. Chicago: Lewis Pub. Co., 1917. 934 pp.

Chillicothe and Ross County, comp. by W.P.A. Columbus: F.J. Heer Pr. Co., 1938. 91 pp.

## Sandusky County

History of Sandusky County, Ohio . . . [partly by Homer Everett]. Cleveland: H.Z. Williams & Bros., 1882. 834 pp.

Twentieth Century History of Sandusky County . . . ed. and comp. by Basil Meek. Chicago: Richmond-Arnold Pub. Co., 1909. 934 pp.

## Scioto County

Pioneers of Scioto County . . . Comprising . . . Historical Matter and Anecdotes of the Early Settlement . . . by James Keyes. Portsmouth: N.p., 1880. 121 pp.

A History of Scioto County . . . with Pioneer Record of Southern Ohio, by Nelson W. Evans. Portsmouth: N.W. Evans, 1903. viii, 322 pp.

Scioto Sketches; an Account of Discovery and Settlement of Scioto County, by Henry T. Bannon. Chicago: A.C. McClurg, 1920. 86 pp. (New issue, with additions and corrections, and index. N.p., n.d.)

Stories Old and Often Told, being Chronicles of Scioto County, Ohio, by Henry T. Bannon. Baltimore: Waverly Pr., 1927. xiii, 275 pp. (Part of Scioto Sketches, *see* above.)

## Seneca County

History of Seneca County . . . Since Its First Settlement . . . to the Present Time . . . by Consul W. Butterfield. Sandusky: D. Campbell, 1848. 251 pp.

History of Seneca County, from the Close of the Revolutionary War to July 1880 . . . by W. Lang. Springfield: Transcript Pr. Co., 1880. 691, xii pp.

History of Seneca County . . . Chicago: Warner, Beers, 1886. 1,069 pp.

A Centennial Biographical History of Seneca County, Ohio. New York: Lewis Pub. Co., 1902. 757 pp.

History of Seneca County . . . by Abraham J. Baughman. 2 vols. Chicago: Lewis Pub. Co., 1911.

## Shelby County

History of Shelby County . . . Philadelphia: N.p., 1883. 406 pp. (Repr. with added index. Sidney: Shelby County Hist. Soc., 1968. vi, 398 pp.)

History of Shelby County, Ohio, by A. Hitchcock. Chicago: Richmond-Arnold Pub. Co., 1913. 862 pp.

## Stark County

History of Stark County, with an Outline Sketch of Ohio [by A.A. Graham], ed. by William H. Perrin. Chicago: Baskin & Battey, 1881. 1,012 pp. (Repr. Evansville, Ind.: Unigraphic, 1977.)

Old Landmarks of Canton and Stark County, ed. and comp. by John Danner. 2 vols. Logansport, Ind.: B.F. Bowen, 1904. 1,511 pp.

A Standard History of Stark County . . . John H. Lehman, supervising ed. 3 vols. Chicago: Lewis Pub. Co., 1916.

History of Stark County, Ohio, from the Age of Prehistoric Man to the Present Day, by Herbert T.O. Blue. 3 vols. Chicago: S.J. Clarke Pub. Co., 1928.

The Stark County Story . . . as Broadcast Over WHBC-WHBC-FM, by Edward Thorndale Heald. 4 vols. in 6 parts. Canton: Stark County Hist. Soc., 1949-59. 782 pp.

History of Stark County; a Digest of Mr. Heald's Six Vols. Canton: Stark County Hist. Soc., 1963. 183 pp.

## Summit County

Historical Reminiscences of Summit County . . . by Gen. L.V. Bierce. Akron: T. & H.G. Canfield, 1854. 157 pp.

History of Summit County . . . ed. by William H. Perrin. Chicago: Baskin & Battey, 1881. 1,056 pp.

Fifty Years and Over of Akron and Summit County, by Samuel A. Lane. Akron: Beacon Job Dept., 1892. xl, 1,167 pp.

Centennial Historical of Summit County, ed. by William B. Doyle. 2 vols. Chicago: Biographical Pub. Co., 1908. 1,115 pp.

Akron and Summit County, Ohio, 1825-1928, ed. by Scott D. Kenfield. 3 vols. Chicago: S.J. Clarke Pub. Co., 1928.

Akron and Summit County, by Karl H. Grismer. Akron: Summit County Hist. Soc. [1952]. 834 pp.

## Trumbull County

History of Trumbull and Mahoning Counties. 2 vols. Cleveland: H.Z. Williams & Bros., 1882.

Biographical History of . . . Trumbull County, 1893, *see* Ashtabula County.

A Twentieth Century History of Trumbull County . . . by Harriet T. Upton. 2 vols. Chicago: Lewis Pub. Co., 1909.

## Tuscarawas County

The History of Tuscarawas County . . . [comp. by J.M. Mansfield, et al.]. Chicago: Warner, Beers, 1884. 1,007 pp.

*Tuscarawas County (cont.)*

A History of Early Tuscarawas County, Ohio . . . by the Tuscarawas Historical Society. New Philadelphia: Acme Pr. Co., 1930. 54 pp.

Valley of the Tuscarawas: a History of Tuscarawas County, by Herbert P. Lahrman. Dover?: Ohio Hills Pubs. [1915]. 78 pp. (Pub. 1930 as A History of Tuscarawas County, *see* above.)

Guide to Tuscarawas County, comp. by Federal Writers' Project of Ohio, W.P.A. [New Philadelphia: Tucker Pr. Co.], 1939. 119 pp.

## Union County

The History of Union County, Ohio, Containing a History . . . 2 vols. Chicago: W. H. Beers, 1883. 562, 694 pp.

Memorial Record of . . . the County of Union, 1895, *see* Delaware County.

## Van Wert County

History of Van Wert and Mercer Counties. . . Wapakoneta: R. Sutton, 1882. 488 pp.

History of Van Wert County . . . ed. and comp. by Thaddeus S. Gilliland. Chicago: Richmond & Arnold, 1906. 803 pp.

History of Van Wert County, Ohio. Van Wert: Van Wert Co. Hist. Co., 1981. 229 pp.

## Vinton County

A Brief History of Vinton County, by Louise O. Biggs. Columbus: Heer Pr., 1950. 184 pp.

History of Vinton County . . . by Lew Ogan. [McArthur: N.p., 1954-55.] 327 pp.

## Warren County

The History of Warren County . . . by J. Morrow. Chicago: W.H. Beers, 1882. 1,070 pp. (Repr. Salt Lake City: Genealogy International, 1978. Name index to biographies, by Nellie M. Sheldon. [San Diego], 1964. 36 pp.)

## Washington County

Biographical and Historical Memoirs of the Early Pioneer Settlers . . . by Samuel P. Hildreth. Cincinnati: H.W. Derby & Co., 1852. 539 pp.

Washington County, and the Early Settlement of Ohio . . . Centennial Address . . . by Israel W. Andrews. Cincinnati: P.G. Thomason, 1877. 83 pp.

History of Washington County, Ohio . . . Cleveland: H.Z. Williams & Bros., 1881. 739 pp. (Repr. with new index. Knightstown, Ind.: The Bookmark, 1976. 833 pp.)

History of Marietta and Washington County . . . ed. and comp. by Martin R. Andrews. Chicago: Biographical Pub. Co., 1902. 1,471 pp.

*Washington County (cont.)*

Washington County, Ohio: a Collection of Topical and Family Sketches. Marietta: Washington County Hist. Soc., 1980. 403 pp.

## Wayne County

History of Wayne County, Ohio, from the Days of the Pioneers and First Settlers to the Present Time, by Benjamin Douglass. Indianapolis, Ind.: Douglass, 1878. 868 pp. (Repr. Evansville, Ind.: Unigraphic, 1973.)

Picturesque Wayne: a History in Text and Engraving . . . with Biographies and a History of Its Settlement and Growth. [Akron: Werner Co., 1900.] 285 pp.

History of . . . Wayne County, 1931, in History of North Central Ohio, *see* p. 283.

## Williams County

County of Williams, Ohio, Historical and Biographical, ed. by Weston A. Good-speed. Chicago: Goodspeed, 1882. 820 pp. (Repr. Evansville, Ind.: Unigraphic, 1975. Surname index. Williams County Gen. Soc., 1982.)

The County of Williams . . . by William H. Shinn. Madison, Wis.: Northwestern Hist. Assoc., 1905. 611 pp.

A Standard History of Williams County, Ohio . . . prepared under ed. supervision of Hon. Charles A. Bowersox. 2 vols. Chicago: Lewis Pub. Co., 1920.

Bryan and Williams County, comp. by Workers of the Writers' Program of W.P.A. [Gallipolis: Downtain Pr. Co., 1941.] 117 pp.

Williams County, Ohio: a Collection of Historical Sketches and Family Histories, comp. by Members and Friends of the Williams County Historical Society. 2 vols. Montpelier: The Society, 1978-80.

## Wood County

Commemorative, Historical and Biographical Record of Wood County, Ohio, Its Past and Present . . . Chicago: J.H. Beers, 1897. xvi, 1,386 pp. (Repr. Evansville, Ind.: Unigraphic, 1980.)

Reminiscences of Pioneer Days in Wood County and the Maumee Valley . . . from papers . . . of Charles W. Evers. [Bowling Green: N.p., 1909.] 264 pp.

Many Incidents and Reminiscences of the Early History of Wood County . . . collected from the papers and material of the late C.W. Evers. Bowling Green: The Democrat, 1910. 264 pp.

## Wyandot County

The History of Wyandot County . . . Chicago: Leggett, Conaway, 1884. 1,067 pp.

Past and Present of Wyandot County, Ohio: a Record of Settlement . . . ed. by Abraham J. Baughman. 2 vols. Chicago: S.J. Clarke Pub. Co., 1913.

# OKLAHOMA

## Regional

Muskogee and Northeast Oklahoma: Including the Counties of Muskogee, McIntosh, Wagoner, Cherokee, Sequoyah, Adair, Delaware, Mayes, Rogers, Washington, Nowata, Craig and Ottawa, by John D. Benedict. 3 vols. Chicago: S.J. Clarke Pub. Co., 1922. 693, 527, 567 pp.

Prairie Fire . . . A Pioneer History of Western Oklahoma. Elk City: Western Oklahoma Hist. Soc., 1978. 688 pp. (Histories of Beckham, Custer, Roger Mills, Washita.)

## Adair County

Adair County: a Comprehensive and Veracious Review of One of the Banner Counties . . . [N.p., 1918?] 164 pp.

[History of] County of Adair, 1922, in Muskogee and Northeast Oklahoma, *see* above.

## Alfalfa County

Our Alfalfa County Heritage, 1893-1976. San Angelo, Tex.: Alfalfa County Hist. Soc., 1976. 608 pp.

## Beaver County

A History of Beaver County Pioneer Families. 2 vols. in 1. Beaver: Beaver County Hist. Soc., 1970-71. 632, 608 pp. (Computerized every-name index. Park City, Utah: Hamilton Computer Service, 1980. 93 pp.)

## Beckham County

[Pioneer History of Beckham County], 1978, in Prairie Fire, *see* above.

## Blaine County

Their Story; a Pioneer Days Album of the Blaine County Area. Oklahoma City: Heritage Book Comm., 1977. xiii, 290 pp.

## Bryan County

The History of Bryan County, Oklahoma, comp. by the Bryan County Heritage Association. Dallas, Tex.: National ShareGraphics, 1983. 596 pp.

## Carter County

The History of Carter County, sponsored by Ardmore Junior Chamber of Commerce. Fort Worth, Tex.: Univ. Supply & Equipment Co., 1957. 240 pp.

Indian Territory and Carter County, Oklahoma Pioneers . . . comp. and ed. by Patty V. Norton and L.R. Sutton. Vol. 1, 1840-1926. Dallas, Tex.: Taylor Pub. Co., 1983. 786 pp.

## Cherokee County

[History of] County of . . . Cherokee, 1922, in Muskogee and Northeast Oklahoma, *see* p. 303.

## Cleveland County

Cleveland County, Oklahoma, Historical Highlights, by John Womack. Noble: Author, 1982. viii, 259 pp.

## Cotton County

A History of Walters and Cotton County, by Dave Boyer. [Walters: Walters Herald], 1953. 24 pp.

History of Cotton County Family and Area Stories. Walters: Cotton County Hist. Soc., 1979. 633 pp.

## Craig County

[History of] County of . . . Craig, 1922, in Muskogee and Northeast Oklahoma, *see* p. 303.

## Custer County

History of Custer and Washita Counties, Oklahoma, 1883-1937. [Clinton:] Clinton Daily News, 1937. 72 pp.

[Pioneer History of Custer County], 1978, in Prairie Fire, *see* p. 303.

## Delaware County

[History of] County of . . . Delaware, 1922, in Muskogee County and Northeast Oklahoma, *see* p. 303.

Heritage of the Hills: a Delaware County History, by Delaware County Historical Society. Cassville, Mo.: Litho Pr., 1979. 1,064 pp.

## Dewey County

Spanning the River, by Dewey County Historical Society. San Angelo, Tex.: The Soc., 1976. 568 pp.

## Ellis County

Our Ellis County Heritage, 1885-1974. Vols. 1-2. Oklahoma City: Ellis County Hist. Soc., 1974, 1979. 544, 352 pp.

## Garfield County

County Faces and Places: a Collection of Cherokee Strip Photographs and Stories, by Velma T. Jayne and S.C. Rockwell. Enid: Harold Allen Pr., 1968. 81 pp.

Garfield County, Oklahoma, 1893-1982. Oklahoma Diamond Jubilee Ed., ed. by Stella C. Rockwell. 2 vols. [Enid:] Garfield County Lib., 1982. 1,120 pp.

## Garvin County

From Bluestem to Golden Trend: a Pictorial History of Garvin County, Covering the Old and New. Fort Worth, Tex.: Univ. Supply & Equipment Co., 1957. (Unpaged)

## Grant County

History of Grant County, Oklahoma, 1811-1870, by Guy P. Webb. [Medford: Grant County Hist. Soc., 1971.] 268 pp.

The History of Grant County Families. Vols. 1-2, 1893-1980. Medford: Grant County Hist. Soc., 1980-82. 704, 568 pp.

## Greer County

A History of Old Greer County, and Its Pioneers. Mangum: Old Greer County Museum & Hall of Fame [1980]. 192 pp.

## Harper County

Sage and Sod: Harper County, Oklahoma. 2 vols. 1885-1973, 1885-1974. Laverne?: Harper County Hist. Soc., 1974-75. 519, 496 pp.

## Jackson County

A History of Jackson County, by Cecil R. Chesser. Altus: Altus Pr. Co., 1971. iv, 296 pp.

## Jefferson County

History of Jefferson County, Oklahoma, by J.M. Dyer. N.p., 1957. 80 pp.

## Johnston County

Johnston County History, 1855-1979. Oklahoma City: Johnston County Hist. Soc., 1979. 472 pp.

# Kay County

Kay County, Oklahoma. Ponca City: Kay County Gas Co., 1919. 75 pp.

The Last Run, Kay County, Oklahoma, 1893: Stories Assembled by the Ponca City Chapter, D.A.R. Ponca City: Curier Prior Co., 1939. 352 pp. (3d ed. Ponca City: Skinner & Son, Pr. Co., 1970.)

Newkirk and Kay County, by Marijane Boone. N.p., 1968. 128 pp.

# Kingfisher County

Pioneers of Kingfisher County, 1889-1976, ed. by Velma Musick. San Angelo, Tex.: Newsfoto Yearbooks, for Kingfisher County Hist. Soc., 1976. 416 pp.

# Kiowa County

Pioneering in Kiowa County, 6 vols. Hobart: Kiowa County Hist. Soc., 1975-1982.

Heritage of an Outlaw: the Story of Frank Nash, by Clyde C. Callhan and B.B. Jones. Hobart: Schoormaker Pubs., 1979. 352 pp. (Vol. 5 of Pioneering in Kiowa County.)

# Le Flore County

The Proud Heritage of Le Flore County; a History of an Oklahoma County . . . by Henry L. Peck. [Van Buren, Ark.: Press Argus, 1963.] x, 402 pp.

# Logan County

Cowboy Flat from Cow Country to Combine, by M.C. Rouse. Coyle: Author, 1972. 71 pp.

The Logan County History, 1889-1977: Logan County, Oklahoma. 2 vols. Guthrie: Hist. Comm., Logan County Extension Homemakers Council, 1978-80. 728, 520 pp.

# Love County

Frontier Days of Love County, by Ralph L. Evans. Marietta: Author, 1966. 36 pp.

The History of Love County, Oklahoma, comp. by the Love County Heritage Commission. Dallas, Tex.: National ShareGraphics, 1983. 371 pp.

# McCurtain County

McCurtain County and Southeast Oklahoma; History, Biography . . . by W.A. Carter. Idabel: Author, and Fort Worth, Tex.: Tribune Pub. Co., 1923. 381 pp.

History, McCurtain County, by Eliza S. Oglesby. [Haworth: N.p., 1973.] 203 leaves.

# McIntosh County

[History of] County . . . of McIntosh, 1922, in Muskogee and Northeast Oklahoma, *see* p. 303.

# Major County

A Pictorial History of Fairview and Major County; Souvenir Book, Fairview Diamond Jubilee. [Fairview: N.p., 1968.] 50 pp.

# Mayes County

[History of] County of . . . Mayes, 1922, in Muskogee and Northeast Oklahoma, *see* p. 303.

Historical Highlights of Mayes County. Pryor: Mayes County Hist. Soc., 1977. 544 pp.

# Murray County

Murray County, Oklahoma, in the Heart of Eden, by Opal H. Brown, in cooperation with Murray County Historical Society. Wichita Falls, Tex.: Nortex Pr., 1977. xviii, 413 pp.

# Muskogee County

[History of] County of Muskogee, 1922, in Muskogee and Northeast Oklahoma, *see* p. 303.

Muskogee City and County, by Odie B. Faulk. Muskogee: Five Civilized Tribes Museum, Western Heritage Books, 1962. 208 pp.

# Noble County

A History of Noble County, Oklahoma, by Fannie L. Eisele. Covington: N.p., 1958. 159 pp.

# Nowata County

[History of] County of . . . Nowata, 1922, in Muskogee and Northeast Oklahoma, *see* p. 303.

History of Nowata County, by Felix M. Gay. Stillwater: Redlands Pr., 1957. 36 pp.

# Oklahoma County

Heart of the Promised Land, Oklahoma County . . . by Bob L. Blackburn. [Oklahoma City:] Oklahoma County Hist. Soc., 1982. 264 pp.

# Okmulgee County

Okmulgee County History Book. Oklahoma City: Oklahoma Hist. Soc., 1984.

## Ottawa County

[History of] County of Ottawa, 1922, in Muskogee and Northeast Oklahoma, *see* p. 303.

The History of Ottawa County, by Velma Nieberding. Marceline, Mo.: Walsworth Pub. Co., 1983. 576 pp.

## Pontotoc County

History of Pontotoc County, Oklahoma, by Pontotoc County Hist. and Genealogical Society. Ada: The Society, 1976.

## Pottawatomie County

Pottawatomie Country and What Has Come of It; a History of Pottawotomie County, by John Fortson. [Shawnee: Pottawatomie County Hist. Soc., 1936.] 90 pp.

Localized History of Pottawatomie County, Oklahoma to 1907, by Charles W. Mooney. Midwest City: Thunderbird Industries, 1971. xiv, 315 pp.

Frontier Lore, 1975. Shawnee: Pottawatomie County Hist. Soc. [1975]. 127 pp.

## Roger Mills County

A Brief History of Roger Mills County, by Nat M. Taylor. [Strong City: Author, 1947.] 64 pp.

[Pioneer History of Roger Mills County], 1978, in Prairie Fire, *see* p. 303.

## Rogers County

[History of] County of Rogers, 1922, in Muskogee and Northeast Oklahoma, *see* p. 303.

The History of Rogers County, Oklahoma, comp. by The Claremont College Foundation. Claremont: Will Rogers Memorial, or Tulsa: Heritage Pub. Co., 1979. 495 pp.

## Sequoyah County

[History of] County of . . . Sequoyah, 1922, in Muskogee and Northeast Oklahoma, *see* p. 303.

The History of Sequoyah County, 1828-1925. N.p.: Sequoyah County Hist. Soc., 1976. 520 pp.

## Tillman County

Origin of Tillman County, by Virginia Warhurst. Norman: Univ. of Oklahoma, 1942. 104 pp. (M.A. thesis)

A Diamond History of Tillman, 1901-1976. 2 vols. Frederick: Tillman County Hist. Soc., 1976-78. 768, 568 pp.

## Tulsa County

The History of Tulsa, Oklahoma . . . with a [History] of Tulsa County . . . by Clarence B. Douglas. 2 vols. Chicago: S.J. Clarke Pub. Co., 1921. 695, 775 pp.

## Wagoner County

[History of] County of . . . Wagoner, 1922, in Muskogee and Northeast Oklahoma, *see* p. 303.

Wagoner County History. [Wagoner?:] Oklahoma Extension Homemakers Council, 1980. 403 pp.

## Washington County

[History of] County of . . . Washington, 1922, in Muskogee and Northeast Oklahoma, *see* p. 303.

History of Washington County and Surrounding Area, by Margaret W. Teague. 2 vols. Bartlesville: Bartlesville Hist. Comm., n.d. 332, 362 pp.

## Washita County

History of Washita County, 1937, *see* Custer County.

Wagon Trucks: 1892-1976: Washita County Heritage. [Cornell?:] Washita County Hist. Comm., 1976. 448 pp.

[Pioneer History of Washita County], 1978, in Prairie Fire, *see* p. 303.

Across the Prairie: the Story of Washita County Pioneer Families . . . and Historical Events. Sentinel: Schoormaker Pubs., 1980. 288 pp.

## Woods County

History of Woods County, Oklahoma, by George R. Crissman and R. Davies. [Alva: N.p., 1930?] 119 pp.

Pioneer Footprints Across Woods County. San Angelo, Tex.: Newsfoto Yearbooks, for Cherokee Strip Volunteer League, 1976. 776 pp.

## Woodward County

Woodward County Pioneer Families Before 1915. Woodward: Plains Indians & Pioneer Hist. Foundation, 1975. 543 pp.

# OREGON

## Regional

History of Southern Oregon, Comprising Jackson, Josephine, Douglas, Curry and Coos Counties . . . Portland: A.G. Walling, 1884. 545 pp.

An Illustrated History of Baker, Grant, Malheur, and Harney Counties . . . [Spokane, Wash.:] Western Hist. Pub. Co., 1902. xxiii, 788 pp.

An Illustrated History of Central Oregon, Embracing Wasco, Sherman, Gilliam, Wheeler, Crook, Lake and Klamath Counties, State of Oregon. Spokane, Wash.: Western Hist. Pub. Co., 1905. xxx, 1,097 pp.

❧   ❧   ❧

## Baker County

Thirty-one Years in Baker County. A History of the County from 1861 to 1893, by Isaac Hiatt. Baker City: Abbott & Foster, 1893. 208 pp. (Repr. Baker City: Baker County Hist. Soc., 1970.)

Illustrated History of Baker County, 1902, *see* above.

## Benton County

History of Benton County, Oregon . . . and Biographical Sketches . . . pub. by David D. Fagan. Portland: A.G. Walling, 1885. 532 pp.

Benton County, Oregon, Illustrated, by Benton County Citizens' League. [Corvallis: N.p., 1901?] 58 pp. (Repr.? 1904.)

## Clatsop County

Clatsop County, Oregon, a History, by Emma G. Miller. Portland: Binfords and Mort, 1958. 291 pp.

## Coos County

History of Coos County, 1884, in History of Southern Oregon, *see* above.

Pioneer History of Coos and Curry Counties, Oregon . . . Orvil Dodge, historian. Salem: Capital Pr. Co., 1898. 468, 103 pp.

A Century of Coos and Curry; History of Southwest Oregon, by Emil R. Peterson, et al. Portland: Binfords & Mort, 1952. 599 pp. (Repr. Coquille: Coos-Curry Pioneer & Hist. Assoc., 1977.)

## Crook County

Illustrated History of . . . Crook County, 1905, *see* Illustrated History of Central Oregon, above.

*Crook County (cont.)*

Old Crook County: the Heart of Oregon, by Frances Juris. Prineville: Juris, 1975. 31 pp.

## Curry County

History of . . . Curry County, 1884, in History of Southern Oregon, *see* p. 310.

Pioneer History of . . . Curry County, 1898, *see* Coos County.

A Century of . . . Curry, 1952, *see* Coos County.

## Douglas County

History of . . . Douglas County, 1884, in History of Southern Oregon, *see* p. 310.

Historic Douglas County, Oregon, with Family Histories. Roseburg: Douglas County Hist. Soc., 1982. 350 pp.

## Gilliam County

Illustrated History of . . . Gilliam County, 1905, *see* Illustrated History of Southern Oregon, p. 310.

## Grant County

Illustrated History of . . . Grant County, 1902, *see* p. 310.

## Harney County

Illustrated History of . . . Harney County, 1902, *see* p. 310.

Harney County, Oregon and Its Range Land, by George F. Brimlow. Port Oregon: Binfords & Mort [1951?]. 316 pp.

## Jackson County

History of . . . Jackson County, 1884, in History of Southern Oregon, *see* p. 310.

The History of Jackson County, by William P. Tucker. Seattle, Wash.: Univ. of Washington, 1931. 251 pp. (M.A. thesis)

## Jefferson County

Jefferson County, Oregon, Reminiscences by Many Hands. Portland: Binfords & Mort [1957]. 384 pp.

## Josephine County

History of . . . Josephine County, 1884, in History of Southern Oregon, *see* p. 310.

## Klamath County

Illustrated History of . . . Klamath County, 1905, *see* Illustrated History of Central Oregon, p. 310.

## Lake County

Illustrated History of . . . Lake County, 1905, *see* Illustrated History of Central Oregon, p. 310.

## Lane County

Illustrated History of Lane County, Oregon, comp. by Albert G. Walling. Portland: A.G. Walling Pr. House, 1884. 508 pp.

## Linn County

History of Linn County, comp. by W.P.A. [Albany: N.p., 1941.] 174 pp.

The Land of Linn; an Historical Account of Linn County, Oregon, by Floyd C. Mullen. Lebanon: Dalton's Pr. [1971]. 352 pp.

## Malheur County

Illustrated History of . . . Malheur County, 1902, *see* p. 310.

Pioneer Days in Malheur County . . . by Jacob R. Gregg. Los Angeles: Priv. pr., by L.L. Morrison, 1950. 442 pp.

## Marion County

Book of Remembrance of Marion County, Oregon Pioneers, 1840-1860, by Sarah H. Steeves. Portland: Berncliff Pr., 1927. 348 pp.

## Morrow County

An Illustrated History of Umatilla County, by Col. William Parsons, and of Morrow County, by W.S. Shiach. [Spokane, Wash.:] W.H. Lever, 1902. xv, 581 pp.

Homesteads and Heritages; a History of Morrow County, Oregon, by Giles French. Portland: Binfords & Mort, 1971. 127 pp.

## Polk County

Polk County Pioneer Sketches, comp. by Sarah Childress. 2 vols. Dallas, Oreg.: Polk Chapter, no. 6, D.A.R., and Polk County Observer, 1927-29. (Repr. 2 vols. in 1. Dallas, Oreg.: Itemizer Observer, 1977.)

## Sherman County

Illustrated History of . . . Sherman County, 1905, *see* Illustrated History of Central Oregon, p. 310.

The Golden Land; a History of Sherman County, Oregon, by Giles French. [Portland:] Oregon Hist. Soc., 1958. 237 pp.

## Tillamook County

History . . . of Tillamook County, Oregon. Portland: W.P.A., 1940. 79 pp.

Tillamook: Land of Many Waters, by Ada M. Orcutt. Portland: Binfords & Mort [1951].

Tillamook Memories; Places We Love Come Back to Us as Sweet Music. Tillamook: [Tillamook Pioneer Assoc.], 1972. 218 pp.

## Umatilla County

An Illustrated History of Umatilla County, by Col. William Parsons. [Spokane, Wash.:] W.H. Lever, 1902. xv, 581 pp.

Way Back When, by Mildred Searcey. Pendleton: East Oregonian Pub. Co. [1972]. 203 pp.

We Remember, by Mildred Searcey. Pendleton: East Oregonian Pub. Co. [1973]. 173 pp.

## Wasco County

Illustrated History of . . . Wasco County, 1905, *see* Illustrated History of Central Oregon, p. 310.

History of Wasco County, Oregon, by William H. McNeal. [The Dalles, N.p., 1953.] 471 pp.

A Brief History of the Old Wasco County, Oregon Pioneers Association . . . by William H. McNeal. [The Dalles] McNeal [1975]. v, 188, 6 pp.

## Washington County

Pioneer Landmarks of Washington County, Oregon, by Robert L. Benson. Hillsboro: Washington County Hist. Soc., 1966. 24 pp.

## Wheeler County

Illustrated History of . . . Wheeler County, 1905, *see* Illustrated History of Central Oregon, p. 310.

# PENNSYLVANIA

## Regional

History of Northampton, Lehigh, Monroe, Carbon and Schuylkill Counties . . . by Israel D. Rupp. Harrisburg: Hickock & Gantine, 1845. xiv, 568 pp. (Repr. [New York:] Arno Pr. [1971]. Every-name computerized index, by Von Gail Hamilton. Park City, Utah: Hamilton Computer Service, 1976. 19 pp.)

Early History of Western Pennsylvania . . . by Israel D. Rupp. With . . . a Topographical Description of the Counties of Allegheny, Westmoreland, Washington, Somerset, Greene, Fayette, Beaver, Butler, Armstrong . . . Harrisburg: Hickock & Gantine, 1846. 352, 406 pp.

The History and Topography of Dauphin, Cumberland, Franklin, Bedford, Adams, Perry, Somerset, Cambria, and Indiana Counties . . . comp. by Israel D. Rupp. Lancaster City: G. Hills, 1848. 598 pp. (Repr. with index, by John C. Fralish, Jr. N.p., 1974. 723 pp. Every-name index of Dauphin, Cumberland, Franklin, Bedford, Adams, and Perry counties, by Von Gail Hamilton. Park City, Utah: Author [1976?]. 38 leaves.)

History and Topography of Northumberland, Huntingdon, Mifflin, Centre, Union, Columbia, Juniata and Clinton Counties . . . by Israel D. Rupp. Lancaster: G. Hills, 1847. 560 pp. (Index, by Mary B. Lontz. Milton: Author [1967]. 10 pp. Computerized index. Park City, Utah: Hamilton Computer Service, 1976. 19 pp.)

History of That Part of the Susquehanna and Juniata Valleys Embraced in the Counties of Mifflin, Juniata, Perry, Union and Snyder . . . ed. by F. Ellis and A.N. Hungerford. 2 vols. Philadelphia: Everts, Peck & Richards, 1886. (Index, by Hilda Chance. Huntsville, Ark.: Century Enterprises, 1969. 82, 80 pp. Repr. 2 vols. Evansville, Ind.: Unigraphic, 1975.)

History of the Counties of McKean, Elk, Cameron and Potter, Pennsylvania [comp. by Michael A. Leeson]. Chicago: J.H. Beers & Co., 1890. 1,261 pp. (Repr. 2 vols. Evansville, Ind.: Unigraphic, 1978.)

A Pioneer Outline History of Northwestern Pennsylvania, Embracing the Counties of Tioga, Potter, McKean, Warren, Crawford, Venango, Forest, Clarion, Elk, Jefferson, Cameron, Butler, Lawrence and Mercer . . . by William J. McKnight. Philadelphia: J.B. Lippincott, 1904. 748 pp.

Annals of Southwestern Pennsylvania, by Lewis C. Walkinshaw. 4 vols. New York: Lewis Pub. Co., 1939. (Includes Histories of Allegheny, Armstrong, Beaver, Bedford, Butler, Cambria, Fayette, Greene, Indiana, Lawrence, Somerset, Washington, and Westmoreland Counties.)

History of Northwestern Pennsylvania, Comprising the Counties of Erie, Crawford, Mercer, Venango, Warren, Forest, Clarion, McKean, Elk, Jefferson, Cameron and Clearfield. 3 vols. New York: Lewis Hist. Pub. Co. [1943].

Southeastern Pennsylvania, a History of the Counties of Berks, Bucks, Chester, Delaware, Montgomery, Philadelphia and Schuylkill, ed. by J. Bennett Nolan. 3 vols. New York: Lewis Hist. Pub. Co. [1943].

## Adams County

History and Topography of . . . Adams County, 1848, *see* p. 314.

History of . . . Adams County, 1886, *see* Cumberland County.

A Glimpse Into Adams County, 1860-1914: a Photographic Record. Gettysburg: Adams County Hist. Soc., 1977.

## Allegheny County

Topographical Description of the County of Allegheny, 1846, in Early History of Western Pennsylvania, *see* p. 314.

History of Allegheny County, Pennsylvania . . . [by Samuel W. Durant]. Philadelphia: L.H. Everts, 1876. 242 pp.

Allegheny County's Hundred Years, by George H. Thursten. Pittsburgh: A.A. Anderson, 1888. 312 pp.

Allegheny County: Its Early History and Subsequent Development, from the Earliest Period Till 1790, by A.A. Lambing. From 1790 Till the Present Time, by Hon. J.W.F. White. Pittsburgh: Snowden & Peterson, 1888. 277 pp. (Another ed., 1888.)

History of Allegheny County . . . ed. by Thomas Cushing. 2 vols. in 1. Chicago: A. Warner, 1889. viii, 758 pp. (Repr. with new index. 2 vols. Pittsburgh: Western Pennsylvania Gen. Soc., 1975. 762, 786 pp. Repr. Evansville, Ind.: Unigraphic, 1979. Repr. Baltimore: Genealogical Pub. Co., 1975. 577 pp.)

Memoirs of Allegheny County, Pennsylvania. 2 vols. Madison, Wis.: Northwestern Hist. Assoc., 1904.

Allegheny County: a Sesquicentennial Review, ed. by George E. Kelly, 1783-1938. Pittsburgh: Sesquicentennial Comm. [1938]. xv, 364 pp. (Rev. and enl. [N.p., 1939?]. xv, 402 pp.)

History of Allegheny County, 1939, in Annals of Southwestern Pennsylvania, *see* p. 314.

## Armstrong County

History of Armstrong County, by Robert W. Smith. Chicago: Waterman-Watkins, 1883. 624 pp.

Biographical and Historical Cyclopedia of . . . Armstrong County, 1891, *see* Indiana County.

Armstrong County: Her People, Past and Present, Embracing a History of the County . . . 2 vols. Chicago: J.H. Beers, 1914.

History of Armstrong County, 1939, in Annals of Southwestern Pennsylvania, *see* p. 314.

## Beaver County

Topographical Description of the County of . . . Beaver, 1846, in Early History of Western Pennsylvania, *see* p. 314.

*Beaver County (cont.)*

Beaver County Centennial Directory. N.p.: Weyand & Reed, 1876. (Repr. Apollo: Closson Pr., 1983.)

History of Beaver County, Pennsylvania, Including Its Early Settlement . . . [by J.F. Richard]. Philadelphia: A. Warner, 1888. 908 pp.

History of Beaver County and Its Centennial Celebration, by Rev. Joseph H. Bausman. 2 vols. New York: Knickerbocker Pr., 1904.

History of Beaver County, 1939, in Annals of Southwestern Pennsylvania, *see* p. 314.

## Bedford County

History and Topography of . . . Bedford County, 1848, *see* p. 314. (Repr. of Bedford County part. Laughlintown: Southwest Pennsylvania Gen. Services, 1983.)

History of Bedford, Somerset and Fulton Counties, Chicago: Waterman-Watkins, 1884. 672 pp. (Index to surnames, by Floyd G. Hoenstine. Hollidaysburg: Author, 1967. 58 pp. Repr. Evansville, Ind.: Unigraphic, 1980.)

History of Bedford and Somerset Counties . . . Bedford County, by E.H. Blackburn. Somerset County, by William H. Welfley. 3 vols. New York: Lewis Pub. Co., 1906. (Repr. 3 vols. Somerset: Somerset Hist. Soc., 1983. x, 1,567, x, 723, x, 595 pp.)

The Annals of Bedford County . . . 1750-1850 . . . by Hon. William P. Schell. Bedford: Gazette Pub. Co., 1907. 90 pp.

History of Bedford County, 1939, in Annals of Southwestern Pennsylvania. *see* p. 314.

The Kernel of Greatness; an Informal Bicentennial History of Bedford County. [Bedford: Bedford County Heritage Comm., 1971.] 272 pp.

Bedford County, by Winona Garbrick. N.p., 1971.

## Berks County

History of the Counties of Berks and Lebanon . . . comp. by Israel D. Rupp. Lancaster: G. Hills, 1844. 512 pp. (Computerized index. Park City, Utah: Hamilton Computer Services, 1976. 38 pp. Repr. Laughlintown: Southwest Pennsylvania Gen. Services, 1983.)

History of Berks County in Pennsylvania, by Morton L. Montgomery. Philadelphia: Everts, Peck & Richards, 1886. x, 1,204 pp. (Repr. Laughlintown: Southwest Pennsylvania Gen. Services, 1984.)

School History of Berks County, by Morton L. Montgomery. Philadelphia: J.B. Rodgers Pr. Co., 1889. 302 pp.

History of Berks County in the Revolution from 1774 to 1783, by Morton L. Montgomery. Reading: C.F. Haage, 1894. 295 pp.

*Berks County (cont.)*

Historical and Biographical Annals of Berks County . . . comp. by Morton L. Montgomery. 2 vols. Chicago: J.H. Beers, 1909. (Originally pub. under title, History of Berks County . . . 1886. Superior index. Park City, Utah: Hamilton Computer Service, 1977. 700 pp.)

The Story of Berks County, by A.E. Wagner. Reading: Eagle Book & Job. Pr., 1913. 253 pp.

Reading and Berks County, Pennsylvania; a History, ed. by Cyrus T. Fox. 3 vols. New York: Lewis Pub. Co., 1925.

The Story of Berks County, by F.W. Balthaser. [Reading: Reading Eagle Pr., 1925.] xvii, 373 pp.

Early Narratives of Berks County, by J. Bennett Nolan. [Reading: N.p., 1927.] 188 pp.

History of the County of Berks, 1943, in Southeastern Pennsylvania, *see* p. 314.

The Berks County Story, by Richard M. Moll, et al. Reading: Superintendent of Schools of Berks County, 1953.

## Blair County

History of the City of Altoona and Blair County . . . by James H. Ewing. Altoona: H. Slep, 1880. 262 pp.

History of Blair County, 1883, *see* Huntingdon County.

A History of Blair County, from Its Earliest Settlement . . . to 1896, by C.B. Clark. Altoona: C.B. Clark, 1896. 116 pp.

Twentieth Century History of Altoona and Blair County, Pennsylvania . . . by Jesse C. Sell. Chicago: Richmond-Arnold Pub. Co., 1911. 972 pp.

A History of Blair County, ed. by Tarring S. Davis. 2 vols. Harrisburg: National Hist. Assoc., 1931.

A History of Blair County . . . Altoona Senior High School Project. [Altoona: School, 1938.] viii, 122 pp.

Blair County's First Hundred Years, 1846-1946, ed. by George A. Wolf. Altoona: Mirror Pr., 1945. xv, 526 pp. (2d ed. Hollidaysburg: Blair County Hist. Soc., 1945.)

## Bradford County

History of Bradford County [by David Craft]. Philadelphia: L.H. Everts, 1878. 492 pp. (Every-name index, by Reid D. Macafee. South Weymouth, Mass.: N.p. [1955]. 255 leaves.)

Outline History of . . . Bradford County, 1885, *see* Tioga County.

History of Bradford County . . . by H.C. Bradsby. Chicago: S.B. Nelson, 1891. 1,320 pp.

*Bradford County (cont.)*

Pioneer and Patriot Families of Bradford County, 1770-1800 . . . by Clement F. Heverly. 2 vols. Towanda: Bradford Star Pr., 1913-15. (Every-name index, prepared by Reid D. Macafee. South Weymouth, Mass.: N.p., 1955. 427 leaves. Expanded, 1770-1825, with index, by E.R. Glueck. 2 vols. in 1. Evansville, Ind.: Unigraphic, 1977.)

History and Geography of Bradford County, 1615-1924 . . . by Clement F. Heverly. Towanda: Bradford County Hist. Soc. [1926]. xi, 594 pp. (Name index, by Ellen R. Glueck. 2 vols. in 1. Towanda: Bradford County Hist. Soc., 1976.)

## Bucks County

History of Bucks County, by William J. Buck. Willow Grove: N.p., 1855. 118, 24 pp.

The History of Bucks County, from the Discovery of the Delaware to the Present Time, by W.H.H. Davis. Doylestown: Democrat Book and Job Office Pr., 1876. xii, 875 pp. (2d ed., rev. and enl. . . . ed. by Warren S. Ely. 3 vols. New York: Lewis Pub. Co., 1905.)

Local Sketches and Legends Pertaining to Bucks and Montgomery Counties, Pennsylvania . . . by William J. Buck. [Philadelphia:] Author, 1887. 340 pp.

History of Bucks County . . . ed. by J.H. Battle. Philadelphia: A. Warner, 1887. 1,176 pp. (Repr. Laughlintown: Southwest Pennsylvania Gen. Services, 1983.)

History of . . . Bucks County, 1943, in Southeastern Pennsylvania, *see* p. 314.

A History of Bucks County. Part 1, to 1776, by Terry A. McNealy. Fallsington: Bucks County Hist. Tourist Comm., 1970.

## Butler County

Topographical Description of the County of . . . Butler, 1846, in Early History of Western Pennsylvania, *see* p. 314.

History of Butler County . . . Chicago: Waterman-Watkins, 1883. viii, 454 pp.

History of Butler County [ed. by Robert C. Brown]. 2 vols. [Chicago:] Brown, 1895. 1,360 pp. (Repr. Evansville, Ind.: Unigraphic, 1980.)

A Pioneer Outline History of . . . Butler County, 1904, *see* p. 314.

20th Century History of Butler and Butler County . . . ed. and comp. by James A. McKee. Chicago: Richmond-Arnold Pub. Co., 1909.

History of Butler County, by Chester H. Sipe. 2 vols. Topeka-Indianapolis: Hist. Pub. Co., 1927.

History of Butler County, 1939, in Annals of Southwestern Pennsylvania, *see* p. 314.

Butler County. (150 Years of History and Development.) Butler: N.p., 1950. 198 pp.

*Butler County (cont.)*

A Concise History of Butler County, 1800-1950, by James Brandon. Butler: Butler County Hist. Soc., 1962. 176 pp.

## Cambria County

History and Topography of . . . Cambria County, 1848, *see* p. 314. (Repr. of Cambria County part. Laughlintown: Southwest Pennsylvania Gen. Services, 1983.)

History of Cambria County . . . by Henry W. Storey. 3 vols. New York: Lewis Pub. Co., 1907.

Cambria County Pioneers; a Collection of Brief Biographical and Other Sketches Relating to the Early History of Cambria County, by James M. Swank. [Philadelphia: Allen, Lane & Scott], 1910. 138 pp.

History of Cambria County, Pennsylvania, by John E. Gable. 2 vols. Indianapolis, Ind.: Hist. Pub. Co., 1926. 1,224 pp.

History of . . . Cambria County, 1939, in Annals of Southwestern Pennsylvania, *see* p. 314.

Sesquicentennial of Cambria County. Ebensburg: Cambria County Hist. Soc., 1954.

## Cameron County

History of the County of . . . Cameron, 1890, *see* p. 314.

A Pioneer Outline History of . . . the County of Cameron, 1904, *see* p. 314.

History of the County of . . . Cameron, 1943, in History of Northwestern Pennsylvania, *see* p. 314.

## Carbon County

History of . . . Carbon County, 1845, *see* p. 314.

History of the County of . . . Carbon, 1884, *see* Lehigh County.

History of Carbon County . . . by Fred Brenckman. Harrisburg: J.J. Nuhgesser, 1913. ix, 626 pp.

## Centre County

History and Topography of . . . Centre County, 1847, *see* p. 314. (Repr. of Centre County part. Laughlintown: Southwest Pennsylvania Gen. Services, 1983.)

Industries and Institutions of Centre County, with Historical Sketches of Principal Villages, etc., comp. by D.S. Maynard. Bellefonte: Republican Job Pr., 1877. 340 pp.

*Centre County (cont.)*

History of Centre and Clinton Counties, Pennsylvania, by John B. Linn. Philadelphia: L.H. Everts, 1883. x, 672 pp. (Index, comp. by J. Thomas Mitchell. Bellefonte: Centre County Lib. & Hist. Museum, 1962. Unpaged. Repr. State College: Centre County Hist. Soc., 1981. x, 1,052, including every-name index.)

Centre County, the County in Which we Live, by J. Marvin Lee. [State College: N.p., 1965.] 234 leaves. (Rev. ed. [State College: N.p., 1974.] 155 leaves.)

## Chester County

History of Chester County . . . by J. Smith Futhey. Philadelphia: L.H. Everts, 1881. 782, xliv pp. (First and last name index, by Constance J. Wilson. Berkeley, Calif.: Wilson, 1983. 171 pp.)

Biographical and Portrait Cyclopedia of Chester County, Comprising an Historical Sketch . . . by Samuel T. Wiley, rev. and ed. by Winfield S. Garner. Philadelphia: Gresham Pub. Co., 1893. 879 pp.

Chester County and Its People, ed. by Wilmer W. Thomson. New York: Union Hist. Co., 1898. 982 pp.

Historic Houses and Institutions, and . . . Personal Memoirs of Chester and Delaware Counties, by Gilbert Cope. 2 vols. New York: Lewis Pub. Co., 1904. 1,198 pp.

A History of Chester County, Pennsylvania, ed. by Charles W. Heathcote. [West Chester: H.F. Temple, 1926.] viii, 129 pp. ([Another ed., with Biographical Sketches.] Harrisburg: National Hist. Assoc., 1932. vii, 479 pp.)

History of the County of . . . Chester, 1943, in Southeastern Pennsylvania, *see* p. 314.

Chester County, Pennsylvania, by Berenice M. Ball. Philadelphia: Horace Temple Inc., 1960.

Chester County and Its Day, by Berenice M. Ball. West Chester: KNA Pr., 1970.

100th Anniversary, Chester County's Daily Local News, 1872-1972. 5 vols. Special Centennial ed. [West Chester: Daily Local News Co.], 1972.

## Clarion County

History of Clarion County . . . ed. by A.J. Davis. Syracuse, N.Y.: D. Mason, 1887. 664, lxxii pp. (Repr. with historical suppl. to 1919. Rimersburg: Record Pr., 1968. 664, lxxii, 180 pp. Repr. with surname index added. Evansville, Ind.: Unigraphic, 1980.)

A Pioneer Outline History of . . . County of . . . Clarion, 1904, *see* p. 314.

History of . . . Clarion County, 1943, in History of Northwestern Pennsylvania, *see* p. 314.

Clarion County and Its Beginnings, ed. by Helen W. Urban. Clarion: Clarion County Hist. Soc., 1975.

# Clearfield County

History of Clearfield County . . . ed. by Lewis C. Aldrich. Syracuse, N.Y.: D. Mason, 1887. 731 pp. (Repr. with every-name index. Laughlintown: Southwest Pennsylvania Gen. Services, 1980. Repr. Evansville, Ind.: Unigraphic, 1980.)

Clearfield County's Centennial . . . Clearfield: Raftsman's Journal [1904]. 88 pp.

Twentieth Century History of Clearfield County . . . by Roland D. Swoope, Sr. Chicago: Richmond-Arnold Pub. Co. [1911]. 981 pp.

Clearfield County, Present and Past, by Thomas L. Wall. Library ed. [Clearfield:] Author [1925]. x, 296 pp. (Computerized index. Park City, Utah: Hamilton Computer Service, 1980.)

Clearfield County, Pennsylvania . . . by Albert Y. Straw. N.p., 1931. (Repr. with added index. Clearfield: Clearfield County Hist. Soc., 1983. 292, 62 pp.)

History of . . . County of . . . Clearfield, 1943, in History of Northwestern Pennsylvania, *see* p. 314.

# Clinton County

History and Topography of . . . Clinton County, 1847, *see* p. 314.

Historical View of Clinton County, from Its Earliest Settlement to the Present Time . . . by D.S. Maynard. Lock Haven: Enterprise Pr. House, 1875. 228 pp.

History of . . . Clinton County, 1883, *see* p. 314.

Historical and Biographical Work, or Past and Present of Clinton County . . . by J. Milton Furey. Williamsport: Pennsylvania Grit Pr. Houses, 1892. 417 pp.

A Picture of Clinton County, comp. by Pennsylvania Writers' Project, W.P.A. [Harrisburg:] Commissioners of Clinton Co., 1942. xiv, 195 pp.

# Columbia County

History and Topography of . . . Columbia County, 1847, *see* p. 314. (Repr. of Columbia part. Laughlintown: Southwest Pennsylvania Gen. Services, 1983.)

Columbia and Montour Counties, by G.H. Walker and C.F. Jewett. New York: F.W. Beers & Co., 1876. 95 pp.

A History of Columbia County, from the Earliest Times, by John G. Freeze. Bloomsburg: Elwell & Bittenbender, 1883. 572 pp.

History of Columbia and Montour Counties, ed. by J.H. Battle. Chicago: A. Warner, 1887. 132, 542, 220 pp.

Historical and Biographical Annals of Columbia and Montour Counties . . . 2 vols. Chicago: J.H. Beers, 1915.

History of Columbia County, Pennsylvania, by Edwin M. Barton. [Bloomsburg:] Columbia County Hist. Soc., 1958.

Columbia County 200 Years Ago, by Edward M. Barton. Bloomsburg: Columbia County Hist. Soc., 1976.

# Crawford County

History of Crawford County, Pennsylvania [by Robert C. Brown]. Chicago: Warner, Beers, 1885. 1,186 pp.

Centennial ed. of the Daily Tribune-Republican . . . 1888, with Historical and Biographical Sketches. Meadville: Tribune Pub. Co. [1888]. 168 pp.

Our County and Its People: a Historical and Memorial Record of Crawford County, by Samuel P. Bates. [Boston?:] W.A. Fergusson, 1899. xv, 972 pp.

A Pioneer Outline History of . . . the County of . . . Crawford, 1904, *see* p. 314.

History of County of . . . Crawford . . . 1943, in History of Northwestern Pennsylvania, *see* p. 314.

# Cumberland County

The History and Topography of . . . Cumberland County, 1848, *see* p. 314. (Repr. of Cumberland County part. Laughlintown: Southwest Pennsylvania Gen. Services, 1983.)

History of Cumberland County, by Rev. Conway P. Wing. Philadelphia: J.D. Scott, 1879. 272, v pp. (Repr. with new index. Carlisle: Cumberland County Hist. Soc. & Hamilton Lib. Assoc., 1982. 275 pp.)

History of Cumberland and Adams Counties . . . Chicago: Warner, Beers, 1886. 132, 588, 516 pp. (Part 1, History of Pennsylvania, by Sam Bates; Part 2, History of Cumberland County, by P.A. Dusant and J.F. Richard; and Part 3, History of Adams County, by H.C. Bradsby, A. Sheely, and M.A. Leeson.) (Index to personal names, by Allice B. Canyon and R.E. Staub. [York], 1941. Repr. Knightstown, Ind.: The Bookmark, 1977. Includes index by Henry Young. Superior index. Park City, Utah: Hamilton Computer Service, 1977. 338 pp.)

Farm Scenes: the Early Years in Cumberland County, Pennsylvania. [Carlisle:] Cumberland County Hist. Soc. and Hamilton Lib. Assoc., n.d.

Two Hundred Years in Cumberland County . . . ed. by D.W. Thompson. Carlisle: Hamilton Lib. & Hist. Assoc. of Cumberland County, 1951. 388 pp. (Index, by Hilda Chance. Liberty: Author [1965]. 10 leaves.)

A Cumberland County Album, by Roger K. Todd, ed. by Gail M. Gibson. Carlisle: Cumberland County Hist. Soc. and Hamilton Lib. Assoc., 1972.

# Dauphin County

History and Topography of Dauphin County, 1848, *see* p. 314. (Repr. of Dauphin County part. Laughlintown: Southwest Pennsylvania Gen. Services, 1983.)

Centennial: the Settlement, Formation and Progress of Dauphin County, from 1785 to 1876, prepared by George H. Morgan. Harrisburg: Telegraph Steam Book and Job Pr., 1877. 239 pp.

History of the Counties of Dauphin and Lebanon . . . by William H. Egle. 2 vols. Philadelphia: Everts & Peck, 1883. ix, 616, 360 pp. (Index to persons in Lebanon County, comp. by Rhea D. Johnson. Lebanon: Lebanon County Hist. Soc., 1962. 217 pp.)

*Dauphin County (cont.)*

History of Dauphin County, by Luther R. Kelker. 3 vols. New York: Lewis Pub. Co., 1907.

Harrisburg and Dauphin County . . . 1900-1925, by George P. Donehoo. 2 vols. Dayton, Ohio: National Hist. Assoc., 1925.

Dauphin County Elements Towards a Twentieth Century History, by G.G. Stoctay [pseud. for George Feigley]. Harrisburg: Author, 1971. 244 pp.

## Delaware County

History of Delaware County from the Discovery of the Territory . . . by George Smith. Philadelphia: H.G. Ashmead, 1862. vii, 581 pp. ([Reissue?], 1907.)

History of Delaware County, by Henry G. Ashmead. Philadelphia: L.H. Everts, 1884. x, 767 pp.

Biographical and Historical Cyclopedia of Delaware County . . . by Samuel T. Wiley. Rev. and ed. by Winfield S. Garner. Richmond, Ind.: Gresham Pub. Co., 1894. 500 pp.

A History of Delaware County and Its People, ed. by John W. Jordan. 3 vols. New York: Lewis Hist. Pub. Co., 1914.

A History of Delaware County, ed. by Charles Palmer. 2 vols. Harrisburg: National Hist. Assoc., 1932. 425 pp.

History of the County of . . . Delaware, 1943, in Southeastern Pennsylvania, *see* p. 314.

Some Aspects of Delaware County History as Presented at Meetings of the Eastern Chapter of the Delaware County Historical Society . . . [Aldan?: N.p.], 1954. 110 pp.

The First 100 Years of Delaware County, by William Sawyer. Chester: Wilber C. Kriebel, 1957.

## Elk County

History of the County of . . . Elk, 1890, *see* p. 314.

Pioneer Outline History of . . . County of . . . Elk, 1904, *see* p. 314.

History of the County of . . . Elk . . . 1943, in History of Northwestern Pennsylvania, *see* p. 314.

## Erie County

The History of Erie County, by Laura G. Sanford. Philadelphia: J.B. Lippincott, 1862. 347 pp. (New and enl. ed. [Erie?:] Author, 1894. 460 pp.)

History of Erie County, by Benjamin Whitman and N.W. Russell. Chicago: Warner, Beers, 1884. 1,006, 239 pp.

Popular History of Erie County . . . Erie: Advertiser Pr., 1895. 192 pp.

*Erie County (cont.)*

Nelson's Biographical Dictionary and Historical Reference Book of Erie County . . . prepared by Benjamin Whitman. Erie: S.B. Nelson, 1896. 922 pp.

A Twentieth Century History of Erie County . . . by John Miller. 2 vols. Chicago: Lewis Pub. Co., 1909.

History of Erie County, Pennsylvania, by John E. Reed. [2 vols.] Topeka, Ind.: Hist. Pub., 1925. 1,288 pp.

Erie: a Guide to the City and the County . . . Federal Writers' Project, W.P.A. Philadelphia: William Penn Assoc. of Philadelphia, 1938. 133 pp.

History of the County of Erie, 1943, in History of Northwestern Pennsylvania, *see* p. 314.

## Fayette County

A Topographical Description of the County of Fayette, 1846, in Early History of Western Pennsylvania, *see* p. 314.

History of Fayette County . . . ed. by Franklin Ellis. Philadelphia: L.H. Everts, 1882. 841 pp. (Index, recomp. by Della R. Fischer. McKeesport: Author, 1970. 345 leaves.)

Nelson's Biographical Dictionary and Historical Reference Book of Fayette County, ed. by Henry E. Shepherd. Uniontown: S.B. Nelson, 1900. 1,225 pp.

History of . . . Fayette County, 1939, in Annals of Southwestern Pennsylvania, *see* p. 314.

## Forest County

History of the County of . . . Forest, 1890, *see* p. 314.

Pioneer Outline History of . . . County of . . . Forest, 1904, *see* p. 314.

History of the County of . . . Forest, 1943, in History of Northwestern Pennsylvania, *see* p. 314.

## Franklin County

The History and Topography of . . . Franklin County, 1848, *see* p. 314. (Repr. of Franklin County part. Laughlintown: Southwest Pennsylvania Gen. Services, 1983.)

Historical Sketch of Franklin County, prepared for Centennial Celebration . . . by I. H. M'Cauley. 2d ed., enl. Harrisburg: Patriot Pub. Co., 1878. 294 pp. (Reissue, with added appendix, by J.L. Suesserott. Chambersburg: D.F. Pyrsel, 1878. 322 pp. Repr. Evansville, Ind.: Unigraphic, 1979.)

History of Franklin County . . . [by J.F. Richard]. Chicago: Warner, Beers, 1887. 968 pp. (Index to personal names. [York:], 1961.)

Historical Sketches of Franklin County and Its Several Towns . . . by Frederick J. Seaver. Albany, N.Y.: J.B. Lyon Co., 1918. 819 pp.

*Franklin County (cont.)*

Historical Papers, Franklin County and the Cumberland Valley, by Jacob H. Stoner, comp. by Lu C. Stoner. Chambersburg: Craft Pr. [1947]. 549 pp.

## Fulton County

History of Fulton County, 1884, *see* Bedford County.

The History of Fulton County, by Elsie S. Greathead. [McConnellsburg: Fulton County News], 1936. 55 pp.

## Greene County

Topographical Description of the County of . . . Greene, 1846, in Early History of Western Pennsylvania, *see* p. 314.

History of Greene County . . . from 1682 until 1781 . . . by Rev. William Hanna. N.p., 1882. 350 pp. (Repr. Apollo: Closson Pr., 1983. 357 pp., with new surname index.)

History of Greene County, by Samuel P. Bates. Chicago: Nelson, Rishforth, 1888. 898 pp. (Repr. Evansville, Ind.: Unigraphic, 1980.)

History of . . . Greene County, 1939, in Annals of Southwestern Pennsylvania, *see* p. 314.

Pioneer History of Greene County [by L.K. Evans]. Waynesburg: Waynesburg Republican, 1941. 177 pp.

## Huntingdon County

History and Topography of . . . Huntingdon County, 1847, *see* p. 314. (Repr. of Huntingdon County part. Laughlintown: Southwest Pennsylvania Gen. Services, 1983.)

History of Huntingdon County . . . from the Earliest Times to the Centennial Anniversary of American Independence . . . by Milton S. Lytle. Lancaster: W.H. Roy, 1876. 361 pp.

History of Huntingdon and Blair Counties, by J. Simpson Africa. Philadelphia: L.H. Everts, 1883. vi, 500, 261 pp.

Souvenir Historical Book Issued in Connection with the Sesquicentennial Celebration of Huntingdon County, 1787-1937, by the Huntingdon County Historical Society. [Harrisburg: Telegraph Pr., 1937.] 113 pp.

Rung's Chronicles of Pennsylvania History, by Albert M. Rung. (Huntingdon County History.) Huntingdon: Huntingdon County Hist. Soc., 1977.

## Indiana County

History and Topography of . . . Indiana County, 1848, *see* p. 314.

*Indiana County (cont.)*

1745-1880: History of Indiana County, Pennsylvania, by Capt. C.T. Adams and E. White. Newark, Ohio: Caldwell, 1880. 543 pp. (Repr. Indiana: Hist. and Gen. Soc. of Indiana County, 1982. 597 pp. Index. Park City, Utah: Hamilton Computer Service, 1976, bound in repr.)

Biographical and Historical Cyclopedia of Indiana and Armstrong Counties . . . managed by Samuel T. Wiley. Philadelphia: J.M. Gresham, 1891. 636 pp. (Repr. Apollo: Closson Pr., 1983.)

Indiana County: Her People, Past and Present, Embracing a History of the County, comp. by Joshua T. Stewart. 2 vols. Chicago: J.H. Beers, 1913.

History of . . . Indiana County, 1939, in Annals of Southwestern Pennsylvania, *see* p. 314.

Sesquicentennial Association Sesquicentennial Celebration of Indiana County. Indiana: The Assoc., 1953.

Indiana County, 175th Anniversary. 3 vols. Indiana: Halldin Pub. Co., 1978-79.

## Jefferson County

Pioneer Outline History of . . . County of . . . Jefferson, 1904, *see* p. 314.

History of Jefferson County . . . ed. by Kate M. Scott. Syracuse, N.Y.: D. Mason, 1888. 753 pp.

A Pioneer History of Jefferson County . . . by E.J. McKnight. Philadelphia: J.B. Lippincott, 1898. 670 pp.

Jefferson County, Pennsylvania, Its Pioneers and People, 1800-1915, by William J. McKnight. 2 vols. Chicago: Beers, 1917.

History of . . . County of . . . Jefferson, 1943, in History of Northwestern Pennsylvania, *see* p. 314.

Jefferson County, Pennsylvania, by the Jefferson County Historical and Genealogical Society. Summerville: The Society, 1982. 380 pp.

## Juniata County

History and Topography of . . . Juniata County, 1847, *see* p. 314.

History of . . . County of . . . Juniata, 1886, in History of . . . the Susquehanna and Juniata Valleys, *see* p. 314.

## Lackawanna County

History of . . . Lackawanna County, 1880, *see* Luzerne County.

Memorial of the Erection of Lackawanna County, Pennsylvania, comp. by Robert H. McKune. Scranton: Walter, 1882. 115 pp.

Jubilee History, Commemorative of the 50th Anniversary of the Creation of Lackawanna County . . . by Thomas F. Murphy. 2 vols. Indianapolis, Ind.: Hist. Pub. Co., 1928.

## Lancaster County

History of Lancaster County . . . comp. by Israel D. Rupp. Lancaster: Gilbert Hills, 1844. 531 pp. (Repr. with new index. Laughlintown: Southwest Pennsylvania Gen. Services, 1984.)

An Authentic History of Lancaster County, by J.L. Mombert. Lancaster: J.E. Barr, 1869. vii, 617 pp.

A Biographical History of Lancaster County . . . by Alexander Harris. Lancaster: J.E. Barr, 1872. 638 pp. (Index, by Hilda Chance. Huntsville, Ark.: Century Enterprises, 1968. 27 pp. Repr. Baltimore: Genealogical Pub. Co., 1977.)

History of Lancaster County . . . by Franklin Ellis and Samuel Evans. Philadelphia: Everts & Peck, 1883. vii, 1,101 pp. (Subject index. [York: N.p., 1942.] Exhaustive index. 4 vols. [York:] N.p., 1941-45.)

A Brief History of Lancaster County . . . by Israel S. Clare, ed. by Anna Lyle. Lancaster: Argus Pub. Co., 1892. 317 pp.

Lancaster County, a History, ed. by Harry M.J. Klein. 4 vols. New York: Lewis Hist. Pub. Co., 1924.

Lancaster County, 1841-1941, by Frederic S. Klein. Lancaster: Lancaster County National Bank, 1941. 198 pp.

Lancaster County Since 1841, by Frederic S. Klein. Rev. [i.e. 2d] ed. Lancaster: Lancaster County National Bank, 1955. 239 pp.

Lancaster County: 200th Anniversary, 1729-1979(?), by G. Terry Madonna, et al. Lancaster: N.p., 1979.

## Lawrence County

History of Lawrence County . . . by Samuel W. Durant. Philadelphia: L.H. Everts, 1877. 228 pp. (Repr. Evansville, Ind.: Unigraphic, 1979.)

Historical Review of the Towns and Business Houses of Lawrence County . . . by Wick W. Wood. New Castle: Author, 1887. 132 pp.

Pioneer Outline History of . . . County of . . . Lawrence, 1904, *see* p. 314.

Twentieth Century History of New Castle and Lawrence County . . . ed. and comp. by Hon. Aaron L. Hazen. Chicago: Richmond-Arnold Pub. Co., 1908. 1,015 pp.

History of . . . Lawrence County, 1939, in Annals of Southwestern Pennsylvania, *see* p. 314.

Lawrence County: a Compact History, by Bart Richards. New Castle: New Castle Area School Dist., 1968. 287 pp.

## Lebanon County

History of the County of . . . Lebanon, 1844, *see* Berks County.

History of the County of . . . Lebanon, 1883, *see* Dauphin County.

The Heritage of Lebanon County, Pennsylvania. Lebanon: Lebanon News Pub. Co., 1960.

*Lebanon County (cont.)*

Lebanon County, Pennsylvania, a History, comp. by Edna Carmean. Lebanon: Lebanon County Hist. Soc., 1976.

## Lehigh County

History of . . . Lehigh County, 1845, *see* p. 314. (Repr. of Lehigh County part. Laughlintown: Southwest Pennsylvania Gen. Services, 1983.)

History of the Counties of Lehigh and Carbon . . . by Alfred Mathews and A. Hungerford. Philadelphia: Everts & Richards, 1884. xi, 802 pp.

A History of Lehigh County, from the Earliest Settlements to the Present Time [by James J. Hauser]. Emmaus: Times Pub. Co., 1901. 93 pp. (2d ed. Allentown: Jacks, 1902. 127 pp.)

History of Lehigh County . . . by Charles R. Roberts. 3 vols. Allentown: Lehigh Valley Pub. Co., 1914.

## Luzerne County

Annals of Luzerne County . . . from Its Settlement at Wyoming to 1860, by Stewart Pearce. Philadelphia: J.B. Lippincott, 1860. 554 pp. (2d ed., with notes, corrections, and additions. Philadelphia: J.B. Lippincott, 1866. 564 pp.)

History of Luzerne, Lackawanna and Wyoming Counties . . . New York: W.W. Munsell, 1880. 540 pp.

History of Luzerne County . . . ed. by Henry C. Bradsby. Chicago: S.B. Nelson, 1893. 1,509 pp.

## Lycoming County

History of Lycoming County . . . Philadelphia: D.J. Stewart, 1876. 132 pp. (Index. Park City, Utah: Hamilton Computer Service, 1981.)

History of Lycoming County, by John F. Meginness. Chicago: Brown, 1892. 1,267 pp. (Repr. N.p.: Lycoming County Hist. Soc., 1974. Index, by Hilda Chance. Liberty: Comp., 1974. Index Park City, Utah: Hamilton Computer Service, 1978. Repr. Evansville, Ind.: Unigraphic, 1980.)

Lycoming County: Its Organization and Condensed History of 100 Years, 1795-1895, by John F. Meginness. Williamsport: Gazette & Bull. Pr. House, 1895. 82 pp.

Official Report of the Proceedings of the Centennial Anniversary of Lycoming County . . . ed. by John F. Meginness. Williamsport: Gazette & Bull Pr. House, 1896. 388 pp.

History of Lycoming County, Pennsylvania, by Col. Thomas W. Lloyd. 2 vols. Topeka: Hist. Pub. Co., 1929.

A Picture of Lycoming County . . . comp. by Pennsylvania Writers' Project of W.P.A. Williamsport: Frank H. Painter, 1939. 223 pp.

## McKean County

History of McKean County, Pennsylvania [by Samuel W. Durant]. Philadelphia: N.p., 1877.

History of the County of McKean, 1890, *see* p. 314.

Pioneer Outline History of . . . County of . . . McKean, 1904, *see* p. 314.

McKean, the Governor's County, by Rufus B. Stone. New York: Lewis Hist. Pub. Co., 1926. 315 pp.

History . . . of the County of . . . McKean, 1943, in History of Northwestern Pennsylvania, *see* p. 314.

## Mercer County

History of Mercer County [by Samuel W. Durant]. Philadelphia: L.H. Everts, 1877. 156 pp.

History of Mercer County, Its Past and Present . . . Chicago: Brown, Funk, 1888. 1,210 pp. (Index. Park City, Utah: Hamilton Computer Service, 1980.)

A Pioneer Outline History of . . . County of . . . Mercer, 1904, *see* p. 314.

A Twentieth Century History of Mercer County . . . ed. by John G. White. 2 vols. Chicago: Lewis Pub. Co., 1909. 1,111 pp.

History of . . . County of . . . Mercer, 1943, in History of Northwestern Pennsylvania, *see* p. 314.

## Mifflin County

History of Mifflin County . . . by Joseph Cochran. Vol. 1 (all pub.). Harrisburg: Patriot Pub. Co., 1879. 422 pp.

History of . . . County of . . . Mifflin, 1886, in History of . . . the Susquehanna and Juniata Valleys, *see* p. 314.

The Genesis of Mifflin County, Pennsylvania . . . by John M. Stroup and R.M. Bell. Lewistown: N.p., 1939. 68 pp. (The Pioneers of Mifflin County, by John M. Stroup. Lewistown: N.p., 1942. Suppl. of 1939 ed. Repr. with additions, by Mifflin County Historical Society. Lewistown: N.p., 1957.)

Two Hundred Years; a Chronological List of Events in the History of Mifflin County, Pennsylvania. Lewistown: Mifflin County Hist. Soc., 1957.

A Pictorial History of Mifflin County in Pictures. Lewistown: Mifflin County Hist. Soc., 1977.

## Monroe County

History of . . . Monroe County, 1845, *see* p. 314.

The History of Monroe County, During the Civil War . . . from 1840-1873, by Le Roy Jenning Koehler. [East Stroudsburg?: N.p., n.d.] xiii, 250 pp.

History of . . . Monroe County, 1886, *see* Wayne County.

*Monroe County (cont.)*

History of Monroe County, by Robert B. Keller. Stroudsburg: Monroe Pub. Co., 1927. 500 pp.

History of Monroe County, Pennsylvania, 1725-1976, by John C. Appel, et al. East Stroudsburg: Monroe County Hist. Soc., 1975.

## Montgomery County

History of Montgomery County Within the Schuylkill Valley . . . by William J. Buck. Norristown: E.L. Acker, 1859. 124 pp.

A History and Geography of Montgomery County, Designed for Schools . . . by J.K. Harley. N.p., 1883. 108 pp. (Rev. ed. N.p., 1891. 114 pp.)

History of Montgomery County, ed. by Theodore W. Bean. Philadelphia: Everts & Peck, 1884. x, 1,197, lxxxviii pp.

The Centennial Celebration of Montgomery County . . . ed. by F.G. Hobson. Norristown: Centennial Assoc. of Montgomery Co., 1884. xi, 467 pp.

Montgomery County: a History by Clifton S. Hunsicker. 3 vols. New York: Lewis Hist. Co., 1923.

A Brief History of Montgomery County . . . for the Use of Schools . . . by Howard W. Kriebel. Norristown: School Directors' Assoc., 1923. 216 pp.

History of the County of . . . Montgomery, 1943, in Southeastern Pennsylvania, *see* p. 314.

The Montgomery County Story, by Everett G. Alderfer. Norristown: Commissioners of Montgomery County, 1951. xv, 301 pp.

Montgomery County: the Second Hundred Years, ed. by Jean B. Toll and M. Schwager. 2 vols. Norristown: Montgomery County Federation of Hist. Societies, 1983. xvi, 1,699 pp. (A continuation of Bean's History . . . 1884, *see* above.)

## Montour County

History of . . . Montour County, 1887, *see* Columbia County.

Historical and Biographical Annals of . . . Montour County, 1915, *see* Columbia County.

A History of Montour County, Pennsylvania, by Fred W. Diehl. Berwick: Keystone Pub. Co., 1969.

## Northampton County

History of Northampton County, 1845, *see* p. 314.

History of Northampton County, Pennsylvania . . . by Capt. Franklin Ellis. Philadelphia: P. Fritts, 1877. 293 pp.

*Northampton County (cont.)*

History of Northampton County and the Grand Valley of the Lehigh . . . ed. under the supervision of William J. Heller. 3 vols. Boston: American Hist. Soc., 1920.

Northampton County Guide, comp. by Federal Writers' Project, W.P.A. Bethlehem: Times Pub. Co. [1939]. 246 pp.

Northampton Heritage: the Story of an American County, by Everett G. Alderfer. Easton: Northampton County Hist. and Gen. Soc., 1953.

## Northumberland County

History and Topography of Northumberland . . . County, 1847, *see* p. 314.

History of Northumberland County . . . Philadelphia: Everts & Stewart, 1876. vi, 161 pp.

History of Northumberland County . . . ed. by Herbert C. Bell. Chicago: Brown, Runk, 1891. 1,256 pp.

## Perry County

History and Topography of . . . Perry County, 1848, *see* p. 314. (Perry County part, repr. Laughlintown: Southwest Pennsylvania Gen. Services, 1983.)

History of Perry County, from the Earliest Settlement to the Present Time, by Silas Wright. Lancaster: Wylie & Griest, 1873. 290 pp.

The History of Perry County, by Philomathean Society of Bloomfield, Pennsylvania. New Bloomfield: The Society, 1882, 146 pp.

History of . . . County of . . . Perry, 1886, in History of . . . the Susquehanna and Juniata Valleys, *see* p. 314.

History of Perry County . . . by Harry H. Hain. Harrisburg: Hain-Moore Co., 1922. 1,088 pp.

Tales of Perry County, by Roy F. Chandler. [Deer Lake: Bacon and Freeman, 1973.] 199 pp.

## Philadelphia County

History of the County of . . . Philadelphia, 1943, in Southeastern Pennsylvania, *see* p. 314.

Old Northeast Philadelphia County, 1609-1854, by Stephen Aaronson. Philadelphia: Pied Typer Pr., Northeast High School, 1969. xi, 202 pp.

## Pike County

History of . . . Pike County, 1886, *see* Wayne County.

Pike County, a Diamond in Northeastern Pennsylvania, by George J. Fluhr. N.p.: Pike County Bd. of Commissioners, 1978.

## Potter County

History of the County of . . . Potter, 1890, *see* p. 314.

Pioneer Outline History of . . . County of . . . Potter, 1904, *see* p. 314.

History of Potter County, by Victor L. Beede. Coudersport: Potter County Hist. Soc., 1934. 280 pp. (Repr. Coudersport: N.p., 1962.)

## Schuylkill County

History of . . . Schuylkill County, 1845, *see* p. 314.

History of Schuylkill County . . . New York: W.W. Munsell, 1881. 405, 60 pp.

Biographical and Portrait Cyclopedia of Schuylkill County, Comprising a Historical Sketch of the County, by Samuel T. Wiley. Rev. and ed. by Henry W. Ruoff. Philadelphia: Rush, West & Co., 1893. 752 pp.

Old Schuylkill Tales; a History . . . of the Early Settlers of Schuylkill County, by Mrs. Ella Z. Elliott. Pottsville: Author, 1906. 344 pp.

History of Schuylkill County . . . ed. by Adolf W. Schalck and D.C. Henning. 2 vols. N.p.: State Hist. Assoc., 1907.

History of the County of Schuylkill . . . Pottsville: Dives, Pomeroy & Stewart, 1911. 104 pp.

History of the County of . . . Schuylkill, 1943, in Southeastern Pennsylvania, *see* p. 314.

The History of Schuylkill County . . . Pottsville: School Dist. of Pottsville, 1950. 107 pp.

## Snyder County

History of . . . the County of . . . Snyder, 1886, in History of . . . the Susquehanna and Juniata Valleys, *see* p. 314.

Snyder County Annals; a Collection of All Kinds of Historical Items Affecting Snyder County . . . 2 vols. Middleburgh: Middleburgh Post, 1919-21.

The Story of Snyder from Its Earliest Times to the Present Day . . . prepared by George F. Dunkelberger. Selinsgrove: Snyder County Hist. Soc. [1948]. xviii, 982 pp.

## Somerset County

A Topographical Description of the County of . . . Somerset, 1846, in Early History of Western Pennsylvania, *see* p. 314.

History and Topography of . . . Somerset County, 1848, *see* p. 314. (Repr. of Somerset County part. Laughlintown: Southwest Pennsylvania Gen. Services, 1983.)

History of . . . Somerset County, 1884, *see* Bedford County.

*Somerset County (cont.)*

History of . . . Somerset County, 1906, *see* Bedford County.

History of . . . Somerset County, 1939, in Annals of Southwestern Pennsylvania, *see* p. 314.

Descriptive History of Somerset, Pennsylvania, by E.S. Martin. [Terre Haute, Ind.?] State Teachers Coll., 1959. (thesis)

## Sullivan County

History of Sullivan County, by Thomas J. Ingham. 3 parts in 1 vol. Chicago: Lewis Pub. Co., 1899.

History of Sullivan County, by George Streby. Dunshore: N.p., 1921.

## Susquehanna County

History of Susquehanna County, from . . . Its Settlement to Recent Times, by Emily C. Blackman. Philadelphia: Claxton, Remsen & Haffelfinger, 1873. x, 640 pp. (Repr. with . . . index to names. Baltimore: Regional Pub. Co., 1980. x, 685 pp.)

Centennial History of Susquehanna County, by Rhamanthus M. Stocker. Philadelphia: R.T. Peck, 1887. x, 851 pp. (Repr. with biography and index to names. Baltimore: Regional Pub. Co., 1974. x, 927 pp.)

The Centennial of Susquehanna County, by James T. Du Bois and W.J. Pike. Washington, D.C.: Clay & Clarkson, 1888. 138 pp.

## Tioga County

History of Tioga County . . . [by J.L. Sexton]. New York: W.W. Munsell, 1883. 366, 35 pp.

An Outline History of Tioga and Bradford Counties in Pennsylvania . . . [by John L. Sexton]. [Elmira, N.Y.: Gazette Co., 1885.] 283 pp.

History of Tioga County, Pennsylvania [by John F. Meginness]. Chicago: R.C. Brown, 1897. 1,186 pp.

A Pioneer Outline History of . . . County of Tioga, 1904, *see* p. 314.

Headwaters Country: the Story of Tioga County, by John C. Heaps. [State College: Himes Pr., 1970.] 177 pp.

## Union County

History and Topography of . . . Union County, 1847, *see* p. 314.

History of . . . the County of . . . Union, 1886, in History of . . . the Susquehanna and Juniata Valleys, *see* p. 314.

Union County, 1855-1965, by Mary B. Lontz. [Milton: Author, 1966?] 426 pp.

Union County, Pennsylvania: a Bicentennial History, by Charles M. Snyder. Lewisburg: Colonial Pr. House, 1976.

## Venango County

History of Venango County . . . ed. by J.H. Newton. Columbus, Ohio: J.A. Caldwell, 1879. 651 pp.

History of Venango County . . . [ed. by Herbert C. Bell]. Chicago: Brown, Funk, 1890. 1,164 pp.

Pioneer Outline History of . . . County of . . . Venango, 1904, *see* p. 314.

Venango County, Her Pioneers and People, Embracing a General History of the County, prepared by Charles A. Babcock. 2 vols. Chicago: J.H. Beers, 1919.

History of . . . County of . . . Venango, 1943, in History of Northwestern Pennsylvania, *see* p. 314.

Venengo County Panorama: a Salute to Its People, a Pictorial History of Venango County, Pennsylvania. Franklin: Venango County Hist. Soc., 1983. 275 pp.

## Warren County

History of Warren County . . . ed. by J.S. Schenck and W.S. Rann. Syracuse, N.Y.: D. Mason, 1887. 692, cxv. (Repr. Evansville, Ind.: Unigraphic, 1980. 807 pp.)

Pioneer Outline History of . . . County of . . . Warren, 1904, *see* p. 314.

History of . . . County of . . . Warren, 1943, in History of Northwestern Pennsylvania, *see* p. 314.

## Washington County

Topographical Description of the County of . . . Washington, 1846, in Early History of Western Pennsylvania, *see* p. 314.

History of Washington County from Its First Settlement to the Present Time . . . by Alfred Creigh. Washington: N.p., 1870. 386, 121 pp. (2d ed., rev. and corrected by Alfred Creigh. Harrisburg: B. Singerly, 1871. 375, 132 pp.)

History of Washington County . . . ed. by Boyd Crumrine. Philadelphia: L.H. Everts, 1882. 1,002 pp. (Repr. with new name index. Evansville, Ind.: Unigraphic, 1974. Index. Pittsburgh: Western Pennsylvania Gen. Soc., 1975. 135 pp. Repr. with new name index. Washington: First United Methodist Church, 1978. Repr. with index. Apollo: Closson Pr., 1984. 1,000 and 135 pp.)

In Our Early Days: Notes and Queries . . . History of Southwestern Pennsylvania, Especially Washington County, under auspices of Washington County Historical Society. Washington: The Society, 1908.

Twentieth Century History of the City of Washington and Washington County . . . by Joseph F. McFarland. Chicago: Richmond-Arnold Pub. Co., 1910. 1,369 pp.

History of Washington County, by Earle R. Forrest. 3 vols. Chicago: S.J. Clarke Pub. Co., 1926.

History of . . . Washington County, 1939, in Annals of Southwestern Pennsylvania, *see* p. 314.

# Wayne County

History of Wayne County, by Phineas G. Goodrich. Honesdale: Haines & Beardsley, 1880. xiv, 409 pp.

History of Wayne, Pike and Monroe Counties, ed. by Alfred Mathews. Philadelphia: R.T. Peck, 1886. x, 1,283 pp.

Centennial and Illustrated Wayne County: Historical and Biographical. 2d ed. Honesdale: B.F. Haines, 1902. xii, 178 pp.

History and Up-to-date Facts of Honesdale and Washington County, Pennsylvania. Honesdale: Bruce Pr., 1961. 80 pp.

Wayne County Before 1870. N.p.: Montrose Pub. Co., 1963.

# Westmoreland County

Topographical Description of County of . . . Westmoreland, 1846, in Early History of Western Pennsylvania, *see* p. 314.

History of the County of Westmoreland . . . ed. by George D. Albert. Philadelphia: L.H. Everts, 1882. 727 pp. (Index, by Charlotte H. Beard, recomp., by D.R. Fischer. McKeesport: Fischer, 1969. 204 pp. Repr. Apollo: Closson Pr., 1983.)

The Biographical and Historical Cyclopedia of Westmoreland County, Pennsylvania . . . comp. by Samuel T. Wiley. Philadelphia: John M. Gresham & Co., 1890. 850 pp. (Repr. with new surname index. Laughlintown: Southwest Pennsylvania Gen. Services, 1980.)

Old Westmoreland: a History of Western Pennsylvania During the Revolution, by Edgar W. Hassler. Pittsburgh: J.R. Weldin & Co., 1900. 200 pp. (Computerized index. Park City, Utah: Hamilton Computer Service, 1980. 6 pp.)

History of Westmoreland County, by John N. Boucher. 3 vols. New York: Lewis Pub. Co., 1906.

Old and New Westmoreland, by John N. Boucher. 4 vols. New York: American Hist. Soc., 1918. (Repr. with new every-name index. Laughlintown: Southwest Pennsylvania Gen. Services, 1982. Index. Park City, Utah: Hamilton Computer Service, 1976. 75 pp.)

History of . . . Westmoreland County, 1939, in Annals of Southwestern Pennsylvania, *see* p. 314.

A Short History of Westmoreland County . . . by C.M. Bomberger. Jeannette: Jeannette Pub. Co. [1941]. 100 pp.

# Wyoming County

History of . . . Wyoming County, 1880, *see* Luzerne County.

## York County

History of York County . . . to the Present Time (1729-1834), by W.C. Carter. York: A.J. Glossbrenner, 1834. 183, 30 pp. (New ed. with additions, ed. by A.M. Aurand, Jr. Harrisburg: Aurand Pr., 1930. xvi, 221 pp. Repr. Baltimore: Regional Pub. Co., 1975. Repr. Evansville, Ind.: Unigraphic, 1980.)

History of York County, from 1719 to 1845 . . . by Israel D. Rupp. Lancaster: G. Hills, 1845. 205 pp. (Repr. [Evansville, Ind.: Unigraphic, 1978.] 230 pp.)

History of York County, from the Earliest Period to the Present Time . . . History, ed. by John Gibson. Chicago: F.A. Battey, 1886. 772, 207 pp. (Index. [York:] N.p., 1940. Part 2 repr. as A Biographical History of York County. Baltimore: Genealogical Pub. Co., 1975. 207 pp.)

A Brief History of York County, Pennsylvania, by George R. Prowell. York: N.p., 1906. 67 pp.

History of York County, Pennsylvania, by George R. Prowell. 2 vols. Chicago: J.H. Beers & Co., 1907. (Subject index to Vol. 1. [York:] N.p., 1949.)

Reminiscences of an Old Man on Life in York County, Pennsylvania During the 19th Century: Diary of Henry Bolt, ed. by Carl E. Hatch and R.E. Kohler. York: Shrine Pub., 1973.

# RHODE ISLAND

## Kent County

History of . . . Kent County, 1889, *see* Washington County.

## Newport County

History of Newport County . . . 1638 to 1887 . . . ed. by Richard M. Bayles. New York: L.E. Preston, 1888. x, 1,060 pp.

## Providence County

History of Providence County, Rhode Island, ed. by Richard M. Bayles. 2 vols. New York: W.W. Preston, 1891. 821, 639 pp.

## Washington County

Washington and Kent Counties, Rhode Island, Including Their Early Settlement and Progress to the Present Time . . . by J.R. Cole. New York: W.W. Preston, 1889. xiv, 1,344 pp.

# SOUTH CAROLINA

## Abbeville County

Abbeville County Bicentennial 1758-1958, Historical Souvenir Program. [McCormick?:] Abbeville County Hist. Soc., 1964.

## Aiken County

A Short History of Aiken and Aiken County. Columbia: R.L.B., 1951. 45 pp.

Ninety Years in Aiken County: Memoirs of Aiken County and Its People. [Charleston: N.p., 1959.] 401 pp.

## Anderson County

Anderson County, Economic and Social, by Olin DeW. Johnston. Columbia: Univ. of South Carolina, 1923. 127 pp.

Traditions and History of Anderson County, by Louise A. Vandiver. Atlanta, Ga.: Ruralist Pr., 1928. viii, 318 pp. (Repr. with new index. Easley: Southern Hist. Pr., 1978.)

History of Anderson County, by Louise A. Vandiver. Rev. ed. Anderson: R.M. Smith, 1970. 327 pp.

## Beaufort County

Beaufort, Now and Then, by J.E. McTear. Beaufort: Book Co. [1971]. x, 143 pp.

## Berkeley County

Some Historic Sports in Berkeley, by Henry R. Dwight. Charleston: J.J. Furlong, 1921. 22 pp. (Repr. Charleston: Walker, Evans & Cogswell, 1944. 48 pp.)

## Charleston County

History of Charleston County, South Carolina, Narrative and Biographical, by Thomas P. Lesesne. Charleston: A.H. Cawston, 1931. 369 pp.

## Cherokee County

The Old Iron District: a Study of the Development of Cherokee County, 1750-1897, by Bobby G. Moss. Clinton: Jacobs Pr. [1972]. vii, 390 pp.

Around the Clock in Cherokee, by Cluggson Black. Gaffney: Southern Renaissance Pr., 1974. 67 pp.

## Chester County

Chester County Heritage History. Chester: Chester County Heritage Comm., 1983. 499 pp., with index.

## Clarendon County

History of Clarendon County, 1700-1961, by Virginia K. Orvin. Manning: N. Pub., 1961. 178 pp.

## Darlington County

Darlingtoniana: a History of People, Places and Events in Darlington County, South Carolina. Columbia: N.p., 1964. xviii, 507 pp. (Repr. Spartanburg: Reprint Co., 1977. xviii, 507 pp.)

## Edgefield County

History of Edgefield County from the Earliest Settlements to 1897 . . . by John A. Chapman. Newberry: E.H. Aull, 1897. 521, vi pp. (Contains also History of Saluda County, which was separated from Edgefield. Repr. Easley: Southern Hist. Pr., 1976. 521 pp. Repr. with new index, by Margaret H. Cannon. Spartanburg: Reprint Co., 1980. 568 pp.)

## Fairfield County

Fairfield County Economic and Social, by Samuel W. Nicholson. Columbia: Univ. of South Carolina, 1924. 83 pp.

Through the Years in Old Winnsboro, by Katharine T. Obear. Columbia: N.p., 1940. (Repr. with index. Spartanburg: Reprint Co., 1980. xx, 258 pp.) (History of Fairfield County and its county seat.)

The History of Fairfield County, South Carolina, by FitzHugh McMaster. Columbia: State Commercial Pr. Co., 1946. 220 pp.

History of Fairfield County, South Carolina from "Before the White Man Came" to 1942, by FitzHugh McMaster. Columbia: State Commercial Pr., 1955. ix, 222 pp. (Repr. with new index, by Margaret H. Cannon. Spartanburg: Reprint Co., 1980. 257 pp.)

History of Fairfield County, South Carolina, by William Edrington and Mrs. B.H. Rosson, Jr. Richard Winn Chapter, D.A.R., Jenkinsville. Tuscaloosa, Ala.: Willo Pub. Co. [196-?]. 95 pp.

## Florence County

Rise up so Early: a History of Florence County, by G. Wayne King. Spartanburg: Reprint Co., for Florence County Historical Comm., 1981. xi, 452 pp.

## Georgetown County

The History of Georgetown County, by George C. Rogers, Jr. Columbia: Univ. of South Carolina Pr. [1970]. xvi, 565 pp.

## Greenville County

Greenville County, Economic and Social, by Guy A. Gullick. Columbia: Univ. of South Carolina, 1921. 89 pp.

*Greenville County (cont.)*

History of Greenville County, South Carolina, Narrative and Biographical, by James M. Richardson. Atlanta: A.H. Cawston, 1930. 342 pp. (Repr. with new index, by Margaret H. Cannon. Spartanburg: Reprint Co., 1980. 368 pp.)

Bridging the Gap; a Guide to Early Greenville, South Carolina, by Laura S. Ebaugh. Greenville: Greater Greenville Chamber of Commerce, 1966. 101 pp.

## Greenwood County

Greenwood County Sketches; Old Roads and Early Families, by Margaret J. Watson. Greenwood: Attic Pr. [1970]. iv, 425 pp.

## Hampton County

Both Sides of the Swamp: Hampton County. [Hampton: N.p., 1970.] xiv, 187 pp.

## Horry County

The Independent Republic of Horry, 1670-1970; Items from the Independent Republic Quarterly, Official Publication of Horry Historical Society, ed. by Florence T. Epps. [Conway: Horry Pubs., 1970?] 100 pp.

## Jasper County

Moving Finger of Jasper. Golden Jubilee ed., by Grace (Fox) Perry. [Ridgeland:] Jasper County Confederate Centennial Comm. [1962]. xi, 218 pp.

## Kershaw County

Kershaw County, Economic and Social, by George H. Wittkowsky. Columbia: Univ. of South Carolina, 1923.

Kershaw County Legacy: a Commemorative History, by L. Glen Inabinet. Camden: Kershaw County Bicentennial Comm., 1976. 87 pp.

## Lancaster County

Lancaster County, Economic and Social, by Ernest A. Beatty. Columbia: Univ. of South Carolina, 1923. 115 pp.

Pictorial History of Lancaster County, by Louise Pettus and M. Bishop. N.p., 1984.

## Laurens County

A Laurens County Sketchbook, by Julian S. Bolick, with a Brief Sketch of the Development of Laurens County, by Edna R. Foy. Clinton: Jacobs Pr., 1973. xiv, 306 pp.

## Marion County

A History of Marion County, South Carolina, from Its Earliest Times to the Present, 1901, by William W. Sellers. Columbia: R.L. Bryan Co., 1902. ix, 647 pp.

## Marlboro County

A History of Marlboro County, with Traditions and Sketches of Numerous Families, by Rev. J.A.W. Thomas. Atlanta: Foote & Davies Co., 1897. 292 pp. (Repr. with an added index. Baltimore: Regional Pub. Co., 1978. 325 pp.)

Sketches of Old Marlboro. [Columbia: State Co., 1916.]

A Short History of Marlboro County, South Carolina 1600-1979, by Margaret M. Kelly. Baltimore: Gateway Pr., 1979. 74 pp.

## Newberry County

The Annals of Newberry, Historical, Biographical . . . by John B. O'Neall. Charleston: S.G. Courtenay, 1859. 413, viii pp. (Also pub. in two parts: Part One, by John B. O'Neall; Two, by John A. Chapman, in 1 vol. Newberry: Aull & Houseal, 1892. 816, vii pp. Part One pub. in 1859. Repr. Baltimore: Genealogical Pub. Co., 1974. 816 pp.)

Newberry County, South Carolina, Historical and Genealogical [by George L. Summer, Sr.]. N.p., 1950. 460, 11 pp. (Repr. Baltimore: Genealogical Pub. Co., 1980. 483 pp.)

History of Newberry County, South Carolina, by Thomas H. Pope. Vol. 1, 1749-1860. (No more pub.?) Columbia: Univ. of South Carolina Pr. [1973]. 389 pp.

## Oconee County

Historic Oconee in South Carolina, by Mary C. Doyle. [Seneca? N.p., 1935.] 56 pp.

Benjamin Hawkin's Journeys Through Oconee County, South Carolina in 1796-1797, by Margaret M. Seaborn. [Columbia: R.L. Bryan Co. Pr., 1973.] 34 pp.

## Orangeburg County

The History of Orangeburg County, from Its First Settlement to the Close of the Revolutionary War, by Alexander S. Salley, Jr. Orangeburg: R.L. Berry, 1898. viii. 572 pp. (Repr. Baltimore: Regional Pub. Co., 1978. 572 pp. Repr. Spartanburg: Reprint Co., 1978.)

## Pickens County

It Happened in Pickens County, by Pearl S. McFall. Pickens: N.p., 1959. 216 pp.

## Richland County

A History of Richland County, by Edwin L. Green. Vol. 1: 1732-1805. (all pub.) Columbia: R.L. Bryan Co., 1932. 385 pp. (Repr. Baltimore: Regional Pub. Co., 1974.)

## Saluda County

History of Edgefield County . . . Newberry: E.H. Aull, 1897. 521, vi pp. (Contains the History of Saluda County, which was separated from Edgefield, 1895.) (Repr. with new index, by Margaret H. Cannon. Spartanburg: Reprint Co., 1980. 568 pp.)

## Spartanburg County

History of Spartanburg County . . . by John B. O'N. Landrum. Atlanta: Franklin Pr. and Pub. Co., 1900. viii, 739 pp. (Repr. Spartanburg: Reprint Co., 1977. 739 pp. Computerized index. Park City, Utah: Hamilton Computer Service, 1978. 88 pp.)

A History of Spartanburg County, comp. by Writers' Program of W.P.A. [Spartanburg:] Band & White, 1940. 304 pp. (Repr. with index. Spartanburg: Reprint Co., 1975. 304 pp.)

Spartanburg County: a Pictorial History, by Philip N. Racine. Virginia Beach, Va.: Donning Co., 1980. 189 pp.

## Sumter County

Sumter County, Economic and Social, by Ralph H. Ramsey. Columbia: Univ. of South Carolina, 1922. 111 pp.

History of Sumter County, South Carolina, by Anne K. Gregorie. Sumter: Lib. Board of Sumter Co., 1954. xvii, 553 pp.

Sumter County Historical Vignettes . . . Sumter? [Sumter:] County Tricentennial Comm., 1970. Unpaged.

Historical Sketches of Sumter County: Its Birth and Growth, by Cassie Nicholes. Vol. 1. [Sumter: Sumter County Hist. Comm., 1975.] 546 pp. (Repr. Easley: Southern Hist. Pr., 1977. 564 pp.)

## Union County

A History of Union County, South Carolina, by William R. Feaster. Greenville: A Press, 1977. 133 pp.

Union County Heritage, South Carolina, ed. by Mannie L. Mabry. Union: Union Co., South Carolina Heritage Comm., 1981. 500 pp.

## Williamsburg County

Narrative of Reminiscences in Williamsburg County, by Samuel D. McGill. Columbia: Bryan Pr. Co., 1897. vii, 304 pp. (Repr. Kingstree: Kingstree Lithographic Co., 1952.)

History of Williamsburg, Something About the People of Williamsburg County, South Carolina, from the First Settlement by Europeans About 1705 Until 1923, by William W. Boddie. Columbia: State Co., 1923. viii, 611 pp. (Repr. with index. Spartanburg: Reprint Co., 1980.)

# SOUTH DAKOTA

## Regional

Memorial and Biographical Record of Turner, Lincoln, Union and Clay Counties . . . and Other Interesting Matters . . . Which Should be Preserved in History . . . Chicago: G.A. Ogle & Co., 1897. 560 pp.

History of Our County and State, comp. by Donald D. Parker. Brookings: South Dakota State Coll., 1959-63. (Social studies reference book for the use of teachers and pupils, sixth grade. State and territorial histories repr. from History of Southeast Dakota, 1881, by Moses K. Armstrong, and Historical Atlas of South Dakota, by Frank E. Peterson.) (County histories are indexed under counties.)

## Aurora County

[History of Aurora County], 1961, 103 pp., in Parker's History, *see* above.

## Beadle County

History of Beadle County, South Dakota . . . N.p.: Beadle County Comm., 1889. 489 pp.

A Social and Economic Survey of Beadle County, South Dakota, by B. Rogers. Chicago: McClaskey, 1940. 260 pp.

Early Beadle County, 1879 to 1900. [Huron?:] F.H. Brown Pr. Co., 1961. 104 pp.

## Bon Homme County

History of Bon Homme County from Early Settlement Until 1921, by Mrs. F.F. Chladek. [N.p., n.d.] 479 pp.

[History of Bon Homme County], 1959, 121 pp., in Parker's History, *see* above.

A History of Bon Homme County, South Dakota, Dakota Territory Centennial, 1861-1961. Scotland: Scotland Journal, 1961. 95 pp.

## Brown County

History of the Finnish Settlement in Brown and Dickey Counties of South and North Dakota, 1881-1955. [2d ed. Savo: Finnish Hist. Soc., S. Dak., 1956.] 128 pp.

Early History of Brown County, South Dakota; a Literature of the People . . . [Aberdeen?: N.p., 1965.] 208 pp.

## Brule County

A Short History of Brule County, by John H. Bingham and N.V. Peters. N.p., 1947. 184 pp. (Repr. from South Dakota Historical Collections, Vol. 23 (1947), pp. 1-184.)

[History of Brule County], 1960, 121 pp., in Parker's History, *see* p. 344.

Brule County History. Pierre: State Pub. Co., 1977. 656 pp.

## Buffalo County

History . . . by the Lady Helpers of the First Congregational Church, Gann Valley. Gann Valley: N.p., 1924. 88, 140 pp. (Sketches of pioneer life in Buffalo County.)

## Butte County

Pioneer Footprints. Black Hills Half Century Club, Belle Fourche. Sioux Falls: Midwest-Beach Co., 1964. iv, 332 pp.

## Campbell County

Early History of Campbell County, by Bob Dale. N.p., 1976. 38 pp.

## Charles Mix County

History of Charles Mix County, South Dakota, comp. by Mr. and Mrs. E. Frank Peterson. Geddes: H.C. Tucker & Sons [1907?]. 184 pp.

[History of Charles Mix County], 1960, 103 pp., in Parker's History, *see* p. 344.

Hollanders in Charles Mix County, 1969, *see* Douglas County.

## Clark County

A History of Southern Clark County and Spirit Lake. N.p., 1976. 434 pp.

## Clay County

Memorial . . . of Clay County, 1897, in Memorial . . . Record, *see* p. 344.

The Early History of Clay County, by Harold E. Briggs. Vermillion: Univ. of South Dakota, 1924. 102 pp. (M.A. thesis)

[History of Clay County], 1961, 135 pp., in Parker's History, *see* p. 344.

History of Clay County, by Herbert S. Schell. Vermillion: Clay County Hist. Soc., 1976. 295 pp.

## Codington County

The Early and Territorial History of Codington County, by Tarbell Wright. In South Dakota Historical Coll., Vol. 24 (1949), pp. 276-449.

*Codington County (cont.)*

"The First 100 Years" in Codington County, South Dakota. Watertown: Codington County Hist. Book Ch., 1979. 486 pp.

## Custer County

Our Yesterdays. Hermosa: Eastern Custer County Hist. Soc., 1970. 920 pp.

Custer County History to 1976, ed. by Jessie Y. Sundstrom. Rapid City: Rapid City Pr., 1977. 440 pp.

## Davison County

[History of Davison County], 1959, 134 pp., in Parker's History, *see* p. 344.

## Day County

History of Day County, from 1873 to 1926, by L.G. Ochsenreiter. Mitchell: Educator Supply Co. [1926]. 258 pp.

[History of Day County], 1960, 130 pp., in Parker's History, *see* p. 344.

## Deuel County

[History of Deuel County], 1960, 141 pp., in Parker's History, *see* p. 344.

Historical Collections of Deuel County, ed. by Eleanor Cochrane. N.p., 1977. 432 pp.

## Douglas County

Douglas County and Centennial Observances, 1961. Stickney: Argus Pr. [1961]. 224 pp.

[History of Douglas County], 1961, 98 pp., in Parker's History, *see* p. 344.

On the Reservation Border - Hollanders in Douglas and Charles Mix Counties [by Henry van der Pol, Sr.]. Stickney: Argus Pr., 1969. 356 pp.

## Fall River County

Fall River County Pioneer Histories. Fall River: Fall River County Hist. Soc., 1976. 358 pp.

## Faulk County

History of Faulk County, South Dakota, by Capt. Caleb H. Ellis. Faulkton: Record Pr., 1909. 508 pp. (Repr. Aberdeen: North Plains Pr., 1973. 508 pp.)

[History of Faulk County], 1961, 209 pp., in Parker's History, *see* p. 344.

# Grant County

History of Grant County, South Dakota, 1861-1937, by Doris L. Black. Milbank: Milbank Herald Advance, 1939. xviii, 98 pp.

100 Years in Grant County, South Dakota, 1878-1978. Milbank: Grant County Hist. Soc., 1979. 528 pp.

# Gregory County

Gregory County Golden Jubilee, 1898-1948, comp. by Katherine Velder. Gregory: Gregory Times Advocate [1948]. 112 pp.

# Haakon County

Pioneers of the Open Range: Haakon County, South Dakota Settlers Before Jan. 1, 1906. N.p.: Midland Pioneer Club of Western South Dakota [1965]. 200 pp.

# Hamlin County

[Hamlin County History], 1963, 311 pp., in Parker's History, *see* p. 344.

Hamlin County, 1879-1979. Hamlin: Hamlin Hist. Comm., 1979. 470 pp.

# Hand County

Early History of Hand County, South Dakota, by Anna M.V.B. Sessions. N.p. [1940]. 53 pp.

[History of Hand County], 1960, 250 pp., in Parker's History, *see* p. 344.

Bring on the Pioneers: History of Hand County, by Scott Heideprien. Pierre: State Pub. Co., 1978. 680 pp.

# Hanson County

[History of Hanson County], 1959, 131 pp., in Parker's History, *see* p. 344.

Hanson Heritage: a History of Hanson County, South Dakota, by Mildred Soladay. Stickney: Argus Pr., 1975. 199 pp.

# Harding County

Building an Empire: a Historical Booklet on Harding County, South Dakota . . . Buffalo: Buffalo Times-Herald [1959]. 107 pp.

# Hughes County

Hughes County History . . . comp. by Bert L. Hall. [Pierre?:] N.p., 1937. 205 pp.

Hughes County History, comp. and ed. by Ruane Pringle. Pierre: State Pub. Co., 1964. 183 pp.

## Hutchinson County

[History of Hutchinson County], 1961, 101 pp., in Parker's History, *see* p. 344.

## Hyde County

History of Hyde County, South Dakota, from Its Organization to the Present Time, by John B. Perkins. [Highmore:] N.p., 1908. 300 pp.

[History of Hyde County], 1961, 198 pp., in Parker's History, *see* p. 344.

Hyde Heritage, 1880s-1977. Pierre: State Pub. Co., 1977. 649 pp.

## Jackson County

Jackson-Washabaugh Counties, 1915-1965, ed. by Lois J. Prokop. [Kadoka:] Jackson-Washabaugh County Hist. Soc., 1965. 345 pp.

## Jerauld County

A History of Jerauld County, South Dakota, from the Earliest Settlement to . . . 1909, by Niles J. Dunham. Washington Springs: N.p., 1910. 441 pp.

A History of Jerauld County, South Dakota . . . 1909-1961 . . . by Fred N. Dunham. [Washington Springs?:] Tamblyn Pr., 1963. 552 pp.

## Jones County

Proving Up: Jones County History. [Murdo:] Book & Thimble Club, 1969. 504 pp.

## Kingsbury County

[History of Kingsbury County], 1960, 186 pp., in Parker's History, *see* p. 344.

## Lake County

[History of Lake County], 1960, 216 pp., in Parker's History, *see* p. 344.

Pioneer Days in Lake County, ed. by Preston E. Tyrrell. Madison: Dakota State Coll., 1980. 190 pp.

## Lawrence County

Lawrence County for the Dakota Territory Centennial, ed. by Mildred Fielder. [Lead?: Lawrence County Centennial Comm., 1960.] 186 pp.

Gold-gals-guns-guts, ed. by Bob Lee. Deadwood-Lead '76 Centennial. N.p., 1976.

Some History of Lawrence County, South Dakota, comp. by Lawrence County Historical Society. Deadwood: Lawrence County Hist. Project, 1981. 723 pp.

## Lincoln County

Memorial of . . . Lincoln . . . County, 1897, in Memorial . . . Record, *see* p. 344.

[History of Lincoln County], 1961, 128 pp., in Parker's History, *see* p. 344.

## Lyman County

Lyman County Pioneers, 1885-1968. Stickney: Argus Pr., 1968. 192 pp.

Early Settlers in Lyman County, ed. by Mrs. Delmer King. Presho: Lyman County Hist. Soc., 1974. 368, 174 pp. (Repr. of Lyman County Pioneers, *see* above.)

## McCook County

[History of McCook County], 1959, 110 pp., in Parker's History, *see* p. 344.

Within These Borders . . . [N.p., 1976.] 84 pp.

## McPherson County

Homesteaders of McPherson County, comp. by W.P.A. [Pierre: N.p., 1941.] 86 pp.

## Marshall County

History of Marshall County, by George Hickman. Britton: Dakota Daylight, 1886. 51 pp. (Repr. Pierre: The Reminder, Inc., 1959.)

Marshall County, South Dakota, by Marshall County Historical Society. Dallas, Tex.: Taylor Pub. Co., for Marshall County Hist. Soc., 1979. 578 pp.

## Meade County

Central Meade County, South Dakota, 1903-1963. Stoneville Steadies Club. [Ella Wahl, ed.] Somerville: The Club [1964]. 416 pp.

Echoes Thru' the Valleys: South Western Meade County. Elk Creek: Pioneer Assoc., 1968. 503 pp.

Mato Paha: Land of the Pioneers; Northwest Meade County, South Dakota. [Marceline, Mo.: Walsworth Pub. Co., for Alkali Community Club, 1969.] 650 pp.

## Mellette County

Mellette County Memories; Golden Anniversary ed., 1911-1961, by Winifred Reautter. Stickney: Argus Pr., 1961. 95 pp.

Mellette County, South Dakota, 1911-1961, ed. by Luree Wacek. White River: Mellette County Central Comm., 1961. 318 pp.

## Miner County

Prairie Tamers of Miner County, prepared by W.P.A. Mitchell: South Dakota Writers' League [1939]. 35 pp.

## Minnehaha County

History of Minnehaha County, South Dakota . . . by Dana R. Bailey. Sioux Falls: Brown & Saenger Pr., 1899. 1,091 pp.

A Comprehensive History of Minnehaha County, South Dakota . . . by Charles A. Smith. Mitchell: Educator Supply Co., 1949. 504 pp.

[History of Minnehaha County], 1960, 177 pp., in Parker's History, *see* p. 344.

## Moody County

A Descriptive Write-up of Moody County. Egan: Express Pr., n.d. 84 pp.

Some Recollections of Moody County History, by Katharine Billie. Flandreau: 20th Century Comm., n.d.

## Pennington County

Eastern Pennington County Memories. Wall: American Legion [1965]. 475 pp.

## Perkins County

Wind and Waving Grass. A Story of Northwestern Perkins County, South Dakota, ed. by Emma Henderson, et al. Dallas, Tex.: Taylor Pub. Co., 1976. 112 pp.

## Roberts County

Homestead Years, ed. by Mr. and Mrs. Lloyd I. Sudlow. Bison: Bison Courier [1958]. 166 pp.

Homestead Years, 1908-1968, by Mrs. Sudlow. Bison: Bison Courier, 1968. 364 pp.

Roberts County History. [Sisseton: Roberts County Centennial Comm., 1961.] 136 pp.

## Sanborn County

Sanborn County History, 1873-1963, by Alice Mitchell. N.p.: Brown & Judy, 1963. 232 pp.

## Spink County

Settlement of Spink County . . . Vermillion: Univ. of South Dakota, 1917. 41 leaves. (M.A. thesis)

Prairie Echoes: Spink County in the Making. [Aberdeen?: Hayes Bros. Pr., 1961.] 436 pp.

## Sully County

History of Sully County. N.p.: Sully County Old Settlers Assoc., 1939. 287 pp.

75 Years of Sully County History, 1883-1958 [ed. by Mrs. E.L. Thompson]. [Onida: Onida Watchman, 1958?] 451 pp.

## Tripp County

Tripp County 50th Anniversary, Winner, 1909-1959, ed. by Mable A. Read. Winner: Sodak [1959]. 208 pp.

Before Homesteads, in Tripp County and the Rosebud, by Gladys W. Jorgensen. [Freeman: Pine Hill Pr., 1974.] x, 138 pp.

## Turner County

Memorial . . . of Turner . . . County, 1897, in Memorial . . . Record, *see* p. 344.

Turner County Pioneer History . . . comp. by William H. Stoddard, et al. Sioux Falls: Brown & Saenger Pr., 1931. 470 pp. (2d ed. Freeman: Pine Hill Pr., 1975. 470 pp., with index.)

[History of Turner County], 1969, 110 pp., in Parker's History, *see* p. 344.

## Union County

Memorial . . . of Union . . . County, 1897, in Memorial . . . Record, *see* p. 344.

Historical Glimpse of the Early Settlement of Union County, comp. by W.H.H. Fate. Sioux City: Perkins Bros., 1924. 144 pp.

[History of Union County], 1959, 120 pp., in Parker's History, *see* p. 344.

## Washabaugh County

Washabaugh County, 1915-1965, *see* Jackson County.

## Yankton County

[History of Yankton County], 1959, 148 pp., in Parker's History, *see* p. 344.

# TENNESSEE

## *Regional*

A. History of Tennessee from the Earliest Times to the Present, Together with an Historical and Biographical Sketch of Carroll, Henry and Benton Counties. Nashville: Goodspeed Pub. Co., 1886. (Biographical index, by Mrs. Leister E. Presley. Searcy, Ark.: Presley, 1971.) (Repr. with full-name index. Easley, S.C.: Southern Hist. Pr., 1978. 176 pp.)

B. History of Tennessee from the Earliest Times to the Present, Together with an Historical and Biographical Sketch of Gibson, Obion, Weakley, Dyer and Lake Counties. Nashville: Goodspeed Pub. Co., 1887. viii, 1,087 pp. (Biographical index, by Mrs. Leister E. Presley. Searcy, Ark.: Presley, 1970. Repr. with full-name index. Easley, S.C.: Southern Hist. Pr., 1978. 352 pp.)

C. History of Tennessee from the Earliest Times to the Present, Together with an Historical and Biographical Sketch of Giles, Lincoln, Franklin and Moore Counties. Nashville: Goodspeed Pub. Co., 1886. viii, 930 pp. (Biographical index, by Mrs. Leister E. Presley. Searcy, Ark.: Presley, 1970. Repr. with full-name index. Easley, S.C.: Southern Hist. Pr., 1978. 181 pp. Repr. with full-name index. Columbia: Woodward & Stinson Pr. Co., 1978?)

D. History of Tennessee from the Earliest Times to the Present, Together with an Historical and Biographical Sketch of Hamilton, Knox and Shelby Counties. Nashville: Goodspeed Pub. Co., 1887. (Repr. Nashville: C. & R. Elder, 1974. 277 pp.)

E. History of Tennessee from the Earliest Times to the Present, Together with an Historical and Biographical Sketch of Henderson, Chester, McNairy, Decatur and Hardin Counties. Nashville: Goodspeed Pub. Co., 1886. (Biographical index, by Mrs. Leister E. Presley. Searcy, Ark.: Presley, 1971. Repr. with full-name index. Easley, S.C.: Southern Hist. Pr., 1978. 111 pp.)

F. History of Tennessee from the Earliest Times to the Present, Together with an Historical and Biographical Sketch of Lauderdale, Tipton, Haywood and Crockett Counties. Nashville: Goodspeed Pub. Co., 1887. viii, 971 pp. (Biographical index, by Mrs. Leister E. Presley. Searcy, Ark.: Presley, 1970. Repr. with full-name index. Easley, S.C.: Southern Hist. Pr., 1978.)

G. History of Tennessee from the Earliest Times to the Present, Together with an Historical and Biographical Sketch of Lawrence, Wayne, Perry, Hickman and Lewis Counties. Nashville: Goodspeed Pub. Co., 1886. (Biographical index, by Mrs. Leister E. Presley. Searcy, Ark.: Presley, 1970. Repr. with full-name index. Easley, S.C.: Southern Hist. Pr., 1979. 129 pp. Repr. with full-name index. Columbia: Woodward & Stinson Pr. Co., 1979? 175 pp.)

H. History of Tennessee from the Earliest Times to the Present, Together with an Historical and Biographical Sketch of Maury, Williamson, Rutherford, Wilson, Bedford and Marshall Counties. Nashville: Goodspeed Pub. Co., 1886. 1,232

*Regional (cont.)*

pp. (Repr. with full-name index. Columbia: Woodward & Stinson Pr. Co., 1978. 483 pp.)

I. History of Tennessee from the Earliest Times to the Present, Together with an Historical and Biographical Sketch of Montgomery, Robertson, Humphreys, Stewart, Dickson, Cheatham and Houston Counties. Nashville: Goodspeed Pub. Co., 1886. 1,402 pp. (Repr. with full-name index. Easley, S.C.: Southern Hist. Pr., 1978. 653 pp. Repr. with full-name index. Columbia: Woodward & Stinson Pr. Co., 1978?)

J. History of Tennessee from the Earliest Times to the Present, Together with an Historical and Biographical Sketch of Sumner, Smith, Macon and Trousdale Counties. Nashville: Goodspeed Pub. Co., 1887. (Repr. with full-name index. Easley, S.C.: Southern Hist. Pr., 1979. 194 pp. Repr. with full-name index. Columbia: Woodward & Stinson Pr. Co., 1979?)

K. History of Tennessee from the Earliest Times to the Present, Together with an Historical and Biographical Sketch of White, Warren, De Kalb, Coffee and Cannon Counties. Nashville: Goodspeed Pub. Co., 1886. (Repr. with full-name index. Easley, S.C.: Southern Hist. Pr., 1979. 195 pp.)

*Although many reprints of Goodspeed's Tennessee works have been published, not all have been found. Biographical indexes by Mrs. Leister E. Presley of Searcy, Ark., are numerous, and not all have been listed.*

Historical Sketches of Adams, Robertson County, Tennessee, and Port Royal, Montgomery County, Tennessee, from 1779 to 1968, by Ralph L. Winters. Clarksville: N.p., 1968. 280 pp.

🌱          🌱          🌱

## Anderson County

A History of Anderson County, Tennessee, by Raymond C. Seeber. Knoxville: Univ. of Tennessee, 1928. 116 pp. (M.A. thesis)

## Bedford County

History of Bedford County, by H.L. Davidson. Chattanooga: Crandall, 1877. 31 pp.

Historical and Biographical Sketch of . . . Bedford County, 1886, *see* H., p. 352.

## Benton County

Historical and Biographical Sketch of . . . Benton County, 1886, *see* A., p. 352.

A History of Benton County, Tennessee to 1900, by Jonathan K. Smith. [Memphis: J. Edge Co., 1970.] 151 pp.

Historic Benton: a People's History of Benton County, Tennessee, by Jonathan K.T. Smith. [Memphis?:] Smith [1975]. iv, 231 pp.

## Bledsoe County

An Educational Economic Survey . . . of Bledsoe County. Knoxville: Univ. of Tennessee, 1927. 39 pp. (M.A. thesis)

A History of Bledsoe County, Tennessee, 1807-1957, by Elizabeth P. Robnett. Nashville: George Peabody Coll. for Teachers, 1957. (Ed.S. dissertation)

## Blount County

History of Blount County, Tennessee; from War Trail to Landing Strip, 1795-1955, by Inez E. Burns. Nashville: Benson Pr. Co., 1957. vii, 375 pp.

## Bradley County

History of the Rebellion in Bradley County, East Tennessee, by J.S. Hurlburt. Indianapolis: [Downey & Brause?], 1866. 280 pp.

A History of Bradley County, by John M. Wooten. 2 vols. Cleveland: Cleveland Chamber of Commerce, Bradley County, 1929. (Repr. Cleveland: Bradley Post 81 American Legion & Tennessee Hist. Comm., 1949. 323 pp.)

An Album of Historical Memories, Chatata-Tasso, Bradley County, Tennessee, 1830-1961, by Lucina E. Hardy. [N.p., 1962.] 84 pp.

A History of Bradley County, Tennessee to 1861, by James L. Slay. Knoxville: Univ. of Tennessee, 1967. (thesis)

## Campbell County

A History of Jellico . . . Containing Information on Campbell County, Tennessee and Whitley County, Kentucky, by James H. Siler. Jellico: N.p., 1938. 44 pp.

The Land of the Lake; a History of Campbell County, Tennessee, by George L. Ridenour. LaFollette: LaFollette Pub. Co. [1941]. 106 pp.

## Cannon County

Historical and Biographical Sketch of . . . Cannon County, 1886, *see* K., p. 353.

History of Woodbury and Cannon County, Tennessee, by Sterling S. Brown. Manchester: Doak Pr. Co., 1936. 235 pp.

## Carroll County

Historical and Biographical Sketch of Carroll County, 1886, *see* A., p. 352.

Sesquicentennial Booklet, Carroll County, by Mary R. De Vault. MacKenzie: MacKenzie Banner, 1972. 192 pp.

## Carter County

Early History of Carter County, 1760-1861, by Frank Merritt. Knoxville: East Tennessee Hist. Soc. [1950]. vi, 213 pp.

# Cheatham County

Historical and Biographical Sketch of . . . Cheatham County, 1886, *see* I., p. 353.

# Chester County

Historical and Biographical Sketch of . . . Chester County, 1886, *see* E., p. 352.

# Cocke County

Over the Misty Blue Hills; the Story of Cocke County, Tennessee, by Ruth O'Dell. [Newport?: N.p., 1951.] 369 pp. (Repr. Spartanburg, S.C.: Reprint Co., 1982. vii, 371 and 25 index pp.)

# Coffee County

Historical and Biographical Sketch of . . . Coffee County, 1886, *see* K., p. 353.

History of Coffee County, Tennessee, by Leighton Ewell. Manchester: Doak Pr. Co., 1936. 85 pp.

Coffee County, from Arrowheads to Rockets; a History of Coffee County, Tennessee, by Corinne Martinez. Tullahoma: Coffee County Conservation Bd., 1969. 360 pp.

# Crockett County

Historical and Biographical Sketch of . . . Crockett County, 1887, *see* F., p. 352.

# Cumberland County

Cumberland County's First Hundred Years, by Helen B. Krechniak and J.M. Krechniak. Crossville: Centennial Comm., 1956. ix, 377 pp.

# Davidson County

History of Davidson County, Tennessee . . . by W. Woodford Clayton. Philadelphia: J.W. Lewis & Co., 1880. 499 pp. (Repr. Nashville: Charles Elder, 1971.)

# Decatur County

Historical and Biographical Sketch of . . . Decatur County, 1886, *see* E., p. 352.

# De Kalb County

Historical and Biographical Sketch of . . . De Kalb County, 1886, *see* K., p. 353.

History of De Kalb County, by William T. Hale. Nashville: F. Hunter, 1915. xii, 254 pp. (Repr. McMinnville: Ben Lomond, 1969. Name index, comp. by Mike Marler. [Nashville:] N.p., 1970. 43 pp. Index, by Alta F.J. Bowman. [Richmond?: N.p., 1974.] 41 leaves.)

## Dickson County

Historical and Biographical Sketch of . . . Dickson County, 1886, *see* I., p. 353.

A History of Dickson County, Tennessee, by Robert E. Corlew. [Nashville:] Tennessee Hist. Comm., 1956. 243 pp.

## Dyer County

Historical and Biographical Sketch of . . . Dyer County, 1887, *see* B., p. 352.

## Fayette County

History of Fayette and Hardeman Counties. (Repr. from Goodspeed's Tennessee Histories, 1887. Easley, S.C.: Southern Hist. Pr., 1979. 167 pp. Repr. Columbia: Woodward & Stinson Pr. Co., 1979?)

Our Portion of Hell: Fayette County, Tennessee; an Oral History of the Struggle for Civil Rights, by Robert Hamburger. New York: Links [1973]. x, 255 pp.

## Fentress County

History of Fentress County, Tennessee . . . [by Albert R. Hogue]. Nashville: Williams Pr. Co., 1916. 165 pp. (Repr. Baltimore: Regional Pub. Co., 1975. xxxii, 165 pp.)

One Hundred Years in the Cumberland Mountains Along the Continental Line, by Albert R. Hogue. McMinnville: Standard Pr. Co., 1933. 96 pp.

## Franklin County

Historical and Biographical Sketch of . . . Franklin County, 1886, *see* C., p. 352.

A Brief History of Franklin County, Tennessee, by Thomas F. Rhoton. Knoxville: Univ. of Tennessee, 1941. 87 pp. (M.A. thesis)

Chuwalee: Chronicles of Franklin County, Tennessee, by William H. McKellar. Winchester: Franklin County Hist. Soc., 1973. 135 pp.

## Gibson County

Historical and Biographical Sketch of Gibson County, 1887, *see* B., p. 352.

Gibson County, Tennessee . . . Gibson County Historical, Descriptive and Biographical, ed. by W.P. Greene. Nashville: Gospel Advocate, 1901. 144 pp.

Gibson County Story . . . from Indian Times . . . to the Present, by Conrad F. Smith. Trenton: Herald Register, 1960. 121 pp.

Gibson County, Past and Present; the First General History of One of West Tennessee's Pivotal Counties, by Frederick M. Culp and Mrs. R.E. Ross. Trenton: Gibson County Hist. Soc., 1961. 583 pp.

# Giles County

A Brief Sketch of the Settlement and Early History of Giles County, Tennessee, by James McCallum. 1876. [Pulaski: Pulaski Citizen, 1928.] 134 pp. (Repr. Spartanburg, S.C.: Reprint Co., 1983.)

Historical and Biographical Sketch of . . . Giles County, 1886, *see* C., p. 352.

History of Giles County, Tennessee, by Elizabeth C. Parker. Murfreesboro: Middle Tennessee State Coll., 1953. (M.A. thesis)

Official Souvenir Program of Giles County, Tennessee Sesquicentennial, 1809-1959. Pulaski: Giles County Sesquicentennial Assoc., 1959. 128 pp.

# Hamilton County

Goodspeed History of Hamilton County, Tennessee. (Repr. from 1887 ed. Easley, S.C.: Southern Hist. Pr., 1979. 220 pp., with full-name index.)

Historical and Biographical Sketch of Hamilton County, 1887, *see* D., p. 352.

The History of Hamilton County and Chattanooga, Tennessee . . . by Zella Armstrong. 2 vols. Chattanooga: Lookout Pub. Co., 1931-40. 553, 342 pp.

# Hardeman County

History of Hardeman County, 1887, *see* Fayette County.

Early History of Hardeman County, Tennessee, by Warner W. Clift. Nashville: George Peabody Coll. for Teachers, 1930. (M.A. thesis)

# Hardin County

A History of Hardin County, Tennessee, by B.G. Brazelton. Nashville: Cumberland Presbyterian Pub. House, 1885. 135 pp. (Repr. Savannah, Ga.: Savannah Pub., 1965. 109 pp.)

Historical and Biographical Sketch of . . . Hardin County, 1886, *see* E., p. 352.

# Haywood County

Historical and Biographical Sketch of . . . Haywood County, 1887, *see* F., p. 352.

# Henderson County

Historical and Biographical Sketch of Henderson County, 1886, *see* E., p. 352.

History of Henderson County . . . by Auburn Powers. [Lexington:] N.p., 1930. 169 pp.

# Henry County

Historical and Biographical Sketch of . . . Henry County, 1886, *see* A., p. 352.

A History of Henry County, Tennessee . . . by E. McLeod Johnson. [Paris?: E.M. Johnson], 1958.

*Henry County (cont.)*

A History of Henry County, Tennessee Through 1865, by Roger R. Van Dyke. Nashville: Univ. of Tennessee, 1966. (thesis)

## Hickman County

Historical and Biographical Sketch of . . . Hickman County, 1886, *see* G., p. 352.

A History of Hickman County, Tennessee, by W. Jerome D. Spence and D.L. Spence. Nashville: Gospel Advocate Pub. Co., 1900. 509 pp. (Repr. Spartanburg, S.C.: Reprint Co., 1981. 532 pp., including index. Repr. Centerville: Edward and Olga Dotson, 1981. Repr. Lawrenceburg: Norval Gilbert, 1955.)

## Houston County

Historical and Biographical Sketch of . . . Houston County, 1886, *see* I., p. 353.

A History of Houston County, by Iris H. McClain. [Columbia?: N.p., 1966.] 241 pp. (thesis)

## Humphreys County

Historical and Biographical Sketch of . . . Humphreys County, 1886, *see* I., p. 353.

A History of Humphreys County, by Jill K. Garrett. [Columbia?:] N.p., 1963. 376 pp.

## Jackson County

Early History of Jackson County, Tennessee, by R. Draper. Gainesboro: Jackson County Sentinel, 1928-29.

## Knox County

Historical and Biographical Sketch of . . . Knox County, 1887, *see* D., p. 352. (Repr. with full-name index. Easley, S.C.: Southern Hist. Pr., 1982. 275 pp.)

The French Broad-Holston Country: a History of Knox County, Tennessee . . . ed. by Mary U. Rothrock. Knoxville: East Tennessee Hist. Soc., 1946. xiii, 573 pp. (Repr. N.p., 1981.)

Historic Treasure Spots of Knox County, Tennessee, by Nannie L. Hicks. Knoxville: Simon Harris Chapter, D.A.R. [1964]. 82 pp.

## Lake County

Historical and Biographical Sketch of . . . Lake County, 1887, *see* B., p. 352.

## Lauderdale County

Historical and Biographical Sketch of Lauderdale County, 1887, *see* F., p. 352.

*Lauderdale County (cont.)*

Lauderdale County from Earliest Times . . . ed. by Kate Peters. Ripley: Sugar Hill Lauderdale County Lib., 1957. 377 pp.

## Lawrence County

Historical and Biographical Sketch of Lawrence County, 1886, *see* G., p. 352.

## Lewis County

Historical and Biographical Sketch of . . . Lewis County, 1886, *see* G., p. 352.

## Lincoln County

Historical and Biographical Sketch of . . . Lincoln County, 1886, *see* C., p. 352. (Repr. of Lincoln County, transcribed by Jane W. Waller. Batavia, Ill.: Lincoln County, Tennessee Pioneers, 1971. 57 pp.)

## McNairy County

Reminiscences of the Early Settlement and Early Settlers of McNairy County, Tennessee, by General Marcus J. Wright. Washington, D.C.: Commercial Pub. Co., 1882. 96 pp.

Historical and Biographical Sketch of . . . McNairy County, 1886, *see* E., p. 352.

## Macon County

Historical and Biographical Sketch of . . . Macon County, 1887, *see* J., p. 353.

## Madison County

Social Survey of the City of Jackson and Madison County, Tennessee, by Augustus F. Kuhlman. Jackson: Jackson-McClaren Chapter, American Red Cross, 1920. 139 pp.

Historic Madison; the Story of Jackson and Madison County, Tennessee, from the Prehistoric Moundbuilders to 1917, by Emma I. Williams. Jackson: Madison County Hist. Soc., 1946. xiv, 553 pp. (Repr. Jackson: Jackson Service Leagues, 1972.)

## Marion County

A History of Marion County, Tennessee, by Gertrude B. Link. Murfreesboro: Middle Tennessee State Univ., 1953. 113 pp. (M.A. thesis)

## Marshall County

Historical and Biographical Sketch of . . . Marshall County, 1886, *see* H., p. 352.

A History of Marshall County, Tennessee, by Mitchel Wright. Franklin: Author, 1963. 144 leaves.

# Maury County

Historical and Biographical Sketch of Maury County, 1886, *see* H., p. 352.

A History of Mount Pleasant, Especially, and the Western Part of Maury County, Generally, as He Remembers It, by Nathaniel W. Jones. Nashville: McQuiddy, 1903. 78 pp. (Repr. Columbia: Maury County Hist. Soc., 1965.)

Century Review, 1805-1905, Maury County, Tennessee [by D.P. Robbins]. Columbia: Bd. of Mayor & Aldermen, 1905. 426 pp. (Rev. ed. Columbia: Maury County Hist. Soc., 1970. 336 pp. Repr. [of 1905 ed.] Spartanburg, S.C.: Reprint Co., 1980. 426 pp., plus new full-name index.)

History of Maury County, Tennessee, by William B. Turner. Nashville: Parthenon Pr., 1955. 404 pp.

Historic Maury County, Tennessee in Pictures. Vol. 1 (all pub.). Columbia: Maury County Hist. Soc., 1966.

Maury County Cousins. Vol. 1 (all pub.?). Columbia: Maury County Hist. Soc., 1967. (Repr. with index. Columbia: Maury County Hist. Soc., 1978. 740 pp.)

Smith's History of Maury County, Tennessee, comp. by Frank H. Smith and Maury County Historical Society. [Columbia: The Society], 1969. 391 pp.

# Meigs County

Meigs County, Tennessee; a Documented Account of the European Settlement and Growth, by Stewart Lillard. Sewanee: Univ. of the South Pr., 1975. 222 pp. (Repr. Easley, S.C.: Southern Hist. Pr., 1982.)

# Monroe County

History of Monroe County, Tennessee, from the Western Frontier Days to the Space Age, by Sandra G. Cox Sands. 2 vols. in 3. Baltimore: Gateway Pr., and Author, Sweetwater, 1982.

# Montgomery County

Historical and Biographical Sketch of Montgomery County, 1886, *see* I., p. 353.

Along the Waterloo, or, A History of Montgomery County, Tennessee, by Ursula Beach. Nashville: Kiwanis Club of Clarksville & Tennessee Hist. Comm., 1964. xii, 390 pp.

Historical Sketches of . . . Montgomery County, 1779-1968, 1968, *see* p. 353.

# Moore County

Historical and Biographical Sketch of . . . Moore County, 1886, *see* C., p. 352.

# Morgan County

A History of Morgan County, Tennessee, by Ethel Freytag and G.K. Ott. [Wartburg:] Specialty Pr. Co. [1971]. 379 pp.

# Obion County

Historical and Biographical Sketch of . . . Obion County, 1887, *see* B., p. 352.

History of Obion County . . . ed. by Edwin H. Marshall. Union City: Daily Messenger, 1941. 272 pp. (Repr. Union City: Lanzer Co., 1970.)

Glory and Tears: Obion County, Tennessee, 1860-1870, by Rebel C. Forrester. Union City: Lanzer Co. [1970]. 222 pp.

# Perry County

Historical and Biographical Sketch of . . . Perry County, 1886, *see* G., p. 352.

# Pickett County

Pioneer Families of Pickett County, Tennessee, by Tim Huddleston. [Collegedale: College Pr., 1968.] 180 pp.

History of Pickett County, Tennessee, comp. by Tim Huddleston. [Collegedale: College Pr., 1973.] viii, 339 pp.

# Polk County

History of Polk County, by R. Haynes. N.p., 1937. 159 pp.

Sketches in Polk County History, by Sadie S. Patton. Hendersonville, N.C.: N.p., 1950.

# Putnam County

A History of Putnam County, Tennessee . . . by Walter S. McClain. Cookeville: Q. Dyer [1925]. 154 pp.

Putnam County, Tennessee, 1850-1970, by Mary J. DeLozier. Cookeville: Putnam County Hist. Soc., 1979. xvii, 377 pp.

# Rhea County

Records of Rhea; a Condensed County History, by Thomas J. Campbell. Dayton: Rhea Pub. Co., 1940. 204 pp.

# Roane County

The History of Roane County, Tennessee, 1801-1870, by Emma H.M. Wells. Chattanooga: Lookout Pub. Co., 1927. 308 pp. (Repr. with new index, by Jessica Budick and A. Comtois. Baltimore: Regional Pub. Co., 1975. 352 pp.)

History of Roane County, Tennessee, 1860-1870, by William J. Fowler. Nashville: Univ. of Tennessee, 1964. (thesis)

A History of Roane County to 1860, by Eugene Pickel. Nashville: Univ. of Tennessee, 1971. (thesis)

## Robertson County

Historical and Biographical Sketch of . . . Robertson County, 1886, *see* I., p. 353.

Historical Sketches of . . . Robertson County, 1779-1968, 1968, *see* p. 353.

## Rutherford County

Historical and Biographical Sketch of . . . Rutherford County, 1886, *see* H., p. 352.

Handbook of Murfreesboro and Rutherford County, Tennessee. Murfreesboro: Mutual Realty & Loan, 1923. 128 pp.

A History of Rutherford County, ed. by Carlton C. Sims. [Murfreesboro: The Editor, 1947.] 236 pp.

## Scott County

County Scott and Its Mountain Folk, by Esther Sanderson. Huntsville: N.p. [1958]. 254 pp.

## Sequatchie County

Sequatchie County: History and Development, by Ora Layne. Dunlap: Author, 1969. 57 pp.

## Sevier County

History of Sevier County, by Fred D. Matthews. [Knoxville:] N.p., 1950. 56 pp. (Rev. ed. [Knoxville:] N.p., 1960. 55 pp.)

## Shelby County

Historical and Biographical Sketch of Shelby County, 1887, *see* D., p. 352. (Repr. with full-name index. Easley, S.C.: Southern Hist. Pr., 1979. 266 pp.)

History of . . . Memphis and Shelby County, Tennessee . . . by John McL. Keating and O.F. Vedder. 2 vols. in 1. Syracuse, N.Y.: D. Mason, 1888.

The Builders of the Pyramid; the Story of Shelby County, Tennessee . . . by Joseph R. Williams. Memphis: De Garis Pr. Co., 1897. 96 pp.

## Smith County

Historical and Biographical Sketch of . . . Smith County, 1887, *see* J., p. 353.

## Stewart County

Historical and Biographical Sketch of . . . Stewart County, 1886, *see* I., p. 353.

A History of Stewart County, Tennessee, by Helen G. Brandon. Knoxville: Univ. of Tennessee, 1944. (thesis)

A History of Stewart County, Tennessee, by Iris H. McClain. [Columbia:] N.p., 1965. 152 pp.

## Sullivan County

Historic Sullivan; a History of Sullivan County, Tennessee . . . by Oliver Taylor. Bristol: King Pr. Co., 1909. xii, 330 pp. (Repr. Nashville: Charles Elder, 1971. 330 pp.)

Memoirs, by Homer H. Smith. Blountville: King Pr. Co. [1948]. 121 pp.

## Sumner County

Historical and Biographical Sketch of Sumner County, 1887, *see* J., p. 353.

Historic Sumner County, Tennessee . . . by Jay G. Cisco. Nashville: Folk-Keelin Pr. Co., 1909. xii, 319 pp.

The Great Leap Westward; a History of Sumner County, Tennessee from Its Beginnings to 1805, by Walter T. Durham. [Gallatin: Sumner County Pub. Lib., 1969.] iv, 224 pp.

Old Sumner: a History of Sumner County, Tennessee, from 1805 to 1961, by Walter T. Durham. [Gallatin: Sumner County Pub. Lib., 1972.] xiv, 530 pp. (Sequel to The Great Leap Westward, above.)

## Tipton County

Historical and Biographical Sketch of . . . Tipton County, 1887, *see* F., p. 352.

## Trousdale County

Historical and Biographical Sketch of . . . Trousdale County, 1887, *see* J., p. 353.

History of Trousdale County, by J.C. McMurtry. Hartsville: Vidette, 1970. 332 pp.

## Unicoi County

The Valley of the Long Hunters, by Roxie A. Masters. Parsons, W. Va.: McClain Pr. Co., 1969. 246 pp.

## Warren County

Historical and Biographical Sketch of . . . Warren County, 1886, *see* K., p. 353.

Early History of Warren County, by William T. Hale. McMinnville: Southern Standard, 1902. 59 pp. (Repr. McMinnville: Standard Pr. Co. [1930].)

## Wayne County

Historical and Biographical Sketch of . . . Wayne County, 1886, *see* G., p. 352.

## Weakley County

Historical and Biographical Sketch of . . . Weakley County, 1887, *see* B., p. 352.

## White County

Historical and Biographical Sketch of White County, 1886, *see* K., p. 353.

History of White County, Tennessee, by Monroe Seals. [Sparta:] Brown Pr., 1935. viii, 152 pp. (Repr. Spartanburg, S.C.: Reprint Co., 1975.)

## Williamson County

Historical and Biographical Sketch of . . . Williamson County, 1886, *see* H., p. 352.

Historic Williamson County; Old Homes and Sites, by Virginia McD. Bowman. [Nashville: Blue & Gray Pr., 1971.] viii, 194 pp. (Repr. of an earlier, undated ed.)

## Wilson County

Historical and Biographical Sketch of . . . Wilson County, 1886, *see* H., p. 352.

The History of Wilson County; Its Land and Its Life, comp. by History Association of Wilson County. [Lebanon: The Association?], 1961. 453 pp.

# TEXAS

## *Regional*

A History of Texas: History of Milam, Williamson, Bastrop, Travis, Lee and Burleson Counties. Chicago: Lewis Pub. Co., 1893. 826 pp.

A Memorial and Biographical History of McLennan, Falls, Bell and Coryell Counties, Texas . . . from the Earliest Period of Its Occupancy to the Present Time . . . Chicago: Lewis Pub. Co., 1893. 999 pp.

A Memorial and Biographical History of Navarro, Henderson, Anderson, Limestone, Freestone and Leon Counties. Chicago: Lewis Pub. Co., 1893. 980 pp.

## Anderson County

A Memorial and Biographical History of . . . Anderson County, 1893, *see* above.

A Centennial History of Anderson County, Texas, by Pauline B. Hohes. San Antonio: Naylor Co., 1936. xviii, 565 pp.

## Andrews County

A Golden Jubilee, 1910-1960: 50 Years, and Solid Growth. Andrews: N.p., 1960. 64 pp.

## Angelina County

History and Description of Angelina County, by R.W. Haltom. Lufkin: N.p., 1888. 66 pp. (Repr. Austin: Pemberton Pr., 1969. 65 pp.)

The History of Angelina County, by Effie M. Boon. Austin: Univ. of Texas, 1937. 245 pp. (M.A. thesis)

## Archer County

A History of Archer County, Texas, by Winnie A. Nance. Austin: Univ. of Texas, 1927. 118 pp. (M.A. thesis)

Archer County Pioneers: a History of Archer County, Texas, ed. by Ruth J. O'Keefe. Hereford: Pioneer Book Pub. [1969]. ix, 133 pp.

## Armstrong County

A Collection of Memories; a History of Armstrong County, 1876-1965. Hereford: Pioneer Pubs. [1965]. 567 pp.

## Atascosa County

Atascosa County Centennial, 1856-1956. Official Centennial Program and History, Atascosa County. Pleasanton: N.p., 1956. 110 pp.

## Austin County

An Historical and Descriptive Sketch of Austin County, Texas . . . by Martin M. Kenney. Brenham: Banner Pr., 1876. 25 pp.

Footprints of Five Generations, by C.M. Schmidt. New Ulm: New Ulm Enterprise, 1930. 76 pp.

## Bailey County

History of Bailey County, by Thelma Stevens. Lubbock: Texas Technical Coll., 1939. 125 pp. (M.A. thesis)

## Bandera County

Pioneer History of Bandera County, 75 Years of Intrepid History, by John M. Hunter. Bandera: Hunter's Pr. House, 1922. 287 pp.

A Brief History of Bandera County, Covering 100 Years of Intrepid History, by John M. Hunter. Baird: Frontier Times Museum, 1949. 76 pp.

100 Years in Bandera, 1853-1953; a Story of Sturdy Pioneers, by John M. Hunter. [Bandera:] N.p., 1953. 91 pp.

## Bastrop County

History of . . . Bastrop County, 1893, in A History of Texas, *see* p. 365.

In the Shadow of the Lost Pines; a History of Bastrop County and Its People. Bastrop: Bastrop Hist. Soc., 1955. 44 pp.

The History of Bastrop, Texas, 1851-1935, by Oliver W. Sumerlin. Austin: Univ. of Texas, 1963. 141 pp. (M.A. thesis)

## Baylord County

The Early History of Baylor County. Dallas: Story Book Pr., 1955. 185 pp.

Salt Pork to Sirloin: the History of Baylor County, Texas, from 1879 to 1930 . . . Quanah: Nortex Offset Pub., 1972. 227, 179 pp.

## Bee County

A History of Bee County . . . by Mrs. I.C. Nadray. [Beeville:] Beeville Pub. Co., 1939. 135 pp.

The History of Bee County, Texas, by Lillian G. Schoppe. Austin: Univ. of Texas, 1939. 218 pp. (M.A. thesis)

*Bee County (cont.)*

Bee County Centennial, 1858-1958. [Beeville:] Bee County Centennial, 1958. 115 pp.

History of Bee County, Texas, by Joseph G. Rountree. [Beeville?: N.p., 1960.] 143, 56 pp.

Historical Study of Bee County, Texas, by Camp Ezell. Beeville: Beeville Pub. Co. [1973]. xii, 258 pp.

## Bell County

A Memorial and Biographical History of . . . Bell County, 1893, *see* p. 365.

The History of Bell County, by George W. Tyler, ed. by Charles W. Ramsdell. San Antonio: Naylor Co., 1936. xxiii, 425 pp.

Bell County History: a Pictorial History of Bell County, Texas . . . Fort Worth: Univ. Supply and Equipment Co., 1958. 220 pp.

History of Bell County, Texas, by Bertha Atkinson. Belton: Bell County Hist. County Survey Comm., 1973. 147 pp. (Originally M.A. thesis, Univ. of Texas, Austin, 1929.)

## Blanco County

A History of Blanco County, by John W. Speer, ed. by Henry C. Ambruster. Austin: Pemberton Pr., 1965. iv, 73 pp.

## Bosque County

A History of Bosque County, by William C. Pool. Austin: Univ. of Texas, n.d. 183 pp. (M.A. thesis)

The History of Bosque County, Texas, by E.W. Smith. Greeley: Colorado State Coll. of Education, 1937. 199 pp. (M.A. thesis)

A History of Bosque County, Texas, by William C. Pool. San Marcos: San Marcos Record Pr., 1954. 74 pp.

## Bowie County

Bowie County: a Descriptive and General History, by an Emigrant. N.p., 1850. 64 pp.

A History of Bowie County, by Barbara S.O. Chandler. Austin: Univ. of Texas, 1937. 97 pp. (M.A. thesis)

History of Texarkana and Bowie [Texas] and Miller [Arkansas] Counties, Texas-Arkansas, by Barbara Chandler and J.E. Howe. Texarkana: N.p., 1939. 375 pp.

De Kalb and Bowie County: History and Genealogy, by Emma L. Meadows. [De Kalb: N.p., 1968.] xiii, 249 pp.

## Brazoria County

History of Brazoria County, by Laura Underwood and Mrs. J.P. Rogers, et al. Brazoria: Brazoria County Federation of Women's Clubs, 1940. 61 pp.

History of Brazoria County, by Elizabeth Lane. Kingsville: Coll. of Arts & Industries, 1948. 68 pp. (M.A. thesis)

A History of Brazoria County, Texas . . . ed. by Travis L. Smith. [N.p., 1958.] 92 pp.

## Brazos County

History of Brazos County, Texas, by Elmer G. Marshall. Austin: Univ. of Texas, 1937. 234 pp. (M.A. thesis)

Pioneers of Brazos County, Texas, 1800-1850, by W. Broadus Smith. [Bryan: Scribe Shop], 1962. vii, 282 pp.

## Brewster County

A History of Brewster County, 1535-1934, by Alice V. Cain. Alpine: Sul Ross State Teachers Coll., 1935. 238 pp. (M.A. thesis)

Life Along the Border . . . 1905-1913, by Charles A. Hawley. Spokane, Wash.: N.p. [1955]. 165 pp.

## Brooks County

The History of Brooks County, by Lloyd Dyer. Kingsville: Texas Coll. of Arts, 1938. 64 pp. (M.A. thesis)

## Brown County

The History of Brown County, by Thomas R. Havins. Austin: Univ. of Texas, 1931. 192 pp. (M.A. thesis)

Frontier's Generation, the Pioneer History of Brown County . . . by Tevis C. Smith. Brownwood: Greenwood Pr. [1931]. 63 pp. (Repr. Comanche: Margaret Waring, 1980. 100 pp.)

The Promised Land: a History of Brown County, Texas, by James C. White. Brownwood: Brownwood Banner, 1941. 123 pp.

Something About Brown, a History of Brown County, Texas, by Thomas R. Havins. Brownwood: Banner Pr. Co., 1958. 208 pp.

## Burleson County

History of . . . Burleson County, 1893, in A History of Texas, *see* p. 365.

## Burnet County

History of Burnet County, by M.G. Bowden. Austin: Univ. of Texas, 1940. 194 pp. (M.A. thesis)

## Caldwell County

The History of Caldwell County, by Maurice M. O'Bannion. Austin: Univ. of Texas, 1931. 259 pp. (M.A. thesis)

## Callahan County

Early Days in Callahan County, by Brutus C. Chrisman. [Baird?: N.p., 1966.] ix, 356 pp.

## Cameron County

An Early History of Cameron County . . . by Maurice S. Pipkin. [Kingsville:] Texas Coll. of Arts [1940]. 130 pp. (M.A. thesis)

A Story of Cameron County, Texas, by Walter W. Hildebrand. Denton: Texas State Coll., 1950. 108 pp. (M.A. thesis)

## Camp County

The Camp County Story, by Artemesia L.B. Spencer. Fort Worth: Branch-Smith, 1974. xii, 192 pp.

## Carson County

A Historical Sketch of Carson County, by George G. Bobbitt. Amarillo: G.E. High Pr., 1948. 68 pp.

A Time to Purpose; a Chronicle of Carson County, ed. by Mrs. Ralph E. Randel and the Carson County Historical Survey Committee. 4 vols. Hereford: Pioneer Book Pub., 1966-1972.

## Cass County

History of Cass County People. Atlanta: Cass County Gen. Soc., 1982. 250 pp.

## Castro County

The Moving Finger, by Lillie M. Hunter. (The Story of Cass County.) Borger: Plains Pr. Co., 1956. 171 pp. (Repr. Dalhart: N.p. [1977?].)

This Land We Hold, by Ernestine L. Bowden. [Wichita Falls: Nortex Offset Pubs., 1971.] 402 pp.

## Chambers County

A History of Chambers County, by Jewel H. Harry. Austin: Univ. of Texas, 1940. 285 pp. (M.A. thesis)

## Cherokee County

A History of Cherokee County, by Hattie J. Roach. Dallas: Southwest Pr., 1934. 184 pp.

*Cherokee County (cont.)*

The Hills of Cherokee: Historical Sketches of Life in Cherokee County, Texas, by Hattie J. Roach. [Rusk?: N.p., 1952.] 216 pp.

## Childress County

The History of Childress County, by LeRoy Reeves. Canyon: West Texas State Coll., 1951. 112 pp. (M.A. thesis)

They Followed the Rails; in Retrospect a History of Childress County, comp. by Susie Ord, et al., ed. by Paul Ord. Childress: Childress Reporter, 1970. 432 pp.

## Clay County

Romance and Dim Trails: a History of Clay County, by Katherine C. Douthitt. Dallas: W.T. Tardy, 1938. 288 pp.

A History of Clay County, by William C. Kimbrough. Abilene: Hardin-Simmons Univ., 1942. 161 pp. (M.A. thesis)

History of Clay County and Northwest Texas, by J.P. Earle. Henrietta: Henrietta Ind. Pr., 1897. 64 pp. (Repr. Austin: Brick Row Book Shop, 1963.)

A History of Clay County, by William C. Taylor. Austin: Jenkins Pub. Co., 1972. xii, 168 pp.

## Cochran County

Texas' Last Frontier; a History of Cochran County, Texas, by Elvis E. Fleming. Morton: Cochran County Hist. Soc. [1965]. 94 pp.

## Coleman County

"Into the Setting Sun," a History of Coleman County, by Beatrice G. Gay. Santa Anna: N.p., 1936. x, 193 pp.

History of Coleman County, by Ernest G. Mitchell. Austin: Univ. of Texas, 1949. 172 pp. (M.A. thesis)

They Came in Peace to Coleman County, by Leona Bruce. Fort Worth: Branch-Smith, 1970. vii, 101 pp.

## Collin County

History of Collin County, by Harold E. Massey. Georgetown: South West Univ., 1948. 128 pp. (M.A. thesis)

A History of Collin County, Texas, by J. Lee Stambaugh and Lillian Stambaugh. Austin: Texas State Hist. Assoc., 1958. 303 pp.

## Collingsworth County

A History of Collingsworth County . . . Wellington: Leader Pr. Co., 1925. xxii, 234 pp.

*Collingsworth County (cont.)*

Survey of the History of Collingsworth County, by C.C. Brown. Boulder: Univ. of Colorado, 1934. 127 pp. (M.A. thesis)

## Colorado County

Flaming Feuds of Colorado County, by John W. Reese. Salado: Anson Jones Pr., 1962. 169 pp.

## Comal County

History of New Braunfels and Comal County, Texas, 1844-1946, by Oscar Haas. [Austin: Steck Co.], 1968. xiv, 338 pp. (2d pr. Austin: Steck Co., 1975.)

A History of Comal County, by Lillian E. Penshorn. San Marcos: Southwest Texas State Teachers Coll., 1950. 82 pp. (M.A. thesis)

## Comanche County

Blazing the Way: Tales of Comanche County Pioneers . . . comp. by Mrs. Eulalia N. Wells. [Blanket: N.p., 1942.] 168 pp.

The History of Comanche County, Texas to 1900, by Billy B. Lightfoot. Austin: Univ. of Texas, 1949. 352 pp. (M.A. thesis)

## Concho County

Concho County History, 1858-1958, by Hazie D. LeFevre. 2 vols. Eden: N.p., 1959.

## Cooke County

Early Days in Cooke County, 1848-1873, by C.N. Jones. Gainesville: N.p., 1936. 88 pp.

The First 100 Years in Cooke County, by Alex M. Smith. San Antonio: Naylor Co., 1955. vii, 290 pp.

## Coryell County

A Memorial and Biographical History of . . . Coryell County, 1893, *see* p. 365.

Coryell County History Stories, by Frank E. Simmons. Oglesby: Author, 1946. 120 pp.

Coryell County Centennial, 1854-1954, with a History of Coryell County. Gatesville: N.p., 1954. 68 pp.

Coryell County Scrapbook. [Waco: Texian Pr., 1963.] xii, 253 pp.

A History of Coryell County, Texas, by Zelma M. Scott. Austin: Texas State Hist. Assoc., 1965. xviii, 278 pp.

History of Coryell County, by Frank E. Simmons. Belton: Dayton Kelley, 1965. 102 pp. (Repr. of a 1936 ed.?)

## Cottle County

Our Roots Grow Deep: a History of Cottle County, by Carmen T. Bennett. Floydada: Blanco Offset Pr., 1970. 214 pp.

## Crockett County

The History of Crockett County, Texas, by W.M. Stoker. Waco: Baylor Univ., 1950. 186 pp. (M.A. thesis)

## Crosby County

The History of Crosby County, Texas, by Roger A. Burgess. Austin: Univ. of Texas, 1937. 111 pp. (M.S. thesis)

Through the Years: a History of Crosby County, Texas, by Nellie W. Spikes and A.E. Temple. San Antonio: Naylor Co., 1952. 493 pp.

A History of Crosby County, 1876-1977; a Collection of Historical Sketches and Family Histories . . . [Crosbyton?:] Crosby County Hist. Comm., 1978. 608 pp.

## Dallam County

History of Dallam County, Texas, by W.F. Mauldin. Austin: Univ. of Texas, 1938. 127 pp. (M.A. thesis)

The Book of Years; a History of Dallam and Hartley Counties, by Lillie M. Hunter. Hereford: Pioneer Book Pubs., 1969. x, 206 pp.

## Dallas County

History of Dallas County, Texas, from 1837-1887, by John H. Brown. Dallas: Milligan, Cornett & Farnham, 1887. 114 pp. (Suppl., *see* below, Cochran.)

Memorial and Biographical History of Dallas County, Texas . . . from the Earliest Period . . . to the Present Time. Chicago: Lewis Pub. Co., 1892. vii, 1,001 pp.

Dallas County; a Record of Its Pioneers and Progress, Being a Supplement to Brown's History of Dallas County (1887) . . . by John H. Cochran. Dallas: A.S. Mathis Service Pub. Co. [1928]. 296 pp. (Brown's History, *see* above.)

A History of Dallas County, by Ann Stark. Austin: Univ. of Texas, 1935. 198 pp. (M.A. thesis)

## Dawson County

The Trail of Years in Dawson County, Texas, by M.C. Lindsay. [Fort Worth?: N.p., 1960.] 266 pp.

## Deaf Smith County

The History of Deaf Smith County, Texas, by Clois T. Brown. Canyon: West Texas State Univ., 1948. 106 pp. (M.A. thesis)

A History of Deaf Smith County, Featuring Pioneer Families, by Bessie Patterson. Hereford: Pioneer Pubs. [1964]. 167 pp.

## Delta County

Loose Leaves; a History of Delta County, by Ikie G. Patteson. Dallas: Mathis Pub. Co., 1935. 228 pp.

## Denton County

History and Reminiscences of Denton County, by Ed. F. Bates. Denton: McNitsky Pr. Co. [1918]. xi, 412 pp.

Geography of Denton County, by Mary J. Cowling. Dallas: B. Upshaw & Co., 1936. xii, 132 pp.

## De Witt County

A History of De Witt County, by Nellie Murphee, ed. by Robert W. Shook. [Thomaston: N.p., 1962.] 212 pp.

## Dickens County

A History of Dickens County . . . by Fred Arrington. [Dickens?:] Nortex Offset Pub., 1971. 355 pp.

## Donley County

History of Donley County, by Dalton Ford. Boulder: Univ. of Colorado, 1932. 122 pp. (M.A. thesis)

## Eastland County

History of Eastland County, Texas, by Mrs. George Langston. Dallas: Aldridge Pr., 1904. 220 pp.

History of Eastland County, Texas, by Robert Y. Lindsey, Jr. Austin: Univ. of Texas, 1940. 200 pp. (M.A. thesis)

History of Eastland County, Texas, by Edwin T. Cox. San Antonio: Naylor Co. [1950]. xii, 95 pp.

Eastland County, Texas; a Historical and Biographical Survey, by Pearl Ghormley. Austin: Rupegy Pub. Co. [1969]. 397 pp.

## Ector County

A History of Ector County, Texas, by Finas W. Horton. Austin: Univ. of Texas, 1950. 167 pp. (M.A. thesis)

## Ellis County

Memorial and Biographical History of Ellis County, Texas . . . Chicago: Lewis Pub. Co., 1892. 573 pp. (*See* below.)

Ellis County History; the Basic 1892 Book (*see* above . . . with Additional Biographies), comp. by Ellis County Historical Museum and Art Gallery. Waxachie: The Museum, 1972. vii, 774 pp. (Has additions and deletions.)

History of Ellis County, Texas, by Edna D. Hawkins, et al. Waco: N.p., 1972. vii, 338 pp.

## El Paso County

A History of El Paso County, Texas to 1900, by Nance L. Hemmons. El Paso: Univ. of Texas at El Paso, 1942. 175 pp.

Official Souvenir Program, El Paso County Centennial, 1850-1950 . . . [El Paso: N.p., 1950.] 64 pp.

## Erath County

A History of Erath County, Texas, by Vallie Eoff. Austin: Univ. of Texas, 1938. 226 pp. (M.A. thesis)

History of Erath County, comp. by Homer Stephen. [Stephenville?: N.p.], 1950. 48 pp.

A History of Erath County, by M.L. Austen. Abilene: Hardin-Simmons Univ., 1951. 240 pp.

Fragments of History: Erath County . . . Stephenville: H. Stephen [1966]. 137 pp.

People-Events and Erath County, Texas, by Arden J. Schuetz. Stephenville: Ennis Favors [1970]. 126 pp.

## Falls County

A Memorial and Biographical History of . . . Falls County, 1893, *see* p. 365.

The History of Falls County, by Walter Brown. Waco: Baylord Univ. [1938]. 167 pp. (M.A. thesis)

History of Falls County, Texas; Old Settlers and Veterans Association of Falls County, ed. by Roy Eddins. [Marlin?:] The Assoc., 1947. viii, 312 pp.

Western Falls County, Texas, by Lillian S. St. Romain. Austin: Texas State Hist. Assoc., 1951. ix, 160 pp.

## Fannin County

History of Fannin County, Texas . . . by W.A. Carter. Bonham: N.p., 1885. 128 pp.

History of Fannin County, by Rex W. Strickland. Dallas: Southern Methodist Univ., 1929. 134 pp. (M.A. thesis)

Sidelights on the History of Fannin County, by Bertha J. Gribble. Commerce: East Texas State Teachers Coll., 1939. 177 pp. (M.A. thesis)

A History of Fannin County . . . by Floyd C. Hodge. Hereford: Pioneer Pubs. [1966]. 267 pp.

# Fayette County

Fayette County (Texas): Her History and Her People, by Frank Lotto. Schulenberg: Author, 1902. xvi, 424 pp.

Early History of Fayette County, 1822-1865, by Leonie R. Weyand. Austin: Univ. of Texas, 1932. 237 pp. (M.A. thesis)

An Early History of Fayette County, by Leonie R. Weyand and Houston Wade. La Grange: La Grange Journal, 1936. 383 pp.

# Fisher County

A Short History of Fisher County, by Lora Blount. Abilene: Hardin-Simmons Univ., 1947. 120 pp. (M.A. thesis)

History of Fisher County, Texas, by E.L. Yeats. [Roby?: N.p., 1971.] 208 pp.

# Floyd County

The Early History of Floyd County, by Claude V. Hall. Austin: Univ. of Texas, 1922. 197 pp. (M.A. thesis) (Another ed.? N.p., 1947. 147 pp.)

One Corner of Heaven, by Blanche S. Rutherford. San Antonio: Naylor Co. [1964]. xi, 294 pp.

# Foard County

They Loved the Land: Foard County History, by Batley Phelps. [Quanah:] Quanah Tribune-Chief, 1969. 289, 106 pp.

# Fort Bend County

History of Fort Bend County, by Andrew J. Sowell. Houston: W.H. Coyle, 1904. xii, 373 pp. (Repr. [Waco: W.M. Morrison, 1964.] xii, 373 pp.)

The Book of Fort Bend County, Texas, by S.K. McMillan. N.p.: McMillan, 1926. 264 pp.

Wharton's History of Fort Bend County, by Clarence R. Wharton. San Antonio: Naylor Co., 1939. xi, 250 pp. (20 Years After: Chapter 17 of Wharton's History. Richmond: N.p., 1939. 48 pp. Repr. Houston: Anson Jones Pr., 1950. 250 pp.)

# Freestone County

A Memorial and Biographical History of . . . Freestone County, 1893, *see* p. 365.

The Early History of Freestone County to 1865, by Philip D. Browne. Austin: Univ. of Texas, 1925. 179 pp. (M.A. thesis)

# Frio County

Historic Frio County, 1871-1971. Frio County Centennial Corporation. [Pearsall: The Corp.? 1971?] 82 pp.

*Frio County (cont.)*

Frio County, Texas: a History, by the Frio Pioneer Jail Museum Association. Dallas: Taylor Pub. Co., 1979. 152 pp.

## Garza County

Wagon Wheels: a History of Garza County, comp. by Garza County Historical Survey Committee, ed. by Charles Didway. Seagraves: Pioneer Book Pubs., 1973. x, 340 pp.

## Gillespie County

History of the German Settlements in Gillespie County, Texas, 1831-1861, by Rudolph L. Biesele. Austin: Von Boeckmann-Jones, 1930. 259 pp.

A History of Gillespie County, Texas, 1846-1900, by Sara K. Curtis. Austin: Univ. of Texas, 1943. 146 pp.

Pioneers in God's Hills; a History of Fredericksburg and Gillespie County, People and Events. Austin: Gillespie County Hist. Soc., by Von Boeckmann-Jones [1960]. 305 pp.

## Glassock County

A Brief History of Glassock County, by Max H. Greenwood. Lubbock: Texas Technical Coll., 1937. 106 pp.

## Gray County

A History of Gray County, by Frances D. Prouse. Austin: Univ. of Texas, 1957. 407 pp.

## Grayson County

A History of Grayson County, Texas, by Mattie D. Lucas. Sherman: Scruggs Pr. Co. [1936]. 212 pp.

History and Business Guide to Sherman and Grayson County, Texas, by Edward H. Anderson. N.p., 1940. 72 pp.

Grayson County: an Illustrated History of Grayson County, Texas, by Graham Landrum and A. Smith. 2d ed. Fort Worth: Hist. Pubs., 1967. 195 pp.

History of Grayson County, Texas, comp. by Grayson County Frontier Village, Denison, Texas. Dallas: National ShareGraphics, 1981. 687 pp.

## Gregg County

A History of Greater Gregg County, by Bailey S. Etheridge. Norman: Univ. of Oklahoma, 1937. 146 pp. (M.A. thesis)

The History of Gregg County. Fort Worth: Longview Chamber of Commerce, 1957. 300 pp.

## Grimes County

Early History of Grimes County, by E.L. Blair. [Austin: N.p., 1930.] 253 pp.

## Guadalupe County

Incidents Connected with the Early History of Guadalupe County, by Andrew J. Sowell. Seguin: C.L. Martin, n.d. 60 pp.

An Authentic History of Guadalupe County, by Willie M. Weinert. Seguin: Seguin Enterprise, 1951. 96 pp.

## Hale County

History of Hale County, Texas, by Mary L. Cox. Plainview: N.p., 1937. xi, 230 pp.

## Hall County

Yesterday in Hall County, Texas, by Inez Baker. Memphis, Tenn.: N.p., 1940. 224 pp.

## Hamilton County

A History of Hamilton County, by Oran J. Pool. Austin: Univ. of Texas, 1954. 241 pp. (M.A. thesis)

Parade of Progress, Hamilton County, 1858-1958; Centennial ed., by Hamilton Herald-News. [Hamilton: Herald-News, 1958.] (Unpaged)

## Hansford County

A Search for Opportunity; a History of Hansford County, by Dotty Jones. Gruver: Jones Pub. Co., 1965. 208 pp.

## Hardeman County

History of Hardeman County, by J. Paul Jones. Denton: North Texas State Coll., 1949. 128 pp. (M.A. thesis)

The Last Frontier: the Story of Hardeman County, by Bill Neal. [Quanah:] Quanah Tribune-Chief [1966]. ix, 276 pp.

## Hardin County

A History of Hardin County, by Mary L. Proctor. Austin: Univ. of Texas, 1950. 94 pp. (M.A. thesis)

## Harris County

The City of Houston and Harris County, Texas, by Charles F. Morse. Houston: Cumming & Son Pr., 1893. 106 pp.

## Harrison County

Historical Hallmarks of Harrison County, by V.H. Hackney. Marshall: N.p. [1964]. (Unpaged)

## Hartley County

The Book of Years; a History of . . . Hartley County, 1969, *see* Dallam County, p. 372.

## Hays County

The History of Hays County, by Annie M. Hall. Greeley: Colorado State Coll. of Education, 1935. 267 pp. (M.A. thesis)

A Brief History of Hays County and San Marcos, Texas, by Dudley R. Dobie. San Marcos: N.p., 1948. 69 pp.

## Hemphill County

The History of Hemphill County, by Glyndon M. Riley. Canyon: West Texas Coll., 1939. 135 pp. (M.A. thesis)

## Henderson County

A Memorial and Biographical History of . . . Henderson County, 1893, *see* p. 365.

Henderson County, by James Easterling, ed. by W.P. Webb. 128 pp. (In Texas History Teacher's Bull., 1924.)

History of Henderson County, Texas, Recording Names of Early Pioneers . . . by James J. Faulk. [Athens?: N.p., 1929.] 322 pp.

The History of Henderson County, by Winnie M. Reynolds. Commerce: East Texas State Teachers Coll., 1952. 128 pp. (M.A. thesis)

## Hidalgo County

History of Hidalgo County, 1749-1852, by Oran R. Scott. Fort Worth: Texas Christian Univ., 1934. 113 pp. (M.A. thesis)

History of Hidalgo County, by W. Clyde Norris. Kingsville: Texas Coll. of Arts, 1952. 127 pp. (M.A. thesis)

## Hill County

Memorial and Biographical History of . . . Hill County, 1892, *see* Johnson County.

A History of Hill County, Texas, to 1873, by James Reese. Austin: Univ. of Texas, 1961. 183 pp.

The Early Settlers' Life in Texas, and the Organization of Hill County. [Waco: Texian Pr., 1963.] 107 pp.

*Hill County (cont.)*

A History of Hill County, Texas, 1838-1965, by Ellis Bailey. [Waco: Texian Pr., 1966.] xii, 269 pp.

## Hockley County

History of Hockley County, by Orville R. Watkins. Lubbock: Texas Technical Coll., 1941. 119 pp. (M.A. thesis)

Hockley County, 1921-1971, the First Fifty Years: an Epilogue, 1971-1976, by Lillian Brasher. Canyon: Staken Plains Pr., 1971-76 [actually 1977]. 412 pp.

## Hood County

History of Hood County, by Thomas T. Ewell. Granbury: Granbury News, 1895. 160 pp. (Repr. Granbury: Junior Woman's Club, 1956.) (Also has a Sketch of the History of Somervell County.)

Hood County History in Picture and Story (covers Hood and Somervell Counties), sponsored by Junior Woman's Club, Granbury. Fort Worth: Hist. Pubs., 1970. (Hood County History, by Thomas T. Ewell, *see* above.)

## Hopkins County

Early History of Hopkins County . . . [by E.B. Fleming]. N.p., 1902. 183 pp.

The History of Hopkins County, by G.G. Oren. Commerce: East Texas State Teachers Coll., 1938. 233 pp. (M.A. thesis)

Heritage from the Past; Sketches from Hopkins County History, by Celia M. Wright. Sulphur Springs: Shining Path Pr., 1959. 50 pp.

A History of Hopkins County, Texas, by Gladys A. St. Clair. Austin: Univ. of Texas, 1940. 164 pp. (Pub. in different form. [Austin: N.p., 1965.] viii, 99 pp.)

## Houston County

The History of Houston County . . . by Armistead A. Aldrich. San Antonio: Naylor Co., 1943. xv, 225 pp.

History of Houston County, Texas, by Eliza H. Bishop. Dallas: National Share-Graphics, 1979. 707 pp.

## Howard County

Howard County in the Making, by John R. Hutto. Big Spring: N.p., 1938. 76 pp.

## Hunt County

A History of Hunt County, by Anne E. Cassles. Austin: Univ. of Texas, 1935. 72 pp. (M.A. thesis)

## Irion County

A History of Irion County, Texas, by Leta Crawford. [N.p., 1966.] vii, 152 pp.

## Jack County

History of Jack County, by Thomas F. Houghton. Jacksboro: Gazette Pr. [1932]. 166 pp.

Ninety-four Years in Jack County, 1854-1948, by Ida Huckabay. [Jacksboro?: N.p., 1949.] xvi, 513 pp.

Jackson County, by Mindora Bogby, ed. by W.P. Webb. (In Texas History Teacher's Bull., 1924. 128 pp.)

The Cavalcade of Jackson County, by Ira T. Taylor. San Antonio: Naylor Co. [1938]. xii, 471 pp.

## Jeff Davis County

The Story of Fort Davis, Jeff Davis County and the Davis Mountains, by Barry Scobee. Fort Davis: M. Hunter, Jr., 1936. 27, 38 pp.

The History of Jeff Davis County, by James H. Lundy. Alpine: Sul Ross State Coll., 1941. 136 pp. (M.A. thesis)

## Jefferson County

History and Progress of Jefferson County, by Lorecia East. Dallas: Royal Pub. Co., 1961. 168 pp.

Time and Shadows, by L.I. Adams. [Lumberton, Miss.?: N.p., 1971.] ix, 297 pp.

## Jim Wells County

The History of Jim Wells County . . . by Neva V. Pollard. Kingsville: N.p., 1945. 3 pp., 119 leaves.

## Johnson County

History and Description of Johnson County . . . by A.J. Byrd. Marshall: Jennings Bros., 1879. 232 pp.

A Memorial and Biographical History of Johnson and Hill Counties, Texas . . . Chicago: Lewis Pub. Co., 1892. 735 pp.

The Building of Johnson County, and the Settlement of the Communities of the Eastern Portion of the County, by F.D. Abernathy. Austin: Univ. of Texas, 1936. 294 pp. (M.A. thesis)

History of Johnson County and Surrounding Areas, by Viola Block. [Waco: Texian Pr., 1970.] vi, 336 pp.

## Jones County

Jones County, by Velma Thomas, ed. by W.P. Webb. (In Texas History Teacher's Bull., 12, 1924.)

## Karnes County

A History of Karnes County and Old Helena, by Hedwig K. Didear. Austin: San Felipe Pr., 1969. 124 pp.

## Kaufman County

A History of Kaufman County, Texas, by Robert R. Butler. Austin: Univ. of Texas, 1940. 172 pp. (M.A. thesis)

History of Kaufman County, by Mabel C. Keller. Denton: North Texas State Coll., 1950. 151 pp.

History of Kaufman County, comp. by Kaufman County Historical Commission. 2 vols. Terrell: The Commission, 1978. 271 pp., and Dallas: National Share-Graphics, 1984. 434 pp.

## Kerr County

A History of Kerr County, Texas, by Matilda M. Real. Austin: Univ. of Texas, 1942. 236 pp. (M.A. thesis)

Kerr County, Texas, 1856-1956, by Bob Bennett. San Antonio: Naylor Co., 1956. xi, 332 pp.

Kerr County, Texas, 1856-1976, by Clara Watkins. Bicentennial ed. Kerrville: Hill Country Preservation Soc., 1975. vii, 343 pp. (Rev. of Kerr County, by Bob Bennett, *see* above.)

## Kimble County

It Occurred in Kimble, by Ovie C. Fisher. Houston: Anson Jones Pr., 1937. 240 pp.

## King County

History of King County, by Lotte Gibson. El Paso: Texas Western Univ., 1954. (M.A. thesis)

## Kinney County

Kinney County, by Mrs. H.J. Manny. Bracketville: N.p., 1947. 80 pp.

## Knox County

Early Days in Knox County, by Mrs. R.D. Gray (Jewel B. Gray). New York: Carlton Pr., 1963. 260 pp.

## Lamar County

The History of Lamar County, by Alexander W. Neville. Paris: North Texas Pub. Co. [1937]. 246 pp.

This Stubborn Soil, by William A. Owens. New York: C. Scribner [1966]. 307 pp. (English ed. London: Faber, 1967.)

*Lamar County (cont.)*

A Season of Weathering, by William A. Owens. New York: Scribner [1973]. xii, 258 pp.

## Lamb County

A History of Lamb County . . . by Evalyn P. Scott. [Sudan: Author, 1968.] v, 281 pp.

## Lampasas County

The History of Lampasas County, by J.R. Elsner. Georgetown: Southwestern Univ., 1950. 304 pp.

Lamplights of Lampasas County, Texas, by Jonnie Elzner. Austin: Firm Foundation House, 1951. 219 pp.

Relighting Lamplights of Lampasas County, Texas, by Jonnie Elzner. N.p.: Hill County, 1974. v, 331 pp.

## La Salle County

Settlement of the Cibolo-Nueces Strip: a Partial History of La Salle County, by Stanley D. Casto. [Hillsboro: Hill Junior Coll. Pr., 1969.] v, 64 pp.

## Lavaca County

The History of Lavaca County, by Paul C. Boethel. San Antonio: Naylor Co., 1936. 156 pp. (Rev. ed. Austin: Von Boeckmann-Jones [1959]. 172 pp.)

Send in Your Craw: Tales of the Early History of Lavaca County, by Paul C. Boethel. Austin: Von Boeckmann-Jones [1959]. 134 pp.

## Lee County

History of . . . Lee County, 1893, in A History of Texas, *see* p. 365.

Lee County, Historical and Descriptive, by Julia Jones. [Houston: Gulf Coast Baptist Pr., 1945.] 69 pp.

History of Lee County, Texas, comp. by Lee County Historical Survey Comm., ed. by Mrs. James C. Killen. [Giddings?:] The Comm. [1974]. x, 458 pp.

## Leon County

A Memorial and Biographical History of . . . Leon County, 1893, *see* p. 365.

Through the Years: a Historical Sketch of Leon County . . . by Frances J. Leathers. Oakwood: N.p. [1946]. 224 pp.

Leon County, Texas Historical Collections. 3 vols. Centerville: Leon County Gen. Soc., 1979-83. (In progress?)

## Liberty County

Historic Liberty County, by Arlene Pickett. [Dallas:] Tardy Pub. Co. [1936]. 120 pp.

The History of Liberty County, by Rosalie Fincher. Austin: Univ. of Texas, 1937. 99 pp. (M.A. thesis)

Liberty, Liberty County, and the Atascosito District, by Miriam Partlow. Austin: Pemberton Pr., 1974. 369 pp.

## Limestone County

A Memorial and Biographical History of . . . Limestone County, 1893, *see* p. 365.

A History of Limestone County, by Ray A. Walter. Austin: Von Boeckmann-Jones, 1959. 159 pp.

## Lipscomb County

The History of Lipscomb County, by Clinton L. Paine. Canyon: West Texas State Teachers Coll., 1961. 85 pp.

## Live Oak County

Live Oak County Centennial, 1856-1956. N.p., 1956. 40 pp.

## Llano County

A History of Llano County, Texas, by T.B.M. Fry. Austin: Univ. of Texas, 1943. 286 pp. (M.A. thesis)

Llano County Centennial, by Llano County Centennial Association. Llano: N.p. [1936]. 36 pp.

Llano, Gem of the Hill Country; a History of Llano County, Texas, by Wilburn Outman. Hereford: Pioneer Book Pubs. [1970]. x, 196 pp.

## Loving County

History of Loving County, Texas, by Robert W. Dunn. Austin: Univ. of Texas, 1948. 164 pp. (M.A. thesis)

## Lubbock County

History of Lubbock County, Texas, by Addie L. Morrison. Greeley: Colorado Coll. of Education, 1939. 236 pp. (M.A. thesis)

History of Lubbock County, Texas, by Murray L. McDonald. Austin: Univ. of Texas, 1942. 146 pp. (M.A. thesis)

## McLennan County

Waco and McLennan County, comp. by John Sleeper and J.C. Hutchins. [Waco:] Waco Pr., 1876. 170 pp. (Repr. [Waco:] D. Kelley, 1966. 171 pp.)

Memorial and Biographical History of McLennan County, 1893, *see* p. 365.

Action on Bullhide Creek, 1897-1908; a Socio-Historical Narrative, by Frank M. Locke. [Waco: Texian Pr., 1970.] vii, 191 pp.

The Handbook of Waco and McLennan County. Waco: D. Kelley, 1972. ix, 307 pp.

## McMullen County

A Vaquero of the Brush Country, by J. Frank Dobie. Dallas: Southwest Pr., 1929. 314 pp. (Much on McMullen County.)

A History of McMullen County, Texas, by Joe P. Smyer. Austin: Univ. of Texas, 1952. 339 pp. (M.A. thesis)

## Marion County

Marion County [History], 1936, *see* Jefferson County.

Marion County, Texas, 1860-1870, by Lucille B. Bullard. Jefferson: N.p., 1965. v, 115 leaves.

Carpetbaggers, Scalawags, and Others, by Traylor Russell. [Waco: N.p., 1973.] x, 137 pp.

## Martin County

Pioneering on the Plains, History of Martin County, Texas, by Vernen Liles. Austin: Univ. of Texas, 1953. 269 pp. (M.A. thesis)

## Mason County

A History of Mason County, Texas, by Katherine Eilers. Austin: Univ. of Texas, 1939. 260 pp. (M.A. thesis)

A History of Mason County, Texas, by Katherine Eilers. Austin: Univ. of Texas, 1959. 261 pp. (M.A. thesis)

Mason and Mason County: a History, by Stella Polk. Austin: Pemberton Pr., 1966. 119 pp.

## Matagorda County

Historic Matagorda County, by Bay City Lions Club. Bay City: Tribune Pr. Co., 1947. 52 pp.

Miss Ella of the Deep South of Texas, by Arda Allen. San Antonio: Naylor Co. [1951]. x, 231 pp.

## Medina County

The History of Medina County, Texas, comp. by the Castro Colonies Heritage Association. Dallas: National ShareGraphics, 1983. 600 pp.

## Menard County

A History of Menard County, by Harvey H. Sutton. San Marcos: Southwest Texas State Univ., 1939. 84 pp. (M.A. thesis)

The Free State of Menard: a History of the County, comp. by N.H. Pierce. Menard: Menard News Pr., 1946. 213 pp.

## Midland County

Land of the High Sky, by John H. Griffin. Midland: First National Bank of Midland, 1959. 212 pp.

## Milam County

History of Milam County, 1893, in A History of Texas, *see* p. 365.

The Early History of Milam County, by Katherine B. Henderson. Austin: Univ. of Texas, 1924. 206 pp. (M.A. thesis)

The History of Milam County, by Margaret E. Langert. Austin: Univ. of Texas, 1949. 225 pp. (M.A. thesis)

History of Milam County, Texas, by Lelia McN. Batte. San Antonio: Naylor Co. [1956]. 257 pp.

## Mills County

A No Man's Land Becomes a County, by Flora Bowles. [Austin?: N.p., 1938.] 332 pp.

## Mitchell County

A History of Mitchell County, Texas, by Giles E. Bradford. Austin: Univ. of Texas, 1937. 170 pp. (M.A. thesis)

History of Mitchell County to 1900, by Omar W. Cline. Commerce: East Texas State Teachers Coll., 1948. 149 pp. (M.A. thesis)

## Montague County

History of Montague County . . . by Fannie C. Potter. Austin: E.L. Steck [1913]. viii, 191 pp. (Repr. Saint Jo: Ipta Pr., 1957. 184 pp.)

100 Years in Montague County, Texas, by Jeff S. Henderson. Saint Jo: Ipta Pr., 1958. 175 pp.

## Montgomery County

The History of Montgomery County, by Robin Montgomery. Austin: Jenkins Pub Co. [1975]. x, 333 pp.

Montgomery County History, 1981, comp. and ed. by Montgomery County Genealogical Society. Conroe: The Society, 1981. 633 pp.

## Moore County

The Windswept Land: a History of Moore County, Texas, by Myrna T. Thomas. Dumas: N.p., 1967. 163 pp.

## Motley County

The Early History of Motley County, by Harry H. Campbell. San Antonio: Naylor Co. [1958]. 74 pp. (2d ed. Wichita Falls: Nortex Offset Pub., 1971. iv, 74 pp.)

Of Such as These: a History of Motley County and Its Families, by Eleanor M. Traweek. Quanah: Nortex Pubs., 1973. 399 pp.

## Nacogdoches County

The Book of Nacogdoches County, Texas, by Nugent E. Brown. Houston: Author, 1927. 96 pp.

History and Description of Nacogdoches County, Texas, by Richard W. Haltom. Nacogdoches: News Pr., 1860. 73 pp. (Repr. Austin: Jenkins Pub. Co., 1972?)

## Navarro County

A Memorial and Biographical History of Navarro County, 1893, *see* p. 365.

History of Navarro, by Annie Carpenter Love. Dallas: Southwest Pr., 1933. 278 pp.

## Newton County

A History of Newton County, Texas, by Josephine C. Peary. Austin: Univ. of Texas, 1942. 123 pp. (M.A. thesis)

## Nolan County

History of Nolan County to 1900, by Lloyd Pyle. Commerce: East Texas State Teachers Coll., 1938. 192 pp.

Our Community: Organization and Development of Nolan County, Heritage of the Great Southwest, by Lelia J. Wade. Sweetwater: Watson-Focht Co., 1960. x, 87 pp.

# Nueces County

An American-Mexican Frontier, Nueces County, Texas, by Paul S. Taylor. Chapel Hill: Univ. of North Carolina Pr., 1934. xiii, 337 pp. (Repr. New York: Russell & Russell [1971]. xiii, 337 pp.)

Nueces Headwater Country; a Regional History, by Allan A. Stovall. San Antonio: Naylor Co. [1959]. 468 pp.

Pioneers on the Nueces, by Lena H. Crofford. San Antonio: Naylor Co. [1963]. xiii, 185 pp.

History of Nueces County, by the Nueces County Historical Society. Austin: Pemberton Pr., 1972. 224 pp.

# Ochiltree County

Wheatheart of the Plains: an Early History of Ochiltree County. N.p.: Texas Hist. Survey Comm., n.d. (Computerized index. Park City, Utah: Hamilton Computer Service, 1976. 43 pp.)

# Palo Pinto County

The Palo Pinto Story, by Mary W. Clarke. Fort Worth: Manney Co., 1956. 172 pp.

Gas as a Grig: Memories of a North Texas Girlhood, by Ellen M. Holland. Austin: Univ. of Texas Pr., 1963. x, 161 pp. (M.A. thesis)

# Panola County

History of Panola County . . . [by Mrs. V.D. Hooker]. Carthage: Circulating Book Club, 1935. 52 pp.

# Parker County

Historical Sketch of Parker County and Weatherford, Texas . . . by Henry Smythe. St. Louis, Mo.: L.C. Lavat, 1877. vii, 476 pp.

Parker County: History, 1895, *see* Tarrant County.

A New History of Parker County . . . by J.S. Grace and R.B. Jones. Weatherford: Democrat Pub. Co., 1906. 206 pp.

"The Double Log Cabin," being a Brief Symposium of the Early History of Parker County . . . comp. by G.A. Holland. [Weatherford:] N.p., 1931. 83 pp.

History of Parker County, and the Double Log Cabin . . . Weatherford: Herald Pub. Co., 1937. 296 pp.

Panorama of the Past; 100 Years of Progress . . . [Weatherford: Parker County Centennial Assoc., 1956.] 44 pp.

## Parmer County

A History of Parmer County, Texas, by Parmer County Historical Society, ed. by Nelson Lewis. Vol. 1 (all pub.). Quanah: Nortes Pr., 1974. 377 pp.

## Pecos County

Pecos County, Its History, by O.W. Williams. N.p., 1908. 96 pp.

## Polk County

The History of Polk County, by Emma Haynes. [Livingston:] N.p., 1937. 160 pp.

## Potter County

Early Records of Potter County, by Della Key. Amarillo: Tyler-Berkley Co., 1961. 388 pp. (2d ed., *see* below.)

In the Cattle Country: a History of Potter County, 1887-1966, by Della Key. 2d ed. [Quanah-Wichita Falls: Nortex Offset Pubs., 1972.] vii, 356 pp.

## Presidio County

The History of Presidio County, by John E. Gregg. Austin: Univ. of Texas, 1933. 231 pp. (M.A. thesis)

Spirit of the Big Bend; Chronology of Presidio's Outstanding Dates, by Evelyn Davis and Thomas C. Davis. San Antonio: Naylor Co. [1948]. 59 pp.

## Rains County

Early Days in Texas and Rains County, by William O. Hebison. Emory: Leader Pr., 1917. 52 pp. (Repr. Garland: Lost & Found, 1977.)

## Randall County

A History of Randall County, by Charles B. McClure. Austin: Univ. of Texas, 1930. 156 pp. (M.A. thesis)

The Randall County Story from 1541 to 1910 . . . Hereford: Pioneer Book Pubs. [1969]. xiii, 360 pp.

## Reagan County

A History of Reagan County . . . 1925-1950, by George H. Rice. Alpine: Sul Ross State Coll., 1950. 122 pp. (M.A. thesis)

## Real County

A History of Real County, Texas, by Grace L. Lewis. Austin: Univ. of Texas, 1956. 191 pp. (M.A. thesis)

## Red River County

The History of Clarksville and Old Red River County, by Pat B. Clark. Dallas: Mathis, Van Nort & Co., 1937. 259 pp.

## Refugio County

Refugio, a Comprehensive History of Refugio County from Aboriginal Times to End of World War II, by Hobart Nuson. 2 vols. in 3. Rufugio: N.p., 1942-46. (Repr. 2 vols. Woodsboro: Rooke Foundation, 1953-56.)

Texas Coastal Bend: People and Places, by Alpha K. Wood. San Antonio: Naylor Co. [1971]. x, 156 pp.

## Robertson County

Historical Recollections of Robertson County, Texas . . . by Richard D. Parker, ed. by Nona C. Parker. Salado: Anson Jones Pr., 1955. 254 pp.

A History of Robertson County, Texas, by John W. Baker. [Waco: Texian Pr., 1970.] vii, 571 pp.

## Runnels County

Runnels Is My County, by Charlsie Poe. San Antonio: Naylor Co. [1970]. xvi, 266 pp.

## Rusk County

In Old Rusk County . . . by Myrtis Watkins and P. Watkins. Henderson: N.p., 1940. 54 pp.

The Realm of Rusk County, by Garland R. Farmer. Henderson: Henderson Times, 1951. ix, 223 pp.

A History of Rusk County, Texas, by Dorman H. Winfrey. Waco: Texian Pr., 1961. 179 pp.

## Sabine County

Memories of Sabine County, Texas, by Robert A. Gomer, comp. by Helen C. Schluter. [Center?:] N.p., 1967. 121 pp.

Sabine County Historical Sketches . . . by Edna McD. White and B.F. Tools. Beaumont: LaBelle Pr. Co. [1972]. 65, 91 pp.

## San Augustine County

Two Centuries in East Texas: a History of San Augustine County and Surrounding Territory from 1685 to the Present Time . . . by G.L. Crockett. Dallas: Southwest Pr. [1932]. xi, 372 pp.

## San Jacinto County

The History of San Jacinto County, 1870-1940, by Ruth Hansboro. Huntsville: Sam Houston State Teachers Coll., 1940. 135 pp. (M.A. thesis)

## San Saba County

The Call of the San Saba; a History of San Saba County, by Alma W. Hamrick. San Antonio: Naylor Co., 1941. x, 331 pp.

## Schleicher County

Schleicher County, or, Eighty Years of Development in Southwest Texas, ed. by R.D. Holt. Eldorado: Eldorado Success, 1930. iv, 110 pp.

## Scurry County

Saga of Scurry, by Kathryn Cotten. San Antonio: Naylor Co. [1957]. 165 pp.

## Shackelford County

Shackelford County Sketches, by Don H. Biggers. Albany: Albany News Office, 1908. 77 pp.

## Shelby County

Legends of the Pineys, by Joseph F. Combs. San Antonio: Naylor Co. [1965]. xi, 100 pp.

## Smith County

Smith County, Texas, Its Background and History in Ante-Bellum Days, by Adele Henderson. Austin: Univ. of Texas, 1926. 118 pp. (M.A. thesis)

A History of Tyler and Smith County, Texas, by Albert Woldert. San Antonio: Naylor Co. [1948]. xi, 165 pp.

## Somervell County

Sketch of the History of Somervell County, 1895, *see* Hood County.

## Stephens County

A History of Stephens County, Texas, by L.W. Hartsfield. Austin: Univ. of Texas, 1929. 271 pp. (M.A. thesis)

Settlers of Stephens County, Texas, comp. by Adelle W. Olney. [Denver City: Three D Illustrators], 1974. 439 pp.

Doodle Bugs and Cactus Berries: a Historical Sketch of Stephens County, by Betty E. Hanna. N.p.: Nortex Pr. [1975]. ix, 144 pp.

## Sterling County

Milling Around Sterling County, a History of Sterling County, ed. by Beverly Daniels. Sterling: Sterling County Hist. Comm., 1976. 382 pp. (2d pr., 1980.)

## Stonewall County

History of Stonewall County, Texas, by George D. Railsback. Abilene: Hardin-Simmons Univ., 1940. 106 pp. (M.A. thesis)

The History of Stonewall County, Texas, by Jerome R. Whitmire. Lubbock: Texas Technical Coll., 1936. 156 pp. (M.A. thesis)

History of Stonewall County, by Willard L. Dent. Commerce: East Texas State Teachers Coll., 1949. 129 pp.

## Tarrant County

History of Texas, Together with a Biographical History of Tarrant and Parker Counties. Chicago: Lewis Pub. Co., 1895. 658 pp.

Reminiscences of the Early Days in Tarrant County, by J.C. Terrell. Fort Worth: Texas Pr. Co., 1906. 101 pp.

History of Tarrant County and the Texas Northwest, by B.B. Paddock. 4 vols. Chicago: Lewis Pub. Co., 1922.

Early History of Tarrant County, by George W. Sergeant. Austin: Univ. of Texas, 1953. 192 pp. (M.A. thesis)

## Taylor County

A Short History of Taylor County, by Emmett Landers. Abilene: Hardin-Simmons Univ., n.d. (M.A. thesis)

## Terry County

History of Terry County, by O.S. Buckner. Lubbock: Texas Technical Coll., 1943. 120 pp. (M.A. thesis)

Early Settlers of Terry: a History of Terry County, Texas, by Terry County Historical Survey Comm. Hereford: Pioneer Book Pubs. [1968]. 118 pp.

## Titus County

The History of Titus County Since 1860, by Norma C. Russell. Commerce: East Texas State Teachers Coll., 1937. 185 pp. (M.A. thesis)

History of Titus County, Texas, 1846-1960, by Richard L. Jurney. Dallas: Royal Pub. Co. [1961]. 193 pp. (M.A. thesis)

History of Titus County, Texas . . . by Traylor Russell. 2 vols. Waco: W.M. Morrison [1965-66].

## Travis County

History of . . . Travis County, 1893, in A History of Texas, *see* p. 365.

A History of Travis County, 1832-65, by Aloise Hardy. Austin: Univ. of Texas, 1938. 256 pp. (M.A. thesis)

History of Travis County and Austin, by Mary Barkley, 1839-1899. [Austin: N.p., 1963.] vii, 388 pp. (2d ed. [Austin: Steck Co., 1967.])

## Trinity County

The History of Trinity County, by Flora G. Bowles. Austin: Univ. of Texas, 1928. 138 pp. (M.A. thesis)

## Upshur County

A Brief History of Upshur County, by G.H. Baird. [Gilmer: Gilmer Mirror, 1946.] 76 pp.

A History of Upshur County, Texas, by Doyal T. Loyd, ed. by Sarah Greene. [Gilmer?: N.p., 1966.] v, 136 pp.

## Upton County

On the Last Frontier; a History of Upton County, Texas, by N. Ethie Eagleton. [El Paso:] Texas Western Pr., Univ. of Texas at El Paso, 1971. xi, 125 pp.

## Uvalde County

The History of Uvalde County, by Lois M. Carmichael. San Marcos: Southwest Texas State Coll., 1944. 89 pp. (M.A. thesis)

## Van Zandt County

Some History of Van Zandt County, by Wentworth Manning. Vol. 1 (all pub.). Des Moines, Iowa: Homestead Co. [1919]. 220 pp.

History of Van Zandt County, by William S. Mills. [Canton?: N.p., 1950.] 237 pp.

A History of Van Zandt County, by Margaret E. Hall. Austin: Pemberton Pr., 1976. 156 pp.

The History of Van Zandt County, Texas, comp. by the Van Zandt County Genealogical Society. Dallas: National ShareGraphics, 1984. 568 pp.

## Victoria County

Some Historical Facts in Regard to the Settlement of Victoria, Texas . . . by Victor M. Rose. Loredo: Daily Times Pr., 1883. 216 pp. (Also, *see* below.)

Pictorial History of Victoria and Victoria County, "Where the History of Texas Began," by Leopold Morris. [San Antonio?: Clemens Pr. Co., 1953.] 104 pp.

*Victoria County (cont.)*

A republishing of the book most often known as Victor Rose's History of Victoria, ed. by J.W. Petty, Jr.; added corrective notes, by Kate S. O'Connor. Victoria: Book Mart, 1961. 249 pp. (Also, *see* above.)

300 Years in Victoria County, ed. by Roy Grimes. Victoria: Victoria Advocate Pub. Co. [1968]. 649 pp.

## Washington County

The History of Brenham and Washington County, by May A.W. Pennington. Houston: Standard Pr. & Lith. Co., 1915. 123 pp.

History of Washington County, by Charles F. Schmidt. San Antonio: Naylor Co. [1949]. xii, 146 pp.

The Blazing Story of Washington County, by Wilfred O. Dietrich. [Brenham: Banner Pr., 1950.] ix, 122 pp. (Rev. ed. [Wichita Falls: Nortex Offset Pubs., 1973.] 190 pp.)

Historic Homes of Washington County, 1821-1860, by Betty Plummer. [College Station?: N.p.], 1969. ix, 244 leaves. (New ed.? San Marcos: Rio Fresco Books [1971]. xi, 129 pp.)

## Webb County

A History of Webb County, by Hermelinda A. Murillo. San Marcos: Southwest Texas State Coll., 1941. 89 pp.

## Wharton County

The Book of Wharton County, Texas, by J.O. Graham. N.p., 1926. 234 pp.

A History of Wharton County, 1846-1961, by Annie L. Williams. Austin: N.p., 1964. 399 pp.

## Wheeler County

Memory Cups of Panhandle Pioneers, by Millie J. Porter. A Belated Attempt at Panhandle's History, with Special Emphasis on Wheeler County . . . Clarendon: Clarendon Pr., 1945. xv, 648 pp.

## Wichita County

The History of Wichita Falls, Including a History of the County, by Jonnie R. Morgan. N.p., 1931. 221 pp.

## Wilbarger County

Early-day History of Wilbarger County [by C.P. Ross and T.L. Rouse]. Vernon: Vernon Times, 1933. 208 pp.

A History of Wilbarger County, Texas, by Torrence B. Wilson. Austin: Univ. of Texas, 1938. 122 pp. (M.A. thesis)

## Williamson County

History of . . . Williamson County, 1893, in A History of Texas, *see* p. 365.

History of Williamson County, 1716-1870, by Walton Hinds. Georgetown: Southwestern Univ., 1928. 115 pp. (M.A. thesis)

Land of Good Water: Takachue Pouetsu; a Williamson County, Texas, History, by Clara S. Scarborough. Georgetown: Williamson County Sun Pubs., 1973. xiii, 530 pp.

## Winkler County

A History of Winkler County . . . by Wink Wednesday Study Club. Wink: Wink Bull., 1942. 52 pp.

## Wise County

Pioneer History of Wise County . . . by Cliff D. Cates. Decatur: N.p., 1907. 471 pp. (Repr. Decatur: Wise County Hist. Soc. & Wise County Hist. Survey Comm., R. Gregg, 1972. 471 pp.)

Centennial History of Wise County, 1853-1953, by Mary C. Moore. Dallas: Story Book Pr., 1953. 189 pp.

Wise County History: a Link with the Past, by Wise County Historical Survey Comm., ed. by Rosalie Gregg. 2 vols. Decatur: Wise County Hist. Survey Comm., 1975-83. xvi, 515, ix, 562 pp.

## Young County

Young County, Texas, by Carrie (Johnson) Crouch. Dallas: N.p., 1937. 339 pp. (Rev. ed. A History of Young County, Texas. Austin: Texas State Hist. Assoc., 1956. xiv, 326 pp.)

## Zapata County

The Kingdom of Zapata, by Virgil N. Lott and M. Martinez. San Antonio: Naylor Co. [1953]. 254 pp.

## Zavala County

History of Zavala County, Texas, by R.C. Tate. Washington, D.C.: Government Pr. Office, 1940. 103 pp.

# UTAH

## Regional

Tullidge's Histories. Vol. 2, Containing the History of All the Northern and Western Counties of Utah, Also the Counties of Southern Idaho . . . by Edward W. Tullidge. Salt Lake City: Pr. of the Juvenile Instructor, 1889. vi, 372 pp. (Oneida and Bear Lake Counties, Idaho; Cache, Box Elder, Summit, Tooele, Davis, Morgan and Wasatch Counties, Utah.) [Vol. 1, The History of Salt Lake City.]

## Beaver County

Monuments to Courage, a History of Beaver County, ed. by Aird G. Merkley. Arranged and pub. by Daughters of Utah Pioneers, Beaver County. [Beaver?: Milford News, 1948.] 367 pp.

## Box Elder County

History of Box Elder County, 1889, in Tullidge's Histories, *see* above.

History of Box Elder County, comp. by Lydia W. Forsgren. Daughters of Utah Pioneers. [Salt Lake City: N.p., 1937.] 390 pp. (Superior index. Park City: Hamilton Computer Service, 1979. 41 pp.)

Box Elder Lore of the Nineteenth Century. Brigham City: Sons of Utah Pioneers, Box Elder Chapter, 1951. 169 pp.

## Cache County

History of . . . Cache County, 1889, in Tullidge's Histories, *see* above.

History of Cache County, ed. by Laveta Wallace. [Logan?:] Utah State Agricultural College Lib., 1955. 132 pp.

History of a Valley, Cache Valley, Utah — Idaho, ed. by Joel E. Ricks, E.L. Cooley. Logan: Utah Centennial Comm., Cache Valley, 1956. xvi, 504 pp.

Bridgerland: Your Land and Mine, by J.A. Christenson. Providence, R.I.: Keith Watkins & Sons, 1976. xii, 210 pp.

## Carbon County

Centennial Echoes from Carbon County, comp. by T.J. Reynolds. Daughters of Utah Pioneers. Price: N.p., 1948.

Castle Country: a History of Carbon County, by Richard G. Robinson. N.p. [1973]. iv, 140 pp.

Carbon County: Eastern Utah's Industrialized Island, by Philip R. Notarianni. Salt Lake City: Utah State Hist. Soc., 1981. x, 174 pp.

## Daggett County

Our Strip of Land: a History of Daggett County, Utah, by Dick Dunham and Vivian Dunham. [Lusk, Wyo.: Lusk Herald, 1947.] 113 pp. (And see below.)

Flaming Gorge Country, by Dick and Vivian Dunham. Denver, Colo.: Eastwood Pr. & Pub. Co., 1977. 384 pp. (Originally Our Strip of Land [see above].)

## Davis County

History of Davis County, 1889, in Tullidge's Histories, *see* p. 395.

East of Antelope Island, ed. by Annie C. Carr. Daughters of Utah Pioneers, Davis Company. N.p. [1948]. 519 pp. (2d ed. [Bountiful?: N.p., 1961.] 519 pp.; 3d ed. [Bountiful?: N.p., 1969.] 536 pp.; 4th ed. Salt Lake City: Pub. Pr., 1971.)

History of South Davis County, by William Robb Purrington. N.p., 1959. (M.A. thesis)

## Duchesne County

Early History of Duchesne, comp. by Mildred M. Dillman. Daughters of Utah Pioneers, Duchesne Company. Springville: Art City Pub. Co., 1948. 548 pp.

## Emery County

History of . . . Emery County, 1898, *see* Sanpete County.

"Castle Valley," a History of Emery County, comp. by Mrs. Stella McElprang. Daughters of Utah Pioneers. [Salt Lake City: D.U.P., 1949.] 343 pp.

Early Exploration and Early Settlement of Emery County, by Lawrence A. Mauerman. Salt Lake City: Univ. of Utah, 1967. v, 56 pp. (M.A. thesis)

Emery County; Reflections of Its Past and Future, ed. by Allan K. Powell. Salt Lake City: Utah State Hist. Soc., 1979. x, 134 pp.

Emery County—1880-1980, by the Emery County Historical Society. [Castle Dale?: The Society, 1981.] 801 pp.

## Garfield County

Golden Nuggets of Pioneer Days: a History of Garfield County, prepared by Ida Chidester and E. Bruhn. Daughters of Utah Pioneers, Garfield Company. [Panguitch?: Garfield County News, 1949.] 374 pp.

## Grand County

"Grand Memories," comp. by Phyllis Cortes. Daughters of Utah Pioneers. Salt Lake City: Utah Pr. Co., 1972. 321 pp.

## Iron County

History of Iron County, Mission and Parowan, the Mother Town, comp. by Mrs. Luella A. Dalton. [Parowan?: N.p., 1963?] 474 pp.

## Juab County

History of Juab County, a History Prepared for the Centennial of the Coming of the Pioneers to Utah, 1847-1947, by Alice P. McCune. [Nephi?:] Juab Company of the Daughters of Utah Pioneers, 1947. 301 pp.

## Kane County

History of Kane County, by Elsie C. Carroll. Daughters of Utah Pioneers. Salt Lake City: Utah Pr. Co., 1960. xxiv, 472 pp. (Rev. ed., comp. by Adonie F. Robinson. Salt Lake City: Kane Company, D.U.P., 1970.)

## Millard County

Milestones of Millard: a Century of History of Millard County, by Daughters of Utah Pioneers. Springville: Art City Pub. Co., 1951. xvi, 806 pp.

## Morgan County

History of . . . Morgan County, 1889, in Tullidge's Histories, *see* p. 395.

Mountains Conquered; the Story of Morgan . . . [Morgan: Morgan County News, 1959.] x, 355 pp.

## Rich County

Rich Memories; Some of the Happenings in Rich County from 1863 to 1960, comp. by Mildred H. Thompson. [Springville: Daughters of Utah Pioneers, Rich Company, 1962.] x, 325 pp.

## Salt Lake City

Tales of a Triumphant People; a History of Salt Lake County, 1847-1900, by Daughters of Utah Pioneers. Salt Lake City: Stevens & Wallace Pr., 1947.

## San Juan County

Saga of San Juan, by Cordelia A. Perkins, et al. Blanding: Daughters of Utah Pioneers, Mercury Pub. Co., 1957.

Hole-in-the-Rock; an Epic in the Colonization of the Great American West, by David E. Miller. Salt Lake City: Univ. of Utah Pr., 1959. xi, 229 pp. (2d ed. Salt Lake City: Univ. of Utah Pr., 1966. xiv, 229 pp.)

Indians and Outlaws; settling of the San Juan Frontier, by Albert R. Lyman. Salt Lake City: Bookcraft [1962]. 198 pp.

San Juan County, Utah: People, Resources, and History, ed. by Allan K. Powell. Salt Lake City: Utah State Hist. Soc., 1983. vii, 352 pp.

## Sanpete County

History of Sanpete and Emery Counties, Utah . . . Ogden: W.H. Lever, 1858. 681 pp.

*Sanpete County (cont.)*

These . . . Our Fathers, a Centennial History of Sanpete County, 1849-1947. Daughters of Utah Pioneers. Springville: Art City Pub. Co., 1947. 253 pp.

The Other Forty-Niners: a Topical History of Sanpete County, Utah, 1849-1983, ed. by Albert C.T. Antrei and R.D. Scow. Salt Lake City: Western Epics, 1982. xxii, 519 pp.

## Sevier County

Thru the Years: Sevier County Centennial History, comp. and ed. by Irvin L. Warnock. Springville: Art City Pub. Co., 1947. 470 pp.

Our Own Sevier: a Comprehensive Centennial Volume, Sevier County, Utah, 1865-1965; comp. and ed. by Irvin L. Warrick and L.D. Warrick. Richfield: Richfield Reaper, 1966. 496 pp.

## Summit County

History of . . . Summit County, 1889, in Tullidge's Histories, *see* p. 395.

Echoes of Yesterday: Summit County Centennial History, comp. by Marie N. Petersen. N.p.: Daughters of Utah Pioneers, 1947.

## Tooele County

History of . . . Tooele County, 1889, in Tullidge's Histories, *see* p. 395.

History of Tooele County. Daughters of Utah Pioneers. Salt Lake City: N.p., 1961. 668 pp.

## Uintah County

Builders of Uintah: a Centennial History of Uintah County, by Daughters of Utah Pioneers. Springville: Century City Pub. Co., 1947. (Repr., 1976.)

## Utah County

Memories That Live: Utah County Centennial History, comp. by Emma N. Huff, et al., and Daughters of Utah Pioneers. [Provo?:] N.p., 1947. 488 pp.

## Wasatch County

History of . . . Wasatch County, 1889, in Tullidge's Histories, *see* p. 395.

Under Wasatch Skies: a History of Wasatch County, 1858-1900, by Daughters of Utah Pioneers [& Leslie S. Raty]. Salt Lake City: Deseret News Pr., 1954.

A History of Wasatch County, 1859-1919, by Leslie S. Raty. Provo: Brigham Young Univ., 1954. (M.A. thesis)

How Beautiful Upon the Mountains; a Centennial History of Wasatch County, comp. and ed. by William J. Mortimer. N.p.: Wasatch County Chapter, Daughters of Utah Pioneers, 1963. xii, 1,198 pp.

## Washington County

An Early History of Utah's Dixie, by Hyrum L. Reid. Provo: Brigham Young Univ., 1931. 201 pp. (M.A. thesis)

Under Dixie Sun: a History of Washington County . . . by Nellie Jenson, ed. by Hazel Bradshaw. [Salt Lake City: Daughters of Utah Pioneers, Washington County Chapter, 1950.] 438 pp. (New ed., with suppl., 1978.)

I Was Called to Dixie, the Virgin River Basin . . . by Andrew E. Larson. Salt Lake City: Deseret News Pr., 1961. 681 pp.

## Wayne County

Rainbow Views: a History of Wayne County, comp. by Ann Snow and Daughters of Utah Pioneers. Springville: Art City Pub. Co., 1953.

## Weber County

Beneath Ben Lomond's Peak, a History of Weber County, 1824-1900, by Milton R. Hunter. Salt Lake City: Deseret News Pr., 1944. xxiv, 606 pp. (2d ed. 1945. 606 pp.)

# VERMONT

## Regional

Successful Vermonters; a Modern Gazetteer of Caledonia, Essex and Orleans Counties, Containing an Historical Review . . . by William H. Jeffrey. East Burke: Historical Pub. Co., 1904. xii, 361, 158, 274 pp.

Successful Vermonters: a Modern Gazetteer of Lamoille, Franklin and Grand Isle Counties, Containing an Historical Review . . . by William H. Jeffrey. East Burke: Historical Pub. Co., 1907. 479 pp.

## Addison County

Statistical and Historical Account of the County of Addison . . . by Samuel Swift. Middlebury: A.H. Copeland, 1859. 132 pp.

Addison County, by Abby M. Hemenway. Ludlow: Hemenway [1860]. 128 pp. [Vermont Quarterly Gazetteer, no. 1, 1860.]

Gazetteer and Business Directory of Addison County, Vt., for 1881-82, comp. and pub. by Hamilton Child. Syracuse, N.Y.: Journal Office, 1882. 541 pp.

History of Addison County, Vermont . . . ed. by Henry P. Smith. Syracuse, N.Y.: D. Mason, 1886. 774, lxii pp.

## Bennington County

Bennington County, ed. by Abby M. Hemenway. Ludlow: Hemenway [1861]. 140 pp. [Vermont Quarterly Gazetteer, nos. 2-3, 1861-62.]

Gazetteer and Business Directory of Bennington County, Vermont, for 1880-81 . . . comp. by Hamilton Child. Syracuse, N.Y.: Journal Office, 1880. 409 pp.

History of Bennington County, Vermont . . . ed. by Lewis C. Aldrich. Syracuse, N.Y.: D. Mason, 1889. 584 pp.

## Caledonia County

Caledonia County, by Abby M. Hemenway. Ludlow: Hemenway [1862]. 192 pp. [Vermont Quarterly Gazetteer, nos. 3-4, 1862.]

Gazetteer of Caledonia and Essex Counties, Vermont, 1764-1887 . . . also Business Directory . . . 1887-88, comp. by Hamilton Child. 2 parts. Syracuse, N.Y.: Syracuse Journal Co., 1887. 492, 289 pp.

Gazetteer of Caledonia County, 1904, in Successful Vermonters . . . *see* above.

## Chittenden County

Chittenden County, by Abby M. Hemenway. Ludlow: Hemenway [1863]. 164 pp. [Vermont Quarterly Gazetteer, nos. 5-6, 1863.]

Gazetteer and Business Directory of Chittenden County, Vermont, for 1882-83, comp. and pub. by Hamilton Child. Syracuse, N.Y.: Journal Office, 1882. 584 pp.

History of Chittenden County . . . ed. by William S. Rann. Syracuse, N.Y.: D. Mason, 1886. 867 pp.

Look Around Chittenden County, Vermont, ed. by Lillian B. Carlisle. Burlington: Chittenden County Hist. Soc., 1976. 494 pp.

## Essex County

Gazetteer of . . . Essex County, 1887, *see* Caledonia County.

Memorial Sketches, Written of Many Friends by George N. Dale. comp. by Porter H. Dale. Island Pond: Essex County Herald Pr., 1903. 384 pp.

Gazetteer of . . . Essex County, 1904, in Successful Vermonters . . . *see* p. 400.

## Franklin County

Gazetteer and Business Directory of Franklin and Grand Isle Counties, Vt., for 1882-83, comp. by Hamilton Child. Syracuse, N.Y.: Journal Office, 1883. 612 pp.

History of Franklin and Grand Isle Counties, Vermont . . . ed. by Lewis C. Aldrich. Syracuse, N.Y.: D. Mason, 1891. 821 pp.

Gazetteer of . . . Franklin County, 1907, in Successful Vermonters . . . *see* p. 400.

## Grand Isle County

Gazetteer and Business Directory of . . . Grand Isle County, 1882-83, *see* Franklin County.

History of . . . Grand Isle County, 1891, *see* Franklin County.

Gazetteer of . . . Grand Isle County, 1907, in Successful Vermonters . . . *see* p. 400.

## Lamoille County

Gazetteer and Business Directory of Lamoille and Orleans Counties, Vermont, for 1883-84, comp. by Hamilton Child. Syracuse, N.Y.: Journal Office, 1883. 658 pp.

Gazetteer of . . . Lamoille County, 1907, in Successful Vermonters . . . *see* p. 400.

## Orange County

Gazetteer of Orange County, Vermont, 1762-1888 . . . and Business Directory . . . comp. by Hamilton Child. 2 parts. Syracuse, N.Y.: Journal Office, 1888.

## Orleans County

Gazetteer and Business Directory . . . of Orleans . . . comp. by Hamilton Child, 1883, *see* Lamoille County.

Gazetteer of . . . Orleans County, 1904, in Successful Vermonters . . . *see* p. 400.

## Rutland County

Gazetteer and Business Directory of Rutland County, Vermont, for 1881-82 . . . comp. by Hamilton Child. Syracuse, N.Y.: Journal Office, 1881. 643 pp.

The History of Rutland County . . . by Abby M. Hemenway. White River Junction: White River Paper Co., 1882. 843 pp. [Vermont Historical Gazetteer, Vol. 3.]

Rutland County Historical Society. 1781. Rutland County. 1881. Centennial Celebration of the Organization of Rutland County . . . comp. by Lyman W. Redington. Montpelier: Argus and Patriot Book Pr., 1882. 196 pp.

History of Rutland County . . . ed. by H.P. Smith and W.S. Rann. Syracuse, N.Y.: D. Mason, 1886. 959 pp.

## Washington County

The History of Washington County, in the Vermont Historical Gazetteer . . . collated and pub. by Abby M. Hemenway. Montpelier: Vermont Watchman and State Journal Pr., 1882. 932 pp.

Gazetteer of Washington County, Vermont, 1783-1889, comp. by Hamilton Child, ed. by William Adams. Syracuse, N.Y.: Syracuse Journal Co., 1889. 544, 280 pp.

## Windham County

Gazetteer and Business Directory of Windham County, Vermont, 1724-1884 . . . comp. by Hamilton Child. Syracuse, N.Y.: Journal Office, 1884. 624 pp.

## Windsor County

Gazetteer and Business Directory of Windsor County, Vermont, for 1883-84, comp. by Hamilton Child. Syracuse, N.Y.: Journal Office, 1884. 666 pp.

History of Windsor County . . . ed. by Lewis C. Aldrich and F.R. Holmes. Syracuse, N.Y.: D. Mason, 1891. 1,005 pp.

# VIRGINIA

## Regional

History of the Lower Shenandoah Valley Counties of Frederick [Va.], Berkeley [W. Va.], Jefferson [W. Va.] and Clarke [Va.], Their Early Settlement and Progress to the Present Time . . . ed. by J.E. Norris. Chicago: A. Warner, 1890. 812 pp. (Repr. with new index. Berryville: Virginia Book Co. [1972]. viii, 925 pp.)

Shenandoah Valley Pioneers and Their Descendants. A History of Frederick County, Virginia, from Its Formation in 1738 to 1908, comp. mainly from original records of Old Frederick County [Va.], now Hampshire [W. Va.], Berkeley [W. Va.], Shenandoah [Va.], Jefferson [W. Va.], Hardy [W. Va.], Clarke [Va.], Warren [Va.], Morgan [W. Va.], and Frederick [Va.], by Thomas K. Cartmell. Winchester: Eddy Pr. Corp., 1909. vii, 587 pp. (Repr. with new index. Berryville: Chesapeake Book Co., 1963. vii, 572 pp.)

## Accomack County

History of . . . Accomac County, 1951, *see* Northampton County.

## Albemarle County

Albemarle County in Virginia . . . by Rev. Edgar Woods. [Charlottesville: Michie Co., 1901.] iv, 412 pp. (Repr. Bridgewater: C.J. Carrier, 1932 and 1964. 412 pp. General index, comp. by Mrs. Anne B. Coddington and E.N. Dunlap. Philadelphia: Magee Pr., 1936. 27 pp.)

Historical Guide to Albemarle County . . . Charlottesville: Colonial Dames & D.A.R., 1924. 64 pp.

Ante-bellum Albemarle: Albemarle County, Historical Sketches, by Mary Rawlings. Charlottesville: Michie Co., 1925. 150 pp.

Beautiful and Historic Albemarle, by Emily E. St. Claire. N.p.: Appeals Pr., 1932. 115 pp.

Jefferson's Albemarle, a Guide to Albemarle County . . . comp. by Writers' Program of W.P.A. [Charlottesville: Jarmans], 1941. vi, 157 pp.

Albemarle: Jefferson's County, 1726-1976, by John H. Moore. Charlottesville: Univ. Pr. of Virginia for Albemarle County Hist. Soc., 1976. xi, 532 pp.

## Alexandria County, *see* Arlington County.

## Alleghany County

A Centennial History of Alleghany County, Virginia, by Oren F. Morton. Dayton: Roebush Co., 1923. 226 pp.

## Amherst County

Amherst and Bedford Counties. Hardesty's Historical and Geographical Encyclopedia. Richmond: Hardesty, 1884.

Amherst County, Virginia, in the Revolution . . . 1773-1782, by Lenora H. Sweeny. [Lynchburg:] N.p., 1951. xiii, 212 pp.

The Amherst County Story: a Virginia Saga . . . Madison Heights: Percy Pr., 1961. 126 pp.

## Appomattox County

The History of Appomattox, by Nathaniel R. Featherstone. N.p.: American Legion, Appomattox, 1948. 440 pp.

A History of Appomattox County, 1845-1965: Appomattox County, Past, Present, Future, by Vera S. Stanley. Appomattox: Times-Virginia [1965]. 92 pp.

## Arlington County

A Brief History of Alexandria County . . . by C.G. Boteler, et al. Falls Church: Newell Pr. Co. [1907]. 56 pp. (Alexandria County became Arlington County in 1920.)

A History of Arlington County, by Dorothy E. Lee. Richmond: Dietz Pr., 1946. xiii, 160 pp.

Arlington Heritage: Vignettes of a Virginia County, by Eleanor Lee (Reading) Templeman. [Arlington: N.p., 1959.] viii, 220 pp.

Arlington County, a History, by C.B. Rose, Jr. Baltimore: Port City Pr., 1976. 274 pp.

## Augusta County

History of Augusta County, by J. Lewis Peyton. Staunton: S.M. Yost, 1882. vii, 387, 7 pp. (2d ed., containing a rev. and enl. index, by Charles R. Carrier. Bridgewater, 1953. 428 pp.)

Annals of Augusta County . . . by Joseph A. Waddell. Richmond: W.E. Jones, 1886. vii, 374 pp. (New ed. Richmond: J.W. Randolph & English, 1888. vii, 460 pp. (Includes separate suppl., pp. 381-460, from 1726 to 1871.) 2d ed., rev. and enl. Staunton: C.R. Caldwell, 1902. x, 545 pp. (Repr. Bridgewater: C.J. Carrier & Co., 1958. Repr. Harrisonburg, 1979.)

Augusta County, Virginia, in the History of the United States, by Boutwell Dunlap. Frankfort: Kentucky State Hist. Soc., 1918. 73 pp. (First pub. in Register of the Kentucky Hist. Soc. (1918), pp. 77-145.)

## Bath County

Annals of Bath County, by Oren F. Morton. Staunton: McClure Co., 1917. vi, 208 pp. (Repr. Harrisonburg: Carrier & Co., 1978. 213 pp.)

## Bedford County

Bedford County, 1884, *see* Amherst County.

Historical Sketch of Bedford County, 1753-1907. [Lynchburg: J.P. Bell Co., 1907.] 121 pp.

The History of Bedford County; the Colorful 200-Year Record . . . Bicentennial ed., 1754-1954, by Lula E. Parker. [Bedford: Bedford Democrat, 1954.] 135 pp.

## Bland County

History of Bland County: Bland County Centennial Corporation. [Bland: The Corp., 1961.] 464 pp.

## Brunswick County

Brunswick Story; a History of Brunswick County, by Edith R. Bell and William L. Heartwell, Jr. [Lawrenceville: Brunswick Times-Gazette, 1957.] 76 pp.

Brunswick County, Virginia, 1720-1795, by Gary Neale, with material by Henry J. Mitchell, Jr. and W.M. Pritchett. Lawrenceville: Brunswick County Centennial Comm., 1975. x, 502 pp.

## Buchanan County

Looking Back One Hundred Years, a Brief Story of Buchanan County and Its People, by Hannibal A. Compton. Grundy: Buchanan Chamber of Commerce, 1958. 86, 6 pp. (Repr. Knightstown, Ind.: The Bookmark, 1979. 112 pp.)

## Buckingham County

A History of Buckingham County, by Eugene A. Maloney. Buckingham: Buckingham Centennial Comm., 1976. 119 pp.

## Campbell County

Campbell Chronicles and Family Sketches, Embracing the History of Campbell County, Virginia, 1782-1926, by Ruth H. Early. Lynchburg: J.P. Bell Co., 1927. xii, 554 pp. (Repr. Baltimore: Regional Pub. Co., 1978. xxiv, 554 pp.)

## Caroline County

A History of Caroline County, from Its Formation in 1727 to 1924 . . . by Marshall Wingfield. Richmond: Pr. of Trevvet Christian, 1924. xv, 528 pp. (Repr. Baltimore: Regional Pub. Co., 1975.)

*Caroline County (cont.)*

Colonial Caroline; a History of Carolina County, by Thomas E. Campbell. Richmond: Dietz Pr. [1954]. xvi, 561 pp.

## Charlotte County

Charlotte County, Virginia: Historical . . . comp. by J. Cullen Carrington. Richmond: Hermitage Pr., 1907. 142 pp.

Charlotte County, 1765-1815, by Catherine L. Knorr. [Pine Bluff, Ark.?:] N.p., 1951. 119 pp.

Charlotte County, Rich Indeed: a History from Prehistoric Times Through the Civil War, comp. by Timothy S. Allsworth. Charlotte Court House: Charlotte County Bd. of Supervisors, 1979. xviii, 588 pp.

## Chesterfield County

Chesterfield County, Virginia: Its History and Present Condition, by T. Bransford Cox. Richmond: Williams Pr. Co., 1907. 45 pp.

Chesterfield, an Old Virginia County, by Francis E. Lutz. Richmond: W. Byrd Co., 1954. xii, 385 pp.

Chesterfield County: a History, by Bettie W. Weaver. Richmond: Lewis Pr. Co., 1957. 64 pp. (Repr. Richmond: N.p., 1970. 95 pp.)

## Clarke County

History of . . . Clarke County, 1890, in History of the Lower Shenandoah Valley, *see* p. 403.

History of . . . Clarke County, 1909, in Shenandoah Valley Pioneers, *see* p. 403.

History of Clarke County, Virginia, and Its Connection with the War Between the States . . . by Thomas D. Gold. [Berryville: C.P. Hughes, 1914.] 337 pp. (Indexed ed. [Berryville: Chesapeake Book Co., 1962.])

Clarke County, a Daughter of Frederick; a History of Early Families and Homes, by Rose M.E. MacDonald. Berryville: Blue Ridge Pr., 1943. 75 pp.

Annals of Clarke County, Virginia. Old Homes, Families, Etcetera, of the Southern (South of U.S. Route 50) Section, by Stuart E. Brown, Jr. Berryville: Virginia Book Co., 1983. 425 pp.

## Culpeper County

Genealogical and Historical Notes on Culpeper County, Embracing a Rev. and Enl. Edition of Philip Slaughter's History of St. Mark's Parish, comp. by Raleigh T. Green. Culpeper: R.T. Green, 1900. (Repr. Baltimore: Southern Book Co., 1958. viii, 120, 160, xxvi pp. Reissued. Baltimore: Regional Pub. Co., 1983.)

*Culpeper County (cont.)*

Historic Culpeper. Culpeper: Culpeper Hist. Soc., 1972. 112 pp.

An 18th Century Prospective: Culpeper County, comp. and ed. by Mary S. Jones. Culpeper: Culpeper Hist. Soc., 1976. 150 pp. (Appendix, errata, and addenda. Culpeper: The Society, 1977. 22 pp.)

Culpeper: a Virginia County's History Through 1920, by Eugene M. Scheel. Culpeper: Culpeper Hist. Soc., 1982. 497 pp.

## Cumberland County

The Story of Cumberland County, by Garland E. Hopkins. Winchester: Author, 1942. 127 pp.

Crucible and Cornerstone — a History of Cumberland County, Virginia, by Michael K. Vaughan. Atlanta: Southern Regional Education Bd., 1969. 86 pp.

## Dickenson County

Meet Virginia's Baby: a Brief Pictorial History of Dickenson County, Virginia . . . 1880-1955, ed. by Elihu J. Sutherland. Clintwood: Dickenson Co. Diamond Jubilee Comm., 1955. 320 pp.

## Dinwiddie County

Dinwiddie County, comp. by W.P.A. [Richmond: Whittet & Shepperson, 1942.] 302 pp.

## Elizabeth City County

History of Hampton and Elizabeth City County, by Lyon G. Tyler. Hampton: Bd. of Supervisors, 1922. 56 pp.

The First Plantation; a History of Hampton and Elizabeth City County, 1607-1887, by Marion L. Starley. [Hampton: Houston Pr. and Pub. House], 1936. 95 pp.

## Essex County

Essex Sketches: an Appreciation, by Virginia Showell. Baltimore: Thomas & Evans Co., 1924. 85 pp.

The History of Essex County, Virginia, 1607-1692, by Pauline P. Warner and T.H. Warner. Dunnsville: Sentinel Pr., 1926. 51 pp.

Tidewater Tales, by William C. Garnett. Dunnsville: Tidewater Pub. Co. [1927]. 237 pp.

History of Old Rappahannock County, 1656-1692 . . . Including the Present Counties of Essex and Richmond . . . by Thomas H. Warner. Rappahannock: P.P. Warner, 1965. 222 pp.

## Fairfax County

Fairfax County, by Jean Geddes. Middleburgh: Denlingers, 1967. 126 pp.

Fairfax County in Virginia . . . 1742-1973. Fairfax: History Program, Office of Comprehensive Planning, 1974. viii, 177 pp.

Fairfax County, Virginia, a History, by Nan Netherton, et al. Fairfax: Fairfax County Bd. of Supervisors, 1978. xiv, 780 pp.

## Fauquier County

Fauquier During the Proprietorship; a Chronicle of the Colonization and Organization of a Northern Neck County, by Harry C. Groome. Richmond: Old Dominion Pr., 1927. 255 pp. (Repr. Baltimore: Regional Pub. Co., 1969.)

An Old Timer in Warrenton and Fauquier County, by Marie L. Evans, ed. by Charles F. Knox, Jr. Warrenton: Virginia Pub. [1955]. 188 pp.

Fauquier County, Virginia, 1759-1959. Warrenton: N.p. [1959]. 335 pp.

Life on a Virginia Farm; Stories and Recollections of Fauquier County, by Robert B. Herbert. [Warrenton: Fauquier Democrat, 1968.] 181 pp.

## Floyd County

Floyd County: a History of People and Places, by A.D. Wood. Willis: Floyd Co. Hist. Soc. [1923]. (Repr. St. Charles, W. Va.: J.D. Dietz, 1981.)

## Fluvanna County

Fluvanna County Sketchbook, by Virginia J. Snead. Richmond: Whittet & Shepperson, 1963. 111 pp.

## Franklin County

Historical Sketches of Franklin County, by Edward H. Davis. Raleigh, N.C.: Edwards & Broughton Co., 1948. 298 pp.

Franklin County; a History, by Marshall Wingfield. Berryville: Chesapeake Book Co., 1964. x, 309 pp.

Pioneer Families of Franklin County, by Marshall Wingfield. Berryville: Chesapeake Book Co., 1964. 373 pp.

## Frederick County

History of . . . County of Frederick, 1890, in History of Lower Shenandoah Valley, *see* p. 403.

History of Frederick County, 1909, in Shenandoah Valley Pioneers, *see* p. 403.

## Giles County

Giles County, by Robert C. Friend. Pearisburg: Giles County Chamber of Commerce, 1956. 46 pp.

*Giles County (cont.)*

Giles County, Virginia: History—Families, by Giles County Historical Society. N.p.: The Society, 1982. 440 pp.

## Gloucester County

Gloucester County, by Mary W. Gray. Richmond: Cottrell & Cooke, 1936. 243 pp.

Records of Colonial Gloucester County; a Collection of Abstracts from Original Documents . . . by Mrs. G.C. Mason. 2 vols. Newport News: Author, 1946-48.

Stories of Old Gloucester, by Caroline B. Sinclair. [Vienna:] McClure Pr. [1974]. xvi, 66 pp.

## Goochland County

The Story of Goochland, by Richard C. Wight. Richmond: Richmond Pr., 1938. 51 pp. (Enl. ed. Richmond: Richmond Pr., 1943. 76 pp. Repr. Richmond: Dietz Pr., 1973. 80 pp.)

Facets of Goochland County's History, by H.B. Agee. Richmond: Dietz Pr., 1962. 227 pp.

## Grayson County

Pioneer Settlers of Grayson County, Virginia, by Benjamin F. Nuckolls. Bristol, Tenn.: King Pr. Co., 1914. xv, 206 pp. (Repr. with new index, by Veronica Schofield. Baltimore: Genealogical Pub. Co., 1982. Repr. Sanford, N.C., 1979.)

## Greensville County

Historical and Biographical Sketches of Greensville County, Virginia, 1650-1967, ed. by Douglas S. Brown. Emporia: Riparian Woman's Club, 1968. xii, 439 pp.

## Halifax County

A History of Halifax County, by Wirt J. Carrington. Richmond: Appeals Pr., 1924. 525 pp. (Repr. Baltimore: Regional Pub. Co., 1975.)

History of Halifax, by Pocahontas W. Edmunds. 2 vols. N.p.: Edmunds [1977?].

## Hanover County

Hanover County; Its History and Legends, by Rosewell Page. [Richmond:] N.p., 1926. 157 pp.

Historical Hanover County, by Herald Progress. 4 parts in 1 vol. Ashland: N.p., 1938. (60th Anniversary. 4 parts in 1 vol. Ashland: N.p., 1941, repr. 1957, Hanover County, 1721-1971. 5 parts in 1 vol. Ashland: N.p., 1971.)

## Henrico County

Henrico County: a Hand-book, Embracing an Outline of Its History . . . Richmond: Whittet & Shepperson, 1893. 46 pp.

The County of Henrico; a History, by Pauline P. Warner. N.p., 1959. 66 pp.

The History of Henrico County, by Louis H. Manarin and C. Dowdey. Henrico County Bicentennial Commission. Charlottesville: Univ. Pr. of Virginia, 1984. 584 pp.

## Henry County

A History of Henry County . . . by Judith P.A. Hill. Martinsville: N.p., 1925. 332 pp. (Repr. Baltimore: Regional Pub. Co., 1983. 329 pp.)

History of Henry County, 1933, *see* Patrick County.

## Highland County

A History of Highland County, by Oren F. Morton. Monterey: Author [1911]. 419 pp. (Repr. with added index. Baltimore: Regional Pub. Co., 1979. 532 pp.)

A Handbook of Highland County [Va.] and a Supplement to Pendleton [W. Va.] and Highland History, by Oren F. Morton. Monterey: Highland Recorder, 1922. 109 pp.

## Isle of Wight County

Isle of Wight County, 1608-1907, by E.M. Morrison. [Norfolk?: N.p., 1907.] 72 pp.

Seventeenth Century Isle of Wight County . . . by John B. Boddie. Chicago: Chicago Law Pr. Co. [1938]. 756 pp. (Repr. Baltimore: Genealogical Pub. Co., 1980.)

## King and Queen County

King and Queen County, by Rev. Alfred Bagby. New York: Neale Pub. Co., 1908. 402 pp. (Repr. Baltimore: Regional Pub. Co., 1974.)

## King William County

Old King William County Homes and Families . . . by Peyton N. Clarke. Louisville, Ky.: J.P. Morton & Co., 1897. 211 pp.

King William County . . . by Elizabeth H. Ryland. Richmond: Dietz Pr., 1955. xiii, 137 pp.

## Loudoun County

History and Comprehensive Description of Loudoun County, Virginia, by James W. Head. [Washington, D.C.:] Park View Pr. [1908]. 186 pp.

*Loudoun County (cont.)*

Legends of Loudoun; an Account of the History and Homes of a Border County . . . by Harrison Williams. Richmond: Garrett & Massie [1938]. xv, 248 pp.

Loudoun County, Past and Present, ed. by Harriet B. Samuels. Princeton, N.J.: Graphics Arts Pr., 1940. 60 pp.

Loudoun Harvest: Faces and Places, Past and Present, in Loudoun County, Virginia: a Collection of Stories and Photographs . . . Leesburg: Carr Pr. and Pub. Co., 1973. 187 pp.

## Louisa County

History of Louisa County, by Malcolm H. Harris. Richmond: Dietz Pr., 1936. viii, 525 pp.

## Lunenburg County

The Old Free State; a Contribution to the History of Lunenburg County and Southside Virginia, by Landon C. Bell. 2 vols. Richmond: William Byrd Pr., 1927. 623, 644 pp. (Criticisms were pub. in a separate vol., 1928. 39 pp. Repr. 2 vols. in 1. Baltimore: Genealogical Pub. Co., 1974. 1,267 pp.)

## Madison County

A History of Madison County, Virginia, by Claude L. Yowell. Strasburg: Shenandoah Pub. House, 1926. 203 pp.

## Mecklenburg County

Land of the Roanoke: an Album of Mecklenburg County, by William B. Hill. Richmond: Whittet and Shepperson, 1957.

Life by the Roaring Roanoke; a History of Mecklenburg County, Virginia, by Susan L. Bracey. Mecklenburg: Mecklenburg County Bicentennial Comm., 1977. 571 pp.

## Montgomery County

The Montgomery County Story, 1776-1957, by Charles W. Crush. Christiansburg: Montgomery County, Jamestown Festival Comm., 1957.

Montgomery County, Virginia — Circa 1790, by Netti Schreiner-Yantis. [Springfield: Author, 1972.] 124 pp.

A Valley and Its People in Montgomery County, by R.L. Lucas. Blacksburg: Southern Pr. Co., 1973.

Sidelights in the Early History of Montgomery County, Virginia, by Patricia G. Johnson. Christiansburg: Author, 1975. 184 pp.

## Nansemond County

The History of Nansemond County, by Jos. B. Dunn. [Suffolk: N.p., 1907?] 71 pp.

History of Suffolk and Nansemond County, by A. Burton. Suffolk: Phelps Ideas, 1970.

## Nelson County

Colonial History of Nelson County, 1734-1807, by J.B. Coincom. N.p.: Amherst Pub. Co., n.d.

## Norfolk County

Historical and Descriptive Sketches of Norfolk and Vicinity, by William S. Forrest. Philadelphia: Lindsay & Blakiston, 1853. 496 pp.

History of Norfolk County, 1637-1900, by William H. Stewart. 1 vol. in 2. Chicago: Biographical Pub. Co., 1902. 1,042 pp.

## Northampton County

Virginia's Eastern Shore: a History of Northampton and Accomack Counties, by Ralph T. Whitelaw. 2 vols. Richmond: Virginia Hist. Soc., 1951. 1,511 pp. (Repr. Gloucester, Mass.: Peter Smith, 1968.)

## Nottoway County

Old Homes and Families in Nottoway, by William H. Turner. [Blackstone: Nottoway Pub. Co., 1932.] 115 pp. (New ed.? [Blackstone: Nottoway Pub. Co., 1950.] Index, comp. by R. Bolling Batte. Richmond: Virginia Gen. Soc. [1961].)

Nottoway County Founding and Development, by A.B. Cummins. Blackstone: Nottoway Pub. Co., 1970.

## Orange County

A History of Orange County, Virginia, from Its Formation in 1734 to . . . 1870 . . . by William W. Scott. Richmond: E. Waddey, 1907. 292 pp. (Repr. Baltimore: Regional Pub. Co., 1974. 292 pp.)

## Page County

A Short History of Page County, Virginia, by Harry M. Strickler. Richmond: Dietz Pr., 1952. xx, 442 pp.

## Patrick County

History of Patrick and Henry Counties, by Virginia G. Pedigo and Lewis G. Pedigo. Roanoke: Stone Pr. and Mfg. Co., 1933. viii, 400 pp. (Repr. Baltimore: Regional Pub. Co., 1977.)

## Pittsylvania County

The History of Pittsylvania County, Virginia, by Maud C. Clement. Lynchburg: J.P. Bell Co., 1929. ix, 340 pp. (Repr. Baltimore: Regional Pub. Co., 1981. ix, 340 pp.)

## Powhatan County

Powhatan: a Bicentennial History, by Richard T. Couture. Richmond: Dietz Pr., 1980. 579 pp.

## Prince Edward County

A History of Prince Edward County, Virginia, from Its Formation in 1753 to the Present . . . by Charles E. Burrell. Richmond: William Pr. Co., 1922. 408 pp.

History of Prince Edward County, Virginia, from Its Earliest Settlements . . . in 1754 to Its Bicentennial Year, by Herbert C. Bradshaw. Richmond: Dietz Pr. [1955]. xxii, 934 pp.

## Prince George County

The Prince George-Hopewell Story, by Earl Lutz. Richmond: William Byrd Pr., 1957. xxii, 314 pp.

## Prince William County

Landmarks of Old Prince William. Richmond: Old Dominion Pr., 1924. 724 pp. (Repr. Berryville: Chesapeake Book Co., 1964.)

History of Prince William County, by Annye B. Clark. [Manassas:] Prince William Co., Va. County School Bd. [1933]. 73 pp.

Prince William, the Story of Its People and Its Places, comp. by Writers' Program, W.P.A. [Richmond: Whittet & Shepperson], 1941. 261 pp.

## Pulaski County

Colonial Days in the Land That Became Pulaski County, by Conway H. Smith. Pulaski: Pulaski County Lib. Bd., 1975. xiii, 150 pp.

## Rappahannock County

History of Old Rappahannock County, 1656-1692, by Thomas H. Warner. Rappahannock: Warner, 1965. 22 pp. (Includes counties of Essex and Richmond.)

Rappahannock County, Virginia: a History: Fact, Fiction . . . and the Fairfax Story [1833-1979], by Elizabeth Johnson and C.E. Johnson, Jr. Sperryville: Authors, 1981. 440 pp.

## Richmond County

History of . . . County of Richmond, 1965, *see* Rappahannock County.

Richmond County, 1776-1976, by Elizabeth L. Ryland. Warsaw: N.p., 1976. 559 pp.

## Roanoke County

History of Roanoke County, Salem, Roanoke City, Virginia, 1734-1900 . . . ed. and comp. by William McCauley. Chicago: Biographical Co., 1902. 560 pp.

History of Roanoke County, by George S. Jack. [Roanoke: Stone], 1912. 255 pp.

Roanoke County Centennial ed., 1838-1938. Salem: Times-Register [1938].

Roanoke, Story of County and City, comp. by Writers' Program, W.P.A. [Roanoke: Stone Pr. and Mfg. Co.], 1942. 390 pp.

## Rockbridge County

A History of Rockbridge County, Virginia, by Oren F. Morton. Staunton: McClure Co., 1920. 574 pp. (Repr. Baltimore: Regional Pub. Co., 1980.)

Historical Significance of Rockbridge County, Virginia, by James W. McClung. Staunton: McClure Co., 1939. 276 pp.

Rockbridge County, Virginia; an Informal History, by Edmund P. Tompkins, ed. by Marshall W. Fishwick. Richmond: Whittet & Shepperson, 1952. 187 pp.

Rockbridge County, Virginia Note Book, comp. from an article by George W. Diehl, as pub. in the News-Gazette, Lexington, Virginia. Additional notes . . . comp. by A. Maxim Coppage. Concord, Calif.: Compiler, 1982. 235 pp.

## Rockingham County

Hardesty's Historical and Geographical Encyclopedia . . . Special Virginia ed. Rockingham County History, by R.A. Brock. New York: H.H. Hardesty, 1884. 430 pp.

A History of Rockingham County, by John W. Wayland. Dayton, Ohio: Roebush-Elkins Co., 1912. 466 pp. (3d pr. Harrisonburg: Carrier & Co., 1980. 673 pp.)

Virginia Valley Records; Genealogical and Historical Materials of Rockingham County, Virginia, and Related Regions . . . by John W. Wayland, et al. Strasburg: Shenandoah Pub. House, 1930. 491 pp. (Repr. Baltimore: Genealogical Pub. Co., 1978.)

## Russell County

Russell County, Virginia's Blue Grass Empire, by Dot C. Pratt. Bristol, Tenn.: King Pr. Co., 1968. xii, 156 pp.

## Scott County

History of Scott County, Virginia, by Robert M. Addington. [Kingsport, Tenn.:] Kingsport Pr., 1932. xiv, 364 pp. (Repr. Baltimore: Regional Pub. Co., 1977. Repr. Kingsport, Tenn.: Dart Crowe, 1979.)

## Shenandoah County

History of . . . Shenandoah County, 1909, in Shenandoah Valley Pioneers, *see* p. 403.

A History of Shenandoah County, Virginia, by John W. Wayland. Strasburg: Shenandoah Pub. House, 1927. 874 pp. (Repr. 2d ed. Baltimore: Regional Pub. Co., 1980.)

## Smyth County

Smyth County History and Traditions, by Goodridge Wilson. [Kingsport, Tenn.: Kingsport Pr., 1932.] xi, 397. (Repr. N.p.: Frank I. Detweiler, 1976. x, 408 pp.)

## Southampton County

Southampton County, by Thomas C. Parramore. Charlottesville: Univ. of Virginia Pr., for Southampton County Hist. Soc., 1978. ix, 283 pp.

## Spotsylvania County

A History of Early Spotsylvania, by James R. Mansfield. Orange: Green Pubs., 1977. xv, 294 pp.

Forgotten Companions: the First Settlers of Spotsylvania County and Fredericksburg Town, with Notes on Early Land Use, by Paula S. Felder. Fredericksburg: Hist. Pubs. of Fredericksburg, 1982. x, 257 pp.

## Stafford County

The Story of Stafford, by John T. Goolrich. N.p., 1939. (Repr. Concord, Calif.: N.p., 1976.)

Stafford County, Virginia, 1800-1850, comp. by A. Maxim Coppage and H.W. Tackitt. Concord, Calif.: Authors, 1980. (2d pr., 1982.)

## Surry County

Colonial Surry, by John B. Boddie. Richmond: Dietz Pr., 1948. xi, 249 pp. (Repr. Baltimore: Genealogical Pub. Co., 1974.)

## Sussex County

Sussex County, a Tale of Three Centuries, comp. by Writers' Program, W.P.A. [Richmond: Whittet & Shepperson], 1942. 324 pp.

## Tazewell County

History of the Settlement and Indian Wars of Tazewell County . . . by George W.L. Bickley. Cincinnati, Ohio: Morgan & Co., 1852. 267 pp.

History of Tazewell County and Southwest Virgina, 1748-1920, by William C. Pendleton. Richmond: W.C. Hill Pr. Co., 1920. xvi, 700 pp.

*Tazewell County (cont.)*

Annals of Tazewell County, from 1800 to 1922 . . . by John N. Harman, Sr. 2 vols. Richmond: W.C. Hill Pr. Co., 1922-25.

## Warren County

History of . . . Warren County, 1909, in Shenandoah Valley Pioneers, *see* p. 403.

Historical Sketches and Reminiscences of an Octogenarian, by Thomas L. Preston. Richmond: Author, 1900. 170 pp. (Sketches of Washington County.)

History of Southwest Virginia, 1746-1786, Washington County, 1777-1870, by Lewis P. Summers. Richmond: J.L. Hill Pr. Co., 1903. 921 pp. (Repr. Baltimore: Regional Pub. Co., 1979. 912 pp.)

## Westmoreland County

Westmoreland County, Virginia [1653-1912] . . . a Short Chapter . . . in Its History . . . comp. by T.R.B. Wright. Richmond: Whittet & Shepperson, 1912. 153, xi pp.

Westmoreland County, Virginia, 1653-1983, ed. by Walter B. Norris, Jr. Montross: Westmoreland Bd. of Supervisors, 1983. xii, 699 pp.

## Wise County

A Narrative History of Wise County, by Charles A. Johnston. Norton: Norton Pr., 1938. xvi, 416 pp.

The Story of Wise County, Virginia, by Luther F. Addington. [Wise:] Centennial Comm. and School Bd. of Wise County [1956]. 296 pp. (Repr. Norton: Norton Pr., 1975.)

## Wythe County

Hardesty's Historical and Geographical Encyclopedia . . . Wythe County. New York: H.H. Hardesty, 1884.

## York County

York County, comp. by Ura A. Bradshaw and V. Watkins. Hampton: N.p., 1957.

# WASHINGTON

## Regional

Historic Sketches of Walla Walla, Whitman, Columbia and Garfield Counties, Washington Territory . . . by Frank T. Gilbert. Portland, Oreg.: A.G. Walling Pr. House, 1882. 488, 66 pp.

An Illustrated History of the Big Bend Country, Embracing Lincoln, Douglas, Adams and Franklin Counties, State of Washington. Spokane: Western Hist. Pub. Co., 1904. xxiv, 1,024 pp. (Histories by Richard F. Steele, assisted by Arthur P. Rose.) (Repr.? [N.p., 1979.])

An Illustrated History of Southeastern Washington, Including Walla Walla, Columbia, Garfield and Asotin Counties, Washington. [Spokane:] Western Hist. Pub. Co., 1906. xxii, 874 pp.

Lyman's History of Old Walla Walla County, Embracing Walla Walla, Columbia, Garfield, and Asotin Counties, by William D. Lyman. 2 vols. Chicago: S.J. Clarke Pub. Co., 1918.

History of Yakima Valley, Washington, Comprising Yakima, Kittitas and Benton Counties, by William D. Lyman. 2 vols. Chicago: S.J. Clarke Pub. Co., 1919.

The Big Bend Country Heritage, by Raymond Thompson. 2 vols. Alderwood Manor: Author, 1975. (Includes Lincoln, Douglas, and Grant Counties.)

🌿     🌿     🌿

## Adams County

Illustrated History of . . . Adams County, 1904, in Illustrated History of the Big Bend Country, *see* above.

## Asotin County

An Illustrated History of . . . Asotin County, 1908, in Illustrated History of Southeastern Washington, *see* above.

History of . . . Asotin County, 1918, in Lyman's History of Old Walla Walla County, *see* above.

Historic Glimpses of Asotin County, Washington, by Judge Elgin V. Kuykendall. Clarkston: Clarkston Herald, 1954. 70 pp.

## Benton County

History of . . . Benton County, 1919, in History of Yakima Valley, *see* above.

## Chelan County

Illustrated History of . . . Chelan County, *see* Stevens County.

## Clallam County

Jimmy Come Lately, History of Clallam County . . . ed. by Jervis Russell. Port Angeles: Clallam County Hist. Soc., 1971. xxvi, 631 pp.

Dungeness, the Lure of the River; a Bicentennial History of the East End of Clallam County, ed. by Virginia Keeting. Port Angeles: Sequim Bicentennial Comm., 1976. 150 pp.

## Clark County

History of Clarke [*sic*] County, Washington Territory, by B.F. Alley. Portland, Oreg.: Washington Pub. Co., 1885. 399 pp.

## Columbia County

Historic Sketches of Columbia County, *see* p. 417.

An Illustrated History of . . . Columbia County, 1906, in Illustrated History of Southeastern Washington, *see* p. 417.

History of . . . Columbia County, 1918, in Lyman's History of Old Walla Walla County, *see* p. 417.

## Cowlitz County

Cowlitz County, 1854-1948, by Mrs. Charles H. Olson. Kelso: Univ. of Washington Pacific Northwest Coll., 1947. 96 pp.

## Douglas County

Illustrated History of . . . Douglas County, 1904, in Illustrated History of The Big Bend Country, *see* p. 417.

[History of Douglas County], 1975, in The Big Bend Country Heritage, *see* p. 417.

## Ferry County

A History of Ferry County, by Mrs. Van B. Putnam. N.p., n.d.

Illustrated History of Ferry County, 1904, *see* Stevens County.

## Franklin County

Illustrated History of . . . Franklin County, 1904, in Illustrated History of The Big Bend Country, *see* p. 417.

## Garfield County

Historic Sketches of . . . Garfield County, 1882, *see* p. 417.

An Illustrated History of . . . Garfield County, 1906, in Illustrated History of Southeastern Washington, *see* p. 417.

*Garfield County (cont.)*

History of . . . Garfield County, 1918, in Lyman's History of Old Walla Walla County, *see* p. 417.

## Grant County

[History of Grant County], 1975, in The Big Bend County Heritage, *see* p. 417.

## Gray's Harbor County

The River Pioneers; Early Days of Gray's Harbor, by Edwin Van Syckle. Seattle: Pacific Search Pr., 1982. 423 pp.

## Island County

Island County, a World Beater, by Ferdinand B. Hawes. Seattle: N.p., 1968. 55 pp.

## Jefferson County

With Pride in Heritage History of Jefferson County . . . Port Townsend: Jefferson County Hist. Soc., 1966. xii, 422 pp.

## King County

History and Progress of King County, Washington . . . [comp. by Henry C. Pigott]. [Seattle:] C.J. Hutchinson, 1916. 53 pp.

History of King County, Washington, by Clarence B. Bagley. 3 vols. Chicago: S.J. Clarke Pub. Co., 1929.

## Kitsap County

Kitsap County History, comp. by Kitsap County Historical Book Committee. Silverdale: Kitsap County Hist. Soc., 1977. 850 pp.

## Kittitas County

An Illustrated History of Kittitas County, 1904, *see* Klickitat County.

History of . . . Kittitas County, 1919, in History of Yakima Valley, *see* p. 417.

Ah Kittitas, by Edna M. Fleming. Yakima: Franklin Pr., 1969. 68 pp.

## Klickitat County

An Illustrated History of Klickitat, Yakima and Kittitas Counties . . . Chicago: Inter-State Pub. Co., 1904. xxiii, 941 pp.

Early Klickitat Valley Days, by Robert Ballou. [Goldendale: Goldendale Sentinel, 1938.] 496 pp. (Index to names and persons and subjects, comp. by Jean A. Smeltzer. Portland, Oreg.: N.p. [1972]. 16 pp.)

Early Days of Klickitat County. Skamania: Tahlkie Books, 1977. 279 pp.

## Lincoln County

Illustrated History of . . . Lincoln County, 1904, in Illustrated History of the Big Bend Country, *see* p. 417.

[History of Lincoln County], 1975, in The Big Bend Country Heritage, *see* p. 417.

## Mason County

History of Mason County, by Harry W. Deegan. Shelton: Author, 1960. 100 pp.

An Illustrated History of Mason County, Washington, by Susan C. Olsen and M. Randlett. Shelton: Mason County Senior Center, 1978. 99 pp.

## Okanogan County

Illustrated History of . . . Okanogan County, 1904, *see* Stevens County.

Early Okanogan History, by William C. Brown. Fairfield: Ye Galleon Pr., 1968. 27 pp.

## Pacific County

Our Pacific County, by Lewis R. Williams. Raymond: Raymond Herald, 1930. 104 pp.

Coast Country, by Lucile MacDonald. Portland, Oreg.: Binford & Mort, 1966. 184 pp.

## Pend Oreille County

Historic Sketches of Pend Oreille County, by Ruby L. Dinges. Newport: Miner Pr., 1930. 35 pp.

Pend Oreille Profiles, by Lee Taylor. Fairfield: Ye Galleon Pr., 1977. 334 pp.

## Pierce County

History of Pierce County, Washington, by William P. Bonney. 3 vols. Chicago: Pioneer Hist. Pub. Co., 1927. (Repr. Evansville, Ind.: Unigraphic, 1979.)

## San Juan County

Pig War Islands, by David Richardson. Eastsound: Orcas Pub. Co., 1971. 352 pp.

## Skagit County

Sebring's Skagit County Illustrated. Historical and Pictorial ed. of Skagit County, by H. Sebring. Mount Vernon: N.p., 1902. 38 pp.

An Illustrated History of Skagit and Snohomish Counties . . . Chicago: Inter-State Pub. Co., 1906. xxvii, 1,117 pp. (Repr. 2 vols. Evansville, Ind.: Unigraphic, 1980.)

*Skagit County (cont.)*

Chechacos All; the Pioneering of Skagit . . . ed. by Margaret Willis. [Mount Vernon: Skagit County Hist. Soc., 1973.] ix, 212 pp.

Skagit Settlers, Trials and Triumphs, 1890-1920, ed. by Margaret Willis. Mount Vernon: Skagit County Hist. Soc., 1975. 228 pp.

Skagit Memories, by Charles Dwelley. Mount Vernon: Skagit County Hist. Soc., 1979. 170 pp.

## Skamania County

Columbia River Gorge History, by Jim Attwell. 2 vols. Stevenson: Tahlkie Books, 1974.

## Snohomish County

Illustrated History of Snohomish County, 1906, *see* Skagit County.

A Text Book of Snohomish County, by Elmer E. Johnston. Everett: Tribune Job Pr., 1909. 54 pp.

Snohomish County, Washington, William Whitfield, supervising ed. 2 vols. Chicago: Pioneer Hist. Co., 1926. (Repr. 2 vols. Evansville, Ind.: Unigraphic, 1979.)

## Spokane County

An Illustrated History of Spokane County, State of Washington, by Rev. Jonathan Edwards. [San Francisco?:] W.H. Lever, 1900. xviii, 726 pp. (Repr. Spokane: Eastern Washington Gen. Soc., 1983.)

The Inland Empire of the Pacific Northwest, by George Fuller. Spokane: H.G. Lindermann, 1928.

History, Government and Resources of the Spokane Area, by Edmund T. Becher. 3d ed. Spokane: Spokane Pub. Schools [1965]. v, 182 pp.

Spokane Corona: Eras & Empires, by Edmund T. Becher. [Spokane: C.W. Hill, Pr., 1974.] vii, 319 pp.

## Stevens County

An Illustrated History of Stevens, Ferry, Okanogan and Chelan Counties, State of Washington. Spokane: Western Hist. Pub. Co., 1904. xxii, 867 pp.

The People's History of Stevens County, by Fred Bohm. Colville: N.p., 1983. 133 pp.

## Thurston County

History of Thurston County, Washington, by John C. Rathbun. Olympia: N.p., 1895. 131 pp.

*Thurston County (cont.)*

Early History of Thurston County, Washington . . . comp. and ed. by Georgiana Blankenship. Olymia: N.p., 1916. 392 pp.

## Wahkiakum County

Wahkiakum County, Washington, by Carlton E. Appelo. Deep River: Author, 1969. 40 pp.

## Walla Walla County

Historic Sketches of Walla Walla County, 1882, *see* p. 417.

An Illustrated History of Walla Walla County. [San Francisco?:] W.H. Lever, 1901. xiv, 510 pp.

An Illustrated History of Walla Walla County, 1906, in Illustrated History of Southeastern Washington, *see* p. 417.

History of . . . Walla Walla County, 1918, in Lyman's History of Old Walla Walla County, *see* p. 417.

The West as I Knew It. Walla Walla County, by Nesmith Ankeny. Lewiston: R.G. Bailey Pr. Co., 1953. 148 pp.

## Whatcom County

Whatcom County, by Lottie R. Roth. 2 vols. Chicago: Pioneer Hist. Pub., 1926.

The Fourth Corner; Highlights from the Early Northwest, by Lelah J. Edson. Bellingham: Whatcom Museum of Hist. and Art, 1951. 298 pp. (Repr., 1968.)

The Trail Through the Woods: History of Western Whatcom County, by Frances B. Todd. Baltimore: Gateway Pr., 1982. xi, 370 pp.

## Whitman County

Historic Sketches of Whitman County, 1882, *see* p. 417.

An Illustrated History of Whitman County. San Francisco, Calif.: Lever, 1901. 469 pp.

## Yakima County

An Illustrated History of Yakima County, 1904, *see* Klickitat County.

History of . . . Yakima County, 1919, in History of Yakima Valley, *see* p. 417.

Valley of the Strong: Stories of Yakima and Central Washington. History, by Joseph C. Brown. Yakima: West Coast Pub. Co., 1974. 111 pp.

They Know Our Valley, by Maurice Holland. Yakima: Author, 1975. 182 pp.

Remembering Yakima, by Those Who Were There. 5 vols. Yakima: Golden Wert Pub., 197?-1980.

# WEST VIRGINIA

## *Regional*

History of the Panhandle; being Historical Collections of the Counties of Ohio, Brooke, Marshall, and Hancock, West Virginia . . . by J.H. Newton, G.G. Nichols, and A.G. Sprankle. Wheeling: J.A. Caldwell, 1879. 450, xxx pp. (Repr. Evansville, Ind.: Unigraphic, 1973.)

Hardesty's Historical and Geographical Encyclopedia, Illustrated, Containing . . . Special History of Virginias [and] Outline Maps and Histories. Chicago: H.H. Hardesty, 1883-84.

> Greenbrier and Monroe Counties. 378, 35 pp.
> Braxton and Gilmer Counties. 397 pp.
> Harrison and Marion Counties. 349 pp.
> Jackson, Wirt, Calhoun Counties, 312, 35 pp.
> Lewis, Upshur, Barbour Counties. 376, 30 pp.
> Mason and Putnam Counties. 266, 34, 45 pp.
> Ritchie and Doddridge Counties. 391 pp.
> Tyler and Wetzel Counties. 337 pp.
> Roane, Calhoun, Jackson, Wirt Counties. 347 pp.

History of the Lower Shenandoah Valley Counties of Frederick [Va.], Berkeley [W. Va.], Jefferson [W. Va.] and Clarke [Va.], Their Early Settlement and Progress to the Present Time . . . ed. by J.E. Norris. Chicago: A. Warner, 1890. 812 pp. (Repr. with new index. Berryville, Va.: Virginia Book Co. [1972]. viii, 925 pp.)

Shenandoah Valley Pioneers and Their Descendants: a History of Frederick County, Virginia from Its Formation in 1738 to 1908, comp. mainly from original records of Old Frederick County, now Hampshire [W. Va.], Berkeley [W. Va.], Shenandoah [Va.], Jefferson [W. Va.], Hardy [W. Va.], Clarke [Va.], Warren [Va.], Morgan [W. Va.], and Frederick [Va.], by Thomas K. Cartmell. Winchester, Va.: Eddy Pr. Corp., 1909. vii, 587 pp. (Repr. with new index. Berryville, Va.: Chesapeake Book Co., 1963. 572 pp.)

West Virginia Heritage Encyclopedia, Supplemental Ser., repr. by Jim Comstock. 8 vols. Richwood: Comstock, 1973. (A repr. of many counties contained in Hardesty's Historical and Geographical Encyclopedia . . . 1883-84.) (The counties are listed below with reference: "In Hardesty's . . . Encyclopedia, and Comstock's repr., Vol. . . . ")

Vol. 1, pp. 1-54. West Virginia History.
1, pp. 55-112. Monroe County.
1, pp. 113-177. Putnam County.
1, pp. 178-239. Tyler County.
2, pp. 1-49. Doddridge County.
2, pp. 50-116. Marion County.
2, pp. 117-168. Upshur County.
2, pp. 169-244. Wetzel County.
3, pp. 1-35. Calhoun County.
3, pp. 36-59. Pocahontas County.
3, pp. 60-140. Braxton County.
3, pp. 141-243. Berkeley County.
4, pp. 1-63. Jackson County.
4, pp. 64-204. Kanawha County.

*Regional (cont.)*

| | |
|---|---|
| 4, pp. 205-244. Barbour County. | 6, pp. 109-164. Wirt County. |
| 5, pp. 1-149. Mercer County. | 6, pp. 165-243. Greenbrier County. |
| 5, pp. 150-193. Pleasants County. | 7, pp. 1-35. Gilmer County. |
| 5, pp. 194-242. Lewis County. | 7, pp. 36-88. Ritchie County. |
| 5, pp. 243-341. Roane County. | 7, pp. 89-148. Lincoln County. |
| 6, pp. 1-84. Harrison County. | 7, pp. 149-239. Wayne County. |
| 6, pp. 85-108. Cabell County. | 8, pp. 1-168. Wood County. |

History of Northern West Virginia Panhandle, Embracing Ohio, Marshall, Brooke and Hancock Counties, by Peter Boyd. 2 vols. Topeka, Kans.: Hist. Pub. Co., 1927.

🌿       🌿       🌿

## Barbour County

History of Barbour County, 1883, in Hardesty's . . . Encyclopedia, and Comstock's repr., Vol. 4, pp. 205-244, *see* pp. 423-424.

The History of Barbour County, from Its Earliest Exploration and Settlement to the Present Time . . . by Hu Maxwell. Morgantown: Acme Pub. Co. [1888]. 438 pp. ([New ed.?] Morgantown: Acme Pub. Co., 1899. 517 pp. Repr. Parsons: McClain Pr. Co., 1968.)

## Berkeley County

History of Berkeley County, 1883, in Hardesty's . . . Encyclopedia, and Comstock's repr., Vol. 3, pp. 141-243, *see* p. 423.

Aler's History of Martinsburg and Berkeley County, West Virginia . . . by F. Vernon Aler. Hagerstown, Md.: Author & Mail Pub. Co. [1888]. 452 pp.

History of . . . County of Berkeley, 1890, in History of the Lower Shenandoah Valley Counties, *see* p. 423.

History . . . of Berkeley County, 1909, in Shenandoah Valley Pioneers, *see* p. 423.

History of Berkeley County, West Virginia, by Willis F. Evans. Wheeling: N.p., 1928. 347 pp.

Chronicles of Old Berkeley, a Narrative History of a Virginia County from Its Beginnings to 1926, by Mable H. Gardiner. Durham, N.C.: Seeman Pr., 1938. ix, 323 pp.

Berkeley County, U.S.A.: a Bicentennial History of a Virginia and West Virginia County, 1772-1972, by William T. Doherty. Parsons: McClain Pr. Co., 1972. xviii, 428 pp.

## Braxton County

History of Braxton County, 1883, in Hardesty's . . . Encyclopedia, and Comstock's repr., Vol. 3, pp. 60-140, *see* p. 423.

*Braxton County (cont.)*

History of Braxton County and Central West Virginia, by John D. Sutton. Sutton: N.p., 1919. 458 pp. (Repr. Parsons: McClain Pr. Co., 1967.)

## Brooke County

History of . . . County of Brooke, 1879, in History of the Panhandle, *see* p. 423.

Brooke County, being a Record of Prominent Events Occurring in Brooke County, West Virginia from the Settlement of the County Until 1882 . . . by J.G. Jacob. Wellsburg: Herald Office, 1882. 193 pp.

History of . . . Brooke County, 1927, in History of Northern West Virginia Panhandle, *see* p. 424.

History of the Cross Creek and Harmon Creek Country, Brooke and Hancock Counties, West Virginia. Morgantown: West Virginia Univ., 1938. 100 leaves. (M.A. thesis)

A History of Brooke County, by Nancy L. Caldwell. Wellsburg: Brooke County Hist. Soc., 1975. 159 pp.

## Cabell County

History of Cabell County, 1884, in Hardesty's . . . Encyclopedia, and Comstock's repr., Vol. 6, pp. 85-108, *see* p. 424.

Cabell County Annals and Families, by George S. Wallace. Richmond, Va.: Garrett & Massie, 1935. xix, 589 pp.

## Calhoun County

History of Calhoun County, in Hardesty's . . . Encyclopedia, and Comstock's repr., Vol. 3, pp. 1-35, *see* p. 423.

Calhoun County Centennial, 1856-1956. Grantsville: Calhoun County Centennial Corp., 1956. 72 pp.

## Clay County

The History of Clay County, by Perry W. Woofter. [N.p., 195-?] 48 leaves. (Typescript)

## Doddridge County

History of Doddridge County, 1883, in Hardesty's . . . Encyclopedia, and Comstock's repr., Vol. 2, pp. 1-49, *see* p. 423.

The History of Doddridge County, West Virginia. West Union: Doddridge County Hist. Soc., 1979. 367 pp.

## Fayette County

History of Fayette County, West Virgina, by J.T. Peters and H.B. Carden. Charleston: Jarrett Pr. Co., 1926. 772 pp. (Repr. Parsons: McClain Pr. Co., 1972.)

Historical Notes on Fayette County, West Virgina, by Clarence S. Donnelly. [Oak Hill:] N.p., 1958. 178 pp.

A Portrait of Fayette County, by Robert M. Holliday. Oak Hill: Fayette Tribune, 1960. 340 pp.

## Gilmer County

History of Gilmer County, 1883, in Hardesty's . . . Encyclopedia, and Comstock's repr., Vol. 7, pp. 1-35, *see* p. 424.

Gilmer: the Birth of a County . . . comp. by Writers' Program, W.P.A. Charleston: West Virginia Writers' Project, 1940. 14 leaves.

## Grant County

History of Grant and Hardy Counties, West Virginia, by Elvin L. Judy. Charleston: Charleston Pr. Co. [1951]. vi, 466 pp. (Repr. Elkins: Caroline B. Wilson, 1983.)

## Greenbrier County

History of Greenbrier County, 1883, in Hardesty's . . . Encyclopedia, and Comstock's repr., Vol. 6, pp. 165-243, *see* p. 424.

Recollections of the Rev. John McElhenney, by His Granddaughter, Rose W. Fry. Richmond, Va.: Whittet & Shepperson, 1893. 291 pp.

History of Greenbrier County, by J.R. Cole. Lewisburg: N.p. [1917?]. 347 pp.

Greenbrier Pioneers and Their Homes, by Ruth W. Dayton. Charleston: West Virginia Pub. Co., 1942. 383 pp.

## Hampshire County

History of Hampshire County, West Virginia . . . by Hu Maxwell and H.L. Swisher. Morgantown: A.B. Boughner, 1897. 744 pp. (Repr. Parsons: McClain Pr. Co., 1972. 778 pp.)

History . . . of Hampshire County, 1909, in Shenandoah Valley Pioneers, *see* p. 423.

## Hancock County

History of . . . County of Hancock, 1879, in History of the Panhandle, *see* p. 423.

History of Hancock County, 1927, in History of Northern West Virginia Panhandle, *see* p. 424.

*Hancock County (cont.)*

History of Hancock County, 1938, *see* Brooke County.

History of Hancock County, Virginia and West Virginia, by Jack Welch. [Wheeling: Wheeling News Pr. & Litho Co., 1963.] 202 pp.

## Hardy County

History . . . of Hardy County, 1909, in Shenandoah Valley Pioneers, *see* p. 423.

History of Hardy County, 1951, *see* Grant County.

History of Hardy County of the Borderland, by Alvin E. Moore. Parsons: McClain Pr. Co., 1963. 303 pp.

## Harrison County

History of Clarksburg and Harrison County from Its Earliest Settlement to the Present Time. N.p., n.d. 123 pp. (Transcript of articles in Clarksburg Telegram, 1875-76.)

History of Harrison County, 1883, in Hardesty's . . . Encyclopedia and Comstock's repr., Vol. 6, pp. 1-84, *see* p. 424.

History of Harrison County, West Virginia, by Henry Haymond; from the Early Days of Northwestern Virginia to the Present. Morgantown: Acme Pub. Co. [1910]. 455 pp.

History of Harrison County, West Virginia, by Dorothy Davis, ed. by E. Sloan. Clarksburg: American Assoc. of Univ. Women, 1970. 986 pp.

## Jackson County

History of Jackson County, 1883-84, in Hardesty's . . . Encyclopedia, and Comstock's repr., Vol. 4, pp. 1-63, *see* p. 423.

Washington's Woods; a History of Ravenswood and Jackson County, West Virginia, by Dean W. Moore. Parsons: McClain Pr. Co., 1971. xiv, 389 pp.

Early History of Pioneer Days in Jackson County: a History of Jackson County Prior to 1900, by Delta Kappa Gamma Society. Marietta, Ohio: Conservco, 1976. 149 pp.

## Jefferson County

History of . . . County of Jefferson, 1890, in History of the Lower Shenandoah Valley Counties, *see* p. 423.

History . . . of Jefferson County, 1909, in Shenandoah Valley Pioneers, *see* p. 423.

A History of Jefferson County, West Virginia, by Millard K. Bushong. Charles Town: Jefferson Pub. Co., 1941. xviii, 438 pp.

Historic Jefferson County, by Millard K. Bushong. Boyce: Carr Pub. Co., 1972. xx, 604 pp.

## Kanawha County

History of Kanawha County, from . . . 1789 Until the Present Time . . . by George W. Atkinson. Charleston: West Virginia Journal Office, 1876. 338 pp.

History of Kanawha County, 1883, in Hardesty's . . . Encyclopedia, and Comstock's repr., Vol. 4, pp. 64-204, *see* p. 423.

History of Charleston and Kanawha County, West Virginia, and Representative Citizens, by W.S. Laidley. Chicago: Richmond-Arnold Pub. Co. [1911]. 1,021 pp.

## Lewis County

History of Lewis County, 1883, in Hardesty's . . . Encyclopedia, and Comstock's repr., Vol. 5, pp. 194-242, *see* p. 424.

A History of Lewis County, West Virginia, by Edward C. Smith. Weston: Author, 1920. 427 pp.

## Lincoln County

History of Lincoln County, 1884, in Hardesty's . . . Encyclopedia, and Comstock's repr., Vol. 7, pp. 89-148, *see* p. 424.

## Logan County

History of Logan County, West Virginia . . . by George T. Swain. Logan: G.T. Swain, 1927.

History of Logan County, by Henry C. Ragland, from the 1896 Files of the Logan Banner. Logan: Clarence H. Frey, 1949. 122 pp.

History of Logan and Mingo Counties, Beginning in 1617, by Nancy S. Smith. [Williamson?: N.p., 1966?] 70 pp.

1880 Logan County, West Virginia Families Old and New, comp. by David Turner and J. Hager. Madison: Turner, 1981. 197 pp.

## McDowell County

McDowell County Centennial, 1858-1958. [Welch?:] N.p., 1958. 94 pp.

McDowell County History . . . D.A.R., Colonel Andrews Donnally Chapter, Welch. Fort Worth, Tex.: Supply & Equipment Co., for the Chapter, 1959. 132 pp.

## Marion County

History and Progress of the County of Marion, West Virginia . . . by George A. Bunnington. Fairmont: Author, 1880. 162 pp.

History of Marion County, 1883, in Hardesty's . . . Encyclopedia, and Comstock's repr., Vol. 2, pp. 50-116, *see* p. 423.

*Marion County (cont.)*

Marion County in the Making, by the Class of the Fairmont High School, West Virginia. Fairmont: J.O. Watson, n.d., and [Baltimore: Meyer & Thalheimer, 1917.] 362 pp.

Now and Long Ago: a History of the Marion County Area [by Glenn D. Lough]. [Morgantown: Morgantown Pr. & Binding Co., 1969.] xix, 698 pp.

## Marshall County

History of . . . County of Marshall, 1879, in History of the Panhandle, *see* p. 423.

History of Marshall County . . . by Scott Powell. Moundsville: N.p., 1925. 334 pp.

History of Marshall County, 1927, in History of Northern West Virginia Panhandle, *see* p. 424.

## Mason County

History of Mason County, 1883, in Hardesty's . . . Encyclopedia, *see* p. 423.

History of Mason County, West Virginia, by Robert H. Ferguson. Mount Pleasant: N.p., 1961. 175 leaves.

## Mercer County

History of Mercer County, 1883, in Hardesty's . . . Encyclopedia, and Comstock's repr., Vol. 5, pp. 1-149, *see* p. 424.

The Story of Mercer County, by Kyle McCormick. [Charleston:] Charleston Pr. Co., 1957. 132 pp.

## Mineral County

Sesqui-centennial of Frankfort, Mineral County, West Virginia . . . [N.p.: Frankfort Sesqui-centennial Comm. and Mineral County Hist. Soc., 1938.] 80 pp.

## Mingo County

An Early History of Mingo County, West Virginia, by Nancy S. Smith. [Williamson?:] Williamson Pr. Co., 1960. 24 pp.

History of Mingo County, 1966, *see* Logan County

## Monongalia County

History of Monongalia County, West Virgina, from Its First Settlement to the Present Time . . . by Samuel T. Wiley. Kingwood: Preston Pub. Co., 1883. 776 pp.

Sesqui-centennial of Monongalia County, West Virginia . . . 1776-1926 . . . Morgantown: Monongalia Hist. Soc., & Charleston: Tribune Pr. Co. [1928]. 275 pp.

*Monongalia County (cont.)*

The 175th Anniversary of the Formation of Monongalia County, West Virginia . . . [Morgantown: Monongalia Hist. Soc., 1954.] ix, 454 pp.

## Monroe County

History of Monroe County, 1883, in Hardesty's . . . Encyclopedia, and Comstock's repr., Vol. 1, pp. 55-112, *see* p. 423.

A History of Monroe County, West Virginia, by Oren F. Morton. Staunton, Va.: McClure Co., 1916. 509 pp. (Repr. Baltimore: Regional Pub. Co., 1980.)

Gleanings of Monroe County, West Virginia History, by Charles B. Motley. Radford, Va.: Commonwealth Pr., 1973. 240 pp. (Repr.? 1983?)

## Morgan County

History of Morgan County, 1909, in Shenandoah Valley Pioneers, *see* p. 423.

Morgan County, West Virginia, and Its People. [Dallas, Tex.: Taylor Pub. Co., 1981.] 261 pp.

## Nicholas County

History of Nicholas County, West Virginia, by William G. Brown. Richmond, Va.: Dietz Pr., 1954. xxx, 425 pp.

## Ohio County

History of . . . County of Ohio, 1879, in History of the Panhandle, *see* p. 423.

History of Wheeling City and Ohio County, West Virginia, and Representative Citizens, ed. and comp. by Hon. Gibson L. Cranmer. 1776-1900. Chicago: Biographical Pub. Co., 1902. 853 pp.

History of . . . Ohio County, 1927, in History of Northern West Virginia Panhandle, *see* p. 424.

## Pendleton County

A History of Pendleton County, West Virginia, by Oren F. Morton. Franklin: Author, 1910. viii, 493 pp. (Repr. Baltimore: Regional Pub. Co., 1980.)

Handbook of Highland County [Virginia] and a Supplement to Pendleton and Highland History, by Oren F. Morton. Monterey, Va.: Highland Recorder, 1922. 109 pp.

## Pleasants County

History of Pleasants County, 1883, in Hardesty's . . . Encyclopedia, and Comstock's repr., Vol. 5, pp. 150-193, *see* p. 424.

A History of Pleasants County, West Virginia, by Robert L. Pemberton. St. Marys: Oracle Pr., 1929. 276 pp.

## Pocahontas County

History of Pocahontas County, 1883, in Hardesty's . . . Encyclopedia, and Comstock's repr., Vol. 3, pp. 36-59, *see* p. 423.

Historical Sketches of Pocahontas County, West Virginia, by William T. Price. Marlinton: Price Bros., 1901. 622 pp. (Repr. Parsons: McClain Pr. Co., 1963.)

## Preston County

History of Preston County, West Virginia, by Samuel T. Wiley. Kingwood: Journal Pr. House, 1882. xv, 529 pp. (Repr. Parsons: McClain Pr. Co., 1968. Index, by Harold F. Powell. Parsons: McClain Pr. Co., 1971. 66 pp.)

A History of Preston County, West Virginia, by Oren F. Morton. 2 vols. Kingwood: Journal Pub. Co., 1914. 885 pp.

Preston County, West Virginia, History. Kingwood: Preston County Hist. Soc., 1979. 514 pp.

## Putnam County

History of Putnam County, 1883, in Hardesty's . . . Encyclopedia, and Comstock's repr., Vol. 1, pp. 113-177, *see* p. 423.

The History of Putnam County, ed. by William D. Wintz and Ivan N. Hunter. Charleston: Upper Vandalia Hist. Soc., 1967. 55 pp.

## Raleigh County

Memoirs of Raleigh County, Historical and Biographical, comp. by Charles B. Hedrick. Beckley: Wood Pr. Co., 1932. 44 pp.

## Randolph County

The History of Randolph County, West Virginia, from Its Earliest Settlement to the Present . . . by Hu Maxwell. Morgantown: Acme Pub. Co., 1898. 531 pp.

A History of Randolph County, West Virginia, from Its Earliest Exploration to the Present Time . . . by A.S. Bosworth. [Elkins: N.p., 1916.] 448 pp. (Repr. Parsons: McClain Pr. Co., 1975. Repr. Beverly, Va.: Mrs. Owen Crickard, 1979. 448 pp.)

Randolph County Profile - 1976: a Handbook of the County, comp. and ed. by Anne D. Kek. Parsons: McClain Pr. Co., 1976. 162 pp.

## Ritchie County

History of Ritchie County, 1883, in Hardesty's . . . Encyclopedia, and Comstock's repr., Vol. 7, pp. 36-88, *see* p. 424.

History of Ritchie County . . . by Minnie K. Lowther. Wheeling: Wheeling News Litho. Co. [1911]. xvi, 681 pp. (Repr. [N.p.: Louise B. Summers, 1967.])

The History of Ritchie County, by Ritchie County Historical Society. [Harrisville?: N.p., 1980.]

## Roane County

History of Roane County, 1884, in Hardesty's . . . Encyclopedia, and Comstock's repr., Vol. 5, pp. 243-341, *see* p. 424.

History of Roane County, West Virginia, from the Time of Its Exploration to 1927, by William H. Bishop. Spencer: W.H. Bishop [1927]. 711 pp.

## Summers County

History of Summers County . . . by James H. Miller. [Hinton: N.p.], 1908. xv, 838 pp. (Index, by Maude V. Clark. [Chillicothe, Ohio?:] N.p., 1973? 44 leaves.

## Tucker County

History of Tucker County, West Virginia, from the Earliest Explorations and Settlements to the Present Time . . . by Hu Maxwell. Kingwood: Preston Pub. Co., 1884. 574 pp. (Repr. Parsons: McClain Pr. Co., 1971. 590 pp.)

History of Tucker County, West Virginia, by Homer F. Fansler. Parsons: McClain Pr. Co., 1962. 702 pp.

Blackwater Country, by John L. Smith. Parsons: McClain Pr. Co., 1972. 59 pp.

. . . and Live Forever: a Compilation of Senior Citizens Articles from the Parsons Advocate, comp. and ed. by M. McC. Smith. Parsons: McClain Pr. Co., 1974. xiv, 521 pp.

Roots in Tucker County, by Ruth C. Allman. Parsons: McClain Pr. Co., 1979. 144 pp.

## Tyler County

History of Tyler County, 1883, in Hardesty's . . . Encyclopedia, and Comstock's repr., Vol. 1, pp. 178-239, *see* p. 423.

## Upshur County

History of Upshur County, 1883, in Hardesty's . . . Encyclopedia, and Comstock's repr., Vol. 2, pp. 117-168, *see* p. 423.

The History of Upshur County, West Virginia, from Its Earliest Exploration and Settlement to the Present Time . . . by W.B. Cutright. [Buckhannon?: N.p., 1907?] xii, 607 pp. (Repr. with family history index, comp. by Hilda L. Sayre. Buckhannon: Upshur County Hist. Soc., 1977. 607, 123 pp.)

## Wayne County

History of Wayne County, 1884, in Hardesty's . . . Encyclopedia, and Comstock's repr., Vol. 7, pp. 149-239, *see* p. 424.

History of Wayne County, West Virginia, by Pearl A. Porter. [Huntington?:] N.p., 1944. 57 leaves.

## Webster County

Moccasin Tracks, and Other Imprints, by William C. Dodrill. [Charleston: Lovett Pr. Co., 1915.] 298 pp. (Sketches relating to pioneer history of Webster County.) (Repr. Parsons: McClain Pr. Co., 1974.)

Webster County History, by R.L. Thompson. Webster Springs: Star Pr., 1942. 200 pp.

Annals of Webster County, West Virginia, Before and Since Organization, 1860, by Sampson N. Miller. [Webster Springs: N.p., 1969.] xiii, 479 pp.

## Wetzel County

History of Wetzel County, 1883, in Hardesty's . . . Encyclopedia, and Comstock's repr., Vol. 2, pp. 169-244, *see* p. 423.

History of Wetzel County, West Virginia, by John C. McEldowney. [Wetzel?:] N.p., 1901. 183 pp. (Repr. New Martinsville: Wetzel County Gen. Soc., 1980. 120 pp.)

History of Wetzel County, West Virignia, 1983. [Marceline, Mo.: Walsworth Pub. Co., 1983.] 296 pp.

## Wirt County

History of Wirt County, 1883, in Hardesty's . . . Encyclopedia, and Comstock's repr., Vol. 6, pp. 109-164, *see* p. 424.

## Wood County

Sketches of Wood County: Its Early History . . . by Stephen C. Shaw. Part 1 (no more pub.). Parkersburg: G. Elletson, 1878. 65 pp. (Repr. Clarksburg: W.G. Tetrick [1932].)

History of Wood County, 1883, in Hardesty's . . . Encyclopedia, and Comstock's repr., Vol. 8, pp. 1-168, *see* p. 424.

Wood County Formation. A Century of Progress, History of Divisions . . . Past and Present . . . by Alvaro F. Gibbens. Morgantown: Acme Pr., 1899. 131 pp.

History of Wood County, West Virginia, by Donald F. Black. Marietta, Ohio: Richardson Pr. Co., 1975. 250 pp.

## Wyoming County

Reference Book of Wyoming County History, by Mary K. Bowman. Parsons: McClain Pr. Co., 1965. 492 pp. (Genealogical index and gazetteer, with corrections and additions to census section, by Agnes B. Pearlman. Santa Ana, Calif.: N.p., 1976. 108 pp.)

# WISCONSIN

## Regional

Historical and Biographical Album of the Chippewa Valley. Chicago: S.J. Clarke Pub. Co., 1891-92. (Index. Madison: Wisconsin State Gen. Soc., 1979. 66 pp.) (Includes Barron, Chippewa, Dunn, Eau Claire, Pepin and Price Counties.)

History of Northern Wisconsin. Chicago: S.J. Clarke Pub. Co., 1881. (Index, Madison: Wisconsin State Gen. Soc., 1981. 124 pp.)

History of the St. Croix Valley, by Augustus B. Easton. 2 vols. Chicago: S.J. Clarke Pub. Co., 1909. (Includes Burnett, Pierce, Polk and St. Croix Counties.)

Portrait and Biographical Album of Green Lake, Marquette and Waushara Counties, Wisconsin. Chicago: S.J. Clarke Pub. Co., 1890. (Index. Madison: Wisconsin State Gen. Soc., 1983.) (Primarily biographical volumes, but the three counties listed have histories.)

Southeastern Wisconsin: a History of Old Milwaukee County, ed. by John G. Gregory. 4 vols. Chicago: S.J. Clarke Pub. Co., 1932. (Index. Madison: Wisconsin State Gen. Soc., 1982. 63 pp.) (Includes Milwaukee, Racine Counties in Vol. 1; Kenosha, Rock, Jefferson, Walworth, Waukesha, Dodge, Washington, and Ozaukee Counties in Vol. 2.)

Southwestern Wisconsin: a History of Old Crawford County, ed. by John G. Gregory. 4 vols. Chicago: S.J. Clarke Pub. Co., 1932. (Index. Madison: Wisconsin State Gen. Soc., 1983. 59 pp.) (Includes Crawford, Iowa, Grant, and Green Counties in Vol. 1; Dane, Sauk, Richland, and Vernon in Vol. 2.)

## Ashland County

Souvenir of Ashland County, Wisconsin. Milwaukee: Stiles Co., 1904. (Unpaged)

## Barron County

The History of Barron County, Wisconsin, comp. by Franklyn Curtiss-Wedge, ed. by N.S. Gordon. Minneapolis: H.C. Copper, Jr. Co., 1922. 1,165 pp.

Historical and Biographical Album of Barron County, 1891-92, *see* above.

## Brown County

History of Brown County, Wisconsin, Past and Present, by Deborah B. Martin. 2 vols. Chicago: S.J. Clarke Pub. Co., 1913.

Birthplace of a Commonwealth: a Short History of Brown County, by Jack Rudolph. Green Bay: Brown County Hist. Soc., 1976. 96 pp.

## Buffalo County

History of Buffalo County, Wisconsin, by Lawrence Kessinger. Alma: N.p., 1888. xvi, 656 pp.

History of Buffalo and Pepin Counties, Wisconsin, by Franklyn Curtiss-Wedge. Winona, Minn.: N.p., 1919. 1,047 pp. (Index. Madison: Wisconsin State Gen. Soc., 1980. 71 pp.)

## Burnett County

History of . . . Burnett County, 1909, in History of the St. Croix Valley, *see* p. 434.

## Chippewa County

Historical and Biographical Album . . . of Chippewa County, 1891-92, *see* p. 434.

Chippewa County, Wisconsin, Past and Present . . . 2 vols. Chicago: S.J. Clarke Pub. Co., 1913. 924 pp.

## Clark County

Neillsville and Clark County, Wisconsin. (In The American Sketch Book, Vol. 1.) La Crosse: N.p., 1875.

Clark and Jackson Counties, Wisconsin Biographical History. Chicago: Lewis, 1891. 387 pp.

History of Clark County, Wisconsin, by Franklyn Curtiss-Wedge. Chicago: H.C. Cooper, Jr. Co., 1918. 748 pp.

The Book of the Years; the Story of the Men Who Made Clark County . . . Clark County Sesquicentennial, 1853-1953 . . . [Neillsville: N.p., 1953.] 96 pp.

## Columbia County

The History of Columbia County, Wisconsin . . . Chicago: Western Hist. Co., 1880. 1,095 pp.

The Family Trees of Columbia County, Wisconsin, by Andrew J. Turner. [Portage: Pr. of the Wisconsin State Register, 1904.] 142 pp.

A History of Columbia County, Wisconsin . . . comp. under ed. supervision of James E. Jones. 2 vols. Chicago: Lewis Pub. Co., 1914. (Index. Madison: Wisconsin State Gen. Soc., 1983.)

Columbia County History Book. Dallas, Tex.: Taylor Pub. Co., for Columbia County Hist. Soc., 1982. 401 pp.

## Crawford County

History of Crawford and Richland Counties, Wisconsin . . . Springfield, Ill.: Union Pub. Co., 1884. 1,308 pp. (Index. Madison: Wisconsin State Gen. Soc., 1981. 28, 36 pp. Repr. Evansville, Ind.: Unigraphic, 1975.)

History of . . . Crawford County, 1932, in Southwestern Wisconsin, *see* p. 434.

## Dane County

Madison, Dane County and Surrounding Towns . . . Madison: W.J. Park & Co., 1877. 664 pp. (Repr. Madison: Dane County Hist. Soc, 1978.)

History of Dane County, Wisconsin . . . C.W. Butterfield, principal ed. Chicago: Western Hist. Co., 1880. 1,289 pp.

History of Dane County, by Elisha W. Keyes. Madison: Western Hist. Assoc., 1906. 423 pp.

History of Dane County . . . Madison: Western Hist. Assoc., 1906. 974 pp. (Index of names. Milwaukee: Wisconsin State Gen. Soc., 1970. 17 pp. 2d ed. 1978. 53 pp.)

History of Dane County, 1932, in Southwestern Wisconsin, *see* p. 434.

This Is Dane County, by John Drury. Chicago: N.p., 1958? 954 pp.

## Dodge County

The History of Dodge County, Wisconsin . . . Chicago: Western Hist. Co., 1880. 766 pp. (Index. Madison: Wisconsin State Hist. Soc., 1970. 48 pp.)

Dodge County, Wisconsin, Past and Present, by Homer B. Hubbell. 2 vols. Chicago: S.J. Clarke Pub. Co., 1913.

History of Dodge County, 1932, in Southeastern Wisconsin, *see* p. 434.

Bicentennial History of Dodge County, Wisconsin. Beaver Dam: Citizen Pub. Co., 1982. 178 leaves.

## Door County

History of Door County, Wisconsin . . . by Charles I. Martin. Sturgeon Bay: Expositor Job. Pr., 1881. viii, 138 pp. (Index. Madison: Wisconsin State Gen. Soc., 1979. 15 pp.)

History of Door County, Wisconsin . . . by Hjalmar R. Holand. 2 vols. Chicago: S.J. Clarke Pub. Co., 1917.

Old Peninsula Days, Tales and Sketches of the Door County Peninsula, by Hjalmar R. Holand. Ephraim: Pioneer Pub. Co. [1925]. viii, 244 pp. (Repr. of 1925 ed. Madison: Wisconsin House [1972]. 5th rev. ed. Ephraim: Pioneer Pub. Co., 1923. 292 pp. 6th ed. Ephraim: Pioneer Pub. Co., 1943. xii, 295 pp. 7th ed. Ephraim: Pioneer Pub. Co., 1946. 319 pp. 8th ed. New York: Twayne Pub. [1959]. 245 pp.)

Door Way: the People in the Landscape . . . by Norbert Blei. Peoria, Ill.: Ellis Pr., 1981. 304 pp.

## Dunn County

Menomonie and Dunn County, Wisconsin, by Belle F. Swisher. (In The American Sketch Book, Vol. 1.) La Crosse: N.p., 1875.

Historical and Biographical Album of . . . Dunn County, 1891-92, *see* p. 434.

History of Dunn County, Wisconsin, by Franklyn Curtis-Wedge, et al. Chicago: H.C. Cooper, Jr. Co., 1925. 966 pp.

History of Dunn County, Wisconsin, by Dunn County Historical Society. Dallas, Tex.: Taylor Pub. Co., 1985.

## Eau Claire County

Historical and Biographical Album of . . . Eau Claire County, 1891-92, *see* p. 434.

History of Eau Claire County, Wisconsin, Past and Present . . . ed. by William F. Bailey. Chicago: C.F. Cooper & Co., 1914. 920 pp. (Index. Madison: Wisconsin State Gen. Soc., 1981. 35 pp.)

## Florence County

Heritage of Iron and Timber, 1880-1980. Florence County Centennial Committee. N.p.: Centennial Comm., 1980? 96 pp.

## Fond du Lac County

History of the County of Fond du Lac, Wisconsin . . . by Martin Mitchell. Fond du Lac: J.A. Smith, 1854. 96 pp.

History of Fond du Lac, Wisconsin . . . Chicago: Western Hist. Co., 1880. 1,063 pp.

Incidents and Anecdotes of Early Days and History of Business in the City and County of Fond du Lac County . . . by A.T. Glaze. Fond du Lac: Haber Pr. Co., 1905. 368 pp.

Fond du Lac County, Wisconsin, Past and Present, ed. by Maurice McKenna. 2 vols. Chicago: S.J. Clarke Pub. Co., 1912.

The History of Fond du Lac County as Told by Its Place Names, by Ruth S. Worthing. Fond du Lac: Author, 1976. 117 pp.

## Forest County

Memories of Forest County: Historical Research Project, Youth Community Conservation Program. N.p., 1980. 310 pp.

## Grant County

History of Grant County, Wisconsin . . . Chicago: Western Hist. Co., 1881. 1,046 pp. (Index, by Norma G. Patterson. Minneapolis: Author, 1976. 126 pp.)

*Grant County (cont.)*

History of Grant County, Wisconsin . . . by Castello N. Holford. Lancaster: Tellar Pr., 1900. viii, 782 pp. (Repr. Marceline, Mo.: Walsworth Pub. Co., 1976.)

History of Grant County, 1932, in Southwestern Wisconsin, *see* p. 434.

Grant County History, 1900-1976. Lancaster: Resource Comm. of Grant Co., 1976. 456 pp.

## Green County

History of Green County, Wisconsin, by Helen M. Bingham. Milwaukee: Burdick & Armitage, 1877. 310 pp.

History of Green County, Wisconsin . . . Springfield, Ill.: Union Pub. Co., 1884. 1,158 pp. (Repr. with added index. Monroe: Green County Hist. Soc., 1978. 1,248 pp.)

History of Green County, 1932, in Southwestern Wisconsin, *see* p. 434.

## Green Lake County

History of Green Lake County, by John C. Gillespy. Berlin: N.p., 1860. 111 pp.

History and Directory of Green Lake and Waushara Counties . . . by Edgar B. Fox. Berlin: N.p., 1869. 142 pp.

Portrait and Biographical Album (and History) of Green Lake County, 1890, *see* p. 434.

## Iowa County

History of Iowa County, Wisconsin . . . Chicago: Western Hist. Co., 1881. 970 pp. (Repr. Marceline, Mo.: Walsworth Pub. Co., 1976. Index. Madison: Wisconsin State Gen. Soc., 1981. 46 pp.)

Memoirs of Iowa County from the Earliest Times Down to the Present, by George Crawford. 2 vols. N.p., 1913.

## Iron County

Diamond Jubilee Edition, Iron County, Wisconsin. Hurley: Iron County Advertising Comm., 1968. (Unpaged)

## Jackson County

Biographical History of Jackson County, 1891, *see* Clark County.

Jackson County: a History by Jackson County Historical Society. Dallas, Tex.: Taylor Pub. Co., 1984. 302 pp.

# Jefferson County

The History of Jefferson County, Wisconsin . . . Chicago: Western Hist. Co., 1879. 733 pp. (Index. Madison: Wisconsin State Gen. Soc., 1981. 32 pp.)

Jefferson County, Wisconsin, and Its People . . . by John H. Ott. 2 vols. Chicago: S.J. Clarke Pub. Co., 1917.

History of Jefferson County, 1932, in Southeastern Wisconsin, *see* p. 434.

Koshkonong Country: a History of Jefferson County, Wisconsin, by Hannah Swart. Fort Atkinson: W.D. Hoard & Sons, 1975. 331 pp.

Koshkonong Country Revisited: an Anthology. 2 vols. Muskego: Marek Lithographics, 1981. 268 pp. Fort Atkinson: Fort Atkinson Hist. Soc., 1983. 288 pp.

# Juneau County

Juneau County, Wisconsin, Old Settlers, by J.T. Manson. Articles in Mauston Star, 1887-1888.

# Kenosha County

The History of Kenosha County, 1879, *see* Racine County.

The City of Kenosha and Kenosha County, Wisconsin . . . by Frank H. Lyman. 2 vols. Chicago: S.J. Clarke Pub. Co., 1916.

History of Kenosha County, 1932, in Northeastern Wisconsin, *see* p. 434.

Kenosha County in the Twentieth Century: a Topical History, ed. by John A. Neuenschwander. Kenosha: Kenosha County Bicentennial Comm., 1976. xvii, 516 pp.

Kenosha Retrospective: a Biographical Approach, by Nicholas C. Burckel and J.A. Neuenschwander. Kenosha: Kenosha County Bicentennial Comm., 1981. 384 pp.

# Kewaunee County

Treasured Memories . . . by Orwin Burmeister. Kewaunee: Kewaunee County Hist. Soc., 1980? 141 pp.

# La Crosse County

History of La Crosse County, Wisconsin. Chicago: Western Hist Co., 1881. 862 pp. (Repr. with added index. Evansville, Ind.: Unigraphic, 1977. 862, 116 pp.)

Memoirs of La Crosse County, by Benjamin F. Bryant. Madison: Wisconsin Hist. Assoc., 1907. 428 pp. (Index, by Virginia Kreyer. La Crosse: Murphy Lib., Univ. of Wisconsin of Wisconsin - La Crosse, 1978. 75 leaves.)

A History of La Crosse County, Wisconsin, 1841-1900, by Albert H. Sanford and H.J. Hirshheimer. La Crosse: La Crosse County Hist. Soc., 1951. xi, 274 pp.

## Lafayette County

History of Lafayette County, Wisconsin . . . Chicago: Western Hist. Co., 1881. (Repr. with added index. Evansville, Ind.: Whipporwill Pubs., 1983. 800, 55 pp.)

Lafayette County, Wisconsin, from the Republican Journal, by Patrick H. Conley. Darlington: N.p., 1910. 103 pp.

Lafayette County Bicentennial Book. Darlington: Lafayette County Bicentennial Comm., 1976. 201 pp.

## Langlade County

History of Langlade County, Wisconsin . . . by Robert M. Dessureau. Antigo: Berner Bros., 1922. 349 pp.

## Lincoln County

History of Lincoln, Oneida and Vilas Counties, by George A. Jones. Minneapolis: H.C. Cooper, Jr. Co., 1924. 787 pp. (Index. Madison: Wisconsin State Gen. Soc., 1980. 55 pp.)

Lincoln County History and Biographies. Merrill: Lincoln County Biographies, 1947. 158 pp.

## Manitowoc County

A History of Manitowoc County, by Ralph G. Plumb. [Manitowoc:] Brandt Pr., 1904. 316 pp.

History of Manitowoc County, Wisconsin, Louis Falge, ed. in chief. 2 vols. Chicago: Goodspeed Hist. Assoc. 1911-12. (Repr. with index. 2 vols. Manitowoc: Manitowoc County Gen. Soc., 1976-79. 1,138 pp.)

Manitowoc: Story of a Century, 1849-1949. Manitowoc County Centennial Committee. Manitowoc: The Comm., 1948. 155 pp.

## Marathon County

The History of Marathon County, Wisconsin . . . by Louis B. Marchetti. 2 vols. Chicago: Richmond, Arnold Pub. Co., 1913. 985 pp. (Every-name index, ed. by Patricia A. Grasse. Wausau: Marathon County Gen. Soc., 1982. 64 pp.)

Woodlot and Ballot Box: Marathon County in the Twentieth Century, by H.R. Klueter and J.J. Lorence. Wausau: Marathon County Hist. Soc., 1977. 414 pp.

## Marquette County

Portrait and Biographical Album (and History) of . . . Marquette County, 1890, *see* p. 434.

## Milwaukee County

History of Milwaukee, Wisconsin, ed. by Frank A. Flower. 2 vols. Milwaukee: N.p., 1881. (Repr. 2 vols. Milwaukee: Milwaukee County Gen. Soc., 1981. 1,663 plus 124 pp.)

Milwaukee County: History of Milwaukee County from Its First Settlement to . . . 1895, by Howard L. Conard. 3 vols. Chicago: N.p., 1896.

History of Milwaukee City and County, by William G. Bruce. 3 vols. Chicago, 1922.

Memoirs of Milwaukee County . . . ed. by Jerome A. Watrous. 2 vols. Madison: Western Hist. Assoc., 1909. (Index. Madison: Wisconsin State Gen. Soc., 1978. 66 pp.)

History of Milwaukee County, 1932, in Southeastern Wisconsin, *see* p. 434.

History of Milwaukee County, by W.P.A. Milwaukee: N.p., 1947. 675 pp.

## Monroe County

History of Monroe County, Wisconsin, ed. by Randolph A. Richards. Chicago: C.F. Cooper & Co., 1912. 946 pp. (Repr. with every-name index. Evansville, Ind.: Unigraphic, 1977. 946, 80 pp.)

Monroe County, Wisconsin, Pictorial History, 1976, by Monroe County Bicentennial Committee. Tomah: Tomah Journal Pr. Co., 1976. 416 pp.

Monroe County, Wisconsin Heritage Book, by Monroe, Juneau, Jackson Genealogical Workshop. Dallas, Tex.: Taylor Pub. Co., 1984. 514 pp.

## Oconto County

Recollections of Oconto County. N.p.: Oconto County Hist. Soc., 1954. 85 pp.

## Oneida County

History of Oneida County, 1924, *see* Lincoln County.

## Outagamie County

The Pioneers of Outagamie County, Wisconsin . . . by Elihu Spencer. Appleton: Post Pub. Co., 1895. 303 pp.

History of Outagamie County, ed. by Thomas H. Ryan. Chicago: Goodspeed Hist. Assoc., 1911. 1,391 pp. (Index. Madison: Wisconsin State Gen. Soc., 1981. 72 pp.)

## Ozaukee County

History of Ozaukee County, 1881, *see* Washington County.

History of Ozaukee County, 1932, in Southeastern Wisconsin, *see* p. 434.

## Pepin County

Historical and Biographical Album of . . . Pepin County, 1891-92, *see* p. 434.

History of Pepin County, 1919, *see* Buffalo County.

## Pierce County

The Story of Pierce County, by XYZ [Allen P. Weld], from the Spring Valley Sun, 1904-1906. N.p., [1906]. 222 pp.

History of . . . Pierce County, 1909, in History of the St. Croix Valley, *see* p. 434.

History of Pierce County, Wisconsin, for Use in . . . Schools. Spring Valley: Spring Valley Pub. Co., 1937. 88 pp.

Pierce County's Heritage. 7 vols. River Falls: Pierce County Hist. Assoc. [1971-80].

## Polk County

History of . . . Polk County, 1909, in History of the St. Croix Valley, *see* p. 434.

Polk County Memories. Balsam Lake: Polk County Hist. Soc., 1978. 48 pp.

Recollections of 1876: Polk County's First Written History, by Timothy L. Ericson. Balsam Lake: Polk County Hist. Soc., 1980. 84 pp.

## Portage County

A Standard History of Portage County, Wisconsin. 2 vols. Chicago: N.p., 1919. (Index. Madison: Wisconsin State Gen. Soc., 1980. 35 pp.)

Our County, Our Story: Portage County, Wisconsin, by Malcolm L. Rosholt. Stevens Point: Portage County Bd. of Supervisors, 1959. 600 pp.

Pioneers of the Pinery, by Malcolm Rosholt. Rosholt: Rosholt House, 1979. 272 pp.

## Price County

Historical and Biographical Album of . . . Price County, 1891-92, *see* p. 434.

## Racine County

The History of Racine and Kenosha Counties, Wisconsin . . . Chicago: Western Hist. Co., 1879. 738 pp. (Repr. with index of biographical sketches. Evansville, Ind.: Unigraphic, for Elisha Raymond Chapter, D.A.R., 1976. 738, 138 pp.)

Racine, Belle City and Racine County, Wisconsin, by Fanny S. Stone. 2 vols. Chicago: S.J. Clarke Pub. Co., 1916. 1,135 pp. (Index. Madison: Wisconsin State Gen. Soc., 1983. 33 pp.)

History of Racine County, 1932, in Southeastern Wisconsin, *see* p. 434.

Racine: Growth and Change in a Wisconsin County, ed. by Nicholas C. Burckel. Racine: Racine County Bd. of Supervisors, 1977. 648 pp.

*Racine County (cont.)*

The Grassroots History of Racine County. Racine: Racine County Hist. Museum, 1978. 660 pp.

## Richland County

History of Richland County, 1884, *see* Crawford County.

History of Richland County, Wisconsin, ed. by Hon. James H. Miner. Madison: Western Hist. Assoc., 1906. 698 pp.

History of Richland County, 1932, in Southeastern Wisconsin, *see* p. 434.

Home for the Heart: Richland County, Wisconsin, an Intimate History, by Francis L. Brewer. 2 vols. Richland Center: Brewer Pub. Lib., 1977. 318 leaves.

Chapters in the History of Richland County, Wisconsin, by Margaret H. Scott. Richland Center: Richland County Pub., 1978. 202 pp.

## Rock County

History of Rock County . . . ed. and comp. by Orrin Guernsey. Janesville: W.M. Doty & Bros., 1856. xii, 350 pp.

The History of Rock County, Wisconsin . . . Chicago: Western Hist. Co., 1879. 897 pp. (Index. Madison: Wisconsin State Gen. Soc., 1969. 33 pp.)

Rock County, Wisconsin: a New History . . . William F. Brown, ed. in chief. 2 vols. Chicago: C.F. Cooper, 1908.

History of Rock County, 1932, in Southeastern Wisconsin, *see* p. 434.

## Rusk County

History of Rusk County, Wisconsin. Ladysmith: Rusk County Hist. Soc., 1983. 372 pp.

## St. Croix County

History of . . . St. Croix County, 1909, in History of the St. Croix Valley, *see* p. 434.

Westward to the St. Croix: the Story of St. Croix County, Wisconsin, by Harold Weatherhead. Hudson: St. Croix Hist. Soc., 1978. 91 pp.

## Sauk County

The History of Sauk County, Wisconsin . . . Chicago: Western Hist. Co., 1880. 825 pp. (Index. Madison: Wisconsin State Gen. Soc., 1982. 50 pp.)

Outline Sketches of Sauk County, Including Its History . . . by William H. Canfield. 2 vols. Baraboo: A.N. Kellogg, 1861 [i.e. 1890-91].

A Standard History of Sauk County, Wisconsin . . . Harry E. Cole, supervising ed. 2 vols. Chicago: Lewis Pub. Co., 1918. (5th ed. Baraboo: Mrs. H.E. Cole, 1946. 112 pp. Index. Madison: Wisconsin State Gen. Soc., 1983.)

History of Sauk County, 1932, in Southeastern Wisconsin, *see* p. 434.

Sauk County, a Centennial History, by August W. Derleth. Baraboo: Sauk County Centennial Comm., 1948. 100 pp.

A County Called Sauk, a Human History of Sauk County, Wisconsin, by Kenneth I. Lange. Baraboo: Sauk County Hist. Soc., 1976. 168 pp.

## Sawyer County

I Remember When—: a Centennial Look at Sawyer County and Its People, 1883-1983. Hayward: Sawyer County Hist. Soc., 1983. 45 pp.

## Sheboygan County

Geschichte von Sheboygan County, by F.D. Franke. Sheboygan: Democrat Pr. Co., 1898. 297 pp.

History of Sheboygan County, Wisconsin, Past and Present, ed. by Carl Zillier. 2 vols. Chicago: S.J. Clarke Pub. Co., 1912. 1,096 pp. (Index. Sheboygan: Mead Pub. Lib., 1974-82. 36, 93 pp.)

Historic Sheboygan County, by Gustave W. Buchan. [Sheboygan: N.p., 1944.] ix, 347 pp.

## Taylor County

Reminiscences and Anecdotes of Early Taylor County, by Arthur J. Latton. N.p., 1947. 224 pp.

## Trempealeau County

History of Trempealeau County, Wisconsin, comp. by Franklyn Curtiss-Wedge, ed. by Eben D. Pierce. Chicago: H.C. Cooper, Jr. Co., 1917. xv, 922 pp. (Repr. with index. Evansville, Ind.: Unigraphic, 1978. 922, 112 pp.)

## Vernon County

History of Vernon County, Wisconsin . . . Springfield, Ill.: Union Pub. Co., 1884. 826 pp. (Repr. with index. Evansville, Ind.: Unigraphic, 1977. 826, 61 pp.)

Memoirs of Vernon County, by Earl M. Rogers. Madison, 1907. 531 pp. (Index, comp. by Janet Roon. Viroqua: comp., 1974. 57 pp.)

History of Vernon County, 1932, in Southwestern Wisconsin, *see* p. 434.

## Vilas County

History of Vilas County, 1924, *see* Lincoln County.

## Walworth County

History of Walworth County, Wisconsin . . . Chicago: Western Hist. Co., 1882. 967 pp. (Index. Madison: Wisconsin State Gen. Soc., 1973. 40 pp.)

History of Walworth County, Wisconsin, by Albert C. Beckwith. 2 vols. Indianapolis, Ind.: B.F. Bowen, 1912.

History of Walworth County, 1932, in Southeastern Wisconsin, *see* p. 434.

## Washburn County

Historical Collections of Washburn County and the Surrounding Indianhead Country, ed. by W.E. Ward Winton and K.B. Winton. 3 vols. Shell Lake: Washburn County Hist. Soc., n.d.

## Washington County

History of Washington and Ozaukee Counties, Wisconsin . . . Chicago: Western Hist. Co., 1881. 763 pp. (Index. Madison: Wisconsin State Gen. Soc., 1982. 36 pp.)

Washington County Past and Present, ed. by Carl Quickert. 2 vols. Chicago: S.J. Clarke Pub. Co., 1912. 633 pp.

The story of Washington County, by Carl Quickert. West Bend: Author [1923]. 230 pp.

History of Washington County, 1932, in Southeastern Wisconsin, *see* p. 434.

## Waukesha County

The History of Waukesha County, Wisconsin . . . Chicago: Western Hist. Co., 1880. 1,006 pp. (Repr. Waukesha: Waukesha County Hist. Soc., 1976. pp. 310-1,006.)

Memoirs of Waukesha County, by Theron W. Haight. Madison: Wisconsin Hist. Assoc., 1907. 701 pp. (Index. Madison: Wisconsin State Gen. Soc., 1978. 33 pp.)

History of Waukesha County, 1932, in Southeastern Wisconsin, *see* p. 434.

## Waupaca County

Early Waupaca County, Wisconsin, by Freeman D.D. Dewey. Waupaca: N.p., 1887. 95 pp.

History of Waupaca County, Wisconsin, by Josephus Wakefield. Waupaca: D.L. Stinchfield, 1890. 219 pp. (Repr. Iola: Chester L. Krause, 1983. 219 pp.)

Standard History of Waupaca County, Wisconsin, by John M. Ware. 2 vols. Chicago: Lewis Pub. Co., 1917. 866 pp.

## Waushara County

History and Directory of . . . Waushara County, 1869, *see* Green Lake County.

*Waushara County (cont.)*

Portrait and Biographical Album (and History) of . . . Waushara County, 1890, *see* p. 434.

## Winnebago County

Geographical and Statistical History of the County of Winnebago . . . Oshkosh: Mitchel & Smith, 1856. 120 pp. (Repr. Oshkosh: Winnebago County Hist. Soc., 1983. 83 pp.)

History of Winnebago County, Wisconsin . . . by Richard J. Harney. Oshkosh: Allen & Hicks, 1880. 348 pp.

History, Winnebago County, Wisconsin . . . by Publius V. Lawson. 2 vols. Chicago: C.F. Cooper, 1908.

Prairie, Pines and People: Winnebago County in a New Perspective, ed. by James I. Metz. Oshkosh: Oshkosh Northwestern Co., 1976. 404 pp.

The History of Winnebago County and the Fox River Valley, 1541-1877, by Reuben G. Thwaites. [Oshkosh: Winnebago County, 1984. 104 pp.] (Originally pub. serially in the Oshkosh Times, 1877.)

## Wood County

History of Wood County, by George A. Jones, et al. Minneapolis: H.C. Cooper, Jr. Co., 1923. 795 pp. (Index. Madison: Wisconsin State Gen. Soc., 1980. 57 pp. Index. Wisconsin Rapids: Heart O' Wisconsin Gen. Soc., 1981. 113 pp.)

# WYOMING

## Albany County

The History of Albany County, Wyoming, to 1880, by Lola M. Homsher. [Lusk: Lusk Herald, 1965.] v, 110 pp. (Originally from Annals of Wyoming, 21:2-3.)

Cow-belles Ring School Bells [Albany School], by Albany County Cow-Belles. Cheyenne: Pioneer Pr. Co., 1976. 490 pp.

## Big Horn County

History of Cheyenne and Northern Wyoming, Embracing the Gold Fields of Black Hills, Powder River and Big Horn County . . . Omaha, Nebr.: Herald Pr. House, 1876. 143 pp.

Big Horn County, Wyoming; the Gem of the Rockies, by Asa S. Mercer. Hyattsville, Md.: A.S. Mercer [1906]. 116 pp.

Big Horn National Forest and Vicinity, by James T. Connor. (Takes in Big Horn, Sheridan, Johnson and Washakie Counties.) N.p., 1940. 120 pp.

History of Big Horn County, by Leonard L. Gregory. Laramie: Univ. of Wyoming, 1959. 123 pp. (thesis)

## Campbell County

Only a Cow Country . . . County of Campbell, 1951, *see* Crook County.

## Carbon County

History of Carbon County, by William R. Barnhardt. Laramie: Univ. of Wyoming, 1969. 226 pp. (thesis)

## Crook County

Only a Cow Country, at One Time; Wyoming Counties of Crook, Weston, and Campbell, 1875-1951. [San Diego, Calif.: N.p., 1951.] 104 pp.

Pioneers of Crook County, by Crook County Historical Society. Pierre, S. Dak.: State Pub. Co., 1981. 593 pp.

## Fremont County

Crossroads of the West: Pictorial History of Fremont County. Riverton: Crossroads of the West, 1965.

Glories and History of Fremont County, by Harry S. Harnsberger. Cheyenne: N.p., 1966.

## Johnson County

Big Horn National Forest . . . Johnson County, 1940, *see* Big Horn County.

The Longest Rope; the Truth About the Johnson County Cattle War, by D.F. Baber, as Told by Bill Walker. Caldwell, Idaho: Caxton Pr., 1940. 320 pp.

## Laramie County

History of Laramie County up to 1890, by Sydney Spiegel. Laramie: Univ. of Wyoming, 1961. 196 pp. (thesis)

Pioneer Parade: a Collection of Newspaper and Magazine Stories of Eastern Laramie County Pioneers. Cheyenne: Logan Pr. Co., 1967. 80 pp.

Hillsdale Heritage [Laramie County], by Hillsdale Homemakers Club. Cheyenne: Pioneer Pr. Co., 1976. 314 pp.

## Natrona County

History of Natrona County, Wyoming, 1888-1922 . . . by Alfred J. Mokler. Chicago: Lakeside Pr., 1923. xiv, 477 pp.

## Niobrara County

Robber's Roost Historical Committee. Pioneering on the Cheyenne River . . . Stories of Pioneers and Early Settlers in Northern Niobrara County and Southern Weston County, Wyoming and Western Fall River County, South Dakota. Lusk: Lusk Herald, 1947.

## Sheridan County

Big Horn National Forest . . . Sheridan County, 1940, *see* Big Horn County.

Historical Sheridan and Sheridan County, by American Association of University Women, Sheridan Branch. Sheridan: Sheridan Chamber of Commerce, 1968.

History of Sheridan County Cow-Belles, 1940-1970, by Clara Fuller. Sheridan: Sheridan County Cow-Belles, 1971.

Sheridan County Heritage, by Sheridan County Extension Homemakers Council. Pierre, S. Dak.: State Pub. Co., 1983. 1,034 pp.

## Sublette County

Tales of the Seeds-ke-Dee, by Sublette County Artists Guild. Denver, Colo.: Big Mountain Pr., 1963.

## Teton County

History of Teton County, by Glenn Burkes. (In Annals of Wyoming, 44:1-2, 1972.)

## Uinta County

Uinta County, Its Place in History, by Elizabeth A. Stone. [Laramie: Laramie Pr. Co., 1924.] 276 pp.

## Washakie County

Big Horn National Forest . . . Washakie County, 1940, *see* Big Horn County.

History of Washakie County, by Its People. A Bicentennial Project. Worland: Northern Wyoming Daily News, 1976. 205 pp.

## Weston County

Pioneers and Early Settlers in . . . Southern Weston County, 1947, *see* Niobrara County.

Only a Cow Country . . . Wyoming County of Weston, 1951, *see* Crook County.